S0-BEA-667

CMC Supporting Papers

The Committee for Economic Development is publishing for the Commission on Money and Credit

THE FEDERAL RESERVE AND THE TREASURY: ANSWERS TO QUESTIONS FROM THE COMMISSION ON MONEY AND CREDIT

and fifty-eight individual essays organized into nine separate volumes, each centered around a particular aspect of monetary and fiscal policy. Their titles and the contributing authors are as follows:

IMPACTS OF MONETARY POLICY

Daniel B. Suits; Robert Eisner and Robert H. Strotz, with a bibliography by G. R. Post; Edwin Kuh and John R. Meyer; Leo Grebler and Sherman J. Maisel; Charlotte DeMonte Phelps; Irwin Friend

STABILIZATION POLICIES

E. Cary Brown, Robert M. Solow, Albert Ando, and John Kareken; Milton Friedman and David Meiselman; Lawrence E. Thompson; Arthur M. Okun; Merton H. Miller; Allan H. Meltzer; Oswald Brownlee and Alfred Conrad

MONETARY MANAGEMENT

Frank M. Tamagna; Warren L. Smith; Clark Warburton; Michael D. Reagan; C. P. Kindleberger; Robert Z. Aliber

FISCAL AND DEBT MANAGEMENT POLICIES

William Fellner; Richard A. Musgrave; James Tobin; James R. Schlesinger; Paul H. Cootner; Irving Auerbach; Ralph K. Huitt; John Lindeman

FEDERAL CREDIT AGENCIES

George F. Break; Jack Guttentag; Ernest Bloch; D. Gale Johnson; Dale E. Hathaway; George S. Tolley; Jack McCroskey

FEDERAL CREDIT PROGRAMS

Stewart Johnson; Warren A. Law; James W. McKie; D. Gale Johnson; James Gillies; Robert C. Turner and Ross Robertson; J. Fred Weston

PRIVATE CAPITAL MARKETS

Irwin Friend; Hyman P. Minsky; Victor L. Andrews

PRIVATE FINANCIAL INSTITUTIONS

Paul M. Horvitz; Deane Carson and Paul Cootner; Thomas G. Gies, Thomas Mayer, and Edward C. Ettin; Lawrence L. Werboff and Marvin E. Rozen; Fred H. Klopstock; E. Gordon Keith

INFLATION, GROWTH, AND EMPLOYMENT

Joseph W. Conard; Jesse W. Markham; Franklyn D. Holzman; John W. Kendrick; Daniel Creamer; Stanley Lebergott; Lawrence R. Klein and Ronald G. Bodkin; Tibor and Anne Scitovsky

IMPACTS OF MONETARY POLICY

PRENTICE-HALL INTERNATIONAL, INC. , London
PRENTICE-HALL OF AUSTRALIA, PTY. , LTD. , Sydney
PRENTICE-HALL OF CANADA, LTD. , Toronto
PRENTICE-HALL OF FRANCE, S. A. R. L. , Paris
PRENTICE-HALL OF INDIA (PRIVATE) LTD. , New Delhi
PRENTICE-HALL OF JAPAN, INC. , Tokyo
PRENTICE-HALL DE MEXICO, S. A. , Mexico City

Daniel B. Suits
Robert Eisner
  and Robert H. Strotz
  bibliography, George R. Post
Edwin Kuh
  and John R. Meyer
Leo Grebler
  and Sherman J. Maisel
Charlotte DeMonte Phelps
Irwin Friend

IMPACTS OF MONETARY POLICY

A SERIES OF RESEARCH STUDIES
PREPARED FOR THE

Commission on Money and Credit

Prentice-Hall, Inc.
Englewood Cliffs, N.J.

COMMISSION ON MONEY AND CREDIT

Members

Frazar B. Wilde, CHAIRMAN
Chairman, Connecticut General
  Life Insurance Company

H. Christian Sonne,
  VICE CHAIRMAN
New York, New York

Adolf A. Berle, Jr.
New York, New York
(Withdrew to serve as Chairman
  of the U.S. State Department
  Latin American Task Force.)

James B. Black
Chairman of the Board, Pacific
  Gas & Electric Company

Joseph M. Dodge
Chairman of the Board, The
  Detroit Bank and Trust Com-
  pany
(Resigned October 7, 1960.)

Marriner S. Eccles
Chairman of the Board, First
  Security Corporation

Lamar Fleming, Jr.
Chairman of the Board, Anderson, Clayton & Co.

Henry H. Fowler
Fowler, Leva, Hawes & Syming-
  ton
(Resigned February 3, 1961, on
  his appointment as Under
  Secretary of the Treasury.)

Gaylord A. Freeman, Jr.
Vice Chairman, The First Na-
  tional Bank of Chicago
(Appointed April 29, 1960.)

Fred T. Greene
President, Federal Home Loan
  Bank of Indianapolis
(Died March 17, 1961.)

Philip M. Klutznick
Park Forest, Illinois
(Resigned February 8, 1961, on
  his appointment as United
  States Representative to the
  Economic and Social Council
  of the United Nations.)

Fred Lazarus, Jr.
Chairman of the Board, Feder-
  ated Department Stores, Inc.

Isador Lubin
Arthur T. Vanderbilt Professor
  of Public Affairs, Rutgers
  University

J. Irwin Miller
Chairman of the Board, Cum-
  mins Engine Company

Robert R. Nathan
President, Robert R. Nathan
  Associates, Inc.

Emil Rieve
President Emeritus, Textile
  Workers of America, AFL-
  CIO
(Appointed May 19, 1960.)

David Rockefeller
President, The Chase Manhattan
  Bank

Beardsley Ruml
New York, New York
(Died April 18, 1960.)

Stanley H. Ruttenberg
Director, Department of Research, AFL-CIO

Charles Sawyer
Taft, Stettinius & Hollister

William F. Schnitzler
Secretary-Treasurer, AFL-CIO
(Resigned April 28, 1960.)

FOREWORD

The Commission on Money and Credit came into being in May 1958 to appraise our monetary and financial system, both public and private, and the governmental regulations and controls that affect it. Based on such an examination, the Commission was to make recommendations on what changes, if any, should be made to improve the structure, operations, regulation and control of our monetary and credit system.

In its early meetings, the Commission blocked out the scope and major subdivisions of its inquiry. It then subdivided itself into topical subcommittees or "task forces," each of which was to identify and spell out the key policy issues related to each task force mission, to develop plans for analyzing these central problems, and to prepare recommendations in relation to each for presentation to the full Commission. When the Commission had reached agreement on the key policy issues to be investigated, the staff then prepared a program of proposed research projects around the issues to be considered by each task force.

The proposed research projects were then discussed at task force meetings, and each project to be undertaken was approved by the Commission. Each research project was to provide for the Commission's deliberations, information that would identify clearly the critical elements which underlay the policy questions under consideration. The projects were to mobilize the relevant facts, analytical findings, and the arguments for and against alternative positions.

One of the earliest sets of projects consisted of a series of papers dealing with the determinants of spending in the various sectors of the economy, with special emphasis on the role of monetary and credit factors in such spending. Extensive research on these matters had been conducted for many years. Various scholars who had contributed significantly to knowledge on such questions were commissioned to prepare papers. The purpose of these papers was to (a) summarize and appraise past research on the factors which determine spending in the major economic sectors, (b) to summarize the present state of knowledge regarding the determinants of such spending, and (c) to indicate the gaps in knowledge and the means by which such gaps might be closed. Six of these papers are included in this volume.

Daniel B. Suits of the University of Michigan was asked to prepare a background memorandum dealing with the determinants of consumer spending. His instructions included, "Within this broad context of the general determinants of consumer spending, the paper will focus on the influence on consumption of monetary and financial variables. It will consider specifically the question—is consumer spending responsive to general monetary policies? If so, through what channels? If not, why not? Attention will be paid to the effects on consumer spending of consumer credit terms, the influence of household liquid assets, the effects of prices of consumer goods on consumer demand, and the influence of income. The analysis will, so far as possible, be disaggregated in terms of expenditure on consumer durables, nondurables, and services."

Robert Eisner and Robert H. Strotz of Northwestern University were asked to develop a background paper dealing with the determinants of business investment spending on plant and equipment and on inventories. Their instructions included, "Within this broad context of the general determinants of investment spending, the paper will focus on the influence of monetary policy and debt management activities on investment outlays and deal with the central question—are plant and equipment and inventory spending responsive to general monetary policies? If so, through what channels? If not, why not? Attention will be paid both to the theory of investment by the individual firm and to aggregate investment in the economy, including a study of the problems and pitfalls involved in moving from knowledge of the individual firm to the economy as a whole."

Edwin Kuh of the Massachusetts Institute of Technology and John R. Meyer of Harvard University were also asked to prepare a paper on the effects of monetary policy on business investment outlays. Their instructions included, "The paper will report the results of an empirical study of quarterly sources and uses of funds data plus McGraw-Hill and National Industrial Conference Board questionnaire results to explore the cyclical variability of sources and uses of funds in major sectors of the economy. The study will be designed to test hypotheses relating to both the interest rate and credit rationing effects of monetary policy on cyclical variations of plant and equipment outlays in the entire economy, as well as the indirect effects stemming from the influence of monetary policy on final consumer demand. It will also consider the longer-run effects of interest rates on investment decisions."

Leo Grebler of the University of California at Los Angeles and Sherman Maisel of the University of California were asked to prepare a background study dealing with the determinants of residential construction. Their instructions included, "Within this broad context the paper will focus on the responsiveness of new housing construction to changes in monetary and credit variables. The study will discuss the influence of the supply and cost of credit on home building, the role of supply factors other than credit, and the significance of the demand for housing in both the short run and the long run. The role of the FHA and VA programs and the influence of the Federal National Mortgage Association on the level of and fluctuations in residential construction will be treated. Since the determinants of the demand for new residential construction cannot be separated analytically or empirically from the determinants of the total demand for housing, the study will also concern itself with the demand for housing of all types."

Mrs. Charlotte DeMonte Phelps of the Cowles Foundation for Research in Economics was asked to prepare a background memorandum dealing with the general determinants of state and local government expenditures and the impact of monetary policy thereon. Her instructions included, "Within this broad context of the general determinants of state and local government expenditures the paper will focus on the specific influence of monetary and debt management policies, particularly the impact of "tight money." Is state and local government borrowing and spending responsive to monetary policy? If so, through what channels? If not, why not?"

Irwin Friend of the Wharton School, University of Pennsylvania, was asked to prepare a study of the determinants of the volume and composition of saving with special reference to the influence of monetary policy. His instructions included, "This study will involve a discussion of the state of existing knowledge on the determinants, especially financial determinants, of the size, composition, and forms of savings and on the influence of monetary and debt management policies on the volume and composition of savings. It will summarize both existing theories relating interest rates, liquidity, price level increases and other variables to categories of savings and the empirical evidence bearing on these relationships. An important concern of the Commission is the effects of possible actions on the part of financial institutions, the monetary authority, and the debt management authority to stimulate or discourage savings; consequently the major purpose of this study is to provide a foundation for these considerations."

These studies were submitted to and used by the Commission and its staff in preliminary form. The authors were then given an opportunity to revise them in the light of comments received from outside readers, the Commission's staff, and readers chosen from the Commission's Advisory Board. The final manuscripts are presented in this volume as they were received from their authors; there has been no final editing by the staff of the Commission. The paper by Mrs. Phelps on state and local government expenditures has been drastically shortened from that originally submitted to the Commission because the bulk of her original paper was contained in her Ph.D. thesis which was published in the <u>Yale Economic Essays</u>, Vol. 1, No. 2, Fall 1961. The other five papers are presented in full.

The Commission is happy to present these research studies among the supporting papers behind its Report. The members of the Commission and its staff are grateful to the authors of the papers for their contributions to the deliberations of the Commission.

Bertrand Fox
Director of Research

Eli Shapiro
August 1962   Deputy Director of Research

CONTENTS

CONTENTS

Research Study One

THE DETERMINANTS OF CONSUMER
EXPENDITURE: A REVIEW OF
PRESENT KNOWLEDGE

Daniel B. Suits
University of Michigan

INTRODUCTION AND SUMMARY

The activities of governments and monetary institutions exercise a wide influence over many aspects of our economic life. Unfortunately the exact nature of the influence exerted by any particular activity is not always well understood. Economic life is an interrelated articulated whole—indeed this is the reason we refer to our institutions as an economic "system"—and the difficulties of disentangling the effects of a particular policy from the play of other events are enormous. It is thus important that any attempt to assess the effectiveness of policy begin with a careful examination of as many other factors as possible in addition to the performance of policy instruments. The purpose of this paper is to explore the present state of our knowledge of the determinants of consumer expenditure from such a point of view.

The present state of our theory of consumer behavior represents a vast improvement over that of a few years ago. We now insist that theoretical propositions imply testable and measurable conclusions. Research along these lines naturally runs in diverse directions, and the resulting picture is confusing. The areas of ignorance are great; nevertheless a number of significant conclusions can be drawn.

1. Consumers do not react on a day-to-day basis. Behavior and its determinants have a relatively long time dimension. What is spent in a given quarter depends on so many accidental short-run variables that its association with even so basic a variable as consumer income is obscured. An association between income and consumption can be observed for periods as short as a year, but it is clear that still longer-run phenomena play an important part in consumer behavior. This is evidenced by the differing behavior of families with the same income, but who differ in educational and occupational background, and are in different stages in the life cycle. Moreover the consumption habits of consumers change with their experience and development. Families with economic reverses tend to sustain their standard of living and will maintain a higher consumption expenditure at a given level of income than families who have always had such incomes.

2. Regression studies of income and expenditure show that, at the margin, one dollar of disposable personal income is associated with about sixty-five cents in additional consumption expenditure and thirty-five cents in additional saving. It is tempting to identify these results with the Keynesian marginal propensity to consume and assert that an additional dollar of disposable income will "generate" or "induce" an additional sixty-five cents in consumption expenditure, but there are two reasons to exercise great caution in this regard.

In the first place there is reason to believe that the response to increases in income depends on their nature as well as their magnitude. For example, the marginal propensity to spend windfalls may be as high as 0.90.

Secondly, one is increasingly impressed with the extent to which a family in a modern prosperous economy has the power actually to control the size of its income. If income is not a datum, but is itself a reflection of family behavior, the implications of a statistically estimated "marginal propensity to consume" are by no means clear. Attempts to control consumption by means of policies (for example taxes) designed to alter disposable income may have much greater incentive and smaller consumption effects than generally supposed.

3. Consumption is much more autonomous than earlier theory had implied. There is strong evidence that varying psychological attitudes of consumers can induce big movements in consumer expenditure independently of traditional economic variables. There are several vehicles that permit this kind of variation in behavior. Even a family that always spends all of its income can temporarily increase its expenditure by resorting to consumer credit. A permanent increase in consumption can derive from increased income via extra overtime, longer hours, more wage earners in the family, etc. For families with liquid saving, extra expenditure can be made by reducing the saving rate or dipping into liquid assets.

4. It appears likely that monetary variables play their primary role in interaction with other variables. The effect of liquid assets plainly shows up in association with income variation. Savings of groups such as businessmen and farmers, whose income is subject to high variability, are much more responsive to the level of liquid assets already possessed than is the case with other people. Moreover, among families with declining incomes, the level of consumption of those with liquid assets is higher than that of those without.

Consumer credit terms can be shown to increase the demand for automobiles on a year-to-year basis. It is estimated that a 1 percent lengthening in credit terms will increase expenditure for automobiles by about one-half of 1 percent. The evidence is not adequate to indicate how much this increase is offset by a decline in expenditure for services and other commodities. As would be expected resort to the use of consumer credit is largely associated with families with low liquid asset holdings.

5. Finally, the determinants of consumer expenditure do not act in a symmetrical fashion. An increase in income is not "just the opposite" of a decrease. The act of accumulating liquid assets is not the "other side" of the act of spending liquid assets. This asymmetry of behavior is not yet well investigated and much more attention needs to be given to it.

The active interest in consumer behavior, the improved data and research tools are rich in promise of a well-developed theory to come. The present state of our knowledge of consumer behavior, however, is not only inadequate, but one may well question its usefulness for the evaluation of monetary policy, beyond the indication of the general direction of possible effects. One important fact should be noted. Crude as our data and approach may be, it seems reasonable to suppose that if such an effect existed--that if monetary policy produced any sizable reaction in consumption-- it would be indicated even by crude measurements. Yet with the possible exception of the automobile market, none of the studies of the effects of monetary factors on consumer behavior has succeeded in showing an unambiguous, statistically significant, important direct effect.

The presentation of material in the following pages is divided into six sections. The definition of consumer expenditure and the definition of the consumer unit take up the first two. Section three is devoted to the historical development of consumption theory with particular emphasis on the Keynesian and post-Keynesian development. Section four deals with empirical findings in general, while section five is devoted expressly to monetary factors, especially to liquid asset holdings and consumer credit. The concluding section is devoted to an evaluation of our present state of knowledge and a brief suggestion of the kind of research that is needed.

I. DEFINITION OF CONSUMER EXPENDITURE

The term "aggregate consumer expenditure" is generally familiar. It constitutes a total over the entire economy of the value of certain classes of transactions. The delimitation of the classes of transactions included in the total is to a certain extent arbitrary. This is the familiar concomitant of any useful definition involving economic behavior, and it is unnecessary to dwell at length on the details. At the same time it is useful to remind ourselves at the outset of the study of some of the limitations of the concept.

There are at least two aspects of consumption that are important. On the one hand, we are concerned with the welfare of the members of the community, and hence in the rate at which benefits flow to them. From this standpoint consumption clearly differs from the act of expenditure by consumers. The purchase of a durable, for example, is an addition to the real wealth of the purchaser; its value represents the value of a stored flow of services. To impute the entire benefit derived from the good to the time of its purchase is a distorted measure of the flow of welfare.

On the other hand, we are often interested in the impact of consumer behavior on production, employment, and on the flow and distribution of income. In this case it is the act of purchase and its relationship to production that is of primary interest. Durability is interesting insofar as it is a factor in the dynamics of consumer expenditure, but it is the purchase itself that we attempt to analyze and explain. From this standpoint consumption is distinguished from other purchases in the effort to group together expenditures that have common determinants. This means, in the first place, that the behavior of households is to be distinguished from that of business firms.

In the second place not all expenditures by households are included in the concept. The purchase of a new house by a family is not included in consumer expenditure, presumably because the decision to purchase the house is sufficiently different from the decision to purchase, say, a new car to require separate analysis. The difference between the purchase of a new car and the purchase of a can of beans is hardly less, although in this case the two are classed together as components of consumer expenditure, and in many analyses no effort is made to distinguish them.

It cannot be too often asserted, however, that the mere fact that we treat consumer expenditure as if it were a single behavioral phenomenon does not make it so. Human behavior is a complex affair--vastly more complicated than the behavior of, say, physical particles--and we must pursue its study without the benefit of laboratory controls. To proceed at all we must employ crude analytical categories, and we do so without apology. But they must not be confused with <u>true</u> behavioral invariants. The study of aggregate consumer expenditure is a useful short-cut device for getting results in the face of complications, but it automatically introduces an error of unknown magnitude into our analysis. The error is further compounded when we add together expenditures not only on different goods, but purchases made by many different consumer units, treating the Joneses and the Smiths, the lawyer and the farmer as if they were so many homogeneous atoms.

All this is true at the conceptual level, even before any attempt to measure the aggregate thus defined; the process of measurement involves further approximation. The entity defined for measurement purposes is not the same as that defined conceptually. This is a familiar property of costly data that must be compiled to be approximately useful for a number of purposes (and hence exactly suited to none). Consumer expenditure as estimated in the national accounts includes some items more properly associated with the welfare, rather than the expenditure concept of consumption. Most notable is the imputation of the value of owner occupied dwellings as part of the income and consumption of home owners. To the extent that we are interested in consumption in terms of current demand and stimulation of production, this item is irrelevant. This is not to say that homeowners and renters have the same behavioral patterns, but the differences might better be analyzed by taking home ownership status directly into account than by altering the definition of consumption expenditure.

A second notable difficulty with the national accounts is the inclusion of nonprofit institutions in the consumer sector and of outlays by nonprofit institutions under the heading of consumption expenditure. The purchase of an operating table by a hospital and a dining room table by a household are counted in the same way. Moreover, since income receipts of nonprofit institutions are treated as part of "personal income," the difference between institutional receipts and outlays is a part of "personal saving."[1]

A second important source of data on consumer behavior is that procured from sample surveys. The definitions of consumer expenditure and saving appropriate to the analysis of survey data differ not only from those of the national accounts, but vary from survey to survey with the specific set of questions asked.

----

[1]An extensive examination of the problems of definition and measurement involved in the national accounts will be found in <u>The National Accounts of the United States</u>, Hearings before the Subcommittee on Economic Statistics of the Joint Economic Committee, 85th Congress, First Session, October 29, 30, 1957.

Finally, regardless of definitions, the actual gathering and compilation of data is subject to errors of various kinds depending on the sources and methods used. To illustrate one specific problem in the national accounts, expenditure of consumers for new automobiles involves first dividing total <u>wholesale</u> value of new car retail sales between households, businesses and governments, secondly estimating the dealers' gross margin over wholesale value to obtain a retail expenditure figure. In view of the legal status of motor vehicles, the necessary information is somewhat more readily available in the case of automobiles than in the case of, say, furniture, but however carefully such estimates are prepared, they clearly involve considerable measurement error. In obtaining information by personal interview in a survey sample, errors obviously arise due to memory failure, misinterpretation of the question by the respondent, misconstruction of the answer by the interviewer, etc. Moreover, the aggregate consumption figures obtained will vary with the way in which questions are phrased. For example, the larger the number of specific items (television set, radio, washing machine, automobile, etc.) mentioned, the larger, in general, the reported expenditure tends to be, since the respondent is reminded of more purchases.

The problems associated with differing concepts and errors of measurement are further complicated by the fact that our analytical methods are necessarily crude. Although we occasionally introduce curvilinearities or interaction terms, we habitually deal with linear approximations to complex relationships. The analysis is restricted to a severely limited number of factors, and we must, as often as not, use methods in the face of their failure to satisfy the requirements of strict statistical validity. Results thus obtained are the crudest reflection of reality; apparent contradictions and ambiguities are to be expected.

II. THE CONSUMER UNIT

The consumer sector of the economy is composed of a collection of units, the precise definition of which depends on the purpose of the analysis. In purely theoretical work we are often uncritical of the exact units of analysis. Indeed we habitually speak of "the" consumer, and the textbook discussion of consumer theory often reads as if the unit of analysis were the individual person. Even in more sophisticated analysis we generally think in terms of a "typical" family: husband, wife and children (the latter all clearly minor) living together. But when we turn to empirical research we are no longer free to deal in casual concepts and the specific problem of definition arises.

The objective in defining a proper unit is to simplify our analysis. There is no "true" definition which we can hope to uncover or somehow approximate. What we look for, rather, is a way of dividing people into groups for which reasonably consistent behavior patterns can be determined with a minimum of concern for the relationship among individuals within the group. A number of such groups can be defined.

The term "family" usually refers to a group of persons, related by blood, marriage or adoption, and residing together. In this connection a single person living alone sometimes constitutes a "one person family" and sometimes is excluded from the definition.

A "household" as defined by the Bureau of the Census consists of all of the persons who occupy a house, an apartment, or other group of rooms that constitutes a dwelling unit. All persons living in the house are counted as members of the household whether related or not. However groups of persons living in institutions, hotels or large rooming houses are classified as "quasi-household."

The difficulty with these two definitions is largely that their use too often entails reference to the internal structure of the unit. When a young married son and wife live with the son's parents, the group constitutes a single family, although its behavior may appear greatly atypical until the particulars of its make-up are examined. Similarly, a household consisting of two unrelated families may require special attention.

Another way to think of the problem is in terms of getting information by interview. In gathering information from a household consisting only of a married couple and their young children, an interview with the husband is generally sufficient to elicit all necessary information about income, expenditure, and similar variables. But if a young couple lives with parents, neither of the two husbands is necessarily well informed about the precise position of the other family, and gathering information on a household or family basis sometimes requires two or more interviews per unit. This strongly indicates that an alternative to the family or household would be more useful as a unit analysis.

It is for a similar reason that the British Survey of Personal Income and Savings employs the "income unit" for data collection and analysis. Each person 18 years of age or older and each married couple is defined as a separate income unit.[2] It is clear

---

[2] A brief description of the survey will be found in Harold Lydall (30). (Numbers in parentheses refer to publications listed in the bibliography appearing at the end of this Research Study.)

that for purposes of income data collection, and certain kinds of income comparison this is a useful unit to employ. On the other hand, the behavior of such a unit — even to a certain extent its employment and income — would frequently require reference to the relationships in which the particular unit stood to others. For example, whether a twenty-year-old man has an income or not may depend in part on whether his parents are sufficiently well off to support him in school.

From the standpoint of consumer theory the most useful classification is the "spending unit." As employed by the University of Michigan Survey Research Center, a spending unit is a group of people, related by blood or marriage, living in the same dwelling, who pool together more than half of their combined incomes for expenditure purposes. It is clear that either the household or the family, as defined above, may contain more than one spending unit, but that all members of a spending unit must belong both to the same household and the same family. But--almost by definition-- the spending unit concept breaks the household and the family into groups more closely approximating autonomous decision-making units. Indeed, the ultimate test of whether a given household or family contains one or several spending units is precisely the extent to which expenditures--hence, by implication, effective decisions to spend--are jointly undertaken.

The theory of consumer behavior is directed toward understanding the relationships among the several decisions made by the spending units, the relationship of these decisions to the several aspects of the environment and, ultimately toward the prediction of what spending units are likely to do in response to changed conditions and how their response is conditioned by circumstances.

III. THE DEVELOPMENT OF CONSUMER THEORY

Classical Theory

In the classical theory of consumer behavior, each spending unit is characterized by a system of tastes or preferences for the objects of expenditure. This system may be represented as an ordering preference relation, as a set of indifference surfaces, or as a utility function; the representation varies from writer to writer, and properly used involves no essential difference in method or conclusions. The behavior of the spending unit is dictated by the attempt to maximize its utility, subject to the constraints placed on its decisions by the limitations of earning power, family resources, prices which must be paid for goods, etc.

The statement that prices and resources given, the spending unit selects the most preferred from among the alternative patterns of expenditure open to it is, taken alone, a completely empty proposition. It is an elaborate statement of the fact that a spending unit does what it does, but provides no insight into its behavior. For it to be more than a tautology, the nature of the utility function must be so restricted that it would, under specified circumstances, predict one mode of behavior rather than another. One such restriction is provided by the law of diminishing marginal utility (or, in other terms, the diminishing marginal rate of substitution). This restriction (i.e. that the more of a thing a spending unit has, the less desirable an additional amount becomes) predicts, among other things, that the lower the price of a good, the more of it a spending unit will normally buy, and the less it will buy of substitutes for the good in question.

The extension of this principle to consumption as a whole yields the proposition that the lower the price of present goods compared to the present price of the same real volume of goods at a future time, the more of the spending unit's resources will be devoted to present expenditure and the less set aside in the form of saving for future enjoyment. The terms on which present and future goods can be exchanged are defined by the interest rate and expected price movements. With expected price stability, the higher the interest rate, the cheaper the present cost of future consumption of a given real good and the more its present consumption will be postponed. It does not necessarily follow from this that no saving would occur at zero interest rate, but it does follow that the supply of savings is interest elastic. It was presumed by classical theorists that this supply elasticity was sufficient, when taken in conjunction with the elasticity of the demand for saving, to permit market equilibrium at any given level of income. Moreover this equilibrium was presumed to occur at full employment. As the supplier of labor services the spending unit must decide how much of its available labor resources to offer on the market. Since labor was supposed to be subject to increasing marginal disutility, its supply would vary with the real wage. Flexibility of prices in the several markets of the economy should therefore be adequate to ensure an equilibrium position at full employment: i.e., a position where all offers of labor at the going real wage are accepted, and the division of income between consumption expenditure and savings matches the investment intentions of business at the going interest rate.

Whether this global prediction is contrary to fact or not is open to question: the theory is static, and refers to an equilibrium position that is not necessarily observable in view of the dynamics of the economy. But it is perfectly clear that the proposition is not a useful guide to specific policy in a world characterized by actually observed problems of unemployment or inflation.

The Keynesian Analysis

The inability of the classical model to lend itself to an explanation of fluctuations in the level of unemployment lead Keynes (19)
to reorient the model in a more useful direction.

The Keynesian alteration of the classical theory of consumer
behavior involved the assumption that the spending unit is not
highly responsive to changes in the rate of interest over the
economically meaningful range, and that its behavior is especially
inelastic at the lower end of the range. Moreover it was explicitly
assumed that saving has utility in its own right. Under these circumstances it is easily shown that diminishing marginal utility
implies that, other things equal, an increase in income will result
in a lesser increase in consumer expenditure. That is, that changes
in income are accompanied by changes in the rate of both consumption expenditure and saving in the same direction. The aggregation of the relationship of consumption to income over the economy
defined the aggregate consumption function; linking the consumption
function to the rest of the economic system via the familiar
Keynesian apparatus produced the desired results: a simple model
that could account for the existence of observed fluctuations in the
general level of employment.

Keynes was well enough aware that consumption expenditure was
determined by factors other than income, and in the three chapters
devoted to the consumption function, he discussed a number of these
and their presumed effect. In chapter 8 "The Propensity to Consume:
I," he listed the six "principal objective factors which influence the
propensity to consume." (p. 19)

(1) The Wage Unit. Keynes argues that spending unit consumption
was a function of real spending unit income, and asserted that--as a
first approximation--a rise in money wages at a given level of
employment would increase money consumption expenditure and
prices in proportion. However, he noted that "in some circumstances
we may have to make an allowance for possible reactions on
aggregate consumption of the change in the distribution of real
income between entrepreneurs and rentiers resulting from a change
in the wage unit." (p. 92) This is simply to say that, unless all
individual spending units have precisely the same real marginal
propensity to consume, the relation between aggregate consumption
and income will depend on the distribution of income among spending
units. Redistribution may be affected not only by inflation and deflation, but also by changes in the composition of output (e.g., as
associated with shifts of production among industries, among
regions, etc.) or by governmental intervention. (cf. (5) below)

(2) Income v. "Net Income." Keynes noted that "it is, by definition, his net income that a man has in mind when he is deciding his

scale of consumption." (p. 42) In view of this "definition" it is not clear why Keynes classified this as an "objective" factor. Discussion at a later point indicates that the distinction Keynes had in mind had to do with allowance for maintenance of capital; the natural extension of "net income" is the currently used "disposable income" concept.

(3) "Windfall" Capital Gains. Keynes observed that "the consumption of the wealth-owning class may be extremely susceptible to unforeseen changes in the money value of its wealth. This should be classified as amongst the major features capable of causing short-period changes in the propensity to consume." (p. 93) This opinion, which is not elaborated, is of particular interest in view of current concern with the role of the real value of liquid assets. The capital gains effect referred to here is in some respects the opposite of the so-called Pigou effect.

(4) The Ratio of Time Discounting. Although the discounting referred to here is broader than the rate of interest, since it allows for expected price changes, risks, etc., Keynes said that "as an approximation we can identify this with the rate of interest" and believed that "the influence of this factor is open to a good deal of doubt."

(5) Fiscal Policy. Under this heading Keynes included primarily the incentive effects of taxation on saving, although he also indicated that "if fiscal policy is used as a deliberate instrument for the more equal distribution of incomes, its effect in increasing the propensity to consume is ... all the greater." (p. 95)

(6) Expectations of the Relation between Present and Future Levels of Income. Keynes listed this factor "for the sake of formal completeness," (p. 95), although again the logic of counting this an "objective" factor is not clear. In this context, Keynes also explicitly suggested an important dynamic aspect of the consumption function: "A man's habitual standard of life usually has first claim on his income, and he is apt to save the difference...between his actual income and the expense of his habitual standard ....Thus a rising income will often be accompanied by increased saving and a falling income by decreased saving, on a greater scale at first than subsequently." (p. 97)

In addition to the "objective" factors, Keynes listed eight "subjective" motives leading individuals to refrain from spending out of their incomes:

(1) To form a contingency reserve.

(2) To anticipate future needs.

(3) To earn income from interest.

(4) To enjoy gradually increasing expenditure.

(5) To have independence and power.

(6) To accumulate business working capital.

(7) To bequeath a fortune.

(8) To satisfy "pure miserliness."

Use of the terms "objective" and "subjective" to categorize these and the foregoing factors was a rather unfortunate choice. Keynes clearly believed that the "subjective" factors were part of the general social background and could change with it only over long periods. The "objective" factors are, on the other hand, more volatile and hence the cause of observable short-run fluctuations. Even so, it is well to recall that Keynes was quite explicit in his opinion that even the "objective" factors were likely to have rather small impact on consumption and that the important aspect of his theory was the relationship between income and consumption.

The overwhelming popularity of the Keynesian reorientation of economic theory was due to several factors. Perhaps most important, the theory was expressly formulated to come to grips with the problem of unemployment, at a time when such a theory was badly needed. In addition, however, the theory easily lent itself to empirical research.

In the first place the Keynesian theory underscored, as the earlier theory did not, the immense practical importance of understanding what spending units did, in fact, do. Whereas the measurement of a particular demand curve is generally of rather limited interest and importance, the measurement of a consumption function could provide an important guide to general policy. At the same time, measurements of income and its expenditure components were becoming available and the Keynesian theory provided a framework for their analysis. Moreover the results of initial attempts showed great promise, as regression lines of consumption expenditure on income revealed a marginal propensity to consume of the predicted size (i.e., less than one) and a correlation very nearly perfect. This appeared to be ample empirical justification for the basic Keynesian thesis that although the determinants of consumer expenditure were complex, the essential single important factor was the level of real income.

The only essential difference between the Keynesian model and the older theory lies in the different restrictions placed on the utility function. Nevertheless there arises a rather subtle change in emphasis, the nature of which has until quite recently been overlooked, and the consequences of which may be far-reaching. Where the older theory concerned itself with the decisions of the spending unit with regard to demand for goods, and the supply of productive services, prices given, the Keynesian model deals almost exclusively with the decision of the spending unit with regard to the demand for consumption goods, prices and income being given. Since the Keynesian theory was propounded at a time of extensive unemployment, and was intended to focus its analytic power on this situation, this shift of emphasis passed without comment: Income was only too tragically effective as a constraint on family behavior. We shall argue later that this same assumption is of highly questionable applicability in the period of high postwar prosperity. The difference in the two assumptions has important consequences both for research methodology and for the interpretation of results.

Subsequent Development of Consumption Theory

The post Keynesian theory of consumption has developed along two main lines. Until quite recently the main effort was directed toward more precise formulation, extension, and elaboration of the Keynesian consumption function in which short-run variation in the level of consumer expenditure is primarily generated by short-run variation in spending unit incomes. Even the so-called Pigou effect, while it raises serious questions about the possibility of economic equilibrium below full employment, implies merely the inclusion of the real value of liquid assets with the other variables that determine consumption. More recently, however, a number of important non-Keynesian contributions to the theory of consumer behavior have moved in the direction of restoring a measure of autonomy to the spending unit and returning some attention to the longer-run aspects of the relationship of consumption to income.

Extension of the Keynesian Consumption Function

The result of actual research on the consumption function soon revealed that satisfactory explanation of consumer behavior would require a somewhat more complex formulation and would involve many variables besides income. Even if the principal interest is measurement of the effect of income variation on consumption, statistical efficiency requires that other factors be taken into account in the analysis. Moreover, when economists turned their attention away from the generalities of utility maximization to the specific problem of how spending units did--in fact--respond under specified circumstances, they began to realize the need for a more useful body of theory. As a result, variables other than those discussed by Keynes have been introduced, dynamic formulations of the function departing somewhat from that originally suggested have been discussed, and extensive empirical investigation has taken place. It goes without saying that these three developments have proceeded hand in hand and that the following attempt to make a rough separation is only an expository convenience.

Additional Variables

(1) Liquid assets. Although Keynes suggested that consumption might depend on capital gains and the price of real wealth, he appeared to neglect the direct effect of accumulation in the form of liquid assets. Inclusion of this variable gives rise to the "Pigou" effect. In essence the Pigou hypothesis is that, like consumption, the real value of liquid assets is subject to diminishing marginal utility. When, therefore, the stock of real purchasing power held in liquid form reaches a proper proportion to real income, the motive for further accumulation is removed, or diminished, and the level of consumption expenditure should rise. The importance of this factor for the theory of business fluctuations is familiar: If wages and prices are flexible and can fall in response to unemployment, the resulting deflation will raise the real value of the existing stock of liquid assets, stimulate consumption and tend to restore the level of employment. It was expected by some that the immediate postwar period would exhibit greatly expanded consumer demand on the part of spending units holding "hot" money and war-bonds, and the wartime accumulation of liquid assets has been referred to as a cause of the apparent upward shift of the U.S. consumption function over its prewar levels.

(2) The stock of wealth. A natural extension of the idea of including the real stock of liquid assets in the consumption function is to include the total real stock of wealth held by consumer units. The spending unit is then imagined as striving to maintain an optimum distribution of its resources among its stock of goods and claims to goods (shares), its real stock of liquid wealth, and the flow of goods for its consumption. It has been pointed out by Ackley (2) that the accumulation of wealth should account for a secular rise in the level of consumption, income given. This would, moreover, imply an apparent difference in the marginal propensity to consume as observed in the short run and in the long run.

(3) Consumer credit. The terms on which consumers are able to borrow, or to finance purchases by use of credit is a natural factor to include in the consumption function. As a monetary factor it will be dealt with in some detail in the following section.

(4) The distribution of income. The distribution of income may influence aggregate consumption expenditure in a number of ways.

(a) Since there is a presumption (and some evidence from cross-section data) that the consumption function is curvilinear (i.e., that the marginal propensity to consume declines with increasing income), a measure of over-all income inequality (e.g. the Pareto α or a similar measure) should exert a significant influence on consumption. Attempts made by Tinbergen (47), Staehle (45), and Pollack (42) to introduce such measures into the consumption function did not, however, prove notably successful.

(b) The functional distribution of income should also be a significant determination of consumption expenditure. Disaggregation of income into wages, farm income, and other property income by Tinbergen, Klein (21), and Klein and Goldberger (23) seeks to accomplish two objectives. First, since functional shares vary by income bracket, taking account of functional distribution makes some allowance for the curvature in the consumption function mentioned above. Secondly, the economic role of the several functional groups gives rise to differential savings-income behavior. For example, farmers and unincorporated businessmen are notable as relatively high savers, presumably because they have the opportunity--if not, indeed, the necessity--to invest directly in their own businesses. (cf. Friend and Kravis (15))

(c) In analyzing the relationship between consumption and income in cross-section data, Duesenberry (9) hypothesized that consumption expenditure may depend on the income rank of the spending unit. (Keeping-up-with the Joneses.) A similar hypothesis has been explored by Brady and Friedman (5).

(d) Finally it is clear that the consumption needs of spending units vary widely according to such factors as the stage of the life cycle attained, region of residence, race, educational attainment, number of children, number of wage earners, and so on. Representative of work in this area is that of Fisher (13), Klein and Mooney (25), and Lippett (29).

(5) Relative prices. There is a strong disposition on the part of economists to deal with the determination of consumer expenditure as a whole. In this view, relative prices merely distribute this total among particular items, and what is not spent on one thing is spent on something else. It is by no means clear that this is entirely correct; it may be that the total outlay of the spending unit is to some extent governed by the structure of prices. The question has been raised (Ackley and Suits (3)) but no empirical light has been shed on the problem.

Dynamic Factors

Keynesian theory was largely static, attempting to depict the behavior of spending units as of a given level of income, at a particular point in time. It is natural, however, to look at the problem from a dynamic point of view, and a number of dynamic or quasi-dynamic factors have been introduced into the consumption function.

(1) Time trend. The most primitive recognition of the dynamics of consumer behavior is the use of a time trend as part of the consumption function. Strictly speaking, of course, the passage of time does not influence the propensity to consume; time serves as a proxy variable for whatever factors may account for the general secular drift of consumer behavior. Its use may be justified on the ground that it permits more accurate measurement of the short-run impact of other factors in the absence of knowledge about the longer-run mechanism.

(2) The rate of increase in income. There is reason to suppose that two spending units with the same current income but with different previous incomes would behave differently. In particular we may suppose that a spending unit whose income is rising feels richer, more optimistic, and in general more inclined to spend than one experiencing a decline in income. This might be particularly the case if the current movement of income is taken as an indication of the future. On the other hand, as Keynes himself suggested, the spending unit may take time to adapt to its new level of income. In this case a spending unit with rising income would exhibit a lower level of consumer expenditure than would one with a falling income.

(3) Lagged income. It is sometimes argued that the decisions of the spending unit are based, not on current income, which is still in the process of being earned, but on past income, already received and available for expenditure. If this point of view is adopted, the income variable in the consumption function should be replaced by income lagged by some period. It may be argued, however, that while current consumption depends to some extent on past income, it is unrealistic to suppose it entirely unrelated to current income, particularly when rather long periods are involved. In this case, lagged income becomes a variable in addition to current income. It should be noted, moreover, that this is mathematically equivalent to use of the difference in income as a variable in addition to current income.[3]

---

[3]I.e., since $Y_{t-1} = Y_t - \Delta Y_t$, a consumption function of the form

$$C_t = aY_t + bY_{t-1} + C \tag{1}$$

can also be written as

$$C_t = (a+b)Y_t - b\Delta Y_t + C \tag{2}$$

But while (1) and (2) are mathematically identical, from a statistical point of view they are not. The high correlation of Y_t with Y_{t-1} may make impossible the accurate estimation of a and b in (1), while (2) poses no such problem.

(4) <u>Previous maximum income</u>. One of the most important contributions to the dynamic theory of consumer behavior were the attempts, made by Duesenberry (9) and Modigliani (32), to allow for some kind of learning process in consumption. According to their theories, a spending unit experiencing new levels of income is relatively cautious in expanding its consumption horizon and exhibits a rather low marginal propensity to consume. When, however, income sinks below levels which the spending unit has experienced, the spending unit clings to its higher standard of living, and consumption expenditures fall less than they have risen, giving rise to a "ratchet" effect. Recovery of income to the old level is accompanied by rapid restoration of the old consumption pattern. Further income increases, however, are accompanied by a return to a more cautious expansion of the standard of living. This ratchet effect can be approximated by including the previous maximum income as a separate variable in the consumption function. A somewhat improved result was obtained by Brown (6) who substituted the previous maximum level of consumption in place of previous maximum income.

(5) <u>Lagged consumption</u>. The use of previous maxima of either income or consumption is subject to the objection that the effect of a maximum, once attained, will persist indefinitely. The theory, in short, encompasses consumer learning, but not forgetting. To permit some reversal of the habituation process, some sort of decay coefficient must be assigned to the previous maximum. The use of lagged consumption by Klein (21), and Klein and Goldberger (23), and others can be considered equivalent to the use of a high speed reversible habituation effect.

Unless considerable care is taken in the analysis of data, however, the apparent influence of lagged consumption is subject to misinterpretation. In the first place since lagged consumption is highly correlated with lagged income, the introduction of lagged consumption may merely re-introduce lagged income in a disguised form. In the second place, it is well known that residuals from the consumption function are autocorrelated; another way of saying this is that the level of the observed consumption function tends to shift from time to time due to the influence of unknown factors not introduced in the analysis. Therefore, as Ackley (1) has pointed out, the role of lagged consumption may merely be that of continually correcting the level of the function for the effect of these unobserved factors.

Finally, it is clear that the short-run effect of past consumer expenditure depends on what was purchased. Since a durable good yields service over a long period of time, its purchase during one year tends to preclude another purchase the next. This influence is clearly distinguishable in certain markets. For example a substantial part of the marked year-to-year variation in automobile demand appears to be associated with their durability. (cf. Suits (46)) Again it should be noted, however, that while the existing stock of durable goods clearly influences the composition of expenditure, it is not so clear that it exercises any substantial influence on the total.

Non-Keynesian Modifications of the Theory of the Consumption Function

The foregoing modifications represent more or less straightforward extensions of the Keynesian thesis that the consumer sector is essentially incapable of acting independently as an economic prime mover. Much of the opposition to the Keynesian position arose in connection with this point. (cf. Burns (7)) It is probably going too far to identify the following important modern developments in consumer theory as "anti-Keynesian," but in view of their emphasis on the autonomy of consumer behavior they are surely "non-Keynesian."

(1) Consumer attitudes. The importance placed on consumer psychology by Katona (17), (18), (37), Mueller (36), and others is a direct restoration of a measure of autonomy to the consumer. To quote directly, the neglect of consumer attitudes "has often been justified by the assumption that consumer spending and saving are governed primarily by income, past and present, and that income fluctuations are determined by forces beyond the power of the consumer ... The postwar period has provided ample evidence that such views are one-sided in our economy in which consumers have high incomes and high asset holdings."[4]

The importance of consumer psychology is two-fold. First, a high level of income and assets gives the consumer room to maneuver on his own. His activity can generate economic disturbances or can counteract contraction or expansion in other parts of the economy. Secondly, the response that is elicited by any given policy is itself conditioned by consumer attitudes.

Katona and Mueller (39) express the relationship between purchase of durable goods and consumer attitudes by a regression

$$D = .135(Y_{-1}) + .412(A_1) - 39.727 \qquad (R^2 = .93)$$
$$\quad\;\; (.009) \qquad\quad (.044)$$

where D is consumer durable goods expenditure during the six months following a survey, Y_{-1} disposable personal income during the six months preceding the survey, and A_1 is the Survey Research Center Index of Consumer Attitudes. The study is based on 17 surveys covering the period November 1952 to May 1960. Not only does

---

[4]Katona and Mueller (37) p. 1.

this represent a close fit to the data (as shown by the value of R^2 and the standard errors of the coefficient estimates) but more important for the present purpose, an impressive part of the explanatory power of the equation lies in the attitudes index. Indeed almost all of the quarter to quarter variation in durable purchases is associated with attitudes; the effect of income is little more than a rising trend over the period. (cf. p. 39)

(2) Income status and the permanent income hypothesis. The second important modification of the theory of consumer behavior is to relate spending unit behavior not to the immediate level of income, but to the unit's income status in some more permanent sense. Several versions of such a hypothesis have been suggested, most familiarly by Milton Friedman (14).

According to Friedman, the consumption status of a spending unit, which he denotes as "permanent consumption," is a function of its income status or "permanent income." The consumption expenditure of a spending unit as observed over any particular period of time will differ in random fashion from its true permanent consumption due to such factors as timing of outlays for lumpy durables, vacations, the impact of emergencies, and similar causes.

In the same way over short periods the observed level of income will differ from the permanent level due to timing of receipts, fluctuations in economic conditions, etc. Moreover, it is hypothesized that there is no correlation between the deviations of observed income and consumption from their (unobserved) permanent levels.

When we lengthen the period over which changes are investigated, the short-run factors begin to smooth out and reveal underlying relationships of a more permanent sort. Thus whereas quarterly variation in consumer expenditure consists largely of "noise," annual data indicate some measure of systematic response. There is considerable evidence now being accumulated that periods considerably longer than a year are of importance in accounting for consumer behavior.

The permanent income hypothesis is a specific formulation of the relationship between expected values of income and consumption. Each spending unit is taken to have a time-pattern of expected income. This time pattern specifies an expected value for income for each period as a function of such personal and demographic factors as education, occupation, skill, race, region, etc., as well as such things as the level of productivity, expected economic events, etc.

The expected time-pattern of consumption is then a function of the expected income pattern. The expected value of consumption at any particular time is a function of the expected value of income at

that time, the life cycle stage of the spending unit, its size and so on.
Neither the expected value of income nor of consumption are directly
observable since they differ from actual current receipts and expenditures in a number of ways. Current income fluctuates around
its permanent level from many causes. In addition to the accidents
of timing, there are such factors as windfalls, losses, etc. Similarly,
the expected level of consumption differs from current outlay because of lumpy purchase of durables, the impact of accidents, illness, etc.

The relationship specified for the consumption function is that
the expected level of consumption is a constant proportion of the
level of permanent income regardless of the level of the latter. The
proportion varies with the ratio of wealth to income, the composition,
and stage in the life cycle of the spending unit.

Formally stated, the permanent income hypothesis is expressed
as

$$C_p = k(i, w, u)Y_p$$

where C_p represents the expected value of consumption; i, the rate
of interest at which the spending unit can borrow; w, the ratio of
nonhuman wealth to income; while u represents a number of other
factors including life cycle status, spending unit tastes, etc.

This relationship can be explored empirically in a number of
ways. In terms of cross-section analysis, it implies that, current
income given, spending unit consumption should depend on the age
and stage of development of the spending unit, race, region, occupation, etc. Extensive testing yields results in substantial agreement
with theory. In time series analysis, the theory predicts a long-run
consumption function in which consumer expenditure is a constant
proportion of income. At the same time since permanent income is
much less volatile than observed income, the short-run marked
fluctuations in observed income are accompanied by less than proportional changes in consumption, yielding the appearance of a
marginal propensity to consume below the long-run average.

Exploration of similar hypotheses, undertaken by Modigliani
and Brumberg (33) and by Watts (48), both relying primarily on
cross-section data, provide general corroboratory evidence that the
behavior of spending units depends on long-run income expectations.

The objections raised to the permanent income hypothesis are
directed at the specific formulation of the theory, rather than at
the basic proposition that behavior must be studied in terms of a
time period longer than a year. Having given only a very brief
presentation of the theory it would be inappropriate to expound at

length on the argument. There are, however, several cogent points which require comment.

(a) In terms of the theory, consumption is defined in terms of actual using up of wealth; a disposition to save the transitory component of income may actually reflect itself in the act of expenditure for durable goods, education, and similar objects of (human or non-human) wealth; thus there may still exist a relationship between current income and current consumption expenditure as usually defined.

(b) In any case it is clear that the extent to which consumption can be sustained during periods of unemployment and low income is subject to the constraint of current income and assets. This may imply the need for an asymmetrical theory, e.g., that behavior during a depression is subject to different constraints than that during a period of full employment and prosperity.

(c) Finally a direct test of the effect of a windfall on consumption expenditure has been published by Bodkin (4). Since the National Service Life Insurance dividends of 1950 constituted an unexpected windfall to the receivers, he could analyze the BLS 1950 Survey of Consumer Expenditures data to assess the effect of this dividend on expenditures during the year. Analysis of the data showed a regression coefficient of 0.97 for the windfall dividend as compared to a figure of 0.75 for family income after taxes. When expenditure on nondurable goods only was considered, the respective regression coefficients are 0.72 and 0.56. The coefficient on the windfall is in each case highly significant statistically, and the conclusion is unmistakable that windfalls tend to increase the level of consumption expenditure and that this increase is not confined to durable goods.

(3) Economic status. The final modification of the concept of the consumption function represents at least a partial denial of the consumption function itself, and a return toward something nearer the classical model of consumer behavior. The essential feature of the consumption function is the role of income as a constraint on, rather than an aspect of, behavior. In the context of unemployment and depression it is clear that income may usefully be treated as a behavioral constraint: Consumption is limited by the extent to which the spending unit succeeds in marketing its labor services. But, however important this may be during a period of serious unemployment, it is dangerous to consider it a general case. For during periods of prosperity and full employment, many spending units are free to offer more or less labor services and hence, within limits, to determine their own incomes. The behavior of the spending unit results in the selection of both a volume of consumption expenditure and a level of income, and the fact that one spending unit has a high standard of consumption expenditure (or saving, or

both) may result in, rather than from, the fact that it has a higher total income.

The secular aspects of this point of view have been beautifully expressed by Ruth P. Mack (31). Moreover there is increasing evidence that even in the relative short run, spending units have considerable choice over their own incomes. There are many vehicles for this behavior. The wife can take or leave a job, the individual wage earners can work harder, opting for overtime, taking extra pay in lieu of vacation, or even working on more than one job.

At the present time between 30 and 40 percent of married women are engaged in at least half-time employment. A Bureau of Census study made during March 1957 showed that of the wives whose husbands had full-time employment, 32.4 percent were in the labor force and about 25 percent were employed.[5]

Although working wives are found in spending units at all income levels, there is a clear inverse correlation between husband's income and the wife's employment status. In fact Sobel (44) has shown that in discriminating statistically between wives who are employed and those who are not, the importance of husband's income is second only to whether there are children under six years old. This inverse correlation suggests that wives tend to take employment when the family "needs the money." But this is merely another way of saying that the family consumption standard cannot be maintained without the wife's income, i.e. that the consumption standard is an important determinant of family income.

Reasons for working given by a random sample of 672 working wives studied by Sobel ran overwhelmingly to financial reasons. Of 862 responses (some women gave two), 307 involved chronic or temporary financial difficulties, and 302 involved the desire to acquire a new asset of some kind--generally consumers' durable goods.

Special efforts by the family to raise its income are sometimes induced by special events. The entrance of a child into college is an important example. Lansing, Lorimer, and Moriguchi (26) report that of a random sample of 338 families with a child in college, 27 percent reported additional work by family members (other than the student himself) to help meet expenses. In about two-thirds of the cases the wife went to work or worked more, in about one-third the husband took another job or worked more.

The employed individual is often free to work on more than one job. The present day work week of roughly 40 hours leaves spare

---

[5]See bibliography no. 10.

time in which additional earnings can be made. During July 1957, over 5 percent of all employed persons held more than one job. Two-thirds of these were full-time employees on at least one of the jobs.[6]

Finally the individual is free within limits to select the kind of employment he wants. Since these often differ substantially in income, the choice of occupation involves to some extent a choice of income. Again, there is little data available on the extent to which such choices can be exercised. We may, however, note that a substantial portion of the staff of any university consists of men and women who remain despite competing opportunities of employment offering substantially higher (not infrequently double or triple) earnings. Many small business proprietors prefer the independence and status of their occupation to the more certain--and often greater --rewards of an employee's position.

The quantitative importance of this aspect of the relationship between consumption and income is an open question. But it is clear that we cannot rely on a model that treats income exclusively as if it consisted of lottery winnings, visited willy-nilly on the spending unit, sweeping all economic behavior before it. To the extent that the association observed between consumption and income is an empirical relationship between two aspects of a single behavior pattern, its bearing on the economic impact of monetary policy, government expenditure, or business investment plans is not clearly defined.

In particular the consequences for the usual multiplier analysis are most serious: To the extent that steps (e.g. tax reduction) taken to raise incomes result in moderating pressure on the spending unit to produce, they may be offset by reduced earning effort. Incomes and consumption will rise less than would be expected from the multiplier analysis.

IV. EMPIRICAL INVESTIGATION OF THE CONSUMPTION FUNCTION

Before embarking on an examination of the statistical analysis of the consumption function, an important and all too often overlooked point must be made. The consumption function is taken to be a relationship between income--as cause--and consumer expenditure-- as a result. This relationship implies a positive correlation between income and consumption, but the converse is not true: The existence of a positive correlation between income and consumption does not validate the causal relationship. The fact is that income, the total

---

[6]See bibliography no. 40.

of consumption and savings, is necessarily correlated with its part.
Moreover, since aggregate consumption constitutes about 90 percent
of aggregate income, we should predict that the correlation between
income and consumption should be somewhere around 0.9 even if
consumption and saving were random variables.[7] This spurious
correlation gives rise to the now familiar least-squares bias in
the estimate of the consumption function. But a more important fact
is that it leads to the impression of a more uniform responsiveness
of consumption to income that is, in fact, the case.

The hypothesis of the consumption function implies more than
merely a correlation between income and consumption, or--by the
same token--a correlation between income and saving. Such correlations would follow directly from the definition of income and are,
to that extent, trivial. More carefully stated, the hypothesis of the
consumption function implies that an increase in income is associated with <u>simultaneous</u> increases in both consumption and saving.
That is, that consumption and saving are not independent random
variables but are themselves positively correlated, and it is the
relationship between saving and consumption that is properly of
primary interest in the study of the consumption function.

The importance of this point is illustrated by the accompanying
figures. In Figure I-1 we have the scatter diagram of aggregate consumer expenditure on disposable income. A glance is sufficient to
assure us that the correlation between the two is well over .9, and
highly significant. Although the postwar level is perhaps somewhat
higher than the prewar, the slopes of the relation in the two periods
are the same. There is a clear impression of highly regular behavior, and it is easy to imagine that we have here a theory of consumer expenditure nearly completely drawn.

----

[7]It is easily shown that if consumption and saving were independent
random variables with variances σ_c^2 and σ_s^2, the correlation of consumption with income would be given by

$$r^2 = \frac{1}{1 + \dfrac{\sigma_s^2}{\sigma_c^2}}$$

Even if the variance of consumption were only four times the variance of saving, the correlation would be 0.9.

The spurious nature of the correlation of consumption with income has been noted among others by Katona (17). Considerable
emphasis is given the point by Ackley (1), pp. 233 ff.

FIGURE I-1

Real Disposable Income and Consumption 1929-1960
(Units are billions of 1954 dollars)

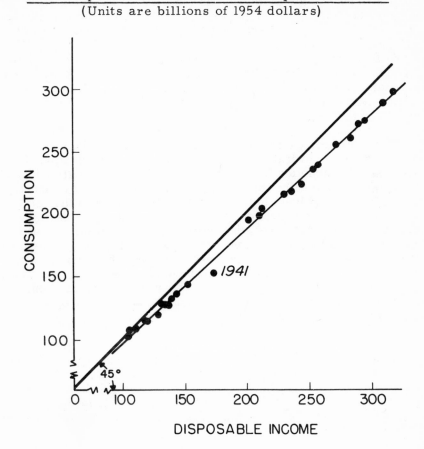

Quite a different impression is gained from Figure I-2. In the scatter between consumer expenditure and saving there remains an obvious tendency for saving and consumption to move together, but clearly the important components of an adequate theory are still missing. The apparent regularity of the prewar period is considerably less than before, while the postwar data indicate very little more than a long-run tendency for saving and consumption to grow together. Indeed, during the ten year period 1951-60 consumption expenditure increased at a steady trend of about $6 billion per year while saving oscillated between $18 and $20 billion in an apparently unrelated fashion.

The direct comparison of consumer expenditure with income can be avoided in several ways. In his extensive examination of the aggregate consumption function, Ferber (11) studied regressions of saving on income rather than regressions of consumption on income. Although this is subject to the same theoretical bias as the relation of consumption with income, the actual correlation of saving with income is somewhat lower, thus reducing somewhat the misleading appearance of the results. Duesenberry (9) avoided the problem by focusing attention on the relationship between the level of income and the percent of income saved. The percent saved is, of course, ultimately determined by the ratio of saving to consumption, and hence is definitionally free of the spurious statistical properties of the consumption-income correlation.

Klein and Goldberger (23) and others have retained the form of the consumption-income relationship, but have employed consistent statistical methods for the estimation of the parameters. A special case of this procedure is that used by Zellner (49) in some of his calculations in which the relation of consumption to income is calculated via a reduced form which actually consists of the regression of consumption on saving.

Summary of Results

The empirical examination of a number of alternative formulations of the aggregate consumption function may be largely summarized by reference to two important studies. Ferber (11) fitted regressions corresponding to a number of alternative hypotheses, using annual data for the period 1923-40, and tested the ability of each to predict the magnitude of consumption for the postwar years 1947-49. He also examined the effect of fitting the functions to different time periods.

In order to minimize the effect of spurious correlation between income and its parts, Ferber substituted saving in place of consumption as the dependent variable in the relations he studied. All told, seven basic alternative formulations of the regression of sav-

FIGURE I-2

Real Consumption and Saving 1929-1960
(Units are billions of 1954 dollars)

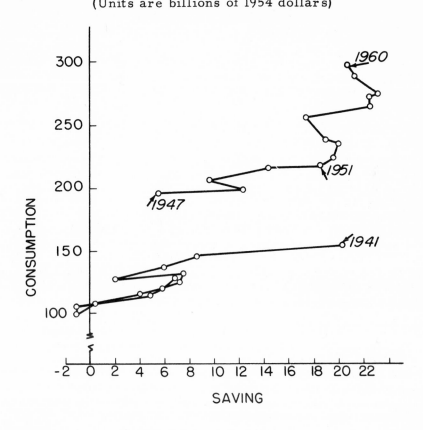

ings on income were analyzed, each being fitted to data for several different periods. The basic formulations involved:

Saving as a function of:

(A) Current income;
(B) Current and lagged income;
(C) Current income and population;
(D) Current income and time trend;
(E) Current and lagged income and time trend.

Ratio of saving to income as a function of:

(F) Ratio of previous peak income to present income;[8]
(G) Ratio of current to previous peak income.

Several variations of these formulations were fitted to data for three periods: 1923-40; 1929-40 and 1923-30; 1935-40. The results were compared as to goodness of fit and as to ability to predict the early postwar years. Interestingly enough, none of the equations provided an accurate forecast of the postwar level of consumer expenditure or saving, despite the fact that correlation coefficients ran well over .9 for many.

The most accurate postwar predictions were those of form (F) and (G), which involved a Duesenberry-type dynamic formulation of the consumption function. These estimates involved absolute errors of 10 to 20 percent. All of the more successful predictions involved some dynamic factors. Nondynamic formulations were notably poorer.

Two conclusions emerge rather clearly from the study. (1) Some recognition of the dynamics of consumer behavior is required if a theory of consumption is to do anything more than merely produce high correlations with past observations. (2) There is an observable difference in behavior of consumers in the postwar period and the prewar period which cannot be imputed to any of the factors investigated.

---

[8]In Ferber's formulation the variable appeared as the difference between present and previous peak income expressed as a fraction of present income. This is, of course, a linear function of the ratio of previous peak to current income, and the real force to the comparison of (F) and (G) is that the independent variable in one is the reciprocal of that in the other. Over the observed range this implies only slight differences in curvature and it is not surprising that the two formulas are about equally reliable.

The second extensive exploration of the behavior of aggregate time series is that of Zellner (49), covering the postwar years 1947-54, using quarterly data. His study followed Ferber in exploring a number of alternative formulations of the consumption function, quarterly consumer expenditures being expressed as a regression on various combinations of variables drawn from among:

(1) Current personal disposable income;
(2) Personal disposable income lagged one quarter;
(3) Previous peak disposable income;
(4) Consumption expenditure lagged one quarter;
(5) Past peak consumption expenditure;
(6) Liquid assets, beginning of the quarter.

Each regression was fitted to the period 1947,QI-1955,QI, with 1950,QIII and 1955,QII omitted. Data were seasonally adjusted.

The results were evaluated by reference to three main criteria:

(a) regression coefficients should agree in sign with a priori expectation, and
(b) should differ significantly from zero.
(c) Residuals should not be autocorrelated. In addition, the performance of each was checked against a naive model. Since the results involve a liquid asset variable, it is useful to reproduce them in some detail in the accompanying table.

The equations were all fitted by least squares except for (1a) and (2a) which were derived from regressions of consumption on saving: equation (1a') and (2a'). The regressions appear in the accompanying table.

At first sight Zellner's equations appear to indicate a wide dispersion of results. The coefficient on Y, disposable income, for example, varies from .747 in (1) to .128 in (3), depending on what other variables are included in the equation. In fact, however, there is much greater consistency than appears.

When a lagged value of income or consumption is included in the equation, its effect must be taken into account in estimating the marginal propensity to consume. For example, in equation (9), the coefficient of income of equation (1) is simply divided between current and lagged income. In an equilibrium position (i.e. $Y = Y_{-1} = Y^{\circ}$) the coefficient on income in (9) would be .756 as compared with .747 in (1). Similar results are obtainable from equations (7), (8), and (10).

The equations including lagged (C_{-1}) or previous maximum (C°) consumption can also be converted into an equilibrium form by setting $C = C_{-1} = C^\circ$ and solving for C. A marginal propensity to consume thus estimated from equation (4) for example is .753, and a similar result is obtainable from (6). Among the ten equations only (3) and (5) are really out of line. These imply a marginal propensity to consume of over .9.

It is interesting to compare the Zellner results with those of Klein and Goldberger.

The consumption function in the Klein-Goldberger model covering 1929-52 appears in the following form:

$$C_t = -34.5 + 0.62(W_1 + W_2 - T_w) + 0.46(P - S_p - T_p) + 0.39(A - T_a)$$

$$+ 0.23C_{t-1} + 0.024L_{t-1} + 0.36N_p$$

where $(W_1 + W_2 - T_w)$, $(P - S_p - T_p)$, and $(A - T_a)$ are, respectively, disposable wage, property, and agricultural income, L_{t-1} is liquid assets at the beginning of the year and N_p is population.

The coefficient on lagged consumption is 0.23, about half the value obtained in the corresponding Zellner equations (4) and (6). On the other hand, the weighted average of the three marginal propensities to consume given by the Klein-Goldberger function is about 0.57, somewhat larger than the magnitudes obtained by Zellner. Nevertheless, when the Klein-Goldberger equation is solved for the equilibrium consumption value we obtain an estimated marginal propensity to consume equal to .740, in clear general agreement with the Zellner results.

In striking contrast to this, it is clear that the liquid asset effect as measured by Zellner for the postwar period is about ten times larger than that derived from the longer period covered by the Klein-Goldberger function. Zellner speculated that this may be due to the fact that the Klein-Goldberger function is heavily weighted by the prewar period and hence that the difference in results reflects a postwar shift in the role of liquid assets. This conjecture is substantiated by the direct comparison of prewar and postwar regressions made below.

In three respects both the Zellner and the Klein-Goldberger equations leave something to be desired. First, since they were produced early, they necessarily cover relatively little of the postwar experience. Secondly, although many alternative formulations were tried, and alternative techniques were used, the real role of the dynamic variables is not brought out. Finally, although fitted to quarterly data, even the Zellner equations fail to provide satisfactory estimates of truly "short-run" behavior, but--as we shall show--apply to annual or larger periods.

TABLE I-1

Zellner's Estimates of Short-Run Consumption Functions*

Estimate (figures in parentheses are standard errors)	R^2
(1) $C = 38.09 + 0.747\ Y$ (0.033)	.944
(1a) $C = 63.53 + 0.620\ Y$	---
(1a') $C = 167.19 + 1.632\ S$ (0.346)	.778
(2) $C = -21.19 + 0.708\ Y + 0.368\ L_{-1}$ (0.021) (0.054)	.979
(2a) $C = -18.52 + 0.665\ Y + 0.396\ L_{-1}$	---
(2a') $C = -55.28 + 1.985\ S + 1.182\ L_{-1}$ (0.216) (0.166)	.784
(3) $C = 0.10 + 0.128\ Y + 0.870\ C_{-1}$ (0.093) (0.127)	.978
(4) $C = -18.96 + 0.375\ Y + 0.489\ C_{-1} + 0.2196\ L_{-1}$ (0.110) (0.160) (0.067)	.984
(5) $C = .35 + 0.165\ Y + 0.825\ C^{\circ}$ (0.112) (0.156)	.971
(6) $C = -23.02 + 0.458\ Y + 0.369\ C^{\circ} + 0.272\ L_{-1}$ (0.114) (0.165) (0.165)	.982
(7) $C = 30.37 + 0.417\ Y + 0.369\ Y^{\circ}$ (0.157) (0.172)	.950
(8) $C = -22.58 + 0.532\ Y + 0.199\ Y^{\circ} + 0.347\ L_{-1}$ (0.099) (0.110) (0.051)	.981
(9) $C = 36.52 + 0.553\ Y + 0.203\ Y_{-1}$ (0.172) (0.176)	.944
(10) $C = -21.96 + 0.582\ Y + 0.133\ Y_{-1} + 0.362\ L_{-1}$ (0.104) (0.108) (0.052)	.979

*Adapted from Zellner (49) Table II, p. 560. Symbols have the following meanings: C = consumption; Y = income; S = savings; L = liquid assets; superscript o indicates previous peak, subscript -1 indicates one quarter lag.

In the following sections the earlier empirical work will be extended to include more recent data. When this is done, the role of lagged consumption can be explored by disaggregation of the consumption function. Finally the behavior of the relationship in the very short run will be examined.

The Consumption Function, 1948-1959

The regression of consumption expenditure on disposable personal income, liquid assets held by households, and lagged consumption expenditure, fitted to annual data for the years 1948-59 is

$$(S_1) \quad C = .837\ Y + .313\ L_{-1} - .122\ C_{-1} - 10.133 \qquad (R^2 = .9999)$$
$$(.053) \quad\ (.042) \qquad (.064)$$

All variables are measured in billions of 1954 dollars.

The high coefficient on income and the high value of R^2 both result from the least squares bias mentioned above. Nevertheless, when interpreted in terms of an equilibrium level of consumption expenditure, as was done above, the marginal propensity to consume becomes .746, a figure quite comparable to those discovered earlier. It is, however, surprising to find a negative coefficient associated with lagged consumption.

The bias in the analysis can be reduced and the estimate greatly improved by casting the regression in first differences. When this is done we find

$$(S_2) \quad \Delta C = .528\ \Delta Y + .549\ \Delta L_{-1} - .432\ \Delta C_{-1} + 3.948 \qquad (R^2 = .92)$$
$$(.085) \qquad (.082) \qquad\ (.098)$$

The use of first differences serves to increase even further the apparent retarding effect of past on present consumption.

The source of this influence is easily seen when the consumption function is disaggregated. For this purpose total consumer expenditure is broken down into four components: Automobiles and Parts (A), Other Durables (D), Non Durables (ND), and Services (S). It is at once apparent that the role of lagged expenditure is not the same in all four components. As has been amply demonstrated elsewhere, the current demand for automobiles is heavily influenced by the number of cars already on the road. Last year's purchases, by adding to the stock, act as a depressant on current sales. A similar argument applies--with less force--to the market for other durables. The older argument for the "ratchet" effect of past consumption applies in the short run only to nondurables and services.

Regression equations fitted to these four components are shown in Table I-2. The variables are expressed in first differences with the exception of the dynamic factors in the Automobile and Other

TABLE I-2

Disaggregated Consumption Equations: Postwar*

		R^2
Automobiles	$\Delta A = .194\ \Delta Y + .220\ \Delta L_{-1} - .551\ A_{-1} + 5.042$ $\qquad\quad (.075) \qquad (.075) \qquad\quad (.136)$	.74
Other Durables	$\Delta D = .178\ \Delta Y + .0709\ \Delta L_{-1} - .0391\ D_{-1} - .363$ $\qquad\quad (.067) \qquad (.016) \qquad\quad (.034)$	.95
Non Durables	$\Delta ND = .207\ \Delta Y + .146\ \Delta L_{-1} + .299\ \Delta ND_{-1} - .085$ $\qquad\quad (.056) \qquad (.060) \qquad\quad (.150)$	.68
Services	$\Delta S = .108\ \Delta Y + .0447\ \Delta L_{-1} + .601\ \Delta S_{-1} + .413$ $\qquad\quad (.028) \qquad (.028) \qquad\quad (.153)$	.76
Total (summed)	$\Delta C = .687\ \Delta Y + .482\ \Delta L_{-1} + \ldots + 5.007$	

*Fitted in first differences to annual data, 1948–59; all variables measured in billions of 1954 dollars.

TABLE I-3

Disaggregated Consumption Equations: Prewar*

		R^2
Automobiles	$\Delta A = .0893\ \Delta Y + .0199\ \Delta L_{-1} - .401\ A_{-1} + 1.243$ $\qquad\quad (.008) \qquad (.0177) \qquad\quad (.076)$	.93
Other Durables	$\Delta D = .0967\ \Delta Y + .0403\ \Delta L_{-1} - .0928\ D_{-1} + .484$ $\qquad\quad (.008) \qquad (.0174) \qquad\quad (.057)$	.93
Non Durables	$\Delta ND = .247\ \Delta Y - .0251\ \Delta L_{-1} + .164\ \Delta ND_{-1} + .870$ $\qquad\quad (.065) \qquad (.132) \qquad\quad (.193)$	.79
Services	$\Delta S = .130\ \Delta Y - .004\ \Delta L_{-1} + .220\ \Delta S_{-1} - .166$ $\qquad\quad (.0265) \qquad (.0501) \qquad\quad (.475)$	.87
Total (summed)	$\Delta C = .563\ \Delta Y + .0311\ \Delta L_{-1} + \ldots + 2.431$	

*Fitted in first differences to annual data, 1930–41; all variables measured in billions of 1954 dollars.

Durables equations. In these equations the lagged volume of expenditure itself is used, representing the accumulation of stock. It is clear that the dynamic effect of accumulating stocks of automobiles and other durables is the source of the negative coefficient on lagged consumption expenditure.

Disaggregation of the function also highlights the importance of automobile demand in the short-run behavior of total consumption. The coefficient on liquid assets is larger in this equation than in any other—indeed almost as large as the other three combined—despite the fact that expenditure for automobiles constitutes only about 5 percent of total consumption. In addition, the constant term—which in a first difference equation measures the trend—constitutes virtually the entire trend in the postwar level of consumer expenditure.

When the four coefficients on income and on liquid assets respectively are summed, we obtain an estimate of the relationship of aggregate consumption to these variables. The marginal propensity to consume, thus estimated, agrees well with other results, although it cannot be readily adjusted as was done above. The coefficient on liquid assets is somewhat higher than those given by Zellner, largely because of the difference in period.

Prewar vs. Postwar

Similar regressions fitted to the prewar period 1929-41 appear in Table I-3. Although the importance of the automobile sector is again apparent, the most striking feature of the comparison is the fact that the coefficients on the liquid asset term in the equations are only about a tenth of their postwar magnitudes, and in the case of nondurables and services are even negative!

One possible explanation of this apparent shift in the coefficient might be an interaction between income and liquid assets. To explore this possibility the liquid asset variable was replaced by an income-liquid asset interaction. The results appear in Table I-4. The primary effect of the introduction of the interaction term is to transfer some of the instability of the liquid assets coefficient to the coefficient on income alone. The sign reversal observed for the liquid assets coefficient is likewise observed for the interaction term. On the other hand, the pre- and postwar equations for automobile expenditure are brought very close together, and it is here that the liquid asset effect is apparently largest. The results obtained from the interaction term must however be pronounced promising but inconclusive.

Long Run and Short Run[9]

In the discussion of long-run and short-run effects two things are sometimes confused: the nature of the problem under investigation,

---

[9] This section is largely an extension of the ideas suggested by Ackley (1), Ch. XI.

TABLE I-4

Disaggregated Consumption Functions with Income-Liquid Asset Interaction

Postwar

Automobile

$$\Delta A = .041 \; \Delta Y + .077 \; \frac{\Delta (L_{-1} Y)}{100} - .320 \; A_{-1} + 2.137$$
$$\quad\quad (.074) \quad\quad (.027) \quad\quad\quad (.143)$$

Other Durables

$$\Delta D = .136 \; \Delta Y + .022 \; \frac{\Delta (L_{-1} Y)}{100} - .023 \; D_{-1} - .655$$
$$\quad\quad (.027) \quad\quad (.007) \quad\quad\quad (.040)$$

Non Durables

$$\Delta ND = .105 \; \Delta Y + .052 \; \frac{\Delta (L_{-1} Y)}{100} + .299 \; \Delta ND_{-1} - .114$$
$$\quad\quad (.084) \quad\quad (.021) \quad\quad\quad (.149)$$

Services

$$\Delta S = .070 \; \Delta Y + .017 \; \frac{\Delta (L_{-1} Y)}{100} + .562 \; \Delta S_{-1} + .547$$
$$\quad\quad (.038) \quad\quad (.010) \quad\quad\quad (.156)$$

Prewar

Automobiles

$$\Delta A = .072 \; \Delta Y + .084 \; \frac{\Delta (L_{-1} Y)}{100} - .407 \; A_{-1} + .883$$
$$\quad\quad (.004) \quad\quad (.015) \quad\quad\quad (.076)$$

Other Durables

$$\Delta D = .061 \; \Delta Y + .040 \; \frac{\Delta (L_{-1} Y)}{100} - .108 \; D_{-1} + .563$$
$$\quad\quad (.013) \quad\quad (.015) \quad\quad\quad (.056)$$

Non Durables

$$\Delta ND = .271 \; \Delta Y - .036 \; \frac{\Delta (L_{-1} Y)}{100} + .177 \; \Delta ND_{-1} + .951$$
$$\quad\quad (.079) \quad\quad (.121) \quad\quad\quad (.200)$$

Services

$$\Delta S = .134 \; \Delta Y - .006 \; \frac{\Delta (L_{-1} Y)}{100} + .224 \; \Delta S_{-1} - .150$$
$$\quad\quad (.032) \quad\quad (.045) \quad\quad\quad (.157)$$

and the nature of the data employed. It is possible to use quarterly data and still analyze a very long-run consumption function. The data set a lower limit to the "length of run" that can be investigated —the Kuznets estimates for decades cannot be used to investigate quarterly variations in consumption—but they do not, of themselves, set an upper limit. A regression fitted directly to annual, quarterly or even monthly data for the period 1865 to the present would yield results essentially no different from that obtained from decade averages. When we use a time span covering nearly a hundred years, the regression analysis is going to be most sensitive to the big over-all changes, to the general drift of the data and not to the rel- atively minor differences between one year and the next. The analysis of the short run can only be carried out by an analytical technique that will focus on the short run and suppress the long-run phenomena.

It does not follow, of course, that when we do this the result is, in fact, a short-run behavioral relation. It may be that the relationship is _only_ one between very broad movements. In the short run the phenomena may be largely dominated by random movements. The actual measurement of any economic flow is necessarily an average over some period of time. The shorter the period, the more complex are the problems of measurement. In the first place, it may be difficult to obtain a useful definition of the variable over short periods. What do we mean, for example, by the disposable income of a family on a "daily" basis? In the second place, the shorter the period taken, the more important becomes the timing of specific events. Expenditure varies according to whether the housewife goes shopping today or tomorrow, whether the vacation is taken this month or next month, whether the new car is bought this year or next year. It is only in terms of the regularities of averages over long periods that economic relationships become meaningful.

This much is clear, but it is by no means clear how short the minimum meaningful period actually is. To attempt literally to relate today's income to today's consumption expenditure—supposing they could be usefully defined and measured—is quite useless. A day or a week is too short a period in terms of the habits, horizons and expectations of spending units. Variations in the data over such short periods involve largely random fluctuations around a mean value determined by longer-run forces. The magnitude of an economic variable can be expressed in terms of a long-run average, and a short-run deviation therefrom. In the particular case of income and consumption, the values observed over a particular short period t can be expressed as $\bar{Y}_t + y_t$ and $\bar{C}_t + c_t$ where $\bar{Y}_t$ and $\bar{C}_t$ are the average rates over some longer period, and y_t and c_t are the deviation of the observed values of the short period from the longer period averages.

We can then restate the foregoing proposition by saying that we can discover useful laws relating $\bar{Y}_t$ and $\bar{C}_t$ over long periods but that for the periods shorter than this, c_t and y_t are not causally related to each other nor to $\bar{C}_t$ and $\bar{Y}_t$. This is the starting point of Friedman's permanent income hypothesis as it must be of any useful theoretical analysis. The important questions then become: How long a period must be taken to obtain meaningful stable relationships? What is the form of the relationship? What are the relevant variables?

The preponderance of evidence is that over periods as long as a quarter, observed consumption expenditure is highly independent of income. To explore this phenomenon we must adopt a technique which focuses the analysis, so far as possible, on the quarterly deviations c_t and y_t, rather than on the longer-run averages $\bar{C}_t$ and $\bar{Y}_t$. There are three ways this can be done:

(1) Since the $\bar{C}_t$ and $\bar{Y}_t$ components of observed consumption and income are slow to change, quarterly first differences will consist primarily in the quarterly differences in the short-term deviations. Thus analysis of first differences provides a ready mechanism for suppressing the longer-run averages. The advantage of this method lies in the fact that the proper length of long-run periods need not be known.

(2) An alternative method is to estimate the values of $\bar{C}_t$ and $\bar{Y}_t$ by averaging observed values over some longer period. Deviations of observed quarterly values from these averages will consist largely of the quarterly deviations. One specific procedure is to calculate the deviation of current quarterly observations from the average of the four preceding quarters.

That is, define $\bar{Y}_t = 1/4 \sum_{i=1}^{i=4} Y_{t-i};\quad \bar{C}_t = 1/4 \sum_{i=1}^{i=4} C_{t-i}$.

then $y_t = Y_t - \bar{Y}_t;\ c_t = C_t - \bar{C}_t$. The values of c_t are then related to y_t.

(3) Any quarterly analysis such as the foregoing must depend on the accuracy of seasonal adjustment in the data, otherwise the deviations in question will reflect not only the random variation of the quarterly data, but will contain a seasonal component as well. A third method can be applied in which the consumption expenditure of each quarter is expressed as a function of quarterly income, the "income status" of the year, and a quarterly seasonal influence. Such regressions have the form

$$C_{it} = a + bY_{it} + d_i + e_t$$

where C_{it}, Y_{it} are consumption and income in quarter i of year t, d_i is the quarterly seasonal effect and e_t is the effect of income and other factors peculiar to year t. In practice this regression is fitted by expressing each quarterly value, say C_{it}, as a deviation from $\bar{C}_{.t}$ the average level of year t, and from $C_{i.}$, the average level (over all years) of quarter i:

$$c_{it} = C_{it} - \bar{C}_{.t} - \bar{C}_{i.} \text{ and } y_{it} = Y_{it} - \bar{Y}_{.t} - \bar{Y}_{i.}.$$

The regression is then fitted to c_{it} and y_{it}. This method amounts to elimination of both seasonal and longer-run effects by application of the analysis of covariance.

Each of these techniques has been applied to seasonally adjusted quarterly data covering the period 1947-58; the results appear in Table I-5.

TABLE I-5

Short-Run Regressions of Consumption on Income and Saving
(All regressions fitted to quarterly data 1948-58)

Quarterly First Differences	R^2
$\Delta C = .118 \ \Delta Y + 1.59$ $(.170)$	*
$\Delta C = .252 \ \Delta Y - .312 \ \Delta C_{-1} + 1.87$ $(.168) (.168)$	.05
$\Delta C = -.495 \ \Delta S + 2.063$ $(.09)$	.43
$\Delta C = -1.632 \ \Delta S + .150 \ \Delta C_{-1}$ $(.10) (.135)$	.47

Adjusted for Year and Quarter Averages

	R^2
$c_{it} = 201.2 + .129 \ y_{it}$ $\phantom{c_{it} = 201.2 + }(.4)$	*
$c_{it} = 246.7 - .865 \ s_{it}$ $\phantom{c_{it} = 246.7 - }(.08)$	.85

Deviations from Preceding 4-Quarter Moving Averages

	R^2
$c_t = 1.755 + .496 \ y_t$ $(.138)$	.30
$c_t = 4.510 - .358 \ s_t$ $(.143)$	.11

$*R^2 < 0$ after adjustment for sample size.

The striking fact is that when the analysis is centered on quarter-to-quarter variations, the correlation between consumption and income vanishes. The movements of consumption in the short run are so nearly independent of income that the usual high correlation between consumption and income is replaced by a substantial negative correlation between consumption and savings.

It is only when we distinguish a given quarter, not from its neighbors, but from the average of the preceding four quarters that a significant correlation between income and consumption appears. Of the three techniques, this method involves the longest "run" phenomenon since we are comparing each quarter with a value centered seven and a half months away from the center of the quarter. This is presumably the reason for the observed improvement in the correlation with income. Even here, however, there remains a significant negative correlation between consumption and savings, indicating that even at this level of analysis substantial independence in consumption behavior remains.

The result of this examination of quarterly behavior in the postwar period is the demonstration that on a true quarterly basis a useful Keynesian-type consumption function does not exist at all! Income is more stable in the very short run than is consumption expenditure. The general level of expenditure in a given quarter is a function of a distributed lag, not only of income, but of other factors as well. The deviations of quarterly expenditure from this general level are the result of such factors as very short-run alteration in consumer attitudes, and accidents in the timing of receipts, requirements, and expenditures. We have already noted (p. 18) the pioneering work done by Katona and Mueller in this area.

V. MONETARY FACTORS IN CONSUMPTION

In the foregoing section monetary variables have been treated only incidentally. We now turn to an explicit examination of monetary factors proper. These are generally taken to include four important variables: the price level, the interest rate, liquid assets, and consumer credit.

The Price Level

There are several avenues by which changes in the general level of prices may exert an influence on consumption expenditure. Most of these are indirect, operating through some other variable, but there are three possibilities for a direct effect of prices on expenditure. The first is the so-called "money illusion." This is the conjecture that some income receivers feel richer with the same real income at higher money prices and hence spend a higher proportion than they otherwise would. Secondly there is the possibility that the fact of rising prices may set off a speculative increase in consumer expenditure, especially on durables, as consumers rush into the market in anticipation of still further price increases. Finally there is the possibility that the process of price inflation may generate price differentials that systematically promote or repress total expenditure. These three direct effect are generally supposed, on balance, to be stimulating, but no empirical evidence of their impact has been produced.

In contrast the indirect effects operate through variables whose impact has been empirically studied. In the first place, under the progressive income tax higher money values of the same real income result in higher tax yields. Thus price increases act to reduce real disposable income, and hence consumer expenditure. Secondly, higher prices imply lower real value to any given money level of liquid assets, and hence, again to depress consumption expenditure. Finally, rising prices are associated with a shift in the distribution of real incomes away from fixed income receivers toward wages and profits. The net effect of this shift depends on the average disposition of the several groups to save. The indirect effects of rising prices are largely depressive of consumer expenditure.

The Rate of Interest

Although it is by no means clear whether the net effect of rising interest rates is more or less consumption, there are several ways the rate of interest can influence consumer behavior. A higher interest rate may directly enhance incentives to save, and hence lead to a reduction in current consumer expenditure. Moreover, higher interest rates may imply restricted consumer credit conditions and hence serve to reduce consumption, particularly on durable items. On the other hand, a higher interest rate, making easier accumulation of a given capital, say for retirement, may actually increase current consumption expenditure. Also, lower interest rates may stimulate home ownership, and hence via repayment of mortgages, serve as a long-run stimulant to saving. In addition, even aside from mortgage repayment, the behavior of home owners in general is somewhat different from that of nonowners. They are prone, other things equal, to save somewhat more. It is, of course, not at all certain to what extent this represents merely the automatic separation of saving-oriented people (who can and will invest in a house) from spending-oriented people (who do not save and hence, inter alia, do not buy houses), and to what extent it represents the actual conditioning brought on by the act of ownership, the saving discipline imposed by the mortgage, and the need for durables associated with ownership.

There are, in addition, a number of ways the interest rate can indirectly influence consumer expenditure via its effect on other variables. For example high interest rates and tight money may increase the need for internal financing and hence reduce the proportion of corporate earnings paid out as dividends. The general braking power of tight money on investment presumably operates in the same direction, but again it should be noted that there is no empirical evidence of such an effect.

In summary, although considerable emphasis on the direct and indirect roles of the interest rate as a determinant of consumer expenditure is found in both classical and Keynesian theory, the preponderance of evidence is that its influence, if any, is negligible in comparison to other factors and any reliance on it as a substantial control weapon is misplaced.

Liquid Assets

The rationale underlying the presumption that liquid assets influence consumption is that the desire to save in liquid form can be saturated. Given a sufficiently large stock of liquid assets, it is argued, the typical spending unit would not only cease saving but would reduce its stock of assets by dis-saving. This argument is surely valid to some extent, but there are two difficulties. In the first place, some liquid assets are earning assets. Even those that are not earning assets can always be exchanged for others, liquid or otherwise, that do yield an income. There is no clear reason, therefore, why a family with large liquid assets should be expected to spend them on consumption. In the second place, the ownership of liquid assets by any particular spending unit is not a "given," but is a matter of choice, and reflects the behavioral pattern of the family. That is, a change in the dollar volume of liquid assets in the hands of consumers is not a datum, but leaving aside the forced accumulation of liquidity during World War II, is an expression of consumer behavior. Possession of liquid assets should, therefore, be intimately associated with the psychological makeup of the individual spending unit, and with its plans. This association is particularly marked when a cross section of families is studied.

Katona has classified holders of liquid assets into (1) those who feel relatively saturated and hence spend more than other people and (2) those who are high savers and by virtue of that fact have higher assets and spend less than other people. For example, "In most income groups the proportion of dis-savers appears to be somewhat larger among those with larger than among those with small liquid assets. (But) the proportion of high savers (more than 30 percent of income saved) is larger among those with large than those with small liquid assets."

One of the most important motives for accumulation of liquid assets is to serve as a buffer between consumption outlays and a

varying income stream, enabling the spending unit to sustain consumption by dis-saving during low income periods. Klein, in a study
of the Survey of Consumer Finances (22), found that the fraction of
income saved was significantly related to the ratio of liquid assets
to income, but that the relationship was much more important for
those spending units who experienced a decline in income than for
those who had experienced an increase.

When S is saving; Y, income; N, spending unit size; L_{-1}, liquid
assets at the beginning of the period, the results were as follows:

$$\Delta Y < 0: \quad \frac{S}{Y} = -1.15 + .47 \ \text{Log} \ \frac{Y}{N} - .31 \ \frac{L_{-1}}{Y} - .54 \ \frac{\Delta Y}{Y_{-1}}$$
$$\qquad\qquad\qquad (.14) \qquad\quad (.03) \qquad\quad (.38)$$

$$\Delta Y > 0: \quad \frac{S}{Y} = -.68 + .26 \ \text{Log} \ \frac{Y}{N} - .06 \ \frac{L_{-1}}{Y} + .02 \ \frac{\Delta Y}{Y_{-1}}$$
$$\qquad\qquad\qquad (.08) \qquad\quad (.03) \qquad\quad (.05)$$

Difference in the constant terms of the two equations indicates a
disposition by those with increasing incomes to save a larger portion of their incomes. Moreover, for those with income decreases,
the proportion saved falls sharply with increases in liquid asset
ownership, while those with increasing income save about the same
proportion of income regardless of their liquid asset holdings.

Additional evidence in this direction is provided by Tobin.[10] In
studying separately the behavior of spending units with large increases in income and those with large decreases, he found that the
proportion of income spent on durable goods rose significantly with
increasing liquid asset ratios of the latter, but fell significantly with
increasing liquid asset ratios of the former. This negative income-
change liquid-asset interaction may reflect the asymmetry of saving
behavior associated with the dual motives for liquid asset behavior:
Liquid assets act to permit expenditure in the face of declining income, and the greater the liquid asset ratio, the more expenditure
is permitted. But among those with rapidly growing incomes the
liquid asset variables identify the high savers and hence is associated with lower expenditure.

A corollary of the proposition that those spending units with the
highest liquid assets are high savers who spend the least, is that
spending units with the largest indebtedness are consumption oriented and should spend the most. This conclusion is in some part
supported by the study of consumer purchases of durable goods by
Klein and Lansing (24). Their study was directed at the problem of

---

[10]Reported by Guthrie (16), pp. 107 ff.

using information available at the beginning of a period to predict which among a sample of spending units would purchase durables during the period. A discriminant function fitted to the data was used to assess the value of the various factors as predictors. They found that predicting durable purchase behavior was significantly dependent on the spending unit's expressed expectations as to purchase and as to prices, on marital status, on age of head, on region, and in addition was significantly positively correlated with the spending unit's debt-to-income ratio. Interestingly enough, the liquid asset-to-income ratio entered the discriminant function with a (non-significant) negative sign.

A later more extensive cross-section study of expenditure for durable goods by Guthrie (16) failed to bring to light any significant liquid asset effect at all.

The accumulation of conflicting empirical evidence from cross-section studies added to the highly unstable coefficient found for liquid assets in the time series analysis of the preceding section is convincing evidence that the role of liquid assets in the consumption function has not yet been discovered.

Part of the trouble doubtless lies in the fact that the dollar volume of liquid assets held by the spending unit at any time is the result of the past behavior of the unit. To this extent, the relationship of consumption to liquid asset holdings is the correlation of one aspect of behavior with another. It is hardly correct to speak of an "effect" on consumption of liquid balances that are deliberately saved up to be spent. (One might as well hold Christmas clubs responsible for the December retail boom.) Nor can we properly impute to liquid assets the expenditure behavior of a business family with widely fluctuating income. There was, of course, one important occasion on which spending units were compelled, willy-nilly, to accumulate liquid assets and then were set free to spend them if they chose. This was during World War II, but a careful study of the immediate postwar period from this point of view has yet to be made.

Consumer Credit

Although including consumer credit among the factors to be investigated in analyzing spending unit behavior is unlikely to arouse comment, there is a wide variety of opinion as to its impact and effect, and as to the appropriate method of testing and measuring it. Clearly, consumer credit can affect the timing of individual purchases. Moreover the opportunity for earlier acquisition of expensive durables may make their purchase more attractive and hence permanently alter the composition of expenditure. On the other hand, it may be that the credit purchase of durable "necessities" (that would be purchased anyhow) serves to enable the spending unit to obtain the good without a sudden cutback in the consumption of other goods. Consumer credit is intimately associated with the short-run dynamics of consumer durable buying: and improvement in credit terms, resulting in concentration of purchases of durables in a short period, is followed by below normal purchases as consumers wear out the goods while repaying the debts. During periods of rising income, consumption may rise more rapidly if consumers can buy on credit in anticipation of continued increases, while after a downturn, consumption must drop more sharply than otherwise, as repayment of inherited debt persists.

In the long run the effect of utilization of consumer credit may be an increase in the proportion of income spent. This might arise from the ease with which certain expenditures can be made. Or the net result may be an increase in saving, as the act of saving to meet repayments leads to a habit of increased thrift, or as the possession of the durables removes the need for expenditure on expensive substitutes, or frees the time of the housewife for outside work, and so on.

If the actual broad effects of consumer credit are open to question, the details of the impact of particular policies are even more in doubt. It is interesting to note that whereas other factors have been widely investigated as to their causal impact on consumption and saving, consumer credit extension has most often been treated as a dependent variable, whose value is determined by consumption and other factors.

The aggregate relationship of consumption to consumer credit can be analyzed in terms of a simple mathematical model:

$$C_t = a + b(Y_t - r_t) + X(T) \qquad\qquad (1)$$

$$E_t = E(T) \qquad\qquad (2)$$

$$Y_t = C_t + I_t \qquad\qquad (3)$$

The first equation relates consumption expenditure (C) to discretionary income: the difference between disposable income (Y) and credit repayments (r). $X(T)$ is the stimulus to consumption provided by credit terms T. The second equation relates E, the level of credit extensions (i.e. consumer borrowing) to credit terms. It should be noted that $X(T)$ is not necessarily equal to $E(T)$. $X(T)$ is the amount by which consumption demand exceeds its "normal" level as a result of easy credit terms, T. Consumers may actually borrow more or less than this. For example, we can imagine that at certain credit terms, say T_0, consumers spend only a "normal" amount on consumption—$X(T) = 0$. But they choose to finance some of this normal expenditure by credit and actually borrow E(T). The third equation is the usual aggregative definition. Since, in long-run equilibrium, repayments are equal to extensions, we can substitute $E(T) = r_t$ and solve for C_0, the equilibrium level of consumption expenditure:

$$C_0 = \frac{a}{1-b} + \frac{b}{1-b} I + \frac{X(T) - bE(T)}{1-b}$$

The impact of credit terms on the equilibrium level of consumption depends on whether the direct stimulus to consumption X(T) exceeds the depressing influence of repayment, bE(T). This in turn depends on whether favorable credit terms induce consumers not only to raise their expenditure by borrowing, but by more than this. If the stimulating effect is only that of increased borrowing, then X(T) = = E(T) and the equilibrium level of consumption is precisely

$$C = \frac{a}{1-b} + \frac{b}{1-b} I + E(T) \ .$$

If the stimulation of consumption is less than the amount of credit extension, the long-run level of consumer expenditure will rise by less than the amount of credit extension. This would arise if credit stimulated consumers simultaneously to consume more and to add to their store of liquid assets. This may appear a remote possibility, but there is nothing particularly irrational about the desire to increase or maintain available liquid assets via borrowing for certain consumption expenditures. In any case, it can be shown that certain types of spending units behave in this way.

Empirical Studies of the Effect of Consumer Credit Terms

A study by Kisselgoff (20) specifically undertook to determine what effect consumer credit terms exerted on total consumer expenditure. Although he succeeded in showing a substantial relationship between credit terms and the demand for credit, i.e. E(T), he was unable to find a reliable relationship between credit terms and the demand for consumer goods in general, i.e. X(T). These results are supported by the findings of Lippett's study (29) of expenditure for household furnishings and equipment. After the effect of disposable income, new marriages, replacement requirements, and related factors are taken into account, an "index of credit ease"— calculated as the ratio of consumer credit outstanding to repayments —did not make a significant contribution to demand for furnishings.

The reverse finding was obtained for the new automobile market. A study of automobile demand (46) showed credit terms to exercise a significant influence on the total number of new vehicles sold. The elasticity of the credit terms was 0.6 in terms of units bought, and presumably greater in terms of dollar expenditure since vari-

ations in demand are associated with corresponding variations in
the quality of cars sold. Since the accumulating stock of automobiles builds up an automatic back pressure on demand the short-run
impact of a liberalization of credit terms is heavily off-set by the
subsequent saturation of the market. It has been argued, however,
that the most important effect of liberalization of credit terms is
an upgrading of demand. This would mean a long-run increase in
the frequency of new car purchase to upgrade the age of cars in
use, and a shift of demand to more expensive cars.

One of the most thorough studies of the impact of consumer
credit is embodied in a study by Lansing and others (27). Their
study was addressed to three problems:

(1) Considering all spending units, who are the spending units
who use consumer credit?

(2) Considering only new car buyers, who are the spending units
who bought on credit?

(3) Considering all spending units who owe consumer debts,
what determines the amount of debt?

The results of the study showed:

(1) Consumers in the middle income range are more likely to
use consumer credit than those with low income (who cannot afford
the goods usually bought on credit) or those with high income (who
pay cash).

(2) Spending units with changing incomes are more likely to
utilize consumer credit than those with stable incomes. It may be
that this is due to the fact that families without liquid assets resort
to credit to sustain their living standard when income falls, while
those with income increases resort to credit to speed up their access to the higher standard of living.

(3) As is to be expected, holders of liquid assets are less likely
to resort to consumer credit than others. This is doubtless a two-
fold effect. Clearly those with available assets need not resort to
expensive credit to purchase desired goods. Moreover, the existence
of the assets to some extent identifies the owner as a habitual high
saver, and one less likely to make the outlay in the first place.

(4) Families in the stage of the life cycle where income is low
but prospects are good and the immediate desirability of durables
is high are likely to resort to credit.

(5) Spending units already owning a home with a mortgage are
likely to resort to credit—probably in connection with the purchase
of durables for home furnishing.

It is clear that in order to employ credit a spending unit must fulfill two sets of criteria. First, it must make a purchase of the kind for which credit can be obtained. Secondly, it must choose to make the purchase on credit and be eligible to do so.

The Lansing study centers attention on the second set of criteria by analysis of a sample of new car buyers. Several important conclusions emerge:

(1) The purchase of a new automobile is highly correlated with spending unit income, but among those who bought cars there is only a weak negative correlation between spending unit income and resort to credit for the transaction. On the other hand,

(2) Among those who purchased cars there is a powerful negative correlation between ownership of liquid assets and resort to consumer credit. Given this fact, use of debt by car buyers was not associated with such factors as life cycle or with region of residence, beyond the fact that farmers appear to be less inclined to resort to credit than other people.

Finally the relationship between the extent of credit utilization and other factors was explored by examination of spending units that did resort to credit. Since the actual size of outstanding debt varies with the age of the contract, the monthly payment was taken as a more reliable index of credit utilization. The study showed that the monthly payments of those spending units that are in debt are related neither to liquid asset holdings nor to income variability. However, the size of total monthly payments rises with spending unit income, but at a slower rate.

A final series of studies relates to the fact, mentioned several times above, that spending unit income is partially an expression of spending unit behavior. This has important implications for the analysis of the effect of consumer credit. For example, the existence of outstanding consumer debt can be shown to be related to the participation of wives in the labor force.

An excellent study by Rosett (43) of data drawn from the Survey of Consumer Finances shows a positive correlation between wive's participation in the labor force and the amount of personal and mortgage debt, after taking into account husbands' income, number and ages of children, wife's education level and number of years married.

Again there is a strong duality in the relationship. The data show, to some extent, that when the husband's salary is low and the family is in debt, the wife's income is "needed." On the other hand, it may be that the wife enters the labor force in order to purchase a new

car or other bulky durable. In this case the debt may be associated
with the purchase of the item in anticipation of the wife's earnings.

An as yet unpublished study by Stanley Lebergott (28) offers
evidence that the latter is often the case. Result of a study by
Marion Sobol (44) of a survey sample of working wives shows that
when asked why they are working, a majority of the women specifically mentioned a particular "target," usually a durable good
to be purchased.

It is also interesting to note that the Rosett study shows that the
wife's participation in the labor force, while positively correlated
with consumer debt, is not related at all to the holding of liquid assets.

VI. GENERAL CONCLUSIONS

Several important conclusions can be drawn from the foregoing
discussion. It is clear from empirical evidence that consumption
expenditure depends on something more than the immediate economic conditions of the spending unit. In fact, in the short run—for
periods as short as a quarter—the variability of consumer expenditure is greater than that of income. Year to year variation in consumer expenditure however bears a sufficiently close relationship
to income and other economic variables to permit a useful estimate
of the marginal propensity to consume, but the relationship is not
nearly as close as is sometimes thought. The techniques employed
with annual data frequently pick up longer-run influences and yield
an appearance of a closer relationship among the variables than is
observed when attention is specifically concentrated on annual variations. Moreover unless considerable care is taken in the analysis
both the estimated marginal propensity to consume and the estimated
correlation between income and consumption are seriously biased.

But even when carefully measured, the mere regression of consumption on disposable income and other variables is a far cry
from a true consumption function. For one thing it is important to
distinguish among different kinds of variation in the independent
variables. A windfall for example appears to have a substantially
larger immediate impact than would be expected of, say, a tax cut
that would produce the same gain in disposable income. In addition
there is conclusive evidence that even in the short run spending units
vary their incomes to provide for varying expenditure requirements.

Similar difficulties surround the analysis of the role of liquid
assets and consumer credit in consumer expenditure. The purpose
of both these instruments is to permit the timing of consumer expenditure to be independent of the receipt of income. It is to be expected, then, that among people with declining incomes—many of

whom have provided themselves with liquid assets for this precise purpose—those possessing liquid assets consume more than those who do not. Moreover we should expect that those who already have at hand one instrument for financing the purchase of a durable good are unlikely to resort to the other. These effects are readily discernible in our data. But the true role, or roles, of liquid assets have not been isolated. The obvious ten-fold increase in the regression coefficient on liquid assets between the prewar and the postwar period may be partially associated with the interaction of liquid assets with income, but the magnitude of the shift leads one to question whether the coefficient is measuring the influence of liquid assets at all. There is a strong presumption that the apparent effect of liquid assets stands as a strong proxy for something else, as yet unidentified.

The role of consumer credit is likewise confounded with other aspects of behavior. The over-all statistical evidence does not indicate any clear cut effect on expenditure. In part this may be due to the rather poor quality of the data available—particularly for credit terms. In part it may be due to the complex interaction of credit with liquid assets and above all with the determination of income itself.

Consumer expenditure is only one aspect of consumer behavior and its proper understanding requires that it be related to other aspects. Broadly speaking the economic behavior of a spending unit is a function of its tastes and attitudes, and of its economic potential.

Tastes are a function of such factors as education level, family size and composition, age, stage in the life cycle, place of residence, and occupation, as well as such economic factors as historical consumption experience, and relative position in the income distribution. We may or may not find it convenient to distinguish between "tastes" and "attitudes," but special attention must be paid to consumer psychology. Consumer behavior is influenced by a variety of factors. Some of these, such as the view the individual has of himself, his environment, and his relationship to it, are deep-seated and change relatively slowly, but their importance is undeniable. Some of the sharply contrasting comparisons of economic behavior among racial and ethnic groups arise because of variation in such factors as the conception that the individual has of the probable success of improving his position in life by hard work and education. Even compulsory education cannot work against the conviction of the child that he has no future as an educated man: that, for example by racial discrimination, he has already been excluded from the possible fruits of effort. Although these factors may be taken as given at any particular time, and hence ignored in short-run analysis, long-run variation in them must be taken into account when longer periods are considered. A proper evaluation of the impact of consumer

credit on consumption expenditure, for example, could hardly ignore
the secular change in the attitude of people toward its use.

Attitudes are also clearly subject to short-run alteration. General feelings of optimism or pessimism, that it is a "good time to
buy" or that it is a "bad time to buy" are associated with variation
in expenditure patterns. Not only do such attitudes generate fluctuations in consumer spending, but they tend to interact with other
factors. It is perfectly clear, for example, that the relationship between easing consumer credit terms and expenditure change depends
upon whether people are well disposed to spend in the first place,
and on whether they view the act of credit liberalization as a har-
binger of good times, or as a signal that things are getting worse.

There is no fine line that can be drawn between psychological
factors and the economic potential of the family. The potential of a
given spending unit at a given time depends on its past behavior: its
education status, its accumulation of assets, etc. Nevertheless it is
useful to identify the range of choices that a spending unit has available to it at any particular time, regardless of how this may be related to the past. The economic potential of a spending unit has two
aspects. On the one hand, the members of the unit are endowed with
a stock of wealth, education, technical skill, experience, etc., that
constitutes the real potential; on the other hand there are the existing market opportunities for the employment of the real endowment,
the accompanying prices and potential earnings, and the alternative
avenues of expenditure.

Both the real and the market component of the economic potential
of the spending unit is subject to variation in three ways. (1) There
is a natural evolution of economic potential over the life cycle.
(2) There are fluctuations in the "level" of the potential due to increased productivity, saving, education, the general state of health
and similar factors, as well as variation in the average level of
remuneration from certain occupations, or (via taxation) variation
in the general level of disposable income from all employments.
(3) Finally, both the real and the market alternatives are subject
to short-run variation associated with accidents, windfalls, illness,
unexpected bargain opportunities. etc.

There is a great difference between a situation where utilization
of potential is a matter of deliberate choice in view of market alternatives—that is, a condition of "full employment"—and one in
which there is rationing of opportunity—unemployment. During
periods of prosperity and expansion, income is an expression of the
behavior of the spending unit, at least at its own margin. During
periods of depression income becomes more nearly a datum. In
periods of prosperity the consumption-income relation is a correlation of one aspect of behavior with another: the two are mutually

caused; in periods of depression the relationship is more directly a causal one. Other things equal, we have every reason to expect the behavior of a spending unit in a period of general unemployment to differ from that in a period of prosperity. This is partly so from the standpoint of the dynamics of behavior (i.e., because it has been conditioned by the experience of better times). It is also true that for many people a serious depression means that a mistaken decision may carry the gravest consequences—loss of the home, for example—while a time of prosperity allows much greater room for error with only minor penalty. In any case, the area of choice is narrower in depressed circumstances. An important research task for the future will be to explore such asymmetry.

There is also reason to believe that many other aspects of the behavioral process are asymmetrical. The act of accumulation is not the same as the act of spending assets. The decision to go to work is not the same as the decision to quit. The decision to buy a refrigerator is not the same as the "decision" to continue to keep a refrigerator once bought. The decision to buy a house rather than rent is not "just the reverse" of the decision to sell a house and start renting. Moreover, the determinants of behavior are subject to a complex set of interactions. How a spending unit reacts to loss of a job by the principal wage earner depends on its life cycle status, its asset holdings, and its current attitude toward the cause of the event and its probable duration.

The financial variables play a part in this complex process, but it is difficult to isolate their effects, and in particular to separate the results of behavior from its determinants and constraints. This greatly increases the difficulty of properly assessing the influence of policy controls on behavior, and it is evident that in our present state of knowledge we must rely for policy guidance primarily on the obvious direction of the effect of the policy step.

In conclusion the general need for research in this area must be emphasized. In many respects, the theory of consumption toward which we are moving owes more to Marshall than to Keynes. It would be wrong, however, to see in it a final retreat from the General Theory back to the classical position. There is an important distinction between present and earlier theory. We increasingly insist that theoretical statements be so formulated as to produce testable consequences. A theory must not only be operational in the sense of implying at least imaginable experiments; if it is to be of real use its terms must be sufficiently explicit and close to experience to permit actual observations to be made. In short, the economist is beginning to insist that economics be a science.

Scientific research in economics is more difficult than research in physics or chemistry. The human being is a vastly more com-

plicated system than the atom; and the behavior of atomic particles
—bewildering as it may be—is now predictable in ways that human
reactions are not. Moreover the simplification of research design
provided by laboratory controls is not available to the economist.
All observations on the economic system must be made in actual
operation, and multivariate statistical analysis must replace experimental control.

In view of these complications there was every justification for
the original use of oversimplified theories; the refinements of the
theoretical model rapidly outstripped the resolving power of existing data and methods. The concept of the consumption function as
a relationship between total consumer expenditure and income is
such a simplification. Aggregate consumer expenditure is the sum
of a number of different kinds of expenditure; aggregate income is
the sum of a number of different kinds of income. There is no
reason to suppose they are really homogeneous.

As we refine our theory it becomes apparent that we must go
beyond global totals to the underlying behavior of individual units.
Cross-section studies yield much greater "leverage" for the study
of many variables: there is more variation in income, liquid assets,
consumption, life cycle status, and debt position from spending unit
to spending unit than there is from time to time in the average of
all. But cross-section data are essentially static. What is revealed
is not a cross section of responses in time, but a cross section of
status as of a given time.

Consumption variations over a cross section do not follow entirely from income variation. To some extent they are a matter of
taste and personality. To some extent they are a function of social
position. To some extent the income variation itself reflects the
same tastes, as does the variation in liquid asset position, debt,
and so on.

Policy evaluation calls for the study of changes over time, not
differences in status. We need to know what change in expenditure
will be accompanied by a change in liquid asset holdings, credit
terms, income or other factors. These changes can only be observed
over time. But because of the greater resolving power of cross-section data, and because behavior varies from spending unit to spending
unit, we need both cross sections and time series over the same units.

The technique of the re-interview sample survey is now developed to a practical level, and experienced research organizations
are equipped to collect precisely the kind of data needed for the
formulation and testing of the theory of consumer behavior. This
technique is currently being applied to a number of problems, and
its use must be greatly extended. We need to observe individual

spending units for periods of five or ten years, and to direct our observation so as to test specific hypotheses. The cost of such surveys—of even a relatively small sample—is great, particularly if any real effort is made to follow spending units who move. But the costs are not unreasonable when compared to the outlays for research in other lines which are of no greater importance to the general welfare. If we are serious about the assessment of public policy—monetary or otherwise—the price of basic research must be paid. There is unhappily no short cut. There is no other way to determine how the causal interrelations operate in the economy.

It is, of course, not sufficient merely to gather better data; they must be used. This means much more elaborate analysis, allowing for more complicated interactions than have hitherto been the case. We must begin to move away from the aggregative habits of thought that lead us to ask about "the" effect of a given factor, and to study instead the circumstances under which the factor has a specified effect. We must recognize that a specific action—for example lengthening credit terms, or payment of a national service dividend—will not affect all families in the same way. The impact of these actions in particular instances depends on the individual family attitudes and environment. It is in the fine structure of interaction that the understanding of economic behavior lies.

BIBLIOGRAPHY

1. Ackley, Gardner, Macroeconomic Theory. New York: The Mac-Millan Co., 1961.

2. ―――――――,"The Wealth-Saving Relationship." Journal of Political Economy, 59 (1951), pp. 154-161.

3. ―――――――,and D.B. Suits, "Relative Price Changes and Aggregate Consumer Demand." American Economic Review, 60 (1950), pp. 785-804.

4. Bodkin, Ronald, "Windfall Income and Consumption." American Economic Review, 49 (1959), pp. 602-614.

5. Brady, Dorothy S., and Rose D. Friedman, "Saving and the Income Distribution." New York: National Bureau of Economic Research, Studies in Income and Wealth, Vol. 10, 1947.

6. Brown, T.M., "Habit Persistence and Lags in Consumer Behavior." Econometrica, 20 (1952), pp. 355-371.

7. Burns, Arthur F., Economic Research and the Keynesian Thinking of Our Times. 26th Annual Report of the National Bureau of Economic Research, New York, 1946.

8. Clark, Lincoln H., ed., Consumer Behavior. New York: Harper and Brothers, 1958.

9. Duesenberry, James S., Income, Savings, and the Theory of Consumer Behavior. Cambridge: Harvard University Press, 1949.

10. "Family Characteristics of Working Wives: March, 1957." Washington, D.C.: Bureau of the Census, Current Population Reports, Series P-50, No. 81 (March 1958).

11. Ferber, Robert, A Study of Aggregate Consumption Functions. New York: National Bureau of Economic Research, Technical Paper No. 8, 1953.

12. ―――――――, Factors Influencing Durable Goods Purchases. Urbana, Ill.: Bureau of Economic and Business Research, University of Illinois Bulletin, Vol. 52, 1955.

13. Fisher, Janet, "Income, Spending, and Saving Patterns of Consumer Units in Different Age Groups." New York: National Bureau of Economic Research, Studies in Income and Wealth, Vol. 15, Princeton University Press, 1952.

14. Friedman, Milton, A Theory of the Consumption Function. New York: National Bureau of Economic Research, Princeton University Press, 1957.

15. Friend, Irwin, and I.B. Kravis, "Entrepreneurial Income, Saving and Investment." American Economic Review, 47 (1957), pp. 269-301.

16. Guthrie, Harold, Changes in the Ratio of Liquid Asset Holdings to Income among Groups of American Consumers between 1947 and 1951 and Some Effects of Liquid Assets on Spending. Unpublished Doctoral Dissertation, University of Michigan, 1954.

17. Katona, George, The Powerful Consumer. New York: McGraw Hill, 1960.

18. _____, Psychological Analysis of Economic Behavior. New York: McGraw-Hill, 1951.

19. Keynes, John Maynard, The General Theory of Employment Interest and Money. New York: Harcourt, Brace, and Co., 1936.

20. Kisselgoff, Avram, Factors Affecting the Demand for Consumer Installment Credit. New York: National Bureau of Economic Research, Technical Paper No. 7, 1952.

21. Klein, Lawrence R., Economic Fluctuations in the United States, 1921-1941. New York: John Wiley & Sons, 1950.

22. _____ , "Estimating Patterns of Saving Behavior from Sample Survey Data." Econometrica, 19 (1951), pp. 439-454.

23. _____ , and Arthur Goldberger, An Econometric Model of the United States, 1929-1952. Amsterdam: North Holland Publishing Co., 1955.

24. _____ , and J. Lansing, "Decisions to Purchase Consumer Durable Goods." Journal of Marketing, 20 (1955), pp. 109-132.

25. _____ , and H. Mooney, "Negro-White Savings Differentials and the Consumption Function Problem." Econometrica, 21 (1954), pp. 425-456.

26. Lansing, John B., T. Lorimer, and C. Moriguchi, How People Pay for College. Ann Arbor: Survey Research Center, 1960.

27. _____ , E. Scott Maynes, and Mordechai Drenin, "Factors Associated with the Use of Consumer Credit," in

Consumer Installment Credit, Part II, Vol. I: Conference on Regulation. Washington, D.C.: Government Printing Office, 1957.

28. Lebergott, Stanley, "Population and Labor Force Relationships." Paper presented at the Conference on Interrelations of Demographic and Economic Change, Princeton, 1958.

29. Lippett, Vernon G., Determinants of Consumer Demand for House Furnishings and Equipment. Cambridge: Harvard University Press, 1959.

30. Lydall, Harold, "The Life Cycle in Income, Saving, and Asset Ownership." Econometrica, 23 (1955), pp. 131-150.

31. Mack, Ruth P., "Trends in American Consumption and the Aspiration to Consume." American Economic Review, 66 (1956), pp. 55-69.

32. Modigliani, Franco, "Fluctuations in the Saving-Income Ration: A Problem in Economic Forecasting." New York: National Bureau of Economic Research, Studies in Income and Wealth, Vol. II, 1949.

33. _____ , and Richard Brumberg, "Utility Analysis and the Consumption Function: An Interpretation of Cross Section Data," in Post Keynesian Economics. New Brunswick, N.J.: Rutgers University Press, 1954.

34. Morgan, James N., "Individual Savings in 1947 and 1949." American Economic Review, 40 (1950), pp. 381-388.

35. Mueller, Eva, "Consumer Attitudes: Their Significance and Forecasting Value." The Quality and Significance of Anticipations Data. New York: National Bureau of Economic Research, Princeton University Press, 1960, pp. 149-181.

36. _____ , "Effects of Consumer Attitudes on Purchases." American Economic Review, 47 (1957), pp. 946-965.

37. _____ , and George Katona, Consumer Attitudes and Demand, 1950-52. Ann Arbor: Institute for Social Research, University of Michigan, 1953.

38. _____ , Consumer Expectations, 1953-1956. Ann Arbor: Institute for Social Research, University of Michigan, 1957.

39. _____ , "The Function of Expectational and Motivational Data," in 1960 Survey of Consumer Finances. Ann Arbor: Survey Research Center, 1961, pp. 171-185.

40. "Multiple Job Holding: July 1957." Washington, D.C.: Bureau of the Census, Current Population Reports, Series P-50, No. 80 (February 1958).

41. The National Accounts of the United States. Hearings Before the Joint Economic Committee, Subcommittee on Economic Statistics, 85th Congress, First Session, October 29, 30, 1957.

42. Pollack, J.J., "Fluctuations in the United States Consumption, 1919-1932." Review of Economic Studies, 19 (1937), pp. 133-143.

43. Rosett, Richard N., Working Wives, An Econometric Study in Studies in Household Economic Behavior. New Haven: Yale University Press, Yale Studies in Economics, Vol. 9, 1958.

44. Sobel, Marion, Correlates of Present and Future Work Status of Women. Unpublished Doctoral Dissertation, University of Michigan, 1960.

45. Staehle, Hans, "Short-Period Variation in the Distribution of Income." Review of Economic Studies, 19 (1937), pp. 133-143.

46. Suits, D.B., "The Demand for New Automobiles in the United States, 1929-1956." Review of Economic Studies, 40 (1958), pp. 273-280.

47. Tinberger, Jan, Business Cycles in the United States of America, 1919-1932. Statistical Testing of Business Cycle Theories, Vol. II, League of Nations, Economic Intelligence Service, Geneva, 1939.

48. Watts, Harold W., "Long Run Income Expectations and Consumer Saving," in Studies in Household Economic Behavior. New Haven: Yale University Press, Yale Studies in Economics, Vol. 9, 1958.

49. Zellner, Arnold, "The Short Run Consumption Function." Econometrica, 25 (1957), pp. 552-567.

Research Study Two

DETERMINANTS OF BUSINESS INVESTMENT

Robert Eisner
and
Robert H. Strotz
Northwestern University

with a Bibliography
by George R. Post

PREFACE

This work was conceived as essentially a critical review of the existing state of knowledge of determinants of business investment. Undertaken for the Commission on Money and Credit, it has tended to ignore or underemphasize issues, admittedly important, not usually felt to be in the domain of the monetary authority. The study was initiated in mid-1959 and submitted in early 1960, with later opportunity for revision in which some account has been taken of very recent work.

It is perhaps more satisfying and defensible, from the standpoint of dispassionate inquiry, only to report evidence, and to avoid judgment. But those who must make policy decisions cannot always wait until tomorrow for the definitive word on today's debatable issues. We feel that the empirical evidence can be made most meaningful within the theoretical framework that we have chosen, a framework around which have been constructed hypotheses with wide application in economics. That the evidence may also be consistent with competing theories which have less appeal to us, though perhaps more appeal to some others, is not a matter to which we have given systematic attention. In any case, we have been concerned throughout with the quest for underlying causal relations, and not simply the record of statistical and historical association.

Each author has scrutinized critically but has not duplicated every effort of the other. It may be noted that Eisner bears primary responsibility for Chapters II and III, Strotz for Chapters I and IV. Only the two distinct parts of the concluding chapter, however, could properly be—and have been—signed separately.

We are pleased to be able to append to our study the quite comprehensive bibliography prepared by Mr. George R. Post of Queens University.

Robert Eisner

Robert H. Strotz

I. THE THEORETICAL FRAMEWORK

A. Introduction

Economics, we like to think, should provide a coherent explanation of the determinants of business investment demand. Starting with first principles pertaining to the decision-making process of the firm, it should proceed to a quantitative statement of the influence of major social changes on the total amount of investment undertaken in an economy. This conception of economic theory is familiar enough, and it probably constitutes the common framework into which most investigators in this area feel their contributions must ultimately fit. We begin at the micro level and in the armchair. We postulate, as pure hypothesis, the principles which guide decision-making units, which in this case are firms, in deciding upon their investment policies. We specify carefully the constraints, technological, financial, and organizational, which condition the choices actually made; and by the careful use of logic we derive significant qualitative propositions regarding how investment decisions are affected by changes in the parameters that define the opportunities open to the firm. Once having articulated the theory of investment at the level of the individual firm, we then imagine that we may proceed synthetically to deduce relationships among broad economic aggregates which govern the investment desires of the business sector as a whole. Firmly rooted in micro theory, a macro theory thus emerges. The macro theory obtained in this way, however, is not supposed to be numerical. Its empirical significance is expected to reside in the identification of those variables that have an important influence on the level of aggregate investment demand and in the specification of so-called "qualitative" properties of an aggregative investment demand function. It is at this point that we suppose we turn to data. On the basis of observation of the relevant economic variables along with our theoretical understanding of how these observations must, in principle, have been generated, we proceed by use of statistical inference techniques to estimate numerically the aggregate investment demand function.

No one pretends, of course, that all this has been achieved to our satisfaction. Rather the theory of investment is a living and developing thing, and we have learned as a methodological principle to welcome the feedback of empirical studies on the theory to be promoted. Thus, we suppose an initial hypothesis enables us to observe and to estimate meaningfully, and that the result of our empirical efforts will in turn modify the initial hypothesis. In this way we lift ourselves by our bootstraps to an understanding of the causes of investment in the economy. Since different economies may be characterized by differing norms and institutions, our theory may

ultimately be culture-bound in that it may be said to apply and to
have been tested only with respect to a particular economy during
a particular portion of historical time. Our interest in this study
is with the American economy, today.

There is, unfortunately, many a serious gap in the sequence
from the a priori theory of the individual firm to the numerical
estimation of the constants in an aggregate investment demand
function. These gaps reflect either how rudimentary our present
knowledge is compared to that which we may hope for or, more
pessimistically, the essentially intractable and capricious character
of the phenomena with which we deal. Some of the main gaps would
appear to be these: investment, entailing as it does by definition
the exchange of one future for another, must depend heavily upon
the expectations of decision makers as to future economic developments. But we lack any very useful theory about the formation of
business expectations and are at best only able to suppose that they
are related to a variety of current and past variables which (to add
to the complications!) enter into our theory in still other ways.
There is, moreover, little understanding of the structural relations
by which expectations are formed, and so, even if we succeeded in
relating expectations intimately to various past observables, we
should have little understanding as to the effects of policy measures,
newly adopted, which might alter the future values of the explanatory variables.[1] Suppose, for example, that the desire for capital
equipment has, historically, been closely related to past profits, the
latter proving a good proxy variable for the expected future return
on capital additions. Does this mean that future changes in the rates
of profit taxation will or will not affect the subsequent desire for
capital?

We pass on to another serious gap in our knowledge. This one
pertains to how we may move from a microeconomic theory of investment of the firm to a macrorelation explaining the investment
of the entire business sector. The micro theory is constructed with
frequent appeal to ceteris paribus assumptions which may have no
validity in the macro theory. The micro theory may, moreover, be
concerned with the typical, average, or representative firm, whereas
the macro theory ought perhaps to stress the importance of the

---

[1] Problems of predicting the effects of basic changes, including
those that are deliberately produced by public policy measures, are
a good deal more difficult than those of forecasting future behavior
under conditions involving no important change in the structure of
behavior relations. On this general subject, see Jacob Marschak,
"Economic Measurements for Policy and Prediction," Ch. I in
W. C. Hood and T. C. Koopmans, Studies in Econometric Method
(New York: Wiley and Sons, 1953).

decisions of "marginal" firms whose behavior may tip the scales
one way or another. Thus, for example, if it were felt that most
firms confront a fairly ideal capital market to start with, we could
foresee no significant effect on investment of improvements in the
capital market if the macro theory we used were built upon a model
of the typical firm. Yet the presence of a small but significant
minority of firms whose capital market was highly imperfect may
at the macro level give great importance to the effect of improvements in the capital market.[2]

A third gap has to do with the application of statistical techniques themselves. We may be forced by problems of computational
know-how to strain any a priori macro theory that we might have
developed by forcing it into a form suitable for statistical inference
procedures. We may be driven to highly special assumptions about
the probability characteristics of a macro model simply because
without those assumptions we do not know how to proceed statistically. And, finally, we may be forced to use data which are themselves highly suspect and unsuitable.

If these foregoing remarks have any important validity, we may
at the outset wonder about how satisfactorily empirical studies
feed back to influence our choice of the underlying theory. When
theory and data are in conflict, shall we trust whatever insights
about aggregate investment demand we can get from our micro
theory—the statistics be damned—or shall we reject our a priorism
and casual empiricism in favor of hard-headed claims about what
the figures show? With our present state of knowledge, we are certain in these circumstances to remain ill at ease. As against the
present-day devotion to econometric studies, however, the present
authors would want to warn against too slavish an acceptance of
anybody's confidence intervals.

B. The Theory of Investment of the Firm

1. Plant and equipment investment

We turn now to the formal theory of the investment of the firm.
To provide some order, we shall group various problems and bits
of analysis under two headings. The first we shall describe as em-
bodying an "interequilibrium approach," involving the concept of

---

[2]It is, of course, not a methodological imperative that a macro
theory be derived from a micro theory. On this, see M.H. Peston,
"A View of the Aggregation Problem," Review of Economic Studies,
xxvii(1), 72 (October, 1959).

an initial equilibrium position for the firm and of a final equilibrium position which differs from the previous one as a result of some change in external circumstances, and involving the further, dynamical notions of the adjustment of the firm from its initial to its final equilibrium state. It will be stressed that models of this sort entail our thinking of the firm as being often in a disequilibrium position, moving from one equilibrium to another. Under the second heading, we shall think of models concerned mainly with "intertemporal allocation." These are the models which imagine the firm to be choosing among a variety of investment <u>projects</u> available to it, the choice being in accordance with some criterion of maximization. The distinction is not clear cut. In the interequilibrium models, the path of adjustment may itself be chosen according to some maximization principle; and in the intertemporal allocation models one may suppose the firm to be allocating resources among calendar dates which separate initial and terminal equilibrium states. The latter models, however, are not truly dynamic. In any case, the purpose of our distinction is not to pose a choice among conflicting theories, but rather to organize the points of view and insights which different approaches provide.

a. <u>The interequilibrium approach.</u> Here we begin with the familiar notion of the long-run equilibrium of the firm. We imagine that the rate of profit has been constant and that the size of plant has been chosen so as to make this constant profit level a maximum. The long-run average cost curve is U-shaped and if the firm is in a competitive industry, it is operating at the minimum point of that curve. Complications of language but not of principle are introduced if multiple products are considered. To avoid those complications, we assume that the firm produces a single product, and, to avoid further complications, we suppose that it operates under conditions of complete certainty as to technology, product demand, and factor supply. We next suppose that there has occurred some change--all of a sudden--which defines a new long-run equilibrium position at which the optimal plant size is now greater than initially. What sorts of changes might have been responsible for this?

The changes which would produce a new long-run equilibrium position for the firm would be (a) changes in demand, (b) changes in factor costs or conditions of supply, and (c) changes in technology.

It is always difficult to state the effects of a change in market conditions upon the equilibrium position of a firm which is in an oligopolistic industry--unless one is willing to assert some definite model of oligopoly behavior. Indeed, even with competitive or monopoly models, the pure theory of the firm yields very little in the way of definite propositions. About all that can be said short of special restrictive assumptions is that under competition in both product and factor markets, the factor demand curves will not be positively inclined. Nevertheless, we may venture some judgments about what would normally be observed. It seems safe to say that, regardless of the form of industrial organization, an increase in demand facing the firm (or, for the competitive firm, an increase in market price) will as a general rule bring about a rise in the equilibrium level of output for the industry as a whole. The effects on the equilibrium output of the firm are less certain. The appearance of new entrants may absorb much or all of the expansion of industry output and, in certain cases, where the expansion of the industry affects the prices of its factors of production, may even lead to a diminution in the output of existing firms. Nevertheless, industry output may be expected to increase in those circumstances. If, by an "increase in demand" we mean either an equal absolute increase or an equal proportional increase in the amount demanded at each possible price, our generalization seems reasonably safe. We should be less sure of our generalization if the increase in demand is coupled with a more complicated alteration in the form of the demand function. In the case of the imperfectly competitive firm, nothing unique can then be said about the possible shift in the marginal revenue function, and it is possible that the increasing and changing demand may lead to a reduction in the output of the firm and of the industry and to an increase in market price.

To relate plant size to the level of demand, we must next suppose that if the equilibrium level of output increases, this will increase the desired stock of capital. This, too, seems to be a reasonable empirical generalization.

It is these considerations which underlie the acceleration principle in some form: The desired stock of capital is assumed to be positively related to the level of expected demand for output. We may usefully note, however, that if the existing stock of capital, because of underutilization, exceeds the desired stock at the new, higher level of expected demand, no acquisition of new capital would be needed. Thus the acceleration principle may be rendered inoperative by less-than-capacity utilization of capital. In this case, of course, the initial position is not one of equilibrium, as we had assumed.

The effects of changes in factor costs are also ambivalent. If the cost of plant and equipment should decline, one would suppose that capital would be substituted for other factors and that the optimal plant size would increase, so that the sales of both the individual firm and the industry would rise. If, however, there were a change in the price of other factors of production--raw materials prices or the wages of labor--one could not state a priori what the effect on the optimal amount of plant and equipment would be. A decline in the cost of other factors may be expected to lead to an expansion of output of the industry as a whole, but this could be achieved either by an expansion of both the amounts of other factors and of plant and equipment employed or by a reduction in the amount of plant and equipment upon the substitution of the other factors which are now relatively cheaper. For the individual firm, there is no certain manner of change in the shape of its long-run average cost curve, and its optimal plant size may become greater or less depending upon the interaction of different factors of production in the production function. In the normal case, however, it seems plausible to assume that a rise in the cost of other factors would lead to a substitution of capital equipment for those factors and that this increase in capital intensity would increase the optimal level of output of the individual firm. The output of the entire industry may, of course, decrease because of the rise in cost.

It is even more difficult to say anything worthwhile at the a priori level about the effect of a change in technology. Technological advance may be either labor saving or capital saving and so, even though it may be expected to result in a diminution of cost and expansion of industry output, it is by no means certain that it must lead to an increase in the amount of capital devoted to the industry.

Much of what we have been able to say thus far has dealt with the effect of a change on the demand or cost side on the optimal level of output. Generally, we may suppose that an increase in output entails an increase in the amount of capital equipment, although this inference is not one of logic, but is based upon one's impressions about actual experience. A very simple version of the acceleration principle, of course, might link the level of sales and the level of capital together in a rigid way, so that if the former increases, so would the latter. Investment, being the time rate of change in capital, would then be linked in fixed proportion to the time rate of change in demand. It is clear that the acceleration principle in this form is a rough and ready empirical rule and not a consequence of the pure theory of the firm. We might note explicitly that from its inception the acceleration principle has been based on the "law of derived demand," and the output changes which were considered relevant were those resulting from changes on the side of demand, not on the side of cost, including technology.

Another rough and ready rule, however, is that whatever causes firms to desire an increase in output also enhances their present profits. Under these circumstances, we should expect to find that investment is correlated with profits as it is with output. But just as investment is not linked by logic necessarily to an increase in output, so investment also is not a logical consequence of present profits. Either profits or sales or both may rise and investment may yet decline. According to the conventional theory of the firm, investment is motivated by profit maximization, but a profit maximization theory does not imply by logical necessity either a profit or an acceleration theory of investment. Nevertheless, under reasonable assumptions and assuming that changes in demand are of most importance, we should expect to find output, profits, and investment moving together over time.

In contrast with the acceleration principle, there are those models that emphasize the causal role of profits in determining investment demand. A prominent work in the theoretical pedigree of this approach is an article by Klein (352).[3] Klein presented alternative models of the firm and derived from each an investment demand function. "Real" profit appears as an explanatory variable in the investment function in one of these models precisely because capital consumption appears in the utility function which the entrepreneur is assumed to maximize. The reason given for this by Klein is that entrepreneurs may "take pride in the size of their establishments." (352, p. 101) It is hard to know how significant this phenomenon may be. Scitovsky (547) has, as a matter of fact, made the opposite assumption in another well-known article. In any case, if the entrepreneur receives satisfaction from the size of his enterprise, then the greater the amount of profit relative to the cost of using capital, the more capital the entrepreneur will be willing to use at the expense of lower profit. This comes down to saying that the more profitable the business, the more it can afford to over-expand. The theoretical basis for this "profit" model of investment demand contradicts the hypothesis of profit maximization.

We now wish to provide our own formulation of a dynamical theory explaining the path taken through time by investment when a firm or industry moves from one long-run equilibrium position to another. In the conventional theory of production, which comes to us through Marshall, the analysis, for all its stress on "time," is essentially one of comparative statics. The adjustment of the firm and the industry from one equilibrium position to another is not formally analyzed precisely because the "short run" and the "long run," the "variable" and the "fixed" factors of production are conceived as technical characteristics of the production process and are independent of the operating variables of the system. Nothing in the theory describes the speed by which interequilibrium movements occur. We propose to provide here a formal analysis of the course of the interequilibrium movement of a competitive firm resulting from an instantaneous and permanent shift in one of the relevant parameters. The parameter shift may, for example, represent an increase in demand for the product, a change in a cost schedule facing the firm, or an improvement in technology, but in any case we assume that an expansion of plant is indicated.

---

[3]Numbers in parentheses refer to publications listed in the Bibliography appearing at the end of this Research Study.

Several other results will flow from this analysis: (1) the distinction between the "short run" and the "long run," between "variable" and "fixed" factors will be made a matter of degree and will be made to depend on economic and not simply technological considerations; (2) a rationalization will be provided for a Koyck-type model (366) of the investment function and for a geometrically decaying distribution of lagged coefficients; (3) a relation between the rate of interest and the distributed-lag coefficients will be developed; and (4) an accelerator-multiplier type model will be formulated in which a Hicks-Goodwin type of ceiling becomes less rigid and is based on economic rather than purely technological considerations.

To be concrete, let us suppose that there is an instantaneous and permanent change in a parameter so that the new long-run equilibrium position for a firm entails a larger plant. We do not expect the new "long-run" equilibrium to come about instantaneously, or we would not refer to it as "long-run." The relative fixity of various factors of production will cause the adjustment to the ultimate, new equilibrium position to take place more or less slowly. In the usual Marshallian analysis, this process is explained by assuming that different productive factors cannot be altered in amount used until a certain length of time has elapsed after an original decision to vary the quantity of each such factor to be employed. The staggering of the lengths of time required to change the quantities of different factors enables one to describe the adjustment process as proceeding by steps and to describe the industry as passing through various states of short- and intermediate-run equilibria before the final adjustment has been made. But the reason for slower rather than more rapid adjustment (in a simple model that excludes uncertainty) is that it costs more (perhaps an infinite amount) to adjust production more rapidly. Indeed, the characterization of productive factors as being more or less fixed in this process ought ultimately to be in terms of the differences in the cost of varying them sooner rather than later, or more rapidly rather than less so.[4] Accordingly, we shall treat a model into which a cost-of-expansion function is specifically introduced in such a way that the adjustment path will be determined not by inflexible technological requirements but by the very principle of profit maximization which determines the equilibrium position itself.

We begin by considering a firm that produces a single product by combining perfectly variable factors of production with another factor of production called its "physical plant." By a "perfectly variable" factor is meant one that can be altered in amount according to a cost schedule which is independent of either the time rate of

---

[4]See in this connection Alchian (7a, p. 33).

change in the amount of that factor used or the time interval between a decision to vary the amount of that factor and its actual variation.

The rate of profit earned by the firm may therefore be regarded as a function of the size of plant, since we may assume that the amounts of the perfectly variable factors used with a plant of given size are always optimally adjusted. We therefore write $p=p(s)$, where p is the rate of profit for a stationary plant of given size s, before deducting interest charges on the plant. Since the size of plant may be regarded as changing through time, t, this may be written out more completely as $p(t)=p[s(t)]$. (When the firm is investing, its net current returns will be less than $p(t)$, however, because, by our definition of "net current returns," we deduct its investment outlay.) Suppose now that the parameter change at time $t=0$ causes this function to attain a unique maximum for a plant size $\hat{s}>s_0$, s_0 being the size of plant at time $t=0$. This we suppose to mean that the entrepreneur wishes that the plant were larger, and we imagine him to draw up a plant expansion program, $s(t)$, at time $t=0$. We next introduce a cost-of-expansion function, $c(t) = c[ds/dt,t]$, where $c(t)$ is a current rate at t. This says that the cost of expansion depends both on the rate of expansion (investment) and on the time that has elapsed between the date at which it was decided to expand, date 0, and the date at which the expansion actually occurs, date t.[5]

If there were no penalty on either the rapidity or promptness of expansion, total investment cost c (a rate), would be proportional to ds/dt, the factor of proportionality representing simply a constant unit cost of the factor called "plant." Total investment cost would then be independent of the time path of plant expansion, and expansion would occur all at once at some most propitious time, t. We assume, however, that the cost of investment increases with the rate of expansion. This means that a cost premium must be paid. Perhaps the best way to look at this is in terms of Figures II-1a and II-1b where investment cost functions are shown. In Figure II-1a, the curve $c[ds/dt,t]$ represents the total cost of various levels of investment at any calendar date t. $c_1=kds/dt$ is a straight line drawn tangent to the function c at the origin, and $c_2[ds/dt,t]$ is simply $c[ds/dt,t]-kds/dt$. c_1 may be defined as the cost component of investment that does not depend upon speed itself. The greater investment, of course, the greater this cost component. But that is because the greater investment (here always regarded as a flow), the greater the amount of additional plant being acquired per unit time. For any increment of plant, Δs (having the dimension of "bricks," not "bricks per unit time"), the cost of this capital will be $k\Delta s$ and this cost is in dollars rather than in dollars per unit time. The rapidity or time path of

---

[5]Considerations underlying the selection of this form of the expansion-cost function are presented later on.

FIGURE II–1a

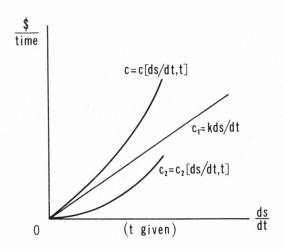

FIGURE II–1b

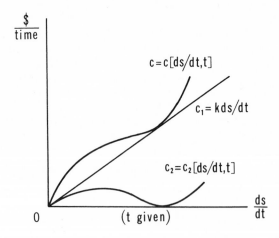

acquiring this additional capital does not affect this cost component. $c_2[ds/dt,t]$ is the cost premium (per unit time) required to elicit a given speed of capital formation. It will be noted that the line $c_1 = kds/dt$ has been chosen tangent to $c = c(ds/dt,t)$ so that the cost component that does not depend upon speed itself (c_1) accounts for as large a share of total expansion cost as possible subject to the condition that c_2 be nonnegative, and therefore so that the component representing the cost premium for speed of expansion (c_2) is minimal. This is the natural meaning of a "premium": what must be paid for an increment of plant (achieved with a given speed) over and beyond what would have to be paid for that same increment if an eternity were available to acquire it. $(c_2$ is, of course, not the premium for the acquisition of a given increment of plant in a given length of time; it is the <u>rate</u> per unit of time at which a premium is being paid for expansion when expansion is taking place at the rate ds/dt. c and c_1 are also <u>rates</u> in this same sense.) In Figure II-1a, however, we have assumed that the speed premium increases monotonically with an increase in ds/dt. In Figure II-1b we do not make this assumption. There we assume that at first it may be more costly to add a given number of bricks slowly than to add them more rapidly, although after a certain point expansion cost is assumed to increase at an increasing rate. In Figure II-1b we have once again chosen the line $c_1 = k\, ds/dt$ so that c_2 represents a premium rate in the sense given above.

The rate of return net of investment cost will therefore be

(1) $p[s(t)] - c[ds/dt,t]$.

We next assume that the firm discounts the net rate of return of all future dates by multiplying (1) by a discounting function which we shall assume is log-linear and represent by $e^{-rt}, r > 0$.[6]

The firm is then assumed to maximize the functional

(2) $$\Phi = \int_0^\infty e^{-rt} \left\{ p[s(t)] - c[ds/dt,t] \right\} dt = \Phi\left\{ s(t) \right\}$$

by choosing the proper function $s(t)$.[7]

---

[6]In the absence of grave imperfections in the credit market, the log-linear assumption here seems reasonable, for the firm is here maximizing a profits stream and not a utility stream and the profits stream does not determine the utility stream uniquely in the presence of borrowing and lending opportunities. (This is also the basis for our subsequent neglect of intertemporal complementarity.)

[7]That a maximum of this integral exists is assured by the fact that $\int_0^\infty e^{-rt}\, dt$ exists and that $p[s(t)] - c[ds/dt,t]$ has an upper bound (under the assumption that if $ds/dt < 0$, $c[ds/dt,t]$ is always finite).

It should be noted that the form of (2) introduces a special assumption regarding the entrepreneur's preferences among future expected streams of returns. Notably it means that the regularization or returns per se is not of consequence to him, or more generally, that there is no intertemporal complementarity in his preference function. Although rather specialized, this is, however, the usual way of thinking about how a future receipts stream is evaluated. If the entrepreneur can borrow or lend at a common rate of interest, the neglect of intertemporal complementarity is evidently justified.

The functional (2) is, of course, to be maximized with respect to the function s(t). To solve this maximization problem we shall assume properties of continuity and of the existence of derivatives that are required for an application of the calculus of variations.

Before proceeding, the reader may wish to look ahead to Figures II-2 and II-3 which portray the relevant functions graphically and show the nature of a solution. In these figures two diagrams with an axis in common are placed side by side. The profit function is shown on the left (with profits plotted horizontally) and maximum profit is shown for plant size $\hat{s}$. If the interest charges on plant were deducted, profit thus redefined would be maximal below $\hat{s}$, say at s^*. The expansion-cost function is plotted against ds/dt and is, for simplicity, assumed in these drawings to be independent of the calendar date t. The expansion path $s(t)$ and its derivative ds/dt are shown on the right. The mathematical conditions for a maximum of (2) are derived in Appendix A and also stated here as:

(10″) $$\frac{\partial^2 d}{\partial(ds/dt)^2} \cdot \frac{d^2s}{dt^2} = \frac{dp}{ds} + r\frac{\partial c}{\partial(ds/dt)} - \frac{\partial^2 c}{\partial(ds/dt)\partial t} \, ,$$

(11″) $$\lim_{t \to \infty} e^{-rt} \frac{\partial c}{\partial(ds/dt)} = 0 \, ,$$

(12″) $$\frac{\partial^2 c}{\partial(ds/dt)^2} \geq 0 \text{ during expansion.}$$

What empirical relationships, if any, are implicit in these results? In particular, what can be said about the nature of that function s(t) that maximizes the discounted stream of future returns? Our first step is to impose certain reasonable a priori conditions on the functions that enter into our problem. We may assume that during the period of expansion (when $ds/dt > 0$) $dp/ds > 0$ because $s < \hat{s}$, i.e., larger plant makes for greater profits; and that $\partial c/\partial(ds/dt) > 0$, i.e., that expansion cost increases with an increase in the rate of expansion. It is conceivable that either or both of these conditions may not hold, but such cases would appear exceptional.

These restrictions, nevertheless, do not permit us to state unequivocally the sign of d^2s/dt^2 - to indicate whether the firm expands at an increasing or decreasing rate. We may, however, point to the factors that determine d^2s/dt^2 best considered in terms of equation (10″). $-\frac{dp}{ds}$ is negative; $+r\ \frac{\partial c}{\partial(ds/dt)}$ is positive and $-\frac{\partial^2 c}{\partial(ds/dt)\ \partial t}$ is indefinite as to sign, although it seems likely that it would be negative, i.e., it is likely that costs related to the speed of expansion would be less for any given rate of expansion with greater lapses of time between the decision to expand and the dates of expansion.

Suppose first that $\frac{\partial^2 c}{\partial(ds/dt)\ \partial t}$ is zero, so that expansion cost depends only on the rate of expansion and not upon the lag involved, and for the moment suppose also that r is so small, the firm hardly discounting future profits at all, that the term $r\ \frac{\partial c}{\partial(ds/dt)}$ does not affect the sign of d^2s/dt^2. Then

$$(10‴) \qquad \text{sign}\ \frac{\partial^2 c}{\partial(ds/dt)^2}\cdot\frac{d^2s}{dt^2}\ =\ -\ \text{sign}\ \frac{dp}{ds}$$

and, since during the expansion period $\frac{dp}{ds}>0$ and $\frac{\partial^2 c}{\partial(ds/dt)^2}\geq 0$, we have $\frac{\partial^2 c}{\partial(ds/dt)^2}>0$ and $\frac{d^2s}{dt^2}<0$. In this simplified case the firm must expand at a slower and slower rate (as the profit attraction of faster and more costly expansion becomes less).

If r is positive as we wish to assume, however, $r\ \frac{\partial c}{\partial(ds/dt)}$ could affect the sign of $\frac{d^2s}{dt^2}$ which could then be positive for a sufficiently great rate of discount. The rationale for the role of this factor is perhaps not very apparent, but can be explained as follows. Suppose we consider the simplest sort of alteration in the expansion plan, that of adding a unit increment to plant one time unit earlier, say at τ rather than at $\tau + 1$ (where the units are very small). Additional cost is given by

$$e^{-r\tau}\ \frac{\partial c}{\partial(ds/dt)}\bigg|_{t\ =\ \tau} \qquad -e^{-r(\tau+1)}\ \frac{\partial c}{\partial(ds/dt)}\bigg|_{t=\ \tau+1}, \text{ additional}$$

profit is given by $e^{-r\tau}\ \frac{dp}{ds}\bigg|_{t=\tau}$. Note that cost is increased at time τ and decreased at time $\tau+1$, but profit is increased at τ without being reduced at any later date. $e^{-r(\tau+1)}$ is approximately equal to $e^{-r\tau}+\frac{d}{dt}e^{-rt}\bigg|_{t=\tau}$

$$\frac{\partial c}{\partial (ds/dt)}\bigg|_{t=\tau+1} \quad \text{is approximately equal to} \quad \frac{\partial c}{\partial (ds/dt)}\bigg|_{t=\tau} \quad +$$

$$+ \frac{\partial^2 c}{\partial (ds/dt)^2}\bigg|_{t=\tau} \cdot \frac{d^2 s}{dt^2}\bigg|_{t=\tau} \cdot$$

The expansion plan does not maximize Φ unless

$$(13) \qquad e^{-r\tau} \cdot \frac{dp}{ds}\bigg|_{t=\tau} \quad -e^{-r\tau} \frac{\partial c}{\partial (ds/dt)}\bigg|_{t=\tau} \quad + e^{-r(\tau+1)} \cdot$$

$$\frac{\partial c}{\partial (ds/dt)}\bigg|_{t=\tau+1} = 0, \text{ or unless}$$

$$(14) \qquad \frac{dp}{ds}\bigg|_{t=\tau} + \frac{\partial^2 c}{\partial (ds/dt)^2}\bigg|_{t=\tau} \cdot \frac{d^2 s}{dt^2}\bigg|_{t=\tau} - r \frac{\partial c}{\partial (ds/dt)}\bigg|_{t=\tau} = 0,$$

the term $-r \dfrac{\partial^2 c}{\partial (ds/dt)^2}\bigg|_{t=\tau} \dfrac{d^2 s}{dt^2}\bigg|_{t=\tau}$ being dropped because

it is small of the second order. It is clear that in evaluating the extra cost of expanding a little more a little sooner, one must add to cost the percentage discount rate, r, times the marginal expansion cost, $\dfrac{\partial c}{\partial (ds/dt)}\bigg|_{t=\tau}$, the latter being the nondiscounted cost trans-

ferred to a slightly earlier date. If this product were sufficiently large, $\dfrac{d^2 s}{dt^2}\bigg|_{t=\tau}$ could be positive; that is to say, the original plan

could call for a <u>rising non-discounted</u> marginal expansion cost (despite the fact that earlier expansion means otherwise greater profits) precisely because this may be consistent with <u>falling discounted</u> marginal expansion cost.

The role of $\dfrac{\partial^2 c}{\partial (ds/dt)\,\partial t}$ in $(10'')$ is more obvious. If $\dfrac{\partial^2 c}{\partial (ds/dt)\,\partial t}$ is negative (the relevant case, we feel), then marginal expansion cost $\dfrac{\partial c}{\partial (ds/dt)}$ decreases with the passage of time. The firm therefore has an incentive to delay its expansion somewhat in order to take advantage of this decline in marginal expansion cost. This consideration may be of sufficient importance to cause $\dfrac{d^2 s}{dt^2}$ to be positive at least during certain phases of the expansion period.

We next show that expansion will not carry the plant to the size $\hat{s}$ at which $p(s)$ is maximal because of the interest burden on plant additions. This is to say that the plant size that maximizes profit net of interest charges on the plant will be smaller than the plant size that maximizes $p(s)$. We pose the question as follows: Is it possible that for some time T it will not pay to expand any further even though $\frac{dp}{ds} > 0$, i.e., even though short-run profits would be greater with a larger plant?

We note that the plan calls for the firm to expand too slowly at date T if

$$\int_T^\infty e^{-rt}\left\{\frac{dp}{ds}\frac{ds}{dt}\right\}\Bigg|_{t=T} dt \equiv \left\{\frac{dp}{ds}\frac{ds}{dt}\right\}\Bigg|_{t=T} \cdot \int_T^\infty e^{-rt} dt >$$

$$> e^{-rT}\left\{\frac{\partial c}{\partial(ds/dt)} \cdot \frac{ds}{dt}\right\}\Bigg|_{t=T}.$$

The term on the left is the rate of addition to the present discounted value of the profit stream with respect to an expansion at the rate $\frac{ds}{dt}$ at date T. The term on the right is the rate at which the present discounted cost of expanding at rate $\frac{ds}{dt}$ at T increases with respect to $\frac{ds}{ds}$ at T. ds/dt should be chosen so that the left and right hand sides above are equal. If the inequality were reversed, the firm would be expanding too rapidly.

The requirement then is that $\frac{dp}{ds} = r\frac{\partial c}{\partial(ds/dt)}$. This means that when expansion ceases $\frac{dp}{ds}$ will still be positive, provided that r is positive and that at ds/dt = 0, the right hand derivative $\frac{\partial c}{\partial(ds/dt)}$ is positive, as is reasonable. This makes sense for $p(s)$ is defined before deducting the interest cost on plant, which is the alternative rate of return on investment. This is to say that the marginal profitability of an "extra brick" must not fall short of the interest charge on the price of an "extra brick."

If the expansion-cost function is as shown in Figure II-1b, the firm will never expand at a rate short of the point at which increasing marginal expansion cost occurs. This imposes a minimum on $\frac{ds}{dt}$ during the expansion period. Consequently the firm will attain plant size s* in a finite length of time. This is illustrated by the two adjacent graphs in Figure II-2 (in which we assume for diagrammatic simplicity that $c[ds/dt]$ is independent of t).

FIGURE II-2

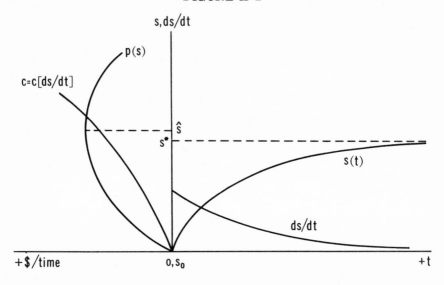

FIGURE II-3

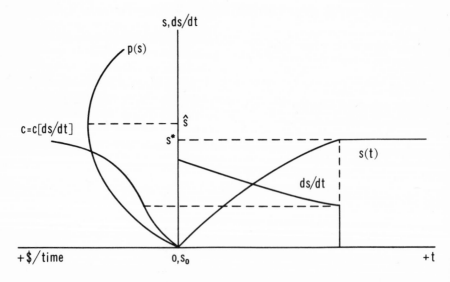

If increasing marginal expansion cost occurs at the very outset (Figure II-1a) so that $\frac{\partial 2c}{\partial(ds/dt)^2}$ is everywhere positive, $\frac{ds}{dt}$ must fall asymptotically to zero as $\frac{dp}{ds} -r \frac{\partial c}{\partial(ds/dt)}$ goes to zero. This will be a continuous process and the new optimal plant size s* will be approached asymptotically as illustrated in Figure II-3.

We turn now to some further remarks about the expansion-cost function, c[ds/dt,t], itself. Surely more involved functions determining c can be concocted, the most general reasonable expression for which would give c as a function of the expansion history $\left\{ ds \left(\int_0^t \right)/d\tau \right\}$ if not of the entire expansion plan $\left\{ ds(\tilde{\tau})_0/d\tau \right\}$. The problem here is similar to (actually an aspect of) that of specifying the static cost function faced by a firm. We focus on two main reasons why a firm may confront greater expansion costs under a program of more rapid expansion: (1) because of a short-run rising supply price in the capital-supplying industry, and (2) because of internal increasing costs associated with integrating new equipment in a going concern: reorganizing production lines, training workers, etc.

A firm that is an important buyer of the product of its capital-supplying industry (or that is integrated vertically so as to supply its own capital) will encounter rising expansion costs on both accounts. To get at the contribution of the first reason to the nature of the expansion-cost function requires that we consider the determinants of the supply function of the capital producing industry. But if expansion endures over any substantial length of time there may be a secondary capital expansion in the supplying industry (the accelerator effect) and to understand this requires an understanding of the technology of the supplying industry as well as of the conditions under which it buys its capital from the industries supplying it. The analytical task can therefore be pressed logically to further and further capital-supplying industries. Throughout, the role of monopolistic and bilaterally monopolistic positions must be taken into account. It is to avoid this and to stay within the bounds of partial-equilibrium analysis that we have simply taken the expansion cost function of our "first-order" firm as given, depending only on ds/dt and t.[8]

A firm that is a competitive buyer in the market for additional plant will not encounter variable expansion costs by reason (1)— rising supply price—if it alone is expanding; but if we are not to

---

[8]For an analysis of the role of time in the supply function of the capital producing industry, see (612a).

fall into a fallacy of composition, we must recognize that during a period of industry-wide expansion an industry which is significant in its market for capital goods will encounter a rising supply price and this will slow down its expansion. There are some subtleties here. A single competitive firm may suppose that it can buy any number of "bricks" for delivery, however rapid or slow, at a fixed price per brick. But if many firms in the economy (or in an industry facing a rising supply curve) were to order above normal quantities of "bricks" for quick delivery, some of them would have to be disappointed. To get these "bricks" quickly, they would have to pay higher prices. It is possible that each of the expanding firms would fail to realize this and would <u>plan</u> its expansion path as if the price of "bricks," even for immediate delivery, were to remain what it has been before the start of general expansion. These plans must then, in a continuous model, be continuously altered, because at all times the price of "bricks" would be changing away from the value that, in their planning, the firms individually took to be fixed. Actual behavior, then, ever based on a false assumption, would not be optimal, and our model would not describe this behavior. But if the individual competitive firms, <u>in their planning</u>, took correct account of the effects of general expansion on factor prices, they would see that it is more expensive to expand sooner rather than later because factor prices would be highest at the beginning of the general expansion (when marginal profitability of plant size is highest) and would subsequently decline (as marginal profitability declines with expanding plant). Our assumption that competitive firms take account of a speed premium function $c_2(ds/dt,t)$ at a time of general expansion does not entail our supposing that each firm imagines that <u>its</u> expansion affects factor prices, but only that each firm has reasonable expectations about the effects of the <u>general</u> expansion on the expansion costs that it confronts. It is difficult to generalize about how these expectations will show up in the function $c(ds/dt,t)$. If each firm assumes simply that the start of general expansion will see higher factor prices, but that those prices will decline as the rate of general expansion abates, then (in the absence of <u>internal</u> speed-premium costs), the expansion-cost function will be $c = k(t) \cdot ds/dt$, where $k(t)$ is the price of a unit increment of plant and declines over time. (We consider this case in greater detail later on.) If, however, each firm supposes that it will not confront a perfect market, but may have to pay premiums to get more rather than fewer "bricks" by a given date, or that it may have to tap more costly or inferior sources of supply to get all it decides it wants by a given date, the expansion-cost function will have to be written in the more general form $c = c(ds/dt,t)$.

These problems of aggregation and of the (ir?-)reconciliation of the parametric character of factor prices in the competitive model with "rational" expectations and optimal plan fulfillment deserve further analysis. It is admittedly a bold stroke for us to regard the individual firm of our model as a miniature of an entire industry or of the economy. But this we do. We suppose that in a tight market for capital goods, individual firms have realistic expectations that price premiums must be paid both for earlier and larger deliveries. This means that expansion cost is an increasing function of the rapidity and promptness of expansion. Moreover, for the model firm we may reasonably assume, as we have, that this function is continuous, because we may think of capital goods as flowing out of the supplying industry to the expanding industry more or less rapidly depending on the demand price for capital of the expanding industry and on the length of time that has elapsed since the expansion began.

This model may be generalized to the case where there are a number of factors that can be varied but where the cost of varying them depends upon either the rate of change or the time lapse between the decision to change and the date of change or both. One would get as a result, however, a system of equations each roughly similar to equations (10"), (11"), and (12"). Here, of course, it may be that during the expansion period some factors would first be increased and then decreased in quantity used, because substitute factors more costly to vary initially may be employed later. The many-factor case is not treated here, however, as it may be developed in a straightforward, albeit complicated, manner from the present model.

What has thus far been shown? Very little perhaps. The effect of an increased desire for capital may lead to expansion at either a decelerating or accelerating rate. Much depends on the role of the magnitude of the terms $\dfrac{\partial c}{\partial(ds/dt)}$ and $\dfrac{\partial 2c}{\partial(ds/dt)\partial t}$ compared to $\dfrac{dp}{ds}$.

We propose next to consider two simple but concrete cases to see what more may be learned about the expansion process. In Case I we suppose that expansion cost depends only on ds/dt. In Case II we think of a competitively structured industry (or economy) that is nevertheless a significant buyer of "plant," and suppose that what deters expansion is only that firms correctly consider the effects of general expansion on the price of capital goods because of a rising capital supply curve.

Case I.

Suppose the functions entering our model are polynomials of the lowest possible degree satisfying the conditions we have imposed upon them. They will then be

$$p = \alpha s - \beta s^2$$

and

$$c[ds/dt] = \gamma(ds/dt)^2 + k(ds/dt),$$

all coefficients positive. The differential equation (10") is then

$$\alpha - \beta s + 2\gamma(d^2s/dt^2) - 2r\gamma(ds/dt) - rk = 0.$$

The general solution is

$$s(t) = A e^{\lambda_1 t} + B e^{\lambda_2 t} + \frac{\alpha - rk}{\beta}$$

where

$$\lambda_1 = \frac{r\gamma + \sqrt{r^2\gamma^2 + 2\gamma\beta}}{2\gamma} ; \quad \lambda_2 = \frac{r\gamma - \sqrt{r^2\gamma^2 + 2\gamma\beta}}{2\gamma} =$$

$$= \frac{r - \sqrt{r^2 + 2\beta/\gamma}}{2} .$$

We note that both roots are real and that

$$\lambda_1 > 0 \text{ and } \lambda_2 < 0.$$

The initial conditions give

$$s_0 = A + B + \frac{\alpha - rk}{\beta}$$

and

$$s^* = \frac{\alpha - rk}{\beta}$$

this being the value of s beyond which the firm does not expand. It is the size of plant at which the marginal profitability equals the price of an extra unit of plant times the rate of interest. That expansion should have occur ed at all implies that $\frac{\alpha - rk}{\beta} > s_0$. We know from subject matter considerations that s does not become infinite as t becomes infinite. Therefore $A = 0$ and $B = s_0 - s^*$. The particular solution is therefore

$$s(t) = (s_0 - \frac{\alpha - rk}{\beta}) \ e^{\frac{r - \sqrt{r^2 + 2\beta/\gamma}}{2} t} + \frac{\alpha - rk}{\beta} .$$

The expansion path of the firm is then a constant minus a decaying exponential, as shown by Figure II-3. If we now consider the effect of $\dfrac{\partial^2 c}{\partial (ds/dt)\, \partial t}$ and suppose that it shows itself primarily in the form of delaying the start of expansion or, better, slowing it down, the expansion path should look approximately like that shown in Figure II-4 by the solid line and may be approximated by an exponentially decaying function starting at some date after 0, as shown by the dashed line in the figure.

Returning to the specific model just treated (in which $\dfrac{\partial^2 c}{\partial (ds/dt)\, \partial t}$ = 0), we want next to ask how an increase in desired capital stock will be translated into investment over a period of time. (We here make contact with the distributed lag models.) This is to ask what determines the ratio of investment in successive periods. This is given by

$$ ds/dt \Big|_{\tau + 1} + ds/dt \Big|_{\tau} = \frac{\lambda_2 (s_0 - \frac{\alpha - rk}{\beta}) e^{\lambda_2 (\tau + 1)}}{\lambda_2 (s_0 - \frac{\alpha - rk}{\beta}) e^{\lambda_2 \tau}} = e^{\lambda_2} $$

e^{λ_2} is therefore the common ratio of investment at dates one unit (year or quarter) apart. According to our model, then, the coefficients of lagged differences between the desired and actual stocks of capital will constitute a declining geometric series. This provides a rationale for the distributed lag formulation of Koyck, which in his work has been proposed largely as a statistically convenient formulation to fit to empirical data.

Others (Stone and Rowe (599); Marc Nerlove, Distributed Lags and Demand Analysis)[9] have also proposed that distributed lag coefficients should decline in a geometrical series, having come to this proposition quite directly from the assumption that the decision maker adjusts his stock to a new level of equilibrium stock demand by adding to stock a fixed proportion of the difference between desired and actual stock each time period. This is an ad hoc proposition which we have now adduced from theoretical considerations —plus some ad hoc simplification of the forms of the functions considered.

How does the common ratio e^{λ_2} change as the rate of time discount (what would correspond to the market rate of interest in a perfect capital market) changes?[10] That is, what is the sign of

[9] Agriculture Handbook No. 141, Agricultural Marketing Service, U.S. Department of Agriculture (June, 1958).
[10] We do not consider here the effect of the change in the rate on optimal plant size itself, though such an effect is to be expected.

$$\frac{de^{\lambda_2}}{dr} = e^{\lambda_2} \cdot \frac{d\lambda_2}{dr} = e^{\frac{r - \sqrt{r^2 + 2\beta/\gamma}}{2}} \quad (1/2)\,[1 - (r^2 + 2\beta/\gamma)^{-1/2}r] =$$

$$(1/2)e^{\frac{r - \sqrt{r^2 + 2\beta/\gamma}}{2}} \quad [1 - \sqrt{\frac{r^2}{r^2 + 2\beta/\gamma}}\,]?$$

The bracketed factor is necessarily positive, as is the other factor so that e^{λ_2} increases with an increase in the rate of interest. This means that investment tends to be spread out more uniformly, the higher the interest rate, ceteris paribus, as one would expect; or, in other words, that a rise in the interest rate delays investment.

On the basis of our analysis of this simple case, we can perhaps acquire some insight into a more complex case. Suppose that t plays some role in c(ds/dt,t), so that the optimal expansion path is that shown by the solid line in Figure II-4. Exponential expansion has there been modified by virtue of the advantages of delaying planned rates of expansion after the initial date at which it has been decided to expand (this is the role ascribed to t). Moreover, the advantage of delaying expansion becomes marginally less the greater the delay. If the interest rate were to rise, the exponential expansion path which has been modified by the advantages of delaying ought itself to be flattened out. Thus, with reference to Figure II-5, if at interest rate r_0, expansion would proceed according to the curve OA in the absence of any advantages in delaying and according to OB in the presence of positive but diminishing marginal advantages to delaying, then at a higher interest rate $r_1 > r_0$, expansion would proceed according to OC in the absence of advantages in delaying and according to OD in their presence. In this more complex case, then, it would seem that a rise in the interest rate would also slow down investment. Suppose that for interest rate r_0, a good approximation to OB is given by OK_BB' (Figure II-6) and for interest rate r_1, a good approximation to OD is given by OK_DD'.

This implies that, in the discrete analog to the continuous case we have considered, a rise in the rate of interest will tend to lower the coefficients of more recent sales changes and raise those of more remote sales changes in a Koyck-type (distributed lag) investment function:

$$I(t) = \sum_{k=0}^{K-1} \varepsilon_k \, \Delta Y(t - k) + \eta \sum_{j=0}^{\infty} \mu^j \Delta Y(t - K - j).$$

FIGURE II-4

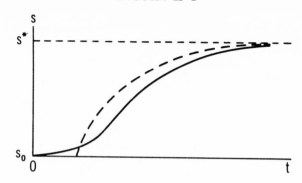

FIGURE II-5

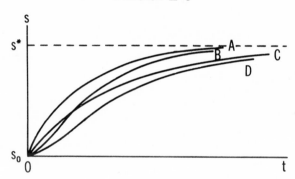

FIGURE II-6

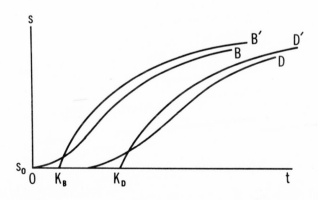

Thus the initial ε_k's will tend to fall. Moreover, the date K beyond which the coefficients can be suitably approximated by a geometrically decaying sequence may be altered (we would judge that K would become greater, as indicated by Figure II-6). μ would be larger; and η most likely smaller. These, at least, are our conjectures about the effect of an increase in the interest rate in this more complex case.

The proposition that if t does not enter the expansion-cost function, so that we may write $c=c[ds/dt]$, investment will decline exponentially rests--it must be stressed--upon a number of simplifying assumptions which were set forth. Our view is that it is plausible, though not logically necessary, that in a distributed lag investment function, the early lags (the ε_k's, above) may be quite arbitrary and several in number, and that only the later coefficients could be approximated by a geometrically decaying sequence.

Case II.

Consider now the case where each of many competitive buyers of plant during a general expansion believes he can buy plant at any rate at a fixed price per unit, but has correct expectations as to how that price will change over time in response to the general expansion. Thus, each firm has the expansion-cost function

$$c = k(t) \cdot ds/dt$$

where $k(t)$ is the actual future time path of the price of a unit of plant. Then equation (10") becomes

$$\frac{dp}{ds} = r\,k(t) - k'(t).$$

Suppose we next consider the linear case where the marginal profitability of plant dp/ds is a linear decreasing function of plant size, thus

$$\frac{dp}{ds} = a - bs \ ,$$

(10") is then $a - bs \quad rk(t) - \dfrac{d\,k(t)}{dt}$.

Moreover, we assume all firms to be identical so that $k(t)$ which depends upon the expansion of the industry can also be written as a function of the rate of expansion of any individual firm. We assume this function to be linear. Thus,

$$k(t) = g + h\,\frac{ds}{dt} \ ,$$

all parameters positive, so that the price of a unit of plant rises linearly with the rate of expansion.

(10″) is then

$$a - bs = rg + rh \cdot ds/dt - \frac{h d^2 s}{dt^2} \; ,$$

a differential equation whose general solution is

$$s(t) = Ae^{\frac{r + \sqrt{r^2 + 4b/h}}{2} t} + Be^{\frac{r - \sqrt{r^2 + 4b/h}}{2} t} + \frac{a - rg}{b} \; .$$

Since the first exponential term has a positive exponent and since the terminal value for $s(t)$ is not infinite, $A = O$. Then, from

$$s(0) = s_0 = B + \frac{a - rg}{b},$$

we have

$$B = s_0 - \frac{a - rg}{b} \; ,$$

so that the particular solution is

$$s(t) = (s_0 - \frac{a - rg}{b}) \; e^{\frac{r - \sqrt{r^2 + rb/h}}{2} t} + \frac{a - rg}{b} \; .$$

s^*, the terminal size of plant, is $\frac{a - rg}{b}$. That expansion occurs at all implies that $B < o$. If r were zero, expansion would proceed to the point at which marginal profitability is zero; but for $r > o$ expansion proceeds only to the point at which the marginal profitability of the last increment of plant is equal to the rate of interest r times the cost of a unit increment of plant.

Once again, the optimal expansion path is a constant minus a decaying exponential and an alternative rationalization of the Koyck-type distributed lag investment function is obtained. The ratio of investment at dates one unit apart

$$ds/dt \big|_{\tau + 1} + ds/dt \big|_{\tau} = e^{\lambda_2} = e^{\frac{r - \sqrt{r^2 + 4b/h}}{2}}$$

is a constant as before; and, moreover $\frac{de^{\lambda_2}}{dr} > 0$, as before.

It appears therefore not to matter for our qualitative results whether firms are slowed down in expanding because a greater rate of expansion costs more per unit than a lesser rate, at any given date, or because of a (correctly) expected change in the price of plant over time. Nevertheless it seems reasonable to allow for the possibility that expansion may be slow at the start because of a more complex expansion-cost function that makes a planning lag almost imperative financially. Hence we still allow for the possibility that the expansion path may be as shown by the solid line in Figure I-4 and that a change in the interest rate is apt to cause it to shift as shown in Figure I-6.

Suppose, next, that we define $s^* - s_0$ as a capital deficiency and call it D_0, or, better, $D(t_0)$ letting t_0 serve as the date at which the deficiency first occurs or at which an investment program intended to remove the deficiency is first activated. Imagine now that new investment deficiencies arise continuously starting at date zero, and as given by some function $D(t_0)$. At the aggregative level $D(0)$ may at first be small, but new deficiencies arise as investment itself proceeds, via a sort of multiplier. In particular, suppose $D(t_0) = \varkappa\, dI(t_0)/dt_0$, where I is the aggregative investment occurring to meet all yet unsatisfied capital deficiencies. We then have, using the model of case I,

$$I(\tau) = -\lambda_2 D(o) e^{\lambda_2 \tau} - \int_0^\tau \varkappa \frac{dI(t_0)}{dt_0} \lambda_2 e^{\lambda_2 (\tau - t_0)} dt_0.$$

Then, $\dfrac{dI(\tau)}{d(\tau)} = -\lambda_2^2 D(o) e^{\lambda_2 \tau} - \varkappa \dfrac{dI(\tau)}{d\tau} \lambda_2$

$$- \int_0^\tau \varkappa \frac{dI(t_0)}{dt_0} \lambda_2^2 e^{\lambda_2 (\tau - t_0)}\, dt_0,$$

or, $\quad \dfrac{dI(\tau)}{d\tau} = \dfrac{\lambda_2}{1 + \varkappa \lambda_2} I(\tau),$

so that, $\quad I(\tau) = K e^{\frac{\lambda_2}{1 + \varkappa \lambda_2} \tau},$

K being determined by the initial disturbance $D(o)$, viz.,

$$I(\tau) = -\lambda_2 D(o) e^{\frac{\lambda_2}{1 + \varkappa \lambda_2} \tau}.$$

This model will be explosive if $\varkappa > -1/\lambda_2$, and it is one of the accelerator-multiplier type. In place of a Hicks-Goodwin ceiling we have continuing and increasing resistance to an increase in the rate of investment in the form of rising marginal expansion cost. But as long as λ is finite, no absolute ceiling will be reached. We might note, however, that if, as investment surged upward, γ, regarded now as a function of time[11] became infinite, λ_2 would go to zero and the expansion would stop.

The explosion in investment could also be kept in check if $\varkappa$ began to fall towards zero, that is, if as investment rose it ceased via the multiplier to increase the profit opportunities for additional capital. It would seem, however, that it is more likely a rise in γ than a decline in $\varkappa$ that would choke off further increases in the level of investment. If $\varkappa < -1/\lambda_2$ to start with, the system will, of course, be damped from the beginning.

Throughout this discussion we have considered the case of expansion, not contraction. A model of contraction would doubtless embody many of the same considerations, but surely not exactly the same functions and parameters.

Returning to the general problem of the path of investment between two equilibria positions, there are considerations beyond those in the model just presented which also enter in. Koyck (366) provides a competent discussion of these considerations. They include the possibility that an increase in output may be obtained first through more intensive use of old machines and the continuation in use of machines which otherwise would be scrapped. With the passage of time, however, these machines age, and age more rapidly the more intensively they are used, so that they must come gradually to be replaced and additional new capacity acquired. Koyck also refers to psychological inertias which must be worn down for the new equilibrium to be approached. These inertias may have some legitimate basis. A change in circumstances leading to a greater equilibrium output may at first be suspected to be temporary. Conviction as to the permanence of the change (and conviction that the increase in long-run equilibrium will not, if it should later recede, be completely undone) may be thought to grow the longer the new equilibrium lasts. Hence long-run adjustments to it may at first proceed cautiously and later gather speed. It is also possible that the firm, industry, or economy may proceed like the paradoxical rabbit cautiously advancing each period of time by some constant fraction of the remaining distance. This version would be more in accord with the received views regarding the distribution of the lag.

b. Intertemporal allocation models. In contrast with the interequilibrium type analysis, the intertemporal allocation models are

---

[11]We are aware that it is, in any strict analysis, improper now to regard γ as a function of I, for this recasts the original model into a nonlinear one. Nevertheless, we think we can discern the properties of the nonlinear model by examining the linear one in this way. (Think of it as piecewise linear with γ rising in jumps.)

not truly dynamic. They do not explain how investment varies over time but are concerned essentially with describing the criteria by which intertemporal allocations are rationally made.

At the most elementary level we can consider the familiar formulation of the investment demand schedule as given by Fisher and Keynes. An expected stream of future returns associated with a given investment program, R_1, R_2, ..., R_n, ... is evaluated by discounting it at some appropriate rate of interest r, thereby giving the present value of the investment program

$$V = \sum_{n=1}^{\infty} R_n/(1 + r)^n .$$

If the appropriate interest rate varies with time, this formula becomes

$$V = \sum_{n=1}^{\infty} R_n/(1 + r_n)^n .$$

If the present value exceeds the cost of the project, the project is expected to be profitable. If the interest rate r is replaced by a variable ρ and ρ is chosen so as to equate the stream of returns discounted at the rate ρ to the cost of the project C, i.e., so that

$$C = \sum_{n=1}^{\infty} R_n/(1 + \rho)^n ,$$

ρ is then defined to be the efficiency of investment. If possible investment projects are ranked with respect to their "efficiencies," a schedule displaying the incremental or marginal efficiency as a function of the level of investment may be defined. If the interest rate r is specified and if investors wish to undertake all profitable projects, the level of desired investment is specified. This same marginal efficiency of investment schedule is then also an investment demand schedule when we think of the rate of interest as the independent variable.

It is important to emphasize that the future returns are expected returns so that the investment demand schedule reflects expectations. In this formulation, however, no explicit account is taken of the investor's feelings about the probability distribution of the possible returns stream. One might slide past this problem by supposing that the investor is interested only in the mathematical expected return of each given date or that the returns which enter into the formulation are "certainty equivalents" to the probability distributions of returns. Even so, the problem becomes complicated if we do not assume that the returns of various dates are statistically independent--an assumption which would appear to be quite unrealistic. What we must then do is to assume that there is some joint probability density function of the returns of all future dates[12]

$$\rho (R_1, R_2, ..., R_N)$$

and define a von Neumann-Morgenstern utility function for a returns stream, i.e.,

$$u = u (R_1, R_2, ..., R_N)$$

so that the investor may be said to maximize the expected value of this function

$$\int_{-\infty}^{+\infty} ... \int_{-\infty}^{+\infty} u(R_1, R_2, ..., R_N) p(R_1, R_2, ..., R_N)$$

$$dR_1, dR_2, ..., dR_N.$$

It would be a further specialization of this function to suppose that it can be written as

$$\sum_{n=1}^{N} \int_{-\infty}^{+\infty} \frac{1}{(1+r)^n} u(R_n) p(R_n) dR_n$$

where $u(R_n)$ is a stationary Neumann-Morgenstern utility function for the return of date n and $p(R_n)$ is an unconditional (marginal) probability density function of R_n.

A further difficulty arises because the probability distribution changes as the scale or volume of investment increases. This means that each project cannot be evaluated in isolation. The more projects that the individual investor (firm) undertakes the less the dispersion about the rate of return. This consideration suggests that larger firms may be more venturesome because of the safety in a large number of projects. This argument requires, however, that the projects considered be sufficiently independent of one another in terms of the probability distributions of their outcomes. It would also suppose that the utility functions of larger firms display no greater risk aversion than those of small firms, which may be untrue.

In computing the present value of an investment project it is also necessary to know what rate of interest to use for discounting. In the case of a perfect capital market--one in which the investor may borrow or lend in any amounts at the same interest rate--the

---

[12]Henceforth we assume that an investment project has a finite duration, terminating in period N.

market rate is the one to use. But the market rate should be regarded as one which prevails for loans of comparable risk. While this point is old hat, it has to be stressed. There is a common impression that the external lending rate for the firm is substantially less than its borrowing rate. This may be true, but one must be careful when contrasting the borrowing rate, the lending rate, and the marginal efficiency of investment of the firm (or what may also be called the marginal internal rate of return) always to consider rates that involve the same risk premium.

It is somewhat neater when evaluating an investment project to include the initial cost C as a return at the starting date ($R_0 = C$), which would, of course, be negative. This is what must also be done when there are project costs to be borne at later dates. Thus R_n may be negative as well as positive. This is what we shall do henceforth. We next consider the curious phenomenon of multiple values for ρ, the efficiency of the project; and indeed some of these values may be positive while others are negative. And it is even possible that all values for ρ may be imaginary. What does this imply about the derivation of the investment demand function? The problem is not simply that the mathematical procedure leads to some spurious roots of the discounting formula and that one must be careful to pick out the economically meaningful root; there may be none or there may be several. For this reason some have concluded that there is something fundamentally unsatisfactory with the concept of the "internal rate of return." We do not agree that the plurality or nonexistence of either positive or of real roots is a cause for concern. We must first note carefully that R's that are positive must be consumed or invested externally (of the project in question). Otherwise, the project and its returns stream have not been unambiguously defined. Suppose that all R's that are positive and which arise before the termination of the project must, if not consumed, be invested externally and that all negative R's must be financed by external borrowing. At the termination of the project the amount of dollars accumulated will be

$$\sum_{n=0}^{N} R_n (1 + r)^{N-n}$$

whose present net value is obtained by dividing by $(1 + r)^N$, so that

$$V = \sum_{n=0}^{N} R_n (1 + r)^{-n},$$

as before. Now, we can always ask: What external (borrowing and lending) interest rate $r = \rho$ would establish the equality

$$0 = \sum_{n=0}^{N} R_n (1 + r)^{-n} ?$$

There may be none, but even this presents no logical difficulty for the derivation of the investment demand schedule. The value of an investment project arises from more than the net interest earnings received from the associated <u>external</u> borrowing and lending. It also pays off <u>internally</u>. It is not at all puzzling conceptually that there could be a returns stream obliging one until the termination of the project to invest externally all positive returns and to borrow externally all funds to be paid in at a common and constant rate of interest, and such that this returns stream would be attractive <u>regardless</u> of the rate of interest. It is simply a sure thing, and one should be happy to seize all such investment opportunities. An example would be the stream $+1, -3, +4.$[13] How would such projects, if they in fact existed, enter in the Keynesian investment demand schedule? They would simply constitute investment projects which would be undertaken at <u>any</u> rate of interest. If such projects exist, the demand schedule would appear as in Figure II-7, with the projects to the left of the vertical asymptote being those in question. Such projects require, however, that the initial return be positive, and are highly unrealistic. What about projects that have multiple positive roots and whose initial payout is negative? The relation between their present value and the interest rate may, for example, be as shown in Figure II-8. Such a project is surely attractive for any interest rate in the region s and unattractive elsewhere. It gives rise to investment demand if the market rate of interest were in the range s and not otherwise. This means simply that the investment demand schedule may be "backward bending," and (in the case of still more positive roots) with as many bends as one pleases. Thus it could, in principle, appear as the one shown in Figure II-9. In principle, then, there is no reason <u>in theory</u> to suppose that investment demand should be sensitive to the rate of interest, or in one way rather than another. After all, investors are both "borrowers" <u>and</u> "lenders." They "borrow" when they commit their funds, and "lend" when they earn the returns. A rise in the present and expected future interest rates may therefore logically cause an <u>increase</u> in the amount of additional capital which firms desire to acquire currently.

More can be said, however, about the empirical importance of the returns streams that have multiple roots; we simply admitted these streams as conceptually possible, because from the standpoint of the <u>pure theory</u> that was all that mattered. One might wish

---

[13]Imagine, for example, a project that would give an initial tax advantage in excess of the initial cost.

FIGURE II-7

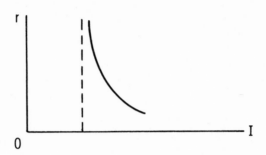

FIGURE II-8

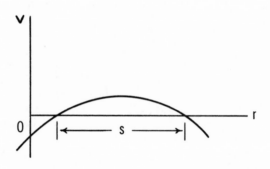

FIGURE II-9

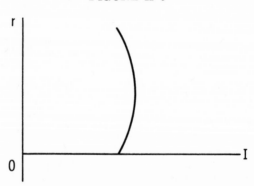

to suppose, however, that if at any date m the remaining portion of the returns stream were of negative value, the investment could and would be costlessly abandoned at that point. This would be to require that for any ρ such that

$$\sum_{n=1}^{N} R_n (1 + \rho)^{-n} \geq 0$$

we would have

$$\sum_{n=m}^{N} R_n (1 + \rho)^{-n} \geq 0 \qquad (m = 1, 2, \ldots, N).$$

By assuming that an investment project defined by a given returns stream can be costlessly terminated at any time that is desirable--with nothing more put in and nothing more taken out--we narrow the class of admissible returns streams, and a backward bending investment demand function is then impossible. (A proof is provided in Appendix B.) This is to ignore "dismantling costs" and the possibility of necessary fixed future contractual obligations that lead to negative returns during the final phase of the project period.

Various rules have been proposed as optimizing criteria for the firm that must choose among alternative investment projects. There is little purpose in our giving them detailed consideration here. Ultimately, the only valid criterion for the case of certainty (and assuming that the firm can be regarded as a single decision maker) is for a utility functional of the decision maker to be maximized subject to constraints displaying both the internal investment opportunities of the firm and the external market opportunities to invest and to raise funds. This is the Fisherian approach and is developed by Hirschleifer (316). For the discrete, two-period case we may, following Hirschleifer, present this as shown in Figure II-10. X_1 and X_2 are pay-outs or income to the entrepreneur in periods 1 and 2. AB is a locus of possible pairs of payouts as given by the internal production possibilities of the firm. Assuming free disposal, all points in the area OAB are possible opportunities. For the moment we suppose the firm can borrow at a fixed rate of interest so that the rate at which the firm can externally exchange X_2 for X_1 is given by the slope of EF. This means that from any point on AB it can move to the southeast along a line parallel to EF, so that the external borrowing opportunities expand the opportunity set to OEHB. Supposing also that the firm can invest externally ("lend"), the X_1, X_2 transfer opportunities being given by the slope of CD, the firm can from any point in OEHB move northwest along a line parallel to CD. This enlarges the opportunity set to the

FIGURE II-10

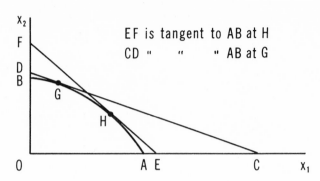

FIGURE II-11

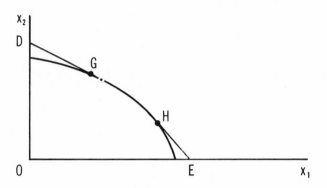

FIGURE II-12

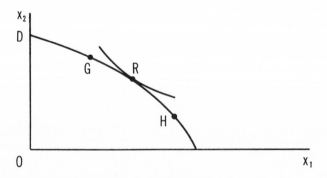

area OEHGD, reproduced in Figure II-11. There is no intrinsic difficulty in supposing that the borrowing and lending rates vary with the amount of the loan or investment so that EH and GD need not be linear.

Next we may superimpose an indifference map on this diagram and determine (uniquely or otherwise) the maximum utility position. If the boundary of the opportunity set is concave from below and the indifference curves are convex, there will be a unique optimum as shown in Figure II-12 by point R.

Depending upon the precise nature of these curves the optimum may lie along HG, as shown, or along EH, in which case the firm borrows, or along GD, in which case the firm invests externally. The internal rate of return will be given by the slope of the locus EHGD at R and it may be equal to the external lending rate, the borrowing rate, or be between the two. In case the lending and borrowing rates are equal, the internal rate of return will equal the two of them. In the multi-period case, the conditions for an optimum just developed must hold for every pair of periods.

We are now in a position (again following Hirschleifer (316)) to point out a serious shortcoming of the use of the internal rate of return as a criterion for selecting investment projects. Given two returns streams, R_0, R_1, ..., R_N and R'_0, R'_1, ..., R'_N, it need not be the case that the one with the higher efficiency or rate of return is the more attractive. If the rate of return differs from the market rates of interest (from either or both), it is necessary in computing present value to apply either the lending or the borrowing rate to any positive or negative return, respectively. To evaluate the returns streams by comparing the roots ρ and ρ' of

$$\sum_{n=0}^{N} \frac{1}{(1+\rho)^n} \cdot R_n = 0 \text{ and } \sum_{n=0}^{N'} \frac{1}{(1+\rho')^n} \cdot R'_n = 0,$$

is misleading, for these formulas assume that the external (market) rate is the same as the internal rate of return. For this to be so, the borrowing and lending rates must be equal and they must be equal to ρ and ρ', i.e., both projects must be marginal.

Let us look further at the two-period diagrams drawn above, and reconsider the nature and meaning of the internal transformation function AB. The very drawing of such a function requires the specification of some "initial conditions," which we may suppose to be a specification of the capital equipment held by the firm at the beginning of period 1. This equipment will define (in the two-period case) a vector $K^\circ = (X^\circ_1, X^\circ_2)$ which may lie inside or on the in-

FIGURE II-13

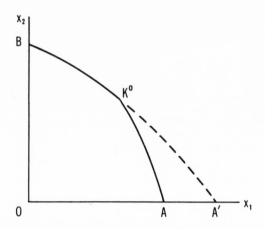

FIGURE II-14

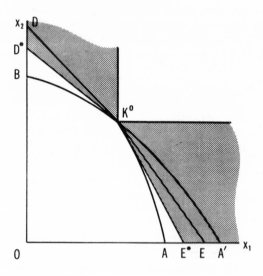

ternal transformation curve AB. We focus on the problem of intertemporal allocation rather than "efficiency" by supposing K° to lie
on AB. It seems natural also to assume that a move away from K°
in the direction of more income next period and less now requires
an accumulation of capital, and that a movement in the opposite
direction entails a capital reduction. Bring in at this point the fact
that a firm's existing capital is often special to it so that it is more
difficult (or costly) for the firm to disinvest than to invest. By this
we mean the following: A firm invests by buying or constructing
plant and equipment. If a firm invests in additional capital and then
immediately decides to disinvest that capital it can do one of two
things: (a) allow the capital to depreciate without replacement,
which is a slow process, or (b) sell the capital used for a lower
price than it has just paid--if the capital is at all special to the
firm. This, at the aggregate level, is a significant element in the
asymmetrical performance of investment in the upswing and the
downswing in the Goodwin and Hicks trade cycle models (255, 312).
Under these conditions the curve AB should appear as in Figure
II-13, being kinked at that intertemporal allocation of internal
earnings for which its existing capital is optimally adjusted, point
K°. Were the capital not at all specific to the firm and were there a
perfect used capital market, the internal transformation function
would be A'B. But under our present assumptions, if the firm is
at K° any effort to increase X_1 (a short-run increase in income)
must entail a substantial sacrifice of X_2--along the segment $K^\circ A$.
The segment $K^\circ B$ rpresents the opportunities via investment to
sacrifice current income X_1 for additional X_2. K° is, as noted
earlier, defined by the existing plant and equipment. We shall use
the symbol k° as the stock of fixed capital (plant and equipment)
corresponding to the position K° on the transformation curve.

If K° is an equilibrium position and if the firm is a borrower,
it must be because (see Figure II-14) the borrowing line through
K° lies in the lower shaded area. If K° is an equilibrium position
and if the firm is a lender, the lending line through K° must lie in
the upper shaded area. In the first case the firm will have reached
its optimum at some point on the borrowing line in the lower shaded
area, say along EK° at a point of tangency with an indifference
curve; and in the second case at some point in the upper shaded
area, say, along $K^\circ D$. Suppose the indifference curves between income of successive periods and the borrowing and lending rates
were stationary, so that we could relabel the horizontal axis X_t and
the vertical axis X_{t+1}. It would then pay the firm, in the first
(borrower) case, in view of its subjective time preference, to
maintain its capital, successive short-term borrowing providing
better terms than depreciation for moving income receipts forward
in time. In the second (lending) case, the firm might never expand
its capital, it being more advantageous, period by period, to invest
externally (lend).

FIGURE II–15

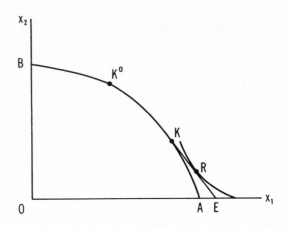

FIGURE II–16

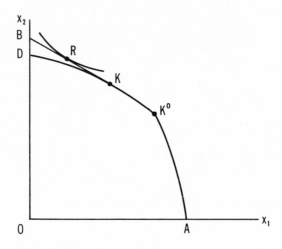

In either equilibrium situation the two interest rates may vary within some range and so long as the borrowing and lending lines through K^{o} remain in the shaded areas, there would be no effect on the optimal plant size. Physical disinvestment is too unremunerative (or costly) to be attractive unless the borrowing rate rises to some upper critical level, and internal investment opportunities would remain unattractive unless the external lending rate fell to some lower critical value.

Consider next a firm that does not have an equilibrium amount of capital. It may have too much (Figure II-15) or too little (Figure II-16). Its present stock of capital we shall call K^{o}. For the case in Figure II-15, the desired amount of capital is K (corresponding to K) and its optimal position is R. Such a firm will borrow and do some disinvesting. Symmetrically, in the case in Figure II-16, a firm would invest and lend.

Suppose that in the aggregate the desired and actual stocks of capital are equal. This might arise either (a) because all firms are in equilibrium or (b) because differences between desired and actual amounts cancel out as between firms that are underexpanded and firms that are overexpanded. Assuming always that changes in the lending and borrowing rates move in the same direction when they move, we find that in situation (a) "small" changes in the rate of interest have no effect on investment and in (b) any change moves both underinvested and overinvested firms in the same direction, i.e., a rise in the interest rate causes aggregate investment to decline, and a decrease in the interest rate causes aggregate investment to rise. Thus, in a position of aggregate equilibrium, the interest elasticity of investment demand may not be zero if and only if there is structural disequilibrium. This analysis would lead us to conclude, then, that there is no reason to find any definite relationship between changes in the rate (or rates) of interest and changes in aggregate investment demand in the neighborhood of the prevailing interest rate. The interest elasticity of aggregate investment will depend on the extent of disequilibrium of individual firms.

The previous drawings may suggest that the lending and borrowing rates must be different for our result. This is by no means the case. In Figure II-17, the borrowing and lending lines are the common line ED which is shown. Firm 1 confronts internal intertemporal allocation possibilities as shown by the curve A_1B_1. Its present internal intertemporal allocation is defined by its stock of capital K^{o}_1 corresponding to K^{o}_1 (remember, capital and investment are not themselves measured on any of these diagrams). Its desired capital stock is K_1 corresponding to K_1. Firm 2 confronts the technical transformation line A_2B_2, has capital in the amount of K^{o}_2 corresponding to K^{o}_2 and desires to be at K_2, with capital in the amount K_2. A change in the interest rate will change the investment demand of both firms in a common direction. Allowance may now be made for the possibility that the transformation function is not perfectly kinked at K°, but merely has a high rate of curvature in the neighborhood of K°. This removes the sharpness from our results, but the general qualitative conclusions still remain. In general, expanding firms and contracting firms are apt to be more responsive to interest rate changes than firms in equilibrium which are apt to be relatively unresponsive to small changes.

FIGURE II-17

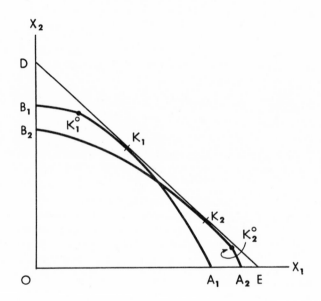

In all the foregoing we have largely abstracted from the presence of risk and uncertainty, and from any critical examination of the firm's own criteria of decision making.

c. <u>Risk, uncertainty, and expectations</u>. There is not much at the formal level to be said under this heading. The utility function or functional to be maximized may be assumed to be of the Neumann-Morgenstern sort, so that it is expected utility which the firm attempts to maximize. Without reference to observations, nothing can be said, however, about the properties of such a function, e.g., whether it would display risk aversion or risk preference. Some investors may be investors simply because of risk preference; others may be investors despite risk aversion because they are attracted by mathematically expected gains. Both types probably exist, although the large corporation would, to common observation, appear to be essentially a risk averter.

A familiar idea is that the firm assigns a very great negative utility to bankruptcy and, more generally, to losses. This can be translated to mean that there is rapidly diminishing marginal utility of income just above the range of negative income.

To explain investment decisions it is important not only to know something about attitudes towards risks, but also about how potential investors come to form judgments as to the probabilities of various possible outcomes of investment decisions, i.e., how expectations are formed. Again, unfortunately, there exists little deductive theory of expectation formation. To the extent that business expectations have been related to economic variables, the hypotheses have been ad hoc and the research empirical. Economists have searched for variables that would play the role in economic models of the expected values of other variables. The substitute variables are the "proxy" variables which have so often appeared in empirical work. But the procedure is experimental. On a priori grounds--the concern of this section of the present paper--nothing can be said. The merits of past and present profit or profit change, sales or sales change, asset value or asset value change, etc. as proxies for the expected return on additional plant and equipment must be appraised in the light of empirical studies and in a later section.

Attempts have been made, of course, to determine business expectations directly by survey methods. Empirical studies employing expectational variables measured in this way will be reported on in Chapters III and IV.

2. Investment in inventories

a. Inventories and the theory of the firm. During recent years there has appeared a growing body of literature concerned with inventory control problems at the level of the individual firm. By and large, this literature is not, at least yet, especially fruitful for problems regarding aggregate inventory investment, for which, of course, it has not been primarily developed. It has, however, focussed more attention than may otherwise have been given on the cost economies to the firm of maintaining a smooth schedule of production through time, a phenomenon which in aggregate dynamic models may not entirely wash out. Emphasis has also been placed on problems of the optimal lot size in which to order inputs, where there are fixed cost components in ordering and in deliveries. As a matter of fact, studies that introduce a flat procurement charge, which is independent of the amount of a stock ordered, are akin to studies emphasizing the benefits of regularity in production. Both

introduce a cost of trying too closely to match production or procurement with current sales.

The optimal procurement problem gives rise to the "square-
root formula" (see 645, p. 33):

$$Q = \sqrt{\frac{2YS}{IC}} \; ,$$

where Q is the "economic purchase quantity," Y is the expected
yearly sales (assumed to occur at a constant rate), I is the constant
inventory carrying cost per unit quantity per year, C is the constant
unit cost of the commodity or factor being purchased, and S is the
fixed cost of a single order. Thus, as sales, Y, rise, Q rises and
the average amount in storage is increased by half the rise in Q
(since sales are assumed to occur at a constant rate). Let this
amount $\frac{Q}{2}$, be J. Then the elasticity of J with respect to Y is +1/2
and with respect to I is -1/2. The qualitative conclusions are that
the stock-sales ratio varies inversely with sales and with inventory
carrying cost, which includes the rate of interest.

Whether a rise in sales would reduce the stock-sales ratio
where the purpose in carrying inventories is not to reduce procurement costs but is rather to schedule production more economically, is another question. The answer would seem to rest
primarily on whether a rise in sales tends to level out percentage
fluctuations in sales over time (e.g., seasonally) or on whether the
probability distribution of expected sales has a smaller coefficient
of variation as mean expected sales rise. A very good analysis of
this matter is provided by Mills (452) who conjectures that when the
mean of expected sales increases the variance increases in lesser
proportion. There are still other considerations. In retailing, for
example, inventories may, as the level of sales changes, tend to be
higher or lower relative to sales because of the marketing considerations that involve the range of choice of colors, sizes, and
designs available to the customer. Whitin (645) finds that, on the
whole, the evidence shows that the stock-sales ratio varies inversely with sales.[14] This conclusion may make us somewhat less
happy with theories that assume the stock sales ratio to be a constant, although such theories may yet have much value as an
approximation.

----

[14]Some of his evidence is cross-sectional in character and this
avoids the great danger of identifying desired with actual stocks
in time-series data.

When inventories are held to avoid the costs of changing production rates, the response of the inventories of the firm to demand changes may be oscillatory. Mills (452) provides a demonstration of this by considering a model in which a cost of changing the rate of production is introduced explicitly. The effect of these costs is to make production sluggish in adjustment to a change in sales with the result that there is also a tendency for inventories to overshoot their new equilibrium, but by less with each oscillation. An analytically similar model is that studied by Morehouse, Strotz, and Horwitz (472) in which inertia coefficients are introduced between the "production department" and the "inventory department," the "inventory department" and the "marketing department," and the "production department" and the "marketing department." These coefficients can be interpreted as reflecting a desire to hold down the rate of change in goods flows, for cost, technical, or psychological reasons. An inventory demand function is ascribed to the firm which exerts a pressure towards readjusting inventories towards their equilibrium levels. Oscillatory responses to a demand function shift are observed.

The reader who is interested in the literature on inventory control problems at the level of the firm is referred to (27, 647, and 645), which also contain adequate bibliographies. A recent reference of much interest is Holt and Modigliani (320a) which surveys and compares several other studies and discusses the possible relation of the microeconomic theory of optimal production scheduling, with its implications for inventory change, to macroeconomic models of aggregate inventory investment.

b. Inventories and the business cycle. The other main body of theoretical literature concerned with the role of inventories in the economy is that dealing with the business cycle. R. G. Hawtrey (see esp., 299a and 299) gave inventories a primary role in his theory of economic fluctuations. Hawtrey regarded the system as being essentially explosive, at least to the extent that there would be sufficient continuing credit creation during the upswing and destruction during the downswing. During an upward explosion an insatiable demand for credit would arise mainly from merchants who would be trying to increase their inventories. But their very efforts would be self-frustrating, for the credit expansion is claimed to result in a continuous upward movement in the demand for goods, and this would hold back inventory accumulation. This process is apt to be terminated only by the curtailment of credit creation and a resulting rise in the interest rate. Hawtrey stressed the importance of the short-term rate of interest and the sensitivity of the desired inventories of merchants to variations in it.

The best-known modern theory of inventories and the business cycle is that of Lloyd Metzler (443, 445, 331).[15] Metzler has presented several models of inventory cycles (443), based mainly on the earlier work of Lundberg (398a). We consider one of the models he presented (which is also the one discussed in Allen (10)). Two aspects of any interesting inventory cycle model are of interest to us: (1) What is the nature of the behavior relation explaining inventory investment? (2) How do inventories behave, according to the theory, over the business cycle? The answer to the second question involves more than simply the nature of the inventory investment function; it involves the other structural relationships in the system as well. These other relations are not the concern of this monograph. Yet they enter critically in any test of a proposed inventory investment function. The kernel of the matter is that a general desire to alter inventories may, at least for a substantial length of time, be self-frustrating (as noted earlier by Hawtrey and stressed more recently by Nurkse (502)). Curtailing of orders in efforts to reduce inventories, for example, may reduce incomes and may lead to unexpected decreases in sales which increase inventories. We have here a much more significant phenomenon for inventory investment than for plant and equipment investment, making it more difficult to formulate or to test an inventory investment function without simultaneously explaining the determinants of sales. The Metzler model provides an excellent illustration of this.

Metzler assumes that the desired stock-to-sales ratio is a constant, α, so that planned inventories are α times expected sales. He assumes further that expected sales are equal to sales of the previous period. Sales in any period are assumed to be proportional to income of that period, the factor of proportionality being β. Thus sales expected for period t are equal to $\beta y(t-1)$, where y is income, and so the desired inventories for period t are $\alpha\beta y(t-1)$. If inventories are represented by k, then planned inventory investment for period t will be $\alpha\beta y(t-1)-k(t-1)$, which is desired inventories minus the inventories of the previous period. Income for period t will consist of planned inventory investment plus production for expected sales for period t plus autonomous investment, i.e.,

$$y(t) = \alpha\beta y(t-1) - k(t-1) + \beta y(t-1) + v_0,$$

where v_0 is autonomous investment.

---

[15] In the literature reviewing the theory of the role of inventories in the business cycle attention is often given to Keynes. His discussion (A Treatise on Money (N.Y.: Harcourt, Brace and Co.), 1930; and The General Theory of Employment, Interest, and Money, (N.Y.: Harcourt, Brace and Co.), 1936) does not, however, appear to add anything, at least to the treatment of later authors.

Inventories of the previous period, k(t-1), will equal planned inventories for that period, $\alpha\beta y(t-2)$ minus any excess of actual over expected sales during t-1. This excess is $\beta y(t-1) - \beta y(t-2)$. Therefore,

$$k(t-1) = \alpha\beta y(t-2) - \left[\beta y(t-1) - \beta y(t-2)\right],$$

so that, substituting in the previous equation, we have

$$y(t) = (2 + \alpha) \cdot \beta y(t-1) - (1 + \alpha) \cdot \beta y(t-2) + v_o.$$

This system leads to oscillations which may be either damped or explosive. (The stability conditions have been analyzed by Metzler (443) and by Allen (10).) A feature of the Metzler model which is of interest is that inventories accumulate past the point at which income turns down and decumulate past the point at which income turns up. As will be seen in Chapter IV, this accords with the facts as reported (note, in this connection, also (3 and 447a)). It is here that we see the self-frustrating character of inventory investment. Though desired inventories may decline, actual inventories may at times rise because the attempt to reduce inventories also reduces income and hence sales. (For a further analysis of this, see Nurkse (502).)

Dynamic small-dimensional business cycle models that ascribe a role to inventories are interesting in certain of their implications, but leave many questions unanswered. The inventory investment equation in the Metzler model is, after all, an extremely simple one: only two behavioral constants appear in it. But inventory investment is a composite of more forces, even in broad outline.

c. Motives for holding inventories. Most commonly, efforts to analyze the motives for holding inventories proceed by first disaggregating inventories into the various forms in which they are held, e.g., purchased materials, goods in process, final goods. Differences in the determinants of these various forms of inventories are postulated, and differences in their behavior are observed.[16] One advantage of casting the analysis in these terms is that available data are classified in this way. The disadvantage is that there are substantial prospects for substitution among these forms or stages of inventory holdings. This is so for the individual firm, which may choose, for example, to hold its inventories in either pre- or post-manufactured form, and for the economy: the raw materials inventories (inputs) of the buyer of them may alterna-

---

[16]Business inventories are also disaggregated by the character of the industry, e.g., durable goods industries and nondurable goods industries.

tively be held by the seller as finished goods inventories (output).
Because technology is here not decisive we prefer, at least at the
theoretical level, to disaggregate by motive rather than by stage.

Any classification of motives for holding inventories is necessarily arbitrary and of arbitrary degree of fineness. We choose,
however, to distinguish four primary ones, though they are, as we
shall argue, not necessarily distinct.[17]   They are:

(1) Technological reasons. The very process of production is
time consuming and certain amounts of inventories must always
be held in the form of "work in process." We may think of the
sausage machine and note that a certain amount of sausage is always
in the machine. The illustration is worth pursuing. If sausage output
is increased by speeding up the operation of the machine, the amount
in the machine at any time nevertheless remains constant. Some
production processes are capable of variation in output rates in
just this way. The addition of more labor to fixed amounts of
capital (especially the addition of more shifts) may increase output
without increasing work in process. On the other hand, the rate at
which sausage is produced may be increased not only by speeding
up the machine or operating it more hours per day, but also by
increasing the number of machines.[18] That involves, pari passu,
increasing work in process. What is to be stressed, however, is that
work-in-process inventories need not be proportional to output.

(2) Procurement and production scheduling reasons. As discussed
at the beginning of this section, inventories may be maintained because of the economies in ordering in "batches," producing in
"batches," or smoothing out variations in production over time.
This implies that inventories will be held in the form of yet-to-be
processed inputs, semi-processed, but idle goods, or final goods.
These inventories are "work not in process." Their existence
arises from the cost structure of ordering, delivering, and production, and from variations in the rate of sales, but not from uncertainty as to sales. If future sales were perfectly known, inventories would still be held for the reasons given here.

We may expect these inventories to vary with sales, but not in
a very simple way. Consider, first, variations in sales that are
seasonal and foreseen. When sales rise in accordance with this
pattern, we may expect such inventories to rise to the extent that
they exist because of procurement costs and the desire not to change

----

[17]An alternative classification by motives is given by Modigliani
in (463).
[18]In his empirical study, Thomas M. Stanback has had occasion to
stress this distinction (582a, p.98).

the rate of output abruptly. But the rise in inventories is apt to occur first, in anticipation of the sales rise, and when sales are high these inventories may then even be depleted, though not necessarily so. This possibility has received serious attention by Modigliani and Sauerlander (462). Consider next a change in the general level of sales that is not a seasonal short-run change but a long-run change, cyclical or secular. The equilibrium level of "not-in-process" inventories would then change in the same direction, although probably by a smaller percentage. That a rise in sales, depending on how well it has been foreseen and how enduring it is expected to be, may lead to a gradual build-up of inventories, or to an anticipatory build-up followed by a depletion, or to a depletion followed by a build-up suggests how difficult it may be to find any stable relationship in time-series data.

(3) Precautionary reasons. If firms take account of the prospect of unforeseen sales changes, inventories may be held to avoid shortages and the necessity of costly unplanned changes in the production schedule. In this way inventories are used as a buffer against unpredictable changes in demand. The volume of inventories to be held for this reason should depend upon the subjective estimates of the probability distribution of future sales. With attention focussed on an equilibrium situation, we may suppose that the variance of the probability distribution of prospective sales is greater, the greater are sales, or that larger inventories would be held as a buffer because of the precautionary motive, the greater the level of sales, though the relation need not be proportionate.

(4) Speculative reasons. If either production and raw materials costs or product prices are expected to rise, and at a rate sufficient to cover storage costs, investors have an incentive to accumulate inventories, and, in the opposite case, to reduce them.[19]

There is not much at the purely theoretical level that can be said, however, to enable us to relate changes in desired inventory holdings for price speculation reasons to observable variables. The problem is that of finding measures of expected price changes. This can, of course, be attempted by questionnaire methods. A proxy variable of dubious merit on theoretical grounds is the price change of the recent past, and it has been tried -- without notable success -- in some empirical inventory studies.

The interest rate probably plays a more important role in determining the speculative and precautionary demands for inven-

---

[19] Consumers, too, have an incentive to accumulate durables, but this, we shall suppose, belongs not in this book, but rather to the topic of a consumer expenditure function.

tories; technological, procurement, and production scheduling causes of demand leave somewhat less flexibility for inventory policy. Indeed, in measuring the interest rate that is relevant to policy, one ought to deflate it by the expected rate of price rise.

A qualification to be noted in passing is that, for some product lines, e.g., automobiles, the capacity to store goods is restricted either by physical limitations or by the prospect of model changes which may make the stored goods obsolete. This limitation may be significant during a period when a substantial inventory accumulation occurs because of strong speculative reasons.

These are the motives for carrying inventories. Keynes wrote his liquidity preference function in a form additive in the cash holdings desired for the transactions and precautionary motives, on the one hand, and the speculative motives on the other hand. May we do the same with inventories and write

$$\hat{I} = I_W + I_n + I_p + I_S$$

where $\hat{I}$ is desired inventories, I_W is work-in-process inventories, I_n is work-not-in-process inventories, I_p is precautionary inventories, and I_S is speculative inventories?

This is dangerous because the same physical goods may serve different purposes. In particular, the presence of inventories held because of a speculative motive may obviate the need to hold still additional inventories for the other reasons. It would seem that inventories are not likely, when $I_S > I_W + I_n + I_p$, to rise much above I_S, nor, in the opposite case, to fall much beneath $I_W + I_n$. This suggests, in our formulation, that if prices are falling sufficiently rapidly (a lower critical value) so that $-I_S > I_p$, desired inventories will be approximately $I_W + I_n$, and that if they are rising at a rate in excess of some upper critical value, the price rise alone will be mainly responsible for the level of inventories. For a rate of price change in between these critical values, the speculative motive will be met by inventories which would be held anyway for other purposes.

Thus far we have given primary attention to <u>desired equilibrium inventories</u>. What will determine inventory investment? Let $\hat{I}(t)$ be desired equilibrium inventories and $I(t)$ be actual inventories at the beginning of period t. Intended inventory investment for period t may then be some fraction of $\hat{I}(t) - I(t)$, the discrepancy not necessarily being corrected within a single period. Intended inventory investment $\tilde{\Delta}I(t)$ is then given by

$$\tilde{\Delta}I(t) = \eta \cdot [\hat{I}(t) - I(t)].$$

But actual inventory investment may be other than what is intended-- as developed in the Metzler model. From $\tilde{\Delta} I(t)$ we must deduct any difference between actual and expected sales.

Let this be $S(t) - S_e(t)$ where $S_e(t)$ is expected sales for period t. We then have

$$\Delta I(t) = \eta - [\hat{I}(t) - I(t)] - K[S(t) - S_e(t)].$$

We have introduced the coefficient K (<1) to allow for the fact that if during the period sales should exceed expected sales some adjustment of production is possible within the period. The difference between expected and actual sales would then not be met entirely out of inventories.

The sort of model sketched in the previous paragraph has been used in several empirical investigations. These are to be discussed in Chapter IV.

We have yet to ask what the effect of a change in the interest rate will be on inventory investment demand, i.e., desired inventories. A rise in the interest rate is presumed to reduce desired inventories and a fall to increase them.[20] It is, of course, the short-term rate which is relevant. The effect of a change in the interest rate on the inventory demand function of the sort considered above may be expected to show itself in a change in the parameters of the inventory investment demand function defined above, although for econometric purposes one might wish to introduce the interest rate as an additive term.

In the first instance inventories should be thought of just like plant and equipment, that is, as physical capital used in the production process, and a rise in the interest rate should tend to economize their use. But as physical capital, inventories do not entail long-term physical commitments. Consequently, inventory holdings should be more responsive to changes in the short-run interest rate than would plant and equipment expenditure. The short-term rate is more readily manipulable by the monetary authorities, and is more volatile over time than the long-term rate. Hence, inventories may be expected to play a more important role in economic fluctuations and in their control than is suggested by the proportion of total capital for which they account, since the latter is, of course, quite small.

---

[20]There could be the opposite effect. A rise in the interest rate (especially the long-term rate) might cause inventories to be substituted for fixed capital.

Of considerable importance is the extent of fixity, for technological reasons, in the ratio of inventories to variable factors and to plant and equipment in the production process. Here is the phenomenon of joint demand. The demand for plant and equipment utilization implies a demand for inventories and other variable factors, and in the case of technologically fixed coefficents, the demand for inventories with respect to the interest rate would be very inelastic, inventory carrying costs being small relative to the fixed costs of plant and equipment and to the cost of other variable factors. In particular, we should expect that the demand for inventories to be maintained as work in process (I_W) would be quite unresponsive to interest rate changes, ceteris paribus. But the less fixed the relation of inventories to plant and equipment utilization and to other factors, the more responsive inventory demand should be to interest rate changes.

Hawtrey aside, it is commonly felt that inventory demand does not respond much to interest rate changes, and from Meade and Andrews (440) to the Radcliffe Committee Report (131a) the responses of businessmen to questionnaires have been advanced as evidence to support this. The evidence is not of a sort that is particularly convincing to us. For a critical review of these studies, and others like them, see William H. White (640, 643) and Eisner (195, 197). Several reasons may be given to explain this view, and some to justify it.

(1) A matter already discussed: the possibility that inventories are technically fixed in ratio to plant and equipment utilization and to other factors of production. Moreover, and in the same vein, if long-term commitments to customers or long-term sales prospects are apt to be jeopardized by a temporary inability to deliver goods, a reduction in inventories beneath some lower critical value can be very costly and not be warranted because of a moderate rise in interest costs.

(2) Interest costs account for but a portion of the total unit costs of maintaining inventories: other costs include those of storage, deterioration, and obsolescence. The smaller interest costs are as a fraction of total unit cost, the less important a change in the interest rate. This is the phenomenon of joint demand, once again.

(3) It is difficult to discern empirically the causes of variation in inventory demand because the behavior of actual inventories does not reflect the behavior of desired inventories, aggregative attempts to change inventories being in some measure self-defeating. The effect of interest rate changes on desired inventories, even if important, does not therefore come readily to light in the behavior of actual inventories.

(4) Speculative and expectational reasons for changing inventory holdings may, in the magnitude of their effects, be much more

important than the effects of the interest rate. This would simply mean that interest rate variations have historically not been great enough to account, alongside waves of optimism and pessimism as to forthcoming rates of sales or variations in expected prices, for but an incidental fraction of changes in inventory demand.

(5) Changes in the terms of credit availability other than the interest rate have been more important than the interest rate changes that have occurred. This may be true and also very misleading. In theoretical discussions one often abstracts from the spectrum of interest rates, thinks of the money market as perfect, as involving no credit rationing, and imagines that the parameters of control by the monetary authorities are effective only in altering the rate of interest on consummated loans. A single (short-term) rate of interest has thus come to be used by theorists as a synedoche for a variety of terms that affect the availability of short-term funds. One ignores the fact that a borrower whose credit has been cut off or reduced, not because he has become a greater credit risk but because of more stringent credit rationing, has had at least his marginal interest rate go to infinity, or at least it has become so high that it is neither reported nor recorded because he does in fact not borrow funds at that rate.[21] The simplification of reducing all the detail of the terms on which funds can be borrowed to the single parameter, the interest rate, may be legitimate enough in theoretical discussions, but it is certainly a dangerous simplification when we move on to empirical appraisal of the importance of the terms of borrowing. What the "interest rate" stands for in theory is not what it is reported to be in collections of financial statistics.

(6) It may be argued that the interest rate and the terms of credit availability are in fact too stationary to account for much change in desired inventories because of the elasticity of supply of trade credit extensions. Although this matter has been of increasing concern to economists during recent years, little is known at the empirical level. We discuss it further in the next chapter.

---

[21] Needless to say, if borrowers are cut off from funds because they now represent greater credit risks, this is not to be interpreted as a rise in the structure of interest rates, even though disappointed borrowers might claim this is the case. At such times as this occurs generally, it is even possible that a borrower who does not represent a greater risk than before can now borrow more on the same terms or better than he could before. The interest rate, in our extended sense, may actually have fallen.

Appendix A

CONDITIONS FOR A MAXIMUM OF (2)

Equation (2) in the main text has the following form:[1]

(3) $\Phi(s(t)) = \int_0^\infty F(s,\dot{s},t)\,dt.$

One end-point is determined: $s(0) = s_0$. The other is free. Let $s(t) = \sigma(t) + \mathcal{E}\eta(t)$, where $\sigma(t)$ is the solution and where $\eta(t)$ is any real-valued function with $\eta(0) = 0$. Then

(4) $\Phi(\mathcal{E}) = \int_0^\infty F[\sigma + \mathcal{E}\eta,\ \dot{\sigma} + \mathcal{E}\dot{\eta},\ t]\,dt$

and

(5) $\Phi'(\mathcal{E}) = \int_0^\infty (F_s\eta + F_{\dot{s}}\dot{\eta})\,dt$

so that a necessary (first-order) condition for a maximum is that

(6) $\Phi'(0) = 0.$

Upon integrating (5) by parts, we obtain

(7) $[F_{\dot{s}}\eta]_0^\infty + \int_0^\infty \eta(F_s - \dfrac{d}{dt} F_{\dot{s}})\,dt = 0 \cdot$

Using $\eta(0) = 0$, $F_{\dot{s}}\eta\big|_{t=0} = 0$, and condition (7) reduces to

(8) $\lim_{t \to \infty} F_{\dot{s}}\eta + \int_0^\infty \eta(F_s - \dfrac{d}{dt} F_{\dot{s}})\,dt = 0.$

Since one admissable function $\eta(t)$ has $\lim_{t \to \infty}\eta(t) = 0$ and (8) must hold for every admissable function $\eta(t)$, (8) requires

(9) $\int_0^\infty \eta(F_s - \dfrac{d}{dt} F_{\dot{s}})\,dt = 0,$

and, by the well-known lemma leading to Euler's differential equation, (9) requires

(10) $\dfrac{\partial F}{\partial s} - \dfrac{d}{dt}\dfrac{\partial F}{\partial \dot{s}} = 0.$

---

[1]The dot on a variable indicates a time derivative; other derivatives are represented in the usual way by subscripts or primes.

But since $\lim\limits_{t \to \infty} \eta(t)$ need not be zero, another necessary condition is that

(11) $\lim\limits_{t \to \infty} F_{\dot{s}} = 0.$

The second order condition for a maximum is given by

(12) $\Phi''(0) = \int_0^\infty (F_{ss} \eta^2 + 2F_{s\dot{s}} \eta\dot{\eta} + F_{\dot{s}\dot{s}} \dot{\eta}^2)\, dt < 0.$

In terms of our problem, conditions (10) - (12) become, respectively:

(10') $p_s + (C_{\dot{s}\dot{s}} \ddot{\bar{s}} + C_{\dot{s}t}^-) - rc_{\dot{s}} = 0,$

(11') $\lim\limits_{t \to \infty} e^{-rt} 0_{\dot{s}} = 0,$

and

(12') $\int_0^\infty e^{-rt} (p_{ss} \eta^2 - c_{\dot{s}\dot{s}} \dot{\eta}^2)\, dt < 0.$

FIGURE II-18

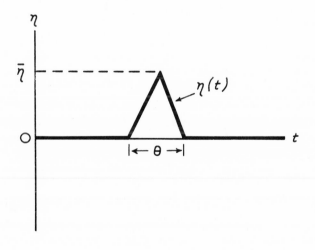

(11') is satisfied provided $c_{\dot{s}}$ does not become infinite. This condition will most certainly hold and so (11') can be henceforth ignored.

From (12') we may obtain the condition that during the period of expansion $c_{\ddot{s}s} \geq 0$, for otherwise we could always choose an $\eta(t)$, such as is shown in Figure II-18, so that $\eta(t)$ is always zero except for a sufficiently small interval θ during which $c_{\ddot{s}s} < 0$. Within that interval $\dot{\eta}^2$ can be as great as we please with η^2 bounded arbitrarily by $\overline{\eta}^2$. The inequality (12') would then be reversed. This means that if the expansion cost function ever displayed diminishing marginal cost, expansion would never proceed in that range of the function, or, it would always pay to expand faster if the rate of increase in expansion cost diminished with an increase in the rate of expansion.

Appendix B

THE SLOPE OF THE INVESTMENT DEMAND SCHEDULE UNDER CERTAIN RESTRICTIVE ASSUMPTIONS

Let $\dfrac{1}{1 + \rho_0}$ be a positive root of the polynomial $\displaystyle\sum_{n=0}^{N} (\dfrac{1}{1+\rho})^n R_n$ which, of course, has a derivative everywhere. We assume that

(1) $\displaystyle\sum_{n=m}^{N} (\dfrac{1}{1+\rho_0})^{n-m} R_n \geq 0$ $\qquad (m = 0,1,2, \ldots, N).$

We note that

$$\sum_{n=m-1}^{N} (\frac{1}{1+\rho})^{n-(m-1)} R_n =$$

$$= R_{m-1} + \frac{1}{1+\rho} \sum_{n=m}^{N} (\frac{1}{1+\rho})^{n-m} R_n .$$

From this equality and (1) we see that if

$$\frac{\partial}{\partial (\frac{1}{1+\rho})} \sum_{n=m}^{N} (\frac{1}{1+\rho})^{n-m} R_n \geq 0 \text{ at } \rho = \rho_0,$$

then

$$\frac{\partial}{\partial \left(\frac{1}{1+\rho}\right)} \sum_{n=m-1}^{N} \left(\frac{1}{1+\rho}\right)^{n-(m-1)} R_n \geq 0 \text{ at } \rho = \rho_0.$$

Since for $m = N$,

$$\frac{\partial}{\partial \left(\frac{1}{1+\rho}\right)} \sum_{n=N}^{N} \left(\frac{1}{1+\rho}\right)^{n-N} R_n = \frac{\partial}{\partial \left(\frac{1}{1+\rho}\right)} R_n = 0,$$

it follows by mathematical induction that

$$\frac{\partial}{\partial \left(\frac{1}{1+\rho}\right)} \sum_{n=m}^{N} \left(\frac{1}{1+\rho}\right)^{n-m} R_n \geq 0 \text{ at } \rho = \rho_0 \text{ for all } m$$

and in particular for $m = 0$. Therefore, at a positive root the graph of $\sum_{n=0}^{N} \left(\frac{1}{1+\rho}\right)^n R_n$ cannot cross the horizontal axis as shown in the

figure,

FIGURE II-19

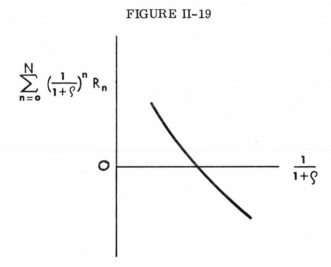

and therefore for all values of $\frac{1}{1+\rho}$ at least as great as any positive root, $\frac{1}{1+\rho_0}$, the project will have a nonnegative value. This

is to say that the project will have a nonnegative value for any $\rho < \rho_0$, and it is then assumed to be at least marginally attractive. Hence, under these assumptions, the investment demand schedule cannot be positively sloped.

II. THE POLICY SIGNIFICANCE OF THE THEORY
OF INVESTMENT

A. Theoretical Framework: A Summary

We now propose to present certain propositions which emerge from the purely theoretical analysis of the determinants of business investment. We shall then proceed to a consideration of the ways in which monetary policy may exert an influence on investment demand according to the theoretical framework which has been set out.

1. Investment: A function of change.

A completely dead economy, in which nothing, not even production, is taking place, would have no investment demand. In a stationary economy, in which the rate of output and all relevant variables are the same at every point of time, production inevitably involves the wearing away of capital. A first major component of investment demand therefore appears as a "replacement" need.

Second, within the limits of an economy that appears stationary at the macroeconomic level there may be microeconomic changes which generate investment. These may include changes in specific product demand or in the supply of specific factors of production. In view of the specificity (as to both physical substance and location) of much capital, changes in particular product demand or factor supply will generate demand for new capital. This constitutes a form of replacement demand at the macro level but not at the micro level, and probably merits distinct treatment from the replacement demand related to output which is unchanged both in aggregate amount and in composition.

A third cause from which we may derive determinants of investment is that involving the values of the relevant aggregative variables. Of key concern would be changes in the level of demand for total output and the total supply of factors of production.

Finally, investment will be generated by independent or exogenously determined changes in the process of production. These we customarily include under the label of "technological change."

Strictly speaking, the four categories indicated above are sufficient to account for changes in the equilibrium amounts of capital. Insofar as we are willing to assume that the amount of capital in existence is always the equilibrium amount, investment, which is the rate of acquisition of capital, is fully explained by the functions defining the equilibria and the rates of change of the arguments of those functions. But there can be little doubt that explanation of the varying rates of investment over periods at least as long as those of the business cycle, if not much longer, cannot proceed far without recognition that the total stock (and composition) of capital in existence is rarely if ever the "equilibrium" amount. Explaining the rate of investment involves then the dynamic problem of rates of adjustment of the capital stock to an ever changing equilibrium demand.

2. Maximization of a future payoff and the process of production.

Of critical importance in the theory of capital and investment is the recognition that the justification for acquiring capital is a "pay-off" in the future, a pay-off which will depend in amount upon future events. Since future events at best can be imperfectly perceived, decisions regarding the acquisition of capital must be made on the basis of uncertain expectations of the future. It is likely that a theory that will be useful in predicting investment must recognize fundamental differences between the behavior that might occur on the basis of known values of explanatory variables and that which occurs in consequence of what decision makers infer from past or current values about the unknown future values that are relevant.

The precise nature of the pay-off which decision makers may be conceived as attempting to maximize will be of some concern. Recognition of the stochastic nature of economic experience forces us to think in terms of businessmen seeking to optimize currently parameters of probability distributions of future variables. It is, of course, not clear that such optimization will consist merely in maximizing the mathematical expectation of future profits. Nor is it clear, however, that such maximization would not account for a great deal of observed investment behavior.

Whatever the nature of the optimization, or the function that businessmen may be most usefully considered to maximize, we can readily indicate some of the constraints under which they operate. Many of these are best encompassed in the concept of a production function which relates inputs of factors of production—stocks or flows or both—at various points of time with output at simultaneous or subsequent points of time. The individual firm "invests" as it acquires goods from other firms and as it creates them by employing factors in the process of production. It disinvests when it sells output. (To the extent that it uses up its capital in the process of production it is also disinvesting but since this is simultaneous with and technologically bound to production it usually amounts merely to a reduction in the investment constituted by production.) Given efficient production, a firm can increase its output at any point of time only by decreasing its output at any other point of time or by increasing its inputs at some point of time. A firm increases its investment (which may be negative) when it adds to inputs or, by delaying the completion of output, postpones its sales.

This implies that a general increase in the rate of output, for all points in time, will require an increase in the rate of input. If there is no change in the time shape of production, that is, in the lags from input to output, such an increase in the rate of input must involve investment. It also follows that a firm that "lengthens" its productive process, that is, substitutes inputs of factors which bring about output further in the future, invests insofar as it is lengthening production (but not after production has been lengthened).

In choosing among inputs the firm is usually assumed to be trying, at least in part, to maximize the mathematical expectation of the discounted value of future returns, measured in profits or, more generally, in utility. To the extent that this is done, and different sets of inputs are associated with different time shapes or distributions of outputs, a change in the rate of discount will lead to substitution among sets of inputs. More specifically, a reduction in "the rate of interest" available in the market will cause businessmen to substitute in favor of inputs, such as capital goods, that lead to outputs that are on the average further in the future, and to substitute against inputs, such as direct labor, that lead to outputs that are on the average nearer in time to their corresponding inputs.[1]

These conditional statements are, however, limited in their applicability by the costs of changing productive processes (including the costs of gathering information and decision making) and by the need to optimize other parameters of the probability distribution of expected returns. Decision makers may desire particularly to minimize the probability of large losses or generally minimize the variance or some other measure of the dispersion of the distribution. This may be interpreted as involving a specific discount for uncertainty, which in turn is an increasing function of distance in time.

3. General propositions about major categories of investment demand.

Without developing them rigorously from the assumptions about business behavior suggested above, there are certain propositions about investment demand which, we feel, can be formulated with reasonable assurance.

a. Replacement investment demand, that is, the gross investment that would be undertaken in a stationary economy, will be larger if output is larger. It will be a larger proportion of output if, with a given longevity of capital, the capital-output ratio is higher. With a given capital-output ratio, however, replacement

---

[1]Cf. J.R. Hicks, Value and Capital, Second Edition (Oxford, 1946), pp. 213-226.

investment demand will on the average be lower if longevity is higher.[2] Thus, the effect of a decrease in the rate of time discount would depend upon the relative magnitude of resulting changes in longevity and in the capital-output ratio, both of which may be expected to increase.

b. The investment demand that may be associated with microeconomic changes in an economy in which the macroeconomic variables do not change will, of course, be related to the amount of microeconomic change. To the extent, for example, that population is moving from one part of the country to another, thus shifting both the location of factors of production and the location of demand for output, investment demand will be generated. Given the rate of microeconomic change in some relevant sense, however, the resultant rate of investment demand will depend upon marginal capital-output ratios. These in turn will be related to the rate of time discount or the rate of interest. A lower rate of interest, which we would associate with higher capital-output ratios, would thus require greater investment to adjust to changes that would bring about a need for different items of specific capital. Qualifying this somewhat, however, it must be observed that higher requirements for capital needed to adjust to new equilibria may slow and inhibit those adjustments in a turbulent economy. The more capital-intensive an economy, the more slowly it may adjust to structural changes.

Changes in the structure of the demand leading to changes in the equilibrium structure of capital need not simply cancel out despite constancy of the macro-variables. There is an asymmetry in the ability of a firm or industry to add to or to reduce its capital. The former entails fabrication, the latter wearing out and disposal. This may affect the time path of the reaction of the economy to structural change. We suppose, in general, as was argued in the previous chapter, that expansion is apt to occur more rapidly than contraction, so that a shift of demand may cause a period of aggregate net expansion followed by a period of aggregate net contraction. This implies a shift of resources first away from the production of consumer goods and then a compensating shift in favor of the production of consumer goods.

Moreover, expanding and contracting industries are apt to be more responsive to changes in the interest rate for, being off dead center, their expansion or contraction targets may be more delicately adjusted to the interest rate. This, too, was elaborated in the previous chapter.

---

[2]See (198, 192, 168).

c. Aggregate investment demand will be greater the faster the rate of growth of demand for the final product and the faster the rate of increase of the supply of factors of production. The higher the capital-output ratio, the greater the ratio of investment demand to output that will be derived from any given percent rate of growth of output. If a lower rate of interest implies a higher capital-output ratio it follows that for any given rate of growth a lower interest rate must also imply a higher ratio of investment demand to output.[3]

d. Technological change cuts a number of ways in its effect upon investment demand. By accelerating the obsolescence of capital specific to outdated processes it has a direct effect in increasing investment demand. However, to the extent that current technological change generates an expectation of further change in the future, the impulse to acquire new capital goods now may be restrained. If longevity of capital is reduced without a corresponding reduction in the capital-output ratio, the effects of technological change will include, in a growing economy, the increase of the ratio of replacement investment demand to total investment demand (as well as output). Insofar as the technological change entails demand for new products with specific capital requirements, investment demand will be generated. And insofar as technological change involves "deepening" or an increase in the capital-output ratio it will imply an addition to investment in order to accomplish this deepening and then a permanently higher rate of investment to maintain the higher capital-output ratio in the face of the replacement and growth requirements discussed above.[4]

4. Investment in inventories.

The above discussion is in principle applicable in large measure to investment in inventories as well as to investment in what are commonly known as capital goods, that is, goods that producers possess for longer periods. A number of particular characteristics of inventory investment may be stressed, however.

The manner in which fluctuations in the disposal of output may induce investment in inventories is varied. Where the fluctuation is unforeseen or where the nature of the productive process is such as to inhibit speedy adjustment, changes in the rate of disposal of

---

[3]This is essentially the theme of the Harrod-Domar growth models. See Eisner, "On Growth Models and the Neo-Classical Resurgence," The Economic Journal, December 1958, pp. 707-721, for a summary of some of the arguments and references to a few of the major works in the literature.

[4]See (198).

output would induce changes in the rate of investment in the opposite direction. Thus, unforeseen increases in sales of finished products will bring about disinvestment in "liquid capital," which may be taken to include both finished goods and in some cases stocks of raw materials accumulated for production.[5] The word "unforeseen" may in fact prove too restrictive. Even in cases where changes in sales are foreseen with substantial probability, firms may find it a better rule to keep production at a constant rate until the change in sales has actually occurred (and hence, is certain), because fluctuation in output is frequently costly, in part as a result of labor immobility and the difficulties attached to laying off workers and recruiting them again or paying premium rates for overtime.

When firms conclude that an increase in sales is "permanent" they will increase the rate of input and consequently invest. Initially, this may not offset the increased rate of disposal of output, but eventually investment must occur if the stock of goods in the possession of producers is to rise to a level which is optimum in terms of the higher rate of output consistent with the new higher rate of sales.

5. A distributed lag accelerator.

While theoretical considerations point to the importance of the acceleration principle, highlighting the derived character of investment demand, the simplest formulation of this principle, namely, that current investment is proportionate to the current rate of change in sales, must surely be much too simple.

When sales are increasing, investment may for a while be negative because of the selling off of inventories. Nor need investment in plant and equipment rise concurrently and proportionately with the rate of sales increase. Plant and equipment may, for a time, be operated more intensively. The less certain the business sector is as to the permanence of the increase in sales, the more slowly it will wish to react by increasing its fixed capital. Only as the higher level of sales persists through time will an increase in capital become more clearly indicated.

It is also possible that a rise in demand may have been preceded by a prior fall to which the business sector has not fully adjusted. Excess capacity then exists to start with, and this nullifies some or all of the need for additional capital to meet the sales rise.

There may, moreover, even when capital expansion is indicated, be lags of an administrative or technical character in making and implementing decisions to expand capital and these too will cause

---

[5]See Eisner (197, p. 569).

the related investment and rates of sales change to be non-synchronous. Even apart from these considerations, the adjustment of capital may not be instantaneous with the rise in sales, simply because of the costs of more rather than less rapid expansion. The optimal path of capital expansion is one requiring the passage of time, a matter analyzed in some detail in Chapter I.

One aspect of the cost of more or less rapid expansion will be the availability of funds. If the financial capital market is significantly imperfect, it may be more economical for the expanding firms to rely upon internal sources of funds and the expansion will then be paced to some extent by the rate at which these funds become available.

We must note, finally, that the technology of expanding (fabricating) and that of contracting (selling out or scrapping) are not symmetrical. Disinvestment and the rate of sales decline may be related quite differently from investment and the rate of sales increase.

In no case, however, can these considerations, which mitigate against the simplest form of the acceleration principle, imply that investment will depend only on the level of sales or be independent of the past time path of sales. Investment can, of course, depend on other things so that, even though sales were to remain stationary, investment may occur because of changes in relative prices, the composition of aggregate demand, or technology. It would certainly be our conjecture, however, that aggregate sales changes would predominate among the actual causes of investment.

All this leads us, however, to a distributed lag accelerator with coefficients dependent upon and varying with actual and equilibrium capital-output ratios. The role of the rate of time discount or interest rate, in such a model, is expressed primarily in the accelerator coefficients which, in turn, derive their effect from changes in demand. As argued in the previous chapter, at least under certain restrictive assumptions, a rise in the interest rate will tend to delay and a decline will tend to speed up the response of investment to a sales change. A change in the rate of interest will, moreover, affect the equilibrium capital-output ratios and alter the accelerator coefficients for this reason as well. The immediate effect of an interest rate change insofar as the acceleration principle is concerned will, of course, be felt only because the non-lagged accelerator coefficient changes. The effects on various specific types of investment of changes in the interest rate depend primarily then on the degree to which response to a sales change is lagged and on the speed of adjustment and sensitivity to interest rate changes of the specific equilibrium capital-output ratios. It is ultimately an empirical question as to how much and how soon investment may be affected by a given change in the rate of interest, or as to the relative proportions of variation in investment that can be accounted for by variation in the rate of interest or the terms of supply of credit, on the one hand, and by variations in the rate of demand or in the rate of change of demand on the other. This, in an appropriate dynamic formulation, is one aspect of the traditional issue of the relative amounts of investment that are to be attributed to the "deepening" and to the "widening" of capital.

6. The role of profits.

It is frequently suggested that investment is a positive function of profits and that the way to increase the rate of investment is to increase the rate of profits. Careful analysis indicates that this is not a hypothesis that can easily be proved.

At the level of the individual firm with free access to capital markets, it should be clear that, to the extent that profit maximization underlies rational investment decisions, neither past profits nor even expected future profits are relevant. What are relevant are expected future profits on investment—"the efficiency of investment." One should not expect a firm, no matter how high its current profits or expected future profits, to wish to invest unless the contemplated addition to capital stock is expected to increase expected profits, or have an expected return higher than that from alternative uses of funds.

Where the firm does not have free access to capital markets or where the supply of funds is in some way tied to current profits or expected future profits, either of those facts, it is true, may cause profits to influence investment. These effects are, however, limited to the extent that large firms, with more elastic and readily available supplies of capital, account for most of aggregate investment. But even if capital markets are significantly imperfect, what remains important is the total supply of funds. Only if higher current profits leads to greater saving, by altering the distribution of income from workers and rentier groups to common shareholders or (if retained rather than distributed) to firms themselves, will it follow that the supply of funds depends on current profits. But the implication then is that a greater average propensity to save and therefore a smaller average propensity to consume will lead to greater actual saving and investment. By virtue of the principle of derived demand, we should expect the reduction in the average propensity to consume to curtail investment. Only if the increased supply of funds can depress the interest rate enough so as to raise sufficiently the desired capital-output ratio could the demand for additional capital rise when consumption would otherwise decline. This may, of course, be the case. But without the assumption of perpetual full employment, it would seem difficult to argue with any assurance that lowering the propensity to consume (by altering the income distribution in favor of profits) would have a greater positive effect on investment as a consequence of lower interest rates (or easier supply of capital) than its negative effect as a consequence of the reduction in consumption demand.[6]

It should also be pointed out that one may acquire a mistaken notion of the importance of aggregate profit on aggregate investment when one looks at the individual firm. Current profits as a source of funds may be very important to the individual firm in an imperfect capital market; but the role of profits might then be primarily to determine which firms will be able to invest. All this is possible and consistent with a situation in which aggregate profit does not count at all. Along the same lines it may be questioned further whether expected profits, as a basis for credit, have much role in influencing aggregate investment even if they do prove significant in many cases at the level of the individual firm. For it seems plausible that, in rationing a given amount of credit, suppliers may choose firms with high profits expectations without affecting the total amount of credit supplied.[7]

This all suggests a certain danger in cross-section studies. In a given year we may well find that it is the profitable firms that are investing, and contrariwise, but this would tell us nothing reliable about the aggregate effects of a change in aggregate profits.

It is possible that the supply of money capital may itself be a function of current profits quite apart from income distribution considerations. For lack of better information, investors of funds may be guided considerably by current and past profits in their estimates of the return and risk on contemplated investment. One might expect that in the case of large firms, however, it would pay the market to sustain the cost of securing better information. It is hard to believe that the market would allow investment opportunities running into hundreds of millions of dollars (with their consequent effect upon values of equity) to be ignored because a firm's current profits were low. The extent to which the small firm finds the capital market so imperfect that it must pass up really profitable opportunities is an empirical question, but in view of the issue of the cost of information gathering, a priori thoughts do not enable us confidently to predict the answer.

---

[6]See on this, of course, Oscar Lange's well-known "The Rate of Interest and the Optimum Propensity to Consume," reprinted from Economica, 1938, in American Economic Association, Readings in Business Cycle Theory, pp. 169-192.

[7]Cf. Eisner (199; 197, pp. 550-557 and 581-582; 195, pp. 27-29 and passim; and 196, pp. 186-187).

7. Depreciation and tax policy.

We attempt no extended analysis of the effects of fiscal policy, in general, upon investment. It is to be hoped that the framework we have set forth will be useful to the reader in evaluating a good many of the great variety of potentially relevant fiscal measures. For example, the propositions we have developed may be seen to suggest that changes in corporate profits tax rates, which would change current and expected profits but have no direct influence on the expected profitability of investment, would not have any direct effect on investment. (Among the indirect effects which might be noted, however, would be the influence on the volume of corporate expenditures, including expenditures for depreciable capital goods, which would reduce taxable income and yet preserve or increase real income enjoyed by owners of corporate equity in the form of entirely or largely untaxed capital gains.)[8]

In view of much popular and professional discussion of the role of depreciation allowances in capital expenditures, it may be appropriate to devote some brief attention to this particular facet of tax policy affecting investment. It should be recognized, initially, that depreciation policy is essentially tax policy. As a first approximation it may surely be argued that, except for tax implications, it makes no difference what the accountant writes in the book for depreciation. It is true, of course, that to some extent individuals who study financial statements, whether they are prospective investors in a firm's securities, trade union leaders engaged in collective bargaining, or management making decisions as to dividend or expenditure policy, may misinterpret changes in reported earnings resulting from changes in depreciation policy for changes in real earnings. But it is difficult to reconcile such action, based on pure illusion, with the main body of consistent economic theory, or to believe that such action can prove quantitatively important. Depreciation policy may of course also be peculiarly relevant in the case of regulated industries where rates or prices are fixed on the basis of costs, including depreciation charges, and earnings on the net accounting value of capital. To consider this adequately would involve us in the vast area of regulatory problems in general, which it would seem inappropriate to encompass in this study.

Drawing on the conclusions of analyses by one of the present writers and a number of others we may indicate the following with regard to depreciation for tax purposes and its role in investment.

_____

[8]For further discussion of this and related issues, see Eisner (199a).

A. Acceleration or "liberalization" of depreciation for tax purposes, such as was accomplished by the introduction of double-rate
declining balance and sum-of-the-years-digits methods in the Internal Revenue Act of 1954, or further liberalization as has been
proposed now, has the effect, under prevailing and anticipated conditions of growth, of increasing the annual rate of depreciation
charges for all future years (not just for an initial period) and hence
decreasing taxable income and tax liabilities for all future years.
If this reduction in tax liabilities is not matched by increases in
other tax rates or a reduction in government expenditures, the consequent increase in the budget deficit (or decrease in the surplus)
must, of course, be expected to be expansionary. It would be reasonable to suppose that some of the resultant increase in demand would
entail increased investment.

B. We may isolate the effects of depreciation reform from the
general effects of budget deficits or surpluses by assuming that
tax rates are changed so that the long-run tax revenues, with long-
run income unchanged, would be the same. We find then that as a
result of accelerated depreciation:

(1) Tax liabilities are increased in periods of low capital expenditures and are decreased in periods of high capital expenditures
(as against what they would be with unaccelerated depreciation).
This can be expected to have destabilizing effects on aggregate demand and investment.

(2) The current discounted value of proposed capital additions
is increased, as for any given addition the near-term expected
after-tax earnings are raised at the expense of expected after-tax
earnings farther in the future. This may be expected to bring about
some substitution of expenditures on depreciable assets for other
types of expenditures (such as labor services, inventories, advertising, and research and development). Various estimates suggest
that the volume of increased capital expenditures which might result
from such substitution would be small relative to the magnitude of
change in current depreciation allowances or other effects that
might be anticipated.

(3) Depending on the accompanying changes in other tax rates,
accelerated depreciation may increase after-tax profits and cash
flow at the expense of other claims against gross national product.
Evaluation of this effect on investment relates again to the issue
of the "optimum propensity to consume," and the relative influence
on investment of the increase in supply of funds and the decrease
in non-investment demand which result from a redistribution of
income in favor of profits. Again we conclude that, without the assumption of full employment, it is difficult to state whether such a
redistribution would increase or decrease investment. Given full

employment it should increase business investment at the expense
of current output for the consumer and government sectors, though
the magnitude of the increase would be in doubt.

(4) If the accelerated depreciation is expected to apply only
temporarily to new capital additions (as was probably the case with
five year accelerated amortization associated with World War II
and the Korean War and their aftermaths, but is not the case with
the 1954 tax law revisions or other proposed changes), one should
expect a short-run increase in capital expenditures. This would
take place during the period when new capital additions are subject
to the accelerated depreciation but would result in a corresponding
reduction in capital expenditures afterward.[9]

An investment tax credit applicable to equipment purchases,
under consideration by the Congress in early 1962, has been advanced as a substitute for accelerated tax depreciation which might
stimulate more investment per dollar of reduced tax revenue. In
its current (March 1962) form, this measure, by offering tax credits
up to 8 percent of the amount of expenditures on equipment in
addition to regular tax depreciation will, other things being equal,
raise the marginal efficiency of investment schedule substantially.
The net effect on investment, however, will depend also upon the
indirect repercussions of any accompanying or consequential changes
in tax rates or in government expenditures, as well as on the elasticity of the marginal efficiency of investment schedule.

The investment tax credit may be viewed essentially as a subsidy
to firms which may encourage them to make certain kinds of capital
expenditures (expenditures for eligible equipment) at the expense
of other kinds of investment (in inventories and plant) and non-
capital expenditures (such as, again, expenditures for labor, services, advertising, and research and development). In its current
form, however, it should be noted that the critical, marginal effect
on investment demand is considerably muted. For the credit, as
currently drafted, is not restricted to expenditures above some
minimum level (say, an average of previous years' expenditures)
which might have been undertaken anyway. A much higher tax credit,

---

[9] For further discussion of these issues and development of the
underlying reasoning, as well as references to other literature,
see Eisner (191; 192; 193; 194). "Changes in Methods of Depreciation and Their Effects," in Joint Economic Committee's Federal
Tax Policy for Economic Growth and Stability (U.S. G.P.O., Washington, 1955), pp. 515-527; and "Effects of Depreciation Allowances
for Tax Purposes," in Tax Revision Compendium, Vol. 2, of the
Committee on Ways and Means of the House of Representatives
(U.S. G.P.O., 1959), pp. 793-799).

say 20 percent, but restricted to marginal expenditures, might have
been expected to have a considerably greater impact on investment
per dollar of cost to the Treasury (or per dollar of redistribution
of tax burden). As currently written, the tax credit is also likely
to be destabilizing in its effects on aggregate demand and on investment. For it will involve greater subsidies to business in years
when equipment expenditures are already high than in years when
they are low, and equipment expenditures of course tend to move
cyclically with capital expenditures as a whole and with the economy in general.[10]

B. The Role of Monetary Policy

Monetary policy impinges upon investment demand, in terms of
the theoretical framework we have provided, by its effect on:

1. rates of time discount,
2. demand for final product,
3. the nature of risks confronting decision makers.

1. Rates of time discount.

Changes in time discount or in intertemporal marginal rates of
substitution as measured by "the rate [or rates] of interest" are
generally expected to affect both the equilibrium capital-output ratio
and, in a changing economy, the rate of investment. Critical issues
are how much monetary policy may be expected to influence relevant
rates of time discount and the quantitative effect of changes of time
discount on investment, issues of which Keynes' General Theory
helped make economists acutely aware.

The monetary authority can much more easily influence the
short-term rate of interest than the long-term rate. This can most
readily be seen upon viewing the long-term rate as a "compounding"
of successive expected short-term rates. More precisely, if all
expectations as to future short-term rates were held with certainty,
then in a perfect market, the long-term rate, R, would be related
to successive short-term rates, r_t, by the formula $(1 + R)^T = (1 + r_1)$
$(1 + r_2) \ldots (1 + r_T)$, where T is the length of the long term divided

---

[10]It may be noted that an investment tax credit raises a number of
substantial issues of distribution and equity, as well as broad questions of economic policy bearing on the desirability of government
intervention designed to alter the existing allocation of resources,
both in general and in this particular case. These matters seem
beyond the scope of this book but they may prove ultimately critical
to an evaluation of the kind of measure under consideration.

by the length of the short term, and the interest rate is measured in percent per "short term." If this relationship did not hold in a perfect market, arbitrage would tend to establish it.

If the monetary authority were to buy or to liquidate a given dollar amount of short-term debt instruments, it would <u>directly</u> effect r_1, the current short-term interest rate. If T is large, this will, <u>ceteris paribus</u>, have only a small effect on R. <u>Indirectly</u>, of course, the monetary authority can affect expected <u>future</u> short-term rates, r_2, r_3, ... r_T, to the extent that its present policy is expected to be a persisting one. If all expected future short-term rates rose or fell with the current short-term rate, then, under the present assumptions, the long-term rate would move in step. Expectations as to future short-term rates are, however, apt to depend less and less upon the current action of the monetary authority the greater the remoteness of the short-term rate being forecast. Thus, a change in r_1 may induce, by its effects on expectations, a nearly equivalent change in r_2, but a lesser change in r_3, and perhaps no change in r_T. A change in the short-term rate may therefore not induce a very significant change in the long-term rate.[11]

Allowance for the role of risk suggests that frequent manipulation of the short-term rate may raise the price and reduce the amount of long-term commitments. This is because it is reasonable to expect that such manipulation would generate expectations of future fluctuations in short-term rates. A monetary authority that raises rates to fight "inflation" may be expected to lower them again after the cyclical turn, to combat recession. Fluctuations in future short-term rates, however, imply fluctuations in the capital value of existing long-term securities. If lenders have risk aversion, as is generally assumed, this must result in a reduction in the supply of funds to long-term borrowers. In itself, this would mean a higher long-term rate of interest. It should be recognized though that borrowers may also have risk aversion and may find that the increased variance in the expectations of future values of long-term bonds increases the variance of expectations with regard to future competition based upon future long-term borrowing. Thus the borrower may manifest a reduction in demand for long-term funds because of the increased risk attached to the long-term physical commitments for which the borrowing is undertaken. The effect of this reduction in demand for long-term funds is of course to reduce further the amount of borrowing (and investing) but also to lower the long-term rate of interest. There may be some reason to believe that borrowers have less risk aversion than lenders. If this is so it would also appear reasonable that the depressing effect of

---

[11]Cf. Hicks, <u>Value and Capital</u>, Second Edition, pp. 258-264.

the reduction in demand for funds will not be so great as the upward pressure of the decrease in supply, and interest rates on long-term lending will tend to rise as a result of the increase in risk generated by countercyclical manipulations by the monetary authority.[12] Thus far we have considered the case in which the monetary authority buys or sells short-term securities. The results will be the same for other categories of action by the central authority. Suppose the monetary authority buys or sells long-term securities. What effect will this have on the long-term interest rate? This depends on the elasticity of supply of long-term securities. (And if the elasticity is expressed with respect to price rather than with respect to the rate of yield, it must first be noted that a given percentage change in the price of long-term securities implies a smaller change in the effective long-term yield than the same percentage change in price would imply for the change in yield on short-term securities.) Our view is that the elasticity of supply of long-term securities will depend primarily on the expectations as to the future short-term rates. If, for example, the purchase of long-term securities by the central bank is thought to be only a temporary policy, holders of these securities will be eager to sell during this temporary period when prices are up, which is to say that the supply will be highly elastic; if it is thought that this policy will continue into the long run, there is then no urgency for anyone to sell, the supply elasticity will be less, and the effect on the long-term interest rate will be greater. Again, doubt (greater or less) as to the permanence of the central bank's policy will serve to insulate (to a greater or lesser extent) the effectiveness of current action on the long-term interest rate.

Should the monetary authority not enter the open market directly, but act instead to stimulate or to discourage commercial banks from lending, the willingness of these banks to lend on long term will depend once again upon whether they expect the change in their reserve position (or the terms on which additional reserves are available) to be relatively permanent. If their reserves have

---

[12]One might suggest, in contradiction of the argument above, that manipulation resulting in increased dispersion in the subjective probability distribution of expected future short-term rates might cause an increased preference on the part of risk-averters for the certain long-term interest commitments of long-term bonds. While this factor must certainly operate, it is hard to believe that it can be comparable in magnitude to that induced by the increased dispersion in the probability distribution of expected short-term or intermediate-term income (or "capital gains") on long term securities. Cf Joan Robinson, "The Rate of Interest," in The Rate of Interest and Other Essays, especially pp. 5-20, 28-30.

increased, for example, and they do not expect a subsequent decrease, they will be more willing to make long-term commitments; otherwise, they will be less willing to.

This all means that if the monetary authority reverses its policy frequently, it will find that it cannot much affect the long-term interest rate; if it does not reverse its policy over long periods of time (which is essentially to have no countercyclical policy), its effectiveness in determining the long-term rate will be greater. Its power to change the long-term rate is the greater, the less it exercises it.

Another way in which the operations of the monetary authority in the markets for short- and long-term securities may affect the interest rate is by their effects on the stocks of securities of various maturities which are in the public's portfolios. By buying or selling long-terms rather than short-terms (or vice versa) it alters the term composition of the public's security holdings and hence the liquidity position of those portfolios. To the extent that policy action tends to bring about a substitution of long-term securities for short-term in their portfolios, this may lead nongovernment lenders to compensate by substituting short-term investments for long-term investments and, if attractive short-term investment opportunities are not available, to hold more of their assets idle. This effect is equivalent to that of raising the long-term rate of time discount.

Probably a more important aspect of the changes in the public's portfolios has to do with their total value. This effect will be discussed in Section 4 entitled "The Assets Effect."

If investment is sensitive to changes in the interest rate, which interest rate is important, the long term or the short term? Physical investment serves essentially to reduce the liquidity of the investor's assets. It involves the commitment of assets in such a way that it is more costly to liquidate those assets in the short run or on abrupt notice than otherwise. The relevant term of the rate of interest is therefore one which, roughly speaking, does not fall short of the horizon of the investment commitment. An opportunity for a manufacturer to borrow money at a near zero rate of interest for a period of one day may be expected to lead him to virtually no real investment outlay. An opportunity to borrow at a low rate of interest for 30, 60, or 90 days may lead him to invest in working capital and other inventories, but not in plant and equipment. The rate of interest relevant for plant and equipment investment is the long-term rate.

2. Monetary policy against inflation.

What about the usefulness of monetary policy in combatting inflationary pressures? It has generally been argued that whatever
its weakness in stimulating investment in time of depression, monetary policy, by raising the rate of interest can certainly choke off
investment during the boom. This asymmetry may, however, be
exaggerated. Conventional monetary policy, it must be recalled,
operates essentially by bringing about the substitution of the obligations of banks for the obligations of individuals and nonbanking
corporations. If the monetary authority makes bank obligations
scarce or expensive (by selling other obligations and raising reserve requirements and discount rates) one might expect producers
to economize on the bank obligations that are available and to substitute other obligations—generally known as trade credit—for
money. In principle, there is nothing to prevent society from turning
entirely to other means of exchange as "money" becomes more and
more scarce and expensive. Rather than pay 10 percent for bank
money why should not General Motors issue its own notes, backed
by its products, to U.S. Steel? And why should U.S. Steel not use
General Motors notes, or issue its own, to pay its suppliers? What
inhibits this under normal circumstances is that bank money is more
convenient than near-monies created by nonbanking corporations,
especially in its function as a medium of multilateral exchange. But
as a component in business portfolios money can to a greater or
lesser degree be replaced by other credit instruments. Consequently,
during periods of monetary stringency the stock of money held by
corporations can come to be redeployed so as to function more
actively to effect transactions. When this occurs new credit instruments—trade credit—will arise, and money will circulate with
greater velocity. What needs to be known is just how readily in
response to rising interest rates this redeployment of funds will
occur. What is the elasticity of trade credit with respect to the interest rate? Or the elasticity of the velocity of circulation with
respect to the interest rate? It is important to know the answers
to these questions, and for a fair range of variation in interest
rates. If in the presence of persistent inflationary forces, interest
rate and monetary policy is to be pursued so as to check the inflation completely, how high must interest rates go? Is it possible that
before such a policy could succeed, there would be not only a substantial increase in the amount of trade credit extended but that
corporate debt instruments would also come to circulate as a medium of exchange? Those who debate (on both sides) whether the
alleged inadequacy of monetary policy is due to the fact that it has
never been applied far enough must face the question of just how
far it can be pushed without providing a new kind of illustration of
Gresham's Law, and the question of whether the issuance of money
substitutes would cancel out contractions in the monetary supply.

Nor does there seem any reason to alter the general character of this analysis upon reflection that the rationing of credit is actually accomplished by means other than the interest rate. Indeed, one wonders whether much "realistic" criticism of the alleged significance of the rate of interest on the grounds that both lenders and borrowers are more concerned with other parameters or "terms" of credit does not miss the point of the theoretical argument. For the "interest rate" is essentially a symbol of the measure of the cost of money. The essential issue in monetary policy is whether it is possible, feasible, and desirable to alter the cost of money sufficiently to affect the level of aggregate economic activity by the desired magnitude. Viewed this way, it matters not whether our conclusion is that the banks do not raise the interest rate enough, do not tighten collateral requirements enough, or do not tighten up on bad risks enough (or still find too many good risks). Whatever rationing technique the creators of money employ, the test of monetary policy must be whether monetary controls, as felt through these rationing techniques, has had or is likely to have the desired effects.

We may mention incidentally here that just as in the theoretical analysis the interest rate is only a symbol for the whole complex of credit rationing techniques, so in statistical analysis the published series on interest rate changes may reflect very inadequately the changes that occur in the availability of funds. It is safer to think of monetary policy as altering the quantity of money available and to regard the changes in the nominal interest rate as only one possible way in which these changes may be reflected.

The type of study needed to deal with the questions discussed here would be one largely in the domain of money and credit per se, and outside the main focus of this study of investment. Such a study would seek to indicate what we might denote as the elasticity of the cost of capital or credit with respect to some parameter under control of the monetary authority, say, the quantity of money. A companion study would seek to cast light on the elasticity of investment demand with respect to the cost of capital or credit. One difficulty of much work that has been done is that it has not been recognized clearly that the independent variable of the investment demand function—what is generally denoted loosely "the rate of interest"— must be the dependent variable in some function involving the parameters controlled by the monetary authority in order for us to have a completely determined, meaningful relation between monetary policy and investment.

3. The fallacy of composition.

Here (as everywhere in economics) one must beware of the fallacy of composition. There is no doubt that the tightening of money may appear to many individual firms as a negative factor in expenditure decisions. How much a tightening of credit to one firm reflects an increased utilization of and creation of credit by another may not be clear to the individual firm. For example, assume the monetary authority, by one or several of the standard techniques, induces banks to reduce the quantity of money. Banks may decide as a result to take action which reduces the amount of loans extended to Firm A. (This may be done by insisting upon more collateral, tightening on terms of repayment, or raising the interest rate.) Firm B, faced with a reduction in orders from Firm A may meet the situation directly by extending additional "trade credit" to Firm A. However, it is also conceivable that Firm A will not get such additional credit and will therefore forego or lose sales because of limited capacity or the higher costs which it tries to pass on. This may result in increased demand for the output of Firm C. Firm C now gives Firm B the orders that Firm A has curtailed and Firm B extends additional trade credit to Firm C. From the standpoint of Firm A, the tightening of credit has clearly curtailed economic activity. From the standpoint of the economy, aggregate demand has been unaffected and there has been a shift in demand from Firm A to Firm C. Indeed it is even possible that such shifts in the allocation of demand and output as a consequence of changed credit availability may increase investment demand. This would occur if Firm C, in our example above, found it desirable to order new equipment to meet demand that Firm A would have been able to meet in part with existing equipment, and if A would not be able to contract as rapidly as C is able to expand.

4. The assets effect.

Implicitly or explicitly, the discussion above relates to the role of monetary policy in affecting the rate of time discount, for it is this which is measured by the "cost of capital or credit." Monetary policy may, however, as was suggested above, also influence investment demand by its effect on the demand for final product, independently of the role of the rate of time discount. It may accomplish this essentially by changing the assets positions of households and firms in such a way as to increase the current demand for goods (or factor inputs). If by monetary policy we mean not only the substitution (or action to induce the substitution) of banking indebtedness for other forms of indebtedness, but also the creation of additional instruments of exchange and their distribution to the economy for nothing or in return for newly created goods or services, we permit a vast new scope to monetary policy. Such addition to the net assets of the private sector of the economy is, however, usually considered to be the domain of fiscal policy. In its simplest form it involves creation of money by the Treasury to finance government expenditures; this may, of course, be conveniently accomplished by having the Treasury first issue (or "sell") its bonds or notes to the monetary authority or the banks and then spend the proceeds.

If we eliminate deficit financing from the "monetary" arsenal, monetary policy may still influence the value of the stock of existing assets. Even if the number of securities in the hands of the public does not change, as the prices of these securities rise or fall their value changes. To the extent that the securities constitute obligations of the private sector of the economy to itself this may be a distributional matter, but it is still not necessarily to be expected that the positive and negative effects on expenditures will cancel out. But, what is more, a substantial portion of assets in the present day American economy are government bonds. Changes in the value of these have nothing to offset them, at least so long as government expenditures and fiscal policy are held to be unaffected.

It should be recognized that monetary policy may affect the value of existing assets by its effect on expected earnings. If monetary policy can generate substantial movements, for example, in the value of securities sold in financial exchanges the increases in individuals' estimates of their net worth may generate increases in expenditures. It may, however, be well to consider this asset effect essentially as an aspect of the role of expectations, which must require serious study in research on determinants of investment demand.

5. The risk effect.

Finally, we should recall the possibility that monetary policy may affect all expenditures and investment demand in particular, both directly and as induced by the increasing rate of demand for output, by altering the set of risks confronting decision makers. It is perhaps here that the monetary authority has a major role when it curtails the supply of money. For as other obligations are substituted for bank credit, firms may find the dispersion of expected returns increased by the uncertainty of payment (or uncertainty of date of payment) of the obligations due them. This may reduce the length of commitments firms are willing to undertake.

Further, it should be noted that to the extent that the monetary authority contributes to changes in the cost of capital or other monetary parameters affecting the firm, it is likely to increase the risks to which decision makers believe themselves subject. An investment that might be undertaken at an "interest rate" of 3 percent, expected with certainty to remain at 3 percent throughout the life of the investment, might not be undertaken if the decision maker has an expectation that the future interest rate will, with equal probability, be either 2 percent or 4 1/2 percent. For at 2 percent competing investments may be such as to wipe out the original firm, and the utility of the corresponding gain if the future rate turns out to be 4 1/2 percent may not be commensurate. Nor is the problem relieved by equity financing. For if the market is on balance risk averting, the existence of uncertainty as to the future rate of interest would tend to increase the required return on equity.

With the framework suggested above, we are prepared to turn to a consideration of relevant empirical information. This is in part qualitative, based upon interview studies and historical and institutional observations, and in part quantitative, based on both broad-gauged analyses of the data and on more narrowly defined econometric studies. We shall attempt to group our findings in such a way as to cast light upon the role of parameters under the control of the monetary authority in affecting investment demand; this will involve in the main a consideration of the way investment demand responds to sets of parameters such as those embodied in "the cost of capital" but will also perforce involve some consideration of how monetary policy may affect these parameters.

III. EMPIRICAL FINDINGS: PLANT AND EQUIPMENT INVESTMENT

Empirical data bearing on the determinants of capital expenditures are numerous and largely unconvincing. They have often been gathered and analyzed in ways more appropriate for purposes of accountancy than for revealing useful economic relations. Alleged findings are frequently inconsistent with the main body of economic theory as well as with each other. Findings that are consistent with theory are usually tentative and lacking in quantitative precision. Much quantitative analysis has followed along a few time-worn but questionable paths. And many if not most pieces of research have suffered from a failure to consider the varying implications of data at macroeconomic, industry, and firm levels.

It may be convenient to divide the empirical work that we shall consider into three main types. We may designate these as: (A) quantitative, econometric (involving parameter estimation); (B) quantitative, noneconometric (not involving parameter estimation); (C) qualitative, including interview and questionnaire studies of the investment process. Our treatment of these last will be summary in nature; readers are referred for detailed analysis to an earlier work by Eisner on this subject (197). Discussion of noneconometric, quantitative work will be highly scattered and selective from the vast body of literature from a variety of fields which touch upon investment. Our critical review of econometric studies, however, will attempt to cover a large proportion of the relatively few pieces of work which presume to say something bearing directly on investment.

Econometric studies which will be considered, in whole or in part, include works (sometimes more than one in number) by Tinbergen (617), Manne (416), Chenery (115), Klein (353, 354), Klein and Goldberger (355), Christ (117), Koyck (366), Meyer and Kuh (450), Kuh (368), Modigliani (461, 463), Kisselgoff and Modigliani (349), Modigliani and Weingartner (467), Taitel (605), Norton (497), Brown and Rosemann (90), Fisher (213), Grunfeld (274), and Eisner (199, 196). Quantitative studies essentially noneconometric in nature which we shall utilize will be gleaned from reports of Gordon (265), Fellner (209), J.M. Clark (124), Kuznets (372), Hickman (309), Foss (220, 221, 223), Foss and Natrella (224, 225, 226), and anonymous Department of Commerce reports, Keezer and Associates (345a), anonymous McGraw-Hill Department of Economics reports, Cohen (130), and anonymous N.I.C.B. reports. Reference will be made, in addition, to the judgments offered by a number of economists on the basis of quantitative data other than that with which we shall deal explicitly.

A. Econometric Studies

Econometric studies have been varied in approach. Some have involved single equation estimates of an investment function. Some have involved estimates of an investment equation as one relation in a system of simultaneous relations. Some have utilized the time series data of firms, industries, or the economy. Others have utilized cross sections of firms within an industry or the economy. In some cases the dependent or "explained" variable has been gross or net expenditures for plant and equipment or some component thereof. In other cases a proxy variable for investment, such as the production of pig iron or capacity, has been used instead. Data have been taken from both the nineteenth and twentieth centuries and from a number of countries in Western Europe, although chiefly from the United States.

Explanatory variables have reflected a number of theories of investment behavior and in some instances a lack of meaningful theory. Specifically, among major variables tested have been current and past output, sales, profits, interest rates, profit rates, depreciation charges, stocks of capital, age of capital, capacity, prices of output, labor and capital goods, "liquidity" stock variables, value of the firm, and a number of expectational variables. Involved in the latter on some occasions has been a "realization function" which related the difference between actual and previously planned or anticipated investment to discrepancies between actual and expected magnitudes of presumably causal variables.

It may be well to reveal at the outset the major note of criticism which shall become apparent in the discussion which follows. This relates to the failure in many of the studies to work with appropriately identified structural relations whose parameters might be expected to remain stable. Explanatory variables have frequently been "proxies" for those that would appear in a correctly specified "true" or basic relation. Such "proxies" may "work" in the sense of predicting so long as the unspecified relation of these proxies to the true causal variables remains unchanged; but we shall be led seriously astray if the side relation involving the proxy variable changes with the passage of time or with the introduction of policy measures.

A contrived example may make the issue clear. Suppose we are interested in predicting and possibly controlling the birth rate. A statistician estimates the parameters of a relation in which the number of births per year is made a function of the number of auto registrations, current and lagged. Whether the estimates are made with time series data for the entire nation or for any of a large number of possible "cross sections," the coefficients of births on auto registrations will prove positive (and significantly so, at any reasonable probability level, if reasonably sized samples are employed). This would be so, of course, because auto registrations in the United States (as well as a number of other countries) have through most of the present century been positively related to the number of adults as well as to income, both of which are appropriately viewed as variables in the structural relation determining births. Clearly this would give us no reason to expect that the production of new low-cost automobiles or the reduction of registration fees or gasoline taxes would increase the birth rate. It is our studied conviction that there is little or no greater substance to many of the investment relations reported by quantitative investigators than there is to the birth-auto relation suggested above.

Returning to our own field of investigation, it is found that econometric studies of investment have usually focussed on the role of profits, the supply of money capital, of which the rate of interest has been assumed to be a critical parameter, and the acceleration principle. Profits, we shall argue, correspond in large part to the auto registrations of our example above. Findings with regard to the role of the rate of interest and the acceleration principle have been confused, as often as not, by improper tests or misleading interpretations.

A final methodological note may be in order. Our review of the empirical evidence is oriented by our theory, which has led us to the view that not current profits or liquidity but changes in the ratio of expected demand to current capacity are likely to prove paramount in the ultimate explanation of investment. The a priori attractiveness of our theory is based upon its consistency with hypotheses of profit maximization which have had wide applicability in economics.

Our view may be misguided, and we have been prepared to find this demonstrated by the studies we have examined. The evidence leaves room for differences in interpretation, and that it may also be construed to be consistent with theories other than ours is not a matter we claim clearly to have refuted. The balance of this chapter suggests, however, that the empirical data may be analyzed usefully in terms of the theoretical framework we have adopted. If this is so, it should point the way to further estimation—still in its early stages—of quantitative relations providing an understanding of the causal structure of major forces influencing business investment.

1. Tinbergen (616, Vol. I)[1]

Probably the classic pioneering work, casting both light and shadow on future efforts, is that of Tinbergen. The data employed fall into two main categories. One relates to aggregative economic activity, using the consumption of iron and steel, the production of pig iron, and, for postwar U.S. data, a Kuznets series on gross capital formation, as the measures of investment. Periods involved covered about 40 years prior to World War I in Germany, the United Kingdom, the United States, and France, and about 15 years of the interwar period in the U.K. and the U.S. The main conclusions of this macroeconomic part of the analysis are: (a) "There is fairly good evidence that the fluctuations in investment activity are in the main determined by the profits earned in industry as a whole some months earlier"; and (b) "The influence of the other factors included is not considerable and is therefore, in many cases, numerically uncertain." (P. 49) In a separate study of net investment in railway rolling stock, utilizing prewar data in four countries, Tinbergen concluded, "the acceleration principle gives a somewhat better explanation than the profit principle but the regression coefficients found are below the theoretical values," and "the influence of interest rates seems to be rather high, except in Germany." (P. 130)

As a pioneering work, Tinbergen's efforts are to be much admired. Both the substantive conclusions and their further implications are, however, to be questioned. In view of the similar pattern of much subsequent work, we shall devote what might otherwise seem a disproportionate space to Tinbergen's studies.

First to be noted is the danger that variables which do appear to be related reflect in their relationship merely a common association

---

[1]Page references not otherwise identified are to the bibliographical item here cited in the heading of the section. Similar practice will be followed in subsequent sections.

with other unspecified factors which are involved in the true (but unrevealed) structural relation. There is always a strong danger that this is true in the case of profit, which represents a measure, albeit imperfect, of much of economic experience and, since change is not always abrupt and is in any event usually imperfectly foreseen, is, in addition, positively associated with the expected values of variables such as future demand, which might also (and more reasonably) be related to investment.

A major difficulty with lengthy time series is that many variables are likely to be moving in the same general direction (usually up) and hence will appear statistically related. Thus positive relations to investment might well have been found for not only profits within the country or industry but also profits in other countries or industries. Or, further, investment could also be found to be positively related to wage income (Tinbergen used "non-wage income" in some of his regressions), birth rates, and attendance at sporting events.

Some of the extremes of the problem of multicollinearity are removed by Tinbergen's technique of generally measuring his variables in terms of deviations (percent or absolute) from their trend or in terms of moving averages. Since investment and profits, however, are both highly cyclical variables, their relationship may still be due largely to their common cyclical characteristics. There may be many other cyclical variables which would evidence a similar relationship with investment. Tinbergen is presumably aware of these difficulties and offers a defense with which we do not differ in principle: "...the greatest importance must be attributed to the a priori argument to include profits in the explanation of investment" (p. 62), but we find that argument weak.

In terms of Tinbergen's specific results a number of observations about matters of detail may help us anticipate later findings. First, while the signs of "profit" coefficients are correct, their magnitude is frequently disconcerting. Thus, for example, the coefficient of iron and steel consumption on lagged non-labor income in the United Kingdom, 1871-1910, when both variables were measured as percent deviations from trend, varied from 1.79 to 3.45, depending upon what other variables were included in the regression. The sensitivity of the coefficients to the inclusion of other variables should be a cause for concern about the extent to which the coefficients do measure a correctly measured and identifiable structural relation. What is more, the magnitude of the coefficient is such as to defy reasonable theoretical explanation. Why should a 1 percent deviation in "profits" induce a deviation of over 3 percent in investment? In data for Germany, the coefficient of iron and steel consumption on dividends as a percent of capital (with the dividend variable an average of current and one year lagged figures and measured in absolute units of percent deviation from trend) varied from 4.96 to 5.80.[2] But for United States interwar data, with the sum of deliveries of producers durables and non-residential building as the dependent variable, the coefficient of the average of current and lagged corporate profits ranged from .16 to only .20.

Of interest is a significantly negative coefficient of share yield which Tinbergen derives from the interwar U.S. data. It implies that a 1 percent drop in share yield would induce about a 7 percent increase in investment. But it is questionable whether this should be taken to mean either that the way to get more investment is to get firms to cut dividends or that investment is highly elastic with respect to the cost of equity capital. What it more likely reflects is the positive association of high investment and the stock market boom of the twenties, associated with the collapse of both investment and stock values in the thirties, enforced, of course, by the relative sluggishness of dividend movements. (See the discussion of Grunfeld's use of the "market value of the firm," below.)

Tinbergen sees considerable "uncertainty... concerning the coefficient of interest rates." (P. 65) Coefficients for France and Germany were close to zero, but those for England were in the neighborhood of .31 for the prewar data and .1 for the interwar period. In terms of the units of measurement the coefficient of .31, for example, would imply that a reduction of 1 percentage point in the long-term interest rate (as from 5 percent to 4 percent) would cause a 31 percent increase in investment. Tinbergen adds: "It should not be forgotten, however, that the largest fall per annum in the long-term interest rate in any cycle before the war was .18 percent, and that in most cases it was far less." (Pp. 65-6)

Tinbergen's estimates of the interest elasticity of investment have been appropriately criticised by Haavelmo (275), who points out that in Tinbergen's regressions the profits variable was measured net of interest cost. Thus the zero partial regression coefficients for interest rates reported by Tinbergen may have reflected merely the fact that changes in the rate of interest had no further effect beyond the one already measured in the profits variable. For the U.K. where, as observed above, the interest coefficient itself was negative, Tinbergen points out that the "non-labor income" which was the measure of "profits" was in that case gross of interest.

At a later date Haavelmo might well have criticized Tinbergen's work on grounds related to the development of simultaneous-equation estimation techniques, later associated with Haavelmo's name.

---

[2]Depending on which other variables were included in the regression.

We refer in particular to the identification problem, which is formidable with regard to estimates of interest rate coefficients. Tinbergen's formulation involves estimating parameters of a relation in which investment is a function of a number of variables including the rate of interest. But suppose it is also true that the rate of interest is a function of the supply and demand for money and the latter depends primarily upon income (transactions demand) which in turn is a function of investment (by the multiplier). We would then find that the rate of interest and the level of investment are interrelated and in opposite ways. This opens the question of which relation Tinbergen estimated. Until a complete model is specified, one cannot know whether the investment demand function is identifiable. His estimate may relate to the liquidity preference function instead of to the investment demand function, or, more probably, to some combination of the two. It might be argued, in principle, that Tinbergen is on safe ground because his interest rate variable was lagged, thus ruling out the possibility that the estimates relate to the liquidity preference function. This, however, is not likely to be true (a) because of the serial correlation of interest rates, so that, using direct least-squares, Tinbergen would almost surely have obtained similar coefficients for the interest rate variable if he had not used a lag. It might further be suggested that (b) interest rate changes might well lead investment changes according to the relation of the liquidity preference function once the roles of expectations and intertemporal substitution are considered. For if investment demand were to rise this could generate an increase in the demand for money as well as the expectation of tight money before actual investment expenditures were completed. We raise point (b) as a plausible possibility, but have no statistical evidence regarding its importance. Point (a) suffices to raise the identification problem even if the interest rate is lagged.

Tinbergen's generally negative conclusions with regard to the acceleration principle may be considered indecisive with regard to current formulations. Writing when he did, Tinbergen did not use the distributed lag formulation considered later by Hicks and utilized in some recent econometric studies. Nor did Tinbergen make any allowance for excess capacity or shortages of capacity which might be expected to prevent the operation of a simple linear accelerator. His negative findings relate therefore to a formulation which was repudiated many years ago by J. M. Clark (123) and which would not be utilized by serious and informed investigators today. Nevertheless, it is interesting to note certain of Tinbergen's results which may now be recognized as a portent of later findings. First, with the U.K prewar data, the coefficient for the rate of change of consumers goods production was in fact positive, varying[3] from .27 to .45. Similarly, this coefficient was positive for

---

[3]Depending on which other variables were included in the regression.

prewar German data, varying from .23 to .36. The one clearly negative set of findings relates to the U.S. interwar data but here it may be noted that share yields were also included in the regression. One may well wonder whether share yields were not likely to reflect, particularly in this period, whatever effect one might expect from the rate of change of consumers goods production. In the years when such production was rising, stock prices were high, and share yields low, and when production was falling during the depression share yields were high and of course investment was low. The inclusion of both share yields and changes in consumer goods production therefore introduces a problem of multicollinearity and this may explain the particular coefficients obtained.[4]

Tinbergen's findings from data on the railroad industry differ somewhat, in ways anticipated by economic theory, from his findings for aggregative investment. The acceleration principle is more clearly operative (although its influence is still judged to be "relatively low" by Tinbergen). Acceleration coefficients with single lags, varying from one and one-half to two and one-half years were uniformly positive and ranged from .15 to .34 for the four countries studied. Tinbergen also finds, with regard to railroads, that "the influence of interest rates seems to be quite clear" and "largest in the United States." "It would seem," he writes, "that for the United States in the period 1919-32 a reduction of this (long-term interest) rate by 1 percent might have led, after about half a year or so, to an increase in investment activity of about 5 per cent of the average level." (P. 131) Tinbergen suggests that the greater apparent interest sensitivity in railroads is due to the greater longevity of rolling stock and that the greater role of the rate of interest in prewar data may in turn be ascribed to the greater role of railroads in aggregative investment.

---

[4]An explanation as to why collinearity among share yields and change in the rate of consumers goods production may be associated with a non-zero coefficient only for share yields relates to the fact that the acceleration principle must operate through effects on the prospective profit on investment. Past and current changes in production are only imperfectly related to expected future levels of demand which in turn are only one determinant, albeit, we claim, a major determinant, of expected profit on investment. But share yields are themselves essentially the inverse of expected profit on investment as indicated by the market, since the relative stability of dividends makes expected future returns, which have a major effect on stock prices, the chief determinant of share yields. Changes in share yields will thus incorporate the role of changes in the rate of change of past production as well as other factors in investment.

Tinbergen's view that accelerator coefficients are below their "theoretical" values depends upon how the theory is formulated. His coefficients, relating to percent deviations from trend, strike us as remarkably large for equations without distributed lags. They imply if desired capital stock is proportionate to output that up to a third of the induced change in capital stock which results from <u>nonsecular</u> variations in final output occur in the first year of adjustment. This view may be strengthened by re-examining some of Tinbergen's findings. For example, with United States prewar data, Tinbergen derives an equation which may be written:

$$V_R = 1.86(Z_R)_{-1.5} + 3.20[(Z_R)_{-1.5} - (Z_R)_{-2.5}],$$

where V_R is investment in railway rolling stock and the Z_R's are profit rates lagged one and one-half and two and one-half years, respectively. Now profit rates and rates of output are quite generally highly correlated in time series of annual data. It is interesting to consider, therefore, that equations with similar signs and relative sizes of parameters would have been obtained if output had been substituted for profit rates. But we then would clearly have had an accelerator with a rather substantial lag at work.

A further bit of evidence in a similar direction may be found in the curious autoregressive relation that Tinbergen reports at one point (Vol. 2, p. 140) with regard to corporate profits:

$$Z_t^c = 0.398Z_{t-1}^c - 0.220Z_{t-2}^c + 0.013Z_{t-3}^c + 0.027Z_{t-4}.$$

Ignoring the last two terms, this may be rewritten,

$$Z_t^c = 0.178Z_{t-1}^c + 0.220(Z_{t-1}^c - Z_{t-2}^c) + \dots .$$

Since profits, investment, and output show marked correlation, the above empirical finding is consistent with the notion that investment in period t is a function of output in period t-1 and the change in output from t-2 to t-1.

Tinbergen declares: "The demand for investment goods seems to be rather inelastic with regard to price; and in any case the adverse influence of a high price will as a rule, and partly as a consequence, be considerably outweighed by the favorable influence of profits occurring usually at the same time." (Vol. 2, p. 188) Once more, however, we must recall the problem of identification of the particular structural relation we have specified, and then it seems uncertain whether the estimates are of the demand function or supply function of investment goods.

2. Manne (416)

Utilizing data largely similar to some of those involved in Tinbergen's work—investment in freight cars, U.S., 1897-1940—Manne threw significant light on the acceleration principle. Relating

yearly percent changes in total freight cars to yearly percent
changes in ton miles of freight carried, Manne obtained, like Tinbergen, a regression coefficient that seemed superficially to be
too low: "the regression coefficient, which should, according to
the rigorous statement of the acceleration principle, equal unity,
is, in fact, + .299." (P. 94) Manne, however, then related percent
changes in freight cars utilized to percent changes in freight car
loadings, thus allowing for idle capacity, and secured a "regression
coefficient of + .578 (which) is much closer to the coefficient of 1.0,
postulated by the acceleration principle, than that obtained when
the factor of excess capacity is neglected." Further, a scatter diagram of the regression of percent changes in the total number of
freight cars on percent changes in freight car loadings is clearly
marred by the points representing the 1933-35 period of excess
capacity, when the number of freight cars continued to decline in
the face of increases in traffic. And finally, of major importance,
when Manne related percent changes in the number of freight cars
to a three year moving average of percent changes in ton miles of
freight carried (centered in the year preceding the investment) the
regression coefficient was raised from the .299 reported above to
.473. As Manne points out, this may be attributed, in part, to the
effect of expectations of future demand, which are strengthened by
the experience of several years of repeated increases. While confirming Tinbergen's reservations with respect to the naive accelerator, Manne's results are thus consistent with what might be
expected from a distributed lag accelerator adjusted for the role
of excess capacity.

3. Chenery (115)

Chenery compared the "acceleration principle" and the "capacity principle" in explaining interwar changes of capacity in six
United States industries: electric power, steel, portland cement,
zinc, petroleum refining, and paper and paperboard. By the "capacity
principle" Chenery meant a relation according to which in any given
year an industry changes its capacity by some proportion, generally
less than unity, of the difference between the actual output-to-capacity ratio and the ratio considered optimal. By the acceleration
principle he meant a relation according to which capacity changed
by some proportion of the change in output, regardless of the existing ratio of output to capacity. Chenery's specific formulations were:

$$\frac{\Delta K_{t+\theta}}{K_{t+\theta-2}} = b_1\left(\frac{X_t}{K_t} - \lambda\right) = b_1\left(\frac{X_t}{K_t}\right) - b_1\lambda$$

for the capacity principle, and

$$\frac{\Delta K_{t+\theta}}{K_{t+\theta-2}} = b_2\left(\frac{\Delta X_t}{X_t}\right) + C$$

for the acceleration principle, where K is capacity, X is output, λ is the optimum (or preferred) output-capacity ratio, to be derived from the data along with the estimate of the reaction coefficient, b_1, and C is a constant introduced to account for non-accelerator induced investment.

Chenery's results were mixed. The correlations tended to be better (although not uniformly so) for the capacity relation. All coefficients, however, had the right (theoretically expected) sign, with accelerator coefficients varying from .015 and .024 in zinc and steel, respectively, to .513 and .546 in the rapidly growing petroleum refining and electric power industries, respectively. The reaction coefficients, in the capacity relation, varied from .071 in steel and .210 in paper and paperboard to .650 and .915 in petroleum refining and electric power.

The somewhat stronger results with the capacity formulation may be due at least in part to the likelihood that the capacity relation approximates a distributed lag formulation of the accelerator in view of the serial correlation of output. Thus, if output rises and remains at its new higher level, according to Chenery's capacity relation, capital stock adjusts gradually over a number of years until the equilibrium output-capacity ratio is again attained. According to a distributed lag formulation of the accelerator one would have the same gradual adjustment of capital stock in successive years as investment responds in accordance with the successive lagged accelerator coefficients, to the increase in output. What is more, the capacity formulation was able to account, as Chenery pointed out, for the failure of capacity to increase in measure with output increases as industries came out of the great depression of the early thirties. It should be noted then that Chenery's "capacity principle" is essentially consistent with the acceleration principle in Hicksian or other flexible, sophisticated form.

One troublesome aspect of Chenery's analysis is the fact that the values of θ, indicating the lag in adjustment of capacity, averaged about unity and zero in a number of cases where coefficients were high. Values of zero or one, however, mean that Chenery was in fact relating changes in output to previous or concurrent changes in capacity. This, along with the higher coefficients in growing industries, suggests the possibility that increases in capacity made possible and hence induced increases in output, rather than the reverse—the identification problem once again.

4. Klein (353, 354)

Klein offers estimates of parameters of investment functions, both as single equations and as elements in systems of simultaneous relations. In the former category falls a considerable amount of work with American railroad data of the interwar period (354).

After a theoretical discussion of the role of "marginal expected profits, marginal with respect to the variation of the capital stock," Klein declares: "Our best substitute for marginal profit is current profit on existing capital," (354, p. 238) and finally: "We have adopted the simplification of looking upon gross operating profits as a main determinant of gross investment expenditures." (P. 250) Klein generally ignores the role of the acceleration principle or the capacity factor but information on these matters may be gleaned indirectly from some of his findings. Typical of these is the following regression fitted by least-squares to 1922-41 Class I railroad data:

$$I = 1596 + 0.75\pi_{-1} -51i - 0.14K_{-1} + u, \text{ where}$$
$$\quad\quad\quad (.08) \quad\quad (18) \quad (.02)$$

I is gross expenditures on road and equipment in 1910-14 prices,
   π is the net railway operating income before depreciation, deflated by a railroad construction cost index, 1910-14: 1.00,
   i is the average yield on new railroad bonds, u is a random disturbance with zero mean, and
   K is the end-of-year stock of fixed capital in road and equipment in 1910-14 prices.
   I, π, and K are in millions of dollars, and i is in percentage.

Thus past operating income (profits) would appear to be clearly significant and its variation appears to account for a major part of the variation in investment. The rate of interest has a negative coefficient, as does the sum of past investment, embodied in the stock of capital. The interest elasticity of gross investment, calculated at the point of means of the relevant variables in this equation is -0.73, which Klein interprets as showing "that although interest definitely influences investment, the influence is very limited" (p. 252), an interpretation that strikes us as surprising. In another regression Klein secures a significantly negative coefficient for a variable measuring the price of railway capital goods and somewhat different values of the other coefficients. In still other experiments Klein fails to get a significant relation for the surplus account, which is presumed to be a measure of available funds, or for nonoperating income. In fact the coefficient for nonoperating income is negative, having a value of -0.90, greater in absolute value than the coefficient of operating income which is taken as a measure of profits.

Close examination reveals inconsistencies and ambiguities of interpretation regarding Klein's coefficients. Some of these difficulties Klein indicates himself. For example, he writes: "The stock of capital, K, serves as a specific trend influence. If this variable were omitted, the coefficient of i would change sign .... If a linear trend is introduced as a fifth variable in equation (1), the coefficient of i is changed to a positive value ..." (P. 250-1) Further it may be noted that when additional variables such as nonoperating income and surplus are introduced into the regression the coefficient of i is changed to -32, which is less than one standard error from zero.

The profit variable itself, however, is open to serious questions of interpretation. We have already observed that the coefficient of nonoperating income proved negative. This would be hard to reconcile with the interpretation that profits per se, regardless of the source, are a factor in bringing about investment expenditures. This is the role given to them in Klein's earlier theoretical work (352). But, further, we may note that operating profits as defined by Klein are in a close, positive relation with output, and this relation is fairly linear within the range of observations. Thus one might have secured essentially the same result if one had substituted a variable which is explicitly a measure of output (as indeed operating revenue may well be, regardless of Klein's interpretation of it). But now we may also note that Klein secures negative coefficients for his stock of capital variables; in one case the coefficient is -0.20. The stock of capital is clearly a measure of capacity. Are Klein's results then so different from those of Chenery and Manne, who find investment positively related to the difference between actual and desired output-capacity ratios? By way of illustration, if we make the simplifying assumption that operating income is about a third of the output of railway services, which is roughly consistent with the data, we might be able to rewrite part of the equation estimated by Klein as:

$$I = \ldots + 0.25Y_{-1} \ldots - 0.14K_{-1}$$

or

$$\frac{I}{K_{-1}} = \ldots 0.25\left(\frac{Y_{-1}}{K_{-1}} - 0.56\right)\ldots,$$

which states, along with Chenery and Manne, that investment is a positive function of the difference between the existing output-capital (capacity) ratio and a ratio of .56 which is crudely (and with undoubted bias) estimated to be the desired or equilibrium output-capital ratio (the ratio at which there would be zero investment). One discrepancy, of course, is that Klein's data relate to net changes in capacity.

Klein has a number of other findings of some interest. He detects no role in investment for liquid assets. He also secures substantially similar results with analysis of cross-section data for a few of the years included in his time series, although coefficients of these different regressions differ by enough to make it clear that the author has not obtained estimates of parameters of structural relations either in the cross section or the time series regressions, or both.

Klein also studied the electric light and power industry (354). For the relation analogous to the one discussed above with regard to railroads, he obtained:

$$I = 1054 + 2.03 \pi_{-1} - 146i - 0.37K_{-1} + u,$$
$$\quad\quad\quad (.43) \quad\quad (37) \quad (.07)$$

where I, π, and K are in millions of 1911 dollars and i is in percent. Ignoring some question that Klein raised with regard to the time shape of the residuals, we may note that the coefficient for operating revenues is now sharply larger and the interest and capital stock coefficients more sharply negative. The interest elasticity of investment is 2.79, at the point of means (p. 280), but all coefficients are apparently acutely sensitive to the inclusion or exclusion of other variables: "the gross correlation between π_{-1} and I is negative." There is also, Klein states, "a very strong linear relation between π and K." While Klein's π is apparently operating revenue net of wages and salaries, it would appear again that this variable would be closely correlated with an explicit measure of output, such as total operating revenues. Thus, Klein's electric light and power results may also be viewed as consistent with a capacity-accelerator explanation of the investment process. Klein also introduced share yields in the regression and secured a negative coefficient, a matter we have discussed above in our treatment of Tinbergen's work.

In his construction of aggregative models of "Economic Fluctuations in the United States, 1929-1941," (353) Klein presented two relations dealing with investment. In Model I,[5] which involves the simultaneous estimation of parameters of relations explaining consumption, investment and the private wage bill, a maximum likelihood estimate of the investment relation is:

$$I = 17.79 + 0.23 \pi + 0.55 \pi_{-1} - 0.15K_{-1} + u_2',$$

where I, π, and K are respectively net investment, profits, and capital stock, each in billions of 1934 dollars. The corresponding limited information estimates, with asymptotic standard errors, give

$$I = 22.59 + 0.08 \pi + 0.68 \pi_{-1} - 0.17K_{-1} + u_2'',$$
$$\quad\quad\quad (.23) \quad (.21) \quad\quad (.04)$$

Klein points out (p. 72) that the standard error of the sum of the profits coefficients is only 0.09, but this may serve to remind us that autocorrelation is high among profits and it is difficult

---

[5]Offered by Klein in large part "to illustrate techniques and methodology," with sacrifice of "details of economic behavior patterns in order to illustrate different methods of structural estimation in dynamic economic systems." (P. 84)

particularly when other lagged variables are introduced into the regression, to use statistical inquiry to determine the relevant lag for profits. Aside from this question of lags, we may recall our earlier observations with regard to the role of profits and, in particular, our remarks with reference to Tinbergen's work and Klein's findings in the railroad and electric power industries. Again it is clear that profits and investment moved in rough synchronization from the boom of the twenties to the depression of the thirties and that there was a high degree of autocorrelation in both series. Yet many other series certainly manifested similar characteristics during this period and one hardly seems warranted in attaching structural properties to this relation. For in the last analysis, as Tinbergen explained in justifying his attachment to the profits variable, "the greatest importance must be attributed to the a priori argument to include profits in the explanation of investment." (616, Vol. I, p. 62) But if the a priori argument is not sound, and we do not in any case find it impressive, the repeatedly positive coefficients found by Klein and others are also not impressive. In any event, we may note with regard to Klein's Model I, that the investment relation may again be transformed to suggest estimates of parameters similar in sign--though somewhat implausible in magnitude--to those offered by Chenery in his capacity version of the accelerator.

In Klein's Model III, involving a large number of simultaneous relations, the investment function, estimated by the method of reduced forms, is

$$I = 2.59 + 0.12 \left(\frac{pX - E}{q}\right) + 0.04 \left(\frac{pX - E}{q}\right)_{-1} - 0.10K_{-1} + u_2',$$

where I is net investment in plant and equipment and the terms within the parentheses are the money values of output of the private sector of the economy net of excise taxes and deflated by a price index of capital goods. Klein regards $\frac{pX-E}{q}$ as a measure of profit. We feel it can just as meaningfully be regarded as a measure of physical output. Much depends on whether changes in this variable over the observations reflect mainly changes in $\frac{p}{q}$ (the ratio of output to input prices) and E—in which case Klein's interpretation may be better—or changes in X, in which case the output interpretation is better. If $\frac{pX-E}{q}$ is thought of as output, we may once more indicate the possible relation of such a function to the capacity formulation by crudely adding the two output coefficients and writing:

$$\frac{I_{t+1}}{K_t} = \frac{2.59}{K_t} + 0.16\left(\frac{Y_t}{K_t} - 0.625\right) + u_2''.$$

Klein estimated a similar regression with data for the railroad industry only and with an added variable to measure liquid assets, namely, the end-of-year current assets minus current liabilities, deflated by an index of railroad plant and equipment prices. The coefficients of income originating in railroads were 0.20 and 0.56 respectively for the unlagged and lagged variables and -0.11 for lagged capital stock, but the coefficient of the liquid assets variable was virtually zero. Utilizing data published by Lutz, Klein also tried to estimate the effect of liquid balances in manufacturing investment. He does secure positive coefficients but standard errors are too large to warrant rejection of the null hypothesis with regard to the role of liquidity. Klein concluded on this point: "The best that we can say at this stage is that the influence of liquidity on investment remains doubtful." (P. 117)

5. Klein and Goldberger (355)

Klein and Goldberger estimated an investment function as one of a large number of simultaneous relations derived from aggregative United States data for the years 1929-41 and 1946-50. With I equal to gross private domestic capital formation including inventory investment, L_2 equal to year-end liquid assets held by entrepreneurs, K equal to year-end stock of fixed capital and R equal to non-wage income, all in billions of 1939 dollars, we may write the Klein-Goldberger equation

$$I_t = -16.8 + 0.76R_{t-1} - 0.14K_{t-1} + 0.14(L_2)_{t-1}.$$
$$\quad\;\; (4.5) \quad (.17) \qquad (.08) \qquad\;\; (.10)$$

A revision using data to 1952, estimated by direct least-squares, left the coefficients virtually unchanged; the most substantial movement was a change in the estimate of the coefficient of K_{t-1} to -0.073. The results in any event are consistent with earlier work by Klein, and consistent as well with our reinterpretation of the data in terms of a capacity formulation of the acceleration principle.

Klein and Goldberger report that they found "no reasonable empirical result for the effect of interest." (Pp. 67-68) Their difficulties included "estimated coefficients with signs contrary to advance expectations, large sampling errors, and sometimes impossibly large coefficients." They suggest, however, that "to some extent these results follow from our failure to distinguish among inventories, construction, and equipment. In a larger model we may expect to find the short-term interest rate significant in inventory outlays, the long-term interest rate significant in construction outlays, and unlagged income significant in either inventory or equipment outlays." Reference to this last variable follows their statement: "We have not found reasonable estimates of the equations with unlagged earnings appearing simultaneously with lagged earnings." (P. 68) It is curious to note, however, that they do report having obtained coefficients of current and lagged income equal, respectively, to 2.1 and -1.4. These are rejected as "explosive." Yet we could rewrite in part an equation with these coefficients as

$$I_t = 0.7R_t + 1.4(R_t - R_{t-1}).$$

This would make it appear that investment is a function of income and the rate of change of income!

6. Christ (117)

In an intensive critique of Klein's Model III, Christ added 1946 and 1947 data as part of an effort to test the extrapolative predictive powers of the model for the year 1948. Of interest to us are the coefficients Christ obtained in the investment function, coefficients which varied substantially with the method of estimation. They may best be presented in tabular form below:

TABLE II-1

Method of Estimation	Variable		
	$\dfrac{pX-E}{q}$	$\left(\dfrac{pX-E}{q}\right)_{-1}$	K_{-1}
Least Squares	0.130 (.04)	-0.041 (.03)	-0.040 (.05)
Limited Information	1.271 (2.0)	-0.846 (1.4)	0.52 (.32)

The limited information, maximum likelihood estimates have high standard errors and appear strange, if not erratic. Considering the least-squares estimates we may note, as does Christ, that the negative coefficient of lagged output suggests that investment is a function of both output and the change in output. We may further modify Christ's rewriting of this relation in order to exhibit a mixed capacity-accelerator formulation of the investment function. We then obtain (see Christ (117, p. 83)):

$$\frac{I}{K_{-1}} = 0.089\left(\frac{Y}{K_{-1}} - 0.439\right) + 0.041\frac{\Delta Y}{K_{-1}} + \frac{0.18}{K_{-1}}.$$

The function above has the reasonable properties of making the percentage change in the capital stock a function of the amount by which the current output-to-capital ratio exceeds some "equilibrium value" (thus reflecting past increases in output for which net investment has not yet taken place), the current increase in output per unit of capital and a factor which may be taken as a measure of a trend toward increasing returns or decreasing capital intensity of production. The coefficients seem very low and imply a very slow rate of adjustment of capital stock to output changes. However, it is interesting to know that this same basic capacity-accelerator relation can be found even in the work of investigators who have not used it. We shall discuss below the results of various investigations that have focussed more directly on this relation.

7. Koyck (366)

Koyck has estimated parameters of a distributed lag investment function in such a way as to offer important evidence on both the determinants of investment and the usefulness of the Hicksian theory of the trade cycle. By assuming that after some point coefficients of successively lagged variables are in a constant ratio to each other and by assuming generally for practical estimation that this geometric progression of coefficients begins immediately after the first coefficient, Koyck is able to restrict himself to estimation of only four parameters. His investment function is generally of the following form:

$$\Delta k_t = \alpha \Delta y_t + \beta \Delta y_{t-1} + \lambda \beta \Delta y_{t-2} + \lambda^2 \beta \Delta y_{t-3}$$

$$+ \ldots + \gamma t + u_t, \qquad 0 \leq \lambda < 1,$$

where k is the logarithm of capital stock (or capacity) and y is the logarithm of output. Thus Δk, the proportionate or percent change in capital stock or capacity may be thought of as the ratio of net investment to the existing capital stock and Δy as the proportionate or percent change in output. With constant factor prices and an unchanging homogeneous production function of degree one (and other appropriate assumptions about expectations and the proportion of capacity industries may maintain idle) a, say, 1 percent increase in output would ultimately be reflected in a 1 percent increase in the capital stock. The larger are α and β, the faster the reaction of capital stock or capacity to changes in output. Where estimates are made subject to the restriction that the sum of the coefficients is fixed (either at unity or, to reflect the possibility of increasing returns at .8, both done by Koyck), then the speed of adjustment can also be measured by the reciprocal of λ. Put otherwise, the lower the value of λ, the faster the adjustment and the more likely that the early coefficients in the Hicksian model will be high enough to generate undamped or explosive cycles. The inclusion of chronological time, t, serves to capture the effects of increasing or decreasing capacity-output ratios over time, which may, of course, be related to the increasing capital stock and capacity over time. Thus a negative value for γ would indicate that as time progresses (and capital stock, capacity and output have increased) the ratio of capacity (and capital stock) to output has decreased or, alternatively, idle or reserve capacity has decreased.

Koyck dealt in turn with parameters of functions determining investment in freight cars, capacity in the electric light and power

industry, grinding capacity in Portland cement, open hearth capacity
in steel, and crude oil capacity in petroleum refining. He used United
States industry data, generally for the interwar period but, in the
case of freight cars, extending from 1894 to 1940. Estimates vary
somewhat, depending upon the assumptions about the serial relation
among residuals and the assumed restrictions upon the sum of the
coefficients. The major findings are not substantially affected by
these matters, however, and, for simplicity of exposition, we shall
present the estimates of the parameters as approximations or as
ranges, without detailing the variation in estimates.

Findings in the railroad industry (for investment in freight cars)
may prove particularly interesting in view of the substantial attention given to this industry by previous investigators. A typical set
of estimates for the entire period is: $\alpha = 0.077$, $\beta = 0.086$, $\lambda = 0.89$,
$\gamma = -0.02$, and $E_L = 0.86$, where $E_L = \alpha + \dfrac{\beta}{1-\lambda}$ is the long-run elasticity
of capital stock to output, that is, the percent by which the capital
stock would eventually increase in response to a 1 percent increase
in output. The sum of $\alpha + \beta$, indicating the proportion of a change in
output eventuating in a change in capital stock within a two-year
period, is estimated to be about .16.

Now this over-all estimate is not large and would seem to dis-
credit the possibility of an explosive cycle. Of particular theoretical
interest, however, are Koyck's separate estimates for an "expansionary period" (1894-1915) and a "contraction period" (1920-39).
Theory should suggest that α and β would be higher in expansionary
periods where there is less excess capacity that would inhibit the
activation of the accelerator in the upswing and fewer declines in
which the accelerator would be curbed by the lower bound to the
possible rate of gross expenditures on plant and equipment. Koyck's
data confirm this suggestion, as indicated by Table II-2 comparing
estimates for the expansionary and contraction periods, under the
alternative assumptions that the long-run elasticity of capital to
output is unity or is 0.8.

TABLE II-2

Estimated Parameter	Expansion Period		Contraction Period	
	$E_L = 1$	$E_L = 0.8$	$E_L = 1$	$E_L = 0.8$
α	.177	.159	.069	.066
β	.214	.200	.053	.051
λ	.741	.689	.943	.930
γ	.029	-.016	-.037	-.033

It is apparent then that in expansionary period, the estimates indicate that upwards of one-third of a percentage increase in output

would be reflected in the percentage increase in capital stock within two years.[6]

Koyck's results in the electric light and power industry for the years 1920-42 indicate that the sum of α and β, which we may dub the "short-run elasticity" of capacity is close to one-third for the entire period. It is to be noted, in particular, that the estimates of β are considerably larger than those for α and, for hydro-electric plants, are somewhat in excess of 0.2. Indeed, in conjunction with the estimates of λ in the neighborhood of 0.75 we may suggest that the investment relation is, for the first four lags, approximately:

$$\Delta k_t = 0.1\Delta y_t + 0.2\Delta y_{t-1} + 0.15\Delta y_{t-2} + 0.11\Delta_{t-3} + \ldots ,$$

thus indicating that between 50 and 60 percent of an increase in output results in induced investment within four years, a result which, as we shall note, is strikingly confirmed in later investigations with a substantially different body of data and mode of analysis.

The α and β coefficients for grinding capacity in the Portland cement industry for the years 1919-40 were quite low, totaling only about 0.13. When the years of sharp contraction, 1932-36, were eliminated, the estimates for the sum of α and β rose to over one-third. Estimates of this short-run elasticity in the steel industry, however, were very low, amounting to only 0.064 for the interwar period, even with the exclusion of the particularly depressed years of 1932 and 1933. On the other hand, estimates of $\alpha + \beta$ for crude oil capacity in the growing petroleum refining industry ran to just under one-third.

One may conclude from the Koyck analysis that the reaction of capital stock or capacity to output is clearly present and that the speed of reaction is greater in more rapidly growing industries and is more rapid in years of expansion than in years of contraction. One may also note, as does Koyck, that the most favorable case for the simple or crude "acceleration principle (though not very favorable after all) is that of railway freight traffic before the first World War ... (which) was first given as an illustration of the acceleration principle by ... J.M. Clark." (P. 109)

8. Meyer and Kuh (450)

Meyer and Kuh used multiple correlation techniques to analyze Securities and Exchange Commission data on capital expenditures

---

[6]This, in terms of existing capital coefficients, does begin to suggest the possibility of an undamped or explosive accelerator. See Hicks (312, pp. 67-94, 184-193, 195-199).

of over 700 registered firms in 12 manufacturing industries in the years 1946 to 1950. Most of their work was with cross sections within industries for a particular year's capital expenditures or with cross sections of the averages for all years of firm variables within the industry. Some effort was made to make industries homogeneous with respect to durability of capital goods. Some attention was given to the role of the interest rate, stock prices, and relative prices of capital goods and labor. This was in the so-called "time series models" in which previous cross-section estimates of profits and sales coefficients were inserted before the coefficients of the other variables were estimated for three industries using the time-series data.

In the cross-section analysis the basic relations used for estimation were:

$$\frac{I_t}{K_{t-1}} = f_1 \frac{(S_t, D_{t-1}, A_{t-1}, S_t{}', C_t, L_{t-1}, u_t)}{K_{t-1}} \text{, and}$$

$$\frac{I_t}{K_{t-1}} = f_2 \frac{(P_t \text{ or } P_{t-1}, D_{t-1}, A_{t-1}, S_t{}', C_t, L_{t-1}, u_t)}{K_{t-1}} \text{, where}$$

I is gross investment in both new and old plant and equipment,
S is sales,
P is net profits, that is, net income to surplus,
D is depreciation expense,
A is depreciation reserves, taken to be a measure of equipment age,
S' is change in sales,
K is gross fixed assets,

C is "needed capacity" defined as $S_t \left(\dfrac{K_m}{S_m} \right)_{max}$ form = 1946, ...,1949, and

L is the stock of net quick liquidity, i.e., current assets less inventory and current liabilities. (Pp. 78-79)

Meyer and Kuh argue that their "empirical work ... suggests a variety of conclusions but all converge in their emphasis upon the importance of internal liquidity." They declare that the accelerator "worked very well in 1946 and 1947 when almost every industry faced a seller's market, had good prospects, and ample liquidity—the presence of the latter being particularly important. On the other hand, the availability of liquidity became the paramount consideration in 1949. By contrast, the years 1948 and 1950 evidenced a mixture of acceleration and liquidity reactions."

(Pp. 190-191) They claim to find a "clear tendency for liquidity and financial considerations to dominate the investment decision in the short run while, in the long run, outlays on plant and equipment seem geared to maintenance of some relation between output and the capital stock." (P. 192) They further assert: "Insofar as short-run investment behavior is concerned, capital markets are of lesser importance than internal funds," and argue that "empirical results of both this and other studies have found that changes in output explain investment less well than the level of output." (P. 195) We have quoted these conclusions directly in order better to make clear our inability to agree with Meyer and Kuh in substantial parts of their analysis.

Let us first note that Meyer and Kuh are led to a number of their conclusions by the better "performance" of P_t (or P_{t-1}) than S_t in accounting for the variance of I_t, where all variables are deflated by gross fixed assets. But the cross-section variance of the current sales to fixed assets ratio can be expected to reflect only in small part factors that should be related to the cross-section variance of the capital expenditures to gross fixed assets ratio. The ratio S/K is essentially an inverse measure of capital intensity. And after all, there is little reason to expect the itinerant salesman of apples, pencils or shoe laces, who is likely to have a relatively high ratio of sales to capital stock (which latter may approach zero) to have a higher proportionate rate of growth of capital stock[7] $(\frac{I}{K} - \frac{D}{K})$. It is only to the extent that the variance in the S/K ratio relates to variance in pressure on capacity that we should expect it to generate capital expenditures. Surely this capacity pressure component of the cross section variance in the S/K ratio would be relatively small compared to the component reflecting differences in capital intensity. And the effect of even this relatively small component would be limited in the cross section for any one year by the lack of time for adjustment of desired capital stock as well as the reasonable tendency of firms to regard as temporary or transitory a substantial portion of any one year's departure from the normal sales to capital ratio. There may also be some positive relation between I/K and S/K because greater sales may generate greater replacement demand by causing capital to wear out more rapidly, but we should hardly expect this either to account for any substantial co-variance in the cross section.

It is interesting to note that Meyer and Kuh in their work with averaged data secured higher correlations between capital expenditures and sales than between capital expenditures and profits. (The

---

[7]Throughout this discussion we refer interchangeably to "gross fixed assets" and to "capital stock," though the reader should recognize that, while related, these are, of course, not identical.

difference is, however, not significant as the .05 probability level.) The averaging over the 1946 to 1950 period would tend to wash out a considerable portion of the year-to-year transitory variance in sales and the length of the period would be such that the effect of distributed lags might be in some part realized.

Those firms whose sales-to-capital ratio during any year or set of years is high would in part be firms whose sales had increased more than the average and firms whose pressure on capacity is greater than the average. Meyer and Kuh, however, find the role of the sales change variable itself "mediocre and patternless" while the "capacity variable ... explains investment very well in the early years, 1946 and 1947, and then abruptly collapses, usually in 1949 but sometimes in 1948." (P. 123) These findings deserve some scrutiny.

First it should be noted that the "sales model" (f_1 above) contains three variables—S_t, S_t', and C_t—which are likely to be collinear because they have components in common. We note that S_t' = $S_t - S_{t-1}$, and in one-fourth of the cases, where m = t-1, $\frac{C_t}{K_{t-1}}$ = $\frac{S_t}{S_{t-1}} = \frac{S_t - S_{t-1}}{S_{t-1}} + 1$. The "capacity variable" is a strange one and will be analyzed further but it should already be clear that the common and collinear elements in the three variables may reduce the opportunity for discovering a statistically significant positive regression coefficient for any one variable. Since, as Meyer and Kuh point out, sales are highly collinear with profits, the substitution of P_t for S_t in the "profits model" (f_2) is not likely to mitigate the difficulty substantially.

Meyer and Kuh attach particular importance to the varying results that they get over time in the behavior of their capacity variable. These results, however, can be shown to flow very largely from the peculiar properties of their definition of this variable. We can make this clear with the aid of Table II-3 which indicates the changing nature of C_t as t varies from '46 to '50 and m takes on the values of '47 or '48 which, according to Meyer and Kuh, are most common.

Inspection of this table makes clear quickly why the "capacity variable... explains investment very well in the early years, 1946 and 1947, and then abruptly collapses, usually in 1949 but sometimes in 1948." In 1946 and 1947 a "capacity variable" was defined to be (100 percent plus) the rate of growth in gross fixed assets, multiplied either by unity or by the reciprocal of the rate of change of sales, which latter variable is presumably less closely related to investment than is the growth of gross fixed assets. In 1948, the "capacity variable" was simply the rate of growth of capital stock (plus 100 percent) — virtually another way of measuring capital ex-

TABLE II-3

Definition of $\dfrac{C_t}{K_{t-1}} = \dfrac{S_t}{S_m} \cdot \dfrac{K_m}{K_{t-1}}$ for t = 46 to 50 and m = 47, 48

t	m = 1947	m = 1948
1946	$\dfrac{K_{47}}{K_{45}} \cdot \dfrac{S_{46}}{S_{47}}$	$\dfrac{K_{48}}{K_{45}} \cdot \dfrac{S_{46}}{S_{43}}$
1947	$\dfrac{K_{47}}{K_{46}}$	$\dfrac{K_{48}}{K_{46}} \cdot \dfrac{S_{47}}{S_{48}}$
1948	$\dfrac{S_{48}}{S_{47}}$	$\dfrac{K_{48}}{K_{47}}$
1949	$\dfrac{K_{47}}{K_{48}} \cdot \dfrac{S_{49}}{S_{47}}$	$\dfrac{S_{49}}{S_{48}}$
1950	$\dfrac{K_{47}}{K_{49}} \cdot \dfrac{S_{50}}{S_{47}}$	$\dfrac{K_{48}}{K_{49}} \cdot \dfrac{S_{50}}{S_{48}}$

penditures—in a large proportion of the cases. In another large proportion of the cases in 1948, however, the "capacity variable" was the rate of growth of sales from 1947 to 1948. In these cases some accelerator effect might be expected but there is no reason to expect the relation for this one brief lag to be strong and it is not surprising that it "collapses ... sometimes." The years 1949 and 1950 clearly present the inverse of "the early years." Now the capacity variable is defined largely as the reciprocal of the rate of growth of capital stock. Since this is certainly negatively related to capital stock it is clear that we must have the reported "collapse." Had Meyer and Kuh reported other results we might indeed have had reason to suspect a computational error.

The essential argument of Meyer and Kuh on behalf of the role of "liquidity" is vitiated by definitional difficulties. The "liquidity" variables on which their conclusions rest are depreciation charges and net profits. But the former is an accounting entry and is unreliable as a measure of funds actually received or available. Cross-section variance in depreciation reflects differences in

durability of capital and differences in accounting practice. Meyer
and Kuh find positive correlations between depreciation charges
and capital expenditures, particularly in 1949 and 1950. They infer
"(1) that the grant of accelerated amortization privileges has an
influence on investment decisions even in noninflationary times—
if not more so; and (2) that the liquidity aspect of depreciation expense seems to be the variable's dominant characteristic." (P. 109)
Meyer and Kuh claim that durability is not a factor in the observed
relation, basing their claim on a negative (but close to zero) rank
correlation of industries ordered by the range of estimated useful
life of industry-specific equipment in the Treasury Department's
Bulletin "F" and of industries ordered by the size of the partial
correlation coefficient of investment with depreciation charges.
The measure seems crude, however, not in small part because
much of the difference in depreciation rates for firms within "industries" relates to differences in the proportions of plant and equipment. Further, it may be argued that if accelerated amortization
were operative, firms investing heavily throughout the period would
have had a high depreciation rate for the years when accelerated
amortization was employed and firms not investing heavily would
have had a low depreciation rate since the accelerated amortization
in the latter case would apply to only a small proportion of assets.
Indeed the use by Meyer and Kuh of Bulletin "F" should emphasize
the role of durability in depreciation charges; Bulletin "F" itself
declares (p. 3): "The amount of the annual deduction allowable for
depreciation is ordinarily dependent upon the expected useful life
of the assets." If, with Meyer and Kuh, we accept Bulletin "F" as
relevant to the problem of depreciation, we might also consider as
relevant this instruction in Bulletin "F" to tie depreciation rates
to estimated useful lives. We might then infer that the bulk of the
variation in depreciation charges which is observed (virtually all
except that due to accelerated amortization) does in fact relate to
differences in expected useful lives as perceived by individual
firms. And differences in durability must of course be reflected in
the ratio of gross capital expenditures to gross fixed assets, which
is the Meyer-Kuh measure of investment.

If for industries having greater interfirm variation in the mean
durability of plant and equipment, the depreciation variable accounted for a greater percentage of the total variation in investment than it did for industries with smaller variance in durability,
this would confirm the role of the depreciation variable as a measure of durability. In the contrary case, however, the evidence cannot be taken as indicating that depreciation does not measure
durability. This is because high or low partial coefficients of
correlation for the depreciation variable for different industries
may merely reflect the relative adequacy among industries of other
variables, as well as the specification of the function and its form,
to account for variation in investment due to other causes.

The second major factor in what Meyer and Kuh label "liquidity" is net profits after taxes (net income to surplus). Here again some question may be raised as to the extent to which it is really liquidity which is measured. Some firms, particularly growing ones, may show high profits but be very short of cash. There is after all no reason why profits must take the form of cash. In many situations (such as the Korean War boom of 1950) they undoubtedly are related directly to such items as increases in inventories or accounts receivable. It is true that profits are believed by some to make it easier for firms to raise outside funds. But Meyer and Kuh did not find evidence of this and seem rather inclined, after examination of data relating to sources and uses of funds, to accept as accurate oft-repeated assertions of a strong business aversion to outside financing.[8]

With the above in mind we are inclined to reinterpret such statements as "ample liquidity is prerequisite to even the capacity accelerator's effectiveness." (P. 130) Depreciation charges change slowly from year to year. Ample liquidity thus means, in the Meyer-Kuh lexicon, high profits. That high profits should be associated with the effectiveness of sales changes in inducing investment should not be surprising. But are we to attribute this to liquidity or to the pressure of demand on capacity and a general situation of expansion, which are likely to exist when profits are high? Both the implications of "main line" economic theory and other empirical investigations would suggest the latter interpretation. In fact, Meyer and Kuh seem themselves aware of this when they state that the " ... capacity formulation of the accelerator provides a reasonably good explanation of investment when the economy is under strong inflationary pressures and expanding rapidly." (P. 117) To the extent, however, that Meyer and Kuh seek to resolve this apparent ambiguity in their findings they support the liquidity explanation, but on the basis of questionable measures of liquidity. With regard to their variable L, "the stock of net quick liquidity," we may note that they find no significant relation with capital expenditures.

Findings of higher relative correlations with accelerator variables in years of expansion and of higher relative correlation with "liquidity" variables in years of leveling or decline are in part consistent with the findings of others and the theory that the accelerator should work best in times when there is little excess capacity. These findings are, however, left confused by the nature of the "capacity" variable used by Meyer and Kuh and their use of depreciation as a measure of "liquidity" because the years of expansion in which Meyer and Kuh found the accelerator working were

---

[8]Cf. Eisner (195, pp. 27, 74, 77, 90, 97; 197, pp. 547-557), who indicates that aversion to outside financing is of uncertain significance in preventing profitable investment.

precisely the years when their "capacity" variable was definitionally related to the growth in the capital stock. Where the "capacity"
variable is in large part a measure of the inverse of that rate of
growth, as in 1949 and 1950, we might expect the depreciation variable to fare better, both as a measure of durability and because of
possibly higher rates of depreciation on new assets which would
make high average depreciation rates in a firm the result of heavy
recent capital expenditures.

Meyer and Kuh give considerable attention to questions regarding
the supply of money capital. They show concern particularly for the
relation between growth and size of firm and various aspects of
this supply of funds. In regard to growth, Meyer and Kuh use
changes in the ratio of depreciation reserves to gross fixed assets
as a measure of "change in age" and growth. They find evidence of
an association between decrease in age and increase in outstanding
debt and equity. Meyer and Kuh consider the change in age a measure
of growth. If this is so it might be argued that growing industries
rely more on outside financing. However, it is in large part age itself, rather than the change in age, which measures growth, for a
growing firm will have a larger proportion of younger assets. The
decrease in age then signifies an increase in the rate of growth.
The fact that firms that increase their rate of growth turn to more
outside financing does not necessarily mean that firms that are growing rapidly, but at the same rate as before, do so. Meyer and Kuh
also adduce evidence that dividend payout is negatively related to the
net investment rate. This may reflect a tendency for firms with good
investment opportunities to allow owners to receive their income in
the form of capital gains with substantial resultant tax savings,
rather than to accord them cash dividends.

Meyer and Kuh offer a variety of data on the relative position of
small firms. They report that "small firms" generally have larger
investment rates than large firms but that their growth rates declined more in the 1949 recession. Particularly, to the extent that
"gross fixed assets" reflect accidents of accounting under original
cost valuations rather than the market value of existing capital
goods, firms classified as "small" by the Meyer-Kuh criterion of
amount of gross fixed assets might have high ratios of capital expenditures to gross fixed assets although the capital expenditures
ratio may be independent of the size of firm measured by other
(and economically more relevant) criteria. They found "little evidence insofar as the over-all figures go, that small firms had
poorer access to external funds than large firms." (P.176) They
do see a "tentative implication" that "liquidity" is more important
in small firms, the accelerator more important in large firms (pp.
176-178), but in addition to the problems relating to definitions of
liquidity and accelerator variables discussed above, it should be
noted in this case that the Meyer-Kuh judgment is based on relative probability levels of statistical significance (found higher for

liquidity in the more numerous small firm sample) rather than on
the relative strengths of the relations (or size of regression coefficients) and hence is not substantiated. One must always be
cautious not to confuse statistical and economic significance.

In a brief time series analysis, in which Meyer and Kuh en-
deavored to test the role of interest rates, measured by the yield
on grade A industrial bonds (unlagged), stock prices lagged, as
measured by an industry index, and the relative price of labor
lagged, as measured by the ratio of labor to capital cost indices.
Their method was to estimate two partial regression coefficients
in each of two relations in which the third coefficients were respectively the estimates of the profits and sales coefficients from
the cross sections of 1946-50 averaged data. The time series estimates were made from first differences of the variables in order
to eliminate collinearity due to common trend. The analysis was
conducted for three separate industries: textiles, pulp and paper,
and rubber.

Coefficients of the interest rate variable had the wrong sign
(were positive) in five out of six cases but standard errors were
high and the coefficients (except for the one positive coefficient
which was in the rubber industry) were clearly not statistically
significant by the usual criteria. Stock price coefficients were also
positive in all but one case and fared better on tests of statistical
significance. "Relative cost of labor was not used, since from the
simple correlations and intercorrelations it became clear that it
was not a statistically strong variable." (P. 187) Meyer and Kuh
declare: "As in previous studies, interest rates proved to be of
negligible significance. In accordance with Tinbergen's findings
about the influence of stock prices, the results ... indicate that these
may well be important dynamic determinants of investment behavior." (P. 180) We are not, however, able to agree with either of
these judgments on the basis of their analysis because our criticisms
of the earlier Tinbergen analysis in these regards apply here with
equal if not increased force. In particular, there is a major problem
of identification of the unlagged interest rate relation in the Meyer
and Kuh model (although even had it been lagged, there might have
been problems stemming from serial correlation). The finding of
positive coefficients for the interest rate variable suggests that the
estimates relate more to the liquidity preference function (so that
increases in investment and income raise the demand for money and
the rate of interest) than to the investment demand function. The
stock price finding is, however, somewhat more impressive in view
of the first differencing technique which was employed.

We may at this point call attention to a general methodological
issue which applies in varying degree to most of the econometric
studies reviewed. It should be realized that since regression co-

efficients relate to variances and co-variances about the mean of a set of observations the nature of this set can be critical. In a cross section of observations at one point of time, we are relating, for example, variations of investment around its mean. We have no direct information, however, on how the mean of investment would be affected if the mean sales change were to be altered. Put another way, we have no way of knowing that if firms with sales changes 10 percent more than the mean, invest 5 percent more than the mean, it will follow that an increase in all sales by 10 percent would raise all investment by 5 percent.

While the issue is, of course, a fundamental one in any attempt to identify and estimate structural relations from cross-section data, it emerges with particular force in the Meyer and Kuh analysis of cross sections within industries, for it seems particularly dubious that industries will react to changed experience in the same way that a firm reacts to the difference between its experience and the mean experience of the industry. In regard to sales changes again, there is the familiar notion that firms think in terms of maintaining their share of industry demand. This does not mean necessarily that a firm would not take such opportunities as it can find to increase its share, but, unless it receives good evidence to the contrary, it may base its plans on expectations of a stable share of a fluctuating industry demand. This may imply that if a firm in one year happens to have a sales experience better than the industry mean it will expect a reversion to the mean the following year. In deciding upon capital expenditures a firm may then be inclined to ignore the deviation of its rate of change of sales from the mean rate of change of sales for the industry as a whole, although a change in its rate of sales which reflects a general change for the industry would be viewed in a quite different light. It is the former phenomenon that Meyer and Kuh measure; it is likely to be the latter that is more relevant to the problem of what determines the level of aggregate capital expenditures.

9. Kuh (368)

Evidence which we may interpret as relevant to this issue is presented by Kuh in a recent article. It should be noted at the outset, however, that Kuh's purpose in this contribution is more to illustrate methodological issues and the differences between cross-section and time-series studies than to present substantive findings regarding the determinants of investment. He compares regression coefficients calculated from cross sections with those calculated from time series of data of "seventy-three capital goods producing firms with complete records on investment and explanatory variables over the period 1935-55, excluding the war years 1942-45," and including for the most part firms which in 1953 "had gross fixed assets valued in the neighborhood of 30 to 50 million dollars."

(P. 199) His regression, with some variation of profits lags, is of the form:

$$I_t = a_0 + a_1 P_t + a_2 K_{t-1} + a_3 C,$$

where I is investment, P is gross retained profit, K is capital stock and

$$C = \frac{1}{3} \left(\frac{S_{48}}{K_{48}} + \frac{S_{52}}{K_{52}} + \frac{S_{53}}{K_{53}} \right) \text{ is a "capital intensity index."}$$

Kuh presents estimates of the coefficients of the profits and capital stock variables taken from "averaged data" and a "weighted regression" of unaveraged data. These estimates turn out to be positive. This is disconcerting in the case of the capital coefficient, but is probably to be explained by the fact that the data are not adjusted either for trend in the case of the time-series nor for differences in firm size in the case of the cross section. This makes the estimates of doubtful value. If one were to divide the regression equation through by the stock of capital to obtain the capacity formulation of Chenery, one would get the wrong sign for the optimal output-to-capital ratio, because of the positive capital stock coefficient Kuh obtained. Why does Kuh get a positive coefficient here when Klein, Klein and Goldberger, and Christ (except for the limited information estimate) did not? In the case of Kuh's time-series estimates, we suspect that this has to do with the period covered. Kuh's regression is over the period 1935-55, from a depression year to a prosperous year, and capital stock would be trend dominated. This is not so decidedly the case for the other investigations. In the case of Kuh's cross-section studies, the positive coefficient of capital can be ascribed to the absence of any adjustment for firm size. It is interesting to note, however, that the estimates of the capital stock coefficients as derived from the cross sections range from 0.016 to 0.033 while those derived from the time series are considerably higher, ranging from 0.049 to 0.098. The cross-section profit coefficients range from 0.477 to 0.646, while the time-series profits coefficients are decidedly lower, ranging from 0.202 to 0.520. The systematic differences between the cross-section and time-series estimates bring into the open perennial problems of interpretation. Under ideal circumstances, the time-series approach is adapted to questions regarding the effects on aggregate investment of changes in macroeconomic variables; and, also under ideal circumstances, the cross-section approach is adapted to the question of how a given aggregate change in investment is apt to be distributed among firms of different characteristics. It may be, as pointed out earlier, that profit would have little power in explaining a change in aggregate investment, but might explain very well which firms will account for a given aggregate investment. The

problem of interest to a monetary authority concerned with affecting the aggregate level of demand is the former one, and time-series
studies would appear to be the more relevant ones. But there are
attendant practical difficulties in using time-series data, and so
cross-section studies are not without interest even for the former
problem. It is best, of course, if the cross-section data also have
a time dimension, observations on firms extending over a few
years, though even then it is difficult to disentangle the aggregative
from the distributional effect of a change in an explanatory variable.
In any case, our general expectation, based upon theoretical considerations, is that profits would be more important in explaining
distributive than aggregative effects. Kuh is expressly concerned
with the different interpretations to be given to cross-section and
time-series regressions, and he ascribes the differences in his
estimates to the greater role played by dynamical, short-run forces
in the time-series formulation and by what he regards as the more
long-run [equilibrium] character of the adjustments of firms reflected in the cross-section data. One would have expected on his
interpretation that the profits variable would have had higher coefficients in the short-run time-series regression than in the longer-
run cross-section regressions. This is contrary to our conjecture
above where we stress the difference between the aggregative and
distributional impact of a change in profits and is contrary to his
results. Yet if the importance of profit in the cross-section regression is to explain which firms will expand relatively more or less
rather than the aggregate expansion resulting from across-the-
board policy measures, then the role of profits is of less importance
for the macroeconomic policy of the monetary authority. Kuh does
quite properly emphasize, nevertheless, some of the difficulties of
interpreting cross-section estimates in a dynamic time-series
context.

10. Kisselgoff and Modigliani (349)

Kisselgoff and Modigliani report a study of investment in the
United States electric power industry from 1924 to 1941 which gives
strong support for a capacity formulation of the acceleration principle. They argue that whatever importance realized profit may have
in determining investment in a competitive industry, it is not likely
to be so useful in sectors where high profits are associated with
monopoly power which expansion would only weaken. In regressions
relating price deflated capital expenditures to price deflated profits
(before interest deduction) and to the rate of interest as measured
by annual yield averages on new bonds, profit coefficients are found
to be negative and interest coefficients positive, although none would
pass the usual significance tests and multiple correlations are quite
low. Like others, Kisselgoff and Modigliani have not, however, faced
up to the identification problem with regard to the rate of interest.

A close relation between investment and changes in capacity, with appropriate lags, is indicated by an equation relating capital expenditures in millions of deflated dollars, I/A, to increase in capacity during the current year, ΔS_t, presumably accomplished by expenditures that complete projects that were commenced earlier, and to capacity increases during the subsequent year, ΔS_{t+1}, associated with expenditures on projects commenced but not completed during the current year. This equation, with estimated standard errors beneath the estimated coefficients, follows:

$$\left(\frac{I}{A}\right)_t = 101 + \underset{(.015)}{.057} \ \Delta S_{t+1} + \underset{(.015)}{.074} \ \Delta S_t, \qquad \bar{R} = .935.$$

This is, of course, a technical relation indicating the apparent consequences of investment but not its determinants. It leads Kisselgoff and Modigliani however to a formulation which relates current deflated capital expenditures to current (or lagged) deflated profits, the ratio of output to capacity lagged two years, the increase in the ratio of output to capacity lagged one year, and a trend factor to take account of increases in the equilibrium ratio of output to capacity resulting from the fact that power companies have been able to operate with less in the way of reserves and idle capacity. They estimate accordingly the equation:

$$\left(\frac{I}{A}\right)_t = -495 + \underset{(.234)}{.661} \left(\frac{\pi}{A}\right)_t + \underset{(.038)}{.253} \left[\left(\frac{P}{S}\right)_{t-1} - \left(\frac{P}{S}\right)_{t-2} \right]$$

$$+ \underset{(.024)}{.225} \left(\frac{P}{S}\right)_{t-2} - \underset{(2.4)}{21.3} \ T, \qquad \bar{R} = .972,$$

where I/A is deflated investment, π/A is deflated profits, and P/S is an output-to-capacity ratio. This implies that a high ratio of output to capacity, P/S, in the year t-2 induces expenditures on capital projects which are commenced in year t-1 and completed in year t. Similarly, a high value of P/S in the year t-1 induces expenditures on projects which are commenced in the year t, but these additional expenditures are reduced in proportion to the expenditures which were initiated in the year t-1 on the basis of a high value of P/S in t-2; hence the appearance of $(P/S)_{t-2}$ with a negative sign in the expression in brackets.

The positive sign for current price-deflated net income plus depreciation, π/A, lends support to the profit theory of investment. The disclaimer would be that the importance in the regression of π/A may reflect in part the fact that depreciation includes some proportion of current investment and a proportion of the sum of past investment, which may be serially related to current investment.

When the equation is altered to include lagged instead of current profits, the relevant coefficient is reduced to .321, with a standard error of .226. On the other hand, quoting Kisselgoff and Modigliani: "The coefficients of regression of the other variables show a high degree of stability. Since at least one year is required to carry out large-scale investment programs, these results are not inconsistent with the hypothesis that profits are not a key variable in major investment decisions." (P. 369)

Kisselgoff and Modigliani also estimated relationships for plant and equipment expenditures separately and the results were consistent with and similar to those achieved for all capital expenditures combined. The positive relation with current profits was conspicuous in the equipment regression but less strong in the plant regression. Attempts to find significant and plausible relations involving other variables were not successful. The coefficient of the ratio of the electric light and power construction cost index to the hourly wage, intended to measure relative prices, had the wrong sign (was positive). The same thing occurred with the interest rate. In both cases, however, we must again note the lack of identification of the relation presumably being estimated.

Kisselgoff and Modigliani conclude that the acceleration principle (in the capacity formulation they employ) is the prime explanation of investment in the electric power industry. Profits have some influence but it is "not very pronounced." (P. 378) They caution, however, that the strength of the acceleration relation in this industry may be due to strong institutional and legal pressures to meet demand and to the support of capitalization by regulatory bodies. Thus, it would "be hazardous to extend our findings" to other unsheltered and unregulated industries.

11. Modigliani and Weingartner (467)

Some further evidence on the role of changes in demand is offered by Modigliani and Weingartner in their analysis of planned and actual capital expenditures reported by the Commerce Department and the Securities and Exchange Commission. Dealing with annual, aggregate data for manufacturing, Modigliani and Weingartner relate actual capital expenditures, I, to planned capital expenditures, X, and the difference between anticipated and actual sales, E, the latter variables adjusted for unforeseen price changes. If the desired capital stock depends upon sales one would expect that sales in excess of those expected would, to the extent firms have time to adjust, lead to some excess of investment over the amount planned, and vice versa. This is confirmed by the following relation estimated by Modigliani and Weingartner:

$$I = 0.91X + 0.031E + 0.98, \qquad\qquad \bar{R} = 0.989,$$
$$\quad (.05) \quad\;\; (.011)$$

all variables in billions of dollars.

12. Taitel (605)

On the basis largely of a series of cross-section analyses in the United States petroleum and steel industries from 1927 to 1938, Taitel concluded: "Factors other than the amount or the rate of profit have been the major determinants of the level of capital expenditures of groups of companies in the same industry and, hence, of business as a whole. Of these other factors, the most important have been the level of output in relation to capacity and the pressure upon business for the introduction of available new technologies." (P. xix) He bases this upon examination of the differences among yearly scatter diagrams of rate of return and net property expansion. Rates of net property expansion for given profits rates differed widely from year to year as the ratio of output to capacity (and other factors) varied.

13. Norton (497)

Norton used 1940 data of essentially the same sample of firms in the petroleum industry employed by Taitel in a cross-section analysis of investment behavior. He reports that "the coefficients of the demand variables may all be considered statistically significant. As for the capacity variable, ... its coefficient is usually significant. The liquidity variables do not meet the test ... Coefficients of the debt-equity variable are never significant." The demand variable employed with repeated success is "change in net sales." All regressions involve three independent variables, and in the one case where sales and sales change were both included, the coefficient of sales was not significant while the coefficient of sales change was. The liquidity variables, all lagged, that failed to pass significance tests were "current assets, liquid assets (= cash balances + marketable securities), cash balances, ratio of current assets to net sales, liquid assets to net sales, cash balances to net sales, current assets - current liabilities = working capital, ratio of working capital to net sales, ratio of current assets to current liabilities, ratio of liquid assets to current liabilities." (P. 332) "The capacity variable is represented by the lagged [net] capital stock of the firm and the debt-equity variable by the lagged ratio of fixed liabilities to net worth." Norton's results are somewhat puzzling, however, because he does not uniformly deflate his variables in such a way as to eliminate the effects of size of firm (investment is not deflated by fixed assets, for example; nor are sales and a number of measures of profits) and he reports rather surprisingly that equations involving profits and all other variables other than those reported upon explicitly "were quite unsatisfactory." (P. 337) The stated reasons were low multiple correlation coefficients, and wrong signs or lack of significance for individual coefficients at the 5 percent level. Norton does not report actual coefficients but does offer a table of t ratios for variables. (P. 337)

Just as Kuh's cross-section estimates seem to be of doubtful value to us because the data are not adjusted for differences in the size of firms, so do Norton's estimates and for the same reason. We are therefore uninspired to try to reconcile their apparently conflicting results, one with the other.

14. Brown and Roseman (90)

Brown and Roseman reported on a "Cross Section Analysis of Manufacturing Investment during 1951-55" which is similar in a number of ways to the work of Meyer and Kuh. They utilized data of 339 firms compiled by the Securities and Exchange Commission and Department of Commerce and took supplementary information from Moody's. Firms were classified into eleven industry groups, each of which was analyzed separately. Their regressions were of the form,

$$\frac{I_t}{K_t} = b_0 + b_1 \frac{\pi_t}{K_t} + b_2 P_t + b_3 \frac{S'_t}{S_t} \ ,$$

relating gross investment divided by capital stock to profits, similarly deflated, a measure of capacity pressure (P) defined as "the ratio of sales to capital stock ... divided by the average of the sales-capital stock ratio for the period 1950-55," (p. 346) and the ratio of expected [future(?)] sales to actual sales. Brown and Roseman used as an alternate form the above regression with $\frac{S_t}{K_t}$ (the sales-to-capital ratio) substituted for the profit rate. Unlike Meyer and Kuh, Brown and Roseman found little to choose between the "profits" and "sales" models and little consistent pattern in the year-to-year differences. They offer sets of multiple and partial correlation coefficients (the latter for profits, sales, and capacity pressure only) and conclude that "sales and profits are significant explanatory variables of investment ... [but] are not consistently significant.... Annual sales expectations are slightly inferior to ex post sales in explaining investment behavior" and the sales change and lagged capacity variables, among others, "do not perform well in our linear form." (P. 350) It is difficult to evaluate these conclusions, however. Sales should be structurally related to investment only insofar as they relate to the capital stock and requirements for its replacement. The formulation of the "capacity pressure" variables seems rather unfortunate, relating as it does, the current sales-capital ratio to both previous and future ratios for most years,[9] but a check of one of the Brown-Roseman tables reveals that this variable had the right (positive) sign in 41 of the 55 industry-year regressions. Indeed, for 1954 and 1955 where the variable related more to the ratio of the current sales-capital ratio to previous ratios, there were 18 positive coefficients and only 4 negative ones.

15. Fisher (213, 217)

Gene H. Fisher has used aggregative data, both of the interwar and of the postwar periods to estimate parameters of the model Samuelson devised to illustrate the interaction of the multiplier and the accelerator. Fisher utilizes the reduced form, expressing income as a function of the income of two previous years, to estimate parameters of both a first order difference equation describing the consumption function and a second order difference equation relating investment linearly to the previous change in income. Using annual U.S. data in 1939 dollars for the period 1929 to 1941, Fisher obtains an estimate of $\beta = 0.5$, where $I_t = \eta + \beta (Y_{t-1} - Y_{t-2})$. (217, p. 530) Then, using similar quarterly data for the period 1947 to 1950, Fisher estimated β to be 0.482, but in this case β is the coefficient of the change in consumption, rather than the change in income, and the lags are measured in quarters instead of years. Fisher interprets his estimates as suggesting that the investment coefficient is too low to give the undamped or explosive cycles called for by the Hicksian trade cycle model, but one can challenge the model which underlies this inference, if only because of the exclusion of distributed lags.

16. Grunfeld (274)

Grunfeld completed a set of time-series analyses of each of 11 large United States corporations, using data from 1935 to 1954. Defining investment to include maintenance and repair expenditures, but excluding investment in inventories, Grunfeld found that the simple correlations between investment and current or realized

---

[9]For example, relatively high values of the "capacity variable" for the early years imply that the sales-capital ratio was declining during the 1950-55 period as a whole. This might reflect the effects of capital expenditures (thus suggesting a relation opposite in direction to the one presumably being measured) or it might reflect a relatively low or a negative rate of growth of sales, which would contribute to a negative relation between the capacity variable and capital expenditures. In neither case could we infer anything clearly about the role of capacity pressure in investment.

profits were accounted for by the stock of plant and equipment and
the market value of the firm, the latter variable being essentially
the sum of debt and the market value of equity. The partial correlation of investment and profits with stock of capital and value of
firm in the regression was -0.01. Partial correlations were similarly not significant with respect to a number of "liquidity" variables: sales, income plus depreciation minus dividends, income to
surplus, and cash and marketable securities. Grunfeld's market
value of the firm is actually a splendid measure of expected profits,
discounted for risk, uncertainty, time--and whatever else may be
relevant. It might be used in a critical test by taking it as the divi-
sor of current profits. To the extent it were current profits rather
than expected future profits which were relevant to investment (it
should really be marginal expected profits on investment, according to standard theory) one should expect a positive relation between
investment and the rate of current profit measured as a ratio of the
market value of the firm. If expected future profits were of more
direct concern one should expect the coefficient of this variable to
be negative. Tinbergen's results with share yields suggest the coefficient might well be negative but the specific test has not to our
knowledge been attempted. Grunfeld's own conclusion is: "The data
that we have examined did not show any indication that the variable
profits can successfully serve as an explanatory variable of corporate investment decisions. Our evidence indicates that ... realized profits fail to incorporate the main expectation factors or
liquidity considerations that determine the investment decisions of
the firm." (P. 3)

17. Eisner (196, 199)

In a cross-section study of 1948 to 1950 McGraw-Hill capital
expenditure survey data, Eisner (196) reported evidence of an
"acceleration component" of investment. Combining questionnaire
responses with accounting data as to sales, profits, and fixed assets,
Eisner worked with sets of firms that varied in number from 122
to 255 in regressions involving investment.

Capital expenditures, capital expenditure plans, and profits were
deflated by 1949 gross fixed assets, and actual and expected sales
were expressed as percentages of 1948 or 1949 sales, thus eliminating heteroscedasticity and multicollinearity associated with size
of firm. The capital expenditure variable, so deflated, was related
to capital expenditure plans, actual sales changes (current and
lagged), expected sales change, profits (current or lagged), and
expansion plans.

The 1950 ratio of capital expenditures to gross fixed assets,
$\frac{I_{50}}{F}$, was found to have regression coefficients of 0.160 with the
1948 to 1949 percentage sales change and 0.099 with the 1949 to

1950 percentage sales change. Both of these coefficients were far in excess of their standard errors (0.023 and 0.017, respectively). They were also relatively insensitive to the inclusion or exclusion in the regression of other variables, such as profits, past investment, or investment plans. When firms were divided into six industry groups--machinery; all other durables; textiles and apparels; food, tobacco, and alcoholic beverages; all other nondurables; and utilities, transportation, and other manufacturing- $\frac{I_{50}}{F}$ was found to be positively related to the 1948 to 1949 percentage sales change within all groups.

Capital expenditures (1950) showed only a slight correlation ($r = .164$) with prior sales change expectations, although this was significant at the .05 level. When firms were divided into three groups on the basis of the direction of expected sales change from 1949 to 1950 (up, no change, or down), the operation of the acceleration principle for actual changes in sales was found to be most clearly operative among firms which had been expecting increases in sales. For firms expecting increases in sales the following relation was estimated:

$$\frac{I_{50}}{F} = 0.091 + \underset{(.084)}{0.286} \frac{S_{50} - S_{49}}{S_{49}} + \underset{(.093)}{0.354} \frac{S_{49} - S_{48}}{S_{48}}$$

thus indicating that some 64 percent of the full adjustment of capital stock to output is accounted for by a "short-run, two-year accelerator." (P. 184) The corresponding figures for firms expecting no change in sales and expecting a decline were 13 percent and 12 percent, respectively. Capital expenditures of 1949 were also positively related to the sales change of 1948 to 1949, but the regression coefficient, while significant at the .05 probability level, was only .063 in a bivariate relation.

A positive relation was also found between 1950 capital expenditures and 1949 profits. The simple correlation was 0.358 and the corresponding regression coefficient was 0.119, significant at the .01 level. It is interesting to note, however, that while the profits relation holds in regressions involving the sales change variables, it then has a partial correlation coefficient of only .107, not statistically significant at the .05 level, when capital expenditure plans, the two previous years' capital expenditures, and the sales variables are included. This is consistent with the possibility that profits are a proxy variable for other factors which are also encompassed in investment plans. It is also consistent with the possibility, however, that profits influence investment plans which in turn are related closely to actual investment, but have little additional effect on investment which is independent of their role in the planning process.

Analysis of firms by size class suggested that large firms were relatively slow to adjust their capital expenditures to the boom in the latter half of 1950 but did adjust very substantially to the decline in 1949. (See Table 3, p. 174.) There is also evidence that in the case of large firms capital expenditure plans are more closely related to corresponding actual expenditures and that sales changes account for little of the variance in capital expenditures which has not already been accounted for by capital expenditure plans.

Finally, Eisner reported a positive relation between the difference of actual and planned investment and the difference between actual and expected sales. This involved the actual and planned or expected values for 1950. Regression coefficients were small but significant at the .05 level for the entire set of firms and for the subsets of firms in the medium-size category and of firms with expectations of higher sales. For all firms the estimated relation was:

$$\frac{I_{50} - I_{50}^{49}}{F} = 0.010 + 0.047 \underset{(.023)}{} \frac{S_{50} - S_{50}^{49}}{S_{49}} \quad ,$$

where I_{50}^{49} and S_{50}^{49} are the investment and sales expected for 1950

in 1949.[10] The regression coefficient for firms expecting a sales increase was 0.093 (standard error of 0.041) and for firms in the medium-size category was 0.094 (standard error of .037).

In a subsequent paper (199) Eisner reported estimates of a distributed lag investment function based on accounting data for large corporations collected by the Board of Governors of the Federal Reserve System.[11] He used two formulations for estimating purposes. In one, called "The Basic Accelerator and Profits Model," the structural form assumed was:

$$\frac{I_t}{F_{53}} = b_0 + b_1 \left(\frac{S_t - S_{t-1}}{S_{53}} \right) + b_2 \left(\frac{S_{t-1} - S_{t-2}}{S_{53}} \right) + b_3 \left(\frac{S_{t-2} - S_{t-3}}{S_{53}} \right)$$

$$+ b_4 \left(\frac{S_{t-3} - S_{t-4}}{S_{53}} \right)$$

---

[10]A very recent work by Eisner confirming this relation in later, cross-sectional McGraw-Hill data and in broad industry, SEC-Commerce quarterly time series is reported in (199b).

[11]As reported by Eisner (p. 4, fn. 3), while gathered by the Federal Reserve for presentation in reports on sources and uses of funds: "The basic data for capital expenditures as well as the other variables are in virtually all cases items included specifically in financial reports and are not residuals calculated in the course of the 'sources and uses' compilation."

$$+ b_5 \frac{P_t}{F_{53}} + b_6 \frac{P_{t-1}}{F_{53}} + b_7 \frac{P_{t-2}}{F_{53}} + b_8 \frac{P_{t-3}}{F_{53}} + b_9 \frac{D_{53}}{F_{53}}$$

$$+ b_{10} \frac{N_{53}}{F_{53}} + u$$

where I is gross capital expenditures,
   F is gross fixed assets,
   S is net sales,
   P is profits before federal income taxes,
   D is depreciation charges,
   N is net fixed assets (gross fixed asset minus the accumulated
        depreciation reserve),
   u is a stochastic disturbance,

and subscripts refer to years; t = 1955, 1954, and 1953. (Three sets of regressions were calculated with this equation, with the dependent variable in turn I_{53}/F_{53}, I_{54}/F_{53}, and I_{53}/F_{53}, and the sales change and profits variables correspondingly lagged in each case.) Eisner reported (pp. 4,5) that a number of observations were eliminated because of firm mergers and extreme values. The latter were defined to include all observations in which the ratio of capital expenditures to gross fixed assets was equal to or greater than .4 or sales change ratios or the ratios of profits to gross fixed assets were greater than 1.0.

The sales change regression coefficients were uniformly positive, whether the estimates related to 1955, 1954, or 1953 capital expenditures. Their sum approximated 0.5 in the 1955 and 1954 regressions; it was 0.325 in the regression relating to 1953 capital expenditures. The profits coefficients, however, summed to approximately zero. These findings could be reconciled with earlier results of other investigators and, to some extent Eisner himself, by noting that the simple or zero order correlations between capital expenditures and profits were positive. These positive relations were entirely accounted for and were not manifested as significantly positive regression coefficients when current and three lagged sales changes were included in the regression. This is clearly consistent with the hypothesis that firms with high profits invest more, not because of the high profits per se, but because firms with high profits tend to be those which have been experiencing sales increases over a number of years and have reason therefore to expand capacity.

The sales change relationship held up reasonably well when estimates were made on the basis of cross sections within industry groups, although sampling variations were greater with the smaller numbers of firms. Among food and tobacco firms (presumably not

growing rapidly) the sum of the sales change regression coefficients was only 0.097. When firms were divided by the direction
of their sales changes in 1954 and 1955, it became clear that it was
firms whose sales were increasing that tended to account for positive sales change investment coefficients. For example, the sum of
the sales change coefficients for 1955 investment for firms whose
sales increased in 1955 was 0.651; for firms whose sales decreased
this sum was only 0.161. Similarly, for firms whose sales increased
in 1954 the sum of the sales change coefficients was 0.807; for those
whose sales decreased the sum was only 0.465.

Similar results were obtained when firms were classified by a
measure of sales over the 1948 to 1955 period, called the "long-run
sales change." In a model including current sales change and six
previous lags, the first five coefficients were positive and totaled
0.92 for that third of the firms that had experienced the greatest
long-run sales expansion; the last two distributed lag coefficients
were negative, although not significantly so by the usual probability
criteria. No clear relation at all appeared for the two-thirds of the
firms that had experienced lower long-run sales changes. When
1955 capital expenditures were related directly to the long-run sales
change variable, which was actually an average of the sales changes
over a seven-year period, the regression coefficient was 0.451.

It may be argued that interfirm heterogeneity in risk and the
value of "normal profits" may have obscured an underlying relation
between expected profits and capital expenditures. However, no
evidence to support this was reported by Eisner. In fact, a further
test by Eisner offered results which would conflict with this argument. Dividing firms into three equal sets whose 1955 and 1954
profits had been respectively high, moderate, and low with regard
to their own 1953 and 1952 profits, Eisner found that, while the
difference was not statistically significant at the .05 probability
level, firms in the "low" current profit group actually invested
more in 1955 than those in the "high" current profits group.

Eisner also reports (p. 12): "The rate of depreciation (a measure
of the reciprocal of durability of capital goods), as expected, accounts
for considerable interfirm variance in capital expenditures.[12] Along
with the positive (although not statistically significant) constant term,

---

[12]Use of fixed assets and depreciation data of 1953 ruled out variance in depreciation due to changes in the tax law in 1954. An attempt
to isolate differences in depreciation due to use of accelerated
amortization failed, however, because of a paucity of reports of such
amortization. Differences on this score, therefore, cannot be ruled
out as a possible contributor, unrelated to durability, to the positive
coefficient for the depreciation variable.

the positive depreciation coefficient (not significantly different from unity) suggests that a substantial part of investment is not related to the variance of individual firms' sales changes."

In preliminary, as yet unpublished work with 1958 McGraw-Hill capital expenditure surveys and related data Eisner (199c) has noted some evidence of persistence of a profits-investment relation in the case of relatively smaller firms (1953 gross fixed assets less than $100,000,000). However, this relation disappears again in the case of larger firms (1953 gross fixed assets $100,000,000 or over), which accounted for the bulk of capital expenditures.[13]

Confirmation of these preliminary findings would suggest that imperfections in the capital market do induce smaller firms to tie their capital expenditures to a certain extent to current profits.

18. General comment on estimation procedures.

One possible difficulty in the use of econometric methods has been advanced by Ta-Chung Liu[14] with particular reference to Klein's work. This is the exclusion of explanatory variables from the investment demand function on the grounds that either their coefficients are too close to zero or have the wrong sign, or else because they are highly correlated with other explanatory variables which already appear and thereby give rise to the problem of multicollinearity.

It is possible that a variable which enters significantly into the structural determination of investment demand may have a near-zero or wrong-signed coefficient because some other explanatory variables have been excluded, and the remedy is to introduce these excluded variables rather than now to exclude a variable which was originally thought to be operative in a particular way. (Thus, the coefficient of a sales-change variable may become more signifi-cant--economically--if an excess capacity variable is introduced.) Moreover, the multicollinearity problem is not one which can safely be overcome simply by eliminating all but one of a set of linearly

---

[13] This work by Eisner (199c) serves generally to confirm the oper-ation of a distributed lag accelerator and to minimize the independ-ent role of profits in cross sections based on McGraw-Hill capital expenditure surveys from 1955 to 1958. It also notes higher coef-ficients of determination and higher accelerator coefficients in between-industry-year-mean regressions which might be expected to reflect more of "permanent" rather than "transitory" variance and covariance.

[14] Ta-Chung Liu, "Underidentification, Structural Estimation, and Forecasting," Econometrica, 28, no. 4 (October 1960), pp. 855-865.

related explanatory variables from the function being estimated. If that is done, the coefficient of the remaining variable may become statistically significant, whereas before it was not, but that does not make it economically significant. Our interest, after all, is to estimate true structural coefficients as best we can and not merely to search out empirically variables which yield contradiction of null hypotheses. Indeed, hypothesis testing has been given too important a role vis-a-vis estimation in many applications of statistics and this can lead to serious mischief in cases where there is multicollinearity among variables which we regard as explanatory on theoretical grounds.

B. Quantitative but Noneconometric

No pretense will be made in this section of surveying comprehensively the vast writings bearing on investment. Rather we shall report on a few, mainly recent works in order to provide some view of contemporary opinion, chiefly of those who have familiarized themselves with empirical data bearing on investment or who report studies involving the analysis of such data. We shall pay particular attention to reports and analyses of several postwar surveys of capital expenditures, capital expenditure anticipations, and capital appropriations.

R.A. Gordon writes (398b): "Instability of private investment [is] associated with the irregular growth of an expanding economy. By 'irregular growth' I mean not only variable time-rates of expansion in aggregate measures of output, but also irregular changes in the composition of output, and in the ways in which that output is produced." (P. 283) Gordon's emphasis is on investment induced by structural changes or expected changes rather than by changes in aggregate output. He argues that with industries at different positions on their S-shaped long-run growth curves, shifts in the composition of output become a source of investment demand. He cites figures of Kuznets and the Department of Commerce to show a declining ratio of construction expenditure to equipment expenditure. One result "has been the rise in the importance of capital consumption in gross capital formation." (P. 292) Along with this has come a shorter period of gestation, a greater relative importance for replacement expenditures, and a greater proportion of investment "financed" by depreciation. The emphasis on machinery and equipment ascribes more importance to the steady flow of small technological changes and less importance to "dramatic innovations that created important new industries." (P. 293) Gordon feels, however, that "replacement" expenditures are cyclically sensitive. (P. 304) Of minor importance in Gordon's view are the prices of capital goods, the prices of complementary and substitutable inputs, and the availability of loanable funds. To the extent that the supply of funds is significant, the issue is one of availability rather than cost--if that is indeed a distinction! Gordon considers earnings but not low interest rates to be significant for a corporation that wants equity capital. He suggests that low interest rates are more stimulating to industries with high capital-output ratios. The increasing emphasis on investment in equipment rather than plant, we may then add, should further reduce the significance of the rate of interest. High prices of capital goods, Gordon declares, work to restrain more the investment of old than of new industries. And the investment boom of the 1946-50 period Gordon attributes to "reconversion, accelerated expansion, and deferred replacement," and to "technological change, high profits, a favorable liquidity position and rising labor costs."

Fellner (398b) accounts for the postwar boom in part with "broadened versions of the 'acceleration principle.'" He reports that "Kuznets' data and rough computations from Department of Commerce estimates" indicate that "the aggregative average capital-output ratio so computed (excluding consumer durables but including residential buildings) fell short of 2.5 (may have amounted to about two-thirds of the prewar ratio). Subsequently there was an increase, although at the outbreak of hostilities in Korea the ratio was still considerably below its prewar level." (Pp. 14-15) Fellner sees investment taking place in response to an inadequacy of the capital-output ratio, but believes that the capital-output ratio for an unchanging composition of output has been declining and feels that we cannot make definite statements about the "true" or "normal" value of that ratio. Fellner does believe that the postwar structure of taxes, with high marginal rates and effects on the willingness to bear risk "had a directly adverse effect on investment." (P. 30)

It may also be worth recording a few scattered comments of non-American economists writing on the basis of experience in their own countries. Preiser and Krelle (398b) report that in West Germany the ratio of changes in capacity to investment was "steadily decreasing" from 1949 to 1951; and "this reflects," according to them, "the rapidly falling natural marginal efficiency of capital, once the worst war and dismantling damage had been made good." (P. 138) They refer, "at least so far as postwar conditions in Germany are concerned, ... (to) the extremely doubtful nature of the dependence of investment upon changes in production; in other words, the question remains whether an accelerator does, in fact, exist at all." (P. 123)

Lundberg (398b) writing on the Swedish situation, declares, "very stringent cash ratios, ... supported by a large budget surplus, have resulted in a sudden and sharp decrease in 'credit availability.' Credit rationing by the banks has become very severe, and the 'fringe of unsatisfied borrowers' has been increasing rapidly. The 'squeezed' situation of many firms ..., which had been made still more serious by the turn taken by prices, rendered them very vulnerable to the restrictive credit policy now pursued, which seemed to be very effective in postponing or stopping altogether the execution of investment plans, and in forcing down costs. One important result of credit scarcity has, for instance, been the selling out of stocks at low prices.... The new feature of Swedish credit policy consists in a desire to concentrate on the purely quantitative aspects of credit restrictions, if possible with little or no effect on the long-term rate of interest (short-term rates have, however, been allowed to rise)." (Pp. 74-75)

E.A.G. Robinson, referring to the United Kingdom of the mid-1950's, declared (398b), "... It would appear that difficulties of short-term liquidity due to rising requirements of inventory finance are having powerful repercussions on plans for long-term investment, and may in the end precipitate so great a reduction of the latter as to cause an industrial depression of the traditional form." (P. 52)

On the basis of a study of quarterly profits of large United States corporations in the interwar period Hultgren writes (480), "In deciding whether or not to invest in land, plant, and equipment, businessmen are presumably motivated by the prospects for profit on new investment rather than by profits already earned on existing investment, but there is an intimate connection between the two. If high profits are earned on existing investment, there is a presumption that additional profits could be earned on additional facilities, at least if the cost of the latter has not risen too much. Especially where conditions are competitive, rising profits are likely to encourage both expansion by existing firms and the entry of new firms; falling profits are likely to discourage them. Moreover, profits place in the hands of businessmen funds they can use to inaugurate projects of whose merits they are convinced on other grounds than the current rate of return. They influence credit ratings and hence the ability of enterprises to borrow. They affect the market value of stocks and hence the ability of stockholders to borrow, perhaps for investment in fields other than those in which the profits were earned....One may note that a decline in profits does not need to be general to influence aggregate investment. Business capital formation may at times be concentrated in a few industries that have unusual technological opportunities or prospects of a long-run shift of demand toward their products. If their profits temporarily change adversely, aggregate investment may decline even though the aggregate profits of all enterprises have been rising." (P. 226)

In discussing the investment boom of the twenties, Gordon (480) suggests that the "failure of electric power investment to expand further after 1924" occurred because "the long-run working of the

acceleration principle was exerting a downward pressure on investment in generating capacity long before the boom ended." (P. 192)
Gordon also offers "tentative conclusions regarding the impact of
electric power on investment outside the electric power industry
during the interwar period. Here again the principle of acceleration
operated to raise the level of investment in the '20's and lower it
during the '30's." (P. 196) Excluding investment induced by electricity and automobiles, Gordon does not think technological change
was "a major cause of the investment boom of the '20's." (P. 199)
Monetary and financial developments, he argues, were important
but "secondary." Factors making for a high marginal efficiency of
capital and a "wave of speculative optimism" were "the active
initiating forces." (P. 206) And finally, we may note Gordon's view
that "attitudes toward liquidity seem to have affected the extent and
direction of capital rationing more than the level of interest rates."
(P. 207)

Before turning to the various surveys of capital expenditures
and capital expenditure plans, we shall treat briefly a few of the
classic and a few of the recent noneconometric studies bearing on
the acceleration principle. In particular, let us recall J. M. Clark's
work on "Business Acceleration and the Law of Demand" (123). The
data he presented there regarding railroad traffic and purchases
of railroad cars from 1901 to 1916 led him to the following conclusions: 1) "The percentage fluctuatons in car manufacturing are
vastly greater than in railroad traffic" although the stock of cars,
nevertheless, does not keep pace with variations in traffic. 2) Orders
for cars fluctuate ahead of the movements in traffic. 3) Car orders
are above average when the rate of growth of traffic is above average and they are below average when the rate of growth of traffic
is below average. 4) Car orders and the rate of growth of traffic
tend to move in the same direction. 5) "The noticeable peaks of
car orders fall (generally) within the years of maximum growth of
traffic." 6) Minimum points for car orders lag behind shrinkages
of traffic and the beginning of recovery shows a similar lag. 7) "The
general trend of car orders is slightly downward, in spite of a great
increase in traffic" but "this may be accounted for by an increase
in the capacity of cars." Clark concluded: "In short, the figures, so
far as they go, bear out the statement that the demand for cars
varies with the rate at which traffic is increasing or diminishing
rather than with the absolute volume of the traffic." (Pp. 247-249)

In his famous critique of the acceleration principle, Kuznets
(370) used data on investment in freight cars, passenger cars, and
locomotives in the United States railroad industry from 1891 to
1930. He charged that the amplitudes of fluctuations in investment
were only from one-fifth to one-half as large as their "theoretical"
values; it may also be observed that the discrepancy from what
Kuznets considered to be the "theoretical" values was greater at

the troughs. And in further criticism Kuznets wrote, "Similarly, the lead of the cycles in the demand for capital goods is far short of that suggested by turning points in the net changes in the demand for finished products. Indeed, the statistical study suggests that the hypothesis is severely qualified, and in respect of timing, almost nullified by other factors, directly or remotely related to its basic assumptions." (Pp. 266-267)

In a reply to Kuznets, Clark pointed out that the version of the acceleration principle that Kuznets presumed to test is a "mechanical" one that Clark himself had mentioned only for heuristic purposes. Kuznets' findings serve rather to confirm qualifications that Clark had stated originally, particularly with regard to the effects of excesses and shortages of capacity. It should be clear from our discussion in the previous section that we consider Clark's rejoinder appropriate. We may add that Kuznets, like others, focussed attention improperly on the question of whether investment leads or lags turning points in output. Lags, including distributed lags, may be such as to give a variety of time relations between output and investment which are consistent with the acceleration principle. Furthermore, it should be pointed out that the acceleration principle per se says nothing about the time relation of investment and output (regardless of J.M. Clark's remarks on the subject). It is true that for a model without lags a sinusoidal cycle in output, for example, would have the rate of increase of output declining as the peak of output is approached, and the rate of decrease of output likewise slackening as the trough is approached. But there is after all no reason to insist on cycles of that regular type and they do not seem conspicuous in the data presented. If, rather, output rises at an increasing pace only to break suddenly and decline, then even without lags investment might be rising until output is at its peak. Output, the rate of change of output, and the rate of investment would then all collapse at once. An increasing rate of decline terminating abruptly in an upturn does seem less likely, but the accelerator is not likely to be fully operative in the downturn because of a lower limit on gross investment, so that the timing hypothesis criticized by Kuznets and others seems in any event not to be implied generally by the acceleration principle.

Bert G. Hickman (309) made a detailed study of capacity and production with 13 time series of "industries" or products, ranging over the period from 1908 to 1951. Hickman's findings include the following. "Capacity change, and by inference fixed investment, in particular industries is dominated by secular growth. In the case of growing industries, the secular expansion of output makes for relative immunity to cyclical contractions. Furthermore in growing industries contractions of production do not usually prevent the expansion of capacity because projects initiated during upswings carry over a year or two into contractions, and because favorable long-run expectations encourage investment even during periods of depressed demand." (P. 246) The rate of change of capacity is modified by cyclical fluctuation in output even if the direction of change in capacity is not. Cyclical contraction of production slows the rate of increase of capacity, even in growing industries. The accelerator does not work in the downswing because capacity rarely declines. Higher levels of utilization of capacity tend to be associated with greater increases in capacity in growing industries. "These results show conclusively that there is a relationship between the level of utilization and the rate of growth of capacity--a relationship which is broadly consistent with the predictions of the modified acceleration principle," but this is not a mechanical relation in which output increases until it is limited by capacity, at which point capacity abruptly increases. "Moderate levels of utilization induce moderate expansions of capacity despite the fact that a substantial margin of unused capacity still exists." (P. 438) Hickman doubts that the acceleration principle holds rigidly enough to warrant ignoring such factors in investment as "the supply prices of assets, the availability and interest cost of funds, and the prospective yield of the investment over its economic life." (Pp. 438-439) He set up as a critical test the extent to which "changes in the rate of growth of output are associated with changes in the rate of growth of capacity in the same direction, and therefore whether the possibility exists that net real investment has changed in the predicted direction" (pp. 439-440), and reported that "no such persistent relationship is discernible in the data, whether simultaneous rates of change are compared or lags are assumed." (P. 440)

In a comment on Hickman's paper, Modigliani declared: "... Such tests as can be carried out from Hickman's data fully support the acceleration hypothesis properly understood and formulated and confirm that this hypothesis is a very useful principle in explaining much of the behavior of investment in fixed capital." (P. 451) Modigliani suggested as a reasonable test of the acceleration principle the formulation:

$$K_t - K_{t-1} = \beta (\alpha_{t-g} \eta 0_{t-g} - K_{t-1}),$$

provided $\alpha_{t-g} \eta 0_{t-g} > K_{t-1}$, where K is capital stock, α is the desired capital-output coefficient, η is the ratio of output expected for the period t to output in the period t - g, 0 is output, and β is the adjustment coefficient indicating what proportion of the shortage in capacity an industry makes up in a single period.

This formulation helps focus on a number of difficulties in Hickman's data and analysis. In particular, the data deal with "capacity" which, because of construction time, is apt to lag behind capital expenditures (and to vary less smoothly over time). Second, as the condition above indicates and as we have suggested (and as Hickman is aware), the acceleration principle cannot be expected to operate freely with regard to decreases in output. But what is more, if change in capacity is used as a proxy for capital expenditures, it should be remembered that one can hardly expect decreases in output to be reflected as adequately. A reduction in capital expenditures, intended over time to reduce capacity, may not result in any prompt reduction of capacity as reported. Instead, the useful life of existing equipment may be extended longer and the reduction of capacity for current output may thereby be deferred. [See Modigliani (464, p. 452).] The timing and extent of decreases in capacity, given a drop in output, would depend in large measure on the pace of retirement of existing assets, which "depends upon many factors, including the age distribution of existing facilities." (464, p. 454) But the main difficulty is that in most of his paper Hickman is beating a straw man, the "naive" acceleration model,

$$K_t - K_{t-1} = \alpha \ (0_{-t} - 0_{-t-1}).$$

With a number of simplifying assumptions, however, Modigliani (464, p. 458) puts his model in the form,

$$\frac{\Delta C}{C} = A \left(\frac{0}{C}\right) - B,$$

where C is capacity, $\underline{0}$ again is output, and A and B are constants. Modigliani then tests Hickman's data to ascertain whether the rate of change of capacity is in fact a positive function of the rate of utilization. His results are decidedly consistent with this hypothesis.

In a later article (310) Hickman again challenges the usefulness of the acceleration principle. This time he uses postwar quarterly data on output and investment in both the aggregate and each of 16 industries in the United States. His main arguments with regard to fixed investment are that the rate of output rather than the rate of change of output seem to be associated with investment, that turning points in investment do not consistently lead turning points in output. Hickman prefers to explain whatever effects of the "retardation" of the rate of growth of output on investment are observed as the result of an increasing proportion of firms which are actually declining during a period when, in the aggregate, only the rate of growth is declining. The declining profits in such firms are believed to bring about a reduction in investment because "retained profits are an important source of investment funds (and) expected returns from investment are doubtless sensitive to current profits ... especially when the latter are declining during a period of general business expansion and are therefore symptomatic of weakness within the industry." (P. 561) To the extent that Hickman's data bear on the acceleration principle they relate once more to crude versions of this principle and to hypotheses about timing which, as we have argued above, are special and not germane. For the rest, Hickman, like Gordon and others, is inclined to emphasize the importance of disaggregation and "autonomous" factors.

In a study of the telephone industry Paul G. Clark (125) finds demand carefully estimated, with field studies in each individual exchange and a tendency to extrapolate the recent trend of output. Investment is found to fit well the pattern of changes in expected demand, particularly when allowance is made for shifts in demand between geographical areas and for technological change. Clark sees his data as offering "considerable support to the ... hypothesis ... that net investment depends, via fixed capital and spare-capacity coefficients, upon changes in expected demand." (P. 285) Clark points out, however, that retirement is not a stable percentage of capital stock and that discretion in the timing of replacements is evident, particularly in the case of the more durable assets. On the issue of the supply of money capital, Clark writes: " ... There have apparently been no instances in which an investment program has been drawn up and then cut back because of lack of funds, or expanded because of the ease of obtaining funds....No serious error seems to be involved in neglecting the influence of the availability of funds upon the final investment decision." (P. 263) Clark argues further, by way of conclusion, that the "capital requirements theory can be extended to other industries" which are capital intensive, have little scope for input substitution, cannot stock inventories for output, have been steadily expanding, have technological developments which are related to their expansion, find it economical to build ahead of demand and are subject to public regulation. (Pp. 293-294)

A mass of data has been collected in continuing surveys of capital expenditures, capital expenditure plans or anticipations, and capital expenditure authorizations. These collections are by the Department of Commerce, the Securities Exchange Commission, the McGraw-Hill Publishing Company, and the National Industrial Conference Board. We shall here touch only very briefly on some of the observations and reports of those who have been working with these data. [Detailed analyses of some of these data have been presented by Friend and Bronfenbrenner (Crockett) and by Eisner and have been reported elsewhere. See 237, 238, 197 .]

Some of this analysis has attempted to explain discrepancies between planned and actual capital expenditures in order to cast light on the determination of actual expenditures. In 1957, Foss and Natrella (223, p. 6) observe, "Downward revisions from anticipated spending may be considered as evidence of the supply difficulties that have prevailed in capital goods markets of 1956." They point to shortages of structural steel as affecting primary metals and transportation equipment, a scarcity of plates affecting car building, and insufficient steel tubing curtailing well-drilling. It may be noted, in the light of the decline in investment and the recession beginning later in 1957, how well these observations fit the Goodwin-Hicks trade cycle model (255, 312) in which the boom is broken by "ceilings" in investment goods industries.

Foss and Natrella observe that the record investment of 1956 was associated with further expected sales increases. They also report "some correlation between signs of the deviations between actual and anticipated sales and actual and anticipated investment" but not so good a correlation as in previous surveys. "Perhaps the most important reason for the poorer general relationship was that supply shortages limited expenditures in 1956." (P. 20)

In an analysis of factors influencing the realization of recent investment anticipations (222) Foss reports that sales rather than earnings predominate among the factors listed by business respondents whose actual investment in 1955 exceeded what had been anticipated. Profits, however, were cited slightly more frequently where investment was less than anticipated. Plant and equipment costs were infrequently cited as a cause of discrepancies, and, in cases where they were, actual investment expenditures were greater in dollar terms than anticipated, suggesting that investment demand was inelastic with respect to the price of capital goods. Outside financing was not a factor mentioned much, but its importance might conceivably be underestimated in this type of analysis since it might have been important in affecting the level of anticipated expenditures without affecting the difference between the anticipated and the actual. "Unexpected delays in equipment deliveries and construction progress was the chief factor given by companies spending less than anticipated." (P. 352) But these, Foss observes (p. 354), would apparently result in subsequent additions. Comparing results with the earlier Friend and Crockett analysis, Foss notes that sales, profits, and working capital requirements were mentioned by 70 percent of respondents whose expenditures were less than anticipated in 1949, but by only 40 percent in 1955. On the other hand, supply shortages were mentioned by only 15 percent of the firms in this category in 1949 but by more than half of the companies in 1955. In terms of the general relation between the deviation of investment anticipations and the deviation of sales expectations, for manufacturing as a whole for the years 1948-56, the correlation coefficient was .88 (and .92 when relative deviations of actual and anticipated profits before taxes were used) but the relationship is very hard to find at the detailed manufacturing industry level.

A paper by Keezer, Ulin, Greenwald and Matulis (345a) as well as various unsigned reports of the McGraw-Hill Department of Economics offer evidence of a relationship between capital expenditures and the utilization of capacity. In 1957 Keezer et al. reported that the McGraw-Hill index of manufacturing capacity "increased sharply in 1951-53, presaging the downturn in expenditures in 1954. And again for the past three years this index has been rising sharply and as reported in the spring 1957 survey, the 1957 year-end index is expected to stand 50 percent above the figure for 1950. Manufacturing output has risen only 30 percent in the same period. This buildup of extra capacity clearly foreshadowed a decline in manufacturing investment in 1958."

Keezer and his associates add that companies spend their depreciation allowances, and they argue that when expansion declines, the decline in investment resulting from the presence of excess capacity will be mild because these depreciation allowances will not decline and because, moreover, the share spent for modernization will increase (according to questionnaire responses). We do not believe, however, that any confidence can be placed in the view that businessmen will spend an amount equal to depreciation charges regardless of business conditions. Detailed analysis of McGraw-Hill data by Eisner (196) indicated that regardless of what businessmen say they will do, when expansion investment declines, total investment declines; "modernization" expenditures take up little or none of the slack.

The paper by Keezer and associates also reports that, on the average, there is a seven year lag from the inception of research on a new product to the time when it is in full scale production, but that improvements in existing products take less time. They view research expenditures as resulting in a rising proportion of investment for new products, which, they claim, reduces the probability of a major depression.

In October 1958, a McGraw-Hill checkup on manufacturing capacity (unpublished) reported:

(1) Manufacturing capacity was then 50 percent greater than at the end of 1950.

(2) There was apparently no general need for a continuation of the past 6 percent per annum expansion of capacity.

(3) High investment in 1959 would have to depend on investment for modernization and new products, because manufacturing companies were operating at about 78 percent of capacity--12 points below their preferred operating rate of 90 percent.

(4) About 48 percent of all manufacturing capacity then in place was installed prior to 1945. It would cost about $35 billion to replace "obsolete" facilities in manufacturing.

(5) "Large companies, as a rule, account for a disproportionately large share of plant expansion. . . ."

In a recent report of their annual survey, Business Plans for New Plant and Equipment, 1959-1962, McGraw-Hill declared:

1. "Industry plans to spend more in 1959 than ever before to modernize obsolete plants and equipment. Two-thirds of the capital expenditures planned by manufacturing companies in the years 1959-62 are for modernization, rather than expansions. . . .

2. "Manufacturing companies were operating at an average rate of 80 percent of capacity at the end of 1958. They plan to increase their capacity during the next four years, but at a modest rate compared with earlier years.

3. "Sales of manufacturing companies are expected to be 9 percent higher this year and to show an additional increase of 18 percent by 1962. If realized, these gains will bring operating rates close to preferred levels and create a need for additional capacity.

4. "Manufacturing employment is expected to rise less than half as rapidly as sales. . . . Industry anticipates substantial gains in productivity over this period.

5. "The flow of funds from depreciation will continue to rise and by 1962 will be 21 percent greater than in 1958. This increasing source of funds will provide strong financial support for business' capital spending. Almost half the companies participating say they would spend more on plants and equipment if depreciation allowances under the tax law were increased substantially." (P. 1)

Finally, a few figures may be offered to give some picture of the relative magnitudes of various components or categories of investment. First, by industry, a total of $32.1 billion of actual plant and equipment investment in 1958 is reported to have been divided as follows:

Manufacturing	$9.8
Petroleum	4.8
Mining	.4
Railroads	.8
Other transportation and communication	3.9
Electricity and gas	6.1
Commercial	7.0

(It is explained that the sum of $32.8 billion does not agree with the total cited above because "petroleum refining, included under both manufacturing and the petroleum industry, is counted only

once in the total.") In regard to types of spending, McGraw-Hill
reports that in 1959 buildings will account for 30 percent, vehicles
for 4 percent, and other machinery and equipment for 66 percent.

Cohen and Gainsbrugh, in the June 1959 issue of The Conference
Board Business Record, National Industrial Conference Board,
report on capital appropriations and associate rising appropriations with rising profits, improving liquidity (as measured by
the ratio of cash and government securities to current liabilities)
and manufacturers' sales and new orders. Again, in the September
1959 issue of the same publication, they report: "Trends in appropriations and in profits, profit margins, and liquidity are closely
associated. Manufacturers' appropriations leveled off in the second
quarter, following a first quarter slackening in profits and liquidity."
(P. 4)

In the light of our earlier discussion of the acceleration principle
and relevant lags it is interesting to note the contrast Cohen and
Gainsbrugh offer of the performance of appropriations, which may
be taken as a measure of capital stock demand, and expenditures.
They declare in their June 1959 report: "In the capital goods cycle,
appropriations generally rise very rapidly in the beginning of the
recovery, hitting an early peak in the rate of increase. The rate
of increase in capital spending reaches a peak much later and has
a lower relative magnitude compared with that for capital appropriations." (P. 10) In another paper (130) Cohen declares: "On the
average the formal planning period is about one year. For some
industries such as iron and steel, electrical machinery and chemicals, it may be as long as a year and a half. The backlog rates do
not indicate any formalized long-range planning of five or more
years.... Long-range budgets are guides to thinking but do not
represent formally approved decisions to proceed." (P. 196)

We have not covered in detail a mass of statistical material
purporting to bear upon the financing of investment. These appear
in the Survey of Current Business, the Federal Reserve Bulletin
and many other publications. In general they indicate, as is well
known, that the bulk of investment is "internally financed" in the
sense that the total of depreciation charges and undistributed profits
equals a major fraction of the amount of investment. These data
do not, however, really bear on any causal mechanism and it is
unwarranted to suggest on the basis of them that the investment
of the firm or the economy depends upon the supply of internal
finance.

C. Qualitative, Including Interview and Questionnaire Studies

As indicated above, we shall not review here the earlier works
on this subject by Eisner. He has analyzed (197) the findings of

studies by Meade and Andrews (440), Andrews (19), Mack (406a), Heller and associates (303 and 303a), Katona and Morgan (344), Gort (267), de Chazeau (113), Andrews and Brunner (20), Friend and Bronfenbrenner (Crockett) (237, 238), the Canadian Government (212; Private and Public Investment in Canada, Outlook for 1952; and... for 1953, Canadian Department of Trade and Commerce, 1952 and 1953), McGraw-Hill, and himself (195). In particular, we may call attention to a number of observations of a methodological nature pointing to limitations in the value of subjective "explanations" by businessmen as to what motivates their investment.

We may call attention as well to a few recent studies, and, in particular, to a paper by Brockie and Grey (84) indicating that investment is interest-inelastic and to a criticism of these results by W. H. White (641; see also 85). We shall not attempt to pass judgment on this interchange, beyond suggesting that it be considered in the light of the earlier survey and methodological observations by Eisner.

D. Conclusions

Our conclusions will be brief. We have imposed our own analytical framework through much of the foregoing paper, both in the theoretical sections and in our critique of the various empirical investigations we have reviewed.

Our essential position, as we have indicated earlier, is that we must, for policy purposes, estimate the structural relations determining investment. This necessitates fitting capital expenditures into the main body of economic theory, as a rate of adjustment of actual to desired capital stock. Clearly a major determinant of the desired capital stock is the expected rate of output. Conceptually important as well are the nature of the production function and of the behavior of relative prices, of which the intertemporal price structure symbolized by the rate of interest warrants prime attention. Past profits and liquidity play little part in this picture, except for imperfections in capital markets and in the flow of information which may affect the rate of adjustment of capital stock (as distinguished from the total amount of capital stock).

Empirical findings, when analyzed critically, seem to support our position. Findings by Tinbergen, Klein, Meyer and Kuh and others which seem to reinforce the view that profits (or output itself) are significant in determining capital expenditures can generally be shown to result from common trend factors or multicollinearity with unspecified variables. In a number of instances such findings seem to be readily convertible to more meaningful theoretical formulations.

On the other hand, results of J. M. Clark, Paul G. Clark, Manne, Chenery, Koyck, Modigliani, Kisselgoff, Eisner, and various capital expenditure surveys point to sophisticated formulations of the acceleration principle, recognizing the role of distributed lags and the necessity of special treatment for downswings and situations involving excess capacity, as a fruitful way of explaining investment. Criticisms by Kuznets and Hickman are generally appropriate not to this but only to "naive" and "crude" or "mechanical" models of the acceleration relation.

Evidence regarding other variables is generally inconclusive. The interest rate has occasionally been found to be negatively related to capital expenditures, but such findings are not general. Coefficients are frequently uncertain, or, more important, so small in relation to the variations of the interest rate which have been allowed to occur as to deny that variable much historical role in influencing the rate of investment. However, procedures for estimating the role of the rate of interest have generally been poor. Econometric studies have commonly failed to identify properly the investment-interest relation, and other studies have failed to recognize that the interest rate may exert its effects, if it has any, in a number of indirect ways, on only some capital-intensive industries rather than on all of those that happen to be in the position of borrowing money.

Investment is, of course, a dynamic phenomenon. Questions of timing and rates of adjustment are likely to prove critical. Such matters may, however, be better discerned as part of an analysis relating business behavior to variables which seem relevant in terms of economic principles. The core of such an analysis must rest on the realization that investment involves the change in a capital stock—in a firm, industry, or the economy—which is related by means of a production function to expected rates of output. To this core may have to be added consideration of the nature and formation of expectations, attitudes toward risk and uncertainty, relative prices including "the rate of interest" and variables associated with it, and the role of technological change. And finally, through all, a clear view must be kept of the varying influence of factors at the firm, industry, and macroeconomic levels.

IV. EMPIRICAL FINDINGS: INVENTORY INVESTMENT

A. The Importance of Inventory Investment

Annual inventory investment tends to be but a fraction of plant and equipment investment. Over the years 1946 to 1961 the peak of total U.S. business expenditure on plant and equipment has been $37 billion in current prices, while the high for business inventory investment has been only $10 billion and at the maximum has accounted for but 23 percent of gross private domestic investment.[1]

Nevertheless, inventory investment has been more volatile than plant and equipment investment. The range of the annual rate of plant and equipment investment has been approximately $22 billion—from $15 billion to $37 billion; that of inventory investment has been $13 billion, in current dollars—from $3 billion to $10 billion. Even more striking is the comparison of maximum year to year changes: +$6.4 billion for plant and equipment investment (1955-56), and + $10.8 billion for inventory investment (1949-50), in current dollars. And the relative volatility of inventory investment is likely to appear still greater if viewed on a quarter-to-quarter or month-to-month basis.

The fact that inventory investment can change more rapidly and is therefore more subject to short-run influences underscores the importance of analyzing data reported on a monthly or quarterly basis. These data have not always been available, although monthly data for the U.S. for the period 1947 to date have now been published.

The short-term variability in inventories has presented some problems for econometric estimation. In the first place, the analysis of inventory investment demand within a context of a simultaneous equation model is ordinarily restricted to the use of annual data because other variables appearing in the model are reported only annually. Secondly, even if all related variables were reported on a monthly or quarterly basis, models dealing with observations so close together may be expected to involve substantial serial correlation among the disturbances, thereby impugning the quality of parameter estimates. Nevertheless, some efforts of this sort have been made, and they will be reviewed later.

The empirical work which has been done on inventories can be separated into two kinds. There is first that which has been done according to the Mitchell-National Bureau methodology for studying business cycles, and secondly that which has involved regression methods. These will be considered in order.

B. The Cyclical Behavior of Inventories

1. Abramovitz (2) and Stanback (582a, 583)

Abramovitz and others have studied time series of inventory investment with special attention being given to the timing of cyclical turning points with respect to the National Bureau reference

---

[1]Data from U.S. Department of Commerce, Business Statistics, 1959 Edition, and Survey of Current Business, January 1962.

cycles. Compared with what has been done by way of regression analysis, this type of study has been far greater in volume. Despite that, we shall give it relatively little attention. The problem is that the questions posed and answered are not especially helpful in identifying the determinants of inventory investment demand. The cyclical performance of inventories is not analyzed very specifically in terms of its possible causes. The theories to which this work is most pertinent are those presenting dynamic models of inventory investment oscillation, for these involve time lags and imply things about the behavior of the turning points of inventory cycles vis-a-vis the turning points of other economic time series. Such theories, however, have as their purpose more the illustration and suggestion of how inventories might react and relate dynamically to consumption and income than to the questions of more detailed causal relationships determining inventory investment. One can, of course, compare the timing of inventory cycles with that of certain other economic variables in order to infer something about causation and lags, but the interdependence of economic variables makes this practice somewhat dangerous.

Studies of the cyclical behavior of inventories are also usually organized so as to display differences in the behavior of different types of inventories—raw materials, goods in process, finished goods—as well as the inventories of different types of industries. Our interest, however, will be primarily in inventory investment in the aggregate.

We turn now to a summary of what is surely the most massive work on this subject, the investigations of Professor Moses Abramovitz (2).[1] In connection with this summary we shall refer to a "preprint" for the Joint Economic Committee (582a) of a forthcoming National Bureau study by Thomas M. Stanback on "Postwar Cycles in Manufacturers' Inventories" (583). In this study Professor Stanback meets a well-recognized need in bringing Abramovitz's work up to date—and with the superior postwar data. In the main, Stanback's findings for the postwar period confirm those of Abramovitz for the prewar period.

So brief a summary as we give must treat Abramovitz's work very sketchily, indeed. It must first be noted that his studies deal mainly with manufacturers' inventories. This omits inventories of transportation and other public utilities, mining and quarrying, farming, and trade. Attention is focused by Abramovitz on the behavior of inventories vis-a-vis general business conditions, and the comparison is primarily with respect to turning points. The turning points which mark the beginning or end of general business

---

[1]For a brief preliminary summary of this work, see (1).

expansion or contraction are those selected by the National Bureau of Economic Research. Abramovitz then determines turning points in the manufacturers' inventories series. These are compared with those of the business cycle and conclusions are drawn with respect to leads or lags.

For the period 1918-38, it is first to be reported that the volume of stocks of manufacturers' inventories measured in current prices tends to have a cyclical pattern conforming to that of the business cycle. (By contrast, inventories of agricultural goods may be expected to change largely because of variations in the harvest and would match changes in business activity less well.) In current prices, during this period, manufacturers' inventories, moreover, tend systematically to lag the business cycle at turning points by from three to six months (see 1, p. 87). These results are based on time series of inventory stocks originally prepared by Kuznets for each of 10 industry groups.[2] The data are reported on an annual basis. This is, of course, unfortunate because, as pointed out above, inventories are sufficiently volatile that one would ideally like to use quarterly or, preferably, monthly data. In addition, the use of annual data presents problems of how best to determine lags between different series where the lags are measured in months. (Abramovitz discusses this problem on pp. 64-68.)

The current value series for the ten manufacturing industry groups were then each deflated by a price index so that the behavior of inventories at constant prices could be observed. Here the lag behind turns in general business activity appears to have been 6 to 12 months, although there is greater variation among the ten groups in the average group lags. The greater lag in constant prices than in current prices suggests that prices tend to change course with business activity more promptly than do physical stocks. For the nine industry groups (the miscellaneous group being omitted), the lag in inventories measured in current prices during the period 1919-38 averaged six months behind sales, (p. 113). When inventories were measured in constant prices the average lag was 7.8 months behind turns in output (p. 118). The constant price figures are probably the more relevant ones, as Abramovitz points out, for a consideration of the acceleration principle.

Stanback, using the Department of Commerce data for all manufacturing for the period 1946-58, found that inventories lagged the

---

[2]Food, beverages and tobacco; textiles and textile products; leather and leather products; rubber and related products; lumber and wood products; paper, printing and publishing; chemicals and allied products; stone, clay and glass products; metals and metal products; and miscellaneous.

turning points of the reference cycle by one to eight months. These figures are based on six observed lags, four of which are for price-deflated value series and two of which are based on current book values. It appears therefore that the postwar lag has been somewhat less than the prewar lag. As for the cause of this shift, Stanback suggests (582a, p. 108): "In part, this earlier timing may be due to the shift in composition toward durables and goods in process, resulting in greater sensitivity and consilience with the cycle. It may also be due to a tighter control of inventories by management."

We turn next to Abramovitz's findings on the behavior of the ratio of inventories to sales. In a simple version of the acceleration principle this ratio would be a constant through time. In a more flexible version, of course, it need not be, but its behavior cyclically and secularly must be in some way systematic to be explainable by a modified accelerator type model.

Abramovitz reports that the average value of the inventory-to-sales ratio over the cycle (trough to trough) during the period from 1919 to 1938 tended to be fairly stable, showing but a slight downward drift. It hovered around .21 (1, p. 133); and, the ratio of inventories to value added in manufacturing ran around .5 (p. 134).

Information on the cyclical behavior of the inventory-sales ratio leaves more uncertainty. Inventories clearly tend to rise relative to sales during the contraction period and to fall relative to sales during expansions, but it is uncertain whether the ratio leads or lags at turning points. The obscurity probably results from the annual character of the data. The inventory-output (not inventory-sales) ratio has a more discernible pattern. It tends to lead business turning points by nearly five months. Abramovitz feels, however, that this result is, at least in part, due to some bias in the analysis and concludes: "This review, therefore, leaves us in doubt about the true timing of inventory-output ratios at the turns of output and business cycles. There may be some tendency to lead by a short interval, but we cannot trust our data to reveal it. I conclude that if inventory-output ratios lead at all, the interval is short, and the ratios remain low at business peaks and high at troughs." (P. 144)

Stanback gives little information on the postwar behavior of the stock-to-sales ratio, except for remarking that it has been lower during the postwar period than during the period Abramovitz considered. This is also noted by Cobren and Liebenberg (127) (see Section 2, below).

So far, we have written in terms of inventories, not inventory investment. What has Abramovitz observed about the cyclical behavior of the latter? First, it may be noted that, like inventories themselves, inventory investment tends to move in rhythm with the business cycle. There is, moreover, little difference in the pattern of inventory investment behavior whether it be measured in current or constant dollars. (P. 341) As for leading or lagging, however, Abramovitz writes (p. 337): "The timing measures do not provide a valid basis for supposing that inventory investment by manufacturers tends either to lead or to lag behind business cycle turns. The average lag for total manufacturing is only 0.2 months." Stanback estimates for the postwar period that inventory investment has a lead over the reference cycle of from 0 to 14 months, averaging about 3 months.

Especially in view of the acceleration principle, it would seem more important to ascertain whether inventory investment leads or lags changes in output. To do this, Abramovitz has selected turning points for the change in output; if things moved smoothly, these would be the inflection points of the output time series (Chapter 15, sec. 2). When inventory investment turning points are contrasted with these, they, of course, lag behind. This must be so or they would clearly lead the turning points in business activity itself (assuming that reversals do not occur when acceleration or deceleration is greatest). One result of this is that this category of investment appears to moderate the business cycle, for when general expansion begins to slow down, inventory investment is rising, and contrariwise. (P. 379) Abramovitz provides a summary picture on p. 417:

> The evidence presented above suggests that the pattern of investment in stocks of individual commodities during cycles in manufacturing activity has the following characteristics: (a) when manufacturing activity turns down, inventory investment turns up sharply; (b) by the middle of contraction the rate of inventory investment reaches a level close to the peak for the cycle; thereafter it may continue to rise at a greatly reduced pace, or even tend to fall; (c) in relatively long contractions the tendency for inventory investment to begin to decline before the revival in business is stronger than in short contractions; (d) these generalizations are statements of tendencies characteristic of most commodities in their average behavior during cycles in manufacturing activity and also of most individual cycles, but many a commodity does not behave in this fashion in some cycles; (e) in expansions of manufacturing activity, the behavior pattern of investment is similar but opposite in direction.

One must be careful about concluding, however, that inventory changes are stabilizing. First, they do not move countercyclically at all times, and secondly, even though inventories may, say, rise at a time of general contraction, the contraction could itself be induced or stimulated by a self-frustrating effort to reduce inventories.

If inventories are disaggregated by type, some differences in behavior appear. Goods in process and inventories of finished goods made to order respond rapidly to changes in output and sales. They account for about 25-30 percent of total manufacturers' inventory holdings. It is evident that they must be geared closely to production. Raw materials inventories also appear to be closely related to production, but because of delays between ordering raw materials and receiving them, they respond less promptly to output changes. They account for about 40 percent of the total. The major remaining category, accounting for 20 to 25 percent of the total, is finished durables sold from stock. Holdings in this category respond much more slowly to sales changes and, at least at some times, respond inversely. This is probably the result of an understandable reluctance to cut production promptly when sales first decline or to expand production—with inventories available—when the trough is just passed.

On these matters Stanback found for the postwar period much the same behavior for the component stages of inventory holdings as did Abramovitz—at least where comparisons are possible. The major difference noted is that goods-in-process inventory investment, which seemed roughly coincident with output changes before the war, has since the war lagged behind the latter (582a, p. 109). This change, Stanback suggests (p. 99) may be due in part to a higher proportion of goods-in-process inventories being held by discontinuous-process industries than previously and with more of these inventories thereby being held idle between stages in the manufacturing process.

It should be stressed that Abramovitz is cautious in all of his conclusions. With only annual data to work with, it is difficult to read the record. Indeed, it is impressive to note that his prewar studies based upon such unsatisfactory data have been so well confirmed by Stanback's postwar study based upon better data.

Finally, one may wonder whether non-manufacturers' nonfarm inventories change so as largely to offset the cyclical pattern of manufacturers' inventory holdings. Abramovitz and Stanback both found that the former behave much as do the latter, so that no important offset appears to occur.[3]

---

[3]For a critical review of Abramovitz's work, see (502).

2. Cobren and Liebenberg (127)

Abramovitz's account of the cyclical behavior of inventories can also be extended to the present date on the basis of a study by Cobren and Liebenberg. They investigated the behavior of nonfarm business inventories vis-a-vis GNP for the years 1947-58, both inventories and GNP measured in constant dollars. We quote their conclusions (p. 4):

1. Apart from cyclical fluctuations, the ratio of nonfarm business inventories to GNP was essentially stable throughout the postwar decade. As compared with the 1920-29 period, the ratio was about one-fourth lower.

2. Although cyclical fluctuations in the total stock of inventories were moderate in percentage terms, the absolute changes were large and volatile and accounted for a substantial fraction of the quarterly changes in national output.

3. The cyclical fluctuations in inventories occurred mainly in durable goods.

4. Inventory movements, in line with the pattern of general business activity, were characterized by extended periods of growth followed by sharp declines confined to relatively short spans of time. In each of the broad inventory waves, liquidation canceled only part of the previous accumulation.

5. The highest rates of accumulation generally occurred well in advance of the peaks of business activity, although inventories continue to grow until after the cyclical downturn took place. In contrast, stock liquidation reached its maximum at or near the trough of the business cycle and thereafter tapered fairly rapidly.

6. The total stock of inventories turned down approximately one quarter after the peak in GNP, and turned up approximately two quarters after the trough in activity.

7. Despite sharp liquidations after business downturns, the relatively larger declines in output resulted in stock-output ratios which remained high throughout the period of contraction and showed substantial improvement only after the recovery of business had begun.

It is interesting to note that inventory fluctuations in durable goods were much more important than those in nondurables. Correspondingly, final purchases of durable goods fluctuated a good deal more than final purchases of nondurables. This suggests that the more volatile are sales, the more volatile will be inventory holdings.

It may also be noted that the ratios of stocks to GNP did not display any trend during this postwar period, but during this period it ran generally lower than during the interwar period.

3. Barber (32)

Clarence L. Barber has recently published a study of Canadian inventories which is methodologically similar to that by Abramovitz. He covered the period 1918 to 1950 for ten manufacturing industries. Not having available for the Canadian economy the comprehensive statistical framework for measurements of the business cycle that has been provided for the U.S. by the National Bureau, he was obliged first to select dates for turning points in the Canadian cycles. He reports (p. 95):

> Investment in non-agricultural inventories shows no consistent timing pattern at cyclical turning points. In the earlier period from 1919 to 1925, data (available for only three industries—manufacturing, railways and public utilities) show a lag of about one year; peaks appeared in 1921 and 1924 and troughs in 1922 and 1925. In 1929, 1937, and 1938 peaks and troughs coincided with those of business activity as a whole, although the peak in 1929 followed an earlier and higher peak in 1927. But its trough in 1932 preceded the general upturn by about one year. In the postwar period investment reached a peak in 1946, declined to a trough in 1948 and reached another peak in 1951, whereas total output continued upward throughout this entire period. In contrast, Abramovitz found that in the United States investment in inventories tends neither to lead nor to lag behind the turning points of business cycles.

Barber also considered the interaction of inventories with prices and the money supply. With reference to the table reproduced below he writes (p. 97):

> There is reason to believe that the value of investment in inventories may be an important factor in aggravating inflation and deflation. The relation is one of both cause and effect. A rise in prices leads to an increase in the value of inventory and if this increase is financed out of additional bank loans the spending of these funds leads to a further rise is prices. If a decline in inventory values leads to the paying off of bank loans, this withdrawal of funds from circulation will contribute to a further decline in prices. Table 24 (reproduced below, see Table II-4) gives some support to this thesis. The data presented there show that in most periods the volume of the bank loans and the value of total inventories have moved in the same direction.

The support which the table gives to any causal relation of bank loans is, of course, quite flimsy. It is not at all surprising that bank loans and inventories valued at current prices move together over the cycle. Causal connections would require a good deal more analysis (nor does Barber imply that they would not).

TABLE II-4

Changes in Public Loans of the Chartered Banks and Changes in the Value of Inventories, Canada, 1926 to 1950

Dec. to Dec.	Current public loans chartered banks (Million dollars)	Value of total inventory* (Million dollars)
1926-29	433	559
1929-33	-505	-870
1933-37	-149	339
1938-41	278	886
1945-48	850	2,304
1948-50	574	1,140

*Excludes farm inventory.
Source: Bank of Canada, Statistical Summary, 1946 Supplement, Canadian Statistical Review; and National Accounts: Income and Expenditure 1926 to 1950 (Ottawa, 1952).

4. Eisemann (189; 190)

Doris M. Eisemann has reported some useful information regarding the extent to which inventory investment appears to be related to short-term bank credit. During the period 1947-55 the average ratio of short-term bank loans to inventories for manufacturing firms was 12 percent. This figure should not, however, be interpreted to mean that 12 percent of inventories were financed by short-term bank borrowing. For one thing, short-term bank loans are also made for other purposes and it would be difficult to impute total borrowings to specific corporate purposes. In particular, indebtedness to banks is to some measure incurred to finance account receivables and this may amount to the extension of trade credit by firms that borrow from banks to their customers so that the latter may carry larger inventories. More illuminating is the extent to which changes in short-term banks loans and in inventories are related. On this, Eisemann reports (190, p. 680): "Between the first quarter of 1950 and the first quarter of 1952, a period of rapid inventory accumulation, the ratio of additional loans to the increase in inventories was a little over 25 percent."

5. Mack (404; 405)

Before concluding this section, we should refer to two papers by Dr. Ruth Mack (404 and 405, the latter being based on her study of the shoe, leather, and hide sequence, 406), in which the nonhomogeneity of the components of inventory investment is stressed. Mack argues that because of the considerable diversity in the behavior of stock holdings by type of material, industry, and stage of processing, real progress in the area of explaining inventory investment must give careful attention to the disaggregation of the inventory time series. It is not at all clear that this must be so. The complaint is one that can be made against all aggregation in economics, but its importance can be determined only by the clear success or failure of aggregative relationships to explain the past and to predict the future. It does not appear that so much work has gone into the formulation of aggregative inventory investment relationships that a definitive judgment on this point could be made at the present time. For more detailed criticisms of Mack's views, see (463) and Hickman's reply to Mack in the same National Bureau volume.

C. Regression Studies

1. Clark (122a)

In 1949, Colin Clark reported the results of his estimation of a system of five behavioral equations (plus two identities) designed to provide an explanation for the U.S. trade cycle. Among these equations was an inventory investment relation which was estimated to be the following:

$$(1) \quad J = -.5X - .113\bar{J}' + .119 \sum_{t=1}^{5} X_{-t}$$

$$+ .186 \left(\sum_{t=1}^{3} X_{-t} - \sum_{t=4}^{6} X_{-t} \right) + .136B' - 4.72,$$

where J is inventory investment, X is sales, $\bar{J}'$ is the deviation of stocks from a linear trend, and B' is the deviation of demand and time deposits from a linear trend. The time unit is the quarter year.

Clark chose to think of inventory investment as the difference between "goods put into stock" and "goods drawn from stock." He felt that goods put into stock would depend upon business expectations as to future sales and that this would depend upon past sales, goods already held, and "the financial situation." This accounts for the appearance of the lagged sales variables, the stock minus trend variable $\overline{J}'$, and the amount of bank deposits minus trend, B', in the regression. He wrote: "In order to obviate the effects of chance fluctuations in individual quarters, we have used $\Sigma_1^5 X_{-t}$ to measure the current level of outlay ... and $(\Sigma_{t=1}^3 X_{-t} - \Sigma_{t=4}^6 X_{-t})$ to measure the rate of change of outlay." (P. 108) He then assumed that goods drawn from stock would be "a given fraction of current outlay or sales, i.e., that proportion consisting of goods which by their nature require a fairly long period of production or storage." (Pp. 93-94) To determine inventory investment, then, one must subtract the amount that is drawn from stock from the terms on the right hand side of (1) that determine the amount put into stock. The amount drawn from stock was regarded as a proportion of current sales, and, as the reader can see, Clark estimated this proportion to be one-half. This estimate was not obtained by regression techniques, but was based on other observations. The other coefficients were then obtained by the least squares regression of J + .5X on the remaining variables.

It is interesting to review Clark's reasons for deciding that the fraction of goods sold which are goods sold out of inventories is approximately one-half. He noted first that industries whose output either cannot be stored or is not likely to be stored for long account for between 60 and 65 percent of national product. He also noted that, according to Professor Kuznets, inventories in 1929 were about 45 percent of annual gross income. He regarded these two figures as incompatible and, suspecting the former more than the latter, reduced the 60 to 65 percent to 50 percent. His sense that these two figures are incompatible rested upon the following analysis. Suppose that 60 to 65 percent of all production is sold in the quarter in which it is produced. Suppose further that the remaining production is sold at a constant rate over n succeeding quarters. If production were stationary, how large would n have to be in order that inventories would be 45 percent of annual gross income? (By our computations, assuming the 65 percent figure, the answer is 8.7 quarters.) Clark presented the answer for the case in which it is supposed that non-stored output constitutes 50, rather than 60-65 percent, of total output. For this case he found n to be approximately 6 quarters. A maximum of six quarters of storage seemed high to him. He wrote (pp. 106-107): "... we have to assume that goods which are placed in inventory may spend anything up to eighteen months there in order to secure a result compatible with Professor Kuznets' ratio." The "eighteen months" would have been "twenty-six months" had he used the figure of 65 percent instead of 50 percent. For this reason, he chose the latter. It is difficult to understand why so much credence should be placed in the assumption that goods that are stored for more than a quarter are then sold at a constant rate through succeeding quarters; and his result is exceedingly sensitive to this simplification. Nor must it be assumed that all inventories arise from the technical delay between production and sales. A portion of inventory holdings may be held for speculative or buffer motives. The more important these considerations are, the less the technical production-sales lag that would be implied by Clark's analysis. In any case, the resulting relation is by no means uninteresting. There is appeal in the idea that inventories vary inversely with current sales because of a technological lag. That is, if current sales increase, we should expect this to result in the drawing down of inventories, and probably in proportion to the fraction of total output that entails a significant production lag. Moreover, we should expect a rise in sales to result, ceteris paribus, in an increase in inventories at a later date. One may object, however, to Clark's having assumed that the coefficient of X is -.5 rather than his having estimated this coefficient, along with others, by regression. If the estimate that would otherwise have been obtained differs significantly from -.5 we should expect that this would reflect itself in (possibly important) differences in the estimates of the coefficients of the other explanatory variables.

The data for the regression covered the period 1921-41. The derivation of the time series for inventories was somewhat involved and will not be explained here. Clark synthesized this series using data from Barger, Gilbert, and Kuznets. The interested reader is referred to Clark's Appendix (pp. 121-123). Sales data were also drawn from Barger and Gilbert. The coefficient of multiple correlation was .903. It should be stressed, however, that Clark worked with an interdependent system but applied least squares directly. This, in addition to the constraint on the coefficient of X cited above, means that the estimates of the regression coefficients are subject to unknown bias.

2. Klein (353)

L.R. Klein estimated a dynamic macroeconomic model consisting of 12 stochastic behavior equations in 12 endogenous variables. One of these was an inventory demand equation, presented below:

(1) $H = \gamma_0 + \gamma_1(X - \Delta H) + \gamma_2 p + \gamma_3 p_{-1} + \gamma_4 H_{-1} + \gamma_5 t + u_3$

where H stands for inventories, X - H stands for sales (production minus inventory change), p stands for an output price index and t represents time. The notion is that inventory variation arises from three sources: (1) inventories may be expected to vary with sales (the acceleration principle); (2) inventories may be expected to vary with price changes (speculative demand); and (3) inventories may be expected to be related to their lagged value because of the time required for adjustment. In addition, a trend term is introduced.

The single equation, limited information estimates of the parameters in this function are shown below:

(2) $H = 1.17 + 0.12(X - \Delta H) + 4.60p + 0.50H_{-1} + u_3'.$ [4/]
          $(1.6) \quad (.02) \qquad\qquad (1.1) \qquad (.07)$

It is to be noted that p_{-1} and t have been dropped because their coefficients proved to be unimportant. Observations were used for the years 1922 to 1941. The inventory figures include agricultural inventories and were obtained from the Survey of Current Business and from Agricultural Statistics. They are in constant 1934 dollars. Production, X, is given by

(3) $X = \dfrac{p(Y + T) - W_2 - R_1 - R_2}{p},$

where p is a price index for output as a whole, $Y + T$ is net national product is 1934 dollars, W_2 is the government wage-salary bill, in current dollars, R_1 is nonfarm rentals, paid and imputed, in current dollars, and R_2 is farm rentals measured the same way. All data are on an annual basis.

(4) $H = 1.06 + 0.13(X - \Delta H) + 4.66p + 0.48H_{-1} + u_3'.$
          $(0.02) \qquad\qquad (1.15) \quad (0.08)$

The von Neumann serial correlation statistic, δ^2/S^2 was 2.26 for the limited-information regression and 2.17 for the least-squares regression, in neither case inconsistent, at the .05 probability level, with the hypothesis of zero serial correlation. The standard error of estimate for the limited-information regression is .55 and for direct least-squares is .57. We may notice the similarity of the coefficients obtained by the two estimation methods and also note that the standard errors by least-squares are at most a small fraction of the coefficient.

It should be pointed out that in Klein's equation inventories are related, in part, to sales rather than production. That is, one of the explanatory variables is $X - \Delta H$ rather than just X. A relation to X would indicate the extent to which inventories are "technically" related to production. But a fixed relation to production need not imply a fixed relation to sales (in the short run). To the extent

---

[4]Standard errors in parentheses given by Christ (117, p. 72).

inventories are used as a buffer they may for a time move inversely with sales. $X - \Delta H$ is, of course, $X - H + H_{-1}$, so that we may rewrite (2) as

$$H = 1.17 + .12X - .12H + .12H_{-1} + 4.60p + 0.50H_{-1} + u_3^!$$

or as

$$H = \frac{1.17}{1.12} + \frac{.12}{1.12}X + \frac{4.60}{1.12}p + \frac{.62}{1.12}H-1 + u_3^!$$

or

$$H = 1.05 + .11X + 4.11p + .55H_{-1} + u_3^!.$$

The coefficient changes are all small compared to their standard errors, however, so that it seems doubtful if the choice between production or sales can be reliably interpreted.

How is the relation obtained to be interpreted? It will be best to express the coefficients as elasticities. The elasticity of inventory holdings with respect to the price index, by our calculations, using the limited-information estimates, is .21; the elasticity with respect to sales is .25, and that with respect to lagged inventories is .49. The "speculative" term therefore appears to be nearly as important as the "sales" term or acceleration principle, although both are dominated by the much greater importance ascribed to the autoregressive term. The latter appears excessive. Suppose that all values were at their sample means. H would then be 25, and H_{-1} would be 24.6. These may be regarded as equilibrium values, H and H_{-1} being almost the same. But then if, because of a disturbance, H were to increase by one unit, the next period H_{-1} would be a unit greater (that is, a unit in excess of its equilibrium value) and this would then cause current inventories to be half a unit in excess of equilibrium. This means that for price and sales constant, inventories would move half the way toward their equilibrium each year. If H_{-1} is introduced—as was the case—to represent the "inertia" in inventory adjustment, the "inertia" as estimated seems too big. This is not to say that over the cycle a displacement of actual inventories from intended inventories would in fact be made up at a rate in excess of one-half that displacement each year; but this is because, over the cycle, unintended inventory surpluses or deficiencies may be fairly persistent because of movement in other factors. Some of the importance ascribed to lagged inventories ought perhaps better be parceled out to the other explanatory variables.

It should be noted that the extended interpretation which we have given to lagged inventories in this regression—an interpretation which says that it represents not only inertia in adjusting inventories, but the cyclical phenomenon of unintended inventories tending to be perpetuated over time because of the income and consumption effects of trying to eliminate them—is the sort of thing which is supposed to be avoided by a simultaneous equation model, for these other effects are presumed to be dealt with elsewhere in the system.

Klein's work was critically reviewed and modified in the light of later data by Carl Christ (117), but Klein has criticized Christ's efforts as not contributing at the substantive (only at the methodological) level (354, pp. 313-18), and in any case, Christ did not find Klein's inventory demand equation to be particularly unsatisfactory. Christ did re-estimate it in the context of a revision of Klein's model, however, changes having been introduced in other relationships. His limited-information results were:

$$(5) \qquad \Delta H = 5.22 + .082(X - \Delta H) + 1.93p + 0.539H_{-1} + u_3'.$$
$$\qquad\quad (1.9)\quad (.02) \qquad\qquad (1.4) \qquad (.12)$$

It is to be noted that the major difference between Christ's estimates and those of Klein was in the coefficient of the price term, Christ obtaining a much smaller value for the coefficient. If Christ's results are to be accredited, a lesser role might be ascribed to the speculative factor in inventory change than Klein's results indicate.

Klein also experimented with the use of quarterly data. The data for inventories were obtained from H. Barger (33a). The least-squares regression for the years 1921 through 1938 was:

$$(6) \qquad H = -0.71 + 1.10p + 0.16(X - \Delta H) + 0.88H_{-1} + u'.$$
$$\qquad\qquad (0.32)\quad (0.04) \qquad\qquad\qquad (0.04)$$

The coefficient of multiple correlation was .98, the standard error of estimate was .41 and δ^2/S^2 was 1.68. It is difficult to compare this quarterly model with the annual model, but this can be done under the assumption that quarterly sales and the quarterly price index were constant during the year. Under these assumptions the quarterly model has coefficients comparing reasonably well with those obtained (either by limited-information or least-squares) for the annual model. The main difference is that the quarterly model (under the special assumptions) has a lower coefficient for price when converted to an annual basis, i.e., plus 3.66, and a higher coefficient for lagged inventories when converted to an annual basis, i.e., .60. On the whole, one can say that Klein's quarterly study does not impugn the results he obtained using annual data.

3. Darling (144)

In a very interesting article, Paul G. Darling uses quarterly data for the period 1947-58 to fit an inventory investment function. The underlying function he has in mind is:

(1) $\Delta H = a_0 + a_1(rS - H)_{-t} + u,$

where ΔH is inventory investment, H is inventories, S is sales, and r may be interpreted as a desired ratio of inventories to sales. a_1 is then a coefficient expressing the speed with which a discrepancy between intended inventories and actual inventories will be made up. The subscript -t is an unspecified response lag.

Darling first combined monthly aggregative inventory data of the Department of Commerce, seasonally adjusted, into quarterly values. Monthly sales data were also summed to obtain quarterly values. None of the variables was deflated for price-level changes, and inventories are measured by their book value. Since FIFO is a much more common accounting practice than LIFO, this means that an increment of inventories reflects fairly well the amount of working capital which has had to be devoted to that purpose. A main danger here is that there might be spurious correlation because both the dependent and explanatory variables reflect price-level changes. Inasmuch as the dependent variable is a time-series difference, however, it may be hoped that this problem is not too important.

Darling then recast equation (1) as:

(2) $H = a_0 + bS_{-1} - a_1 H_{-2} + u,$

where $b = a_1 r$, all lags being expressed in quarter years. This form of the equation was apparently chosen, after trying various possibilities, on the basis of how well it fit. This equation says that what causes firms to change their inventory position is a discrepancy between the inventories desired on the basis of the sales of the immediately preceding quarter and the mean value of end-of-month inventories for the quarter preceding the quarter for which sales occur.

The estimates obtained were:

(3) $\Delta H = -.625 + .581S_{-1} - .299H_{-2}$.
                    (0.46) (0.22)

The coefficient of multiple regression was .896, the standard error of estimate was .508, and δ^2/S^2 was 1.49, which was "somewhat low." These estimates imply a desired stock-sales ratio of about 1.9 which conforms fairly well to what was observed over the period, although it is just a trifle high.

Darling then considered the possibility that the stock-sales ratio, r, is itself variable. He conjectured that r would be greater when new orders received by firms exceed sales, and otherwise smaller. He therefore decided to make r a linear function of the ratio of the change in unfilled orders to sales, lagged one quarter. Thus:

(4) $r = b_0 + b_1 (\Delta O/S)_{-1}$,

where ΔO is the change in unfilled orders. Equation (4) substituted into equation (1) yields:

(5) $\Delta H = a_0 + c_1 S_{-1} + c_2 \Delta O_{-1} - a_1 H_{-2} + u$,

where $b_0 = c_1 a_1$ and $b_1 = c_2/a_1$. The result obtained for this regression was:

(6) $\Delta H = -.387 + .415 S_{-1} + .324 \Delta O_{-1} - .212 H_{-2}$.

The coefficient of multiple correlation was .945, the standard error of estimate was .375, and δ^2/S^2 was 1.85. For $\Delta O = 0$ the value of r is 1.95, conforming fairly closely with what was obtained for the previous regression.

The high coefficient of multiple correlation has led Darling to declare that: "It appears that aggregation may be pushed much further in inventory analysis than has heretofore been generally felt justified." (P. 958) This is, of course, apropos the criticisms of Ruth Mack. The proof of the pudding is, of course, in how well the regression predicts future values and in whether it provides us with pertinent and reliable information about the structure of inventory behavior.

We should comment next on the improvement which resulted when the desired stock-sales ratio was allowed to change depending upon whether unfilled orders were rising or falling. The estimate of b_1 is approximately 1.5, and so r is greater during the revival. In view of the fact that inventory adjustment proceeds with a lag, this is in effect to say that intended inventories exceed actual inventories to a greater extent (than if r were constant) during the upswing, and vice versa during the downswing. This can, of course, reflect a speculative motive as well as the indirect effects, via income and sales, of efforts to increase inventories in perpetuating the discrepancy these efforts seek to remove.

After completing this basic work, Darling was able to use his regressions, ex post, to predict inventory investment for the fourth quarter of 1958 and the first and second quarters of 1959. Equation (6) predicted a decline of 170 (all figures in millions of dollars), whereas the actual drop was 90 for the fourth quarter of 1958. For the first quarter of 1959 the predicted change was plus 710; the actual change was plus 1,250. For the second quarter of 1959, the predicted change was plus 1,310; the actual change was plus 1,630. Darling also fitted equation (5) for the full period, 1947-58, with two badly behaving quarters omitted, and also for the latter half of the total period. The results were somewhat better than they had been for the full period.

In (570a), Mabel A. Smith brings Darling's regression up to date by computing it for quarterly data over the period from the first quarter of 1948 through the first quarter of 1961. She obtained (in Darling's notation) (570a, p. 158)

$$\Delta H = -.038 + .327 S_{-1} + .149 \Delta \underline{O}_{-1} - .173 H_{-2},$$

with $R = .9$. Though the individual coefficients seem to differ importantly from those Darling obtained, the value of r, the desired stock-sales ratio when there has been no change in unfilled orders, remains much the same (falls slightly from 1.95 to 1.89). The coefficient for b_1, however, falls from 1.5 to .86.[5]

Somewhat similar regression studies were reported in (83a) by Lawrence Bridge and Clement Winston for retail trade and for wholesale trade. Their results were given in detail only for the regression of stocks on lagged sales. High coefficients of correlation were obtained, but both series were heavily trend dominated.

In a more recent publication (146), Darling has reported some further regressions of much the same sort as those commented upon above. We report his most elaborate regression here without any detailed analysis of the theoretical considerations underlying it, for the basic ideas are essentially the same as those underlying his previous work. The regression is:

$$\Delta H_t = 6.297 + 0.040 S_{t-1} + .035 \underline{O}_{t-1} + .055 \Delta Q_{t-1} - .265 H_{t-1}$$
$$\quad\;\; (.020) \qquad (.011) \qquad (.028) \qquad\;\; (.076)$$
$$+ .383 \Delta H_{t-1} + .062 T$$
$$(.086) \qquad\quad (.022)$$

for quarterly data deflated to 1954 prices, for the period 1948, first quarter, through 1960, fourth quarter.

---

[5]It appears, though, that the data employed differed in that Darling's quarterly inventory series consisted of the monthly mean for the quarter, whereas Smith used end-of-quarter inventories.

For the period of 1952, third quarter, through 1958, fourth quarter, which eliminates the Korean War period as well as the 1959 steel strike, the results are much the same. For the regression reported here the coefficient of determination was .811. The regression coefficients appear to have been quite significantly affected, however, by the differences between this study and the previous one. The model is an appealing one, but the estimates are apparently not very robust in view of the differences obtained by Mabel Smith in her up-dating of Darling's earlier model and by Darling in his more recent version.

In his recent publication (146, esp. Sections III and IV), Darling stresses the "feed-back" of inventory investment on aggregate demand and hence the desire to invest further in inventories, and he endorses the notion that inventories likely play a strong role in the business-cycle mechanism. But "feed-back" is not explicitly taken into account in his regression studies. If it were, a simultaneous system of equations would be required, and the standard argument would then be that the regression he fitted by least-squares, as one of a system of simultaneous relationships, was subject to estimation bias from that cause.

4. Bassie (40a)

V. Lewis Bassie fitted several inventory regressions to data for the period 1921-42 and 1947-54. We report here on the regression which he found most satisfactory. It was:

(1) $\Delta H = -0.598 + 0.251G - 0.562H'_{-1}$ $(R^2 = .721)$.

ΔH is the change in nonfarm inventories in billions of 1947 dollars for the year (all data used were on an annual basis). G represents a time series which consists of Gross National Product minus personal services, minus gross government product, minus foreign investment, minus one-half of new construction, and minus change in business inventories. H' is an adjusted figure for stocks at the beginning of the year. The adjustment is affected by matching a trend in inventories with the trend in G, the trends being loglinear. This is to remove the element of a secular change in the stock to goods-flow ratio. The theory behind the equations being estimated is the simple acceleration principle. Bassie begins with the relation:

(2) $H = a + bG$,

which can be rewritten as:

(3) $\Delta H + H_{-1} = a + bG$.

He then writes: "By simple algebra, the statistical form [sic] of the relationship then becomes:

$$\Delta H = a + bG - cH_{-1}."$$

By his hypothesis, c as estimated ought to equal 1, which it is far from doing.

There is, however, another interpretation for what he has obtained. Suppose, following Darling, we begin by postulating that the change in inventories is a linear function of the difference between desired inventories and adjusted actual inventories at the beginning of the period. Let desired inventories be measured by rG. We then have:

(4) $\Delta H = a + c(rG - H'_{-1})$,

which becomes:

(5) $\Delta H = a + crG - cH'_{-1}$.

Bassie's b is then our cr, so that r would be estimated to be $0.251/0.562 = .45$. This then is an estimate of the desired stock to goods-flow ratio. The actual ratio of adjusted beginning-of-year inventories to the total flow of goods averages .4 more closely. Bassie's estimate of c could, in this model, be interpreted as the rate at which a discrepancy between desired and actual inventories would be made up during the course of the year. This corresponds very closely to Klein's result (which is not too surprising because their data have much in common); and it is not out of accord with Darling's result which states (depending upon the regression used) that between 20 percent and 30 percent of the discrepancy would be made up in the first quarter. Acknowledging that Bassie's result conforms with the others, we are led to repeat the criticism previously advanced, namely, that this adjustment coefficient appears to us to be too low and possibly reflects some speculative or "runaway" factors operating typically during upswings and downswings. In short, the low adjustment coefficient need not be pure "inertia" but may be in part the result of cumulative elements which partially counteract efforts to catch up.

5. Lovell (396)

In a recent article, Michael Lovell has developed three inventory behavior functions, one for purchased-goods and goods-in-process inventories, one for finished-goods inventories, and one for total inventories, the last being the sum of the first two.

Estimates of the constants in these functions were made, using quarterly data for the period 1948 to 1955, for durable goods manufacturing, nondurable goods manufacturing, and all manufacturing. Variables expressed in money values were deflated for price changes and the inventory data were seasonally adjusted.

We consider first Lovell's model for purchased-goods and goods-in-process inventories. This model assumes that the change in these inventories in any period, $\Delta S_t = S_t - S_{t-1}$, is proportional to the discrepancy between an equilibrium level of stocks, S_t^e, and the actual level at the end of the previous period, S_{t-1}. Thus

$$S_t - S_{t-1} = \delta (S_t^e - S_{t-1}),$$

where δ is the quarterly adjustment coefficient. Note the assumption that for these categories of inventories a stable (presumably desired) quarterly adjustment rate can be regularly achieved. There is no distinction between planned and unplanned increments of purchased-goods and goods-in-process inventories. Lovell assumes that the equilibrium level of these inventories is a linear function of output, Q_t, the recent change in output, ΔQ_t, the rate of change in prices, p, and the level of unfilled orders. Thus

$$S_t^e = \alpha + \beta_1 Q_t + \beta_2 \Delta Q_t + \beta_3 \frac{p_t - p_{t-1}}{p_t} + \beta_4 U_t.$$

Substituting the right hand side of the foregoing into the previous equation, Lovell obtains

$$S_t = \delta \alpha + \delta \beta_1 Q_t + \delta \beta_2 \Delta Q_t + \delta \beta_3 [(p_t - p_{t-1})/p_t] + \delta \beta_4 U_t +$$
$$+ (1 - \delta) S_{t-1} + \varepsilon_t,$$

where ε_t is a disturbance term. This is a flexible accelerator model in which firms effect only a partial adjustment of inventories during the period. Estimating the coefficients in the regression, it is then possible to decompose them into the original parameters. We report the estimates for all manufacturing later on.

For finished-goods inventories a somewhat different model is used. In this case, the distinction between planned and unintended inventories is used. Planned finished-goods inventories, I_t^p, are assumed to be a weighted mean of equilibrium finished-goods inventories, I_t^e, and those at the beginning of the period, I_{t-1}:

$$I_t^p = \delta' I_t^e + (1 - \delta') I_{t-1}, \quad u < \delta' \leq 1$$

(our notation in part), where δ' is a reaction coefficient. The equilibrium level is next assumed to be a linear function of expected sales, $\hat{X}_t$, thus:

$$I_t^e = \alpha' + \beta_1' \hat{X}_t .$$

(Note that this is a simpler function than the comparable one for purchased-goods and goods-in-process inventories.) Planned finished-goods inventories are therefore

$$I_t^p = \delta' \alpha' + \delta' \beta_1' \hat{X}_t + (1-\delta') I_{t-1} .$$

Ideally, Lovell would like to regard unplanned finished-goods inventories as a proportion λ of the difference between expected and actual sales, i.e., as

$$\lambda (\hat{X}_t - X_t),$$

the proportion λ allowing for the possibility of some adjustment of production during the period t to meet the discrepancy between planned and actual sales. The inclusion of λ as a parameter to be estimated, however, makes it impossible to decompose the later regression coefficients into the structural coefficients, and so λ is in effect taken to be unity. Therefore, the unintended component of finished-goods inventories is simply $\hat{X}_t - X_t$ and total (planned and unintended) inventories will be

$$I_t = \delta' \alpha' + \delta' \beta_1' \hat{X}_t + (1-\delta') I_{t-1} + \hat{X}_t - X_t .$$

It remains for expected sales to be explained. This Lovell does by assuming that expected sales are a weighted mean of the sales that actually develop and those of the past period. Thus,

$$\hat{X}_t = \rho (X_{t-1}) + (1-\rho) X_t, \qquad\qquad 0 \le \rho \le 1;$$

the smaller ρ the better the forecast. Substituting this in the previous equation, Lovell obtains

$$I_t = \delta' \alpha' + \delta' \beta_1' X_t - (\delta' \beta' + 1) \rho \Delta X_t + (1-\delta') I_{t-1} + \mathcal{E}_t',$$

$\mathcal{E}_t'$ being a disturbance term. This model couples the flexible accelerator model with an unintended inventory investment component representing the "buffer stock" role of inventories. We report the estimates later on.

To obtain a model for inventories of all stages, Lovell adds the final equations for purchased-goods and goods-in-process inventories and for finished-goods inventories. He first, however, substitutes sales, X_t, for output, Q_t, in the first of these component equations. The result is (partially in our notation)

$$H_t \equiv S_t + I_t = da + db_1 X_t + (1 - d)H_{t-1} - (db_1 + 1)r\Delta X_t$$
$$+ db_2 U_t + db_3 \frac{\Delta p_{t+1}}{p_t} + e_t,$$

where

$$d = \delta \frac{S_{t-1}}{H_{t-1}} + \delta' \frac{I_{t-1}}{H_{t-1}},$$

$$da = \delta\alpha + \delta'\alpha',$$

$$db_1 = \delta\beta_1 + \delta'\beta_1',$$

$$(db_1 + 1)r = \delta\beta_2 - (\delta'\beta_1' + 1)\rho,$$

$$db_2 = \delta\beta_4,$$

$$db_3 = \delta\beta_3, \text{ and}$$

$$e_t = \varepsilon_t + \varepsilon_t'.$$

The coefficients of this all-inventory equation may be estimated either by use of the above equalities, being thereby derived from the estimates of the two component equations, or by direct estimation, using least squares. The estimates obtained are shown in Table II-5.

Reasonably good conformity is obtained for all coefficients except that for the rate of change in prices, the only coefficient that also was far from being statistically significant.

Lovell has made a similar comparison, but his is a comparison of the "structural" coefficients themselves. These results are presented in Table II-6.[6] Lovell writes:

> First of all, one would surmise that the total inventory reaction coefficient obtained for each sector would be a rough average of the sector's stock and inventory reaction coefficients obtained under the separate regressions utilizing the stage of fabrication breakdown. This indeed proves to be the case.... Again, remembering that sales are now being utilized as a proxy for output, we should find the total marginal desired inventory coefficient to be roughly the sum of the coefficient for purchased materials and goods in process stocks and that for finished goods inventory; this indeed holds, the approximation being particularly good for total manufacturing and total durables. Also, for total manufacturing and total durables, if not for the nondurables,

---

[6] These values were computed by us. Lovell's comparisons were "rough."

TABLE II-5

Variable	$X_t^{(a)}$	Lagged inventory $(S_{t-1}, I_{t-1}, H_{t-1})$	$\Delta X_t^{(b)}$	U_t	$\Delta p_{t+1}/p_t$	Constant
Purchased-goods and goods-in-process inventories	$\delta\mathcal{E}_1$ .0620	$1 - \delta$ .5424	$\delta\beta_2$ -.0097	$\delta\beta_4$ .0609	$\delta\beta_3$ -.3204	$\delta\alpha$ 4004
Finished-goods inventories	$\delta'\beta_1'$ .0419	$1 - \delta'$ .8479	$-(\delta'\beta_1' + 1)\rho$ -.1315	Excluded	Excluded	$\delta'\upsilon'$ -258.2
Total inventories (obtained by regression)	$\delta\beta_1 + \delta'\beta_1'$ .1039	$1 - \delta\dfrac{S_{t-1}}{H_{t-1}} - \delta'\dfrac{I_{t-1}}{H_{t-1}}$ .6524$^{(c)}$	$\delta\beta_2 - (\delta'\beta_1' + 1)\rho$ -.2312	$\delta\beta_4$ .0609	$\delta\beta_3$ -.3204	$\delta\alpha + \delta'\upsilon'$ 3745.8
Total inventories (obtained by adding components)	db_1 .1672	$1 - d$ .5699	$-(db_1 + 1)r$ -.1679	δb_2 .0618	δb_3 -1.6852	da 3066

(a) Actually, Q_t for purchased-goods and goods-in-process inventories.
(b) Actually, ΔQ_t for purchased-goods and goods-in-process inventories.
(c) Estimated by present authors assuming that $S_{t-1}/H_{t-1} = .64$ and $I_{t-1}/H_{t-1} = .36$, their mean values for the sample period.

TABLE II-6

	δ	β_1	β_2	β_3	β_4	α
Purchased-goods and goods-in-process inventories	δ .4576	β_1 .135	β_2 −.218	β_3 −.7002	β_4 .1331	α 8,750
Finished-goods inventories	δ' .1521	β_1' .275	ρ .1262			α' −1,698
Total inventories (obtained by adding components)	$\delta\frac{S_{t-1}}{H_{t-1}} + \delta'\frac{I_{t-1}}{H_{t-1}}$ .3476	$\dfrac{\beta_1\delta\frac{S_{t-1}}{H_{t-1}} + \beta_1'\delta'\frac{I_{t-1}}{H_{t-1}}}{\delta\frac{S_{t-1}}{H_{t-1}} + \delta'\frac{I_{t-1}}{H_{t-1}}}$ .158	$\dfrac{\delta\beta_2 - (\delta'\beta_1' + 1)\rho}{-(\delta\beta_1 + \delta'\beta_1' + 1)}$ .2094	$\dfrac{\delta\beta_3}{\delta\frac{S_{t-1}}{H_{t-1}} + \delta'\frac{I_{t-1}}{H_{t-1}}}$ −.9217	$\dfrac{\delta\beta_4}{\delta\frac{S_{t-1}}{H_{t-1}} + \delta'\frac{I_{t-1}}{H_{t-1}}}$ .1752	$\dfrac{\delta\alpha + \delta'\alpha'}{\delta\frac{S_{t-1}}{H_{t-1}} + \delta'\frac{I_{t-1}}{H_{t-1}}}$ 10,776
Total inventories (obtained by regression)	d .4301	b_1 .3887	r .1438	b_3 −3.918	b_2 .1437	a 7,129

the unfilled orders coefficient is remarkably stable.
The estimates of the coefficient of anticipations obtained when the stage-of-fabrication breakdown is
neglected quite closely approximate those obtained
with the finished goods regression; even the largest
discrepancy, that for total manufacturing, is only a
contrast of 0.13 versus 0.15 in estimating the anticipations coefficient. Only the coefficient of the rate of
change in prices of purchased materials and goods in
process shows a marked sensitivity to the level of
aggregation; we find them larger in absolute value and
all negative, implying that total inventories are smaller
when prices of purchased materials are on the increase.

With the exception of a possible distortion of the
role of prices, the estimates obtained when the data
on finished goods inventory are combined with the
figures for stocks of purchased materials and goods
in process are remarkably consistent with the earlier
estimates utilizing the breakdown.

Let us ask specifically what interpretation could be given to
either a good or a bad conformity of the least-squares estimates
of the total-inventories coefficients and the coefficients calculated
by adding the two component regressions. That there should be a
difference can arise only from three specific causes. Let us note
first that it is a property of least-squares regression that if

$$y_1 = \hat{\alpha}_1 + \sum_k \hat{\beta}_{1k} x_k$$

and

$$y_2 = \hat{\alpha}_2 + \sum_k \hat{\beta}_{2k} x_k$$

are least squares regressions, then for the regression

$$y \equiv y_1 + y_2 = \hat{\alpha} + \sum_k \hat{\beta}_k x_k ,$$

$\hat{\alpha} = \hat{\alpha}_1 + \hat{\alpha}_2$ and $\hat{\beta}_k = \hat{\beta}_{1k} + \hat{\beta}_{2k}$, necessarily. Lovell's models
would fit this framework under three assumptions: (1) S_t and I_t are
always in fixed proportion; (2) X_t and Q_t are always in fixed proportion; and (3) U_t and $\Delta p_{t+1}/p_t$ would have had estimated coefficients of zero had they been included in the finished-goods inventory
regression. A good conformity of the two sets of estimates for the
total-inventories equation would mean that these assumptions are
approximately satisfied (or that the errors introduced by them cancel out). What is of most interest is the result of accepting the first

two assumptions and examining the third. Lovell's comparison of the two sets of estimates for the total-inventories equation is then essentially a test of the importance of leaving unfilled orders and relative price change out of the finished-goods inventory regression. Had these variables appeared in this regression, the two sets of estimates of the coefficients in the total inventories equation would, under our present assumptions, have been necessarily equal. That they are judged to be close is therefore essentially a judgment that if U_t and $\Delta p_{t+1}/p_t$ had been introduced in the finished-goods equation, their coefficient estimates would have been close to zero and there would have been very little difference in the estimates of the other coefficients. This could, of course, have been tested directly by trying out U_t and $\Delta p_{t+1}/p_t$ in the finished-goods inventory equation. But it is simple to determine what the least-squares estimates would then have been. This can be done by subtracting the regression for purchased goods and goods in process from the regression for total inventories (ignoring the difference between X_t and Q_t). This gives the following coefficients: $\delta' \beta_1' = .1052$; $1-\delta' = .6190$; $-(\delta'\beta_1'+1)\rho = .2694$; coefficient of $U_t = .0009$; coefficient of $\Delta p_{t+1}/p_t = -1.3648$; and $\delta'\alpha' = -938$. The estimates of the structural parameters are then: $\beta_1' = .2761$; $\delta' = .3810$; $\rho = -.2437$; and $\alpha' = -2470$. The coefficient of U_t is certainly close to zero, and its absence from Lovell's equation has made little difference. But the same cannot be said for the coefficient of $\Delta p_{t+1}/p_t$—and it does not help that in Lovell's regressions this coefficient had substantial standard errors.

In any case, the test can hardly shed any light on the validity of the two distinct models used by Lovell for the two inventory components. Both models would lead to the same set of explanatory variables except that in the purchased-goods and goods-in-process model U_t and $\Delta p_{t+1}/p_t$ enter into the equation determining the equilibrium level of stocks, whereas they are excluded in the finished-goods model from the equation determining the equilibrium level. This distinction seems arbitrary from the theoretical point of view, even though U_t appears on the statistical evidence to be unimportant for finished goods inventories. It is doubtful, therefore, if Lovell's results would justify our concluding that different models, especially as regards the "buffer stock" motive,[7] are needed for these two

---

[7] There are no a priori grounds for supposing that the "buffer stock" motive may not also play a role in determining purchased-goods and goods-in-process inventories, for unintended changes can occur in these inventories as well. It may be noted that Eisner (197, p. 569) has pointed out circumstances, illustrated by acquisition of iron ore by steel companies, predetermined during limited periods of the year when Great Lakes shipping is open, where stocks of purchased inventories will in fact be inversely related to current output. Where demand and output are greater than anticipated it is then stocks of these purchased materials, rather than finished inventories, which are run down.

inventory components, or that much has been learned about whether inventories differing by stage of manufacture can or cannot be safely aggregated for an econometric study of total inventories. The real test for this is whether the two component equations differ significantly in their coefficients, and the observed differences appear to fall within the margins of error that Lovell has allowed for his own comparison of the two ways of estimating the coefficients of the total inventory equation. But the Lovell study seems highly worthwhile because the estimates seem reasonable and the correlation coefficients are high. Both kinds of models that he has used appear to give good results. It is nevertheless also unfortunate that we cannot really distinguish between them (identify them) on the basis of the statistical results. Any of Lovell's regressions could have come from either type of model.

Lovell's work does not take account of simultaneous relationships. In particular, the feed-back of inventory investment on the level of sales and sales and price changes is ignored. The model is in this sense perhaps critically incomplete and the estimates subject to simultaneous equation bias.

6. Bakony (29a)

In an unpublished doctoral dissertation L. I. Bakony estimated an inventory investment function as a part of a simultaneous equation model. The estimates provided were, however, direct least-squares estimates, and therefore the simultaneity in the model was ignored in the estimation procedure and the familiar source of least-squares bias was present. This work was done with quarterly data for the Canadian economy for the period 1947-58.

The theory underlying Bakony's choice of an inventory investment function was the following: Inventory investment is divided into two parts, intended and unintended. Intended investment is postulated to be equal to the difference between stocks at the beginning of the quarter and desired stocks, the latter being in fixed proportion to expected sales. Thus,

(1) $\Delta I^i = a X^e - I_{-1}$,

where I_{-1} is inventory stocks at the end of the previous quarter, and X^e is sales expectations for the current quarter.[8] Expected sales are assumed to be a weighted mean of sales for past quarters, where the weights diminish in geometrical proportion. Unintended inventory investment is postulated to be a constant times the dif-

---

[8]Our notation differs slightly from Bakony's.

ference between expected sales and actual sales of the current quarter. Thus,

(2) $\Delta I^u = b(X^e - X)$,

where ΔI^u is unintended inventory investment and X is current quarter sales. The reason the unintended component is not postulated to <u>equal</u> this difference is because some adjustment of inventories to an unexpected change may be possible <u>within</u> the quarter.

Total inventory investment is therefore given by the equality:

(3) $\Delta I = (a + 2b)wX_{-1} - (1 - w)I_{-1} - bX + u$,

where ΔI is inventory investment, w is the constant defining the geometrical sequence of weights, and u is a disturbance term. (Incidentally, u, according to the theory, would be serially correlated, a fact noted by Bakony and one which has troubled many in various contexts. It may also be noted that Bakony's method is similar to Koyck's and that Koyck did not find estimates to be much affected by introducing an autoregressive disturbance term.)

All variables were seasonally adjusted and deflated by the ratio of GNP in current dollars to GNP in constant dollars. The inventory data are for business inventories only and are obtained from the Dominion Bureau of Statistics' publication <u>National Accounts, Income and Expenditure</u>. X is GNP in constant dollars.

The resulting regression is:

(4) $\Delta I = -0.894 - 0.049X_{-1} - 0.109I_{-1} + 0.160X$,

where all variables are expressed as quarterly rates. The coefficient of determination, R^2, was .33, and the regression coefficients — except for the coefficient of I_{-1} — were not statistically significant, and the sign of b (see equation (2)) is wrong. The intercept constant estimated to be -.894, ought, according to the model underlying the regression function, to be zero. It is in fact sufficiently small compared to the mean value of inventory investment that it can be regarded as negligible.

The parameter a (see equation (1)) is estimated to be +.265, b is estimated to be -.160, and w (the constant defining the geometrical sequence of weights determining expected sales) is estimated to be +.891. w does not appear on a priori grounds to be unreasonable, but it is disturbing that a, the desired stock-GNP ratio is so low. The actual stock-GNP ratio increased secularly during the period from a low of about +.05 to a high of about +.8, and its average was nearly double the estimated value of the desired

ratio. One difficulty, especially important for the Canadian economy, is that agricultural output is included in Gross National
Product but is not included in the inventory figures. It would be
better for it to be excluded from the variable X. Bakony conjectures
that the difficulty arises from the extent of aggregation, but no
evidence is as yet available on this question.

7. Modigliani and Sauerlander (462)

Modigliani and Sauerlander report some interesting exploratory
investigations of the usefulness of sales expectations data as a
basis for predicting future inventory holdings. The authors construct
a model of the behavior of the firm which rests heavily on the desire
of the firm to schedule production over time in an efficient way.
It abstracts, for example, from the desire to alter inventory holdings
because of a speculative motive concerning future price changes.
Because the model which is formulated is fairly elaborate, we do
not consider it in further detail here, but refer the interested
reader to the authors' work. Let it suffice now to say that on the
basis of this model (plus a number of bold simplifications), the
authors derive a linear relationship to be estimated by regression
techniques.

Using Dun and Bradstreet Survey Reports on business expectations for August 1949, the authors obtained estimates for the
apparel industry. The regression and the coefficients obtained
(with their standard errors) are presented below:

$$(1) \quad X_1 = 0.95X_2 + 0.48X_3 - 0.21X_4 + 0.01, \quad R = 0.88,$$
$$ (\pm 0.10) \quad (\pm 0.08) \quad (\pm 0.05)$$

where the X's represent the successive variables in the relation
(pp. 330-331):

$$(2) \quad "\frac{H(A)}{H'(A)} = \frac{S_A(Q_4)}{S'(Q_4)}$$

$$+ u\left[\frac{H(J)}{H'(J)} - \frac{a}{a+b}\frac{S(A)}{S'(A)} + \frac{b}{a+b}\frac{S_A(Q_4)}{S'(Q_4)}\right]$$

$$+ v\left[\frac{H'(D)}{S'(Q_4)} \div \frac{H_A(D)}{S_A(Q_4)} - 1\right],$$

$$\text{or } X_1 = X_2 + uX_3 + vX_4$$

where $\dfrac{H(A)}{H'(A)} =$ ratio of stocks at the end of August 1949 to stocks at the end of August 1948

$\dfrac{S_A(Q_4)}{S'(Q_4)} =$ ratio of sales expected in August 1949 for the fourth quarter of 1949 to sales in the fourth quarter of 1948

$\dfrac{S(A)}{S'(A)} =$ ratio of sales in August 1949 to sales in August 1948

$\dfrac{H(J)}{H'(J)} =$ ratio of stocks at the end of June 1949 to stocks at the end of June 1948

$\dfrac{H'(D)}{H_A(D)} =$ ratio of stocks at the end of December 1948 to stocks expected for the end of December 1949."

Let us try to interpret this relation and these results. X_1 gives the ratio of end-of-August 1949 inventories to those of the year before. It is the end of August 1949 inventories which one wishes to predict. X_2 stands for the expectation in August 1949 of what fourth quarter sales will be that year relative to the fourth quarter sales of 1948. This term alone (with its unit coefficient) says that the desired end-of-August stocks will be higher or lower in direct proportion with the expectations about fourth quarter sales. In the regression the coefficient of X_2 is not constrained to be unity, but was estimated at .95 with a standard error of .10. This result should be reassuring. X_3 is a measure of the extent to which stocks at the end of June 1949 were out of equilibrium. The measure of this disequilibrium is given by the difference of the ratio of stocks at the end of June 1949 to stocks the year before and a weighted average of the ratio of sales in August 1949 to sales the year before and the ratio of expected sales as of August 1949 for the fourth quarter to fourth quarter sales in 1948. In other words, one would expect that equilibrium stocks at the end of June 1949 would be higher or lower than those at the end of June in 1948 according to whether or not August 1949 sales and the expected fourth quarter 1949 sales were higher or lower than the corresponding sales of the previous year. It is not clear to the present writers how the weights for the weighted average in X_3 were ascertained. The appearance of this term arises from the authors' view that if stocks are above their equilibriim value one would expect that stocks at the end of August 1949 would also be above their equilibrium value and vice versa. This is to indicate the significance of the variable X_3 and to assert that its coefficient should be positive.

It is possible, of course, that stocks at the end of August 1948 were themselves out of equilibrium. Suppose they were above equilibrium. Then, since adjustment is slow, we should expect that stocks at the end of December 1948 would have been still above equilibrium. Initial inventories for 1949, namely H'(D), would then be above the equilibrium value. If we ignored this element of disequilibrium, X_2 by itself would tend to overstate X_1. Something must be deducted, and that something is X_4. Accordingly v must be negative. How does X_4 measure this disequilibrium element? First, it is assumed that the expected year-end inventories for 1949 and the expected fourth quarter sales of 1949 will be in an equilibrium relationship. That value is $H_A(D)/S_A(Q_4)$. This is then used to deflate the year-end inventories of 1948 by the last quarter sales of 1948 (which, for the case we are considering, was above equilibrium) and the number one is deducted to provide a measure of relative error.

The coefficient u, as estimated, is positive and v, as estimated, is negative, which is in accord with the theoretical prescriptions. In addition, a constant term was introduced in the statistical regression even though the relation was assumed to be homogeneous. This term, however, turns out to be as small as .01 with a standard error of .05, and that once again is reassuring. This all constitutes one bit of evidence in support of the hypothesis that sales anticipation data may be used to explain future inventories.

8. Robinson (526)

In a recent article, N.Y. Robinson reports on inventory regression functions obtained from department store data. The data, which were on a monthly basis, were obtained from the Federal Reserve System. The study covered the months of March 1920 to July 1941, October 1948 to June 1950, and November 1951 to March 1956, the gaps being periods that were disturbed by war. Department store inventory figures were deflated by a price index consisting of two components of the CPI: apparel prices with a weight of two and house furnishings prices with a weight of one. As the dependent variable, Robinson used the monthly change in deflated inventories as a percentage of the average of end-of-month inventory holdings over the previous year. A comparable percentage measure was used for the change in sales. Robinson tried regressions with various lagged values of sales changes and with lagged absolute values of sales changes (the latter in order to introduce different coefficients for sales increases and sales decreases). It is difficult to report his many results. We consider the regression:

$$\Delta I_n = \Delta S_n + a_1 \Delta S_{n-1} + \ldots + a_5 \Delta S_{n-5} + a_6(\Delta S_{n-6} + \Delta S_{n-7}$$

$$+ \Delta S_{n-8}) + b_1 |\Delta S_{n-1} + \Delta S_{n-2}| + b_2 |\Delta S_{n-3} + \Delta S_{n-4}| ,$$

where ΔI is change in inventories and ΔS is change in sales. For the period of March 1920 through July 1941 he obtained a coefficient of multiple correlation of .611, and for the combined period a coefficient of .587. The most important lag was one of two months (a coefficient, a_2, of around $+.27$), the coefficients of other lagged sales changes tapering off in both directions from a_2. The sum of the acceleration coefficients for sales changes lagged 0 to 5 months was approximately 1.6. This means, roughly, that if sales rise by 1 percent and stay at the higher level for six months, inventories during the final month will be 1.6 percent higher than before the sales increase. The interpretation is actually more complicated, however, because of the fact that the percentages have as their base the means of monthly values over the previous year.

Other explanatory variables were also tried along with the lagged sales changes. These included past inventory changes, the rate of interest on prime commercial paper, an index of wholesale prices, deflated sales lagged two months, deflated stocks lagged two months, and the average stocks-to-sales ratio lagged one, two, and three months. In general, none of these variables had coefficients which were statistically significant.

D. Conclusion

Of the work reviewed in this chapter, that which appears potentially most fruitful in explaining industry investment consists of the statistical regression studies. The main conclusion of relevance to be drawn from the cycle analysis of Abramovitz is that inventories lag systematically and significantly at the cycle turning points, and that this confirms the theoretical notion that unintended inventory changes are an important component of inventory investment.

The sort of general formulation of an inventory investment equation that one would want to specialize further for econometric research states that inventory investment during any period is a proportion of the difference between desired and actual inventories minus a proportion of the difference between actual sales and expected sales, with desired inventories in some way related to expected output and sales. Such a relation need not be linear, of course.

Of the time-series studies, the investigations by Clark, Lovell and Bakony are the only ones that get all these ingredients into the model. Clark's and Lovell's results are generally encouraging, and Bakony's are not. Technical criticisms can be advanced against all three of these studies, however, so that we cannot count much upon Clark's and Lovell's successes and Bakony's failure as an indication of what fate may be met by similar future investigations. Lovell's results seem unquestionably to be the most satisfactory, however.

In any case, the studies reported on here, viewed as experiments, yield some suggestive results:

1. Bakony attempted to make expected sales a function of past sales with geometrically diminishing coefficients. We cannot conclude from his results that there is any support for this particular sort of distributed lag relationship, although it might have worked better if other difficulties had been overcome. Lovell made expected sales a weighted mean of actual and lagged sales—and with greater apparent success. Modigliani and Sauerlander used survey data on business expectations, in a cross-section study, and though the assumptions of their model were in some ways as tenuous as they were ingenious, they got positive results; and this bolsters the hope that as expectational data are compiled over a longer period of time they can be fruitfully brought to use in time-series studies as well.

2. Klein introduced a price index in order to allow for the role of speculative inventory accumulation, and the index appeared important. It became somewhat less important when Klein turned to quarterly data, however, and much less important in Christ's modification of Klein's model. Since a set of estimates tend to all hang together or to hang separately, the other criticisms advanced against his model impugn somewhat the reliability even of this particular result. Lovell also found a role for price changes, but the coefficient was not clearly significant in all cases.

3. Strikingly enough, Clark is the only one working with aggregate data to have given attention to "the financial situation." He found some role for the amount of existing bank money, but it is hard to assess its importance as no confidence interval is reported for it, and a biased estimation procedure was used. Robinson in his study of department store inventories tried out the rate of interest on prime commercial paper and it did not prove to be a statistically significant variable.

4. A point of interest in Bassie's work is that he tried to remove from his sales variable those components which would not lead to the holding of inventories, and to retain only that component which requires inventories in the production process. While various rules of thumb must be used to do this, it is a procedure which commends itself to the attention of future researchers.

5. Darling experimented with a nonlinear relation between desired stocks and sales, and got encouraging results.

The various studies reported in this chapter are all primitive and pioneering, and for this reason we have, in summarizing, called attention to various novel features to be found among them. The area of econometric research on the determinants of inventory investment is comparatively new, and for more definitive results we shall have to wait for further research. Thus far, the results obtained do not upset any of the theoretical predilections which we have reviewed and advanced earlier in this paper.

V. CONCLUSIONS WITH RESPECT TO MONETARY POLICY

The "conclusions" which follow, unlike the preceding body of this book, are presented separately by each of the authors. This is not to proclaim an inability to formulate a joint expression of our views. It may be useful, however, to set forth, undiluted by the effects of mutual persuasion, the various nuances and points of emphasis with respect to monetary policy to which each of us may individually be inclined after our concerted consideration of theory and data relating to investment.

A. Conclusions with Respect to Monetary Policy: Eisner

Our analysis has done little to support the view that variation of parameters at the control of the monetary authority is likely to mitigate cyclical fluctuations in investment or to increase the aggregate amount of investment. This essentially nonpositive conclusion is, however, easier to support with available data than the corresponding negative view that monetary policy will not accomplish these objectives. We can say that neither theory nor data support the broad claims of monetary policy proponents. We are not in a position to say that these claims are all unambiguously refuted.

Theoretical considerations suggest that even abstracting from the effect of alterations of the rate of interest upon risk and uncertainty, in (prevalent) situations where lending and borrowing rates are different and both differ from internal rates of return, changes in the rate of interest may have little or no effect upon the rate of investment. What effect such changes may have would seem to relate more to the rate at which investment will react to other causal factors rather than to consequences of variations in the rate of interest itself.

Theoretical considerations also suggest that even where a well-defined role can be traced for effects of monetary policy these effects are likely to be small in magnitude. The major potential role of monetary policy would appear to be in influencing the rate of investment in long-lived goods. What are of consequence here are the terms of long-term commitment of capital and their epitomy, the long-term rate of interest. But for reasons well known in monetary theory, the long-term rate of interest is subject to only very modest influence by monetary policy. For the long-term rate must in large part reflect expectations of future short-term rates. While the monetary authority can surely have substantial effects upon short-term rates it can only affect long-term rates to the extent it can alter expectations of future short-term rates. Here a paradox quickly emerges. If the monetary authority is to lower rates in the face of inadequate (recessionary) investment demand and raise interest rates in the face of excess (inflationary) investment demand, it will generate the very attitudes and expectations which will defeat its own purpose. For the investing public can only conclude if the monetary authority "loosens" the monetary controls to combat a recession that it will similarly "tighten" money when in the next phase of the cycle the economy moves toward "inflation." Thus, in time of recession the public will retain its expectation that future short-term interest rates will be high and the current long-term rate will hence remain high.

The fluctuations in interest rates that the monetary authority may be able to bring about by the conscious application of counter-cyclical policy may aggravate the problem of maintaining high average rates of investment over the entire cycle and may thus serve to frustrate policies aimed at maximizing employment and the rate of economic growth. This would result from any tendency of fluctuations in the rate of interest to intensify the speculative motive for holding cash and avoiding long-term commitments. Fluctuation in short-term rates as a result of attempted counter-cyclical policy might tend to keep the long-term rate of interest higher over the cycle as a whole and thus, to the extent that the rate of interest plays any substantial part in investment, to lower the rate of investment.

Empirical evidence, while frequently confused in orientation, does little or nothing to shake these theoretical implications. Investment in plant and equipment is shaped by underlying economic factors of which changes in current and expected demand for product are major. Other variables such as, in particular, the rate of current or past profits, although believed significant by a number of investigators, can quite generally be shown to be only spuriously related to investment. Evidence of any role for monetary policy is restricted to a few tentative findings involving rates of interest and even in these cases the magnitude of the apparent effects taken in the context of historical variation in the rate of interest is small. It should of course be recognized that "the rate of interest" may be only a poor measure of the "tightness" of monetary control and that statistical investigations which have focussed on this may therefore miss much of the potential role of monetary policy. This reservation, along with the largely unanalyzed role of monetary policy in affecting the key factor of "expectations," accounts for my choice of a nonpositive rather than a strictly negative position with regard to the possible impact of monetary measures.

Any significant impact of monetary policy on the substantial fluctuations in investment in inventories must even more surely be restricted to its effect on expectations of future demand and prices. By its nature, investment in inventories, which is essentially short run, cannot be affected sufficiently by fluctuations in the rate of interest for there to be much damping effect upon the large independent fluctuations in expected price and demand. There is no empirical evidence that fluctuations in monetary policy have had any such damping effect.

We have, it is true, in large part considered only the direct effects of changes in the monetary parameters upon investment. One may wonder whether monetary policy may not, however, have powerful indirect effects upon investment. We have already alluded to possible effects via the role of "expectations." Certainly more must be known of the formation and role of the critical expectational factors in virtually all economic decisions. In effect, expectations appears in most models as an unknown stochastic variable — of huge variance. But lacking adequate information at this time, we see little reason to attribute to "expectations" the role of a deus ex machina which permits monetary policy to accomplish all of the things its supporters may claim but for which accomplishments no evidence has yet been found.

Similarly, we might argue that while we find little or no evidence of the role of monetary policy in affecting business investment directly, it may operate through its effects upon other components of the national product. Thus it is possible that easing of monetary controls might encourage installment buying by consumers and the increase in consumer demand may then stimulate investment. Perhaps more likely, easier money might encourage expenditures by state and local governments which are sensitive to the terms at which they borrow. Along the same lines, lower interest rates or easier mortgage terms might increase the demand for houses and the resultant increase in the market prices of houses might stimulate residential construction. Both of these increases in demand might then have accelerator effects upon the rate of investment.

Thus the failure to find a significant direct role for monetary policy among the determinants of business investment does not preclude the possibility that control of the monetary parameters may affect investment indirectly by influencing other components of demand. Our own investigations suggest that some at least of the critical elements frustrating the direct effects of monetary controls on investment may operate in similar frustrating fashion with regard to these other components. But since the determinants of these other components of aggregate demand have not been our present subject of inquiry we shall refrain from any judgments in this regard.

One note that does emerge is that while monetary policy is of doubtful efficacy as a countercyclical device, it may well have some effect upon the average rate of investment over the cycle and hence over the average rate of employment and the rate of economic growth. In particular, monetary institutions and policy can contribute a framework which will reduce risk and uncertainty and reduce imperfections in capital markets. In so doing they would contribute to that lowering of the cost of capital which was urged by Keynes as a much desired aid to the attainment of both high levels of employment and a more equitable distribution of income. And by thus encouraging investment in plant, equipment, inventories, and the human skills and knowledge produced by education and research, a long-run policy of promoting easy money and low rates of interest would contribute substantially to the economic growth which currently is an object of national concern.

B. Conclusions with Respect to Monetary Policy: Strotz

So ?   No one has ever computed a regression of investment on the parameters of action of the monetary authority. Any inference about the effects of monetary controls on the level of investment in the economy must be indirect. Moreover, such inference must proceed along both of two paths. We need to know, first, the extent to which business investment responds to changes in the sources and terms of capital funds; and we need to know, secondly, the sensitivity of investment to product demand, past, present, and expected, including thereby its changes over time. And if we knew the effects of the sources and terms on which capital funds can be obtained, we must then know further how the sources and terms can be affected by the dials the monetary authority can turn. Likewise, it is not enough to know the importance for investment of product demand and its changes; we must know also how product demand can be altered by central bank action.

Even with this another dimension would still have to be added in our analysis: that of time and expectations. Would a particular change in policy by the Federal Reserve System be thought by the private community to be prospectively of short or long duration? The effects of the policy change would depend upon these expectations.

With regard to the classification of the structural relations just formulated, our concern in this study has been not with the effects of monetary policy on the sources and terms of funds nor on final demand. Rather, we have restricted ourselves to the way in which these effects, whatever they may be, would in turn determine investment.

There is also an area of analysis that falls outside this scheme. Investment may be influenced by spontaneous changes in the structure of product demand, the structure of factor supply, technology, and fiscal policy. While noting in this study what we could about these influences, in short compass, we have regarded them as separable from the influences of monetary policy, at least for analytical convenience.

What does the research of economists on the effects of changes in product demand on plant and equipment investment add up too? Is the acceleration principle valid? Is it important? Do business profits explain investment better? Are they important? My view of the evidence presented in Chapter III, coupled with the persuasiveness to me of the theoretical arguments, is that the acceleration principle deserves the center of the stage. It is, of course, a complex and not the simple version of the accelerator that is most supported by the empirical evidence. The accelerator takes time to work out; it is probably quantitatively different in the downswing than in the upswing; and it is partially aborted in the presence of excess capacity. But the role of profit per se (in contrast to the marginal profitability of investment) succumbs as an explanation in the presence of a reasonably well formulated accelerator, and otherwise works mainly as a surrogate for a missing or inadequately formulated accelerator. The evidence is, of course, not thoroughly convincing; but that in support of the accelerator is preponderating enough to persuade me to the view expressed, in the context of our present knowledge.

There is even less doubt that sales changes are the principal cause of inventory investment, if only because of the unintended component in inventory change. The picture is muddied, however, both for plant and equipment and for inventory investment, mainly by the question of the relation of past sales changes to expected future sales. Here our knowledge is most primitive, and it is to be hoped that with the benefit of further survey studies of business expectations a useful theory of expectation formation may in the future be devised, or, alternatively, that regular survey reports of business expectations can be suitably used in time-series type econometric studies and prediction.

Anything that monetary policy can do to affect the level of final demand would appear to be important for investment behavior. This is to say that investment is in the main neither autonomous nor determined only by economic variables that isolate it from consumer expenditure, but that it is instead very much induced by changes in consumer outlays. We have not in this study considered how effective monetary policy can be in altering these outlays, but whatever effects it may have are much amplified (over time) by the accelerator.

What of the effect of changes in the sources and terms of credit on investment? Here less is known; I should say, practically nothing. Using the empirical studies, one cannot amass any impressive amount of evidence to support the motion that the terms of credit are particularly important. It might be that the absence of substantial evidence here is simply because the terms of credit offered by the monetary system are not important. Successful attempts to restrict the amount of money may or may not alter the rate of interest by what would be judged to be significant amounts, but in any case such changes in the quantity of money may fail to change investment by very much because of a high elasticity of supply of nonbank sources of idle funds. When banks are forced to contract during a time of rising product demand, there may simply ensue an increase in trade credit extensions and a redeployment of liquid balances, sufficient to maintain investment much at the level where it otherwise would have been. It seems plausible to me that liquid balances will not be so readily redeployed to finance long-term physical commitments as to finance short-term commitments. Trade credit extensions may more effectively serve to nullify the depressing effects of higher interest rates on inventory investment than on plant and equipment investment. Inventories by virtue of their minor status as one of many joint factors of production, may, however, be relatively less sensitive to interest rate changes than plant and equipment investment. Plant and equipment investment should therefore be more sensitive to interest rate changes both because interest changes exert greater leverage on the profitability of adding plant and equipment and because nonbanking sources of liquidity may be more costly to tap for long-term commitments. But the banking system can less easily alter the long-term rate of interest than the short-term rate unless its policy changes are viewed as secular rather than as countercyclical.

In contrast to all this, however, the absence of substantial evidence supporting the notion that the terms of credit are important may result simply from the fact that we do not look at the correct variables. On a couple of occasions in the present study we have pointed to the possibility that the interest rate may serve as a very poor index of credit availability. In a market in which the amount demanded is made to conform to an amount supplied mainly by consumer rationing, where the commodity is not homogeneous, and where various consumers may have to pay premiums, reported price may be of little use in estimating the demand curve. So may it be here. Changes in the terms of credit may be poorly represented by the tabulated changes in interest rates, and econometric studies may have missed the importance of a change in the availability of funds simply by using an unsatisfactory measure of it.

To gain a better understanding of the efficacy of monetary policy in controlling investment, these two areas should have high research priority: the process and causes of the extension of trade credit and other private sources of liquidity to potential investors, and the causes and effects of credit rationing.

It is a pity that in our empirical studies we are usually trying to select among alternative hypotheses to explain investment: e.g., should we throw out the accelerator? the role of profits? the rate of interest? price changes? etc.? As if one hypothesis were valid and the others false! The real problem is to assess the magnitudes of the effects of changes in sales, in profits, in interest rates, in prices, and thus to acquire genuine quantitative information. But our data and our statistical techniques will not bear the weight. We are reduced instead to classifying explanatory variables: important or unimportant. Perhaps with improvement in our raw materials, and advances in our statistical methods and our theories we can some day turn away from hypothesis testing and begin estimating in earnest. Though I think they are important I should at present dread to have to tell you what the true accelerator coefficients are!

INVESTMENT BIBLIOGRAPHY

Compiled by George Post

I. Coverage

Investment in fixed assets and inventories has been the subject of a great volume of recent writing by economists and business analysts. The selection and arrangement of a bibliography of these writings is necessarily quite arbitrary. The next few paragraphs will describe the objectives and methods that were employed in the selection of these titles. Since there is a wide range of subject matter, some aspects of the investment literature have been omitted. These omissions will be briefly catalogued. A statement of the techniques of compilation and a list of the sources consulted may also help the reader to assess the contents. All of the titles included have been classified into a few broad groups according to subject matter covered.[1] This classification scheme is briefly described below.

This bibliography was conceived as part of a study of the expenditures for durable producers' goods and inventories by private businesses. Expenditures for durable assets may involve new buildings, equipment, and such items as exploration for resources or the construction of roads and dams. Inventories include finished goods, goods in process, and stocks of raw materials. Interest centers on the nature and relative strength of the various influences which determine the timing and amount of these investment outlays.

There are two questions to be answered. How is an investment decision made? What factors determine how much will be spent? With this focus in mind, it was decided to omit references to articles and books which dealt with investment in connection with agriculture, private housing, and federal, state and local government projects. The topics of capital accumulation in underdeveloped countries and of international movements of capital were also judged to be outside the present context, even when private companies were involved. In addition, many statements about investment were excluded because they appeared in references which

---

[1]A small number of titles of very recent works, or works to which reference has been made in the final version of the text of this book but which had not been included in the bibliography, have been added without classification to Mr. Post's bibliography. These are identified by numbers followed by lower case letters (as 440a), and have been inserted in appropriate positions in the alphabetic listing. [R.E. and R.H.S.]

were primarily concerned with another topic. Not to have made
this last type of exclusion would have made the bibliography so
ponderous as to be useless. For example, most of the literature
on business cycles, monetary policy and aggregate income analysis
would have to be included if all casual and incidental references
to private investment were noted.

The titles cited were compiled from journals and periodicals.
The publications listed in Table II-1a were systematically examined
for the period 1945 to the most recent issue available in the summer of 1961. Some of these periodicals commenced publication
during the period. The index of each journal was examined and
articles whose titles appeared relevant were looked up and examined more closely. Many titles were also obtained by cross
reference while studying related articles. Whenever possible, the
cross references were checked. The titles of books were obtained
from the book review sections of the publications surveyed. Whenever possible, the books were consulted directly to check for
further bibliographical references and to make sure of the relevance of the contents. Book titles were also obtained from cross
references.

Because of prior decisions to exclude certain subject matter,
some journals were not examined. For example, The Journal of
Farm Economics and Land Economics were bypassed because of
the decision to exclude capital formation in agriculture.

The comment or annotation which appears with most references
is an attempt to add to and clarify the nature of the content of the
article beyond the information given by the title. A comment is
not given for some articles either because the title is considered
to indicate the content adequately or because the reference was
obtained from a cross reference and was not checked at first hand.

The bibliography contains about 666 separate listings. There
are approximately 400 authors included. In cases where two or
more authors are credited with a certain book or article the detailed reference appears under the name of the author whose name
appears first in the title. The names of the other authors appear
in alphabetical sequence with a cross reference to the bibliographical entry given under the name of the first author.

When the collection of references as described above had been
completed, an effort was made to check the listings with the authors
whose work is involved. The original reference and a description
of the purpose and content of the bibliography as well as a copy
of the classification scheme was mailed to each author. This material was sent to most of the writers covered—the remainder
being deceased or of unknown address. The authors were invited

to make any corrections required in the original listing, to provide annotations where these were not already included, and to supply any further references to their own work which were not originally included.

Replies were received from more than 200 of the authors to whom the original references were mailed. The majority of these replies were from authors with changes or additions to suggest. This assistance from the authors has contributed greatly to the bibliography and is gratefully acknowledged.

The classification of articles by content which is offered with the bibliography is even more arbitrary than the choice of articles to be included. No classification scheme could suit the needs of all users, so it is likely that the classifications applied will be helpful to the user only by generally narrowing the search for references on a particular topic.

There are four types of information given about each reference by the classification scheme. Under each of the four general headings, there are a number of sub-groups and each article was assigned to one or more of these sub-categories. Each of the four groups contains a sub-category entitled "not classified" which indicates merely that the references so designated do not fit into any of the sub-categories listed or that this particular type of information is not relevant for the reference in question. The skeleton classification is given in Section II of this introduction.

The first classification was according to the methodological approach of the reference and whether or not it contained empirical data. The second classification concerns the scope of the reference. That is, it indicates if the primary emphasis is on individual firms, on industries, on the entire economy, or on some large sector of it. The third classification is designed to reveal special topics of particular interest which recur frequently. The fourth classification indicates the nature of the investment dealt with in the reference.

With this four-way classification scheme, each reference has been assigned to at least four sub-groups. The four classification numbers are separated by dashes. When the reference is included in two sub-groups, these numbers are separated by commas.

TABLE II-1a

List of Journals and Periodicals Consulted

The American Economic Review
Proceedings of the Business and Economic Statistics Section of
  the American Statistical Association
Bulletin of the Oxford University Institute of Statistics
Canadian Journal of Economics and Political Science
Economia Internazionale*
Economica
Econometrica
The Economic Journal
The Economic Record
The Federal Reserve Bulletin
Harvard Business Review
International Economic Papers
International Economic Review
International Monetary Fund Staff Papers
Journal of the American Statistical Association
The Journal of Business
The Journal of Finance
The Journal of Industrial Economics
The Journal of Political Economy
The Journal of the Royal Statistical Society, Series A (General)
Kyklos*
Lloyd's Bank Review
Management Science
The Manchester School of Economic and Social Studies
Metroeconomica*
Oxford Economic Papers
The Quarterly Journal of Economics
The Review of Economics and Statistics (earlier called The Review
  of Economic Statistics)
The Review of Economic Studies
The Scottish Journal of Political Economy
The South African Journal of Economics
The Southern Economic Journal
The Survey of Current Business
The Three Banks Review
Weltwirtschaftliches Archiv*
The Yorkshire Bulletin of Economic and Social Research

---

*Only articles appearing in English are included.

II. Classification[1]

A. Type of Study
   1. Theoretical and non-empirical
   2. Empirical, qualitative: interview, questionnaire and case studies
   3. Empirical, quantitative, but not involving parameter estimation
   4. Empirical, quantitative, econometric

   0. Not classified

B. Scope

   1. Individual firm
   2. Industry
   3. Aggregate

   0. Not classified

C. Subject Matter

   1. Capacity-output relations, acceleration principle
   2. Role of internal funds, past and current profits, depreciation charges, liquidity
   3. Role of external funds; cost and availability
   4. Factor supply conditions, locational factors, and prices and supply of capital goods
   5. Technological change
   6. Replacement policy
   7. Decision-making
   8. Capital budgeting, anticipations and forecasting
   9. Tax policy

   0. Not classified

D. Type of Investment

   1. Plant and equipment
   2. Inventories
   3. Plant and equipment and inventories

   0. Not classified

---

[1]All titles are described by at least four digits; there are many multiple listings, particularly within the subject matter classification. Classifications are separated by dashes; multiple listings within a classification are separated by commas.

Example: 1-0-6,7-0 signifies:
Type of study	– theoretical and non-empirical
Scope	– not classified
Subject matter	– replacement policy, decision-making
Type of investment	– not classified

TITLES LISTED ALPHABETICALLY BY AUTHOR

1. Abramovitz, Moses, The Role of Inventories in Business
   Cycles. New York: National Bureau of Economic Research, Occasional Paper No. 26, 1948. Emphasizes the difference between
   the movements of different kinds of stocks. Uses a type of accelerator model to explain observed cycles. 3-1,2-2.

2. Abramovitz, Moses, Inventories and Business Cycles with
   Special Reference to Manufacturing Inventories. New York:
   National Bureau of Economic Research, Studies in Business
   Cycles, no. 4, Princeton University Press, 1950. A compre-
   hensive statistical investigation of the influence of inventory
   movements in business trends. 3-1,2-1-2.

3. Abramovitz, Moses, "Influence of Inventory Investment on
   Business Cycles" and "Further Comment," in Conference on
   Business Cycles. New York: National Bureau of Economic
   Research, 1951. 3-1,2-0-2.

4. Abramovitz, Moses, "Whitin's Inventory Theory," Kyklos, 7
   (1954), 287-289. A review of The Theory of Inventory Management by T. M. Whitin. Princeton: Princeton University Press,
   1953. 1-1-0-2.

5. Abramovitz, Moses, "Inventory Policy and Business Stability,"
   Universities—National Bureau Committee for Economic Research, Regularization of Business Investment, Princeton
   University Press, 1954, pp. 285-296. The stimuli to stabilize
   inventory levels may be greater than those to stabilize changes
   in fixed assets. 3-2-1-2.

   Abramson, A. G. et al. See Woodward, 661.

6. Alchian, A. A., Economic Replacement Policy, Santa Monica,
   California: The Rand Corporation, Special Report No. R-224,
   (1952). A rigorous but practical study of the theory of replacement expenditures with demonstration of the techniques of
   computation. 1-1-6-1.

7. Alchian, A. A., "Review of The Investment Decision by Meyer
   and Kuh." Journal of Business, 32 (July 1959), p. 287. Is
   extremely critical of the logical basis of the study and the
   statistical and economic inferences drawn therefrom. 1-0-1,2-1.

7a. Alchian, Armen, "Costs and Outputs," in The Allocation of
    Economic Resources: Essays in Honor of Bernard Francis
    Haley, edited by Moses Abramovitz et al., Stanford, California:
    Stanford University Press, 1959.

8. Alexander, S.S., "The Accelerator as a Generator of Steady Growth." Quarterly Journal of Economics, 63 (May 1949), pp. 174-197. Examines the requirements for stability in an accelerator model. 1-3-1-1.

9. Alexander, S.S., "Issues of Business Cycle Theory Raised by Mr. Hicks." American Economic Review, 41 (December 1951), pp. 861-878. Reviews the development of the multiplier-accelerator doctrine. Elaborates Hick's model by modifying the definition of the coefficients. Says that Hick's theory appears new because he has only erected a skeleton. 1-3-1-3.

10. Allen, R.G.D., Mathematical Economics. London: Macmillan, 1959. Chapter 3 deals with "The Acceleration Principle" and Chapters 7 and 8 with "Trade Cycle Theory." 1-3-1-3.

11. Allen, R.G.D., "The Structure of Macro-Economic Models," Economic Journal, (March 1960), pp. 38-56. Sets out some very simple models and uses them to demonstrate the importance of lags and interdependencies. 1-3-1-0.

12. American Management Association, Capital Equipment Replacement. Special Report No. 1, American Management Association, New York, 1954. 0-1,2-6-1.

13. Anderson, Clay J., "Trends in the Supply of Equity Capital." Harvard Business Review, 28 (September-October 1950), pp. 79-90. "Analyzes trends in equity and debt sources of funds. Concludes equity capital problem reflects mainly a shift in distribution, such as a reduced flow from new stock issues and an increase in retained earnings, rather than a general shortage of capital funds." 3-1-2,3-3.

14. Anderson, Oskar, Jr., "The Business Test of the IFO-Institute for Economic Research, Munich, and its Theoretical Model." Review of the International Statistical Institute, 20 (1952), pp. 1-17. 3-2-8-3.

15. Anderson, Oskar, Jr., Rainald K. Bauer, and Eberhard Fels, "On the Accuracy of Short-Term Entrepreneurial Expectations." Proceedings of the Business and Economic Statistics Section of the American Statistical Association, 1955, pp. 124-147. A report on the analysis of expectations data collected by the IFO-Institute for Economic Research in Munich. Contains charts and tables. 3-2-8-3.

16. Anderson, Oskar, Jr., Rainald K. Bauer, H. Fuhrer, and J.P. Petersen, "On Short-Term Entrepreneurial Reaction Patterns." Weltwirtschaftliches Archiv, 81. (February 1958), pp. 243-264.

A report on deviations between anticipated and actual values of variables for the textile industry, 1950-53. There is some attempt to spell out the reappraisal and adjustment carried out by businessmen. A study from the Munich IFO-Institute for Economic Research. 3-2-8-3.

17. Anderson, Paul S., "Financing of Large Corporations in 1954." Federal Reserve Bulletin, 41 (June 1955), pp. 623-630. Sources and uses of investment expenditures for the sample of companies surveyed by the Research and Statistics Division. 3-2-2,3-3.

18. Andrews, P. W. S., "Summary of Replies to Questions on Effects of Interest Rates." Oxford Economic Papers, No. 1 (1938). Finds that short-term rates of interest do not directly affect investment either in stocks or in fixed capital; long-term rates do not affect investment directly, but may have some indirect effects. 3-1-2,3-3.

19. Andrews, P. W. S., "A Further Inquiry into the Effects of Rates of Interest." Oxford Economic Papers, 3 (February 1940), pp. 32-73. 3-1-3-3.

20. Andrews, P. W. S., and Elizabeth Brunner, Capital Development in Steel. A study of the United Steel Companies, Limited. Oxford: Basil Blackwell, 1951. A case study of the factors influencing investment in this single firm. Concludes that interest rates do not affect the decision to make a particular capital expenditure, but that they did affect cash resources and so the ability to invest in total earnings; criteria are found to be more important in "replacement" than in "policy" decisions; the level of demand appears to be the most important single influence. 1,2-1-2,3,7-1.

Andrews, P. W. S., and J. E. Meade. See Meade, 440.

Andrews, P. W. S., and T. Wilson. See Wilson, 653.

21. Angell, J. W., Investment and Business Cycles. New York, (1941). A study, mainly non-quantitative, of the role of expectations in investment decisions, and of the two-way interactions among expectations, investment decisions and business cycles. 1-1-7,8-1.

22. Angell, J. W., "Uncertainty, Likelihoods and Investment Decisions." Quarterly Journal of Economics, 75 (February 1960), pp. 1-28. Offers generalizations about the subjective process by which individuals and businessmen make investment decisions under uncertainty. Adopts an hypothesis similar to Shackle's

where the investor focuses his attention on some "most likely" outcome but disagrees with some of Shackle's postulates and with a part of his central conclusions. 1-1-7-0.

23. Anthony, Robert N., "Re: Depreciation in Investment Decisions." Harvard Business Review, 33 (January–February 1955), pp. 75-76. An elaboration of the Eisner article in the same issue. 1-1-2-1.

24. Arndt, H. W., "Mr. Hick's Trade Cycle Theory." Canadian Journal of Economics and Political Science, 17 (August 1951), pp. 394-406. A favorable expository review. 1-3-1-3.

25. Arrow, Kenneth J., "Alternative Approaches to the Theory of Choice in Risk-Taking Situations." Econometrica, 19 (October 1951), pp. 404-437. An extensive discussion of various theories of choice under uncertainty with reference to other works. 1-1-7-0.

26. Arrow, Kenneth J., Theodore Harris, and Jacob Marschak, "Optimal Inventory Policy." Econometrica, 19 (July 1951), pp. 250-271. Sets up models for known and uncertain demand; derives best maximum stock and re-order points as a function of the demand distribution and the costs of ordering and being sold out. Has several cross references with other works. 1-1-7-2.

27. Arrow, Kenneth J., Samuel Karlin, and Herbert Scarf, Studies in the Mathematical Theory of Inventory and Production. Stanford, California: Stanford University Press, 1958. Derives optimal inventory policy under a wide variety of assumptions about demand (known, varying, and random), delivery lags, and costs of ordering and being sold out; includes brief history of inventory theory and extensive bibliography. 1-1-7-0.

28. Bailey, Martin J. "Formal Criteria for Investment Decisions." Journal of Political Economy, 67 (October 1959), pp. 476-488. A general analysis of investments which yield returns for more than two periods and of methods of ranking these investments using different criteria. He considers especially the implications of the rate of return and the present value criteria. 1-1-7-1.

29. Bain, Joe S., "The Relation of the Economic Life of Equipment to Reinvestment Cycles." Review of Economic Statistics, 21 (May 1939), pp. 79-88. Reinvestment cycles need to take account of the fact that service life of equipment is variable and may be influenced by cyclical factors. The "pure echo" effect may be very weak. 1-3-6-1.

29a. Bakony, L.I., A Quarterly Econometric Model of the Canadian Economy. Unpublished doctoral dissertation, University of Washington, 1959.

Ball, R.J. and L.R. Klein. See Klein, 358.

30. Baldwin, R.H., "How to Assess Investment Proposals." Harvard Business Review, 37 (May–June 1959), pp. 98-104. Offers criticism of techniques for calculating present value of an investment project. Specifically attacks assumption that earnings will be reinvested at same rate as original project. 1-1-2-1.

31. Balogh, T., "Investment in Britain and the United States." Bulletin of the Oxford University Institute of Statistics, 14 (June 1952), pp. 183-188. 3-3-0-3.

32. Barber, Clarence L., Inventories and the Business Cycle with Special Reference to Canada. Toronto: University of Toronto Press, 1958. Contains considerable data on industry and aggregate inventory fluctuations in Canada, 1918-50. 3-2,3-1-2.

33. Barber, Clarence L., "Inventory Fluctuations in Canada, 1918-1950." Canadian Journal of Economics and Political Science, 18 (August 1952), pp. 372-378. Concludes that changes in the value of inventories over cycles have reinforced those cycles and are as important as changes in inventory volume. Further inventory changes in Canada have been irregular and unpredictable, sometimes counteracting and sometime aggravating movements in other series. 3-2,3-1-2.

33a. Barger, H., Outlay and Income in the United States, 1921-38. New York: National Bureau of Economic Research, 1942.

34. Barger, Harold, and L.R. Klein, "A Quarterly Model for the U.S. Economy." Journal of the American Statistical Association, 49 (September 1954), pp. 41-437. 4-3-2-0.

35. Barna, T., "The Replacement Cost of Fixed Assets in British Manufacturing Industry in 1955." Journal of the Royal Statistical Society, Series A, 120 (January 1957), pp. 1-36. Contains discussion about the basis of revaluation, relation of value added to assets and the current rate of investment. Data based mainly on fire insurance declarations. 4-2,3-3-1.

36. Barna, T., "Investment in Industry--Has Britain Lagged?" The Banker, (April 1957), p. 219. A comparison of capital formation, stock of capital, capital-output ratios in U.K., U.S., and Germany over about 30 years. 3-3-1-1.

37. Barna, T., "Industrial Investment in Britain and Germany." The Banker (January 1958), pp. 12-23. A comparison of the pattern of investment, 1948-56, and its relationship to the pattern of exports. 3-2,3-0-1.

38. Barna, T., "On Measuring Capital," in Lutz and Hague (eds.) The Theory of Capital, London: Macmillan, 1961. A paper read at the Corfu Conference. Contains data on the value of manufacturing assets and on the length of life of assets, based on a questionnaire survey. 3-2,3-1-1.

39. Barna, T., Investment and Growth Policies of British Industrial Firms, National Institute of Economic and Social Research, London, Occasional Paper No. 20, 1962. A study of a sample of firms by interview and by statistical analysis of accounts. 2,3-1,2-2,3,7,8-3.

40. Barritt, D. P., "Accelerated Depreciation Allowances and Industrial Investment." Journal of Industrial Economics, 8 (October 1959), pp. 80-98. A general review of experiments in the use of accelerated depreciation to stimulate investment. Makes general comments about the differential impact and probable influence of such policies. 3-2-2,6-1.

40a. Bassie, V. Lewis, Economic Forecasting. New York: McGraw-Hill, 1958.

41. Bator, Francis M., "Consumption and Investment Propensities: Comment." American Economic Review, 43 (March 1953), pp. 139-145. A comment on the article by Ta Chung Liu and Ching-Gwan Chang, American Economic Review (September 1950). 4-3-1-1.

Bauer, Reginald K., et al. See Anderson, 15, 16.

42. Baumol, W. J., "Income Effect, Substitution Effect, Ricardo Effect," Economica, 17 (February 1950), pp. 69-80. 1-3-0-0.

43. Baumol, W. J., "Acceleration Without Magnification." American Economic Review, 46 (June 1956), pp. 409-412. Argues that in fact the change in investment resulting from a change in output need not be larger in magnitude than the change in output. 1-3-1-1.

44. Baumol, W. J., Business Behavior Value and Growth. New York: Macmillan, 1959. Discusses the long-run investment decisions between firms and their effect on the rate of growth of the economy. 1-3-0-1.

45. Beckmann, M. and R. Muth, "An Inventory Policy for a Case of Lagged Delivery." Management Science, 2 (January 1956), pp. 145-155. Studies ordering policy when there is a long delivery period and uncertainty of demand. 1-1-7-2.

Beekler, Bernard, and Lawrence Bridge. See Bridge, 75.

46. Belfer, Nathan, "Implications of Capital-Saving Inventions." Social Research, 16 (September 1949), pp. 353-365. Outlines the investment decreasing aspects of innovation and makes a general statement of the stagnation thesis. With maturity and technical development greater and greater expansions of consumer buying are required to maintain a steady level of output in the capital goods sector. 1-0-5-1.

47. Bennion, Edward G., "The Multiplier, The Acceleration Principle and Fluctuating Autonomous Investment." Review of Economics and Statistics, 27 (May 1945), pp. 85-92. An elaboration and qualification of Samuelson's model with some discussion of the assumptions. 1-3-1-1.

48. Bennion, Edward G., "Capital Budgeting and Game Theory." Harvard Business Review, 34 (November-December 1956), pp. 115-123. A discussion of the possibilities of improving capital budgeting and investment evaluation by using game theory techniques. 1-1-8-3.

Berman, Edward B., and Robert N. Grosse. See Grosse, 270.

49. Bickerdike, C. F., "A Non-Monetary Cause of Fluctuations in Employment." Economic Journal, 23 (September 1914), pp. 357-370. An early discussion of an accelerator relation. 1-3-1-1.

50. Bierman, H., Jr., and S. Smidt, The Capital Budgeting Decision. New York and London: Macmillan, 1960. Sets out for businessmen various criteria for assessing the profitability of investment projects. States a preference for the present value method of calculation. Discusses replacement and alternative methods of financing capital projects. 1-1-3,7-1.

51. Bilimovich, Alexander D., "Investment and Employers' Reactions." Economia Internazionale, 4 (November 1951), pp. 847-866. A simplified model of the formation of entrepreneurs' expectations from observed profit data incorporating the concept of a normal level of profit. Investment is assumed to be a function of past investment and the deviation of actual from normal profit. 1-1-2,1-1.

52. Black, J., "Investment Allowances, Initial Allowances and Cheap Loans as Means of Encouraging Investment." Review of Economic Studies, 27 (October 1959), pp. 44-49. This article compares the relative effectiveness of these three techniques under various assumptions about tax rates, interest rates and length of life of capital goods. 1-1,2-2,3,9-1.

53. Blyth, Conrad A., "The United States Cycle in Private Fixed Investment, 1946-1950." Review of Economics and Statistics, 38 (February 1956), pp. 41-49. Emphasizes the importance of secular expansion and investment deferred on account of the war. Discounts the importance of technological development. 3-3-1,5-3.

54. Boiteux, M., "The Role of Amortization in Investment Programming." International Economic Papers, 10 (1960), pp. 147-162. Points out how the traditional procedures of calculating amortization periods can be made equivalent to discounting procedures. In cases of imperfect foresight and uncertainty, amortization procedures become important because they allow for the presence of ignorance about the future. 1-1-2-1.

55. Boot, J. C. G., and G. M. De Wit, "Investment Demand: An Empirical Contribution to the Aggregation Problem." International Economic Review, 1 (January 1960), pp. 3-30. Studies the results of aggregation on the coefficient of an empirical relation calculated by Grundfeld from time series for several large U.S. Corporations. 4-3-0-0.

56. Borenstein, I., Capital and Output Trends in Mining Industries, 1870-1948. National Bureau of Economic Research, Occasional Paper, No. 45, 1954. Analyzes the past trends in investment and the relationship between investment and output. 3-2-9-1.

Borenstein, I., et al. See Creamer, 137.

57. Boschan, Paul, "Productive Capacity, Industrial Production and Steel Requirements." Long Range Economic Projection, Studies in Income and Wealth, Vol. 16, National Bureau of Economic Research and Princeton University Press, 1954, pp. 233-272. Use of the short-term and long-term (capacity determined) component of the production index applied to the analysis of steel demand. A model based on the data for 1919-40 is used to predict for 1950. 4-2-1-1.

58. Boulding, K. E., "The Theory of a Single Investment." Quarterly Journal of Economics, 49 (May 1935), pp. 475-494. Develops the concept of an internal rate of return. 1-1-2-3.

59. Boulding, K.E., "Time and Investment." Economica, N.S. 10, (May 1936), pp. 196-220. Develops a formula for calculating the internal rate of return. 1-1-0-3.

60. Boulding, K.E., "Time and Investment: A Reply." Economica, (November 1936), pp. 436-440. A reply to C.A. Wright, clarifying use of compound interest. 1-1-0-3.

61. Boulding, K.E., "Professor Knight's Capital Theory: A Note in Reply." Quarterly Journal of Economics (May 1936), pp.524-531. Distinguishes between physical and valuational processes in investment. 1-1-0-1.

62. Boulding, K.E., "A note on the Theory of Investment of the Firm" Kyklos, 6 (1954), p. 77. A review of the F. and V. Lutz book, in which he criticizes the marginal approach of investment analysis. 1-0-3-1.

63. Bowman, M.J. (ed.), Expectations, Uncertainty and Business Behaviour. New York, 1958. The papers delivered at a conference sponsored by the Social Science Research Council held at Carnegie Institute of Technology, October, 1955. 0-0-7,8-3.

64. Bowman, Raymond T., and Almarin Phillips, "Conceptual and Statistical Problems in Estimating Capital Coefficients for Four Metal Fabricating Industries." National Bureau of Economic Research, Studies in Income and Wealth, Vol. 19, Princeton University Press, 1957. pp. 347-74. 4-2-0-1.

65. Bowman, Raymond T. and Almarin Phillips, "The Capacity Concept and Induced Investment." Canadian Journal of Economics and Political Science, 21 (May 1955), pp. 190-203. Concerned with a dynamic input-output model which contains capital stocks. These stocks vary with output when the industry is producing at "capacity." The discussion concerns the definition and question of independence of capacity. Under the best conditions coefficients and capacity ranges derived empirically would be extremely suspect. 1-2-1-1.

66. Bratt, Elmer C., "Business-Cycle Forecasting," Journal of Business 21 (January 1948), pp. 1-11. Studies methods for making short-term projection of the various aggregates contained in GNP. 1-3-8-3.

67. Bratt, Elmer C., "Data Needed to Forecast the Business Cycle." Journal of Business, 21 (July 1948), pp. 168-179. Suggestions about requirements of detail for forecasts to be reliable. 1-3-8-3.

68. Bratt, Elmer C., "Short and Long-Term Capital Requirements." Journal of Finance, 7 (May 1952), pp. 128-137. Reviews alternative methods for forecasting capital requirements
and the factors which are likely to be important in determining
future capital requirements. 1-1-3,8-0.

69. Brems, Hans, "How Induced is Induced Investment?" Review
of Economics and Statistics, 37 (August 1955), pp. 267-277.
A theoretical macroeconomic model. Capital depends on output
and output on expected sales. Points out the importance of
the length of the planning and expectations horizon for stability
of the model. 1-3-1,8-1.

70. Brems, Hans, "Response Lags and Non-price Competition
with Special Reference to the Automobile Industry." Expectations, Uncertainty and Business Behaviour, M.J. Bowman
(ed.) 1958, pp. 134-43. Develops a dynamic profit maximizing
model to explain non-price competition and its advantages for
oligopolists. Lists numerous examples. 2-2-0-0.

71. Brems, Hans, "Stability and Growth." Economic Journal, 65
(December 1955), pp. 615-625. A non-mathematical version
of the main idea in "How Induced is Induced Investment?"
from the Review of Economics and Statistics, 1955. 1-3-1,8-1.

72. Brennan, M.J., "A Model of Seasonal Inventories." Econometrica, 27 (April 1959), pp. 228-244. Presents a model to
bridge the gap between optimal inventory levels for individual
firms and the determination of aggregate industry inventory
levels. An iterative dynamic solution is applied to predict
inventory levels for butter, cheese and shell eggs. 4-2-0-2.

73. Brennan, M.J., "The Supply of Storage." American Economic
Review, 47 (March 1958), pp. 50-72. A general analysis of
inventory holdings as determined by the marginal cost of
storage. Takes into account risk premiums as a function of
price spreads. Draws empirical evidence from data about
stocks of agricultural commodities. 1-1-2-2.

74. Bridge, Lawrence, "Capital Requirements of New Trade
Firms." Survey of Current Business, 28 (December 1948),
pp. 18-24. Report on a survey of more than 1000 new firms
(retail and wholesale) that arose between 1945 and 1948.
3-3-0-1.

75. Bridge, Lawrence, and Bernard Beekler, "Capital Investment
Programs and Sales Expectations in 1950." Survey of Current
Business, 30 (April 1950), pp. 6-10. 3-3-8-1.

76. Bridge, Lawrence, and Lois E. Holmes, "Capital Requirements of New Manufacturing Firms." Survey of Current Business, 30 (April 1950), pp. 11-18. Based on information from 1100 new firms that started up between 1946 and 1948. Tells sources and uses with some industrial detail. 3-3-0-1.

77. Bridge, Lawrence, and Lois E. Holmes, "Sales and Investment Trends of New Manufacturing Firms." Survey of Current Business, 30, (June 1950), pp. 19-23. 3-3-0-1.

78. Bridge, Lawrence, "Business Investment and Sales Expectations in 1951." Survey of Current Business, 31 (April 1951), pp. 11-15. 3-3-8-1.

79. Bridge, Lawrence, "Capital Expenditure by Manufacturing Industries in the Postwar Period." Survey of Current Business, 31 (December 1951), pp. 15-22. Also contains information for 1939. 3-3-0-1.

80. Bridge, Lawrence, "Business Investment and Sales in 1952." Survey of Current Business, 32 (April 1952), pp. 13-18. 3-3-8-1.

81. Bridge, Lawrence, and V. Natrella, "Capital Expenditures by Non-manufacturing Industries." Survey of Current Business, 32 (August 1952), pp. 19-22. 3-2-0-1.

82. Bridge, Lawrence, "The Financing of Investment by New Firms." National Bureau of Economic Research, Conference on Research in Business: Finance, 1952, p. 65. A survey of studies of how new firms raise the money required to get started. 3-3-0-1.

83. Bridge, Lawrence and V. Natrella, "Investment Programs and Sales Expectations in 1953." Survey of Current Business, 33 (April 1953), pp. 7-11. 3-3-8-1.

83a. Bridge, Lawrence and Clement Winston, "Inventory Investment in Trade," Inventory Fluctuations and Economic Stabilization, Part I, Joint Economic Committee, 87th Congress, 1st Session, pp. 165-180.

84. Brockie, M.D., and A.L. Grey, "The Marginal Efficiency of Capital and Investment Programming." Economic Journal, 66 (December 1956), pp. 662-675. A discussion of factors influencing the investment decision. States that other factors overshadow the rate of interest. 2-1-3-1.

85. Brockie, M.D., and A.L. Grey, "The Rate of Interest, Marginal Efficiency of Capital and Investment Programming—A Rejoinder." Economic Journal, 69 (June 1959), pp. 333-43. A

reply to White's criticism in Economic Journal, March 1958. 2-1-2-1.

Broida, Sylvia P., and Walter W. Jacobs. See Jacobs, 331.

Bronfenbrenner, J., and Irwin Friend. See Friend, 237,238.

86. Broster, E.J., "An Economic Analysis of Fixed Investment." Economic Journal, 68 (December 1958), pp. 768-79. Classifies types of investment: to expand, to cut costs; to develop, renew or reorganize; and by effects on firm's cost structure and pricing policy. 1-1-1,5-1.

87. Brown, E. Cary, "Business Income Taxation and Investment Incentives." Income, Employment and Public Policy: Essays in Honour of Alvin H. Hansen. New York: W.W. Norton, 1948, pp. 300-316. 1-1-9-1.

88. Brown, E. Cary, "Purposes and Functions of Depreciation Under the Income Tax," in Depreciation and Taxes, a Symposium of the Tax Institute, 1959, pp. 5-16. A review, both aggregative and for the individual firm, of depreciation manipulation on investment. 1-1-9-1.

89. Brown, Murray, "Profit, Output and Liquidity in the Theory of Fixed Investment." International Economic Review, 2 (January 1961), pp. 110-121. Derives a number of simple hypotheses from the theory of investment and considers the controversy between those who support profits and those who emphasize output as the main determinant of investment. 1-1-1,2-1.

90. Brown, Murray and H. Roseman, "A Cross-Section Analysis of Manufacturing Investment During 1951-1955." Proceedings of The Business and Economic Statistics Section of the American Statistical Association (1957), pp. 344-51. Primarily an application of the Meyer and Kuh models for the later period but with slightly different variables. Gets different results. 4-1-1,2-1.

91. Brown, Weir M., "Measuring Physical Inventories." Journal of the American Statistical Association, 43 (September 1948), pp. 377-390. 1-3-0-2.

92. Brown, William H., "Innovation in the Machine Tool Industry." Quarterly Journal of Economics, 71 (August 1957), pp. 406-425. A discussion of calculated obsolescence and the process of development to maintain a relatively steady level of machine tool sales. 2-2-5,6-1.

93. Brownlie, A.D., "Private Investment in New Zealand, 1950-56."
Economic Record, 35 (April 1959), pp. 67-74. A review of
Klein's derivation of investment demand by the firm. An
empirical estimation of an aggregate private investment function for New Zealand. 4-3-2-1.

94. Brozen, Yale, "Adapting to Technological Change." Journal
of Business, 24 (April 1951), pp. 114-26. A discussion of the
impact of new developments and obsolescence on new investment. 1-1-5-1.

95. Brozen, Yale, "Determinants of the Direction of Technological
Change." American Economic Review, 43, Proc. (May 1953),
pp. 288-302. Argues that much technological change is en-
dogenously determined except in the very short run. 1-1-5-1.

96. Brozen, Yale, "Invention, Innovation and Imitation." American
Economic Review, 41 Proc. (May 1951), pp. 239-257. Discusses optimum rates of progress and divergence of actual
rates from these optima on account of the existence or absence
of competitive conditions. 1-1-5-1.

97. Brozen, Yale, "The Role of Technological Change in Regu-
larizing Private Investment," Universities — National Bureau
Committee for Economic Research, Regularization of Business
Investment, Princeton University Press, 1954, pp. 299-318.
Indicates how technological changes might stabilize or de-
stabilize investment. 1-1-5-1.

Brunner, Elizabeth, and P.W.S. Andrews. See Andrews, 20.

98. Buckley, Kenneth, "Capital Formation in Canada." National
Bureau of Economic Research, Studies in Income and Wealth,
Vol. 19, Princeton University Press, 1957, pp. 91-128. This
article is primarily an historical study of estimates of capital
formation. 3-3-0-1.

99. Burns, A.F., "Hicks and the Real Cycle," Journal of Political
Economy, 60 (February 1952), pp. 1-24. A review of the Trade
Cycle in which he sharply criticizes the usefulness of accelerator models and puts forward an alternative explanation
of the investment cycle. 1-0-1-3.

100. Bushaw, D.W., and Robert Clower, Introduction to Mathematical Economics. Homewood, Illinois: R.D. Irwin, Inc.,
1957. Chapter 6 contains a theoretical analysis of micro-
dynamic aspects of investments in stock-flow models of
business behavior. 1-1-7-3.

101. Butler, William F., "Capacity Utilization and the Rate of
Profitability in Manufacturing." American Economic Review,

48 Proc. (May 1958), pp. 239-248. A study of the capacity-output relation for manufacturing industries and an attempt to make a long-term projection of investment expenditures under various assumptions. Concludes that the 1958 slump in investment is unlikely to last. 1-3-1-1.

102. Butler, William F., and Robert P. Ulin, "Business Needs for Venture Capital." Harvard Business Review, 28 (July-August 1950), pp. 52-66. The need for improved methods of channeling savings into business is urgent. If this method is not found, the public may well conclude that investment in industry cannot remain entirely a matter of private initiative. 1-3-0-1.

103. Butlin, N.G., "Some Structural Features of Australian Capital Formation, 1861-1938/39." Economic Record, 35 (December 1959), pp. 389-415. Develops historical series for capital formation in Australia. Gives a breakdown between public and private and between broad industrial classes. 3-3-0-3.

Butters, J. Keith, and Robert Schlaifer. See Schlaifer, 544.

104. Caff, J.T., "A Generalization of the Multiplier Accelerator Model." Economic Journal, 71 (March 1961), pp. 36-52. Extends the Samuelson-Hicks model to any number of sectors and any number of time lags, and considers dropping the assumption of linear relationships. 1-3-0-1.

105. Carter, Anne P., "Capital Coefficients as Economic Parameters: The Problem of Instability." National Bureau of Economic Research, Studies in Income and Wealth, Vol. 19, Princeton University Press, 1957, pp. 287-310. Attributes differences in capital/output ratios for the expansions of capacity among plants in a given industry to grade of product, scale of plant and the specific technology adopted. These factors are discussed and illustrated with information from the chemical industry. 1,3-1,2,3-1-1.

106. Carter, Anne P., "Investment, Capacity Utilization and Changes in Input Structures in the Tin Can Industry." Review of Economics and Statistics, 42 (August 1960), pp. 283-291. An attempt to study empirically how input coefficients change as capital expenditures which embody newer technologies are undertaken. Uses capital outlays between 1951 and 1953 to explain changes in input and coefficients for the tin can and tinware industry. 5-1,2-1,5-1.

107. Carter, C.F., G.P. Meredith, and G.L.S. Shackle, Uncertainty and Business Decisions. Liverpool: The University Press of Liverpool, 1954. 1-1-7-0.

108. Carter, C.F., and Williams, B.R., Investment in Innovation. New York: Oxford University Press, 1958. Relates to the making of capital investment decisions involving substantial innovations. Based on case studies. 2-1-5,7-1.

109. Carver, T.N., "A Suggestion for a Theory of Industrial Depressions." Quarterly Journal of Economics, 17 (May 1903), pp. 497-500. The first formulated theory of the business cycle based on the accelerator. 1-3-1-1.

110. Chamber of Commerce of the United States, "Management Action to Promote Business Stability." A report of the Committee on Economic Policy, Washington, 1961. The report recommends countercyclical planning of pricing, promotion, innovation and research. Short-run and speculative changes in capital outlays are to be discouraged. The government should improve and increase the statistics and economic information as well as maintain appropriate monetary and fiscal policies. 1-1,3-0-3.

111. Chambers, S.P., "Taxation and the Supply of Capital for Industry." Lloyds Bank Review (January 1949), pp. 1-20. A criticism of the adverse effects of the postwar tax structure in the light of the drastic inflation that occurred. 1-3-9-0.

112. Champernowne, D.G., "Capital Accumulation and the Maintenance of Full Employment." Economic Journal, 68 (June 1955), pp. 211-244. A rigorous model of capital accumulation and the changes which become necessary when labour is fully employed in order not to have a fluctuation of employment. 1-3-0-0.

Chang, Ching-Gwan, and Ta-Chung Liu. See Liu, 391.

113. Chazeau, Melvin G. de, "Regularization of Fixed Capital Investment by the Individual Firm," Universities — National Bureau Committee for Economic Research, Regularization of Business Investment, Princeton University Press, 1954, pp. 75-109. Regularization of private investment outlays is possible in the aggregate because of timing variations in cyclical fluctuations among industries. It depends on the development of government policies that lengthen perspective of managerial decisions. 2-1-7-1.

114. Chazeau, Melvin G. de, "Can We Avoid Depression in a Dynamic Society?" Harvard Business Review, 32 (July-August 1954), pp. 37-44. Noncyclical (not procyclical and not counter-cyclical) capital outlays geared to growth potentials of the firm are the hope (and the prospect) for a strong private

enterprise in a society committed to maintaining high productive employment. 1-1-7-1.

115. Chenery, Hollis B., "Overcapacity and the Acceleration Principle." Econometrica, 20 (January 1952), pp. 1-28. An attempt to demonstrate empirically the importance of capacity utilization as a variable in the accelerator relation. 4-2-1-1.

116. Chenery, Hollis B., "The Application of Investment Criteria." Quarterly Journal of Economics, 67 (February 1953), pp.76-96. A general discussion of criteria for choosing between projects with special reference to underdeveloped countries. Emphasizes duration of turnover, balance of payments and social marginal product effect. 1-3-8-1.

117. Christ, Carl F., "A Test of an Econometric Model for the United States, 1921-1947," Universities — National Bureau Committee for Economic Research, Conference on Business Cycles, Princeton University Press, 1951, pp. 35-107. Presents an aggregate model for the U.S. with several alternative equations for plant and equipment investment, several for inventory investment, and several for residential construction. 4-3-0-3.

118. Christ, Carl F., "Aggregate Econometric Models." American Economic Review, 46 (June 1956), pp. 385-408. A review of the Klein-Goldberger study. 1-3-0-3.

119. Christ, Carl F., "On Econometric Models of the U.S. Economy." International Association for Research in Income and Wealth, Income and Wealth Series 6. London: Bowes and Bowes, 1957, pp. 1-23. Reviews the theoretical grounds of Tinbergen-type models and their dynamic properties. Reviews nine studies which applied models of this sort to the U.S.: Tinbergen, Clark, Klein, Christ, Barger, Goldberger, and Valavanis-Vail are the authors reviewed. 1-3-0-3.

120. Churchill, Betty C., "Age and Life Expectancy of Business Firms." Survey of Current Business, 35 (December 1955) pp. 15-19. Based on observations over the period 1944-54. Three-fifths of present firms have been acquired by their present owners since World War II. Half of the firms started in this period were sold or liquidated within two years. 3-3-0-0.

121. Churchill, Betty C., "Survival Patterns of the Post-war Business Population." Survey of Current Business, 32 (December 1952), pp. 12-19. Gives the age distribution of all existing corporations. 3-3-0-0.

Ciaccio, Jack N., and Loughlin F. McHugh. See McHugh, 437.

122. Clark, Clifford D., "Economic Appraisal of Depreciation Policy." Journal of Business, 29 (January 1956), pp. 28-40.
Discusses various types of depreciation procedures and
outlines the influence of accelerated depreciation compared
to alternative schemes. Has considerable reference to the
accelerated depreciation controversy. 1-1-6,9-1.

122a. Clark, Colin, "A System of Equations Explaining the United
States Trade Cycle, 1921 to 1941." Econometrica, 17, No. 2
(April 1949).

123. Clark, J.M., "Business Acceleration and the Law of Demand."
Journal of Political Economy, 25 (March 1917), pp. 217-235.
Reprinted (with "Additional Note") in American Economic
Association's Readings in Business Cycle Theory, Blakiston
(Irwin), 1944, pp. 235-260. The classic original of the ac-
celerator literature. 1-3-1-1.

124. Clark, J.M., "The Effects of Public Spending on Capital
Formation." Capital Formation and Its Elements, National
Industrial Conference Board, 1939, pp. 54-72. An analysis
of the role of government in an economy that must grow to
maintain full employment. 1-3-9-1.

125. Clark, Paul G., "The Telephone Industry: A Study in Private
Investment." Studies in the Structure of the American
Economy, Leontief (ed.), pp. 243-94. An empirical test of a
theory of private investment. The theory is called the
capital-requirements theory and has output as an important
independent variable. 2,4-1-1-1.

126. Clower, R.W., "An Investigation into the Dynamics of Investment." American Economic Review, 44 (March 1954),
pp. 64-81. An abstract model of investment behavior in a
competitive market for a single durable good. Traces the
time path of prices and stocks. 1-3-0-2.

      Clower, R.W., and D.W. Bushaw. See Bushaw, 100.

127. Cobren, George M., and Maurice Liebenberg, "Inventories in
Postwar Business Cycles." Survey of Current Business, 39
(April 1959) pp. 3-8. The ratio of postwar inventories to GNP
is about one quarter lower than in the period 1920-29. There
have been considerable cyclical fluctuations in stocks, especially of durable goods. Total stock of inventories lagged
peaks of GNP by one quarter and troughs by two quarters.
3-3-0-2.

128. Cochran, Thomas C., "The Entrepreneur in American Capital

Formation." Universities—National Bureau Conference, Capital Formation and Economic Growth, Princeton University Press, 1955, pp. 339-73. A historical account of the role of entrepreneurship with some attention to the change in the nature and status of the entrepreneur in recent years. 2-3-7-1.

129. Cohen, J., "Sector Investment and the Availability of Finance." Southern Economic Journal, 27 (January 1961). Attempts to apply a circular flow hypothesis to investment by business sectors and by consumers. Investment is explained in terms of the nonfinancial and financial sources of funds to the sector. These sources of funds are in turn explained by the tendency to spend and save out of income. 1-3-2,3-1.

Cohen, Kalman J., and Franco Modigliani. See Modigliani, 465, 466.

130. Cohen, Morris, "Anticipations Data in the Capital Goods Field." Proceedings of the Business and Economic Statistics Section of the American Statistical Association (1957), pp. 193. An analysis of quarterly appropriations for durable assets based on a distinction between general ex-ante plans to invest and actual appropriation of funds to projects. 4-3-8-3.

131. Colm, Gerhard, "Tax Policy and Capital Formation." Capital Formation and Its Elements, National Industrial Conference Board (1939), pp. 73-85. Primarily concerned with the balance between the incentive and discouraging aspects of taxes. 1-3-9-1.

Combs, C. H., and R. M. Thrall. See Thrall, 614.

131a. Committee on the Working of the Monetary System (Radcliffe Committee), Report, London, Her Majesty's Stationery Office, 1959.

132. Coppock, D. J., "The Periodicity and Stability of Inventory Cycles in the U.S.A." Manchester School of Economic and Social Studies, Part I, 27 (May 1959), pp. 140-174: Part II, 27, (September 1959), pp. 261-299. An examination of the historical data of 1894-1957 to see if the periodicity and stability of Metzler-type models of the inventory cycle, fitted with realistic parameters, are consistent with those of the observed short cycles in the U.S.A. Has quite elaborate inventory models; separates trading and manufacturing sectors. 3-3-0-3.

133. Coughlan, J. W., "Contrast Between Financial Statement and Discounted-Cash-Flow Methods of Comparing Projects." N.A.A. Bulletin, 41 (June 1960), pp. 5-17. This whole issue devoted to capital outlay evaluation. This paper concludes that the discounted-cash-flow method is superior for choosing between projects or appraising past performance. 1-1-2-1.

134. Cox, Garfield V., "Forecasting Expenditures for Plant and Equipment." Journal of Business, 27 (January 1954), pp. 22-51. A statement of the importance of this sector for GNP and of methods for estimating it in advance from business surveys. 3-3-8-1.

135. Creamer, Daniel B., Capital and Output Trends in Manufacturing Industries, 1880-1948. National Bureau of Economic Research Occasional Papers, No. 41 (1954). 3-2-1-1.

136. Creamer, Daniel B., "Postwar Trends in the Relation of Capital to Output in Manufactures." American Economic Review, 48 Proc. (May 1958), pp. 249-259. Analysis of changes in capital-output ratios for 17 sub-groups of manufactures between 1948 and 1956. 3-2-1-1.

137. Creamer, Daniel, Sergei Dobrovolsky, and Israel Borenstein, Capital in Manufacturing and Mining: Its Formation and Financing. New York: National Bureau of Economic Research, Princeton University Press, 1960. The study compares trends in stock of capital and in output and measures the changing contribution of various sources of financing. 3-3-2,3-1.

138. Crockett, Jean Bronfenbrenner, "Effects of Current Operating Experiences on the Realization of Investment Plans." Abstract in Econometrica, 22 (October 1954). 4-3-1,2-1.

139. Cunningham, N. J., "Business Investment and the Marginal Cost of Funds." Metroeconomica, Part I, 10 (August 1958), pp. 60-73; Metroeconomica, Part II, 10 (December 1958), pp. 155-81. Principle of increasing risks when outside finance is required. 1-1-3-1.

140. Cyert, Richard M., Herbert A. Simon, and Donald B. Trow, "Observation of a Business Decision." Journal of Business, 29 (October 1956), pp. 237-48. A generalization of "non-programmed" decision-making based on a case study of a firm considering the installation of an electronic computer. 2-1-8-0.

141. Dale, Ernest, "New Perspectives in Management Decision-Making." Journal of Business, 26 (January 1953), pp. 1-8.

A general discussion of changes in the goals and nature of decision processes with the growth of large businesses. 1-1-8-0.

142. Daly, D. J., "Seasonal Variations and Business Expectations." Journal of Business, 32 (July 1959), pp. 258-270. Analyzes the discrepancies between the forecasts made by businessmen and actual developments. Attributes a considerable part of the discrepancy to the fact that many businessmen do not base their estimates on seasonally adjusted current information. 2-1-7,8-1,2.

143. Daly, James P., "A Review of Existing Estimates of Business Investment in Inventories." National Bureau of Economic Research Studies in Income and Wealth, Vol. 19, Princeton University Press, 1957, pp. 57-90. 3-3-0-2.

144. Darling, Paul G., "Surrogative Measurements of Expectations: An Example in Estimating the Liquidity Influence on Investment." Review of Economics and Statistics, 38 (November 1956), pp. 413-426. An attempt to reconstruct estimates of expectations ex post. Develops a theory of the significance of liquidity. Tests this theory with data aggregates of U.S. firms. 4-3-2-1.

145. Darling, P.G., "Manufacturers' Inventory Investment, 1947-1958." American Economic Review, 49 (December 1959), pp. 950-962. Subjects the accelerator theory of inventory changes of Metzler to a test against manufacturers' inventory, sales and unfilled orders data. He is particularly concerned with aggregation problems, the variability of desired stock-flow ratios over time and the stability of economic structures over time. 4-3-1-2.

146. Darling, Paul G., Inventory Fluctuations and Economic Stabilization. A study of the Joint Economic Committee of the Congress of the United States, Washington, 1961. Mr. Darling directed this study which consisted of eleven papers and a bibliography. 0-2,3-0-2.

Davis, R. L. and R. M. Thrall. See Thrall, 614.

147. Dean, Joel, Capital Budgeting. New York: Columbia University Press, 1951. 1-1-8-1.

148. Dean, Joel, "Capital Rationing and the Firm's Demand for Capital." Zeitschrift fuer Oekonometrie, December 1951. An economic approach to management's capital rationing problem through projection of a firm's demand schedule for capital. 1-1-1,3-1.

149. Dean, Joel, "Controls for Capital Expenditures." Financial Management Series, No. 105. New York: American Management Association, 1953. A survey statement of a comprehensive battery of managerial controls of a firm's business investment. 1-1-0-1.

150. Dean, Joel, "The Role of Economic Forecasting in Capital Expenditure Planning." National Planning Association, May, 1953. A survey of the kinds of economic predictions required for management of a firm's business investments. 1-1-8-1.

151. Dean, Joel, "Better Management of Capital Expenditures through Research." Journal of Finance, 8 (May 1953), pp. 119-128. Statement of the need for businessmen to analyze capital projects to attain better forecasts, better comparison of projects, and sounder estimation of capital funds. Discusses alternative means of evaluating projects. 1-1-8-1.

152. Dean, Joel, "Measuring the Productivity of Capital." Harvard Business Review, 32 (January-February 1954), pp. 120-130. A general review of the alternative methods for project evaluation and criteria for acceptance. 1-1-8-1.

153. Dean, Joel, "The Concept and Economic Significance of Regularization of Business Investment." Universities—National Bureau Committee for Economic Research, Regularization of Business Investment, Princeton University Press, 1954, pp. 37-63. Outlines an economic analysis of a firm's benefits, costs, and probable success from reducing cyclical fluctuations of investment outlays. 1-1-0-3.

154. Dean, Joel, "Break-even Analysis and the Measurement of Capital Productivity." Advanced Management, 20 (April 1955), pp. 26-28. A short general review of break-even analysis as a tool of practical application in business decisions. 1-1-2,8-1.

155. Dean, Joel, and Winfield Smith, "Has MAPI a Place in a Comprehensive System of Capital Controls." Journal of Business, 28 (October 1955). An analytical comparison of discounted-cash-flow vs. MAPI criteria of optimum replacement as developed by Terborgh, pp. 261-274. 1-1-6-1.

156. Dean, Joel, "Four Ways to Write Off Capital Investment, Management Should Have a Wider Tax Choice." Journal of Business, 29 (April 1956), pp. 79-90. A plea for a reappraisal of the economic effects of present tax legislation. 1-1-9-1.

157. Dean, Joel, "Profitability Indexes for Capital Investment."

The Controller (February 1958), pp. 64-ff. Reviews the main indexes of profitability which may be used in measuring the desirability of capital expenditures. 1-1-2-1.

158. Denison, Edward F., "Theoretical Aspects of Quality Change, Capital Consumption and Net Capital Formation." National Bureau of Economic Research, Studies in Income and Wealth, Vol. 19, Princeton University Press, 1957, pp. 215-60. 1-1-5-1.

159. Dennison, Harry S., "Decision-Making at the Top Executive Level." American Economic Review, 41 Proc. (May 1951), pp. 98-105. A case-study of decision in a paper specialty firm. 2-1-8-0.

160. Derrickson, Gardner F., "Trend of Corporate Profits, 1929-1945." Survey of Current Business, 26 (April 1946), pp. 9-20. A summary of corporate profits, sales, taxes and dividends with considerable industrial detail. 3-2-0-0.

161. Devons, E., "The Case for Investment and Productivity." Lloyds Bank Review, 38 (October 1955), pp. 19-31. 1-3-0-1.

162. Dieterlen, Pierre, L'Investissement. Paris: Librairie Marcel Riviere et Cie., 1957. A survey of theories and the literature. Contains an 80-page annotated bibliography. 1-1,3-0-3.

163. Dobrovolsky, S. P., "Depreciation Policies and Investment Decisions." American Economic Review. 41 (December 1951), pp. 906-914. Outlines the nature of depreciation and tax procedures for corporations. Indicates that the incentive features of accelerated depreciation could be achieved by tax changes to permit the deduction of unrecovered costs and the carry-over of operating losses. 1-1-9-1.

164. Dobrovolsky, S. P., "The Effect of Replacement Investment on National Income and Employment." Journal of Political Economy, 55 (August 1947), pp. 352-358. A model to examine the effect of changes in replacement requirements on prices, consumption and investment expenditures, and total output. 1-3-6,9-1.

165. Dobrovolsky, S. P., "Economics of Corporate Internal and External Financing." Journal of Finance, 13 (March 1958), pp. 35-47. Considers the general implications of the customary tendency for internal financing on corporate growth, total capital expenditure, and cyclical stability. 1-2,3-2-1.

166. Dobrovolsky, S. P., "Capital Formation and Financing Trends in Manufacturing and Mining, 1900-1953." Journal of Finance,

10 (May 1955), pp. 250-265. A preliminary report on a larger study carried out for the National Bureau of Economic Research. 3-2-2,3-3.

Dobrovolsky, S. P., and Daniel B. Creamer. See Creamer, 137.

167. Domar, Evsey D., "Accelerated Depreciation: A Rejoinder." Quarterly Journal of Economics, 69 (May 1955), pp. 299-304. 1-3-9-1.

168. Domar, Evsey D., "Depreciation, Replacement and Growth." Economic Journal, 63 (March 1953), pp. 1-32. Emphasizes the importance of investment for replacement and the possibility of speeding up the process. 1-3-1,6-1.

169. Domar, Evsey D., "The Case for Accelerated Depreciation." Quarterly Journal of Economics, 67 (November 1953), pp. 493-519. Provisions for guaranteed realization on investment is one means of encouraging growth in an economy with a large governmental sector with resultant high taxes. 1-3-9-1.

170. Domar, Evsey D., "The Problems of Capital Accumulation." American Economic Review, 38 (December 1948), pp. 777-794. Defines the optimum rate of accumulation in terms of the propensity to consume and the ratio of output to capital. 1-3-1-1.

171. Donachie, Robert J., "Determining Rate of Return on Projects by Discounted-Cash-Flow Technique." N.A.A. Bulletin, 41 (June 1960), pp. 31-39. This whole issue is devoted to capital outlay evaluation. 1-1-2-1.

172. Dorfman, Robert, P.A. Samuelson, and R.W. Solow, Linear Programming and Economic Analysis. New York: McGraw-Hill Book Company, 1958. Chapter 12 deals with the topic, "Efficient Programs of Capital Accumulation." 1-1-8-1.

173. Dryden, M.M., "The MAPI Urgency Rating as an Investment Ranking Criterion." Journal of Business, 33 (October 1960), pp. 327-341. Deals with a formula set out in Business Investment Policy by Terborgh (1958). Points out some of the limitations of Terborgh's new formula and its relationship to more familiar formulae. 1-1-8-1.

174. Duesenberry, James., Business Cycles and Economic Growth. New York: McGraw-Hill Book Co., 1958. An aggregative cycle model based on a revised version of the accelerator and multiplier. 1-3-1-3.

175. Duesenberry, James, "Innovation and Growth." American Economic Review, 46 Proc. (May 1956), pp. 134-41. Discusses the importance of innovation for investment in certain sectors of the economy. Criticizes the concept of autonomous investment. 1-3-5-3.

176. Durand, D., "The Cost of Capital in an Imperfect Market: A Reply to Modigliani and Miller." American Economic Review, 49 (September 1959), pp. 639-654. Criticizes the assumptions on which Modigliani and Miller base their analysis—especially the partial exclusion of risk, the imperfections of the capital market and the exclusion of dynamic expectational factors. 1-1-2,3-0.

177. Dvoretzky, A., J. Keifer, and J. Wolfowitz, "The Inventory Problem: 1. Case of Known Distribution of Demand." Econometrica, 20 (April 1952), pp. 186-222. 1-1,3-7-2.

178. Dvoretzky, A., J. Keifer, and J. Wolfowitz, "The Inventory Problem: II. Case of Unknown Distribution of Demand." Econometrica, 20 (July 1952), pp. 450-466. 1-1,3-7-2.

179. Dvoretzky, A., J. Keifer, and J. Wolfowitz, "On the Optimal Character of (s, S) Policy in Inventory Theory." Econometrica, 21 (October 1953), pp. 586-596. 1-1,3-7-2.

180. Eckaus, R.S., "The Acceleration Principle Reconsidered." Quarterly Journal of Economics, 67 (May 1953), pp. 209-230. 1-3-1-1.

181. Edge, C.G., The Appraisal of Capital Expenditures. The Society of Industrial and Cost Accountants of Canada, Special Study No. 1, Hamilton, Ontario, 1959. A study of alternative means of evaluating investment projects, using compound interest formulae. Considers Discounted-Cash-Flow, Present Worth and Investors' Method as well as administrative procedures for handling appropriation requests. 1,3-1-8-1.

182. Edmunds, Stahl, "Financing Capital Formation." Harvard Business Review, 28 (January-February 1950), pp. 33-42. Rate of capital formation in U.S. over past 100 years has been high. Technologically, it could have been higher. Capital requirements in the future will be greater than in the past. 3-3-5-1.

183. Edwards, W., "The Theory of Decision-Making." Psychological Bulletin, 51 (1954), pp. 380-417. A summary article of work being done by psychologists and sociologists. 1-0-8-0.

184. Egerton, R.A.D., "Investment, Uncertainty and Expectations."

Review of Economic Studies, 22 (1954-55), pp. 143-150. A
treatment of uncertainty using Shackle's model. 1-0-8-0.

185. Egerton, R.A.D., Investment Decisions Under Uncertainty.
Liverpool: University Press, 1960. 1-1-7,8-0.

186. Einarsen, Johan, "Reinvestment Cycles and their Manifestation
in the Norwegian Shipping Industry," Publication No. 14,
University Institute of Economics, Oslo, 1938. Theory of
reinvestment cycles explained. Statistics, partly treated by
actuarial methods, show age distribution of replaced ships
and give probabilities of sale and of replacement for ships
of various ages and for various phases of the business cycle.
3-2-6-1.

187. Einarsen, Johan, "Reinvestment Cycles." Review of Economic
Statistics, 20 (February 1938), pp. 1-10. A short resume of
the main points of the above publication. 3-2-6-1.

188. Einarsen, Johan, "Replacement in the Shipping Industry."
Review of Economic Statistics, 28 (November 1946), pp. 225-
230. Statistics of replacement in the Norwegian shipping
industry for the years 1932-39. Life characteristics for oil
tankers, motor ships and steamships. 3-2-6-1.

189. Eisemann, Doris M., "Bank Credit and Inventory Cycles."
American Statistical Association, Proceedings of the Business
and Economics Statistics Section, 1957, pp. 75-86. Attempts
to discover the importance of bank lending for inventory
purchases. Looks at the differential impact of lending policy
between different firms and different industries. 2,3-2-2,3-2.

190. Eisemann, Doris M., "Manufacturers' Inventory Cycles and
Monetary Policy." Proceedings of the Business and Economics
Statistics Section of the American Statistical Association,
(1958), pp. 680-688. Monetary policy is a very broad instrument with which to control inventory changes. Those industries where savings are greatest are not necessarily
those on which credit restrictions impinges most. 1-3-3-2.

191. Eisner, Robert, "Accelerated Amortization, Growth and Net
Profits." Quarterly Journal of Economics, 66 (November
1952), pp. 533-44. 1-3-2,9-1.

192. Eisner, Robert, "Depreciation Allowances, Replacement Requirements and Growth." American Economic Review, 42
(December 1952), pp. 820-831. Analyzes the relative size
of depreciation allowances and replacement outlays in a
growing economy under various assumptions of price changes,

durability of assets and rates of change of investment. 1-3-6,9-1.

193. Eisner, Robert, "Depreciation Under the New Tax Policy." Harvard Business Review, 33 (January-February 1955), pp. 66-74. Spells out the implications of depreciation changes made in the Internal Revenue Code of 1954. The changes make capital outlay more attractive in many instances. 1-3-9-1.

194. Eisner, Robert, "Accelerated Depreciation: Some Further Thoughts." Quarterly Journal of Economics, 69 (May 1955), pp. 285-96. 1-3-9-1.

195. Eisner, Robert, "Determinants of Capital Expenditures: An Interview Study." Studies in Business Expectations and Planning, No. 2, University of Illinois, 1956. 2-3-1,2-1.

196. Eisner, Robert, "Expectations, Plans and Capital Expenditures, A Synthesis of Ex Post and Ex Ante Data." Expectations, Uncertainty and Business Behavior, M. J. Bowman (ed.), pp. 165-188. An econometric study of actual investment and the influence of sales, profits and expectations for a cross section of firms. 4-3-1,2-1.

197. Eisner, Robert, "Interview and other Survey Techniques and the Study of Investment." National Bureau of Economic Research, Studies in Income and Wealth, Vol. 19, Princeton University Press, 1957, pp. 513-584. A survey of the theoretical constructs, results and their interpretation. 2-3-0-1.

198. Eisner, Robert, "Technological Change, Obsolescence and Aggregate Demand." American Economic Review, 46 (March 1956), pp. 92-105. Elaborates a model to demonstrate that technological developments may increase the volume of investment demand. Page 666, American Economic Review, September 1956, corrects a mistake in the formulation. 1-3-5,6-1.

199. Eisner, Robert, "A Distributed Lag Investment Function." Econometrica, 28 (January 1960), pp. 1-29. An empirical study of capital expenditures by 250 large corporations. Uses sales changes and profit changes over several preceding years as independent variables in a multiple regression analysis. Concludes that the acceleration component of capital expenditure is significant, particularly with growing firms. 4-1-1-1.

199a. Eisner, Robert, "An Appraisal of Proposals for Tax Differentials Affecting Investment," in Income Tax Differentials,
Tax Institute, Princeton, 1958, pp. 154-171.

199b. Eisner, Robert, "Investment Plans and Realizations," American Economic Review, 52 (May 1962), pp. 190-203.

199c. Eisner, Robert, "Capital Expenditures, Profits and the
Acceleration Principle," for Conference on Research in
Income and Wealth, National Bureau of Economic Research,
February 1962.

200. Epstein, J.B., "Electric Power Output and Investment."
Survey of Current Business, 29 (May 1949), pp. 11-17. An
analysis of increases in output and expansion of capacity
extending back to 1922. 3-2-1-1.

201. Ezekial, Mordecai, "Statistical Investigations of Saving,
Consumption and Investment." American Economic Review,
32 (March 1942), pp. 22-50; (June 1942), pp. 272-308. A study
based on aggregate data for the U.S., 1920-40. 4-3-1,2,3-3.

202. Ezekial, Mordecai, "Statistical Determination of the Investment Schedule," Econometrica, 12 (January 1944), pp. 89-90.
4-3-1,2,3-1.

203. Fabricant, Solomon, "Employment Growth and Price Levels."
U.S. Congress 86-1, Joint Economic Committee Hearings.
Testimony on April 8, 1959 contains several historical series
of output and capital growth by industries. 3-3-1-1.

204. Federal Reserve Board, "Capital Outlays and Security Offerings." Federal Reserve Bulletin, 40 (April 1954), pp. 339-
344. A review of recent developments. 3-3-3-1.

205. Federal Reserve Board, "Statistics of Business Inventories;
Report of the Consultative Committee on Inventory Statistics." Board of Governors, Federal Reserve System, October,
1955. 3-3-0-2.

206. Federal Reserve Board, "Financing of Business Expansion."
Federal Reserve Bulletin, 42 (June 1956), pp. 553-558. An
analysis of capital expenditure, inventories and new issues
in 1955. 3-3-0-3.

207. Federal Reserve Board, "Financing Business Investment."
Federal Reserve Bulletin, 44 (June 1958), pp. 641-647. Gives
most recent data available on actual investment, inventories,
profits and new issues. 3-3-0-3.

208. Feinstein, C. H., "Income and Investment in the United Kingdom, 1856-1914," Economic Journal, 71 (June 1961), pp. 367-385. Sets out some new historical series of fixed capital outlays and national income for this period. 3-3-0-1.

209. Fellner, William, "Long-Term Tendencies in Private Capital Formation." National Bureau of Economic Research Conference on Research in Income and Wealth, Vol 16, Long-Range Economic Projection, Princeton, Princeton University Press, 1954, pp. 275-331. Reviews the theory and techniques of investment projection. Discusses the distinction between short-term and long-term projections. 1-3-8-1.

Fels, Eberhard, and Oskar J. Anderson. See Anderson, 15.

210. Ferber, Robert, "Measuring the Accuracy and Structure of Businessmen's Expectations." Journal of the American Statistical Association, 48 (September 1953), pp. 385-413. Relates primarily to sales and shipments expectations. 3-3-8-0.

211. Fetter, R. B., and T. P. Goodman, "An Equipment Investment Analog." Operations Research, 5 (October 1957). 1-1-0-1.

212. Firestone, O. J., "Investment Forecasting in Canada," National Bureau of Economic Research Studies in Income and Wealth, Vol. 17, Short-Term Economic Forecasting, Princeton: Princeton University Press, 1955, pp. 113-249. A statement of the accuracy of investment intentions data collected in Canada. 3-2-8-1.

213. Fisher, Gene H., "A Simple Econometric Model for the United States, 1947-1950." Review of Economics and Statistics, 34 (February 1952), pp. 46-48. A model using quarterly data with results that are questionable because of multicollinearity. 4-3-1,2,3-1.

214. Fisher, Gene H., "A Survey of the Theory of Induced Investment, 1900-1940." Southern Economic Journal, 19 (April 1952), pp. 474-494. A brief survey of the literature of the acceleration principle with emphasis on the gradual shift from micro- to macroeconomic orientation. The other significant development is the substitution of a nonlinear for a linear relation. 1-3-1-1.

215. Fisher, Gene H., "Endogenous and Exogenous Investment in Macro-Economic Models." Review of Economics and Statistics, 35 (August 1953), pp. 211-220. An investigation of the theoretical differences between endogenous and exogenous investment and a discussion of the statistical problems involved

in attempting to include this distinction in aggregative econometric models. 1-3-1-1.

216. Fisher, Gene H., "Hicks' 'Elementary Case' Economic Model for the United States, 1929-1941." Journal of the American Statistical Association, 47 (September 1952), pp. 541-549. An attempt to derive statistical estimates of the parameters in a Hicksian type macroeconomic model for the United States, 1929-41. 4-3-1-3.

217. Fisher, Gene H., "Some Comments on Stochastic Macro-Economic Models." American Economic Review, 42 (September 1952), pp. 528-539. 4-3-1-3.

218. Foldes, Lucien, "Uncertainty, Probability and Potential Surprise." Economica, 25 (August 1958), pp. 246-254. A criticism of Shackle's theory and Knight's distinction between risk and uncertainty. Holds that objective probability concepts are relevant even to unique choices. 1-0-7-0.

219. Foss, Murray F., and Lois E. Holmes, "Trends of Inventories in the Mobilization Period." Survey of Current Business, 31, (April 1951), pp. 16-24. Contains a model relating inventories to sales two quarters earlier. 3-3-0-2.

220. Foss, Murray F., "Investment Programs and Sales Expectations in 1954." Survey of Current Business, 34 (March 1954), pp. 9-12. 3-3-8-1.

221. Foss, Murray F., "Investment and Sales Anticipations in 1955." Survey of Current Business, 35 (March 1955), pp. 4-8. 3-3-8-1.

222. Foss, M., "Factors Influencing the Realization of Recent Investment Anticipations." American Statistical Association, Proceedings of the Business and Economics Section, 1957, pp. 351-364. An investigation to find out why manufacturers departed from their plant and equipment expenditure anticipations in 1955. It is based on the results of a questionnaire but also analyzes relations between investment predictions and sales forecasts. 2-1-8-1.

223. Foss, Murray F., (or Foss and V. Natrella), "Commerce-SEC Annual Survey of Business Investment and Sales Anticipations." Survey of Current Business, (March issue) Presents the findings of the latest annual survey, reviews recent developments in fixed investment, compares anticipations from previous annual surveys with actual expenditures. Some articles give special tabulations and analyses not presented on a regular basis. 3-2,2-8-1.

224. Foss, Murray F., and V. Natrella, "Investment Plans and Realization: Reasons for Differences in Individual Cases." Survey of Current Business, 37 (June 1957), pp. 12-18. Unexpected changes in sales and earnings were responsible for most changes of plans in 1955. Supplies of investment goods were next most important, especially for larger firms. 3-3-8-1.

225. Foss, Murray F. and V. Natrella, "Ten Year's Experience with Business Investment Anticipations." Survey of Current Business, 37 (January 1957), pp. 16-24. Forecasts, on the whole, have a good record especially with respect to turning points. Size of firm and scale of project have significance for accurancy, that of the latter being greater. Utilities have a record superior to manufacturing and transportation. 3-3-8-1.

226. Foss, Murray F., and V. Natrella, "The Structure and Realization of Business Investment Anticipations," in The Quality and Economic Significance of Anticipations Data. Princeton University Press for the National Bureau of Economic Research, 1960, pp. 387-445. A study of the realization of individual firms' anticipations, by industry, scale of investment and stage of the business cycle. 3-1,2,3-8-1.

227. Foss, Murray F., and Walter Leibowitz, "Investment in Fuel and Power Industries," Survey of Current Business, 40 (June 1961) pp. 18-24. 3-2-1,5-1.

228. Foss, Murray F., "Manufacturers' Inventory and Sales Expectations." Survey of Current Business, 41 (August 1961), pp. 27-31. Presents results of a new quarterly survey of manufacturers' inventory and sales expectations, started in late 1957. 3-3-8-2.

229. Fox, Karl A., "Econometric Models of the United States," Journal of Political Economy, 64, (April 1956), pp. 128-142. Contains a critical appraisal of the Klein-Goldberger study and suggests further adaptations of econometric models of the United States to the appraisal of economic policies. 1-3-0-0.

230. Frankel, Marvin, "Obsolescence and Technological Change in a Maturing Economy." American Economic Review, 45 (June 1955), pp. 296-319. Discusses the criteria for innovation with particular reference to the position of the U.K. as a modern manufacturing nation handicapped by an early start. 1,2-3-5-1.

Frankovich, John M., and A.S. Manne. See Manne, 417.

231. Frazer, William J., Jr., "Some Factors Affecting Business Financing." Southern Economic Journal, 25 (July 1958), pp. 33-47. Discusses those factors which limit and determine the form of corporate fund raising. Also considers the impact of interest rate and corporate income tax changes. 1-1-3,9-1.

232. Friday, Frank A., "The Problem of Business Forecasting." Journal of Industrial Economics, 1 (November 1952), pp. 55-71. 1-0-8-0.

233. Friend, Irwin, and Louis J. Paradiso, "Plant and Equipment Expenditures of U.S. Business." Survey of Current Business, 26 (January 1946), pp. 17-18. Describes the inauguration of the investment and sales expectations surveys. 3-3-8-1.

234. Friend, Irwin, "Business Financing in the Postwar Period," Survey of Current Business, 28 (March 1948), pp. 10-16. Sources and uses of corporate funds in 1946 and 1947. Examines equity to debt ratio of new funds. 1-3-2,3-1.

235. Friend, Irwin, "Critical Evaluation of Surveys of Expectations Plans and Investment Behavior." Expectations, Uncertainty and Business Behaviour, M.J. Bowman (ed.), pp. 189-198. 3-3-8-1.

236. Friend, Irwin, "Statistics on Business Plant and Equipment Expenditure Expectations: Report of the Consultative Committee on Business Plant and Equipment Expenditures." Board of Governors, Federal Reserve System, July 1955. 3-3-8-1.

237. Friend, Irwin, and Jean Bronfenbrenner, "Business Investment Programmes and Their Realization." Survey of Current Business, 30 (December 1950), pp. 11-22. Analyzes the importance of various variables in accounting for the discrepancy between anticipated and actual investment. All firms tend to underestimate; large firms most accurate as forecasters; large scale projects tend to be better estimated; for all firms taken together changes in sales and earnings were not a statistically significant explanation. 3-3-8-1.

238. Friend, Irwin, and Jean Bronfenbrenner, "Plant and Equipment Programs and Their Realization." National Bureau of Economic Research, Studies in Income and Wealth, Vol. 17, Princeton University Press, 1955, pp. 53-96. A study of the accuracy of investment anticipations surveys and an attempt to explain deviations from actual investment. 3-3-8-1.

239. Friend, Irwin, and Irving B. Kravis, "Entrepreneurial Income, Saving, and Investment." American Economic Review, 47 (June 1957), pp. 269-301. A study of saving and investment behavior of unincorporated nonfarm businesses for 1950. 3-3-0-1.

240. Frisch, R., "Propagation Problems and Impulse Problems in Dynamic Economics," in Essays in Honour of Gustav Cassel, London: G. Allen and Unwin, 1933. 1-0-5-3.

241. Froehlich, Walter, "The Role of Income Determination in Reinvestment and Investment." American Economic Review, 38 (March 1948), pp. 78-91. Argues for a gross investment concept instead of one referring only to new outlays. The difficulties involved in defining income and profit with price changes and interest rate changes make the former concept the more important. 1-3-1,2,3-3.

242. Froehlich, Walter, "Some Problems of Income Determination and Welfare." Zeitschrift für Nationalökonomie, 19 (1959), pp. 246-261. The dangers inherent in net income concepts are further explored and discussed strengthening the case against using these concepts in analysis in general and in regard to investment specifically. 1-3-1,2-1.

Fuhrer, H., and Oskar J. Anderson. See Anderson, 16.

243. Fujino, Shozaburo, "Some Aspects of Inventory Cycles." Review of Economics and Statistics, 42 (May 1960), pp. 203-209. An empirical analysis of inventory cycles based on Japanese quarterly data between 1950 and 1955. Considers inventory-sales ratio, price and output adjustments, relations between inventory cycles and fixed capital outlays and the influence of cash balances. 4-2,3-1-2.

244. Gainsbrugh, Martin R., "Capital Investment." Hearings before the Joint Economic Committee on the January 1959, Economic Report of the President. Reviews briefly the role of investment in three postwar downturns. 3-3-1-1.

245. Galbraith, J.K., "Market Structure and Stabilization Policy." Review of Economics and Statistics, 39 (May 1957), pp. 124-133. Expresses doubts about the efficacy and equity of monetary policy where competition is not perfect. 1-3-3-3.

246. Gallaway, Lowell E., and Paul E. Smith, "A Quarterly Econometric Model of the United States." American Statistical Association Journal, 56 (June 1961), pp. 379-383. Uses quarterly data 1948 through 1957, seasonally adjusted in

current prices to fit a simple four equation system by least squares. Several lagged values of predetermined variables are included and first differences are used to reduce auto correlation and multicollinearity. An accelerator relationship appears significant. 4-3-0-0.

247. Gehrels, F., and S. Wiggins, "Interest Rates and Manufacturers' Fixed Investments." American Economic Review, 47 (March 1957), pp. 79-92. An economic study of the influence of interest rate changes on investment in the U.S., 1948-55. 3-2-3-1.

248. Gertler, Sidney, "Construction and Business Cycles," Survey of Current Business, 26 (November 1946), pp. 7-14. A projection of prewar and postponed construction expenditures. Speculates about the influence of this on a postwar depression. 3-2-0-1.

Goldberger, A.S., and L.R. Klein. See Klein, 355.

249. Gonzalez, Richard J., "Regularizing Petroleum Investment," Universities — National Bureau Committee for Economic Research Regularization of Business Investment, pp. 137-45. No likelihood of stability or anticyclical outlays in this industry. 2-2-0-1.

250. Goode, Richard, "Accelerated Depreciation Allowances as a Stimulus to Investment." Quarterly Journal of Economics, 69 (May 1955), pp. 191-220. Points out that this is a selective means of alleviating the effect of taxation on investment. 1-3-9-1.

251. Goode, Richard, "Special Tax Measures to Restrain Investment." International Monetary Fund Staff Papers, 5 (February 1957), pp. 434-448. A discussion of the possibility of substituting tax changes for interest rate changes as a means of regulating investment which might cause inflation. 1-3-3,9-1.

252. Goode, Richard, The Corporate Income Tax. New York: John Wiley and Sons, Inc., 1951. Includes a discussion of the influence of the tax on investment decisions and financing. 1-3-9-1.

Goodman, T.P., and R.B. Fetter. See Fetter, 211.

253. Goodwin, R.M. "Innovation and the Irregularity of Economic Cycles." Review of Economics and Statistics, 28 (May 1946), pp. 95-104. A model which generates cycles in response to random innovations and investment disturbances. 1-3-5-1.

254. Goodwin, R.M., "Econometrics in Business Cycle Analysis." Chapter 22 in A.H. Hansen, Business Cycles and National Income. New York: W.W. Norton, 1951, pp. 417-468. 1-1-1,2-1.

255. Goodwin, R.M., "The Non-Linear Accelerator and the Persistence of Business Cycles." Econometrica, 19 (1951), pp. 1-17. 1-3-1-1.

256. Goodwin, R.M., "A Model of Cyclical Growth," in The Business Cycle in the Post War World, ed. E. Lundberg. London: International Economic Association, 1955, pp. 203-221. 1-3-0-0.

257. Goodwin, R.M., "Secular and Cyclical Aspects of the Multiplier and the Accelerator" in Income, Employment and Public Policy, Essays in Honour of Alvin H. Hansen. New York: W.W. Norton, 1948, pp. 118-121. 1-3-1-1.

258. Gordon, Donald F., "Obsolescence and Technological Change: A Comment." American Economic Review, 46 (September 1956), pp. 646-652. A restatement of and critical comment on Frankel's article, American Economic Review (June 1955). 1-3-5-1.

259. Gordon, M.J., The Dynamics of Risk and Investment. Unpublished Ph.D. thesis, Harvard University, 1952. Deals with the problems of capital budgeting in large corporations. Points out that a corporation must have a required rate of profit in order to decide on the inclusion of a project in its capital budget, and presents a model for arriving at a corporation's required rate of profit on the assumption that the objective is to maximize the corporation's value. 1-3-8-1.

260. Gordon, M.J., "Depreciation Allowances, Replacement Requirements and Growth: A Comment." American Economic Review, 43 (September 1953), pp. 609-614. A comment on an article by the same title by Eisner in American Economic Review (December 1952). Eisner has a rejoinder with new data, pp. 614-621. 1-3-9-1.

261. Gordon, M.J., "The Payoff Period and the Rate of Profit." Journal of Business, 28 (October 1955), pp. 253-260. A detailed discussion of one type of investment evaluation procedure. This whole issue of the journal is devoted to the topic of Capital Budgeting. 1-1-8-3.

262. Gordon, M.J., and Eli Shapiro, "Capital Equipment Analysis: The Required Rate of Profit." Management Science, 3 (October 1956), pp. 102-110. Assumes that the objective of a corporation

is to achieve and maintain a satisfactory level of security. The corporation's net debt to equity ratio is taken as an index of security, and the investment that maintains or achieves this level of security is derived. 1-1-2,8-1.

263. Gordon, M. J., "Security and a Financial Theory of Investment." Quarterly Journal of Economics (August 1960), pp. 472-492. Measures degree of risks as the ratio of "net debt" to equity. Net debt is total liabilities minus monetary assets. States that risk as measured by this indicator will influence the scale of investment because the firm will only invest in risky assets so long as its security or desired financial position is kept within certain limits. 1-1-2-1.

264. Gordon, R. A., Business Leadership in the Large Corporations. The Brookings Institution, Washington, D.C., 1945. Discusses the role and residence of the entrepreneurial function in large widely held companies in the U.S. 1-1-7-0.

265. Gordon, R. A., "Investment Behavior and Business Cycles." Review of Economics and Statistics, 37 (February 1955), pp. 23-34. Emphasizes the importance and complexity of investment changes for the cycle. 1-3-0-1.

266. Goris, Hendrieke and L. M. Koyck, "The Prices of Investment Goods and the Volume of Production in the United States." Review of Economics and Statistics, 55 (February 1953), pp. 59-66. A study of the relation between the volume of production and the prices of investment goods in the United States for the period 1919-40. Looks specifically for bottlenecks in the supply of investment goods. 4-3-4-1.

267. Gort, M., "The Planning of Investment: A Study of Capital Budgeting in the Electric Power Industry." Journal of Business, 24, I (April 1951), pp. 79-95, and II (July 1951), pp. 181-202. A report on management interviews with 25 electric power companies, examines budgeting procedures, length of investment plans, and flexibility of decisions. Also considers the methods of forecasting demand expenditures on new capacity, on replacement and the role of financial factors. 2-1-8-1.

Grey, A. L., and M. D. Brockie. See Brockie, 84, 85.

268. Griliches, Zvi, and Yehuda Grunfeld, "Is Aggregation Necessarily Bad?" Review of Economics and Statistics, 42 (February 1960), pp. 1-13. Studies the effect of aggregation on two studies where micro-relations are available. The first example is the investment behavior of single firms as studied by Grunfeld. Concludes that the results of aggregation are

not necessarily bad when one is interested in the aggregate relationships. 1-1,3-0-1.

269. Grosse, Robert N., "The Structure of Capital." in Studies in the Structure of the American Economy, Leontief (ed.), pp. 185-242. Presents a set of empirical relations between stock of capital and rate of output possible for a series of industries. 3-2-1-1.

270. Grosse, Robert N., and Edward B. Berman, "Estimating Future Purchases of Capital Equipment for Replacement." National Bureau of Economic Research, Studies in Income and Wealth, Vol. 19, Princeton University Press, 1957, pp. 389-414. 3-3-8-1.

271. Grosse, Robert N., Capital Requirements for the Expansion of Industrial Capacity. U.S. Bureau of the Budget, November 30, 1953. 0-2-1-1.

272. Grosse, Robert N., The Value of American Manufacturing Plant and Equipment. The RAND Corp., RM-1474, April 28, 1955. 3-2-0-1.

Grosswald, E., and Hans Neisser. See Neisser, 493.

273. Grunfeld, Yehuda, "A Review of Meyer and Kuh, The Investment Decision." Journal of Political Economy, 66 (October 1958), p. 450. 0-0-1,2-1.

274. Grunfeld, Yehuda, The Determinants of Corporate Investment. Doctoral Dissertation, the University of Chicago. Examines the investment outlays of eight large corporations and applies parametric and non-parametric techniques to the relations between investment and profits, sales, liquidity and "the value of the firm." This latter derived from stock prices is assumed to reflect expectations. 4-1-1,2-1.

Grunfeld, Yehuda, and Zvi Griliches. See Griliches, 268.

275. Haavelmo, T., "The Effect of the Rate of Interest on Investment: A Note." Review of Economic Statistics (February 1941), pp. 49-52. This is a review of Tinbergen's book on estimation of aggregate investment in the U.S. 1-3-3-1.

276. Haavelmo, T., "A Note on the Theory of Investment." Review of Economic Studies, 16 (1949-1950), pp. 78-81. Derives an aggregate model of the economy which explains the amount of investment in terms of a consumption function, a labor supply function, a liquidity preference schedule and a given supply of money. 1-3-0-1.

277. Haavelmo, T., A Study in the Theory of Investment. Chicago: University of Chicago Press, 1960. Presents a systematic analysis of the investment process based on fundamental laws of economic behavior. Emphasizes capital as a factor of production and investment behavior in a market economy but also deals with investment in a centralized economy. 1-1,2-0-1.

278. Haberler, Gottfried, "The Interest Rate and Capital Formation." Capital Formation and Its Elements. National Industrial Conference Board, 1939, pp. 119-133. A restatement of arguments developed in Prosperity and Depression. 1-3-3-1.

279. Haberler, Gottfried, Prosperity and Depression. New York: United Nations, 1946. 1-3-0-3.

280. Hadley, G., and T.M. Whitin, "An Optimal Final Inventory Model." Management Science, 7 (January 1961), pp. 179-183. A model is developed which allows the determination of the optimal inventory level for any item at any time if no further procurements are to be made. 1-1-0-2.

281. Hadley, G., and T.M. Whitin, "Family of Inventory Models." Management Science, 7 (July 1961), pp. 351-371. Develops a general inventory control model where the system is reviewed only at discrete time intervals; includes costs for review, procurement holding inventory and stockouts. 1-1-4-2.

282. Hahn, Dorothy, "Investment Repercussion: A Comment." Quarterly Journal of Economics, 63 (August 1949), pp. 430-432. A criticism of an article by Lachmann in Quarterly Journal of Economics, (November 1948). 1-3-0-1.

283. Hahn, F.H., "Expectations and Equilibrium." Economic Journal, 62 (December 1952), pp. 802-819. Discusses the nature of the expectational structure which will lead businessmen to stable behavior. 1-3-8-1.

284. Hamberg, D., "Investment and Saving in a Growing Economy." Review of Economics and Statistics, 37 (May 1955), pp. 196-201. 1-3-0-3.

285. Hamberg, D., "Steady Growth and Theories of Cyclical Crisis." Metroeconomica, Part I, 6 (April 1954), pp. 11-30, Part II, 6 (August 1954), pp. 55-68. A review of cycle and growth models with some emphasis on investment theories and the assumptions involved. 1-3-0-3.

286. Hamberg, D., "The Accelerator in Income Analysis: Comment." Quarterly Journal of Economics, 66 (November 1952),

pp. 592-596. A discussion of an article by Tsiang in August 1951, same journal. 1-3-1-1.

287. Hansen, Alvin H., Business Cycles and National Income. New York: W.W. Norton and Co., 1951. Deals with the role of investment and determinants, especially pp. 184-186, and 471-476 where minor cycles are attributed to inventory investment and disinvestment. 1-3-1-2.

288. Hansen, Alvin H., Fiscal Policies and Business Cycles. New York: W.W. Norton and Co., 1941. 1-3-9-3.

289. Haring, J.E., "The Investment Horizon." Metroeconomica, 13 (August 1961). An essay in investment theory with an analysis of the formation and role of time horizons in investment decisions. 1-1-7-1.

Harris, Theodore, and Kenneth J. Arrow. See Arrow, 26.

290. Hart, A.G., "Anticipations, Business Planning and The Cycle." Quarterly Journal of Economics, 51 (February 1937), pp. 273-297. Stresses that firms almost continually find themselves in a state of disequilibrium in which present values of variables are not expected to remain unchanged. Those factors which influence expectations are complex and anticipations are probably destabilizing forces in the aggregate. 1-3-8-3.

291. Hart, A.G., Anticipations, Uncertainty and Dynamic Planning. Chicago: University of Chicago, 1940. The classic work on entrepreneurial decision-making. (Also, New York: A.M. Kelly, 1951.) 1-1-7,8-0.

292. Hart, A.G., "Assets, Liquidity and Investment." American Economic Review, 39 Proc. (May 1949), pp. 171-181. A statement of the problems involved in formulation of a theory of investment and suggestions for information to be collected. 1-3-2,8-1.

293. Hart, A.G., "Government Measures Designed to Promote Regularization of Business Investment." Universities-National Bureau Committee for Economic Research, Regularization of Business Investment, Princeton University Press, 1954, pp. 451-457. Government action has a strong influence on private decisions and wisely used should promote stability. 1-3-9-1.

294. Hart, A.G., "Uncertainty and Inducement to Invest." Review of Economic Studies, 8 (October 1940), pp. 49-53. A criticism of Shackle's theory of investment in the same issue. Criticizes

Shackle's omission of any consideration of dispersion of expected values. 1-0-8-1.

295. Hartley, Robert W., and Associates, America's Capital Requirements—Estimates for 1946-1960. New York: Twentieth Century Fund, 1950. An attempt at predicting aggregate requirements for producers durables. The predictions were quite out of date at time of publication. Contains data on sources and statistics of capital formation. 3-3-8-3.

296. Hastay, Millard, "The Cyclical Behavior of Investment." Universities—National Bureau Committee for Economic Research, Regularization of Business Investment, Princeton University Press, 1954, pp. 3-35. Based on an analysis of industry and aggregate time series presented in charts. 3-2,3-0-3.

297. Hastay, Millard, "The Dun and Bradstreet Survey of Businessmen's Expectations." Proceedings of the Business and Economic Statistics Section of the American Statistical Association, 1955, pp. 93-123. A re-evaluation of the qualitative accuracy of these short-term surveys. Asks if they indicate the direction of changes. Contains many charts and tables. 3-3-8-3.

298. Hawkins, E.K., "Investment and the Demand for Electricity." Oxford Economic Papers, N.S. 9 (February 1957), pp. 14-29. A review of the increasing demand and capital deepening of the power industry in the U.K. which has led to a large volume of investment expenditures from 1925-54. 3-2-1-1.

299. Hawtrey, R.G., Capital and Employment. 2nd edition. London: Longmans, Green and Co., Ltd., 1952. 1-3-0-3.

299a. Hawtrey, R.G., Trade and Credit. London: Longmans, Green and Co., 1928.

300. Hawtrey, Sir Ralph, "Fixed Capital and the Interest Rate." The Bankers Magazine, 189 (May 1960), pp. 410-418. Reviews the evidence and report of the Radcliffe Commission respecting the influence of interest rates on decisions to purchase new assets and to change inventory holdings. 1-3-3-3.

301. Hawtrey, Sir Ralph, The Pound at Home and Abroad. London: Longmans, Green and Co., Ltd., 1961. Chapters 15 and 16 are devoted to the question of the influence of the short-term rate of interest on inventories. 1-3-3-2.

Hazlewood, A., and L.R. Klein. See Klein, 357.

302. Healy, K.T., "Regularization of Capital Investment in Railroads." Universities-National Bureau Committee for Economic Research, Regularization of Business Investment, Princeton University Press, 1954, pp. 147-212. 3-2-2,4,5,8-1.

303. Heller, Walter W., "The Anatomy of Investment Decisions." Harvard Business Review, 29 (March 1951), pp. 95-103. The report of an interview survey of executives in manufacturing companies in St. Paul and Minneapolis during 1950. Discusses the expanding role of capital budgeting and the importance of availability of funds and managerial talent. 2-1-2,4,8-1.

303a. Heller, Walter W., and Associates, The Minneapolis Project—A Pilot Study of Local Capital Formation, University of Minnesota, 1950.

304. Henderson, H.D., "The Significance of the Rate of Interest." Oxford Economic Papers, 1 (October 1938), pp. 1-13. General discussion of the manner in which the rate of interest influences expenditures by consumers, public authorities and businessmen. 1-3-3-1.

305. Henderson, R.F., "Industrial Investment in Fixed Capital: A Reconsideration." Scottish Journal of Political Economy, 3 (October 1956), pp. 177-187. Investment by industries is less subject to cyclical forces than commonly believed. Changes in over-all confidence in products and technology are more important. 1-3-3-1.

306. Henderson, R.F., The New Issues Market and the Finance of Industry. Bowes and Bowes and the Harvard University Press, 1951. 0-0-2,3-1.

307. Henderson, R.F., and Brian Tew, Studies in Company Finance. Cambridge University Press, 1959. 0-0-2,3-1.

308. Hetrick, J.C., "Mathematical Models in Capital Budgeting." Harvard Business Review, 39 (January-February 1961), pp. 49-64. A plea for more abstract planning and analysis of where capital expenditures are most beneficial. Uses a linear programming model to illustrate the problem. 1-1-8-1.

309. Hickman, B.G., "Capacity, Capacity Utilization and the Acceleration Principle." National Bureau of Economic Research, Studies in Income and Wealth, Vol. 19, Princeton University Press, 1957, pp. 419-449. An analysis of cyclical and secular changes in capacity by industries. Cites evidence that long-term trends are more important than short-run changes in sales. 3-2-1-1.

310. Hickman, B.G., "Diffusion, Acceleration, and Business Cycles." American Economic Review, 49 (September 1959), pp. 535-565. Argues that investment in individual industries depends on level instead of rate of change of individual outputs, and that apparent accelerator relation between aggregate investment and rate of national output change is due to positive correlation between latter and proportion of industries experiencing output increases. 1,3-2,3-1-3.

311. Hicks, Everett M., "Regularization of Business Investment for Industrial Machinery and Equipment Manufacturers." Universities-National Bureau Committee for Economic Research, Regularization of Business Investment, Princeton University Press, 1954, pp. 133-136. There is no hope for this industry to take the lead in promoting more stable investment although it would benefit from a smoother flow. 2-2-0-3.

312. Hicks, J.R., A Contribution to the Theory of the Trade Cycle. Clarendon Press, Oxford, 1950. Chapter 4 contains a modified accelerator model which explains the turning points of the cycle. 1-3-1-3.

313. Hieser, R., "Another Look at the Acceleration Relationship and Equilibrium Growth." Economic Record, 34 (August 1958), pp. 238-248. Claims that the valid accelerator is a general one between increases of income and increases of investment. 1-3-1-1.

314. Higgins, Benjamin, "Government Measures to Regularize Private Investment in Other Countries than the United States." Universities-National Bureau Committee for Economic Research, Regularization of Business Investment, Princeton University Press, 1954, pp. 459-481. Relates experience with depreciation allowances, tax rates and insurance schemes in Canada, Switzerland, Sweden, the U.K., and Italy. 2-3-9-3.

315. Hill, Horace C., Jr., "Capital Expenditure Management." Journal of Business, 28 (October 1955), pp. 285-290. A study of the administrative procedures of capital budgeting and investment planning using an idealized case study. 2-1-8-1.

316. Hirshleifer, J., "On the Theory of Optimal Investment Decision." Journal of Political Economy, 66 (August 1958), pp. 329-352. A comparison and criticism of the "internal rate of return" rule and the "present value" rule for choosing investment projects, in the light of economic theory. 1-1-7,8-0.

317. Hirt, Francis L., "Growth Characteristics of the Economy Illustrated by the Chemical Industry." Survey of Current

Business, 34 (September 1954), pp. 10-14. Data on output, growth rates of chemical products and new investment required in this industry. 2-2-1,5-1.

318. Hoadley, Walter E., Jr., "Regularization of Fixed Investment in the Building Materials Industry." Universities-National Bureau Committee for Economic Research, Regularization of Business Investment, Princeton University Press, 1954, pp. 117-130. 2-2-0-1.

319. Hodges, John E., "A Report on the Calculation of Capital Coefficients for the Petroleum Industry." National Bureau of Economic Research, Studies in Income and Wealth, Vol. 19, Princeton University Press, 1957, pp. 375-387. 2-2-1-1.

320. Hogan, W., "The Equality of Replacement and Depreciation." Economic Record, 35 (August 1959), pp. 196-208. Discusses the problems of estimating the net capital stock which arises from the fact that retirements are not equal to depreciation charges. A continuation of the Eisner, Domar studies in 1952 and 1953. 1-1-2,6-1.

Hohn, F.E., and Franco Modigliani. See Modigliani, 461.

Holmes, Lois E., and Lawrence Bridge. See Bridge, 76, 77.

Holmes, Lois E., and Murray F. Foss. See Foss, 219.

320a. Holt, Charles C., and Franco Modigliani, "Firm Cost Structures and the Dynamic Responses of Inventories, Production, Work Force, and Orders to Sales Fluctuations," in Inventory Fluctuations and Economic Stabilization, Part II, Joint Economic Committee, 87th Congress, 1st Session, Washington, 1961, pp. 3-55.

321. Hoover, Edgar M., "Capital Accumulation and Progress." American Economic Review, 40 Proc. (May 1950), pp. 124-135. A discussion of the controversy over what limits progress: the rate of saving or the rate of spending and technological development. 1-0-5-0.

322. Hoover, Edgar M., "Research in the Area of Productive Capacity and Investment." American Economic Review, 39 Proc. (May 1949), pp. 444-452. Study of research areas and problems on the topic of private investment. 1-0-0-1.

323. Hoover, Edgar M., "Some Institutional Factors in Business Investment Decisions." American Economic Review, 44 Proc. (May 1954), pp. 201-213. A general statement of the nature

and complexity of factors which bear on the investment decision. 1-1-3,4,5-1.

324. Hoover, Edgar M., and B.H. Klein, "Factors Influencing the Demand for Funds by Business Enterprises," National Bureau of Economic Research, Conference on Research in Business Finance, Princeton University Press, 1952, pp. 89-120. 1-1-8-1.

Horwitz, S.J., and N.F. Morehouse. See Morehouse, 472.

325. Hultgren, Thor, American Transportation in Prosperity and Depression. New York, 1948. On pages 157 ff. performs a statistical test of the accelerator. 4-3-1-1.

326. Hultgren, Thor, Cyclical Diversities in the Fortunes of Industrial Corporations. National Bureau of Economic Research, Occasional Paper No. 32, New York, 1950. 1-1-0-0.

Hunt, Pearson, and Robert Schlaifer. See Schlaifer, 544.

327. Hurwicz, L., "Review of Meyer and Kuh The Investment Decision," American Economic Review, 49 (March 1959), p. 162. 1-0-1,2-1.

328. Hurwicz, L., "Theory of the Firm and of Investment." Econometrica, 14 (April 1946), pp. 109-137. An analysis of decisions to invest derived from entrepreneurs' utility functions both with certainty and stochastic expectations. 1-1-7-1.

329. Interstate Commerce Commission, Bureau of Transport Economics and Statistics, Postwar Capital Expenditures of the Railroads, March 1947. 3-2-0-1.

330. Istvan, D.F., "The Economic Evaluation of Capital Expenditures." Journal of Business, 34 (January 1961), pp. 45-51. Based on interviews with 48 large corporations to determine how decisions respecting capital expenditures are made. Concludes that the decision procedures of most companies do not accord with accepted theories of investment. 2-1-8-1.

331. Jacobs, Walter W., and Sylvia F. Broida, "Current Inventory Developments." Survey of Current Business, 29 (April 1949), pp. 14-19. An analysis that seeks to put the large growth of inventories after the war into the perspective of customary prewar levels of inventories. 3-3-0-2.

332. Jacoby, Neil H., and J. Fred Weston, "Financial Policies for Regularizing Business Investment." Universities-National Bu-

reau Committee for Economic Research, Regularization of Business Investment, Princeton University Press, 1954, pp. 369-449. Argues that there is room in this field for fiscal and institutional developments that would be stabilizing. 1-3-9-1.

333. Jacoby, Neil H., and J. Fred Weston, "Factors Influencing Managerial Decisions in Determining Forms of Business Financing: An Exploratory Study." National Bureau of Economic Research, Conference on Research in Business Finance, New York, 1952, pp. 145-197. A comprehensive classification of influential variables. Indicates that intensive study of dynamics of decision-making is the most fruitful research approach, and that the available forms of financing affect the amount of funds demanded. 1-1-7-0.

334. Jensen, Arne, "Application of Stochastic Processes to an Investment Plan." Metroeconomica, 5 (December 1953), pp. 129-137. A model which has been successfully used to determine the optimum capacity installation of telephone equipment in Copenhagen when the demand for service is uncertain. 4-2-8-1.

335. Johnston, J., "Econometric Models and the Average Duration of Business Cycles." Manchester School of Economic and Social Studies, 23 (September 1955), pp. 193-227. Points out the need for separate models for the various sectors of the economy. The general theme of the article is to test the results of linear models against empirical data. 4-3-0-1.

336. Joint Economic Committee, Inventory Fluctuations and Economic Stabilization. A study prepared for the Joint Economic Committee of the Congress of the United States, Washington, 1961. Mr. Paul G. Darling had the major staff responsibility for formulating and directing the study. The three major parts are entitled: I "Postwar Fluctuations in Business Inventories," II "Causative Factors of Movements in Business Inventories," III "Inventory Fluctuations and Economic Instability." 3-2,3-0-2.

337. Jung, Clarence, "Investment Decisions and the Non-Linear Cycle." Journal of Industrial Economics, 4 (October 1955), pp. 33-44. Suggests that the behavior of entrepreneurs is not like that implied by nonlinear theories (e.g. accelerator) but that investment tends to be quite regular except when monetary stringency or panics occur. 1-3-1,7-3.

338. Kaldor, N., "Mr. Hicks on the Trade Cycle." Economic Journal, 61 (December 1951), pp. 833-847. Contains a sharp criticism of Hicks' use of the accelerator. 1-0-1-3.

339. Kalecki, M., "The Principle of Increasing Risk." Economica,
      N. S. 4 (November, 1937), pp. 440-447. A statement of the
      factors which determine the amount of investment given a
      stream of net income, an interest rate and a risk factor
      expressed as a percentage. Argues that rate of risk itself
      changes as investment increases. 1-1-3-1.

340. Kalecki, M., Essays in the Theory of Economic Fluctuations.
      London, 1939. 1-3-0-3.

341. Kalecki, M., Theory of Economic Dynamics, London: Allen
      and Unwin, 1954. 1-3-6-1.

      Karlin, Samuel, and Kenneth J. Arrow. See Arrow, 27.

342. Katona, George, "Psychological Analysis of Business Deci-
      sions and Expectations." American Economic Review, 36
      (March 1946), pp. 44-62. A general article seeking to es-
      tablish the area of interest common to economics and
      psychology. Expectations, their nature and formation are
      discussed. Finds definite expectations stabilizing while
      "cumulative" expectations are destabilizing. 1-1-7,8-0.

343. Katona, George, Psychological Analysis of Economic Behav-
      ior. New York: McGraw-Hill Book Co., 1951. 1-1,3-7-0.

344. Katona, George, and James N. Morgan, "The Quantitative
      Study of Factors Determining Business Decisions." Quarterly
      Journal of Economics, 66 (February 1952), pp. 67-90. Con-
      tains a section on investment decisions. 1-1-7-1.

345. Keezer, Dexter M., "The Short-Run Outlook for Business
      Investment in New Plant and Equipment." Journal of Business,
      28 (July 1955), pp. 165-168. A report on the McGraw-Hill
      Survey for 1955-1956. 3-3-0-1.

345a. Keezer, Dexter M., Robert P. Ulin, Douglas Greenwald, and
      Margaret Matulis, "Surveys of Business' Plans for New
      Plants and Equipment" in (487).

346. Keezer, Dexter M. and Associates, New Forces in American
      Business. New York: McGraw-Hill Book Co., 1959. Chapter II
      deals with prospects for investment in new plant and equip-
      ment in the 60's and Chapter III deals with effects of research
      and development on investment and the economy generally.
      1-1,3-0-1.

347. Kervyn, A., "A Note on the Accelerator and Constant Growth."
      Review of Economic Studies, 22 (1954-1955), pp. 61-66.

Concerned with the internal consistency of a Harrod-Domar growth model in unstable equilibrium. 1-3-1-3.

Kiefer, J., and A. Dvoretzky. See Dvoretzky, 177,178,179.

348. Kimmel, Lewis H., Taxes and Economic Incentives, Washington, D.C.: The Brookings Institution, 1950. A discussion of tax effects based on a mail questionnaire. 2-3-9-0.

349. Kisselgoff, Avram, and Franco Modigliani, "Private Investment in the Electric Power Industry and the Acceleration Principle." Review of Economics and Statistics, 39 (November 1957), pp. 363-380. An empirical analysis of investment by private power companies in the U.S. Concludes that changes in output are the most influential variable on account of rate regulation and the inelasticity of demand for output in view of the condition that all demand must be met. 3-2-1-1.

Klein, B.H., and Edgar M. Hoover. See Hoover, 324.

350. Klein, L.R., "Pitfalls in the Statistical Determination of the Investment Schedule," Econometrica, 11 (July-October 1943), pp. 246-258. A critical review of attempts to derive an aggregate investment function. Emphasizes the identification problem. 1-1-0-1.

351. Klein, L.R., "The Use of Econometric Models as a Guide to Economic Policy." Econometrica, 15 (April 1947), p. 127. 1-3-0-0.

352. Klein, L.R., "Notes on the Theory of Investment." Kyklos, 2 (1948), pp. 97-117. Derives a demand function of the firm for capital goods from entrepreneurs' utility functions and technical production functions. 1-1-2-1.

353. Klein, L.R., Economic Fluctuations in the United States, 1929-1941, Cowles Commission Monograph 11, New York: John Wiley and Sons, Inc., 1950. 4-3-2-1.

354. Klein, L.R., "Studies in Investment Behavior," National Bureau of Economic Research Conference on Business Cycles, New York 1951, pp. 233-277. An analysis of investment by firms. An empirical time-series and cross-section study of investment by American railroads. A time-series study of the electric power industry emphasizes the difference between the growth of this industry and maturity of the railroads. 4-2-2-1.

355. Klein, L.R., and A.S. Goldberger, An Econometric Model of the United States, 1929-1952. Amsterdam: North-Holland, 1952. 4-3-2-1.

356. Klein, L.R., "Econometric Models and the Evidence of Time
Series Analysis." Manchester School of Economic and Social
Studies, 24 (May 1956), pp. 197-201. A comment on an article
by J. Johnston in the same journal, September 1955. 4-3-0-1.

357. Klein, L.R., A. Hazlewood, and P. Vandome, "Re-estimation
of the Econometric Model of the U.K. and Forecasts for
1961." Bulletin of the Oxford University Institute of Statistics,
323 (February 1961), pp. 49-66. Elaborates and extends a
simultaneous equation model of the U.K. economy based on
quarterly data for 1948 to 1958. 4-3-0-0.

358. Klein, L.R., R.J. Ball, A. Hazlewood, and P. Vandome,
An Econometric Model of the United Kingdom. Oxford: Blackwell, 1961. 4-3-0-0.

Klein, L.R., and Harold Barger. See Barger, 34.

359. Knight, Frank, H., "Diminishing Returns from Investment."
Journal of Political Economy, 52 (March 1944), pp. 26-47.
An abstract argument that it is very unlikely that the rate of
return on investment should ever fall to zero. 1-0-3-3.

360. Knox, A.D., "On a Theory of the Trade Cycle." Economica,
17 (August 1950), pp. 317-327. A review of Hicks' The Trade
Cycle in which he examines the theory of investment used
by Hicks and its implications for Hicks' cycle analysis.
1-0-1,2,3-3.

361. Knox, A.D., "The Acceleration Principle and the Theory of
Investment: A Survey." Economica, 19 (August 1952), pp. 269-
297. Examines the usual criticisms of the concept and suggests
the inclusion of profit expectations as well as output changes.
1-1,3-1,2-1.

362. Koch, Albert R., The Financing of Large Corporations, 1920-
1939. National Bureau of Economic Research, Princeton
University Press, 1943. 3-1-2,3-0.

363. Koch, Albert R., "A Method of Projecting Expenditures and
Financial Requirements of Manufacturing Corporations under
Full Employment Conditions." National Bureau of Economic
Research, Conference on Research in Business Finance,
Princeton University Press, 1952, pp. 121-137. 1-3-0-1.

Koch, Albert R., and Doris P. Warner. See Warner, 635.

364. Koopmans, Tjalling C., "Measurement Without Theory."
Review of Economics and Statistics, 29 (August 1947), pp. 161-

172. A review article on Burns and Mitchell, Measuring Business Cycles. 1-0-0-3.

365. Koopmans, Tjalling C., "The Econometric Approach to Business Fluctuations." American Economic Review, 39 Proc. (May 1949), pp. 64-72. A historical discussion of successive stages in the development of econometric techniques for business cycle analysis. 4-0-0-3.

366. Koyck, L.M., Distributed Lags and Investment Analysis. Amsterdam: North-Holland Publishing Co., 1954. Develops a model which explains investment outlays in terms of past changes in sales. Devises a method of estimation where errors are serially correlated. Applies the model to aggregate investment in several industries. 4-2-1-1.

Koyck, L.M., and Hendrieke Goris. See Goris, 266.

Kravis, Irving B., and Irwin Friend. See Friend, 239.

367. Kuh, Edwin, "A Time-Series Approach to Cross-Sectional Investment Behavior." Econometrica, 25 (October 1957), p. 609. An abstract of a paper. 4-1-1,2-1.

368. Kuh, Edwin, "The Validity of Cross-Sectionally Estimated Behavior Equations in Time Series Applications." Econometrica, 27 (April 1959), pp. 197-214. Compares the statistical results obtained for three investment functions based on gross internal funds and the capital stock using cross-section and time-series sample data for individual firms. 4-1-1,2-1.

369. Kuh, Edwin, "Capital Theory and Capital Budgeting." Metroeconomica, 12 (December 1960), pp. 64-80. Approaches the problem of capital budgeting assuming as an objective that the market value of the previously outstanding equity should be maximized. Considers the determination of the optimum debt-equity combination. 1-1-3,8-1.

Kuh, Edwin, and J.R. Meyer. See Meyer, 448,449,450.

370. Kuznets, Simon, "Relation Between Capital Goods and Finished Products in the Business Cycle." Economic Essays in Honor of Wesley Clair Mitchell. New York: Columbia University Press, 1935, pp. 209-269. Contains an empirical test of the acceleration hypothesis based on investment in railroads. 3-3-1-1.

371. Kuznets, Simon, Commodity Flow and Capital Formation. New York: National Bureau of Economic Research, 1938. 3-3-1-1.

372. Kuznets, Simon, "Proportion of Capital Formation to National Product." American Economic Review, 42, Proc. (May 1952), pp. 507-526. A study of the long-term trends in saving, income and capital formation in various types of facilities. 3-3-1-1.

373. Kuznets, Simon, "International Differences in Capital Formation and Financing," in M. Abramovitz (ed.) Capital Formation and Economic Growth. Princeton University Press, for National Bureau of Economic Research, 1956, pp. 19-111. 3-3-2,3-1.

374. Kuznets, Simon, "Quantitative Aspects of the Economic Growth of Nations: V. Capital Formation Proportions: International Comparisons for Recent Years," Economic Development and Cultural Change, 8 (July 1960), pp. 1-96. 3-3-1-1.

375. Kuznets, Simon, "Quantitative Aspects of the Economic Growth of Nations: VI. Long-Term Trends in Capital Formation Proportions." Economic Development and Cultural Change, 9 (July 1961), pp. 1-124. 3-3-1-1.

376. Kuznets, Simon, Capital in the American Economy: Its Formation and Financing. New York: National Bureau of Economic Research, 1961. Number 9 of the Series Studies in Capital Formation and Financing. An analysis of long-term trends in the United States organized primarily around the principal capital-using sectors of the economy. The analysis also attempts to isolate the factors that determine the trends that are observed. 3-2-0-1.

377. Lachman, L. M. "Complementarity and Substitution in the Theory of Capital." Economica, 14 (May 1947), pp. 108-119. Argues that capital goods can be treated meaningfully only as disaggregated separate factors of production and that the concept of profit is too general. 1-1-2-1.

378. Lachman, L. M. "Investment Repercussions." Quarterly Journal of Economics, 62 (November 1948), pp. 698-713. A theoretical study of the interdependence of investment decisions. Points out the way in which one outlay may affect the marginal efficiency of another project. 1-3-0-1.

379. Lachman, L. M., Capital and Its Structure. London: The London School of Economics and Political Science and G. Bell and Sons, Ltd., 1956. Emphasizes the nonhomogeneity of real capital. Units of equipment are indivisible and are related to other units as complements and as substitutes. Is thereby led to discard the concept of marginal productivity of capital but does not offer a replacement. 1-1-2,7-1.

380. Laderman, J., S. B. Littauer, and Lionel Weiss, "The Inventory Problem." Journal of The American Statistical Association, 48 (December 1953), pp. 717-732. An expository article setting out the model of Dvoretzky, Kiefer and Wolfowitz in Econometrica, 1952. 1-3-0-2.

381. Lanzillotti, R. F. "Pricing Objectives in Large Corporations." American Economic Review, 48 (December 1958), pp. 921-940. The results of intensive interview surveys of 20 large companies at two different times. Reports the "Objectives" which managers claimed to be pursuing. 2-1-7-0.

382. Latane, Henry Allen, "Criteria for Choice Among Risky Ventures." Journal of Political Economy, 67 (April 1959), pp. 144-155. A simple model for choosing rationally with a given payout matrix and a subjective probability distribution of events. 1-1-7,8-0.

383. Leaderach, Paul A., "Applying Sound Principles to Equipment Replacement Practice." N.A.A. Bulletin, 40 (April 1959), pp. 70-79. A review of alternative formulae and techniques used in making replacement decisions. 1-1-6-1.

Leibowitz, Walter, and Murray Foss. See Foss, 227.

384. Lent, Charles W., Jr., "Why the Discounted-Cash-Flow Method is Better and How it Works." N.A.A. Bulletin, 41 (June 1960), pp. 21-30. This whole issue is devoted to capital outlay evaluation. 1-1-2,8-1.

385. Leontief, W., et al., Studies in the Structure of the American Economy, Theoretical and Empirical Explorations in Input-Output Analysis. New York: Oxford University Press, 1953. 1,2,3-3-0-1,3.

386. Levine, Robert A., Plant and Equipment Expenditure Surveys: Intentions and Fulfillment. Cowles Foundation Discussion Paper 17, (October 1956) 4-2,3-0-1.

Liebenberg, Maurice, and George M. Cobren. See Cobren, 127.

387. Liebling, Herman I., "Financing the Expansion of Business." Survey of Current Business, 37 (September 1957), pp. 6-14. Analyzes structures of investment and sources of financing in post-World War II period in six major nonfinancial industries including manufacturing and mining, railroads, nonrail transportation, public utilities, communications and trade. 1-2-3-1.

388. Liebling, Herman I., "Financing Business In Recession and Expansion." Survey of Current Business, 38 (October 1958), pp. 15-20. Points out cyclical changes in investment patterns of industries, especially with respect to fixed and working capital requirements; and in financing patterns, especially with respect to shares of internal and external funds. 1-0-3-0.

389. Lindsay, Robert, "The Stability of Business Capital Outlays." Review of Economics and Statistics, 40 (May 1958), pp. 159-163. Disagrees with those who believe that fluctuations of investment have narrowed in the postwar era and are likely to remain quite stable due to policies of maintaining high employment and consumer purchasing power. 1-3-0-1.

390. Lintner, John, "Effect of Corporate Taxation on Real Investment." American Economic Review, 44 (May 1954), pp. 520-534. Concludes that the effects of taxes on investment can be seriously discouraging. 1-3-9-1.

Littauer, S.B., and J. Laderman. See Laderman, 380.

391. Liu, Ta-Chung, and Ching-Gwan Chang, "Consumption and Investment Propensities: Prewar and Postwar, U.S." American Economic Review, 40 (September 1950), pp. 563-582. A statistical fitting of these two relations. Has investment related to income and corporate profits. $I = 0.221Y + 0:339F - 11.20$. 4-3-2-1.

392. Liu, Ta-Chung, "A Simple Forecasting Model for the U.S. Economy." International Monetary Fund Staff Papers, 4 (August 1955), pp. 434-466. A statistical model of the economy to forecast GNP consumption and private investment in plant equipment, based on 1929-52 data. The model is used to predict for 1953 and 1954. Contains an appendix on the estimation procedures. 4-3-1,2-1.

393. Livingston, S. Morris, "The Demand for Producers' Durable Equipment." Survey of Current Business, 29 (June 1949), pp. 8-18. A long-term analysis of investment expenditures with particular attention to telephone, electricity and transportation companies. Attempts to estimate the duration of the backlog of demand created by the war. 3-2-1-1.

394. Lorie, James H., and Leonard J. Savage, "Three Problems in Rationing Capital." Journal of Business, 28 (October 1955), pp. 229-239. A discussion of criteria for selecting among investment projects. This whole issue of the Journal is devoted to the subject of Capital Budgeting. 1-1-8-1.

395. Lorie, James H., "Two Important Problems in Sales Forecasting." Journal of Business, 30 (July 1957), pp. 172-179. Discusses the adaptation of statistical forecasts by subjective judgment and the need to evaluate alternative forecasts. 1-1-8-0.

396. Lovell, Michael C., "Manufacturers' Inventories, Sales Expectations, and the Acceleration Principle." Econometrica, 29 (July 1961), pp. 293-314. The response of manufacturers' inventory holdings to changes in the volume of sales and the backlog of unfilled orders is examined on a quarterly basis for the period 1948-55. 4-2-1-2.

397. Lowe, Adolph, "Structural Analysis of Real Capital Formation." Universities-National Bureau Committee for Economic Research, Capital Formation and Economic Growth, pp. 581-634. An abstract three-sectoral model of the production process for consumer and capital goods in the aggregate. Traces out the implications of innovation and capital additions. 1-3-1,5,6-1.

398. Lundberg, E., "Profitability of Investment." Economic Journal, 69 (December 1959), pp. 653-677. An analysis of the criteria for allocation of aggregate investment expenditure to achieve maximum social benefit. The article is based on questions raised by planning experience in Sweden. 1-3-7-1.

398a. Lundberg, Erik, Studies in the Theory of Economic Expansion. King, 1937.

398b. Lundberg, Erik, ed., The Business Cycle in the Post-War World. New York: Macmillan, Co., 1955.

399. Lutz, Friedrich, "The Criterion of Maximum Profits in the Theory of Investment." Quarterly Journal of Economics, 60 (November 1945), pp. 56-77. Review of the Literature. Distinguishes total profits, internal rate of return, and profit over cost. 1-1-2,3-1.

400. Lutz, Friedrich, "The Interest Rate and Investment in a Dynamic Economy." American Economic Review, 35 (December 1945), pp. 811-830. A discussion of the lack of empirical relations between investment and the level of the interest rate. Discusses the dynamic factors which vitiate the ceteris paribus assumptions of static interest rate analysis. There are other factors which are more influential than the rate of interest in a dynamic model. 1-3-3-1.

401. Lutz, Friedrich and Vera, The Theory of Investment of the Firm. Princeton: Princeton University Press, 1951. 1-1-2,3-1.

402. Lydall, H. F., "The Impact of the Credit Squeeze on Small and Medium-Sized Manufacturing Firms." Economic Journal, 67 (September 1957), pp. 415-431. An examination of the influence of interest rate changes. Probably has most of its influence through sales expectations and availability of financing. Reports on a questionnaire survey. 2-3-3-1.

403. Mack, Ruth P., "Business Expectations and the Buying of Materials." Expectations, Uncertainty and Business Behavior. M. J. Bowman (ed.), 1958, pp. 106-118. A study of materials, purchases and stocks held by individual firms. Observes that purchases are subject to definite fluctuations and that additions to stocks tend to be bunched. 1-1-1-2.

404. Mack, Ruth P., "Characteristics of Inventory Investment: The Aggregate and Its Parts." National Bureau of Economic Research, Studies in Income and Wealth, Vol. 19, Princeton University Press, 1957, pp. 471-487. Argues that the total effect of inventories may be greater than the aggregate volume would suggest. 1-3-0-2.

405. Mack, Ruth P., "The Process of Capital Formation in Inventories and the Vertical Propagation of Business Cycles." Review of Economics and Statistics, 35 (August 1953), pp. 181-198. Statements about aggregative behavior with respect to stocks are precarious because inventory changes are influenced by non-inventory decisions and because of interrelations in the decisions of separate firms. 1-3-8-2.

406. Mack, Ruth P., Consumption and Business Fluctuations: A Case Study of the Shoe, Leather, Hide Sequence. New York: National Bureau of Economic Research, Princeton University Press, 1956. Analyzes changes in inventories for retailers, manufacturers and tanners and the factors that are associated with these changes. 2-2-4-2.

406a. Mack, Ruth P., The Flow of Funds and Consumer Purchasing Power. New York: Columbia University Press, 1941.

407. Mack, Ruth P. and Victor Zarnowitz, "Cause and Consequence of Changes in Retailers' Buying." American Economic Review, 48 (March 1958), pp. 18-49. Elaborates a model of the transmission and magnification of sales changes to production changes with special reference to retailing. Cites evidence from the merchandising experience of department stores. The argument emphasizes the importance of advance ordering for future sales. 1-2-1-2.

Mack, Ruth P. and D. B. Woodward. See Woodward, 661.

408. Maclaurin, Rupert W., "The Process of Technological Innovation: The Launching of a New Scientific Industry."

American Economic Review, 40 (March 1950), pp. 90-112. A study of the radio industry with emphasis on the key entre- preneurial functions and decisions. 2-2-5,7-3.

409. Maclaurin, Rupert W., "Innovation and Capital Formation in Some American Industries." Universities-National Bureau Committee for Economic Research, Capital Formation and Economic Growth, Princeton University Press, 1955, pp. 551-572. Discusses innovation in the automobile, electrical, radio and television, aviation and housing industries. 2-2-5-1.

410. Magee, John F., "Guides to Inventory Policy. I. Functions and Lot Sizes." Harvard Business Review, 34 (January-February 1956), pp. 49-60. The first of three articles on the nature of a rational inventory policy. 1-1-8-2.

411. Magee, John F., "Guides to Inventory Policy. II. Problems of Uncertainty." Harvard Business Review, 34 (March-April 1956), pp. 103-116. 1-1-8-2.

412. Magee, John F., "Guides to Inventory Policy. III. Anticipating Future Needs." Harvard Business Review, 34 (May-June 1956), pp. 57-70. 1-1-8-2.

413. Magee, John F., Production, Planning and Inventory Control. New York: McGraw-Hill Book Co., 1958. A book describing the basic functions of inventories and the different policies and costs which affect inventory and production planning decisions. 1-1-8-2.

414. Maisel, Sherman J., Fluctuations, Growth and Forecasting: The Principles of Dynamic Business Economics. New York: John Wiley and Sons, Inc., 1957. A textbook which contains sections on decision-making, forecasting and the theory of fluctuations. 1-1,3-7,8-3.

415. Malissen, Marcel, Investissement et Financement, Paris: Li- brairie Armand Colin, 1957. An analysis of capital outlays and their financing for 53 French firms over a period of 7 years, 1949-55. 3-1,3-1,2-1.

416. Manne, A.S., "Some Notes on the Acceleration Principle." Review of Economics and Statistics, 27 (May 1945), pp. 93-99. A statistical testing of the principle and some qualifications as to why the results should not conform to the rigid formu- lation. 4-3-1-1.

417. Manne, A.S., and John M. Frankovich, "Electronic Calculating Methods for Handling the Excess Capacity Problem." Review

of Economics and Statistics, 35 (February 1953), pp. 51-58.
A computer simulation model dealing with the effect of excess
capacity and bottlenecks on the volume of investment expenditures. 4-3-1,4-1.

418. Manne, A. S., "Capacity Expansion and Probabilistic Growth."
Econometrica, 29 (October 1961), pp. 632-649. An optimizing
model concerned with the interplay between economics of
scale and an anticipated probabilistic growth in demand for
capacity. 3-1-7-1.

419. Mansfield, Edwin, and Harold H. Wein, "A Study of Decision-
Making Within the Firm." Quarterly Journal of Economics,
72 (November 1958), pp. 515-536. Constructs a model from
an empirical study of railroad operations in which the goal
is not profit maximization. Some uncertainty exists and the
internal complexity of organizations is recognized. 2-1-7-0.

420. Mansfield, Edwin, "Technical Change and the Rate of Imitation." Econometrica, 29 (October 1961), pp. 741-766. A study
of the factors influencing how rapidly firms introduce new
types of equipment. 3-1-5-1.

421. MAPI, Replacement Manual. Machinery and Allied Products
Institute, Washington, D.C., 1950. 0-1-6-1.

422. Marks, B. J., The Prediction and Analysis of Demand for
Replacement Parts. Doctoral Dissertation, University of
Minnesota, 1960. 1-1,2-6-1.

Marschak, Jacob, and Kenneth J. Arrow. See Arrow, 26.

423. Massell, B. F., "Capital Formation and Technological Change
in United States Manufacturing." Review of Economics and
Statistics, 42 (May 1960), pp. 182-188. Attempts to attribute
increases in output per man hour in the U.S. between 1919
and 1955 to increases in amount of capital used per man-hour
or to improvements in technology or methods. Attributes
most of the increase to technological development. 3-3-5-3.

424. Massell, B. F., "Is Investment Really Unimportant?" The
RAND Corporation, Paper P-2088, (June 1961). A theoretical
and empirical re-examination of the hypothesis that the contribution of investment to increases in output per man-hour
is minimal, as suggested by earlier studies. Using time
series and cross-section data, evidence is provided of the
interrelationship of investment and technical change. This
suggests that the role of investment is larger than previously
indicated. To be published in Metroeconomica. 4-3-5-3.

425. Massell, B. F., "A Disaggregated View of Technical Change." Journal of Political Economy (December, 1961). An attempt to measure the relative importance of "intraindustry" and "interindustry" technical change. The latter, which results from factors of production shifting among industries, leads to a discrepancy between the aggregate rate of technical change and a weighted sum of industrial rates. Nearly one-third of aggregate technical change is accounted for by interindustry change, mostly a result of capital mobility. 4-3-5-3.

426. Massell, B. F., "Investment, Innovation, and Growth." The RAND Corporation, Paper P-2149 (January 1961). Examines the evidence that the major part of the increase in average labor productivity in the U.S. over the past 40 years has resulted from technical progress. The relationship between investment and technical progress is considered in the context of a simplified model, and an attempt is made to reassess the contribution of investment to economic growth. To be published in Econometrica. 1-3-5-3.

427. Massell, B. F., "Another Small Problem in the Analysis of Growth." The RAND Corporation, Paper P-2194 (January 1961). Discusses the evidence that the observed increase in the average productivity of labor has been primarily a consequence of technical progress, as contrasted with capital deepening. Indicated another procedural difficulty involved in the apportionment of productivity increase between technical progress and capital deepening and presents a partial solution to the problem. To be published in The Review of Economics and Statistics. 1-3-5-3.

428. Matthews, R. C. O., "Professor Gordon on 'Underlying Investment Opportunities'." Review of Economics and Statistics, 38 (November 1956), pp. 482-484. A criticism of Gordon's article, Review of Economics and Statistics, 37 (February, 1955), pp. 23-34. 1-3-0-1.

429. Matthews, R. C. O., The Business Cycle. Chicago: University of Chicago Press, 1958. Chapters III — V contain a survey of the acceleration principle and other aspects of the theory of investment relevant to business cycles. 1-3-1-3.

430. Mayer, T., Input Lead Time for Capital Coefficients. Washington, D.C.: U.S. Bureau of Mines, Inter-Industry Research Item Number 52, 1953. Provides data on the length of the construction period for most S.I.C. manufacturing industries and on the percent and types of capital equipment put into place in each stage of the construction period. 2-2-4-1.

431. Mayer, T., and Sidney Sonenblum, "Lead Time for Fixed Investment." Review of Economics and Statistics, 37 (August 1955), pp. 300-304. Presents estimates of the time needed to construct and equip new plants for 108 specific S.I.C. industries. Based on data collected during World War II and the Korean War. 2-2-4-1.

432. Mayer, T., "The Inflexibility of Monetary Policy." Review of Economics and Statistics, 40 (November 1958), pp. 358-374. Has data for the construction period, planning period and lag between changes in credit availability and start of construction for most types of investment. 2-0-3,4,7,8-3.

433. Mayer, T., "Plant and Equipment Lead Times." Journal of Business, 33 (April 1960), pp. 127-132. Reports the results of a questionnaire answered by more than 100 companies which had made substantial capital expenditures. The questions dealt with the number of months between initial planning and the start of construction and between start and completion of construction. 2-1-0-1.

434. McClelland, W.G., "The Least-Cost Level of Stocks and the Rate of Interest." Journal of Industrial Economics, 8 (March 1960), pp. 151-171. This paper briefly describes and assesses the techniques that have been developed for determining optimum inventory levels. Considers the influence of changing storage and interest cost. 1-1-4-2.

435. McHugh, Loughlin F., "Financing Corporate Expansion." Survey of Current Business, 40 (October 1960), pp. 13-17. Reviews corporation finance in the recent period. An annual feature on this same topic. 3-3-2,3-1.

436. McHugh, Loughlin F., "Financing Small Business in the Post-war Period." Survey of Current Business, 31 (November 1951), pp. 17-23. A study based on a mail questionnaire. Two out of three firms used exclusively internal funds. Most of the remainder supplied by banks. 3-3-2,3-1.

437. McHugh, Loughlin F. and Jack N. Ciaccio, "External Financing of Small and Medium Size Business." Survey of Current Business 35 (October 1955), pp. 15-22. Results of a survey based on the 12-month period ending June 30, 1954. 3-3-2,3-1.

438. McHugh, Loughlin F. and Leonard G. Rosenberg, "Financial Experience of Large and Medium Size Manufacturing Firms, 1927-1951." Survey of Current Business, 32 (November 1952), pp. 7-13. Prepared from a sample of 100 large firms. Gives balance sheet information about sales, profit, liquidity and interest payments. 3-3-2,3-1.

439. McLean, J.G., "How to Evaluate New Capital Investments."
      Harvard Business Review, 36 (November-December 1958),
      pp. 59-69. Describes the application of discounting cash
      returns to an industrial situation. Argues that this technique
      is superior to most common procedures such as years-to-
      payout. Uses the Continental Oil Co. experience as basis for
      article. 1,3-1-2-1.
440. Meade, J.E., and P.W.S. Andrews, "Summary of Replies
      to Questions on Effect of Interest Rates." Oxford Economic
      Papers, 1 (October 1938), pp. 14-31. Report on interviews
      by the Oxford Economists Research Group with 37 business-
      men. 2-1-3-3.

      Meredith, G.P. and C.F. Carter, See Carter, 107.

440a. Meiselman, David, The Term Structure of Interest Rates,
      unpublished manuscript, April 1961. Based on unpublished
      Ph. D. dissertation, University of Chicago.

441. Merrett, Anthony and Allen Sykes, "Calculating the Rate of
      Return on Capital Projects." Journal of Industrial Economics,
      9 (November 1960), pp. 98-115. Considers the relative merits
      of conventional accounting methods and of theoretical eco-
      nomic methods for calculating the rate of return on capital
      projects. Concludes that an "implied rate of return" calcu-
      lation is superior. 1-1-2-1.

442. Merriam, Malcolm L., "Current and Prospective Plant and
      Equipment Expenditures." Survey of Current Business, 28
      (April 1948), pp. 12-14. 3-3-8-1.

443. Metzler, L.A., "The Nature and Stability of Inventory Cycles."
      Review of Economic Statistics, 23 (August 1941), pp. 113-129.
      The first attempt to show how the desire of businessmen
      to keep their inventories at some optimal level in relation
      to sales introduces a cyclical element into economic fluctua-
      tions. Based upon the dynamic sequence suggested by Erik
      Lundberg, The Economics of Expansion. 1-3-1-2.

444. Metzler, L.A., "Business Cycles and the Modern Theory of
      Employment." American Economic Review, 36 (June 1946),
      pp. 278-291. A verbal formulation of the cycle mechanism
      as waves of adaption to exogenous shocks. Has a consider-
      able application of this principle to inventory fluctuations.
      1-3-1,5-3.

445. Metzler, L.A., "Factors Governing the Length of Inventory
      Cycles," Review of Economics and Statistics. 29 (February

1947), pp. 1-15. An analysis of the influence of consuming habits, the inventory accelerator, or what Nurkse calls the size of the pipeline, and produces expectations upon the average duration of inventory cycles. 1-3-1-2.

446. Metzler, L.A., "The Rate of Interest and the Marginal Product of Capital." Journal of Political Economy, 58 (August 1950), pp. 289-306. A rigorous development of the relation between these concepts. Argues that the rate of interest is only by accident equal to the marginal social product of capital. 1-3-3-1.

447. Metzler, L.A., "The Rate of Interest and the Marginal Product of Capital: A Correction." Journal of Political Economy, 59 (February 1951), pp. 67-68. Refers to an error in an article in the same Journal, August 1950. 1-3-3-1.

447a. Metzler, Lloyd A., "Comment" (on paper by Abramovitz), in Conference on Business Cycles, National Bureau of Economic Research, 1951.

448. Meyer, J.R., and Edwin Kuh, "Acceleration and Related Theories of Investment; an Empirical Inquiry." Review of Economics and Statistics, 37 (August 1955), pp. 217-230. 4-2-1,2-1.

449. Meyer, J.R., and Edwin Kuh, "Further Comments on the Empirical Study of Investment Functions." Review of Economics and Statistics, 39 (May 1957), pp. 218-22 . A rejoinder to criticisms by Morrissett in the February issue. 4-2-1,2-1.

450. Meyer, J.R., and Edwin Kuh, The Investment Decision: An Empirical Study. Harvard University Press, 1957. 4-2-1,2-1

451. Miller, John Perry, "The Pricing Effects of Accelerated Amortization." Review of Economics and Statistics, 34 (February 1952), pp. 10-17. Accelerated amortization permits not only relief from taxes but in some instances also increases revenue when prices are based on costs and the amount of depreciation expense is regarded as a cost. 1-1-9-1.

Miller, M.H., and Franco Modigliani. See Modigliani, 468,469.

452. Mills, Edwin S., "Expectations, Uncertainty and Inventory Fluctuations." Review of Economic Studies, 22 (1954-1955), pp. 15-22. Discusses the implications of uncertainty and

different patterns of firm behavior for inventory fluctuations. 1-3-7,8-2.

453. Mills, Edwin S., "Professor Nurkse on Inventory Cycles." Oxford Economic Papers, N.S. 7 (February 1955), pp. 226-228. Explores some implications of Nurkse's article, Oxford Economic Papers, 1954, pp. 203-225. 1-3-0-2.

454. Mills, Edwin S., "Expectations and Undesired Inventory." Management Science, 4 (October 1957). Attempts to estimate undesired inventories in the postwar U.S. economy within the framework of a formal decision model. 4-3-7,8-2.

455. Mills, Edwin S., "The Theory of Inventory Decisions." Econometrica, 25 (April 1957), pp. 222-238. An attempt to determine whether firms can be assumed to behave as if they were using a rational inventory policy. 1-3-8-2.

456. Mills, G., "The Marginal Efficiency of Capital and the Present-Value Rule." Yorkshire Bulletin of Economic and Social Research, 12 (March 1960), pp. 28-31. Indicates that these two methods for calculating the profitability of a capital asset are not the same when the asset may have a negative yield in some periods. 1-1-0-1.

457. Mills, G., "Fixed Asset Valuation and Linear Programming." Journal of Farm Economics, 42 (May 1960), pp. 378-384. Elementary exposition showing that on the assumptions of the linear programming model, the profit-maximizing firm should adjust its stock of fixed assets in finite jumps as factor and product prices changes gradually. 1-1-4-1.

458. Minsky, Hyman P., "Monetary Systems and Accelerator Models." American Economic Review, 47 (December 1957), pp. 859-883. Considers the restraints imposed on the multiplier-accelerator by the institutional framework of the monetary system. Particularly emphasizes the study of the upper turning point and the possibility of steady growth. 1-3-1,3-1.

459. Mitchell, Wesley C., What Happens During Business Cycles: A Progress Report. New York: National Bureau of Economic Research Inc., 1951. A summary of Mitchell's contribution to cyclical quantitative analysis. 3-3-0-3.

460. Modigliani, Franco and N. Zeman, "The Effect of the Availability of Funds and the Terms Thereof on Business Investment." National Bureau of Economic Research Inc., Conference on Research in Business Finance, Princeton University Press, 1952, pp. 263-308. Develops a model to

show the amount of investment that will be undertaken under different assumptions about expectations and risk and the division of financing between equity and debt. Tests the model with data from large corporations. 4-3-2,3,8-1.

461. Modigliani, Franco and F.E. Hohn, "Production Planning Over Time and The Nature of the Expectation and Planning Horizon." Econometrica, 23 (January 1955), pp. 46-66. A program for meeting certain output requirements at least cost given production and inventory cost functions. 1-3-7-0.

Modigliani, Franco, and Charles C. Holt. See Holt, 320a.

Modigliani, Franco, and Avram Kisselgoff. See Kisselgoff, 349.

462. Modigliani, Franco, and Owen H. Sauerlander, "Economic Expectations and the Plans of Firms in Relation to Short-Term Forecasting." National Bureau of Economic Research Inc. Studies in Income and Wealth, Vol. 17, Princeton University Press, 1955, pp. 261-351. This is a survey of anticipatory data on investment, sales and inventories. It attempts to assess these data for forecasting. 4-3-1,8-3.

463. Modigliani, Franco, "Business Reasons for Holding Inventories and Their Macro-Economic Implications." National Bureau of Economic Research Inc., Studies in Income and Wealth, Vol. 19, Princeton University Press, 1957, pp. 495-506. 1-1,3-8-2.

464. Modigliani, Franco, National Bureau of Economic Research Inc., Studies in Income and Wealth, Vol. 19, Princeton University Press, 1957, pp. 450-462. Comment on Hickman, Bert G., "Capacity, Capacity Utilization and the Accelerator Principle," pp. 419-449. 1-3-1-1.

465. Modigliani, Franco, and Kalman J. Cohen, "The Significance and Uses of Ex-Ante Data," in Expectations, Uncertainty, and Business Behavior, M.J. Bowman (ed.), pp. 151-164. A discussion of the nature of the decision-making process. Hypothesizes that decisions are made a step at a time so as to maximize the value of the firm and to maintain latitude for future decisions. 1-3-7,8-0.

466. Modigliani, F., and K.J. Cohen, The Role of Anticipations and Plans in Economic Behavior and their use in Economic Analysis and Forecasting. Bureau of Economic and Business Research, University of Illinois, 1961. 3-2,3-8-2.

467. Modigliani, Franco and H.M. Weingartner, "Forecasting Uses of Anticipatory Data on Investment and Sales." Quarterly

Journal of Economics, 72 (February 1958), pp. 23-54. An analysis of the predictive accuracy of anticipations data collected in the U.S. The analysis employs time-series techniques on data for nine years. The results are judged more satisfactory than previous cross-section studies. 4-3-8-1.

468. Modigliani, Franco and M.H. Miller, "Cost of Capital, Corporation Finances and the Theory of Investment." American Economic Review, 48 (June 1958), pp. 261-297. Develops several theorems about the financing of investment under assumed capital market conditions. Elaborates the conditions under which a firm would prefer one type of financing rather than another. 1-1,3-3-1.

469. Modigliani, F., and M.H. Miller, "The Cost of Capital, Corporation Finance, and the Theory of Investment: Reply." American Economic Review, 49 (September 1959), pp. 655-669. A reply to criticisms of an article by the same name made by J.R. Rose and D. Durand in this same issue. 1-1-2-0.

470. More, Frederick T., "Capital Coefficients in Mineral and Metal Industries." National Bureau of Economic Research Inc., Studies in Income and Wealth, Vol. 19, Princeton University Press, 1957, pp. 311-346. 3-2-1-1.

471. Morehouse, Edward W., "Regularization of Business Investment in the Electric Utility Industry." Universities-National Bureau Committee for Economic Research, Regularization of Business Investment, Princeton University Press, 1954, pp. 213-281. Believes there is considerable latitude for stabilizing investment programs. Has 34 pages of tables and charts on operating data of utility companies. 3-2-0-1.

472. Morehouse, N.F., R.H. Strotz and S.J. Horwitz, "An Electric-Analog Method for Investigating Problems in Dynamic Economics: Inventory Oscillations." Econometrica, 18 (October 1950), pp. 313-328. 1-0-0-2.

Morgan, James N., and George Katona. See Katona, 344.

473. Morin, F., "Note on an Inventory Problem Discussed by Modigliani and Hohn." Econometrica, 23 (October 1955), pp. 447-450. 1-3-7-0.

474. Morrissett, Irving, "A Note on the Empirical Study of Acceleration and Related Theories of Investment." Review of Economics and Statistics, 39 (February 1957), pp. 91-93. Note on Meyer and Kuh's article in the same review. Critical of the economic reasoning and the wideness of the conclusions drawn by Meyer and Kuh. 4-2-1,2-1.

475. Morse, Philip M., Queues, Inventories and Maintenance, New York: John Wiley and Sons, 1958. 1-3-0-2.

476. Mueller, Willard F., "A Case Study of Product Discovery and Innovation Costs." Southern Economic Journal, 24 (July 1958), pp. 80-86. Attacks the "myth" that it cost a great deal for du Pont to bring nylon into being and to the market and that a smaller company could not have borne the expense for research and development. 2-1-5-0.

Muth, R., and M. Beckmann. See Beckmann, 45.

477. Naddor, Eliezer, "Some Models of Inventory and An Application." Management Science, 2 (July 1956), pp. 299-312. Develops several simple inventory situations with an application to a company making metal castings. 1-1-1-2.

478. Nassimbene, Raymond and Donald G. Wooden, "Producers' Equipment-Growth, Repacement, and Stock," Survey of Current Business, 33 (June 1953), pp. 12-16. Covers the period 1929-52 and presents data on (a) extent to which business equipment purchases were for replacement and (b) the increase in the various types of stock of equipment. 3-3-1-1.

479. Nassimbene, Raymond and Donald G. Wooden, "Growth of Business Capital Equipment 1929-1953, Measures of Purchases, Depreciation, Retirements and Stocks." Survey of Current Business, 34 (December 1954), pp. 18-26. Gross stocks of business equipment in constant dollars showed little change between the end of 1928 and 1941 but doubled between 1941 and 1953. Output per unit of equipment fluctuated widely over the period 1929-53 but without apparent trend. 3-3-1-1.

480. National Bureau of Economic Research, Universities—National Bureau Committee for Economic Research, Vol. 2, Conference on Business Cycles, New York, Princeton University Press, 1951. 1,3-0-0-3.

481. National Bureau of Economic Research, Universities—National Bureau Committee for Economic Research, Vol. 3, Conference on Research in Business Finance, New York, 1952. 1,3-2,3-0-1.

482. National Bureau of Economic Research, Universities — National Bureau Committee for Economic Research, Vol 4, Regularization of Business Investment, Princeton University Press, 1954. 1,3-0-0-3.

483. National Bureau of Economic Research, Conference on Research in Income and Wealth, Vol. 16, Long-Range Economic Projection, Princeton University Press, 1954. 1,3-0-8-1.

484. National Bureau of Economic Research, Conference of the Universities-National Bureau Committee on Economic Research, Vol. 6, Capital Formation and Economic Growth, Princeton University Press, 1955. 1,3-0-0-3.

485. National Bureau of Economic Research, Conference on Research in Income and Wealth, Vol. 17, Short-Term Economic Forecasting, Princeton University Press, 1955. 1,3-0-8-0.

486. National Bureau of Economic Research, Conference on Research in Income and Wealth, Vol. 19, Problems of Capital Formation: Concepts, Measurement and Controlling Factors, Studies in Income and Wealth, Princeton University Press, 1957. 1-3-0-0-1.

487. National Bureau of Economic Research, Conference of the Universities — National Bureau Committee for Economic Research, Vol. 10, The Quality and Economic Significance of Anticipations Data, Princeton University Press, 1960. Reports on a 1957 Conference. 0-0-8-0.

488. National Bureau of Economic Research, Capital in Manufactures and Mining: Its Formation and Financing by D. Creamer, S.P. Dobrovolsky and I. Borenstein, Princeton University Press, 1960. 3-2-0-1.

489. National Industrial Conference Board, Capital Formation and Its Elements. New York: National Industrial Conference Board, 1939. A set of papers presented at a symposium by: A.H. Hansen, S. Kuznets, J.M. Clark, G. Colm, R.S. Tucker, R. Nugent, G. Haberler and C.O. Hardy. 1-3-0-1.

490. National Industrial Conference Board, Controlling Capital Expenditures. Studies in Business Policy, No. 62. An exhaustive study of the factors influencing capital budgeting by a large number of U. S. companies. 3-3-8-1.

491. Natrella, V., "Forecasting Plant and Equipment Expenditures from Businessmen's Expectations," Proceedings of the Business and Economic Statistics Section of the American Statistical Association, 1956, pp. 121-132. Statement of the accuracy of the SEC-Department of Commerce intentions surveys and the factors which affect their accuracy. 3-3-8-1.

Natrella, V., and Lawrence Bridge. See Bridge, 81-83.

Natrella, V., and Murray F. Foss. See Foss, 224, 225, 226.

492. Neisser, Hans, "Critical Notes on the Acceleration Principle." Quarterly Journal of Economics, 68 (May 1954), pp. 253-274.

An analysis of the difference between expansion of demand and the increase of output as accelerators. The substitution of the second for the first is said to break down at the ceiling. An increase of income due to preceding autonomous investment is shown not to induce further investment, and the Hicksian formula for the super-multiplier is correspondingly modified for the elementary case. 1-3-1-1.

493. Neisser, Hans, and E. Grosswald, "Gross Capital Stock and Net Capital Stock: The Simplest Case." Review of Economics and Statistics, 42 (February 1960), pp. 94-96. Considers the size of the gross capital stock at any point of time on the assumption that depreciation allowances are reinvested in equipment and that items of the stock have a fixed useful life. 1-1,3-2-1.

494. Nerlove, S.H., "Inventories and the Business Situation in 1954." Journal of Business, 27 (January 1954), pp. 41-50. Examines the level of total inventories at the end of 1953 in relation to theoretical desired levels and suggests repercussions from attempts to change inventory levels. 3-0-0-2.

495. Nevile, J.W., "Professor Hicks' Theory of Investment and Post-War Investment Figures in Australia and the United States." Economic Record, 34 (August 1958), pp. 249-253. Fits a modified form of Hicks' investment relations with autonomous and induced investment to aggregate data for these two countries. Finds an accelerator coefficient less than one and the absence of a secular trend of autonomous investment. 4-3-1-1.

496. Norris, V.P., "The Costing of Investment Decisions." Journal of Industrial Economics, 5 (March 1957), pp. 112-123. The return from a particular investment is difficult to estimate, particularly since some of the effects are of a qualitative nature, e.g., expected labor scarcity, improvement in product, and the psychological effect on employees. Relates the technique for calculating present value of measurable items and the effect of tax policy. 1-1-8-1.

497. Norton, Frank E., "Some Cross-Sectional Explorations in Investment Behavior." Southern Economic Journal, 22 (January 1956), pp. 330-338. A report on an econometric study in the petroleum industry. Uses the same sample of firms as Taitel. Investment expenditures are hypothesized to depend on demand for output, capital stock in existence, the quantity of liquid assets and the debt-equity ratio. Demand and capital stock variables are most significant. 4-2-1,2-1.

498. Norton, Frank E., "The Accelerator and the Overinvestment and Underconsumption Models." Economic Journal, 66 (March 1956), pp. 49-65. A study of the relationship between the accelerator and more traditional theories. 1-3-1-1.

499. Norton, L.G., and J.E. Wall, "The Control and Oversight of Capital Expenditure within Unilever." Journal of Industrial Economics, 1 (July 1953), pp. 241-253. A case study of capital budgeting in this mammoth corporation. 2-1-8-1.

500. Novozhilov, N.N., "On Choosing Between Investment Projects." International Economic Papers, 6 (1956), pp. 66-87. Translation from transactions of the Leningrad Industrial Institute 1939 and of the Leningrad Polytechnical Institute of 1946. The investment decision is complicated because of the many variables involved, quality of product, effect on other projects, and economic development in general. Goal is to achieve minimum social costs of output. 1-3-8-1.

501. Nurkse, Ragnar, "Period Analysis and Inventory Cycles." Oxford Economic Papers, N.S. 6 (September 1954), pp. 203-225. A macro-dynamic model of fluctuations built around a simple structure of business motives. 4-3-8-2.

502. Nurkse, Ragnar, "The Cyclical Pattern of Inventory Investment." Quarterly Journal of Economics, 66 (August 1952), pp. 385-408. A review of Abramovitz's book. Emphasizes differences in investment at different points of the cycle. 1-0-0-2.

Ohlin, Goran, and John P. Shelton. See Shelton, 564.

503. Oxenfeldt, Gertrude E. and Afred R., "Businessmen's Information about Profitability of Local Enterprises." Journal of Political Economy, 55 (June 1947), pp. 257-261. The results of a questionnaire survey in Boulder, Colorado. Found amazing disagreements about which businesses were profitable. 2-1-2-0.

504. Pankhurst, K.V., "Investment in the West Riding Wool Textile Industry in the 19th Century." Yorkshire Bulletin of Economic and Social Research, 7 (September 1955), pp. 93-116. A historical case study of the accumulation of capital in a growing industry subject to technological change of methods and products. 2-2-5-1.

505. Paradiso, Louis J., "Significance of Inventories in the Current Economic Situation." Journal of the American Statistical Association, 43 (September 1948), pp. 361-376. An examination

of inventory activity in relation to other investment items. 3-3-0-2.

Paradiso, Louis J., and Irwin Friend. See Friend, 233.

506. Parker, H.R., "Some Notes on Risk." Metroeconomica, 5 (December 1953), pp. 138-144. Elaborates on the factors tending towards conservatism under uncertainty. Emphasizes that previous success and experience have great influence on choice. 1-0-7-0.

507. Parkinson, J.R., "The Effectiveness of Changes in Interest Rates." Scottish Journal of Political Economy, 4 (October 1957), pp. 165-176. A general discussion of the marginal influence of interest rate increases. 1-3-3-0.

508. Peck, Merton J., "Marginal Analysis and the Explanation of Business Behavior under Uncertainty: A Case Study of Inventory-Output Behavior in the Aluminum Industry." Expectations, Uncertainty and Business Behavior, M. J. Bowman (ed.), pp. 119-133. Develops a compromise theory of uncertainty from which he concludes that marginal analysis can make some contribution. 2-2-1,7-3.

509. Pegrum, Dudley F., "Investment in the Railroad and Other Transportation Industries under Regulation." American Economic Review, 47 Proc. (May 1957), pp. 416-429. A criticism of the lack of an up-to-date transportation policy to allocate investment properly in the light of recent technological developments. 1-2-5-1.

510. Pegrum, D.F., Public Regulation of Business. Homewood, Ill.: R.D. Irwin Inc., 1959. The effects on investment are considered in Chapters 3, 20, 21, 25, and 26. 1-2-5-1.

511. Peston, M.H., "Acceleration and Magnification," American Economic Review, 47 (December 1957), pp. 1000-1003. A comment on an article by Baumol, American Economic Review, (June 1956). 1-3-1-1.

512. Peters, William, "Notes on the Theory of Replacement." Manchester School of Economic and Social Studies, 24 (September 1956), pp. 270-288. Points out that a decision to replace existing assets is one of a series of such decisions. Considers the problem of forecasting demand and revenue as well as the minimization of production costs. Contains an illustrative appendix. 1-0-6,8-1.

Peterson, J.P., et al. See Anderson, 16.

Phillips, Almarin and Raymond T. Bowman. See Bowman, 64,65.

513. Platt, D.R., "Capital Expenditure Analysis Procedure." Advanced Management, 22 (October 1957), pp. 20-24. Sets out a method for calculating present-value of return from investment projects. 1-1-2-1.

Polak, J.J. and J. Tinbergen. See Tinbergen, 618.

514. Predetti, A., "The Inventory Problem: A New Model with Uncertainty." Weltwirtschaftliches Archiv, 86 (1961), Heft 2, pp. 286-300. Considers a model for a periodic ordering of stocks when the timing and volume of sales are subject to uncertainty. Takes into account storage costs, order costs and depletion costs. 1-1-4-2.

515. Preinreich, G.A.D., "Models of Taxation in the Theory of the Firm." Economia Internazionale, 4 (May 1951), pp. 372-392. Introduces a tax into an abstract model of the firm to show the influence on investment in a capital good that will not be replaced. This article supplements "The Mathematical Theory of the Firm," same journal, May 1949, pp. 492-508. 1-1-7,9-1.

Puglisi, Marie L. and Clement Winston. See Winston, 659.

516. Puthercheary, J., "Investment Incentive and Income Tax." Public Finance, 14 (No. 3-4, 1959), pp. 218-233. Applies the model for decision-making under uncertainty developed by Shackle to the question of the effect of taxes on investment decisions. Concludes that in uncertainty the tax results in less discouragement to investment than usually believed. 1-1,3-9-1.

517. Ravenscroft, E.A., "Return on Investment: Fit the Method to your Need." Harvard Business Review, 38 (March-April 1960), pp. 97-109. Defines three separate rates of return and indicates that each has particular applications. Operating return = profit/assets employed. Cash return = cash income/cash invested. Equity return = net earnings/common stockholders equity. 1-1-2-1.

518. Redfern, P., "Net Investment in Fixed assets in the United Kingdom, 1938-1953." Journal of the Royal Statistical Society, Series A, 118 (1955), pp. 141-182. Starting from official estimates of gross capital formation, attempts to estimate net additions, by broad industry groups. Uses tax allowed depreciation rates to make the adjustments. Considers price changes. 3-2,3-0-1.

519. Renshaw, E., "A Note on the Arithmetic of Capital Budgeting Decisions." Journal of Business, 30 (July 1957), pp. 193-201. Discusses a conflict between methods of ranking investment projects by rate of return and by present value. 1-0-8-1.

520. Reul, Ray I., "Profitability Index for Investment." Harvard Business Review, 35 (July-August 1957), pp. 116-132. Describes a method for evaluating the return expected from an actual investment project. 1-0-8-1.

521. Reynolds, P.D., "Control of Capital Expenditure," Accountancy, 72 (July 1961), pp. 397-404. The series of articles of which this is the first discusses current methods of controlling capital expenditures, with particular emphasis on actuarial techniques for assessing future profits. 1-1-0-1.

522. Rhys-Williams, Lady, Taxation and Incentive. New York: Oxford University Press, 1953. A study with particular reference to the effect of personal and corporate income taxes on incentives and effort in Britain. 1-0-9-0.

523. Robinson, Joan, The Accumulation of Capital. Homewood, Illinois: R.D. Irwin, Inc., 1956. Provides a dynamic analysis of accumulation, employment and profits intended to supercede the traditional static theory. 1-3-0-3.

524. Robinson, Joan, Collected Economic Papers. Oxford: Blackwell, Volume II, 1960. Contains a number of articles on aspects of the theory of capital, distribution and the production function. 1-0-0-1.

525. Robinson, Joan, "Some Problems of Definition and Measurement of Capital." Oxford Economic Papers, 11 (June 1959), pp. 157-166. Deals with some of the problems of measuring a stock of capital at a given moment. These problems arise primarily because the capital has value and is useful through several periods of time. 1-3-0-0.

526. Robinson, N.Y., "The Acceleration Principle: Department Store Inventories, 1920-1956." American Economic Review, 49 (June 1959), pp. 348-358. Indicates that inventory investment is statistically related to recent changes in sales, but not to the rate of interest. 4-2-1-2.

527. Roos, Charles F., and Victor S. Von Szeliski, "The Demand for Durable Goods." Econometrica, 11 (April 1943), pp. 97-122. Develops a general theory of demand for durables. In Part 3, explicitly applies this to the demand for producers' capital goods. 1-1-0-1.

528. Roos, Charles, "The Demand for Investment Goods." American Economic Review, 38 Proc. (May 1948), pp. 311-320. Builds a model that will predict investment for the economy as a whole from both the level of profit and the ratio of output to capacity. The relation with the second variable becomes nonlinear after 85 percent of capacity is in use. 4-3-1,2-1.

529. Roos, Charles, "Survey of Economic Forecasting Techniques." Econometrica, 23 (October 1955), pp. 363-395. Contains an extensive bibliography and survey of forecasting techniques. 1-0-8-0.

Roseman, H., and Murray Brown. See Brown, 90.

Rosenberg, Leonard G., and Loughlin McHugh. See McHugh, 438.

530. Rosenblatt, M., "An Inventory Problem." Econometrica, 22 (April 1954), pp. 244-247. Refers to situations where the production of the item to be carried over is not directly controlled. Uses the example of surplus grain in the hands of the government. 2-2-0-2.

531. Rostow, W. W., "Some General Reflections on Capital Formation and Economic Growth." Universities-National Bureau Conference, Capital Formation and Economic Growth, pp. 635-652. 1-3-0-1.

Rowe, D. A., and Richard Stone. See Stone, 599.

532. Salant, W. A., "Saving, Investment and Stability." American Economic Review, 46 Proc. (May 1956), pp. 87-96. A general discussion of the factors which operate to make desired saving equal to desired investment and hence promote stability. 1-0-2,3-3.

533. Salter, W. E. G., "The Production Function and the Durability of Capital." Economic Record, 35 (April 1959), pp. 47-66. Discusses the importance for investment of the existing stock of capital and the way capital stock and investment enter into the production function. 1-1-0-1.

534. Samuelson, P. A., "Some Aspects of the Pure Theory of Capital." Quarterly Journal of Economics, 51 (May 1937), pp. 469-496. 1-0-0-0.

535. Samuelson, P. A., "Interaction Between the Multiplier. Analysis and the Principle of Acceleration." Review of Economic Statistics, 21 (May 1939), pp. 75-78. This article is the basic

rigorous formulation of the implications of the existence of a "naive" acceleration relation. 1-3-1-3.

536. Samuelson, P.A., "A Synthesis of the Principle of Acceleration and the Multiplier." Journal of Political Economy, 47 (December 1939), pp. 786-797. A review of the controversy about the nature of business cycles which may arise with different values of these two relations. 1-3-1-3.

537. Samuelson, P.A. and R.M. Solow, "A Complete Capital Model Involving Heterogenous Capital Goods." Quarterly Journal of Economics, 70 (November 1956), pp. 537-562. 1-0-0-0.

Samuelson, P.A., et al, See Dorfman, 172.

538. Saposnik, Rubin, Models for the Analysis of Capital Equipment Purchase Policies. Doctoral Dissertation, University of Minnesota, 1960. 1-1-0-1.

Sauerlander, Owen H., and Franco Modigliani. See Modigliani, 462.

Savage, Leonard J., and James H. Lorie. See Lorie, 394.

Scarf, Herbert, et al. See Arrow, 27.

539. Scheuble, Philip A., Jr., "How to Figure Equipment Replacement." Harvard Business Review, 33 (September-October 1955), pp. 81-84. A summary of the various schemes for calculating the most profitable replacement policy and of putting this aspect of operations into perspective with alternative opportunities. 1-1-6-1.

540. Schiff, Eric, "A Note on Depreciation, Replacement and Growth." Review of Economics and Statistics, 36 (February, 1954), pp. 47-53. A review of Eisner's and Domar's work and a suggestion for caution because of the importance of the assumptions usually made. 1-1-2,6-1.

541. Schiff, Eric, "Reinvestment Cycles and Depreciation Reserves Under Straight-Line Depreciation." Metroeconomica, 9 (April 1957), pp. 23-41. Examines a model in which a large number of new machines have the same average service life but actual retirements are distributed around this life. Examines the process by which replacement outlay becomes damped. Cites example of light bulbs. 1-1-2,6-1.

542. Schiff, Eric, "Reinvestment Cycles and Depreciation Reserves Under Declining-Balance Depreciation." Metroeconomica, 10

(April 1958), pp. 7-15. Examines a model analogous to the one analyzed in the article listed above, except that declining-balance depreciation rather than straight-line depreciation is assumed. 1-1-2,6-1.

543. Schiff, Eric, "Gross Stocks Estimated from Past Installations." Review of Economics and Statistics, 40 (May 1958), pp. 174-177. A statistical method for estimating stocks of durable assets when only the series of new purchases are available. 4-0-0-1.

544. Schlaifer, Robert, J. Keith Butters, and Pearson Hunt, "Accelerated Amortization." Harvard Business Review, 29 (May 1951), pp. 113-124. Criticizes the use of this measure as an incentive to expansion, and points out that it does not apply evenly to all firms. Suggests the alternative of government guarantee against losses. 1-3-9-1.

545. Schmidt, Emerson P., "Promoting Steadier Output and Sales," Universities-National Bureau Committee for Economic Research. Regularization of Business Investment, pp. 319-368, Princeton University Press, 1954. 1-3-1-0.

546. Schreder, H.X., "Impact of Business Conditions on Investment Policies." Journal of Finance, 7 (May 1952), pp. 138-172. 1-3-7-3.

547. de Scitovsky, T., "A Note on Profit Maximization and Its Implications." Review of Economic Studies, 11 (Winter 1943), pp. 57-60. 1-1,3-7-0.

548. Schwan, H.T., "Replacement of Machinery and Equipment." in Industrial Engineering Handbook. New York: McGraw-Hill, 1956. 1,2-1-6-1.

549. Scott, J.A., "Comment on the Marginal Efficiency of Capital and Investment Programming." Economic Journal, 67 (September 1957), pp. 543-545. Comment on Brockie and Grey. 1-1-3-1.

550. Shackle, G.L.S., Expectations, Investment and Income, Oxford, 1938. 1-0-7,8-0.

551. Shackle, G.L.S., "The Nature of the Inducement to Invest." Review of Economic Studies, 8 (October 1940), pp. 44-48. The concepts of potential surprise and range of non-surprise outcomes are developed. 1-1-7,8-0.

552. Shackle, G.L.S., "A Theory of Investment Decisions." Oxford Economic Papers, 6 (April 1942), pp. 77-94. Where X is

output and Y is potential surprise — concept of potential surprise: Y = F (X); or Focus function: = (X,F (X)). Investment will be retarded when: (1) critical event is coming; (2) when a surprise occurs, requires reappraisal; (3) an event changes focus—gains or losses need assimilation. 1-1,3-7,8-0.

553. Shackle, G. L. S., "Interest Rates and the Pace of Investment." Economic Journal, 61 (March 1946), pp. 1-17. Argues that interest does influence investment for instruments which assuredly will continue to earn for a long period (e.g. houses). The influence of interest will be smaller or non-existent for instruments whose earnings are uncertain especially when the reaction to uncertainty is to reduce future earnings at an annual rate of discount (or some other strongly increasing function of time). 1-1-3-1.

554. Shackle, G. L. S., Expectation in Economics. Cambridge: Cambridge University Press, 1949. The complete statement of Shackle's theory of decision-making. 1-1,3-7,8-0.

555. Shackle, G. L. S., "The Nature and Role of Profit." Metroeconomica, 3 (December 1951), pp. 101-107. 1-3-1,2-0.

556. Shackle, G. L. S., "On the Meaning and Measure of Uncertainty." Metroeconomica, 4 (December 1952), pp. 87-105. 1-3-2,7-0.

557. Shackle, G. L. S., "The Meaning and Measure of Uncertainty." Metroeconomica, 5 (December 1953), pp. 97-115. 1-3-2,7-0.

558. Shackle, G. L. S., "Business Men on Business Decisions." Scottish Journal of Political Economy, 2 (February 1955), pp. 32-46. A novel experiment in questionnaire technique. 3-0-7,8-0.

559. Shackle, G L. S., "Recent Theories Concerning the Nature and Role of Interest." Economic Journal, 71 (June 1961), pp. 209-254. 1-1-2,3-0.

560. Shackle, G. L. S., "Expectation and Liquidity." Chapter 2 of Expectations, Uncertainty and Business Behavior, ed. Mary Jean Bowman, New York: Social Science Research Council, 1958. 0-0-2,3-1.

561. Shackle, G. L. S., Uncertainty in Economics and Other Reflections. Cambridge, England: Cambridge University Press, 1955. Reprints a number of the above articles. 1-1-3-1.

Shackle, G. L. S., et al. See Carter, 107.

Shapiro, Eli, and M. J. Gordon. See Gordon, 262.

562. Shaw, William H., "How Good are Current Statistics for Following Economic Changes." Proceedings of the Business and Economic Statistics Section of the American Statistical Association, 1956, pp. 193-198. An evaluation of the reliability of present series to reflect turning points. 3-3-0-3.

563. Sheard, P.M., "A Note on Depreciation and Industrial Expansion." Yorkshire Bulletin of Economic and Social Research, 7 (March 1955), pp. 59-68. In a period of growth and rising prices, the depreciation reserves of expanding industries will be adequate. Non-growing industries will not have adequate reserves. 1-3-2-3.

564. Shelton, John P., and Goran Ohlin, "A Swedish Tax Provision for Stabilizing Business Investment." American Economic Review, 42 (June 1952), pp. 375-380. A scheme whereby corporations may evade certain taxes on income by putting profits into funds which are controlled by the government and hence are available for countercyclical investment. 1-3-2-1.

565. Shubik, M., "Approaches to the Study of Decision-Making Relevant to the Firm." Journal of Business, 34 (April 1961), pp. 101-118. A general discussion of problems of analyzing individual decisions and of the development of new theories and techniques to meet these problems. 1-1-8-0.

566. Siegel, Irving H., "Technological Change and Long-Run Forecasting," Journal of Business, 26 (July 1953), pp. 141-156. Points out that the dynamics of change spell disaster for the accuracy of forecasts. 1-3-8-0.

567. Siegel, Irving H., "Scientific Discovery, Invention and the Cultural Environment." Patent, Trademark and Copyright Journal of Research and Education, 4 (Fall, 1960), pp. 233-248. Considers interrelations of discovery and invention in the larger economic and social setting and through time. 0-0-5-1.

Silaner, Fred S., and Paul Wasserman. See Wasserman, 636.

568. Simmons, Gustave, "New Techniques for Capital Formation in a Free Enterprise System." The Conference Board Business Record, (May 1950). Suggests a countercyclical investment incentive plan for the U.S. similar to one operative in Sweden. 1-3-2-1.

569. Simon, Herbert A., "Theories of Decision-Making in Economics and Behavioral Science." American Economic Re-

view, 49 (June 1959), pp. 253-283. A survey of the literature.
1-0-7-0.

Simon, Herbert A., et al. See Cyert, 140.

Smidt, S., and Bierman, H. Jr. See Bierman, H. Jr., 50.

570. Smith, Howard R., "The Status of Stagnation Theory." Southern
Economic Journal, Part I, 15 (October 1948), pp. 191-204;
Southern Economic Journal, Part II, 15 (January 1949).
Distinguishes between "dated" or contemporary institutional
tendencies and general or "nondated" tendencies to stagnation.
Contains a general review of the argument that technological
change is inadequate to maintain the present rate of growth.
1-0-5-1.

570a. Smith, Mabel A., "Factors Influencing Manufacturers' Inventories," Inventory Fluctuations and Economic Stabilization,
Part I, Joint Economic Committee, 87th Congress, 1st Session, pp. 149-163.

Smith, Paul E., and L. E. Gallaway, See Gallaway, 246.

571. Smith, V. L., "Economic Equipment Policies: An Evaluation."
Management Science, 4 (October 1957), pp. 20-37. Summarizes the result of an empirical study of equipment policy
as applied to motor truck users. Studies replacement policies
and choice of original equipment and compares actual with
optimal policies. 2,4-1-4-1.

572. Smith, V. L., "The Theory of Investment and Production."
Quarterly Journal of Economics, 73 (February 1959), pp. 61-
87. Sets out to integrate the theory of production with the
theory of investment. Uses a number of models to explore
the investment and replacement policies that a rational firm
would follow in simplified circumstances. Shows that equipment policy is tied to choice of technique and that "overcapacity" is sometimes desirable. 1-1-1-1.

573. Smith, V. L., "Problems in Production-Investment Planning
Over Time." International Economic Review, 1 (September
1960), pp. 198-216. Considers the dynamic aspects of an
integrated theory of production and investment as set out in
his article in the Quarterly Journal of Economics in 1959.
1-1-1-1.

574. Smith, V. L., Investment and Production: A Study in the Theory
of the Capital-Using Enterprise. Harvard University Press,
1961. 1-1,2-1,5,6,7-3.

Smith, Winfield, and Joel Dean. See Dean, 155.

575. Smithies, A., "Economic Fluctuations and Growth." Econometrica, 25 (January 1957), pp. 1-52. Develops a general model to explain fluctuations and growth through the operation of endogenous forces. Emphasizes the relation between total productive capacity and total demand for output. The investment function in the model is similar to those of Tinbergen and Klein in depending on the level of present and past profits. 1-1,2-1,2-1.

576. Solomon, Ezra, "Measuring a Company's Cost of Capital." Journal of Business, 28 (October 1955), pp. 240-252. Outlines a rational procedure by which management may order and evaluate investment projects. 1-1-8-1.

577. Solomon, Ezra, "The Arithmetic of Capital Budgeting Decisions." Journal of Business, 29 (April 1956), pp. 124-129. Sets out standards for selecting among investment projects to maximize present value of the firm. 1-1-8-1.

578. Solomon, Ezra (ed.), The Management of Corporate Capital. Graduate School of Business, The University of Chicago. Illinois: Free Press of Glencoe, 1959. Reprints of twenty-two essays. 1,3-1-8-0.

579. Solow, Robert M., "Technical Change and the Aggregate Production Function." Review of Economics and Statistics, 39 (August 1957), pp. 313-320. 1-0-5-0.

580. Solow, Robert M., "Investment and Technical Progress." Chapter 7 in Mathematical Methods in the Social Sciences, 1959, by Arrow, Karlin and Suppes (eds.), Stanford, California: Stanford University Press, 1960. 4-3-5-3.

Solow, R. M., et al. See Dorfman, 172.

Solow, R. M., and P. A. Samuelson. See Samuelson, 537.

Sonenblum, Sidney, and Thomas Mayer. See Mayer, 431.

581. Spiro, Alan, "Empirical Research and the Rate of Interest." Review of Economics and Statistics, 40 (February 1958), pp. 52-58. A study of the importance of the interest rate for aggregate investment in construction, durable machinery and inventories in the U.S. during the period 1869-1929. Takes long-run moving averages to reduce cyclical influences. The results are significant but weak. 4-2,3-3-1.

582. Stanback, T. M., Jr., "Cyclical Behavior of Manufacturers'
      Inventories Since 1945." American Statistical Association,
      Proceedings of the Business and Economics Statistics Section,
      1957, pp. 87-95. 3-2,3-0-2.

582a. Stanback, Thomas M., Jr., "Postwar Cycles in Manufacturers'
      Inventories," in Inventory Fluctuations and Economic Stabili-
      zation, Part I, Joint Economic Committee, 87th Congress,
      1st Session, 1961, pp. 1-143. To be republished by the National
      Bureau of Economic Research.

583. Stanback, T. M., Jr., Postwar Cycles in Manufacturers'
      Inventories. National Bureau of Economic Research, Occa-
      sional Paper, New York, 1961. Examines the importance of
      inventories in business cycles with special reference to
      manufacturers' inventories. Cyclical behaviour is examined
      at each stage of fabrication and a theory of manufacturers'
      inventory behaviour is developed. The final chapter contains
      a critique of Metzler's inventory cycle theory. 3-2-0-2.

584. Stanback, T. M., Jr., "A Critique of Inventory Forecasting
      Techniques." Proceedings of American Statistical Associa-
      tion, Business and Economic Statistics Section. 1960. Seeks to
      establish criteria for assessing the validity of certain ap-
      proaches to short-term forecasting of aggregate inventory
      investment. In addition, measures are made of forecasting
      accuracy of the several approaches during recent years.
      4-3-0-2.

585. Stauss, James H., "The Entrepreneur: The Firm." Journal
      of Political Economy, 52 (June 1944), pp. 112-127. A rigorous
      redefinition of the term "entrepreneur" and a discussion of
      where the function is carried on in a modern firm. 1-1-7-0.

586. Steger, Wilbur A., "Countercyclical Corporate Tax Rates."
      Southern Economic Journal, 25 (July 1958), pp. 97-101.
      Argues that one long-run effect of countercyclical changes
      in corporate income tax might be a reduction in economic
      growth. 1-1,3-9-0.

587. Steger, Wilbur A., "The Taxation of Unrealized Capital Gains
      and Losses: A Statistical Study." National Tax Journal, 10
      (September 1957). The effect upon different forms of in-
      vestment in capital assets and on the mobility of capital
      assets of a substantial change in the tax laws regarding
      capital gains and losses. 1-1-2-1.

588. Steger, Wilbur A., "Simulation and Tax Analysis: A Research
      Proposal." National Tax Journal, 14 (September 1961). A

proposed methodological investigation of the effects of various changes in the capital gains tax structure on the different capital markets. 1-1-2-1.

589. Steindl, J., Maturity and Stagnation in American Capitalism. Oxford University, Institute of Statistics, Monograph No. 4, Oxford: Basil Blackwell. Develops a theory of investment in terms of micro- and macro-variables. The independent variables are the change of retained earnings, the ratio of total business assets to equity capital and the degree of excess capacity. 1-3-1,2-1.

590. Steindl, J., "On Risk." Oxford Economic Papers, 5 (June 1941), pp. 43-54. A discussion of the formulation of expectation in the case of uncertainty on the basis of subjective experience. 1-0-7-0.

591. Stern, Ernest H., "Capital Requirements in Progressive Economies." Economica, 12 (August 1945), pp. 163-171. A general study of the relation between capital formation and national income for the U.S. 1878-1928, the U.K. 1924-38. 3-3-1-3.

592. Stern, Ernest H., "The Problem of Capital Accumulation." American Economic Review, 39 (December 1949), pp. 1160-1172. Article emphasizes cyclical importance of changes in composition of investment as against usual emphasis on changes in mere size of investment. 1-3-0-1.

593. Stockfisch, J.A., "Uncertainty, the Capitalization Theory and Investment Behaviour." Metroeconomica, 7 (August 1955), pp. 73-84. A review of methods of capitalization of future earnings. Deals with uncertainty and points to complications of assuming that all assets can be capitalized to a comparable money value. 1-0-8-1.

594. Stockfisch, J.A., "The Capitalization, Allocation and Investment Effects of Asset Taxation." Southern Economic Journal, 22 (January 1956), pp. 317-329. An extensive discussion of the implications and incidence of business taxes with many references to the literature. Sets out the allocation effects of asset taxation, and its simultaneous possible effects on investment incentive. 1-3-9-1.

595. Stockfisch, J.A., "The Relationships Between Money, Cost, Investment and the Rate of Return." Quarterly Journal of Economics, 70 (May 1956), pp. 295-302. Questions the customary assumption of a downward sloping marginal efficiency schedule when much of the economy is devoted to the production of capital goods. 1-0-4,7-0.

596. Stockfisch, J.A., "Investment Incentive, Taxation and Accelerated Depreciation." Southern Economic Journal, 24 (July 1957), pp. 28-40. Since revenue must be raised in some manner, doubts that this particular tax concession can have any permanent incentive effect and indicates that it may even have adverse incentive effects. 1-3-9-1.

597. Stokes, K.C., "Financial Trends of Large Manufacturing Corporations, 1936-1946." Survey of Current Business, 27 (November 1947), pp. 16-24. An analysis of 1000 corporation balance sheets broken into the durable goods and nondurable goods industries. During the war years the 200 largest firms made smaller relative gains than other firms. 3-2-2-0.

598. Stolper, W., "The Logic of Investment Planning." Weltwirtschaftliches Archiv, 85 (No. 2, 1960), pp. 69*-80*. A review of a book by the same title by S. Chakravarty which deals with investment criteria for planning in an open, multisectoral economy. 1-3-0-1.

599. Stone, Richard, and D.A. Rowe, "The Market Demand for Durable Goods." Econometrica, 25 (July 1957), pp. 423-443. 4-2-1-1.

600. Streeten, Paul, "The Effect of Taxation on Risk-Taking." Oxford Economic Papers, 5 (October 1953), pp. 271-287. A general discussion which is critical of the usual simple direct argument which ignores the effects of government expenditure. 1-0-9-0.

601. Streeten, Paul, "Taxation and Enterprise." Toronto Quarterly, (January 1958), pp. 137-147. Shows how tax avoidance in Britain can undermine the tax system. 3-0-9-0.

602. Streeten, Paul, "Tax Policy for Investment." Rivista di diritto finanziario e scienza delle finanze, (June 1960), pp. 117-137. A theoretical discussion of various methods of encouraging investment through tax measures, in relation to and critical of the Report of the U.K. Royal Commission of the Taxation of Income and Profits (1955). 1-0-9-0.

603. Streever, Donald, Capacity Utilization and Business Ivestment. University of Illinois, Bureau of Economic and Business Research, Bulletin No. 86, 1960. Defends the importance of the accelerator as a determinant of investment once the possibility of excess capacity is taken into account. He reviews a number of interview studies then fits a model including a capacity utilization variable to data for four major industrial classifications. 2,4-1,2-1-1.

Strotz, R. H., et al. See Morehouse, 472.

604. Strumilin, S. G., "The Time Factor in Capital Investment Projects." International Economic Papers, 1 (1951), pp. 160-185. Reprint from the Bulletin of the Academy of Science of the U.S.S.R., 1946. Describes the problems of allocating in an economy where product prices are set and where there is a universal need for capital. 1-3-8-1.

Sykes, Allen, and Anthony Merrett. See Merrett, 441.

605. Taitel, Martin, "Profits, Productive Activities and New Investments." TNEC Monograph 12, Washington, 1941. A cross-sectional study of the relation between investment and profit in the oil and steel industries. The statistical relation improves when variables are lumped for several years. Discovered that the relation between investment and profitability was not so good as between investment and output. 4-2-1,2-1.

606. Tannenbaum, Robert, "Managerial Decision-Making." Journal of Business, 23 (January 1950), pp. 22-39. A general discussion of the psychological aspects of decision-making and the subsidiary restraints of information-gathering and administrative execution. 1-0-7-0.

607. Terborgh, George W., Dynamic Equipment Policy, New York: McGraw-Hill, 1949. 1-1,3-6-1.

608. Terborgh, George W., "Business Investment for Stability and Growth." American Economic Review, 47 Proc. (May 1957), pp. 132-134. A comment that capital outlays may be becoming more stable with improved forecasting and planning. 1-0-8-1.

609. Terborgh, George W., Business Investment Policy — a MAPI Study and Manual. Washington, D.C.: Machinery and Allied Products Institute, 1958. 1-1-4-1.

610. Terborgh, George W., Studies in the Analysis of Business Investment Projects. Washington, D.C.: Machinery and Allied Products Institute, 1960. 1-1,3-6-1.

611. Terleckyj, Hestov E., "Measure of Inventory Conditions." Technical Paper No. 8, National Industrial Conference Board, 1960. 3-1,2-0-2.

612. Tew, Brian, "The Finance of Investment." Oxford Economic Papers, 4 (July 1952), pp. 108-120. A restatement of Kalecki's increasing risk thesis. Argues that the restriction placed on investment by the availability of funds will differ among

industries, regions, and firm sizes so that there may be businesses that are chronically wanting to spend more than they can raise. 1-3-3-0.

Tew, Brian, and R. F. Henderson. See Henderson, 307.

612a. Thalberg, Bjorn, "The Market for Investment Goods. An Analysis where Time of Delivery Enters Explicitly." Review of Economic Studies, 27 (February 1960), pp. 99-108.

613. Thomas, David A., Accelerated Amortization. Ann Arbor: University of Michigan, 1958. 1-3-9-1.

614. Thrall, R. M., C. H. Combs, and R. L. Davis (eds.), Decision Processes. New York: John Wiley and Sons, 1954. 1-0-7-0.

615. Tinbergen, J., "Statistical Evidence on the Acceleration Principle." Economica, N.S. 5 (May 1938), pp. 164-176. An empirical study of investment and changes in output in several industries and national economies. Concludes that the relationship is not as good as that between investment and profit. 4-3-1,2-1.

616. Tinbergen, J., Statistical Testing of Business Cycle Theories. Vol. I: A Method and Its Application to Investment Activity; Vol. II: Business Cycles in the United States, 1919-1932, Geneva: League of Nations, 1939. Vol. I tries to explain movements in investment volume with the aid of profits, interest rates, prices of investment goods and the acceleration principle. Figures for U.K., Germany, France and U.S. 4-3-1,2-1.

617. Tinbergen, J., "An Acceleration Principle for Commodity Stockholding and a Short Cycle Resulting From It," in O. Lange, et al., Studies in Mathematical Economics and Econometrics, Chicago, 1942. Tries to show that the acceleration principle applies to investment in stocks of raw cotton, sugar, and wood, in the United Kingdom and stocks of finished goods in the United States. 1,4-3-1-2.

618. Tinbergen, J., and J. J. Polak, The Dynamics of Business Cycles. A Study in Economic Fluctuations. Chicago: University of Chicago Press, 1950. A translation by Polak of a book written in 1942. Tinbergen stresses the importance of profits and financial considerations for investment decisions. 4-3-1,2-3.

Trow, Donald B., et al. See Cyert, 140.

619. Tsiang, S. C., "Rehabilitation of Time Dimension of Investment in Macrodynamic Analysis." Economica, 16 (August 1949), pp. 204-217. Discusses the concept of capital output ratio and period of construction in an aggregate income model, not from the usual point of view of induced investment in a

process of acceleration, but from the point of view of the
generation of an expanded stream of real output to meet the
flow of effective demand. 1-3-1-1.

620. Tsiang, S. C., "Accelerator, Theory of the Firm and the Business Cycle." Quarterly Journal of Economics, 65 (August
1951), pp. 325-341. A critical examination of the accelerator
relation. Because of the limitation of investible funds, investment tends to be more closely related to the level of income
than to its rate of change. 1-3-1-1.

621. Ulin, Robert P., "Are We Building Too Much Capacity?"
Harvard Business Review, 33 (November-December 1955),
pp. 41-47. Takes note of the tremendous increases in productive
capacity since 1950 and questions if this implies a forthcoming
period of price wars and low investment. Believes instability
will result without rapid technical changes. 3-3-1-1.

Ulin, Robert P., and William F. Butler. See Butler, 102.

622. Ulmer, Melville, J., "Plant and Equipment Programs and
Sales Expectations in 1949." Survey of Current Business, 29
(April 1949), pp. 9-13. 3-3-8-1.

623. Ulmer, Melville J., "Autonomous and Induced Investment."
American Economic Review, 42 (September 1952), pp. 587-
589. Questions the existence of this dichotomy so far as the
decisions and motivations of businessmen are concerned.
1-3-7-1.

624. Ulmer, Melville J., Trends and Cycles in Capital Formation
by United States Railroads, 1870-1950, National Bureau of
Economic Research, Occasional Paper No. 43, 1954. 3-2-0-1.

625. Ulmer, Melville J., Capital in Transportation, Communications, and Public Utilities: Its Formation and Financing. New
York: National Bureau of Economic Research, Princeton
University Press, 1960. Studies the long-term trends in the
regulated industries of the U.S., 1870-1950. Trends in output,
capital-output coefficients, and methods of financing are
analyzed. 3-2-0-1.

626. Unilever, Capital Investment, London, 1960. The Chairman's
address at the 1960 annual meeting of the Unilever corporation
contains data and description of how this large complex attempts to allocate capital expenditures. 3-1-8-1.

627. United Nations, National and International Measures for Full
Employment. New York, 1949. Has a discussion of methods

by which governments might stabilize private investment through tax and other measures. 1-3-0-1.

628. Usher, Abbot Payson, "Technical Change and Capital Formation." Universities-National Bureau Committee on Economic Research. Capital Formation and Economic Growth, Princeton University Press, 1955, pp. 523-550. Emphasizes the importance of innovation and the need to include it as an influence on investment. 1-0-5-1.

629. Valavanis-Vail, Stefan, "An Econometric Model of Growth: U.S.A., 1869-1953." American Economic Review, 45 Proc. (May 1955), pp. 208-221. A simultaneous equation system model with 12 structural relations. The author feels that the results are significant. Uses maximum-likelihood estimates. 4-3-1,2-1.

Vandome, P., A. Hazlewood, and L.R. Klein. See Klein, 357.

630. Veno, Hiroya, "Investment Behavior in the Japanese Cotton Spinning Industry, 1916-1934." Econometrica, 29 (January 1961), pp. 44-57. An empirical study of the total data for several large cotton spinning firms. He finds that profits earned are a better explanatory variable than sales and also finds that cash balances were statistically significant. 4-2-1,2-1.

Von Szeliski, Victor S., and Charles F. Roos. See Roos, 527.

631. Wagner, H.M. and T.M. Whitin, "Dynamic Version of the Economic Lot Size Problem." Management Science, 5 (October 1958), pp. 89-96. 1-1-0-2.

632. Walker, David, "Some Economic Aspects of the Taxation of Companies." Manchester School of Economic and Social Studies, 22 (January 1954), pp. 1-36. A discussion of the repercussions of corporate profits taxes in the U.K. since World War II. Concludes that it does not lower pressures to inflation or adversely affect company investment. The main burden has been on the income of shareholders. 3-3-9-1.

633. Walker, Ross G., "The Judgment Factor in Investment Decisions." Harvard Business Review, 39 (March-April 1961), pp. 93-99. Focuses on the basic assumptions and principles that must underly formulas and technical methods for evaluating investment projects. 1-1-7-1.

Wall, J. E., and L.G. Norton. See Norton, 499.

634. Wallich, Henry C., "Effect of Taxation on Investment." Harvard Business Review, 23 (Summer 1945), pp. 442-450. A general discussion in which the desirable influence of government re-expenditure is weighed against the disincentive of taxation. 1-3-9-1.

635. Warner, Doris P., and Albert R. Koch, "Estimated Durable Goods Expenditures, 1939-1945." Federal Reserve Bulletin, 32 (September 1946), pp. 967-973. Gives two digit industry detail. 3-2,3-0-1.

636. Wasserman, Paul, and Fred S. Silaner, Decision Making. An Annotated Bibliography. Ithaca, New York: Cornell University, 1958. 0-0-7-0.

637. Wasson, Robert C., "Investment in Production Equipment: 1929-1952." Survey of Current Business, 33 (November 1953), pp. 11-20. Gives considerable detail about the type of equipment purchased. 3-3-0-1.

Wasson, Robert C., and Donald G. Wooden. See Wooden, 660.

Wein, Harold H., and Edwin Mansfield. See Mansfield, 419.

Weingartner, H.M., and Franco Modigliani. See Modigliani, 467.

Weiss, Lionel, et al. See Laderman, 380.

638. Wellisz, Stanislaw H., "Entrepreneur's Risk, Lender's Risk and Investment." Review of Economic Studies, 20 (1952-1953), pp. 105-114. A reconsideration of Kalecki's principle of increasing risk. 1-1-3-1.

639. Wells, A.S., "Economic Analysis for Better Investment Decisions." N.A.A. Bulletin, 40 (October 1958), pp. 5-14. A review of general criteria involved in planning new projects. 1-1-0-1.

Weston, J. Fred, and Neil H. Jacoby. See Jacoby, 332, 333.

640. White, W.H., "Interest Inelasticity of Investment Demand: The Case From Business Attitude Surveys Re-examined." American Economic Review, 46 (September 1956)., pp. 565-587. A survey of this type of study with critical comments. Holds that the questions and answers do not support the interpretation given. 2-3-3-1.

641. White, W.H., "The Rate of Interest, Marginal Efficiency of Capital and Investment Programming." Economic Journal, 68

(March 1958), pp. 51-59. A criticism of the survey results reported by Brockie and Grey, especially that investment is interest-inelastic. There is a further "Reply" in Economic Journal, 70 (March 1960), pp. 154-157. 2-1-3-1.

642. White, W.H., "The Flexibility of Anticyclical Monetary Policy." Review of Economics and Statistics, 43 (May 1961), pp. 142-147. 1,3-3-7-1.

643. White, W.H., "Inventory Investment and the Rate of Interest." Banca Nazionale del Lavore Quarterly Review, 57 (June 1961), pp. 141-183. 1,2-1-2,3,7-2.

644. Whitin, T.M., "Inventory Control in Theory and in Practice." Quarterly Journal of Economics, 66 (November 1952), pp. 502-521. A study of inventory control models for different types of goods with empirical examples. 1-1-1-2.

645. Whitin, T.M., Theory of Inventory Management. Princeton: Princeton University Press, 1953, second edition, 1957. Discusses alternative methods of inventory control for individual firms and also the aggregative significance of inventories for the economy. 1-1,3-0-2.

646. Whitin, T.M., "Inventory Control and Price Theory." Management Science, 2 (October 1953), pp. 61-68. Most inventory analysis has been concerned only with cost-minimization. Extends this analysis to include price changes and introduces the concept of the demand function. 1-1-0-2.

647. Whitin, T.M., "Inventory Control Research: A Survey," Management Science, 1 (October 1954), pp. 32-40. Cites the significant literature on the topic and refers to the lags and problems of adapting new theoretical models to actual use. 1-0-0-2.

Whitin, T.M., and G. Hadley. See Hadley, 280.

Whitin, T.M., and H.M. Wagner. See Wagner, 631.

Wiggins, S., and F. Gehrels. See Gehrels, 247.

648. Wilson, D. Stevens, "Planned Capital Outlays by Manufactures." Survey of Current Business, 25 (June 1945), pp. 5-9. A preliminary report on the survey of postwar investment plans. Uses 1939 as a bench mark. 3-3-8-1.

649. Wilson, D. Stevens, "Planned Capital Outlays and Financing." Survey of Current Business, 25 (July 1945), pp. 15-23. Dis-

cusses inventories, receivables, and the sources of funds for all capital outlays. Includes a section on the income expectations of utilities and the railroads. 1-2-8-2.

650. Wilson, J. S. G., "Investment in a Monetary Economy." Economica, 16 (November 1949), pp. 321-335. Qualifies the abstract theory of investment by emphasizing the differential availability of capital and the fact that certain interest rates are more relevant to a particular borrower than others. 1-0-7-1.

651. Wilson, J.S.G., "Credit Rationing and the Relevant Rate of Interest." Economica, 21 (February 1954), pp. 21-31. Elaborates the theme outlined in Economica, 1949 article and anticipates certain aspects of the United Kingdom Radcliffe Committee Report of 1959. 1,2-0-3-1.

652. Wilson, T., Fluctuations in Income and Employment. London, 1948. On pp. 114 ff. performs a statistical test of the accelerator. 4-3-1-1.

653. Wilson, T., and P.W.S. Andrews (eds.), Oxford Studies in the Price Mechanism. Oxford: Clarendon Press, 1952. Chapter I deals with the rate of interst and Chapter II deals with price theory and business behavior (Hall and Hitch). 2-3-3-1.

654. Wilson, T., "Cyclical and Autonomous Inducements to Invest." Oxford Economic Papers, N.S. 5 (March 1953), pp. 65-89. General statement of the factors which influence investment. A criticism of econometrics for attempting simple aggregate models. 1-0-3,7-1.

655. Wilson, T., Inflation. Cambridge, Massachusetts: Harvard University Press, 1961. Analyzes the inducements to invest and examines statistics for investing and saving in the U.S. and the U.K. since the War. 3-1,3-1,2,3,5,6,7-3.

656. Wilson, T., "Inflation and Growth." Three Banks Review, (September 1961). Asks whether inflation fosters growth by stimulating investment. 3-1,3-7-1.

657. Wimsatt, Genevieve B., "Expenditure for New Plant and Equipment in 1946." Survey of Current Business, 26 (December 1946), pp. 14-17. Surveys the period 1929-46 and gives a breakdown into manufacturing and mining, service and other commercial firms and utilities and transportation. Gives sales data for the same classification. 3-2-0-1.

658. Winding, Poul, Some Aspects of the Acceleration Principle. Amsterdam: North-Holland Publishing Co., 1957. A thorough

elaboration of the principle and the qualifications. Deals with both inventories and capital goods in algebraic models and arithmetic examples but has no empirical applications. 1-0-1-3.

659. Winston, Clement, and Marie L. Puglisi, "Inventory Turnover in Retail Trade." Survey of Current Business, 28 (June 1948), pp. 16-21. 3-2-0-2.

Winston, Clement and Lawrence Bridge. See Bridge, 83a.

De Wit, G.M., and J.C.G. Boot. See Boot, 55.

Wolfowitz, J., et al. See Dvoretzky, 177,178.

660. Wooden, Donald G., and Robert C. Wasson, "Manufacturing Investment Since 1929 in Relation to Employment Outcome and Income." Survey of Current Business, 36 (November 1956), pp. 8-20. Detail given by type of asset purchased but not by industrial classification. 3-2-0-3.

Wooden, Donald G., and Raymond Nassimbene. See Nassimbene, 478, 479.

661. Woodward, D.B., A.G. Abramson, and Ruth P. Mack, "General Appraisal of the Conference." Universities-National Bureau Committee on Economic Research, Regularization of Business Investment, Princeton University Press, 1954, pp. 485-502. 1-3-0-3.

662. Wright, D.M., "A Neglected Approach to the Acceleration Principle." Review of Economics and Statistics, 23 (May 1941), pp. 100-101. The accelerator relation exists between any autonomous increase of expenditures and increases of total capacity. It is a mistake to let it refer only to increases in consumption outlays. A change in the business outlays for innovation has a similar effect. 1-0-1-1.

663. Wright, D.M., The Economics of Disturbance. New York: Macmillan, 1947. This work deals with investment models especially the acceleration of acceleration and the "back-log" problem. Also considers the practical difficulties of applying these models. 1-1,3-1-1.

664. Yance, Joseph, Investment Behavior in the Railroad Industry. Ph.D. thesis, Harvard University, 1955. 3,4-2-0-1.

665. Youngson, A.J., "Investment Decisions, Trade Cycle and Trend." Oxford Economic Papers N.S. 6 (September 1954),

pp. 285-305. A review of investment theory and some propositions about cycle and trend with illustrations from the Scottish coal industry in the second half of the 19th century. 2-2-0-1.

666. Youngson, A.J., "The Disaggregation of Investment in the Study of Economic Growth," Economic Journal, 66 (June 1956), pp. 236-243. A review of the various categories of investment for analysis of the investment process. 1-0-0-1.

Zarnowitz, Victor, and Ruth P. Mack. See Mack, 407.

Zeman, N., and Franco Modigliani. See Modigliani, 460.

ARTICLES GROUPED BY CLASSIFICATION NUMBERS

A. Type of Study

1. Theoretical and Non-Empirical

Abramovitz, 4; Alchian, 6,7; Alexander, 8,9; Allen, 10,11; Andrews, 20; Angell, 21,22; Anthony, 23; Arndt, 24; Arrow, 25,26,27; Bailey, 28; Bain, 29; Baldwin, 30; Baumol, 42,43, 44; Beckman, 45; Belfer, 46; Bennion, 47,48; Bickerdike, 49; Bierman, 50; Bilimovich, 51; Black, 52; Boiteux, 54; Boulding, 58,59,60,61,62; Bowman, 65; Bratt, 66,67,68; Brems, 69,71; Brennan, 73; Broster, 86; Brown, 87,88; Brown, 89; Brown, 91; Brozen, 94,95,96,97; Burns, 99; Bushaw, 100; Butler, 101,102; Caff, 104; Carter, 105; Carter, 107; Carver, 109; Chamber of Commerce, 110; Chambers, 111; Champernowne, 112; de Chazeau, 114; Chenery, 116; Christ, 118, 119; Clark, 122; Clark, 123,124; Clower, 126; Cohen, 129; Colm, 131; Coughlan, 133; Cunningham, 139; Dale, 141; Dean, 148, 149, 150,151,152,153,154,155,156,157; Denison, 158; Devons, 161; Dieterlen, 162; Dobrovolsky, 163,164, 165; Domar, 167,168,169,170; Donachie, 171; Dorfman, 172; Dryden, 173; Duesenberry, 174,175; Durand, 176; Dvoretzky, 177,178,179; Eckaus, 180; Edge, 181; Edwards,183; Egerton, 184, 185; Eisemann, 190; Eisner, 191,192,193,194,198; Fellner, 209; Fetter, 211; Fisher, 214,215; Foldes, 218; Fox, 229; Frankel, 230; Frazer, 231; Friday, 232; Friend, 234; Frisch, 240; Froehlich, 241, 242; Galbraith, 245; Goode, 250,251,252; Goodwin, 253,254,255,256,257; Gordon, 258; Gordon, 259, 260, 261, 262, 263; Gordon, 264,265; Griliches, 268; Haavelmo, 275,276,277; Haberler, 279; Hadley, 280, 281; Hahn, 282,283; Hamberg, 284,285,286; Hansen, 287, 288; Haring, 289; Hart, 290,291,292,293,294; Hawtrey, 299; 300; Henderson, 304; Henderson, 305; Hetrick, 308; Hickman, 310; Hicks, 312; Hieser, 313; Hirshleifer, 316; Hogan,

320; Hoover, 321, 322, 323, 324; Hultgren, 326; Hurwicz, 327,
328; Jacoby, 332, 333; Jung, 337; Kaldor, 338; Kalecki, 339,
340, 341; Katona, 342, 343, 344; Keezer, 346; Kervyn, 347;
Klein, 350, 351, 352; Knight, 359; Knox, 360, 361; Koch, 363;
Koopmans, 364; Kuh, 369; Lachman, 377, 378, 379; Laderman,
380; Latane, 382; Leaderach, 383; Lent, 384; Leontief, 385;
Liebling, 387, 388; Lindsay, 389; Lintner, 390; Lorie, 394, 395;
Lowe, 397; Lundberg, 398; Lutz, 399, 400, 401; Mack, 403, 404,
405, 407; Magee, 410, 411, 412, 413; Maisel, 414; Marks, 422;
Massell, 426, 427; Matthews, 428, 429; McClelland, 434;
McLean, 439; Merrett, 441; Metzler, 443, 444, 445, 446, 447;
Miller, 451; Mills, 452, 453, 455; Mills, 456, 457; Minsky, 458;
Modigliani, 461, 463, 464, 465, 468, 469; Morehouse, 472;
Morin, 473; Morse, 475; Naddor, 477; National Bureau of Eco-
nomic Research, 480, 481, 482, 483, 484, 485, 486; National
Industrial Conference Board, 489; Neisser, 492, 493; Norris,
496; Norton, 498; Novozhilov, 500; Nurkse, 502; Parker, 506;
Parkinson, 507; Pegrum, 509, 510; Peston, 511; Peters, 512;
Platt, 513; Predetti, 514; Preinreich, 515; Puthercheary, 516;
Ravenscroft, 517; Renshaw, 519; Reul, 520; Reynolds, 521;
Rhys-Williams, 522; Robinson, 523, 524, 525; Roos, 527, 529;
Rostow, 531; Salant, 532; Salter, 533; Samuelson, 534, 535,
536, 537; Saposnik, 538; Scheuble, 539; Schiff, 540, 541, 542;
Schlaifer, 544; Schmidt, 545; Schreder, 546; de Scitovsky, 547;
Schwan, 548; Shackle, 550, 551, 552, 553, 554, 555, 556, 557,
559, 561; Sheard, 563; Shelton, 564; Shubik, 565; Siegel, 566;
Simmons, 568; Simons, 569; Smith, 570; Smith, 572, 573, 574;
Smithies, 575; Solomon, 576, 577, 578; Stauss, 585; Steger, 586,
587, 588; Steindl, 589, 590; Stern, 592; Stockfisch, 593, 594,
595, 596; Stolper, 598; Streeten, 600, 602; Strumilin, 604; Tannenbaum, 606; Terborgh, 607, 608, 609, 610; Tew, 612; Thomas,
613; Thrall, 614; Tinbergen, 617; Tsiang, 619, 620; Ulmer,
623; United Nations, 627; Usher, 628; Wagner, 631; Walker,
633; Wallich, 634; Wasserman, 636; Wellisz, 638; Wells, 639;
White, 642, 643; Whitin, 644, 645, 646, 647; Wilson, 649;
Wilson, 650, 651; Wilson, 654; Winding, 658; Woodward, 661;
Wright, 662, 663; Youngson, 666.

2. Empirical, Qualitative: Interview, Questionnaire and Case
Studies

Andrews, 20; Barna, 39; Brems, 70; Brockie and Grey, 84, 85;
Brown, 92; de Chazeau, 113; Clark, 125; Cochran, 128; Cyert,
140; Daly, 142; Dennison, 159; Eisemann, 189; Eisner, 195,
197; Foss, 222; Frankel, 230; Gonzalez, 249; Gort, 267; Heller,
303; Hicks, 311; Higgins, 314; Hill, 315; Hirt, 317; Hoadley,
318; Hodges, 319; Istvan, 330; Kimmel, 348; Lanzillotti, 381;
Leontief, 385; Lydall, 402; Mack, 406; Maclaurin, 408, 409;
Mansfield, 419; Mayer, 430, 431, 432, 433; Meade and Andrews,

440; Mueller, 476; Norton and Wall, 499; Oxenfeldt, 503;
Pankhurst, 504; Peck, 508; Rosenblatt, 530; Schwan, 548;
Scott, 549; Smith, 571; Streever, 603; White, 640, 641, 643;
Wilson, 651; Wilson and Andrews, 653; Youngson, 665.

3. Empirical, Quantitative But Not Involving Parameter Estimation

Abramovitz, 1, 2, 3, 5; Anderson, 13, 14, 15, 16; Anderson, 17;
Andrews, 18, 19; Balogh, 31; Barber, 32, 33; Barna, 36, 37,
38, 39; Barritt, 40; Blyth, 53; Borenstein, 56; Bridge, 74, 75,
76, 77, 78, 79, 80, 81, 82, 83; Buckley, 98; Butlin, 103; Carter,
105; Churchill, 120, 121; Cobren, 127; Coppock, 132; Cox, 134;
Creamer, 135, 136, 137; Daly, 143; Derrickson, 160; Dobrovolsky, 166; Edge, 181; Edmunds, 182; Einarsen, 186, 187, 188;
Eisemann, 189; Epstein, 200; Fabricant, 203; Federal Reserve
Board, 204, 205, 206, 207; Feinstein, 208; Ferber, 210; Firestone, 212; Foss, 219, 220, 221, 223, 224, 225, 226, 227, 228;
Friend, 233, 235, 236, 237, 238, 239; Gainsbrugh, 244; Gehrels,
247; Gertler, 248; Grosse, 269, 270, 272; Hartley, 295; Hastay,
296, 297; Hawkins, 298; Healy, 302; Hickman, 309, 310; Inter-
state Commerce Commission, 329; Jacobs, 331; Joint Eco-
nomic Committee, 336; Keezer, 345; Kisselgoff and Modigliani,
349; Koch, 362; Kuznets, 370, 371, 372, 373, 374, 375, 376;
Leontief, 385; Livingston, 393; Malissen, 415; Manne, 418;
Mansfield, 420; Massell, 423; McHugh, 435, 436, 437, 438, 439;
Merriam, 442; Mitchell, 459; Modigliani and Cohen, 466;
Moore, 470; Morehouse, 471; Nassimbene, 478, 479; National
Bureau of Economic Research, 481, 482, 483, 484, 485, 486,
488; National Industrial Conference Board, 490; Natrella, 491;
Nerlove, 494; Paradiso, 505; Redfern, 518; Shackle, 558; Shaw,
562; Solomon, 578; Stanback, 582, 583; Stern, 591; Stokes, 597;
Streeten, 601; Terleckyj, 611; Ulin, 621; Ulmer, 622, 624, 625;
Unilever, 626; Walter, 632; Warner, 635; Wasson, 637; White,
642; Wilson, 648; Wilson, 655, 656; Wimsatt, 657; Winston, 659;
Wooden, 660; Yance, 664.

4. Empirical, Quantitative Involving Econometric Estimation

Barger, 34; Barna, 35; Bator, 41; Boot and De Wit, 55; Boschan, 57; Bowman, 64; Brennan, 72; Brown and Roseman, 90;
Brownlie, 93; Carter, 106; Chenery, 115; Christ, 117; Clark,
125; Cohen, 130; Crockett, 138; Darling, 144, 145; Eisner, 196,
199; Ezekial, 201, 202; Fisher, 213, 216, 217; Fujino, 243; Gallaway and Smith, 246; Goris and Koyck, 266; Grunfeld, 274;
Hultgren, 325; Jensen, 334; Johnston, 335; Klein, 353, 354, 355,
356, 357, 358; Koopmans, 365; Koyck, 366; Kuh, 367, 368;
Levine, 386; Liu and Chang, 391; Liu, 392; Lovell, 396; Manne,
416; Massell, 424, 425; Meyer and Kuh, 448, 449, 450; Mills,

454; Modigliani and Zeman, 460; Modigliani and Sauerlander, 462; Modigliani and Weingartner, 467; Morrissett, 474; Nevile, 495; Norton, 497; Nurkse, 501; Robinson, 526; Roos, 528; Schiff, 543; Smith, 571; Solow, 580; Spiro, 581; Stanback, 584; Stone and Rowe, 599; Streever, 603; Taitel, 605; Tinbergen, 615, 616, 617, 618; Valavanis, 629; Veno, 630; Wilson, 652; Yance, 664.

B. Scope

1. The Individual Firm

Abramovitz, 1, 2, 3, 4; Alchian, 6; American Management Association, 12; Anderson, 13; Andrews, 18, 19, 20; Angell, 21, 22; Anthony, 23; Arrow, 25, 26, 27; Bailey, 28; Baldwin, 30; Barna, 39; Beckman, 45; Bennion, 48; Bierman, 50; Bilimovich, 51; Black, 52; Boiteux, 53; Boulding, 58, 59, 60, 61; Bratt, 68; Brennan, 73; Brockie and Grey, 84, 85; Broster, 86; Brown, 87, 88; Brown, 89, 90; Brozen, 94, 95, 96, 97; Bushaw and Clower, 100; Carter, 105, 106; Carter, Meredith and Shackle, 107; Carter and Williams, 108; Chamber of Commerce, 110; de Chazeau, 113, 114; Clark, 122; Clark, 125; Coughlan, 133; Cunningham, 139; Cyert, 140; Dale, 141; Daly, 142; Dean, 147, 148, 149, 150, 151, 152, 153, 154, 155, 156, 157; Denison, 158; Dennison, 159; Dieterlen, 162; Dobrovolsky, 163; Donachie, 171; Dorfman, 172; Dryden, 173; Durand, 176; Dvoretzky, 177, 178, 179; Edge, 181; Egerton, 185; Eisner, 199; Fetter, 211; Foss, 222, 226; Frazer, 321; Goodwin, 254; Gordon, 261, 262, 263; Gordon, 264; Gort, 267; Griliches, 268; Grunfeld, 274; Haavelmo, 277; Hadley, 280, 281; Haring, 289; Hart, 291; Heller, 303; Hetrick, 308; Hill, 315; Hirshleifer, 316; Hogan, 320; Hoover, 323, 324; Hultgren, 326; Hurwicz, 328; Istvan, 330; Jacoby, 333; Kalecki, 339; Katona, 342, 343, 344; Keezer, 346; Klein, 350, 352; Knox, 361; Koch, 362; Kuh, 367, 368, 369; Lachman, 377, 379; Lanzillotti, 381; Latane, 382; Leaderach, 383; Lent, 384; Lorie, 394, 395; Lutz, 399, 401; Mack, 403; Magee, 410, 411, 412, 413; Maisel, 414; Malissen, 415; Manne, 418; Mansfield, 419, 420; Machinery and Allied Products Institute, 421; Marks, 422; Mayer, 433; McClelland, 434; McLean, 439; Meade, 440; Merrett, 441; Miller, 451; Mills, 456, 457; Modigliani, 463, 468, 469; Mueller, 476; Naddor, 477; Neisser, 493; Norris, 496; Norton and Wall, 499; Oxenfeldt, 503; Platt, 513; Predetti, 514; Preinreich, 515; Puthercheary, 516; Ravenscroft, 517; Reynolds, 521; Roos and Von Szeliski, 527; Salter, 533; Saposnik, 538; Scheuble, 539; Schiff, 540, 541, 542; de Scitovsky, 547; Shackle, 551, 552, 553, 554, 559, 561; Shubik, 565; Smith, 571; Smith, 572, 573, 574; Smithies, 575; Solomon, 576, 577, 578; Stauss, 585; Steger, 587, 588; Terborgh, 607, 609, 610; Terleckyj, 611; Unilever, 626; Wagner, 631; Walker, 633; Wellisz, 638; Wells, 639; White, 641, 643; Whitin, 644, 645, 646; Wilson, 655, 656; Wright, 663.

2. The Industry

Abramovitz, 2, 3, 5; American Management Association, 12; Anderson, 15, 16; Anderson, 17; Barber, 32, 33; Barna, 35, 37, 38, 39; Barritt, 40; Black, 52; Borenstein, 56; Boschan, 57; Bowman and Phillips, 65; Brems, 70; Brennan, 72; Bridge, 81; Brown, 92; Carter, 105, 106; Chenery, 115; Creamer, 135, 136; Darling, 146; Derrickson, 160; Dobrovolsky, 165, 166; Einarson, 186, 187, 188; Eisemann, 189; Epstein, 200; Firestone, 212; Foss, 223, 226, 227; Fujino, 243; Gehrels, 247; Gertler, 248; Gonzalez, 249; Grosse, 269, 271, 272; Haavelmo, 277; Hastay, 296; Hawkins, 298; Healy, 302; Hickman, 309, 310; Hicks, 311; Hirt, 317; Hoadley, 318; Hodges, 319; Interstate Commerce Commission, 329; Jensen, 334; Joint Economic Commission, 336; Kisselgoff and Modigliani, 349; Klein, 354; Koyck, 366; Kuznets, 376; Levine, 386; Liebling, 387; Livingston, 393; Lovell, 396; Mack, 406, 407; Maclaurin, 408, 409; Marks, 422; Mayer, 430, 431; Meyer and Kuh, 448, 449, 450; Modigliani and Cohen, 466; Moore, 470; Morehouse, 471; Morrissett, 474; National Bureau of Economic Research, 481, 488; Norton, 497; Pankhurst, 504; Peck, 508; Pegrum, 509, 510; Redfern, 518; Robinson, 526; Rosenblatt, 530; Smith, 574; Smithies, 575; Spiro, 581; Stanback, 582, 583; Stokes, 597; Stone, 599; Streever, 603; Taitel, 605; Terleckyj, 611; Ulmer, 624, 625; Veno, 630; Warner, 635; White, 643; Wilson, 649; Wimsatt, 657; Winston, 659; Wooden, 660; Yance, 664; Youngson, 665.

3. Aggregate

Alexander, 8, 9; Allen, 10, 11; Arndt, 24; Bain, 29; Balogh, 31; Barber, 32, 33; Barger, 34; Barna, 35, 36, 37, 38; Bator, 41; Baumol, 42, 43, 44; Bennion, 47; Bickerdike, 49; Blyth, 53; Boot and De Wit, 55; Bratt, 66, 67; Brems, 69, 71; Bridge, 74, 75, 76, 77, 78, 79, 80, 82, 83; Brown, 91; Brownlie, 93; Butler, 101, 102; Butlin, 103; Caff, 104; Carter, 105; Carver, 109; Chamber of Commerce, 110; Chambers, 111; Champernowne, 112; Chenery, 116; Christ, 117, 118, 119; Churchill, 120, 121; Clark, 123, 124; Clower, 126; Cobren, 127; Cochran, 128; Cohen, 129; Cohen, 130; Colm, 131; Coppock, 132; Cox, 134; Creamer, 137; Crockett, 138; Daly, 143; Darling, 144, 145, 146; Devons, 161; Dieterlen, 162; Dobrovolsky, 164, 165; Domar, 167, 168, 169, 170; Duesenberry, 174, 175; Dvoretzky, 177, 178, 179; Eckaus, 180; Edmunds, 182; Eisemann, 190; Eisner, 191, 192, 193, 194, 195, 196, 197, 198; Ezekial, 201, 202; Fabricant, 203; Federal Reserve Board, 204, 205, 206, 207; Feinstein, 208; Fellner, 209; Ferber, 210; Fisher, 213, 214, 215, 216, 217; Foss, 219, 220, 221, 223, 224, 225, 226, 228; Fox, 229; Frankel, 230; Friend, 233, 234, 235, 236, 237,

238, 239; Froehlich, 241, 242; Fujino, 243; Gainsbrugh, 244;
Galbraith, 245; Gallaway, 246; Goode, 250, 251, 252; Goodwin,
253, 255, 256, 257; Gordon, 258; Gordon, 259, 260; Gordon,
265; Goris and Koyck, 266; Griliches, 268; Grosse, 270;
Haavelmo, 275, 276; Haberler, 278, 279; Hahn, 282, 283; Ham-
berg, 284, 285, 286; Hansen, 287, 288; Hart, 290, 292, 293;
Hartley, 295; Hastay, 296, 297; Hawtrey, 299, 300, 301;
Henderson, 304; Henderson, 305; Hickman, 310; Hicks, 312;
Hieser, 313; Higgins, 314; Hultgren, 325; Jacobs, 331; Jacoby,
332; Johnston, 335; Joint Economic Committee, 336; Jung, 337;
Kalecki, 340, 341; Katona, 343; Keezer, 345, 346; Kervyn, 347;
Kimmel, 348; Klein, 351, 353, 355, 356, 357, 358; Knox, 361;
Koch, 363; Kuznets, 370, 371, 373, 374, 375; Lachman, 378;
Laderman, 380; Leontief, 385; Levine, 386; Lindsay, 389;
Lintner, 390; Liu, 391, 392; Lowe, 397; Lungberg, 398; Lutz,
400; Lydall, 402; Mack, 404, 405; Maisel, 414; Malissen, 415;
Manne, 416, 417; Massell, 423, 424, 425, 426, 427; Matthews,
428, 429; McHugh, 435, 436, 437, 438; Merriam, 442; Metzler,
443, 444, 445, 446, 447; Mills, 452, 453, 454, 455; Minsky, 458;
Mitchell, 459; Modigliani, 460, 461, 462, 463, 464, 465, 466,
467, 468; Morin, 473; Morse, 475; Nassimbene, 478, 479; Na-
tional Bureau of Economic Research, 481; National Industrial
Conference Board, 489, 490; Natrella, 491; Neisser, 492, 493;
Nevile, 495; Norton, 498; Novozhilov, 500; Nurkse, 501; Paradiso, 505; Parkinson, 507; Peston, 511; Puthercheary, 516;
Redfern, 518; Robinson, 523, 525; Roos, 528; Rostow, 531;
Samuelson, 536; Schlaifer, 544; Schmidt, 545; Schreder, 546;
de Scitovsky, 547; Shackle, 552, 554, 555, 556, 557; Shaw, 562;
Sheard, 563; Shelton, 564; Siegel, 566; Simmons, 568; Solow,
580; Spiro, 581; Stanback, 582, 584; Steger, 586; Steindl, 589;
Stern, 591, 592; Stockfisch, 594, 596; Stolper, 598; Strumilin,
604; Terborgh, 607, 610; Tew, 612; Tinbergen, 615, 616, 617,
618; Tsiang, 619, 620; Ulin, 621; Ulmer, 622, 623; United
Nations, 627; Valavanis, 629; Walker, 632; Wallich, 634;
Warner, 635; Wasson, 637; White, 640, 642; Whitin, 645;
Wilson, 648; Wilson, 652, 653, 655, 656; Woodward, 661;
Wright, 663.

C. Subject Matter

1. Capacity-Output Relationships; the Acceleration Principle

Abramovitz, 1, 2, 5; Alchian, 7; Alexander, 8, 9; Allen, 10, 11;
Arndt, 24; Barber, 32, 33; Barna, 36, 38; Bator, 41; Baumol,
43; Bennion, 47; Bickerdike, 49; Bilimovich, 51; Blyth, 53;
Boschan, 57; Bowman, 65; Brems, 69, 71; Broster, 86; Brown,
89, 90; Burns, 99; Butler, 101; Carter, 105, 106; Carver, 109;
Chenery, 115; Clark, 123; Clark, 125; Creamer, 136, 137;
Crockett, 138; Darling, 145; Dean, 148; Domar, 168, 170;

Duesenberry, 174; Eckaus, 180; Eisner, 195, 196, 199; Epstein, 200; Ezekial, 201, 202; Fabricant, 203; Fisher, 213, 214, 215, 216, 217; Foss, 227; Froehlick, 241, 242; Fujino, 243; Gainsbrugh, 244; Goodwin, 254, 255, 257; Grosse, 269, 271; Grunfeld, 273, 274; Hamberg, 286; Hansen, 287; Hawkins, 298; Hickman, 309, 310; Hicks, 312; Hieser, 313; Hirt, 317; Hodges, 319; Hultgren, 325; Hurwicz, 327; Jung, 337; Haldor, 338; Kervyn, 347; Kisselgoff and Modigliani, 348; Knox, 360, 361; Koyck, 366; Kuh, 367, 368; Kuznets, 371, 372, 374, 375; Liu, 392; Livingston, 393; Lovell, 396; Lowe, 397; Mack, 403, 407; Malissen, 415; Manne, 416, 417; Metzler, 443, 444, 445; Meyer and Kuh, 448, 449, 450; Minsky, 458; Modigliani and Sauerlander, 462; Modigliani, 464; Moore, 470; Morrissett, 474; Naddor, 477; Nassimbene, 478, 479; Neisser, 492; Nevile, 495; Norton, 497, 498; Peck, 508; Peston, 511; Robinson, 526; Roos, 528; Samuelson, 535, 536; Schmidt, 545; Shackle, 555; Smith, 572, 573; Smithies, 575; Steindl, 589; Stern, 591; Stone and Rowe, 599; Streever, 603; Taitel, 605; Tinbergen, 615, 616, 617, 618; Tsiang, 619, 620; Ulin, 621; Valavanis, 629; Veno, 630; Whitin, 644; Wilson, 652, 655; Winding, 658; Wright, 662, 663.

2. The Role of Internal Funds, Past and Current Profits, Depreciation Charges and Liquidity

Abramovitz, 1, 3; Alchian, 7; Anderson, 13; Anderson, 17; Andrews, 18, 20; Anthony, 23; Baldwin, 30; Barger, 34; Barna, 39; Barritt, 40; Bilimovich, 51; Black, 52; Boiteux, 54; Boulding, 58; Brennan, 73; Brockie and Grey, 85; Brown, 89, 90; Brownlie, 93; Cohen, 129; Coughlan, 133; Creamer, 137; Crockett, 138; Darling, 144; Dean, 154, 157; Dobrovolsky, 165, 166; Donachie, 171; Durand, 176; Eisemann, 189; Eisner, 191, 195, 196; Ezekial, 201, 202; Fisher, 213; Friend, 234; Froehlich, 241, 243; Goodwin, 254; Gordon, 262, 263; Grunfeld, 273, 274; Hart, 292; Healy, 302; Heller, 303; Henderson, 306, 307; Hogan, 320; Hurwicz, 327; Klein, 352, 353, 354, 355, Knox, 360, 361; Koch, 362; Kuh, 367, 368; Kuznets, 373; Lachman, 377, 379; Lent, 384; Liu, 391, 392; Lutz, 399, 401; Malissen, 415; McHugh, 435, 436, 437, 438; McLean, 439; Merrett, 441; Meyer and Kuh, 448, 449, 450; Modigliani and Zeman, 460; Modigliani and Miller, 469; Morrissett, 474; Neisser and Grosswald, 493; Norton, 497; Oxenfeldt, 503; Platt, 513; Ravenscroft, 517; Roos, 528; Salant, 532; Schiff, 540, 541, 542; Shackle, 555, 556, 557, 559, 560; Sheard, 563; Shelton, 564; Simmons, 568; Smithies, 575; Steger, 587, 588; Steindl, 589; Stokes, 597; Taitel, 605; Tinbergen, 615, 616, 618; Valavanis, 629; Veno, 630; Wilson, 655.

3. The Role of External Funds; Cost and Availability

Anderson, 13; Anderson, 17; Andrews, 18, 19, 20; Barna, 35, 39; Bierman, 50; Black, 52; Boulding, 62; Bratt, 68; Brockie and Grey, 84; Cohen, 129; Creamer, 137; Cunningham, 139; Dean, 148; Dobrovolsky, 166; Durand, 176; Eisemann, 189, 190; Ezekial, 201; 202; Federal Reserve Board, 204; Fisher, 213; Frazer, 231; Friend, 234; Froehlich, 241; Galbraith, 245; Gehrels, 247; Goode, 251; Haavelmo, 275; Haberler, 278; Hawtrey, 300, 301; Henderson, 304; Henderson, 305, 306, 307; Hoover, 323; Kalecki, 339; Knight, 359; Knox, 360; Koch, 362; Kuh, 369; Kuznets, 373; Liebling, 387, 388; Lutz, 399, 400, 401; Lydall, 402; Mayer, 432; McHugh, 435, 436, 437, 438; Meade, 440; Metzler, 446, 447; Minsky, 458; Modigliani and Zeman, 460; Modigliani and Miller, 468; Parkinson, 507; Salant, 532; Scott, 549; Shackle, 553, 559, 560, 561; Spiro, 581; Tew, 612; Wellisz, 638; White, 640, 641, 643; Wilson, 651; Wilson and Andrews, 653; Wilson, 654, 655.

4. Factor Supply Conditions: Locational Factors and the Prices and Availability of Capital Goods

Goris and Koyck, 266; Hadley and Whitin, 281; Healy, 302; Heller, 303; Hoover, 323; Mack, 406; Manne, 417; Mayer, 430, 431, 432; McClelland, 434; Mills, 457; Predetti, 514; Smith, 571; Stockfisch, 595; Terborgh, 609.

5. Technological Change

Belfer, 46; Blyth, 53; Broster, 86; Brown, 92; Brozen, 94, 95, 96, 97; Carter, 106; Carter, 108; Denison, 158; Duesenberry, 175; Edmunds, 182; Foss, 227; Frankel, 230; Frisch, 240; Goodwin, 253; Gordon, 258; Healy, 302; Hirt, 317; Hoover, 321, 323; Lowe, 397; Maclaurin, 408, 409; Mansfield, 420; Massell, 423, 424, 425, 426, 427; Metzler, 444; Mueller, 476; Pankhurst, 504; Pegrum, 509, 510; Siegel, 567; Smith, 570; Smith, 574; Solow, 579, 580; Usher, 628; Wilson, 655.

6. Replacement Policy

Alchian, 6; American Management Association, 12; Bain, 29; Barritt, 40; Brown, 92; Clark, 122; Dean, 155; Dobrovolsky, 164; Domar, 168; Einarsen, 186, 187; Eisner, 192, 198; Hogan, 320; Kalecki, 341; Leaderach, 383; Lowe, 397; MAPI, 421; Marks, 422; Peters, 512; Scheuble, 539; Schiff, 540, 541, 542; Smith, 574; Terborgh, 607, 610; Wilson, 655.

7. Decision Making

Andrews and Brunner, 20; Angell, 21; Arrow, 25, 26, 27;
Bailey, 28; Barna, 39; Beckmann, 45; Bierman, 50; Bowman,
63; Bushaw and Clower, 100; Carter, 107; Carter, 108;
de Chazeau, 113, 114; Cochran, 128; Daly, 142; Dvoretzky,
177, 178, 179; Egerton, 185; Foldes, 218; Gordon, 264; Haring,
289; Hart, 291; Hirshleifer, 316; Hurwicz, 328; Jacoby, 333;
Jung, 337; Katona, 342, 343, 344; Lachman, 379; Lanzillotti,
381; Latane, 382; Lundberg, 398; Maclaurin, 408; Maisel,
414; Manne, 418; Mansfield, 419; Mills, 452, 454; Modigliani
and Hohn, 461; Modigliani and Cohen, 465; Morin, 473; Parker,
506; Peck, 508; Preinreich, 515; Schreder, 546; de Scitovsky,
547; Shackle, 550, 551, 552, 554, 556, 557, 558; Simon, 569;
Smith, 574; Stauss, 585; Steindl, 590; Stockfisch, 595; Tannenbaum, 606; Thrall, 614; Ulmer, 623; Walker, 633; Wasserman,
636; White, 642 643; Wilson, 650; Wilson, 654, 655, 656.

8. Capital Budgeting, Anticipations and Forecasting

Anderson, 14, 15, 16; Angell, 21; Barna, 39; Bennion, 48;
Bowman, 63; Bratt, 66, 67, 68; Brems, 69, 71; Bridge, 75,
78, 80, 83; Chenery, 116; Cohen, 130; Cox, 134; Cyert, 140;
Dale, 141; Daly, 142; Dean, 148, 150, 151, 152, 154; Dennison,
159; Dorfman, 172; Dryden, 173; Edge, 181; Edwards, 183;
Egerton, 184, 185; Fellner, 209; Ferber, 210; Firestone,
212; Foss, 220, 221, 222, 223, 224, 225, 226, 228; Friday,
232; Friend, 233, 235, 236, 237, 238; Gordon, 259, 261, 262;
Gort, 267; Grosse, 270; Hahn, 283; Hart, 290, 291, 292, 294;
Hartley, 295; Hastay, 297; Healy, 302; Heller, 303; Hetrick,
308; Hill, 315; Hirshleifer, 316; Hoover, 324; Istvan, 330;
Jensen, 334; Katona, 342; Kuh, 369; Latane, 382; Lent, 384;
Lorie, 394, 395; Mack, 405; Magee, 410, 411, 412, 413;
Maisel, 414; Mayer, 432; Merriam, 442; Mills, 452, 454, 455;
Modigliani, 460, 462, 463, 465, 466, 467; National Bureau of
Economic Research, 483, 485, 487; National Industrial Con-
ference Board, 490; Natrella, 491; Norris, 496; Norton, 499;
Novozhilov, 500; Nurkse, 501; Peters, 512; Renshaw, 519;
Reul, 520; Roos, 529, Shackle, 550, 551, 552, 554, 558; Shubik,
565; Siegel, 566; Solomon, 576, 577, 578; Stockfisch, 593;
Strumilin, 604; Terborgh, 608; Ulmer, 622; Unilever, 626;
Wilson, 648, 649.

9. Tax Policy

Black, 52; Borenstein, 56; Brown, 87, 88; Chambers, 111;
Clark, 122; Clark, 124; Colm, 131; Dean, 156; Dobrovolsky,

163, 164; Domar, 167, 169; Eisner, 191, 192, 193; Frazer, 231; Goode, 250, 251, 252; Gordon, 260; Hansen, 288; Hart, 293; Higgins, 314; Jacoby, 332; Kimmel, 348; Lintner, 390; Miller, 451; Preinreich, 515; Puthercheary, 516; Rhys-Williams, 522; Schlaifer, 544; Steger, 586, 587,588; Stockfisch, 594, 596; Streeten, 600, 601, 602; Thomas, 613; Walker, 632; Wallich, 634.

D. Type of Investment

1. Plant and Equipment

Alchian, 6, 7; American Management Association, 12; Andrews, 20; Angell, 21; Anthony, 23; Bailey, 28; Bain, 29; Baldwin, 30; Barna, 35, 36, 37, 38; Barritt, 40; Bator, 41; Baumol, 43, 44; Belfer, 46; Bennion, 47; Bickerdike, 49; Bierman, 50; Bilimovich, 51; Black, 52; Boiteux, 54; Borenstein, 56; Boschan, 57; Boulding, 61, 62; Bowman, 64, 65; Brems, 69, 71; Bridge, 74, 75, 76, 78, 79, 80, 81, 82, 83; Brockie and Grey, 84, 85; Broster, 86; Brown, 87, 88; Brown, 89, 90; Brown, 92; Brownlie, 93; Brozen, 94, 95, 96, 97; Buckley, 98; Butler, 101, 102; Caff, 104; Carter, 105, 106; Carter, 108; Carver, 109; de Chazeau, 113, 114; Chenery, 115, 116; Clark, 122; Clark, 123, 124; Clark, 125; Cochran, 128; Cohen, 129; Colm, 131; Coughlan, 133; Cox, 134; Creamer, 135, 136, 137; Crockett, 138; Cunningham, 139; Darling, 144; Dean, 147, 148, 149, 150, 151, 152, 154, 155, 156, 157; Denison, 158; Devons, 161; Dobrovolsky, 163, 164, 165; Domar, 167, 168, 169, 170; Donachie, 171; Dorfman, 172; Dryden, 173; Eckaus, 180; Edge, 181; Edmunds, 182; Einarsen, 186, 187, 188; Eisner, 191, 192, 193, 195, 196, 197, 198, 199; Epstein, 200; Ezekial, 202; Fabricant, 203; Federal Reserve Board, 204; Feinstein, 208; Fellner, 209; Fetter and Goodman, 211; Firestone, 212; Fisher, 213, 214, 215; Foss, 220, 221, 222, 223, 224, 225, 226, 227; Frankel, 230; Frazer, 231; Friend, 233, 234, 235, 236, 237, 238, 239; Froehlich, 242; Gainsbrugh, 244; Gehrels, 247; Gerthler, 248; Gonzalez, 249; Goode, 250, 251, 252; Goodwin, 253, 254, 255, 257; Gordon, 258; Gordon, 259, 260, 261, 262; Gordon, 263; Goris and Koyck, 266; Gort, 267; Griliches and Grunfeld, 268; Grosse, 269, 270, 271, 272; Grunfeld, 273, 274; Haavelmo, 275, 276, 277; Haberler, 278; Hahn, 282, 283; Hamberg, 286; Hart, 292, 293, 294; Hawkins, 298; Healy, 302; Heller, 303; Henderson, 304; Henderson, 305, 306, 307; Hetrick, 308; Hickman, 309; Hieser, 313; Hill, 315; Hirt, 317; Hoadley, 318; Hodges, 319; Hogan, 320; Hoover, 322, 323, 324, 325; Hurwicz, 327, 328; Interstate Commerce Commission, 329; Istvan, 330; Jacoby, 332; Jensen, 334; Johnston, 335; Kalecki, 339, 341; Katona, 344; Keezer, 345, 346; Kisselgoff and Modigliani, 349; Klein, 350,

352, 353, 354, 355, 356; Knox, 361; Koch, 363; Koyck, 366;
Kuh, 367, 368, 369; Kuznets, 370, 371, 372, 373, 374, 375,
376; Lachman, 377, 378, 379; Leaderach, 383; Lent, 384;
Levine, 386; Liebling, 387; Lindsay, 389; Lintner, 390; Liu,
391, 392; Livingston, 393; Lorie, 394; Lowe, 397; Lundberg,
398; Lutz, 399, 400, 401; Lydall, 402; Maclaurin, 409; Malissen, 415; Manne, 416, 417, 418; Mansfield, 420; Machinery
and Allied Products Institute, 421; Marks, 422, Matthews,
428; Mayer, 430, 431, 433; McHugh, 435, 436, 437, 438;
McLean, 439; Merrett, 441; Merriam, 442; Metzler, 446,
447; Meyer and Kuh, 448, 449, 450; Miller, 451; Mills, 456,
457; Minsky, 458; Modigliani, 460, 464, 467, 468; Moore,
470; Morehouse, 471; Morrissett, 474; Nassimbene, 478,
479; National Bureau of Economic Research, 483, 486, 488;
National Industrial Conference Board, 489, 490; Natrella,
491; Neisser, 492, 493; Nevile, 495; Norris, 496; Norton,
497, 498; Norton, 499; Novozhilov, 500; Pankhurst, 504;
Pegrum, 509, 510; Peston, 511; Peters, 512; Platt, 513;
Preinreich, 515; Puthercheary, 516; Ravenscroft, 517; Redfern, 518; Renshaw, 519; Reul, 520; Reynolds, 521; Robinson,
524; Ross, 527, 528; Rostow, 531; Salter, 533; Saposnik,
538; Scheuble, 539; Schiff, 540, 541, 542; Schlaifer, 544;
Schwan, 548; Scott, 549; Shackle, 553, 560, 561; Shelton,
564; Siegel, 567; Simmons, 568; Smith, 570; Smith, 571,
572, 573; Smithies, 575; Solomon, 576, 577; Spiro, 581;
Steger, 587, 588; Steindl, 589; Stern, 592; Stockfisch, 593,
594, 596; Stolper, 598; Stone, 599; Streever, 603; Strumilin,
604; Taitel, 605; Terborgh, 607, 608, 609, 610; Thomas, 613;
Tinbergen, 615, 616; Tsiang, 619, 620; Ulin, 621; Ulmer,
622, 623, 624, 625; Unilever, 626; United Nations, 627; Usher,
628; Valavanis, 629; Veno, 630; Walker, 632; Walker, 633;
Wallich, 634; Warner, 635; Wasson, 637; Wellisz, 638; Wells,
639; White, 640, 641, 642; Wilson, 648; Wilson, 650, 651;
Wilson, 652, 653, 654, 656; Wimsatt, 657; Wright, 662, 663;
Yance, 664; Youngson, 665, 666.

2. Inventories

Abramovitz, 1, 2, 3, 4, 5; Arrow, 26; Barber, 32, 33; Beckman and Muth, 45; Brennan, 72, 73; Brown, 91; Clower,
126; Cobren, 127; Daly, 142; Daly, 143; Darling, 145, 146;
Dvoretzky, 177, 178, 179; Eisemann, 189, 190; Federal
Reserve Board, 205; Foss, 219, 228; Fujino, 243; Hadley
and Whitin, 280, 281; Hansen, 287; Hawtrey, 301; Jacobs,
331; Joint Economic Committee, 336; Laderman, 380; Lovell,
396; Mack, 403, 404, 405, 406, 407; Magee, 410, 411, 412,
413; McClelland, 434; Metzler, 443, 445; Mills, 452, 453,
454, 455; Modigliani, 463, 466; Morehouse, 472; Morse,
475; Naddor, 477; Nerlove, 494; Nurkse, 501, 502, Paradiso,
505; Predetti, 514; Robinson, 526; Rosenblatt, 530; Stanback,

Research Study Three

INVESTMENT, LIQUIDITY, AND MONETARY POLICY

Edwin Kuh[1]
Massachusetts Institute
of Technology

John R. Meyer[1]
Harvard University

I. INTRODUCTION AND SUMMARY OF CONCLUSIONS

A. The Analytical Framework

Analysis of the effects of monetary policy on plant and equipment outlays can be posed in two basic questions. First, what is the relation of business liquidity and the availability of financing to investment outlays? Second, how can monetary policy affect business liquidity and financing? In this paper attention is focused almost exclusively on the first question, and it is taken, almost as a matter of belief, that business liquidity and financing can be influenced by monetary policy. This is not entirely satisfactory, but time and other constraints prevent a more extensive study.

Subsequent material dwells mainly on those determinants of business behavior which lead to or influence business contracts with external financial markets. Particular emphasis has been placed on the relations between the supply of financing and how

---

[1]Carlos Diaz provided valuable research assistance in the preparation of this paper.

management's financial policies may influence investment decisions. Attention is also given, however, to the important topic of the demand for capital assets.

The major issues of investment theory and their relationship to monetary policy can be posed within a simple supply and demand framework.[2] The supply of funds schedule, comprising both internal and external sources, can be described to a first approximation as a function of the "cost of money," including relevant opportunity costs. Demand, on the other hand, can be hypothesized to depend on the level or changes in the level of economic activity, as these influence prospective profitability and utilization of productive facilities, and interest rates. Thus, just as price and a level of activity variable, income, normally are considered to be determinants of consumer demand so both price and activity are assumed to be potential influences on investment demand.

The exact specification of variables to be entered into investment demand functions is, however, a matter of some dispute. For example, some economists feel that changes in the level of activity, particularly if entered with appropriate lags, are the best measure of activity effects on investment demand. Others, including the present authors, prefer that the level of activity be taken relative to some ability to produce as, say, by some measure of capacity utilization. Generally speaking, empirical evidence suggests that the capacity formulations tend to be more closely associated with investment than the other alternatives, but the point is debatable and certainly contested.

A good deal of controversy also exists over the price or interest elasticity of demand for investment goods. Some, for example, those adhering to simple acceleration theories of investment, implicitly or explicitly impute a zero elasticity to price effects. Basically, the position is that short-run variations in investment never are made — at least to any important extent — for purposes other than expansion of productivity capacity. Other reasons for investing like cost reduction and product improvement, are assumed to be trend-related or autonomous; yet, if these other objectives do influence short-run investment, they would seem to be potentially more interest sensitive than investment aimed simply at expansion. It is difficult to say how sensitive the investment-interest rate relationship is likely to be in the short run, other than presuming it is something greater than zero. Available evidence, none of which is terribly satisfactory, suggests that the interest elasticity of

---

[2]Both graphs, and much of the analysis, presented here are in accord with the position of James S. Duesenberry, Business Cycles and Economic Growth, 1958.

demand is not large, at least in the historically relevant range of roughly 3 to 10 percent per annum charged for long-term capital. On the other hand, it seems entirely possible, indeed probable, that the relationship could become more elastic beyond these limits.

A three-dimensional diagram containing the main elements of at least one relevant formulation of the supply-demand relationships for manufacturing investment decisions is shown, for illustrative purposes, in Diagram III-1. On the vertical axis are interest rates or, more specifically, the cost of funds (including opportunity costs) and the rate of return measured as a percent per period; the horizontal axis shows investment divided by the capital stock or the gross rate of growth per period in the capital stock; and the axis coming "out of the page" has a percentage measure of capacity utilization of fixed capital. The capacity axis in actuality is much more complicated than we have presented it here since, in fact, induced plant and equipment investment may follow a distributed lag pattern. We should therefore think of the capacity axis as representing the average lag relevant to the current period's investment, perhaps capacity utilization of one year back.[3]

The shapes of these functions and how they might shift over time establish a framework within which the potential influence of monetary policy can be evaluated. The shifts in the functions strongly depend, of course, on cyclical phenomena. Unfortunately, the interactions between the supply of funds and demand for new assets functions are extremely complicated and not yet fully understood. As in the case of interest elasticity measurements, existing knowledge is regrettably slight.

---

[3] In "Lags for Fiscal and Monetary Policy" (Research Study One in Stabilization Policies) prepared for the Commission on Money and Credit by E. Cary Brown, Robert M. Solow, Albert Ando, and John Kareken, it was found that the production of equipment has, roughly speaking, an average delay of a year between production and orders. If the production of capital goods precedes their installation by an amount assumed to be three months, the average lead time will be about fifteen months. In addition, Solow and Brown found high positive correlation between current percent of capacity utilization and new orders for equipment. The lag structure may, nevertheless, be asymmetrical during periods of increasing capacity utilization and decreasing capacity utilization. It is to be supposed that it takes considerably longer to effectuate a large-scale investment program during a period of increasing capacity pressures than it does to curtail a program when capacity utilization is decreasing. This matter requires further detailed investigation.

Diagram III-1

Hypothetical Individual Firm Supply and Demand for Investment Funds

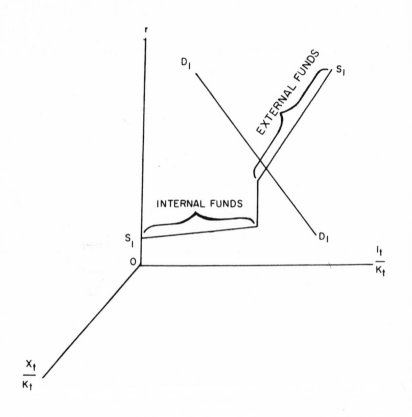

r   = Per Cent Cost of Funds

$\dfrac{I_t}{K_t}$ = Gross Investment divided by Gross Capital Stock

$\dfrac{X_t}{K_t}$ = Output divided by Gross Capital Stock, or Measure of Capacity Utilization

D_1D_1= Demand for Investment, for a given capital stock and level of output as a function of fund costs.

S_1S_1 = Supply of Funds, for given capital stock, level of output and monetary policy as a function of fund costs.

The strongest case for monetary policy effectiveness would exist, however, when the following conditions held:

(1) investment demand is highly interest elastic;

(2a) investment is heavily financed from external sources; <u>or</u>

(2b) the demand for investment funds is not positively synchronized with the availability of internal funds;

(3) businessmen (at least in the aggregate) do not look upon external funds as considerably more expensive than any and all internal funds, so that no discontinuity exists where external funds are joined to the internal fund segment of the supply schedule;

(4) the valuation businessmen place on internal funds is positively and sensitively related to market rates for external funds.

A diagrammatic representation of these circumstances is shown in Diagram III-2; because the demand curve is quite elastic and continuous in relevant ranges, a shift of the supply of funds function from, say, tight money at position (S_1) to easier money at (S_2) causes a substantial increase in investment.

A key assumption, of course, is the elasticity of the demand function. Without some positive elasticity of demand, no monetary or supply effects could be effective. As already noted, it is our belief that for short-run cyclical variations (which are the main concern of this paper) there is some positive interest elasticity of demand for investment, but not much. But this point is not well documented.

Furthermore, demand elasticity is a necessary but not a sufficient condition for effectiveness of monetary policy. Specifically, if internal sources of funds predominate, contrary to assumption (2a) above, an extremely heavy burden is thrust on the remaining supply assumptions (2b), (3) and (4). Furthermore, if condition (4) does not hold (that is, the valuation of internal funds is <u>not</u> sensitive to the general level of market interest rates) and if either (2b) (that shifts in the demand for investment are unrelated to shifts in internal funds) or (3) (that businessmen do not consider external funds to be more expensive than internal funds) also are violated, monetary policy may be ineffective <u>even</u> if the relevant part of the investment demand function is highly elastic. That is, with elimination of condition (2a), internal funds are the dominant source of financing (always assuming that internal funds are considered at least as cheap as external funds) and these by hypothesis cannot be

DIAGRAM III-2

Investment Supply and Demand Functions Favorable to Monetary Policy

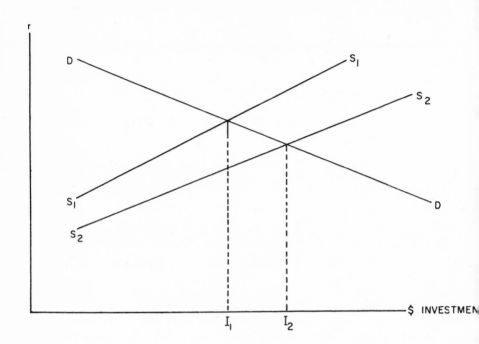

influenced by monetary policy because condition (4) has been reversed. Similarly, failure of (3) implies that discontinuity appears
in the supply of funds schedule at the point where internal funds are
exhausted and external funds are considered. If monetary policy
is assumed to have no effect on the valuation of internal funds because (4) is inoperative, monetary policy can affect investment
only if the demand function shifts sharply to the right beyond the
vertical portion or discontinuity in the supply of funds function. At
a minimum, a rather substantial barrier to the effectiveness of
monetary policy would be created by the presence of any sizable
supply discontinuity. Furthermore, if both (2b) relating to synchronization in supply and demand shifts, and (3) relating to supply
function continuity, do not hold, monetary control instruments almost necessarily will be ineffectual regardless of the elasticity
of demand for investment goods, even if the valuation of internal
funds is sensitive to external interest rates. Under these circumstances the demand function would intersect the supply function along
a vertical or discontinuous portion much of the time, except, for

practical purposes, when investment demand is strong during cyclical upswings. The cost of internal or external funds would be irrelevant during periods when investment demand is weak; only the amount of internal funds and secondarily their costs would matter. Furthermore, with some discontinuity in the supply of funds schedule, just approximate synchronization of the supply and demand functions is required to limit monetary policy severely.

As already noted, knowledge about the shape of the supply of funds function and its interactions with the investment demand function is not as complete as might be desired. However, considerably more is known about these relationships than about the interest elasticity of demand. The available information strongly suggests, moreover, that the three supply conditions, (2b), (3), and (4), required for the effectiveness of monetary policy are rarely met in full.

The non-synchronization condition, (2b), seems particularly dubious, at least in any strict form. Internal business funds can be described to a fair degree of approximation as the sum of retained earnings, depreciation expense, and excess cash assets. The most volatile portion of this sum is retained earnings and this tends to be closely tied to the level of activity which, in turn, is the main determinant of shifts in the investment demand schedule. Changes in depreciation allowances, which, except for tax policy changes usually behave like a linear trend, and the availability of liquid assets are not so directly or sensitively tied to shifts in activity and the investment demand function. Only occasionally, then, do sharp shifts take place in depreciation policies and business liquid assets. The latter, however, sometimes have been known to change quickly to highly abundant or deficient positions independently of output levels. In short, while something less than perfect synchronization of internal fund flows and investment demand shifts probably is the usual case, a generally strong tendency toward synchronization exists.

Arguments in favor of condition (4), that market rates of interest do influence valuations placed on internal funds, are more persuasive but not overwhelmingly convincing. Apparently, at least some businessmen making investment decisions to be financed internally do take into account prevailing monetary conditions. The spread of formal capital budgeting techniques throughout industry supports this contention. However, the quantitative importance of these considerations probably is not great in comparison with the explicitly dynamic and institutional variables emphasized in this paper. And theories about decision making under uncertainty are still in a highly exploratory stage. Therefore, heavy reliance on qualitative implications derived from unsure theory, which may exclude phenomena important to actual decisions, seems injudicious.

The discontinuity in the supply of funds schedule that would occur if (3) is reversed has been widely commented upon in recent discussions of business financial behavior. It is difficult to know, however, how important it might be in the aggregate since the valuations placed on external and internal funds and the position of the discontinuity might vary so widely among different firms that even if every firm had a discontinuity in its own schedule, the aggregate schedule could still appear essentially continuous. This unquestionably mitigates the policy relevance of any discontinuity argument, but it seems doubtful that it actually eliminates such relevance entirely. Specifically, it seems highly probable that most firms value retained earnings well below external funds; for example, internal funds may have an imputed cost of 5 to 8 percent per year, and external funds might be valued at between 10 and 20 percent. The ultimate result would seem to be a reasonably continuous aggregate supply of funds function but one which, while not totally inelastic, is relatively more inelastic in the range beyond 8 or 10 percent. A high degree of inelasticity in this range would be sufficient, of course, to reduce the potential effectiveness of monetary policy.

B. Summary of Conclusions

A primary conclusion of subsequent analysis is that the financial supply conditions entering into manufacturer's investment decisions are such that manufacturer's plant and equipment outlays would be little influenced by monetary policy, even if the demand for manufacturing investment were highly interest elastic. However, manufacturing investment is not totally beyond the control of monetary policy. In particular, financing problems in the manufacturing sector have quite different characteristics depending upon the cycle phase. In the early recovery from a recession, liquidity stocks are relatively ample and increase because of extremely rapid accumulation of internal funds. This accumulation occurs because dividend payouts are relatively low, profit margins are high, and net profits are sharply increasing. Inventory accumulation provides the principal financial problem in the early part of the business cycle recovery. However, internal financing, the quasi-automatic finance provided by trade payables and tax accruals, and the typically easy money policy of the Federal Reserve System at this cyclical phase makes funds so amply available that little real difficulty is normally encountered.

During the later part of the cyclical recovery, by contrast, paying for newly acquired fixed assets is the dominant financial concern of manufacturing firms. This is usually a much more severe problem than the inventory financing encountered in the early recovery. The extent of the problem is normally reflected both in a rising importance of external financing and in a decline of manufacturer's liquid balances in the late recovery phase. If monetary policy is ever to influence manufacturing investment, it is most likely to have an impact during this late phase of recovery.

Financial or supply stringency effects of monetary policy in the late recovery phase might be reinforced, moreover, by direct controls of the monetary authorities over consumer credit if these substantially diminished final demand for consumer durables. Such direct controls as, for instance, restricting the duration of automobile finance paper and increasing required down payments, could lead to excess capacity by choking off final demand and excess capacity in turn could lead to substantial curtailments in plant and equipment outlays. Such a policy, though, requires delicate timing of decisions so it is not obvious that it would lead to greater stability in investment outlays.

In a cyclical downswing, on the other hand, a condition of monetary ease is unlikely to reverse a decline in manufacturer's demand for investment goods. In such periods, the dominant cyclical motive to accumulate assets, capacity pressures, is weak. The major motives for investing in fixed assets at such times appear to be cost reduction and introduction of new products. External finance is not in strong demand since internal finance is usually adequate for these limited asset requirements and for dividend payments. Inventory disinvestment in such periods will also make the problem less burdensome.

In the long run, manufacturing investment outlays may become increasingly insulated from external finance, and hence from the effects of monetary policy. One important factor diminishing the relative importance of capital markets in recent years has been the rapid increase in depreciation caused both by increases in the real capital stock and, more importantly, the replacement of older assets carried at prewar prices by higher priced postwar assets. There has also been a downward trend in fixed capital requirements per unit of output from the 1920's until the 1940's, when the decline leveled out. Should this trend be resumed even at a decreasing rate, the demand for capital assets and financing would lessen. The critical determinants of the demand for funds in the long run are the rate of growth of output and the availability of new technology, either for cost reductions or new products. Only if the rate of growth of assets increases appreciably above present levels or if some important "technological breakthroughs" occur is the decreasing dependence upon external funds likely to be reversed. Moreover, if manufacturers seek to maintain a limited dependence on external capital markets, even a greater rate of growth might not cause greater reliance on external funds. This would be especially true if tax policy were changed so as to give businessmen greater control over the selection of their depreciation rates.

These negative conclusions about the potential influence of
monetary policy on manufacturing investment outlays also apply
to public utility investment. However, the reasons are considerably
different than for manufacturing. Public utilities rely more heavily
on capital markets than the manufacturing sector but because of a
particular institutional structure, utilities are unlikely to be much
affected by monetary policy actions.

A widely accepted doctrine by which public utility regulatory
commissions set customer tariffs enables increased capital costs
caused by higher interest rates to be passed on in the form of tariff
increases. Furthermore, the price elasticity of demand for public
utility services in the short run is probably low, and since rates
may be below the equilibrium monopoly utility price because of
regulation, increased capital costs probably could be shifted forward
in the form of higher rates, with only slight effects on the quantity
demanded. Therefore, variations in interest rates are unlikely to
influence significantly the investment policies of public utilities in
the short run.

In addition, it is not clear that changing the cyclical pattern of
public utility investment should be a major objective of monetary
policy because the investment policies of electrical utilities are
already countercyclical to at least a degree. Electric utilities usually continue to invest at high rates after the peak in the business
cycle and investment in manufacturing has sharply declined. Also,
public utilities have a tendency to reduce investment when manufacturing investment is beginning to recover after a slump. Only
during the late upswing do both public utility and manufacturing investment demands coincide and, at this phase, electrical utility
investment clearly is not countercyclical.

The same reasons which suggest that public utilities will be
largely immune to shorter-run interest rate variations hold in the
long run, too. An additional consideration arises, however, because
the long-run price elasticity of demand is almost certainly greater
than the short-run elasticity. A high long-run income elasticity of
demand also appears likely, though, and this should provide a
counter-balancing support for price increases and increased revenues should capital costs rise.

The analysis which follows and on which these conclusions are
based is highly aggregative, regrettably so since the high level of
aggregation precludes investigation of several interesting hypotheses about monetary policy and investment. Specifically, the supply
factors considered are: business dividend policies, profit margins,
and depreciation (which in combination establish the rate of gross
retained earnings), and trade accruals and the stock of quick assets.
On the demand side, inventories and plant and equipment have been
the main objects of investigation.

The analysis has been confined, moreover, to manufacturing, public utilities (including electricity and gas), and communications (further restricted to American Telephone and Telegraph Company). These sectors account for a major share of private business investment in our economy although the excluded sectors, transportation, mining, wholesale and retail trade, obviously are important. Furthermore, these excluded industries may well be among those most sensitive to monetary policy.

While some reference is made to long-term trends, most of the historical data used in this study are for the postwar period and particularly the two business cycles since the Korean War. These are extremely brief periods in our recent economic history, but nevertheless ones which often reveal enough regularities so that cautious generalizations appear warranted.

II. DATA[1]

A. Sources

Data were collected on two major categories of enterprise, manufacturing and public utilities (specifically, electrical utilities, gas utilities and American Telephone and Telegraph Company). The information is quarterly for the manufacturing sector and annual for the public utilities. The lack of volatility in investment and fund flows in public utilities over the period studied, coupled with the paucity of data in quarterly form for this industry, made the use of annual information both mandatory and, hopefully, also not seriously harmful.

The basic quarterly information for manufacturing was mainly (though not exclusively) derived from the Securities and Exchange Commission-Federal Trade Commission Quarterly Financial Reports for U.S. Manufacturing Corporations. Basic reliance was placed on these SEC-FTC manufacturing data because of one overriding advantage—internal consistency. The data from the SEC-FTC reports, beginning in 1947, had to be rectified for sample changes in 1952 and again in 1956. For the three years 1947, 1952, and 1956 in which the samples were originated or were revised, the sample information was benchmarked on the best available census information. Between these benchmark dates, however, the relation-

---

[1]Important Note:
Moving averages and totals are recorded in tables at the latest included quarter, but interpretation in the text is based upon centered data. The charts have been drawn with centered data.

ship between sample and universe drifted. In order to correct for the drift, the three sample sub-periods were spliced into continuous series.[2]

Other sources which report more limited though similar information to the SEC-FTC Quarterly Financial Reports were used in particular instances where these alternatives provided direct information on data that could be only approximated from the SEC-FTC data by a sources and uses of funds analysis. A prime example of such an alternative series is the new plant and equipment expenditure reports of the Department of Commerce. For purposes of comparison, appendix tables present fund flows estimated by sources and uses of funds techniques and, where available, the most preferred alternative sources of information.

There are several other deficiencies in the SEC-FTC data beyond those already noted. Details and necessary qualifications on the SEC-FTC sample and data are reported in the various issues of the SEC-FTC Quarterly Financial Report, and will not be reproduced fully here. Certain qualifications should be emphasized, however, given the purposes of this particular study. First, important valuation changes occur from quarter to quarter which affect the net profit figures, particularly if these are estimated directly from balance sheet changes. To overcome this potentially serious pitfall, the net retained profit figure was obtained from the income statement itself and not by first differencing the earned surplus account. Similarly, the data for new security issues were taken simply as the first differences in the "capital stock, capital surplus, and minority interest" balance sheet account instead of from the Securities and Exchange Commission new securities flotation reports. Thus if a convertible debenture is converted into common stock, this will appear as a decrease in debt flow and an increase in equity flow so that when distinctions are drawn between these categories, spurious flows sometimes will be recorded. However, for numerous purposes a useful category is simply long-term external finance taken to be long-term debt issues (obtained from the first difference in long-term debt account) plus the first

---

[2]This was done by Locke Anderson using an IBM 704 program. In the first quarter of overlap between the new and old samples, the absolute difference between the two samples for that quarter was calculated. This difference was then distributed proportionally over the time intervals between benchmarks, on the assumption that the new sample benchmark was absolutely correct and the old sample had drifted. This assumption is not likely to hold perfectly since sampling errors are involved in both benchmarks, although the preponderant error is almost certain to orginate from drifting of the old sample.

difference in the capital account and the debt conversion process will not cause any distortion for this total.

All short-term liabilities (such as trade accounts and notes payable, federal income tax accrued, short-term loans from banks, etc.) were obtained by straightforward first differencing. Similarly, the first differences in short-term assets were used to obtain estimates of asset change flows.

Estimates of outlays on plant and equipment were obtained both directly from Department of Commerce-SEC survey data and indirectly by taking the change in net fixed assets and adding to this the current charge to depreciation from the income statement. When major asset revaluations occur (for example, through capital gains and losses which are charged to income but which do not involve a cash flow), the fund flow will be distorted. However, a comparison of fund flow estimates with Department of Commerce-SEC estimates (shown in the appendix tables) indicate that the discrepancies are not too gross for present purposes, and the Department of Commerce estimates actually were used in this study.

B. Transformations

At first it seemed desirable to use strictly quarterly information. This approach was quickly abandoned when it became apparent that two major types of disturbances, so large as to preclude affective analysis, could be eliminated if the quarterly data were seasonally adjusted. First, there were numerous series with pronounced seasonal variations. Plant and equipment outlays and dividend payments have a fourth quarter peak and tax liabilities have an especially large decrease in the second quarter. Second, a number of series were subject to an annoyingly large amount of erratic or random variation.

To overcome both difficulties in the simplest and quickest possible manner, four period moving averages were used to smooth the data. Four quarter moving totals were used for flow data, such as investment and sales, and four quarter averages or totals were calculated for all balance sheet items. Hence, flows are on an annual rate basis. While these smoothing devices facilitate interpretation, through reduction of short-term disturbances, interpretation has been complicated in other respects. Quarterly changes in a series composed of four period moving averages are generated by dropping one quarter and adding another four quarters later, while retaining three quarters in common, so that all the difference in the two quarterly observations is attributable to year to year differences between the current quarter and its seasonal equivalent the year before. This is obviously different from observing the full quarter to quarter change, seasonal effects and all, using the original series. In short, smoothing may sometimes eliminate more than unwanted seasonal and random influences, so that interpretation of the smoothed data must be correspondingly qualified.

III. THE CYCLICAL DETERMINANTS OF INTERNAL FINANCING IN MANUFACTURING

A. Introduction

Manufacturing sector financing is characterized by heavy reliance on internal funds (in contrast with public utilities which use capital markets to a much greater relative extent). Specifically, about three-quarters of total funds used in the manufacturing sector during the postwar period originated from internal sources. In a rough way this proportion also characterizes the historical records of earlier periods. However, manufacturers' dependence on external funds has displayed marked cyclical variability: external funds are used mainly in the later stages of the cyclical upswing and relatively little in the early stages of an upswing and downswing. This cyclical pattern suggests, in terms of the earlier supply and demand analysis, either that there is fair synchronization between the flow of internally generated funds and investment demand over most of the cycle or that external funds appear so much more expensive to manufacturers than internal funds that external funds are seldom used, the only exception being the late recovery phase when investment demand is often particularly strong. In reality, of course, both the synchronization and supply inelasticity effects may exist.

A survey of some of the more relevant evidence for the postwar period follows, starting in Section B with a presentation of evidence on liquid asset stocks. In Section C certain relative liquidity measures like the current ratio, the quick ratio, and the quick assets to sales turnover ratio are reported. In Section D consideration is given to profit margins, dividends, and the determinants of net retained earnings. Finally, all internal finance, including depreciation expense, is reviewed in Section E.

B. The Pattern of Liquidity Stock Holdings in the Postwar Period

Large stocks of liquidity, defined as cash plus government obligations, were built up during World War II when capital assets were heavily rationed and inventories were held below normal working levels because of war-induced scarcities. The excess liquid assets accumulated during the war were largely dissipated by the beginning of 1947.[1] Then, as shown in Chart III-1, the Korean War, which for a surprisingly long period after its termination

---

[1] (See footnote on following page)

shaped the postwar financial scene, created a drastic alteration in the liquidity position of the manufacturing sector. During the Korean emergency period, liquidity stocks leaped by almost 50 percent from previous levels. The effects of this sharply raised initial condition lasted well into the next business cycle. The mid-1951 peak in the liquidity stock was slightly exceeded at the end of 1953, when a brief spurt occurred in the level of activity, and then fell slightly during the 1954 recession. Liquid assets then rapidly accumulated to reach peak levels in the third quarter of 1955. From this level manufacturing liquid assets became steadily depleted throughout the remainder of the 1954-58 (trough to trough) cycle, reaching their lowest value in the first quarter of 1958, coincident with the cyclical trough. Liquid assets then began to increase, although the peak value recorded had not exceeded the 1955 maximum by the end of the first quarter in 1960.

C. Relative Liquidity Stock Holdings

The same cyclical pattern, even in greater contrast, is discernible in the behavior of relative liquidity measures. Three of the more pertinent of these — the current ratio (current assets divided by current liabilities), the quick ratio (cash plus Government bonds divided by current liabilities) and the money asset turnover ratio (the ratio of cash plus Governments to sales) — are graphed in Chart III-2. In these normalized data, the cyclical tendency to build up liquidity stocks in the very early stages of recovery and, to a lesser extent, near the trough of the recession is quite evident. Thus, the last quarter of 1949 and the first two of 1950, the last of 1954, and the first half of 1958 are all periods of recession coupled with initial recovery from a cyclical trough and were characterized by steep increases in relative business liquidity.

---

[1] (Footnote to previous page)
Year-end liquid balances (cash plus government obligations) were:

Manufacturing — Total Quick Assets
($ billions)

1944	23.2
1945	22.3
1946	18.2
1947	19.0
1948	19.3

Source: Corporate Tax Returns, Bureau of Internal Revenue. All returns with Balance Sheets.

In the text, the terms "quick assets," "liquid assets," and "liquidity" will be used interchangeably to denote cash plus government obligations.

CHART III-1

Manufacturing Cash Plus Government Securities (Quick Assets)
Four Quarter Moving Averages (million $)

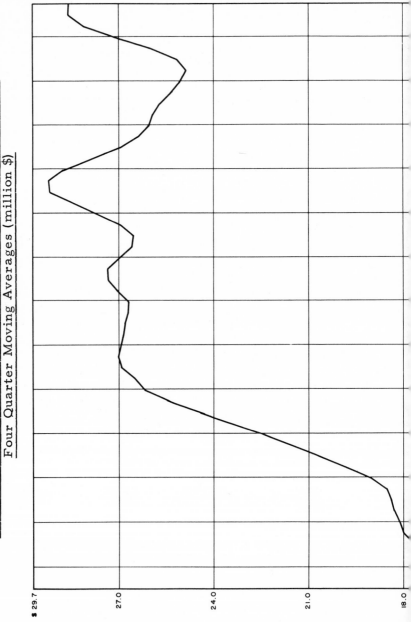

Manufacturing Quick Ratio, Current Ratio and Quick Assets to Sales Ratio

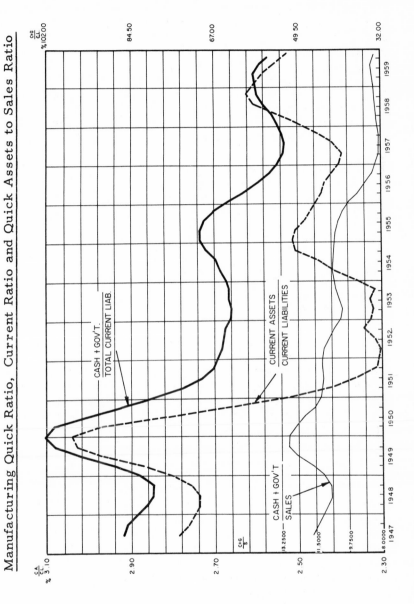

For example, the manufacturing current ratio reached a maxi-mum early in 1950 and then fell drastically to a low of 2.3 in 1952, although still well above the apparently magic number of 2.0. Simi-larly, the current ratio reached another local maximum early in the upswing beginning late in 1954 and then steadily declined until the first quarter of 1957. In the ensuing recession the current ratio definitely improved, reaching a peak in the middle of 1958 shortly after the recovery had begun, whereupon it began to decline. The quick ratio has a fairly similar cyclical pattern but tends to lag slightly behind the current ratio, beginning its recovery later (usually after the trough) and reaching a maximum about two quar-ters later in the revival period.

It is highly interesting, moreover, that the trends of the current and quick ratio series are radically different. There has been a declining trend in the quick ratio since 1953 in contrast to a distinct upward trend in the current ratio from 1952-53. By construction, accounts receivable and inventories, the more illiquid components of current assets included in the current ratio but excluded from the quick ratio, have become relatively more important over the past decade. However, this pattern is no longer evident, the most recent (1958-60) recovery displaying a sharp reversal.

The early 1950 deterioration in the quick ratio is partially attributable to a sharp accumulation of net trade credit. This is apparent from Chart III-3 graphing a single time series for accounts receivable minus accounts payable. Throughout the 1954-57 boom, receivables were accumulated at a more rapid rate than during the remainder of the postwar era. Obviously, the excess of trade credit granted over trade credit received must be financed by a net fund inflow. Since supporting finance is unlikely to arise entirely from other accruals, this particular form of asset accumulation almost certainly required a net inflow of cash funds.[2]

The ratio of cash plus Governments to sales is perhaps an even more pertinent single measure of liquidity than any balance sheet ratio. This relation, like the quick ratio, has been steadily declin-ing — indeed, more than either of the other two ratios.

In summary, two of the three relative measures of liquidity re-ported here, the quick ratio and the quick asset to sales turnover ratio, have trended downward for the past decade, while all three ratios showed noticeable increases during the early upswing of the business cycle and declines during the later part of the upswing

---

[2] By definition, long-term finance would not affect the denominator of this ratio.

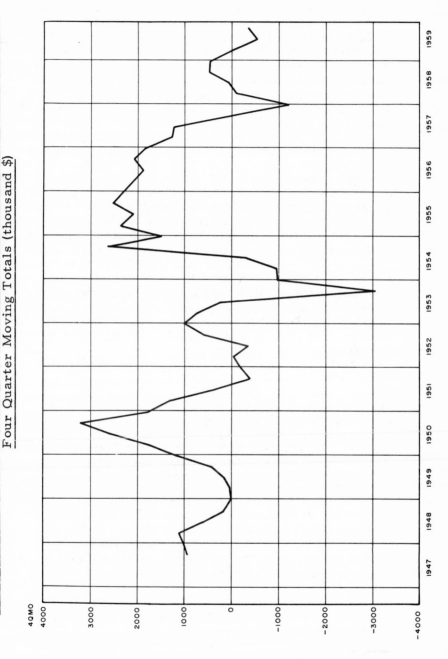

Manufacturing Changes in Accounts Receivable minus Changes in Accounts Payable
Four Quarter Moving Totals (thousand $)

These observations are, however, based on an impressionistic reading of the charts and highly aggregative data. As something of a check, linear least squares regressions have also been fitted to the same SEC-FTC data for individual (2 digit SIC) manufacturing industries to determine "normal" or average relationships between business liquidity and different classes of assets and levels of operation during the years 1947 to 1958.[3] Discrepancies of actual levels from these normal or average relationships for any one period then provide a very rough index of financial stringency, availability, or need in that period.

Specifically, money and marketable securities were estimated as a linear function of sales, in the level of federal tax accruals, short-term bank debt, and the change in sales. Generally speaking, the first two explanatory variables, sales and the level of federal tax accruals, by themselves accounted for about 90 percent of the variation in quick assets during the 1947 to 1958 period. Short-term bank debt proved to have a weak relationship with quick assets; furthermore, it was consistently negative suggesting that short-term bank borrowing is caused by scarcity of cash rather than being a reason for holding cash, despite the widespread practice of compensating balances being tied to bank loans. The change in sales variable had a generally negligible and negative influence. All this suggests that a more "reasonable" model might have included only sales and federal tax accruals as explanatory variables but the influence of the other two variables was so slight that no major changes in the conclusions would have been dictated by such a revision.

Percentage discrepancies between the values predicted by the equation and actual values of quick assets should indicate periods when financial patterns deviated sharply from the norm. The percentage discrepancies listed in Table III-1 are considered to be of particular interest because they correspond to five quarters either very early or very late in cyclical recovery phases.

These data lend useful detail and generally confirm the earlier discussion. Particularly noteworthy is the way in which the second quarters of 1950 and 1957 seem to have been contrasting extremes in business liquidity. At mid-1950 quick assets exceeded "normal levels" in most industries. The second quarter of 1952, on the other hand, coming late in the Korean boom contrasts sharply with the second quarter of 1957, also a late boom period. Clearly, business liquidity was relatively much greater at the end of the earlier upswing, again indicating the importance of the liquidity legacy left by the Korean War.

---

[3]The remainder of this section is based on some current research of John R. Meyer.

TABLE III-1

Estimated Percentage Excess (+) or Deficiency (-) of Cash and Marketable Securities For Selected Quarters by Industry*

Industry	Early Recovery Cycle Stage			Late Recovery Cycle Stage	
	2nd Quarter 1950	3rd Quarter 1955	4th Quarter 1958	2nd Quarter 1952	2nd Quarter 1957
Iron & Steel	6.6%	1.8%	11.6%	-11.5%	-17.6%
Non-Ferrous Metal	3.7	1.9	-14.4	-14.6	-23.4
Elec. Machinery	-7.8	5.8	.2	9.5	-12.4
Other Machinery	1.6	6.5	- 6.3	6.2	- 6.4
Motor Vehicles	9.0	22.5	-25.1	-11.1	-23.2
Other Transportation	-2.2	2.2	15.6	2.2	- 1.6
Stone, Clay and Glass	6.8	-1.0	.7	6.0	- 2.3
Food	4.3	2.2	- 1.1	6.5	- 3.9
Textiles	-4.2	-2.7	11.9	3.8	1.1
Paper	4.7	2.1	- .5	8.9	- 9.1
Chemicals	1.1	5.0	- 9.4	8.6	- 8.3
Rubber	14.5	-5.7	-16.1	11.2	-14.9
Petroleum & Coal	1.8	-5.6	14.0	- .1	- 1.1

*These percentages were computed by using the formula $\frac{M-\hat{M}}{M}$ where M = actual money and marketable securities, $\hat{M}$ = an estimate of M obtained from the linear least squares function M = f(S, G, B, ΔS) where S = sales, G = federal income tax liabilities, B = short term bank borrowing, and ΔS = change in sales.

From the policy standpoint, tight money obviously had less
opportunity to restrict business plans in the 1950-55 period than
it did later. Indeed, tight money probably did exert a dampening
influence in 1957 since the "large cushions" of corporate liquidity
had by then been heavily eroded. A pertinent question for future
policy is whether "deflated" or "inflated" liquidity cushions will be
in existence at some future time when restraint is deemed desirable. This, in turn, raises such questions as what determines the
liquidity stock and, in particular, what creates the cyclical pattern
of fluctuations in liquidity. The level of liquidity is the net resultant
of course, of a great many activities: e.g., accumulation and decumulation of nonliquid assets, dividend policy, profit rates, etc
An analysis of some of these activities follows.

D. Profit Margins and Dividends

Time series for both the net profit margin, defined as net profits
(after both tax and depreciation) divided by sales, and the dividend
payout, defined as cash dividends divided by net profits, are plotted
in Chart III-4. While the excess profits tax during the Korean War
partly obscures a quite regular cyclical relationship between
operating profit divided by sales and the level of sales, certain
important cyclical characteristics in the net margin can be readily
discerned. First, the margin increases sharply during recovery
from a cyclical trough. This "augmented margin" is then whittled
away steadily for the remainder of the business cycle upswing,
dropping abruptly in a cyclical trough and rebounding strongly in
the early part of the next recovery.[4] In short, profit margins are
squeezed in the later part of cyclical upswings and this is apparently one casual factor accelerating the decline in liquid balance
during the upswing.

In the same vein, the dividend payout has had a strong negative
correlation with the net profit margin.[5] During the business cycl

---

[4]Detailed analysis of this relationship will be found in Edwin Kuh
"Profits, Profit Markups and Productivity: An Examination of
Corporate Behavior Since 1947," Study Paper No. 15, materials
prepared in connection with the Study of Employment, Growth
and Price Levels for consideration by the Joint Economic Commit
tee, Congress of the United States, January 25, 1960.

[5]It is incorrect to argue that this is necessarily a spurious cor
relation since net profits is the numerator of one series and the
denominator of the other. Even though dividends form an extremely
smooth, usually steadily increasing time series, the same is no
true of sales which displays a great deal of volatility, certainly
much more than dividends although considerably less than profits

CHART III-4

Manufacturing Net Profit Margin and Dividend Payout

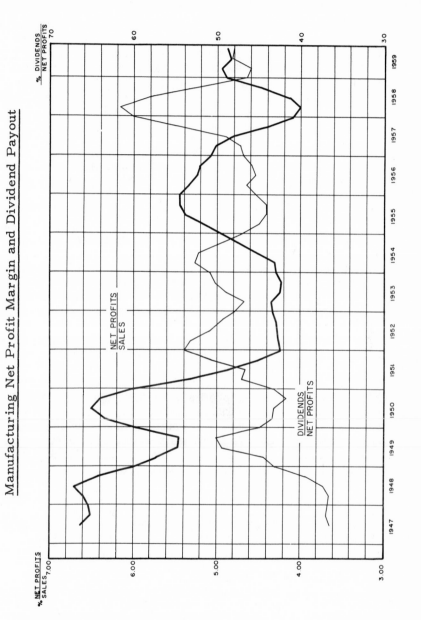

trough, the dividend payout is at a maximum, a fact explained by
the relatively immobility of dividends and the sharp decline in
profits. The percentage payout then falls quickly until about the
middle of the cyclical upturn, then rises slowly and finally increases
rapidly as profits fall during the next downturn. Put somewhat
differently, profits (in absolute terms) in postwar business cycles
have increased rapidly for four to six quarters from the trough and
then remained approximately constant. Simultaneously, dividends
increase during upswings, slowly at times, more rapidly at others,
and flatten out or sometimes decline slightly during downturns.
Irrespective of the cause, net retentions are squeezed as the boom
progresses. By the same token, funds available for additions to
liquidity or other assets are potentially much greater during the
earliest part of the cyclical recovery when the dividend payout falls
to its lowest levels.

E. Internal Finance

   Internal finance (net retained earnings plus the current charge
to depreciation) has generally fluctuated with the level of business
activity about a steadily rising trend. However, the composition
of internal finance has undergone profound change over the postwar
period as Chart III-5 reveals. Depreciation charges have risen
at a steady, even impressive, rate while net retained earnings have
fluctuated at the same level, in rough correspondence with fluctuations in net profits (because of the extremely slow adjustments
in dividend payments). Maximum retained earnings reached in the
1956-57 period only slightly exceeded the Korean War boom peak
which in turn were modestly above the retained profit peak in
1948-49. Net retained profits exceeded depreciation for only a
brief period during the 1954-57 recovery, whereas prior to 1952
even the most depressed net retained profit level exceeded the
depreciation charge. The changing relative importance of each
internal source is readily observable in Chart III-6, showing the
ratio of depreciation expense to internal funds.

   Clearly, as postwar assets replaced and added to prewar assets,
depreciation allowances have reflected the changed price level
composition of the assets. The importance of depreciation has been
further enhanced not only by temporary Korean wartime grants
of accelerated depreciation but by the permanently more liberal
depreciation rates permitted by the 1954 Revenue Code.

   In the early prewar period internal finance began to decline
at the end of 1948, coincident with the cyclical downturn, only to
rebound sharply during the 1950-51 boom. Net retained earnings
then fell abruptly, partly because of the excess profits tax and partly
because of the short-lived decline in the level of output. This was
followed by another increase in retained earnings in 1953. Further-

Manufacturing Total Internal Finance, Net Retained Earnings and Depreciation
Four Quarter Moving Totals (million $)

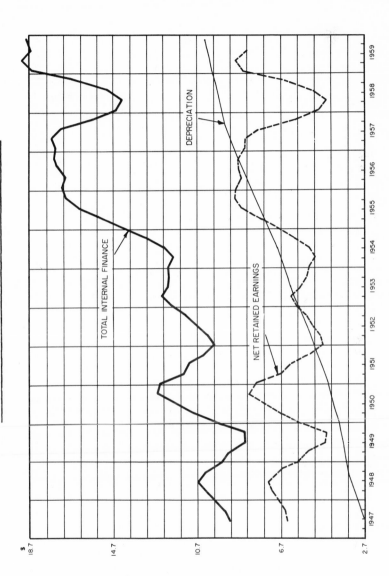

CHART III-6

Manufacturing Ratio of Depreciation to Internal Finance

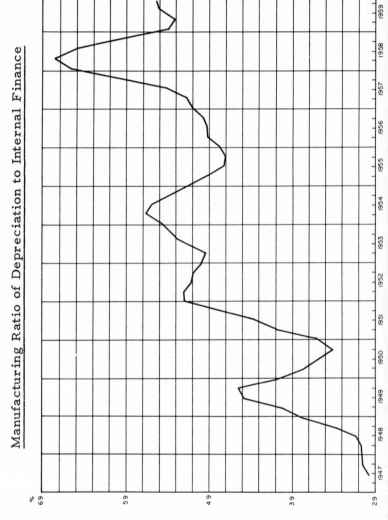

more, all swings in retained earnings up to mid-1953 were fully reflected in corresponding fluctuations in total internal finance.

Then an abrupt change took place in internal manufacturing corporation financing. In particular, total internal finance hardly decreased in the recession of 1953-54, despite the comparatively sharp drop in net retained earnings as very rapid increases in depreciation almost offset the decline in net retained earnings during this mild recession.

While net retained earnings and total internal funds increased steeply after the 1954 trough, total internal finance remained on a plateau with a mild upward gradient from 1956 to mid-1957. Even though net retained earnings fell. gross retentions were approximately stable, again because of offsetting depreciation expense increases. During the 1957-58 slump, however, the abrupt fall in net retained earnings was indeed reflected in total internal financial availability because depreciation charge increases were far from adequate to counterbalance the net retained earnings slump. In this regard, the 1957-58 recession resembles that of 1948-49 more than the 1953-54 slump.

Some implications for monetary policy of this particular behavior can be stated. First, asset financing from internal sources has steadily increased despite the stationary character of net retained earnings, mainly because assets accumulated postwar have become a larger fraction of total assets, and therefore, depreciation charges reflect postwar costs more adequately. Also, the more liberal depreciation provisions of the 1954 Revenue Code have contributed in recent years to the growth in depreciation charges. Of course, the real capital stock increased as well. Should these trends continue, it may tend to make monetary policy a less potent tool of restraint in the future, although the price level "changeover" and initial liberalization effects on depreciation should diminish.

Also, monetary and fiscal policy were working at cross purposes throughout much of the 1955-57 period. Basically, more liberal tax allowances for depreciation incorporated in the 1954 tax law tended to offset monetary policy effects on business liquidity. With the possible exception of early 1953, a really noticeable bind in business liquidity didn't begin to develop until about mid-1956. To the extent that the 1954 tax reform was a once-and-for-all change in the tax laws, monetary policy was operating during this period under a handicap that might be avoided in the future. Of course, the presence, already noted, of relatively large business cash balances left from Korean War experiences only heightened the handicap. On balance, the rapid trend increases in depreciation allowances may create as many difficulties for monetary policy in the near future as the special circumstances of high liquidity and tax law revisions did in the recent past.

IV. THE DETERMINANTS OF MANUFACTURING INVESTMENT
AND THE DEMAND FOR EXTERNAL FUNDS

A. Introduction

In the preceding section an analysis was presented of some
highly aggregative data on the internal funds component of the
supply schedule entering into manufacturer's investment decisions.
These findings suggest that manufacturer's need for external financing is likely to be greatest in periods late in the recovery phase
of the cycle. This would be particularly true if there is a high degree of synchronization in the shift of the supply and demand schedules for manufacturing investment, that is, if investment demands
do the plausible and also rise late in the cyclical upturn. The findings of the last section also suggest the existence of a relatively
inelastic section of the supply curve beyond the point at which
internal funds are exhausted.

As noted in Section I, such supply characteristics make it
probable that even with a highly interest elastic investment demand
function monetary policy will have only a limited influence on manufacturing investment. In a certain sense, therefore, these characteristics of the supply function justify (or at least, rationalize)
emphasizing the influence of activity levels on investment demand
and minimizing the study of the interest or cost elasticity of investment demand. Even with such justifications, empirical investment studies have tended in this direction because of the relatively
greater availability of good data on business activity and the avoidance of numerous other difficulties associated with attempts to
estimate the interest elasticity of investment demand. Nevertheless,
in the investment demand analyses that follow, an attempt has been
made to evaluate the interest elasticity of demand for manufacturing
investment, as well as the effects of levels of activity.

First, however, a brief treatment is presented in Section B on
the accumulation of inventories and their financing in terms of a
simple acceleration model. It is found that inventories typically
accumulate very rapidly early in recovery and then in smaller
magnitudes later in the cyclical recovery, while during a downswing, there is heavy inventory decumulation. This is, of course,
an almost classic acceleration model pattern. It seems, moreover,
that the financing of inventories in the phase of most rapid accumulation, even though assisted by bank lending, could proceed at a
rapid rate without much borrowing because of very large concurrent
generation of internal funds.

Section C presents an additional exposition of the fixed asset
investment demand theory which underlies much of the analysis
and the policy implications of this study. Also, the difference

between the costs of internal and external funds is examined and the nature and extent of synchronization between internal fund flows and the demand for assets is further discussed. Section D reviews in greater detail the postwar relation between capital outlays, liquid assets, and finance including a summary of results obtained from a formal statistical investigation of manufacturing investment for the period from 1950 to 1958. It is shown that liquid assets begin to decline about the middle of the cyclical recovery, at a time when external finance is at its greatest and that there is at least some limited evidence of an interest elasticity of demand for manufacturing investment. The relationship between external financing and capital outlays is also such that even when external financing is being acquired in great quantities, the stock of liquid assets will be considerably reduced in a large investment boom at the time of peak capital outlays. Accordingly, the availability of external finance may be of major importance at this late stage of the cycle.

In Section E, an effort is made to evaluate some effects of external finance reductions on manufacturing investment and liquidity. Hypothetical models are established under various assumptions about reductions in external finance imposed by the monetary authorities. It is seen that even when external finance is reduced by very large amounts, the liquidity stock would not appear to suffer greatly, nor would it seem necessary to greatly curtail the rate of investment.

B. Short-Term Assets and Short-Term Finance

In the first four or five quarters out of the trough, postwar as well as numerous prewar cycles have been characterized by extremely rapid inventory accumulation and a simple acceleration theory of inventory investment has found clear support.[1] Comparison of Chart III-7, showing the percent rate of change in the index of industrial production with Chart III-8 showing the change in inventories, provides some relevant evidence. A sharp increase in the rate of change in production usually leads to a sharp increase in inventories one to three quarters later, while corresponding relations hold for output declines.

---

[1]To be more precise, total finance is defined to be the change in accruals, the change in long-term borrowing and short-term borrowing as well as the change in the paid-in-capital account, plus the charge to depreciation and the net retained earnings figure, both of the latter figures obtained from the income statement. Because of very substantial valuation changes, it was inadvisable to take the simple change in the retained earnings figure as a valid description of internal funds available from that source.

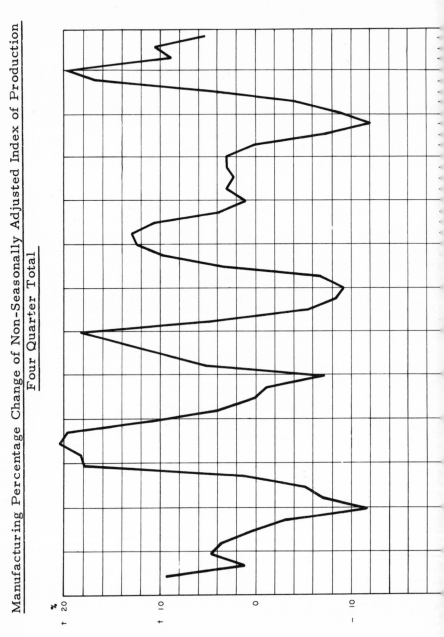

CHART III-7

Manufacturing Percentage Change of Non-Seasonally Adjusted Index of Production
Four Quarter Total

CHART III-8

Manufacturing Changes in Inventories, Short-Term Borrowing, Changes in Accounts Payable Plus Short-Term Borrowing Four Quarter Moving Totals (thousand $)

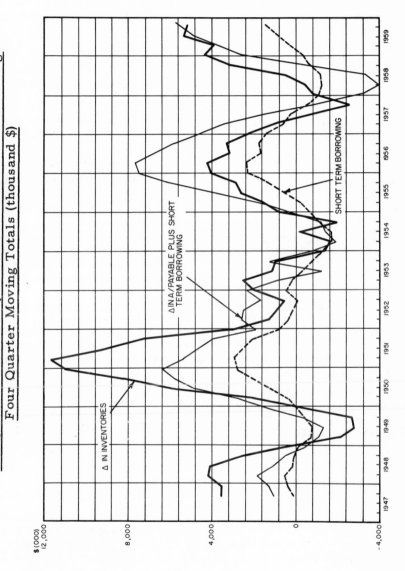

Conventional short-term financial sources, accounts payable and bank borrowing, often by themselves have been insufficient to finance the inventory increment during periods of most rapid inventory accumulation. Since rapid inventory accumulation typically coincides with periods of low dividend payouts and heavy internal fund flows (see Section IV-D and IV-E) inventory investment can be readily financed without extensive long-term external financing. Indeed, there is a very high correlation between total internal finance and inventory accumulation during early upswings, although inventory accumulation tapers off before internal finance declines in the later phases of a recovery.

From the standpoint of monetary policy, it appears that during the early phase of a business cycle recovery, the monetary authorities ordinarily are willing to provide finance in order to encourage the incipient recovery, and financial institutions too are eager to increase high yield business loans. Even if they were not, manufacturing firms are ordinarily in a comfortable position to finance the greatest part of their requirements from internal sources because a rapid inflow of internal funds and a very sharp increase in accounts payable normally coincides with inventory accumulation. A tight monetary policy at this juncture of events not only would normally be considered undesirable but if put into operation would presumably have small effect.

However, should monetary restraint take effect with, say, an average twelve-month delay, it might be desirable to reduce business liquidity through the imposition of monetary restriction early in the cyclical recovery so that plant and equipment outlays later in the cycle would be curbed. Obviously the timing of the response requires detailed investigation before policy inferences can be drawn. Moreover, if a stringent monetary policy is called for very early in a cyclical recovery, it will have to be put into operation by monetary authorities who have extremely high confidence in their own predictive capabilities.

C. Capital Outlays - The Postwar Experience

Outlays on plant and equipment by the manufacturing sector during the period since 1947 have typically reached a peak toward the upper turning point of the business cycle. It is instructive to compare Chart III-9, showing percent capacity utilization based upon the index of industrial production, with Chart III-10 depicting plant and equipment expenditures. The percent capacity utilization measure is the ratio of the FRB index of industrial production (shifted to a 1947 base) divided by the Department of Commerce estimates of the real net capital stock in manufacturing, also indexed on a 1947 base.[2]

The rapid increase of capacity utilization occurring early in the cycle leads to capacity pressures generating demand for new capital assets which appear on the average about six months to a year later. At the same time that quick recovery in output from the cyclical trough leads to capacity pressures, increased activity early in the cyclical upswing also generates supplies of internal finance with which capital outlays may be financed relatively readily.

A basic and unresolved question concerns the nature and extent of any inelasticity in the cost of capital schedule occurring where external funds begin to be used. If the inelasticity of the external funds segment of the supply curve is quite significant, fairly large shifts in the demand schedule for investment can occur with only small variations in the rate of investment and the quantity demanded of investment will be approximately equal to the supply of internal funds. As a matter of fact, rough equality between gross investment and gross retained earnings actually holds for the trough rate of investment in numerous postwar cycles. Similarly, the much sharper decline that occurred in plant and equipment outlays in 1958 compared to the decline in the late 1951 and early 1952, as well as the 1954 slump, might be imputed at least partly to the fact that internal funds fell more sharply in 1958 than in the earlier recessions. The recession of 1954 had comparatively small impact on total internal finance because of continued swift increases in depreciation charges. It is therefore significant that though investment fell off quite sharply in 1954, it recovered quite quickly. By contrast total internal finance declined abruptly in 1957 and 1958, following the pattern of and reinforcing the decline in capacity utilization. This strongly suggests that while capacity utilization rates may dominate investment decisions in the upswing of the cycle, their role might be less important on the downswing. On the view that the supply of external funds is considered inelastic by manufacturers, the availability of internal finance would be an important determinant of investment rates during the slide to the recession trough. Accordingly, the recent trend toward increased depreciation allowances might be construed as a hopeful sign for the future. However, the 1957-58 experience indicates that this trend is not an absolute guarantee against sharp downward swings in manufacturing investment outlays. At best, the increased depreciation allowances (see Chart III-8) would seem to have placed a potentially higher floor or minimum under manufacturing investment.

---

[2]This fact will be reflected in quick ratio and current ratio computations.

CHART III-9

Manufacturing Capacity Utilization

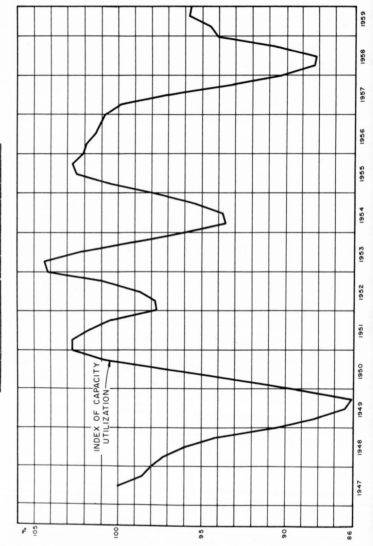

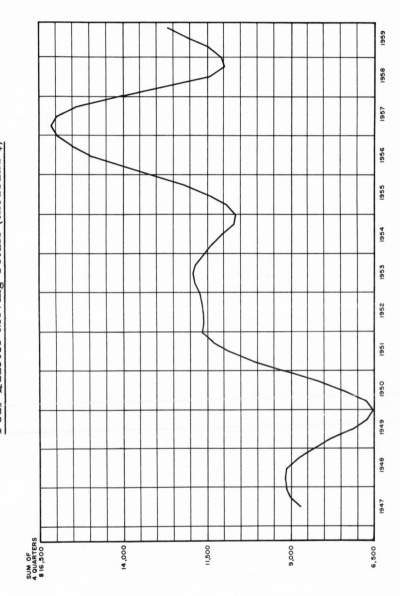

CHART III-10

Manufacturing New Plant and Equipment Expenditures
Four Quarter Moving Totals (thousand $)

A supply-demand synchronization also can lead to rough equality between investment outlays and internal finance at the cyclical trough. As noted earlier, synchronization found together with an inelastic supply function for external funds would provide a powerful insulation between monetary policy and manufacturing investment decisions. Obviously, it makes a considerable difference for the design of fiscal policy if the synchronization is more responsible than external fund supply inelasticity for the approximate equality of investment and internal financing in recession.

A comparison of plant and equipment outlays (Chart III-10) with quick assets (Chart III-1) shows that the liquidity stock has approximately a three to six quarter lead over plant and equipment investment. During a slump, liquid assets do not decline appreciably and sometimes even begin to accumulate. Early in the cyclical recovery liquid balances continue to accumulate. They then diminish when plant and equipment outlays are rising later in the recovery. Hence, liquid balances often actually increase during much of the rapid inventory accumulation phase in the early upswing, and decrease only later when inventory accumulation tapers off. This sequence can be readily discerned in the 1954-57 recovery and is hazily observable in the 1950-53 recovery, though the tremendous liquidity generated by the Korean War boom obscures the relationship somewhat. In part, of course, the two different liquidity patterns of 1949-53 and 1954-57 also reflect a difference between "easy money" and "hard money" policies. Bank lending was generally supported by the Federal Reserve System in 1950-52 while the 1954-57 period (except for a short, early interlude) was a period of relative monetary restraint.

These comments are conveniently summarized in Chart III-11 which shows two curves, one for the ratio of liquid assets to plant and equipment expenditures, and the other for the ratio of liquid assets to total finance. The liquid asset to plant and equipment expenditure ratio reached its lowest value for the 1950-53 upswing at the peak of the boom, towards the end of 1953. The ratio then increased sharply during the slump in 1953-54 to a peak value of 2.6. It fell drastically to 1.8 during the 1954-57 cyclical upswing. There is also a downward trend: each successive peak in the quick asset to plant and equipment ratio is lower than the preceding one. However, the successive troughs do not decline quite so regularly. The trough in 1948 was lower than that in 1953 because of the tremendous liquidity generated during the Korean War, while the lowest trough of all occurred in 1957.

Clearly, manufacturing firms begin the cyclical recovery in a strongly liquid position which initially is reinforced by sizable increases in internal funds. However, when the time arrives to finance and acquire substantial increments of durable assets in the

CHART III-11

Manufacturing Quick Assets to Plant and Equipment Outlay Ratio
and Quick Assets to Total Finance Ratio

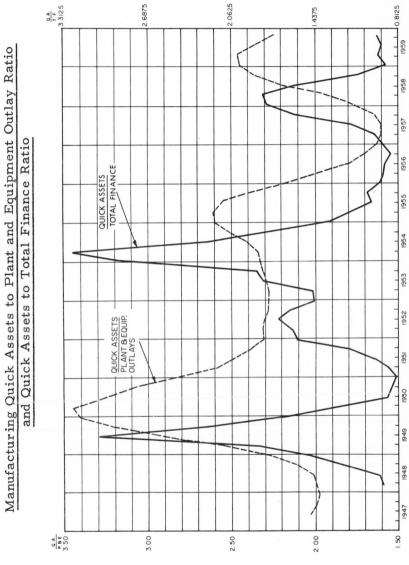

later phases of the cyclical upswing the liquidity position deteriorates, despite large quantities of simultaneous external financing. External finance is most heavily accumulated prior to cyclical peak in plant and equipment outlays, partly because of business cycle dynamics other than external financing and partly because of business desires to acquire financial resources prior to the time of disbursement. Therefore, one should not interpret a rapid decline in the liquid balance (or in the liquid balance relative to plant and equipment outlays) as a sign of distress or as necessarily undesired.

Chart III-12 shows a time series of external cash financing (no accruals are included) divided by total finance. This external finance fraction begins rising from the trough at about the same time as investment expenditures, but reaches a peak two to four quarters prior to the plant and equipment investment peak and about two quarters after the inventory investment maximum. The maximum value, 35%, was similar in the three cycles. Even though the external finance fraction rises from the trough concurrently with liquid assets and then drops off rather abruptly about a half year after liquid assets begin to decline, deterioration in the liquidity position is not halted by increased external financing. The relative importance of external finance as pictured in Chart III-12 has an obvious inverse correlation with the liquid asset to investment ratio in Chart III-11, especially when liquid assets are running down most rapidly in the late upswing. Undoubtedly, a causal relation exists. As the strain on liquid assets, measured by the liquid asset to investment ratio increases, so too does the pressure to acquire external finance. As liquid balances diminish at the peak of the boom, by design in large measure, funds acquired in anticipation of purchasing capital assets are converted into fixed assets. Of course, there may be an involuntary component in liquid asset reduction late in the boom as projected fund flows fall below expectations or capital outlays are unexpectedly heavy.

Chart III-13 portrays total finance and four of its major constituents: short-term borrowing, long-term external finance, internal funds and accruals. Strongly influencing total finance movements are changes in tax liabilities and trade payables, the two most important accruals. Tax liability changes respond to profit changes, increasing swiftly early in a business cycle, dropping close to zero as profits stabilize and finally turning heavily negative when profits drop off in the slump. Trade payable changes follow a similar pattern, so that these two highly volatile accruals heavily shape the path of total finance.

Total finance, as shown in Chart III-13, also can be compared with the plant and equipment outlays shown in Chart III-10. Total finance usually declined two to four quarters prior to the peak in plant and equipment outlays. Also, long-term external finance,

CHART III-12

Manufacturing Ratio of External Cash Finance to Total Finance

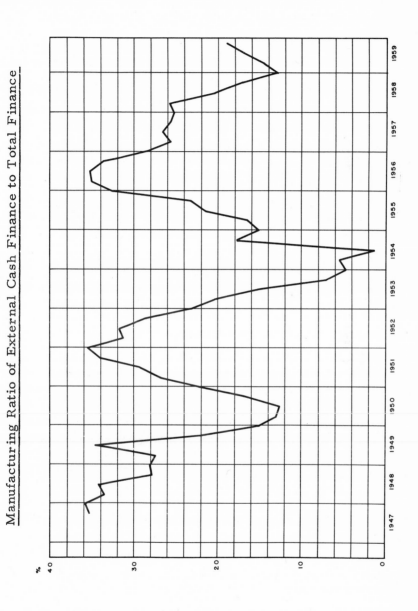

CHART III-13

Manufacturing Total Finance (million $)

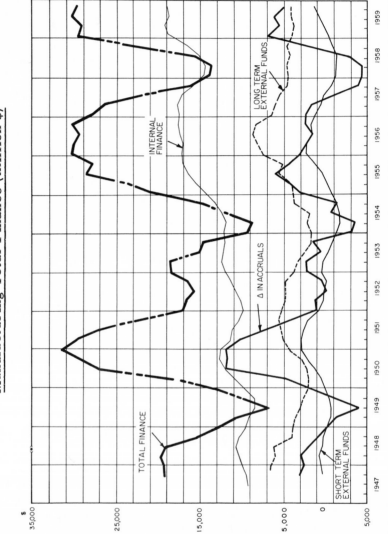

which lagged behind short-term finance, still led the peak in plant and equipment outlays by two to three quarters.

These heuristic impressions are in large measure also formally substantiated by the results obtained from an extensive statistical regression study of quarterly time series observations for the period from 1950 through 1958 inclusive.[3] The data used in this study were essentially the same as those described earlier in this paper: investment data were obtained from the SEC-OBE sample surveys, and the financial data on income and balance sheet statistics from the SEC-FTC Quarterly Reports. In addition, information gathered by the McGraw-Hill Department of Economics on levels and utilization of capacity was employed.

Approximately 15 different models or regression equations were tested against the time series data. These regression equations ranged widely, representing a large, if not exhaustive, sample of suggested theories. For example, several different formulations of the acceleration principle were tested, including explicit change in sales and distributed lag models, capacity models represented by the ratio of current or recent production levels to previous peak production levels, and the ratio between current production levels and capacity as estimated by the McGraw-Hill data. Similarly, a number of different measures of profits and the level of free retained earnings were used; these encompassed a wide variety of adjustments for inventory financing, current assets, and other financial needs. A large number of different lag structures for the different explanatory variables were also tested. In fact (including lagged values), over forty different explanatory variables for investment were tested.

Of the many possibilities tested, the equation that seemed to provide the best performance, both in terms of consistently highest multiple correlation and regression coefficient signs most in agreement with a priori expectations, was the following:

$$I_t = a + b_1 C_{t-1} + b_2 R_{t-1} + b_3 \frac{\Delta SP_{t-1}}{SP_{t-2}} +$$

---

[3]This time series study was undertaken by one of the present authors, John Meyer, as part of a broader series of studies financed by a grant from the Rockefeller Foundation to Professor John Lintner at the Harvard Business School for Research in the general area of Profits and the Functioning of the Economy. Regression analysis results reported earlier on excesses or deficiencies in corporate cash holdings were also part of this same study.

$$+ b_4 r_{t-3} + b_5 I_{t-2} + \begin{bmatrix} \text{Seasonal Correc-} \\ \text{tion by Use of} \\ \text{Dummy Variables} \end{bmatrix} + e_t$$

where

I = investment in plant and equipment (SEC-OBE);

C = capacity utilization as measured by the ratio of the relevant FRB production index to the McGraw-Hill annual capacity index interpolated quarterly with the SEC-OBE quarterly series on investment;

R = cash throw-off from operations as measured by net profits plus depreciation less dividends;

$\dfrac{\Delta SP}{SP}$ = the percentage change in the Standard and Poor's price index for all industrials;

r = Moody's bond yield on AAA corporate bonds (assumed to be the same for all industries);

e = error term;

and t = the current quarter from which all lags are measured by subtraction.

This model, quite gratifyingly, is very similar to one developed by the present authors in earlier work.[4] This consistency tends to minimize the possibility, moreover, that the model is merely an empirical artifact that emerged primarily ex post from experimentation with the data.

The model was fitted to individual time series for most of the component manufacturing industries, as well as to aggregate data for all manufacturing. In order to present the results in as relevant and directly comparable fashion as possible, elasticities have been calculated for all of the variables that were consistently significant or relevant to the present study; these are presented in Table III-2.[5]

---

[4]Meyer and Kuh, op. cit., particularly Chapter XII.

[5]The change in stock price variable almost invariably had the expected positive relationship with investment but was seldom significant and, therefore, has been omitted here. Also, space limitations preclude presentation of all of the regression coefficients.

TABLE III-2

Estimated Investment Elasticities in Manufacturing Industries[a]

Industry	Cash Throw-off Elasticity	Interest Elasticity	Simple or Short-Term Capacity Elasticity	Long-Term Capacity Elasticity-- Inclusive of Distributed Lag[b]
Iron and Steel	.126	-.322	.395	2.55
Non-Ferrous Metals	.424**	-.545	.587	5.32
Electrical Machinery	.183*	-.210	.592**	8.49
Other Machinery	.588**	-.489	.043*	.14
Motor Vehicles and Equipment	-.085	-.342	.365	3.32
Other Transportation Equipment	.345**	-.567**	-.064	.58
Stone, Clay and Glass	.308**	-.276	.613	2.95
Food	.207*	+.391	2.240**	2.67
Textiles	.255**	-.538**	-.405	-1.07
Paper	.829**	-.597*	-.970	-2.95
Chemicals	.119*	+.230	2.416**	24.20
Rubber	.276*	-.645**	.557	2.56
Petroleum and Coal	.268**	-.342	1.253*	6.60
All Manufacturing	.257**	-.165	.685*	2.28

[a]Calculated at mean values for the variables.

[b]No significance tests are reported for this column since the reported elasticities are based on a composite calculation from two regression coefficients.

*The regression coefficients used in calculating these elasticities were significant at the 5% level in a conventional one-tail test of significance.

**The regression coefficients used in calculating these elasticities were significant at the 1% level in a conventional one-tail test of significance.

All of the elasticities were calculated at mean values for the 1950 to 1958 period.

The only figures in Table III-2 that might be somewhat difficult to interpret are those found under the heading "Long-Term Capacity Elasticity Inclusive of Distributed Lag." These numbers were derived by attributing to capacity that portion of the explanation accounted for by the lagged investment variable, I_{t-2}, and were calculated by methods developed by Koyck.[6] These "all inclusive" capacity elasticities are recorded here as much for the record as because of any firm belief in their validity, since both statistical and conceptual questions could be raised about these numbers.

The numbers in Table IV-1 do more or less make sense, however, and are essentially consistent with many previous studies of manufacturing investment. The only really major departure from most previous findings is the reporting of relatively large interest elasticities. Furthermore, the coefficients for the interest variables, though not significant for most industries, are at least negative, as hypothesized by economic theory. This agreement between hypotheses and results, to say the least, has not always been true in most empirical studies of manufacturing investment behavior.[7] The

[6]Koyck, Distributed Lags and Investment Analysis (Amsterdam: North Holland Publishing Company, 1954). The estimates reported here were not corrected for statistical inconsistency described by Koyck because the multiple correlation R_2 was quite high, so that the correction would have been small, and further, some basic doubts could exist about the legitimacy of a distributed lag model in the present context.

[7]While the aggregate manufacturing interest elasticity is -.16, the median industry elasticity is -.34. Two other studies have found statistically relevant interest elasticities. Gehrels and Wiggins, "Interest Rates and Fixed Investment," American Economic Review, March, 1957, pp. 79-92, find statistically significant interest effects, although the interest elasticity cannot be readily established from their article.

Brown, et al, op. cit., p.85, find an interest elasticity of new orders for non-electrical machinery to be -.30 when the explanatory variables additional to interest rates are the index of industrial production and gross corporate profit, and -.40 when net instead of gross corporate profits are used. As these authors point out, these partial elasticities do not imply strong gross monetary effects since the remaining variables, with stronger positive elasticities, will often more than offset the interest effect. "Thus, even if the interest-elasticity of investment demand were as high as .40, it would be a difficult, if not impossible, struggle to keep New Orders from slipping badly in a cyclical recession." (p. 86) Long-run interest elasticities, when the full distributed lag effect is taken into account, come to .45 for the new profits equation and approximately .50 in the gross profits equation.

interest elasticities are small, however, compared to those reported for the two activity level variables, R_{t-1} and especially C_{t-1}. Furthermore, the regression coefficients for the latter two variables are consistently more significant in a statistical sense.

In addition, a closer analysis reveals that most of the statistical significance of the interest variable is in predicting investment in the last seven quarters of the sample period, that is from the second quarter of 1957 through the fourth quarter of 1958. This was revealed by an inspection of the regression error terms before and after inclusion of r_{t-3}. If r_{t-3} is excluded, the errors for the last seven quarters are very large (by far the largest in the whole sample), while if r_{t-3} is included, the errors for the last seven quarters are small and about the same as for other time periods. Furthermore, using the Durbin-Watson coefficient as a measure of error term autocorrelation, significant autocorrelation for most of the regressions is indicated without r_{t-3} and mostly insignificant autocorrelations with r_{t-3} included. Since the last seven quarters were a period of decline from a cyclical peak, this change in the pattern of the error terms with and without r_{t-3} lends additional corroboration to the view expressed earlier that monetary policy is likely to be most effective as a tool for reducing investment demand late in the recovery phase and, allowing for lags, in the early period of decline from the peak. In addition, the sharply diminished liquidity stock levels characterizing this period could have led to the increased interest sensitivity of investment.

In summary, major financing problems seem to strike manufacturing firms most often late in a cyclical recovery when large-scale plant and equipment outlays are being financed. To some extent the financing is anticipated, as reflected in the rapid increase in the relative importance of external finance even when plant and equipment outlays are only beginning to rise. Thus, considerable financial provision is made prior to the actual investment outlay, perhaps on the average two to four quarters ahead. Moreover, a final quantity of financing, apparently unavailable from either internal fund flows or external financing, is acquired through sharp reductions in liquid balances at the end of the cyclical upswing.

Obviously, there are limits to the willingness to draw down liquid balances. If firms knew that a severe curtailment of finance was in the offing they could calculate how much the reductions in financing would affect liquid balances, should capital outlays continue unabated. As noted, internal funds are not generated in increasing quantities after the middle of the cyclical recovery so that only weak reliance can be placed on this source. Hence, the availability of external finance may be of critical importance at this late stage of the cycle, particularly if the liquidity stock is low.

D. Policy Effects of External Finance Reductions

In order to evaluate the impact of financial availability on the liquidity position of the firm, a limited attempt will be made to evaluate some effects of reduced external finance on liquidity and investment policies of manufacturing firms. It should be made clear at the very outset that this cannot be wholly satisfactory without a reasonably complete econometric model but, even with the informal techniques that will be used here, it is possible to emerge with relevant impressions about the possible effects of reduced external funds.

In the hypothetical examples that follow, it has been assumed that proportional reductions in external cash financing of different intensity — 10 percent, 25 percent, and 50 percent, — have been put into effect each period. Actual 1947-59 data have been used so that these reductions are additional to those actually operative during the historical period, 1947 through 1959.

Of course, more sophisticated variants might be considered. For example, instead of flat proportional reductions each period, the postulated reductions could be more severe at some times than at others. However, for more complex approaches to yield additional insights, it would be necessary to know more about the structure than is presently known.

In earlier sections it has been argued that corporations acquire real assets mainly in response to demand factors. Adequacy of finance, however, can strongly condition the amount of investment actually undertaken as a result of demand-generated desires. Internal flows plus moderate reductions in liquid balances can adequately finance the early part of a cyclical recovery during which inventory accumulation is most prominent. During the later stages of the cyclical recovery, however, major financing problems, associated with rapid fixed asset accumulation, are encountered as internal finance plus liquidity stock reduction may be insufficient to finance adequately intended investment. When internal funds cease to supply "sufficient" finance, there are definite limits beyond which further reductions in liquidity might result in severe financial repercussions. In these circumstances firms will seek external funds. At this juncture the monetary authorities could most strongly influence plant and equipment as well as other investment outlays by restricting the supply of funds to the manufacturing sector, although lags in investment response require early monetary action.

The first of the two different monetary policy "experiments" to be considered here (and described in Table III-3) shows the effects of reduced financial availability on the assumption that the burden of reduced external finance is shared equally by liquid

TABLE III-3

Effects of Reduced External Funds:
Reduction Shared by Liquidity and Plant and Equipment Outlays

Year	Quarter	EXTERNAL FUNDS (million $)						TOTAL FINANCE (million $)				EXTERNAL FINANCE / TOTAL FINANCE			
				Reductions of:					Less Reductions According to:			Col.1 + Col.7	Col.1 Minus Col.3 + Col.8	Col.1 Minus Col.5 + Col.9	Col.1 Minus Col.6 + Col.10
		Actual (1)	5% (2)	10% (3)	12½% (4)	25% (5)	50% (6)	Actual (7)	Col.3 (8)	Col.5 (9)	Col.6 (10)	(11)	(12)	(13)	(14)
1947	1														
	2														
	3														
	4														
1948	1	6788	339	679	849	1697	3394	19209	18530	17512	15815	0.353	0.330	0.921	0.215
	2	6905	345	691	863	1726	3453	19287	18596	17561	15834	0.358	0.334	0.295	0.218
	3	6622	331	662	828	1656	3311	19715	19053	18059	16404	0.336	0.313	0.215	0.202
	4	6543	327	654	818	1636	3272	19130	18476	17494	15858	0.342	0.319	0.280	0.206
1949	1	4269	213	427	534	1067	2135	15340	14913	14273	13205	0.278	0.258	0.224	0.162
	2	3630	182	363	454	908	1815	12947	12584	12039	11132	0.280	0.260	0.226	0.163
	3	2914	146	291	364	729	1457	10674	10383	9945	9217	0.273	0.253	0.220	0.158
	4	2354	118	235	294	589	1177	6788	6553	6199	5611	0.347	0.323	0.285	0.210
1950	1	2118	106	212	265	530	1059	9606	9394	9076	8547	0.220	0.202	0.175	0.124
	2	2019	101	202	252	505	1010	13346	13144	12841	12336	0.151	0.146	0.118	0.082
	3	2377	119	238	297	594	1189	18225	17987	17631	17036	0.130	0.119	0.101	0.070
	4	3397	170	340	425	849	1699	27038	26698	26189	25339	0.126	0.115	0.093	0.067
1951	1	4883	244	488	610	1221	2442	29285	28797	28064	26843	0.167	0.153	0.130	0.091
	2	7005	350	701	876	1751	3503	31413	30712	29662	27910	0.223	0.205	0.177	0.126
	3	7960	398	796	995	1990	3980	29708	28912	27718	25728	0.268	0.248	0.215	0.155
	4	7891	395	789	986	1973	3946	27019	26230	25046	23073	0.292	0.271	0.236	0.171
1952	1	7747	387	775	968	1937	3874	22770	21995	20833	18896	0.340	0.317	0.279	0.205
	2	6092	305	609	762	1523	3046	17138	16529	15615	14092	0.355	0.332	0.293	0.216
	3	5194	260	519	649	1299	2597	16673	16154	15374	14076	0.312	0.289	0.253	0.184
	4	4968	248	497	621	1242	2484	15684	15187	14442	13200	0.317	0.294	0.258	0.188
1953	1	4680	234	468	585	1170	2340	16374	15906	15204	14034	0.286	0.265	0.231	0.167
	2	4278	214	428	535	1070	2139	18419	17991	17349	16280	0.232	0.214	0.185	0.131
	3	3754	188	375	469	939	1877	18507	18132	17568	16630	0.203	0.186	0.160	0.113
	4	2259	113	226	282	565	1130	14970	14744	14405	13840	0.151	0.138	0.118	0.082

TABLE III-3 (continued)

Year	Quar-ter	(1)	(2)	(3)	(4)	(5)	(6)	(7)	(8)	(9)	(10)	(11)	(12)	(13)	(14)
1954	1	1023	51	102	128	256	512	14587	14485	14331	14075	0.070	0.064	0.054	0.036
	2	453	23	45	57	113	227	9391	9346	9278	9164	0.048	0.044	0.043	0.025
	3	494	25	49	62	124	247	8913	8864	8789	8666	0.055	0.050	0.042	0.029
	4	160	8	16	20	40	80	11875	11859	11835	11795	0.013	0.021	0.010	0.001
1955	1	2597	130	260	325	649	1299	14584	14324	13935	13285	0.178	0.163	0.140	0.098
	2	3125	156	313	391	781	1563	20614	20301	19833	19051	0.152	0.139	0.118	0.082
	3	3918	196	392	490	980	1959	23799	23407	22819	21840	0.165	0.151	0.129	0.090
	4	6139	307	614	767	1535	3070	28530	27916	26995	25460	0.215	0.198	0.171	0.121
1956	1	6431	322	643	804	1608	3216	27831	27188	26223	24615	0.231	0.213	0.184	0.131
	2	9759	488	976	1220	2440	4880	30055	29079	27615	25175	0.325	0.302	0.265	0.194
	3	10486	524	1049	1311	2622	5243	29963	28914	27341	24720	0.350	0.326	0.288	0.212
	4	10339	517	1034	1292	2585	5170	29404	28370	26819	24234	0.352	0.328	0.289	0.213
1957	1	10154	508	1015	1269	2539	5077	30181	29166	27642	25104	0.336	0.313	0.275	0.202
	2	7856	393	786	982	1964	3928	27734	26948	25770	23806	0.283	0.262	0.229	0.165
	3	6683	334	668	835	1671	3342	26131	25463	24460	22789	0.256	0.236	0.205	0.147
	4	5774	289	577	722	1444	2887	21803	21226	20359	18916	0.265	0.245	0.213	0.153
1958	1	4083	204	408	510	1021	2042	15951	15543	14930	13909	0.256	0.236	0.205	0.147
	2	3518	176	352	440	880	1759	13945	13593	13065	12186	0.252	0.233	0.202	0.144
	3	3511	176	351	439	878	1756	13665	13314	12787	11909	0.257	0.237	0.206	0.147
	4	3210	161	321	401	803	1605	15795	15474	14992	14190	0.203	0.187	0.161	0.113
1959	1	4000	200	400	500	1000	2000	23077	22677	22077	22877	0.173	0.159	0.136	0.087
	2	3751	188	375	469	938	1876	29405	29030	28467	27529	0.128	0.116	0.099	0.068
	3	4208	210	421	526	1052	2104	28962	28541	27910	26858	0.145	0.133	0.113	0.078
	4	5112	256	511	639	1278	2556	30130	29619	28852	27574	0.170	0.155	0.133	0.093
1960	1	5581	279	558	698	1395	2191	29566	29008	28171	27375	0.189	0.173	0.149	0.102

TABLE III-3 (continued)

Year	Quarter	PLANT AND EQUIPMENT OUTLAY (million $)	Less Reductions According to:			REVISED PLANT & EQUIP. UNREVISED PLANT & EQUIP,			LIQUID ASSETS (million $)	Less Reductions According to:		
		Actual (15)	Col.2 (16)	Col.4 (17)	Col.5 (18)	Col.16 + Col.15 (19)	Col.17 + Col.15 (20)	Col.18 + Col.15 (21)	Actual (22)	Col.2 (23)	Col.4 (24)	Col.5 (25)
1947	1											
	2											
	3											
	4	8702							17670			
1948	1	9025	8686	8176	7328	0.962	0.906	0.812	17991	17652	17142	16294
	2	9154	8809	8291	7428	0.962	0.906	0.811	18114	17769	17251	16388
	3	9170	8839	8342	7514	0.964	0.910	0.819	18296	17965	17468	16640
	4	9134	8807	8316	7498	0.964	0.910	0.821	18370	18043	17552	16734
1949	1	8788	8575	8254	7720	0.976	0.939	0.878	18527	18314	17993	17460
	2	8352	8170	7898	7444	0.978	0.946	0.891	19034	18852	18580	18126
	3	7843	7697	7479	7115	0.981	0.954	0.907	19826	19680	19462	19097
	4	7149	7031	6855	6561	0.983	0.959	0.918	20670	20552	20376	20081
1950	1	6738	6632	6473	6208	0.984	0.961	0.921	21538	21432	21273	21008
	2	6578	6477	6326	6074	0.985	0.962	0.923	22426	22325	22175	21921
	3	6782	6663	6485	6188	0.982	0.956	0.912	23412	23293	23115	22818
	4	7491	7321	7066	6641	0.977	0.943	0.887	24430	24260	24005	23581
1951	1	8204	7960	7594	6984	0.970	0.926	0.851	25411	25167	24801	24190
	2	9233	8883	8357	7481	0.962	0.905	0.810	26202	25852	25326	24451
	3	10112	9714	9117	8122	0.961	0.902	0.803	26479	26081	25484	24489
	4	10852	10457	9866	8880	0.964	0.909	0.818	26926	26531	25940	24953
1952	1	11317	10930	10349	9381	0.966	0.914	0.829	27004	26617	26036	25067
	2	11641	11336	10879	10117	0.974	0.935	0.869	26930	26625	26108	25407
	3	11609	11349	10960	10311	0.978	0.944	0.888	26904	26644	26255	25605
	4	11633	11385	11012	10391	0.979	0.947	0.893	26812	26564	26191	25570
1953	1	11679	11445	11094	10509	0.980	0.950	0.900	26700	26466	26115	25530
	2	11710	11496	11175	10640	0.982	0.954	0.909	26699	26485	26164	25629
	3	11862	11674	11393	10924	0.984	0.960	0.921	27049	26861	26580	26110
	4	11908	11795	11626	11344	0.991	0.976	0.953	27326	27213	27044	26761

TABLE III-3 (continued)

Year	Quar-ter	(15)	(16)	(17)	(18)	(19)	(20)	(21)	(22)	(23)	(24)	(25)
1954	1	11809	11758	11681	11553	0.996	0.989	0.978	27331	27280	27203	27075
	2	11570	11547	11513	11456	0.998	0.995	0.990	26939	26916	26882	26826
	3	11357	11332	11295	11233	0.998	0.995	0.989	26578	26553	26516	26454
	4	11038	11030	11018	10998	0.999	0.998	0.990	26535	26527	26515	26495
1955	1	10718	10588	10393	10068	0.988	0.970	0.939	26935	26805	26610	26286
	2	10654	10498	10263	9872	0.985	0.963	0.927	27692	27536	27301	26911
	3	10908	10712	10418	9928	0.982	0.955	0.910	28401	28205	27911	27421
	4	11442	11135	10675	9908	0.973	0.933	0.866	29164	28857	28397	27629
1956	1	12151	11829	11347	10543	0.974	0.934	0.868	29210	28888	28406	27602
	2	13090	12602	11870	10650	0.963	0.907	0.814	28737	28249	27517	26297
	3	14025	13501	12714	11403	0.963	0.907	0.813	27882	27358	26571	25260
	4	14954	14437	13662	12370	0.965	0.914	0.827	26953	26436	25661	24368
1957	1	15501	14993	14232	12963	0.967	0.918	0.836	26370	25862	25101	23831
	2	15950	15557	14968	13986	0.975	0.938	0.877	26049	25656	25067	24085
	3	16126	15792	15291	14456	0.979	0.948	0.896	25930	25596	25095	24259
	4	15959	15670	15237	14515	0.982	0.955	0.910	25709	25420	24987	24265
1958	1	15352	15148	14842	14332	0.987	0.967	0.934	25340	25136	24830	24319
	2	14108	13932	13668	13228	0.988	0.969	0.938	25079	24903	24639	24199
	3	12762	12586	12323	11884	0.986	0.966	0.931	24882	24706	24434	24004
	4	11433	11272	11032	10631	0.986	0.965	0.930	25161	25000	24760	24358
1959	1	10991	10791	10491	9991	0.982	0.955	0.909	26008	25808	25508	25008
	2	11073	10885	10604	10135	0.983	0.958	0.915	27159	26971	26690	26221
	3	11428	11218	10902	10376	0.982	0.954	0.908	28125	27915	27599	27073
	4	12067	11811	11428	10789	0.979	0.947	0.894	28577	28321	27938	27299
1960	1	12657	12378	11959	11261	0.978	0.945	0.890	28565	28286	27867	27170

TABLE III-3 (continued)

Year	Quar-ter	REVISED LIQUID ASSETS / UNREVISED LIQUID ASSETS Col.23 + Col.22 (26)	Col.24 + Col.22 (27)	Col.25 + Col.22 (28)	QUICK RATIO Actual (29)	Col.23 + Col. 9 Table 4 (30)	Col.24 + Col.10 Table 4 (31)	Col.25 + Col.11 Table 4 (32)	CURRENT ASSETS (Million $) Actual (33)	Less Reductions According to: Col.2 (34)	Col.4 (35)	Col.5 (36)
1947	1											
	2											
	3											
	4				0.865				56840			
1948	1	0.981	0.953	0.906	0.850	0.878	0.926	1.028	58416	58077	57567	56719
	2	0.981	0.952	0.905	0.830	0.858	0.905	1.005	59947	59602	59084	58221
	3	0.982	0.955	0.909	0.810	0.839	0.889	0.995	61741	61410	60913	60085
	4	0.982	0.955	0.911	0.796	0.825	0.874	0.980	63154	62827	62336	61518
1949	1	0.989	0.971	0.942	0.795	0.830	0.889	1.017	64114	63901	63580	63047
	2	0.990	0.976	0.952	0.823	0.860	0.923	1.057	64683	64501	64229	63775
	3	0.993	0.982	0.963	0.876	0.916	0.983	1.126	64867	64721	64503	64138
	4	0.994	0.986	0.972	0.944	0.986	1.059	1.211	64870	64752	64576	64281
1950	1	0.995	0.988	0.975	0.999	1.043	1.119	1.275	65238	65132	64973	64708
	2	0.995	0.989	0.977	1.021	1.065	1.141	1.297	66700	66599	66448	66195
	3	0.995	0.987	0.975	1.004	1.046	1.118	1.265	69304	69185	69007	68710
	4	0.993	0.983	0.965	0.936	0.974	1.037	1.167	73439	73269	73014	72590
1951	1	0.990	0.976	0.952	0.862	0.896	0.968	1.074	78307	78063	77697	77086
	2	0.987	0.967	0.933	0.794	0.825	0.878	0.990	83297	82947	82421	81546
	3	0.985	0.962	0.925	0.732	0.762	0.814	0.927	87507	87109	86512	85517
	4	0.985	0.963	0.927	0.695	0.727	0.782	0.903	90948	90553	89962	88975
1952	1	0.986	0.964	0.928	0.669	0.701	0.759	0.888	93295	92908	92327	91358
	2	0.989	0.972	0.943	0.659	0.694	0.756	0.896	94249	93944	93487	92726
	3	0.990	0.976	0.952	0.651	0.687	0.750	0.894	95154	94894	94505	93855
	4	0.991	0.977	0.954	0.647	0.684	0.748	0.893	95886	95638	95265	94644
1953	1	0.991	0.978	0.956	0.644	0.680	0.744	0.889	96590	96356	96005	95420
	2	0.992	0.980	0.960	0.634	0.670	0.734	0.880	97864	97650	97329	96794
	3	0.993	0.983	0.965	0.632	9.669	0.734	0.881	99197	99009	98728	98558
	4	0.996	0.990	0.979	0.638	0.677	0.745	0.897	99577	99464	99295	99012

TABLE III-3 (continued)

Year	Quarter	(26)	(27)	(28)	(29)	(30)	(31)	(32)	(33)	(34)	(35)	(36)
1954	1	0.998	0.995	0.991	0.636	0.674	0.741	0.891	99572	99521	99444	99316
	2	0.999	0.998	0.996	0.643	0.682	0.749	0.897	98798	98775	98741	98685
	3	0.999	0.998	0.995	0.655	0.692	0.757	0.898	97812	97787	97750	97688
	4	0.999	0.999	0.998	0.664	0.700	0.761	0.892	97770	97762	97750	97730
1955	1	0.995	0.988	0.976	0.685	0.717	0.772	0.887	98388	98258	98063	97739
	2	0.994	0.986	0.972	0.695	0.725	0.776	0.882	99963	99807	99572	99182
	3	0.993	0.983	0.965	0.695	0.723	0.770	0.867	102197	102001	101707	101217
	4	0.989	0.974	0.947	0.688	0.713	0.755	0.840	105116	104809	104349	103581
1956	1	0.989	0.972	0.945	0.668	0.693	0.735	0.821	107886	107564	107082	106278
	2	0.983	0.958	0.915	0.639	0.661	0.699	0.779	110438	109950	109218	107998
	3	0.981	0.953	0.906	0.604	0.627	0.665	0.749	112530	112006	111219	109908
	4	0.981	0.952	0.904	0.574	0.597	0.636	0.723	114192	113675	112900	111607
1957	1	0.981	0.952	0.904	0.549	0.572	0.613	0.703	115953	115445	114684	113414
	2	0.985	0.962	0.925	0.532	0.558	0.603	0.705	117470	117077	116488	115506
	3	0.987	0.968	0.936	0.523	0.551	0.597	0.703	118663	118329	117828	116992
	4	0.989	0.972	0.944	0.521	0.549	0.599	0.711	119070	118781	118348	117626
1958	1	0.992	0.980	0.960	0.526	0.556	0.609	0.730	118144	117940	117634	117123
	2	0.993	0.982	0.965	0.535	0.566	0.621	0.744	116986	116810	116546	116106
	3	0.993	0.982	0.965	0.547	0.578	0.633	0.755	116083	115907	115644	115205
	4	0.994	0.984	0.968	0.565	0.596	0.652	0.775	116051	115890	115650	115248
1959	1	0.992	0.981	0.962	0.577	0.608	0.660	0.776	117961	117761	117461	116961
	2	0.993	0.983	0.965	0.582	0.611	0.661	0.770	121314	121126	120845	120376
	3	0.993	0.981	0.963	0.584	0.612	0.661	0.765	124385	124175	123859	123333
	4	0.991	0.978	0.955	0.573	0.600	0.646	0.745	127316	127060	126677	126038
1960	1	0.990	0.976	0.951	0.556	0.582	0.627	0.725	129878	129599	129180	128483

TABLE III-3 (continued)

Year	Quar-ter	CURRENT RATIO				LIQUID ASSETS SALES				LIQUID ASSETS PLANT & EQUIP, OUTLAYS			
		Actual	Col.34 + Col.9 Table 4	Col.35 + Col.10 Table 4	Col.36 + Col.11 Table 4	Actual	Col.23 + Sales	Col.24 + Sales	Col.25 + Sales	Actual	Col.23 + Col.16	Col.24 + Col.17	Col.25 + Col.18
		(37)	(38)	(39)	(40)	(41)	(42)	(43)	(44)	(45)	(46)	(47)	(48)
1947	1												
	2												
	3												
	4	2.782				0.116				2.031			
1948	1	2.760	2.889	3.110	3.578	0.113	0.111	0.108	0.103	1.994	2.032	2.097	2.224
	2	2.748	2.877	3.099	3.570	0.110	0.108	0.105	0.100	1.979	2.017	2.081	2.200
	3	2.735	2.869	3.099	3.591	0.107	0.105	0.102	0.097	1.995	2.032	2.094	2.215
	4	2.737	2.872	3.106	3.604	0.106	0.104	0.101	0.096	2.011	2.049	2.111	2.232
1949	1	2.753	2.896	3.143	3.672	0.106	0.105	0.103	0.100	2.108	2.136	2.180	2.262
	2	2.796	2.941	3.189	3.721	0.110	0.108	0.107	0.104	2.279	2.307	2.352	2.435
	3	2.867	3.011	3.258	3.781	0.116	0.115	0.113	0.111	2.528	2.557	2.602	2.684
	4	2.962	3.108	3.357	3.878	0.123	0.122	0.121	0.119	2.891	2.923	2.972	3.061
1950	1	3.027	3.171	3.417	3.927	0.128	0.127	0.126	0.124	3.197	3.232	3.286	3.384
	2	3.036	3.178	3.419	3.917	0.128	0.127	0.126	0.125	3.409	3.447	3.505	3.609
	3	2.972	3.108	3.337	3.809	0.125	0.124	0.123	0.121	3.452	3.496	3.564	3.687
	4	2.814	2.940	3.154	3.593	0.120	0.119	0.117	0.115	3.261	3.314	3.397	3.551
1951	1	2.658	2.780	2.988	3.421	0.114	0.113	0.113	0.109	3.098	3.162	3.226	3.464
	2	2.523	2.645	2.856	3.301	0.111	0.110	0.107	0.104	2.838	2.910	3.031	3.268
	3	2.418	2.545	2.764	3.238	0.111	0.109	0.106	0.102	2.619	2.685	2.795	3.015
	4	2.349	2.480	2.711	3.220	0.110	0.109	0.106	0.102	2.481	2.537	2.629	2.810
1952	1	2.310	2.447	2.690	3.235	0.111	0.109	0.107	0.103	2.386	2.435	2.516	2.672
	2	2.305	2.447	2.700	3.271	0.111	0.109	0.107	0.104	2.314	2.349	2.405	2.511
	3	2.302	2.446	2.701	3.279	0.110	0.108	0.107	0.104	2.318	2.348	2.396	2.483
	4	2.315	2.461	2.717	3.307	0.107	0.106	0.104	0.102	2.305	2.333	2.378	2.461
1953	1	2.329	2.475	2.735	3.323	0.104	0.103	0.102	0.099	2.286	2.312	2.354	2.429
	2	2.323	2.470	2.731	3.322	0.101	0.100	0.099	0.097	2.280	2.304	2.341	2.409
	3	2.318	2.466	2.727	3.327	0.100	0.099	0.098	0.096	2.275	2.301	2.333	2.390
	4	2.325	2.473	2.734	3.320	0.102	0.101	0.099	0.099	2.295	2.307	2.326	2.359

TABLE III-3 (continued)

Year	Quar-ter	(37)	(38)	(39)	(40)	(41)	(42)	(43)	(44)	(45)	(46)	(47)	(48)
1954	1	2.316	2.459	2.710	3.268	0.103	0.103	0.103	0.102	2.315	2.320	2.329	2.344
	2	2.359	2.501	2.751	3.299	0.104	0.104	0.104	0.104	2.328	2.331	2.335	2.342
	3	2.411	2.550	2.792	3.317	0.105	0.105	0.105	0.104	2.340	2.343	2.348	2.355
	4	2.446	2.578	2.806	3.290	0.105	0.105	0.105	0.104	2.404	2.405	2.407	2.409
1955	1	2.503	2.629	2.845	3.299	0.104	0.103	0.103	0.101	2.513	2.532	2.560	2.611
	2	2.509	2.628	2.830	3.249	0.104	0.103	0.102	0.101	2.599	2.623	2.660	2.726
	3	2.502	2.615	2.808	3.201	0.103	0.102	0.101	0.099	2.604	2.633	2.679	2.762
	4	2.481	2.590	2.773	3.147	0.102	0.101	0.099	0.096	2.549	2.592	2.660	2.789
1956	1	2.468	2.580	2.769	3.160	0.100	0.098	0.097	0.094	2.404	2.442	2.503	2.618
	2	2.454	2.572	2.773	3.198	0.096	0.095	0.092	0.088	2.195	2.242	2.318	2.469
	3	2.440	2.566	2.785	3.257	0.092	0.091	0.088	0.084	1.988	2.026	2.090	2.215
	4	2.433	2.566	2.800	3.311	0.088	0.086	0.084	0.079	1.803	1.831	1.878	1.970
1957	1	2.415	2.554	2.800	3.346	0.084	0.083	0.080	0.076	1.701	1.725	1.764	1.838
	2	2.399	2.544	2.802	3.379	0.082	0.081	0.079	0.076	1.633	1.649	1.675	1.722
	3	2.394	2.542	2.804	3.392	0.081	0.080	0.078	0.076	1.608	1.621	1.641	1.678
	4	2.413	2.565	2.835	3.445	0.080	0.079	0.078	0.076	1.611	1.622	1.640	1.672
1958	1	2.451	2.608	2.886	3.510	0.081	0.080	0.079	0.078	1.651	1.659	1.673	1.697
	2	2.496	2.654	2.935	3.569	0.082	0.081	0.080	0.079	1.778	1.787	1.803	1.829
	3	2.551	2.710	2.992	3.625	0.082	0.082	0.081	0.079	1.950	1.963	1.984	2.020
	4	2.604	2.763	3.044	3.667	0.083	0.082	0.081	0.080	2.201	2.218	2.244	2.291
1959	1	2.619	2.772	3.039	3.627	0.083	0.082	0.081	0.080	2.366	2.364	2.431	2.503
	2	2.599	2.743	2.993	3.534	0.083	0.082	0.082	0.080	2.453	2.478	2.517	2.587
	3	2.582	2.722	2.965	3.486	0.084	0.084	0.083	0.081	2.461	2.488	2.532	2.609
	4	2.552	2.690	2.928	3.439	0.085	0.084	0.083	0.081	2.368	2.398	2.445	2.530
1960	1	2.527	2.666	2.907	3.428	0.083	0.083	0.081	0.079	2.257	2.285	2.330	2.413

SOURCES:
Col. 1:   External funds are made up by two main components: Short term and Long term. Δ in S.T.L. make up short term external funds. Δ in L.T.D.B. plus Δ in OLTD plus Δ in E make up long term external funds.
Col. 7:   Total finance is defined as: External funds plus Internal funds plus Δ in Accruals. Internal Funds are made up of RE plus DÉ. Δ in Accruals is made up of ΔA/P plus Δ FYTA plus ΔOCL plus Δ ONCL.
Col. 15: See Appendix Table III-3C, Col. 22.
Col. 22: See Appendix Table III-3B, Col. 8.
Col. 29: Quick Ratio is defined as C + G (Liquid Assets) ÷ Current Liabilities, i.e., Col. 22, Table III-3 ÷ Col. 8, Table III-4.
Col. 33: See Appendix Table III-3B. Current Assets = Col. 8 plus Col. 9 plus Col. 10 plus Col. 11 of that table.
Col. 37: Current Ratio is defined as Current Assets ÷ Current Liabilities, i.e., Col. 33, Table III-3 ÷ Col. 8, Table III-4.
Col. 41: Col. 22, Table III-3 ÷ Col. 1, Appendix Table III-3A.
Col. 45: Col. 22, Table III-3 ÷ Col. 22, Appendix Table III-3C.

balances and plant and equipment outlays. The second experiment (in Table III-4) shows the effects of various cuts in external funds assuming that the total burden is carried by liquid balances alone. It will be hypothesized that in each period external finance is reduced by different fractions according to the severity of monetary action. One column shows effects for each period of a 10 percent cut in external cash finance, another for a 25 percent cut, and a third column for a 50 percent cut in external cash finance. The 50 percent reduction would seem to be the absolute upper limit of possible action, the cut of one-quarter quite stringent, and a more probable actual upper limit than one-half. While the 10 percent cut appears to be more in keeping with actually feasible practice or possibilities since direct bank lending to manufacturing, both long-and short-term, is seldom more than 10 percent of total finance.

As shown in (Chart III-14) bank lending also bears a close resemblance to the pattern of total finance. The liquidity of other sectors which supply funds to manufacturing is, of course, partly controlled by the banking system. Accordingly, it seems appropriate to assume that all external cash financing has been equally affected by actions of the monetary authorities. To the extent, though, that non-bank fund suppliers are less subject to monetary control than the commercial banking system, the results that follow overstate the potential influence of monetary policy. The results are reported in four columns, the first showing the original time series while the remaining three columns show the time series adjusted downward by the three different percentages. It will be recalled that these data report four quarter averages for liquidity and other stock figures, while the flow figures are simply seasonally adjusted annual rates, achieved by adding up four quarters.

Table III-3 is based upon the following assumptions: (1) external finance is assumed cut by 10 percent, 25 percent, and 50 percent, respectively; (2) the reduction in external finance is split equally between reductions in plant and equipment outlays and liquid balances; and (3) equi-proportional reductions in external finance occur in short-term and long-term sources.

Immediate interest for the purposes of this paper centers on the effect of reductions in external financing on investment. Assuming that half of the external finance cut is reflected in reduced plant and equipment outlays, a 10 percent cut in financial availability shows up hardly at all in investment as shown in column 16. The ratio of plant and equipment adjusted for fund cuts seldom drops below 97 percent of the actual plant and equipment outlays. For a 25 percent cut in external availability, which is probably a plausible upper limit to feasible policy actions, the maximum impact, achieved in 1956, shows a 10 percent reduction in plant and equipment outlays (see column 20). This, it must be noted, refers to maximum

CHART III-14

Manufacturing Bank Loans (million $)

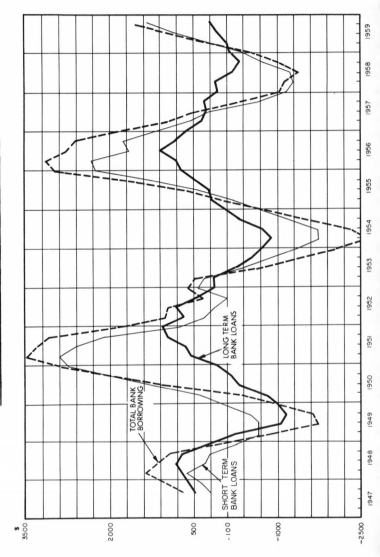

mpact, not the average over the cycle which amounts to only a
5 percent reduction. The most drastic results appear, of course,
when it is assumed that a 50 percent cut in external finance has
been made; the maximum investment cutback is about 20 percent
and the average reduction over the cycle about 12 percent.

As shown in columns 26-28, liquid balances would not have been
greatly influenced even with the most severe monetary action assumed. The maximum effect in 1956 leads to a 10 percent reduction
from the then existing stock of liquid assets, and on the average
over the cycle the adjusted liquid assets are, in the worst possible
case, 5 percent less than the actual totals. The more "moderate"
25 percent reduction in external finance hardly affects the liquid
asset total in a relative sense while the 10 percent cut has a barely
visible impact. Because of the small relative impact on liquid balances, the postulated 50 percent cut in plant and equipment outlays
might not actually be undertaken.

Indeed, columns 29-32 recording the quick ratio show that the
assumed reductions in external finance cause the quick ratio to
improve. The revised ratios are typically 20-30 percentage points
above the actual quick ratio. The higher quick ratio is mainly a
consequence of the fact that proportional reductions take place in
short-term finance as well as in liquid balances. The current ratio,
recorded in columns 37-40, shows behavior comparable to that of
the quick ratio, becoming larger the greater the cuts in external
finance since both liabilities and assets are reduced, but liabilities
by proportionately more than current assets as a result of the reduction in external finance. In short, financial stringency has been
reduced, according to conventional balance sheet ratios when external finance is squeezed.

The ratio of liquidity to sales shows a downward trend throughout
the period in its unadjusted form as indeed it must when revised
according to the methods used here, as recorded in columns 41-44.
However, the quick asset to sales ratio is only slightly affected even
with the most drastic external fund cuts. A 7 percent or 8 percent
reduction in a few quarters is the maximum observable reduction.

The last set of columns, 45-48, shows the ratio of quick assets
to plant and equipment. Because both quick assets and plant and
equipment have shared equally in the reductions, the ratio of quick
assets to plant and equipment has either remained unchanged or,
indeed from the point of view of liquidity, has improved. If it is
believed that the ratios actually experienced were tolerable to manufacturing corporations, then equal sharing of the reduction by plant
and equipment outlays seems unlikely. Accordingly, different assumptions about manufacturing reactions to external finance cuts
might be considered. For example, it might be more realistic to

replace assumption (1) with: (1a) the <u>entire</u> burden of the reduction in external financing is borne by liquid assets.

Under this assumption, recorded in Table III-4, even with a 50 percent over-all reduction in external finance hypothesized the percentage reduction in quick assets is not striking. In 1956 when the maximum hypothetical reductions would have taken place quick assets would have been about 18 percent below the levels actually prevailing. For a 25 percent reduction in external finance the maximum reduction in quick assets is only about 10 percent.

The quick asset to sales turnover ratio under the maximum reduction (column 27) seldom declines more than 12 percent and appears to be of similar magnitude to the figures actually prevailing. The liquid assets to plant and equipment ratio shows (columns 29-31) a 19 percent reduction below the actual figure in a single quarter in mid-1956 when the most stringent policy cut is imposed. During subsequent quarters the revised ratio did not drop by more than 8 percent to 10 percent below the actual. On the average during a cyclical recovery this ratio would decline by only 5 percent or 6 percent with the heaviest curtailment. For such an extremely large reduction in finance, this decline is not especially impressive.

If the view that a 25 percent reduction is strong but feasible is correct, the effects of monetary stringency will be secondary, or so it appears according to the hypothetical experiments presented here. The comparative impotence of monetary policy implicit in these results originates, of course, in the fact that external finance, to begin with, is simply not tremendously important in the manufacturing sector. While this was known at the outset, there might still have been cycle phases when monetary policy could be expected to exert great leverage.[8] Even for these more limited intervals, however, restrictive effects of a strong monetary policy would appear to be quite mild.

Three qualifications are, however, in order. First, the actually observed minimum quick asset to plant and equipment ratio might be lower than that which would have been observed had business expectations been fulfilled. If the degrees of monetary stringency actually experienced in 1947-59 upswings, particularly in 1956-57, have been underestimated, outlays might have been less than those

---

[8]That monetary policy effects are potentially appropriate for (weak) control over investment does <u>not</u> imply such action is desirable from an over-all point of view. If plant and equipment outlays are reduced in the late phase of a cycle, when the rate of increase in real output is low, effective demand will be cut back when contrary policies may be desirable.

TABLE III-4

ts of Reduced External Funds: Reduction Only in Liquidity Stock

Year	Quarter	LIQUID ASSETS (million $) Actual (1)	Col.3 Table 3 (2)	Col.5 Table 3 (3)	Col.6 Table 3 (4)	Col.2 + Col.1 (5)	Col.3 + Col.1 (6)	Col.4 + Col.1 (7)	Actual (8)	Col.8 minus 10% of short term borrowing (9)	Col.9 minus 25% of short term borrowing (10)	Col.10 minus 50% of short term borrowing (11)
947	1											
	2											
	3											
	4	17670							20435			
948	1	17991	17312	16294	14597	0.962	0.906	0.811	21164	20102	18509	15853
	2	18114	17423	16388	14661	0.962	0.905	0.809	21818	20716	19063	16308
	3	18296	17634	16640	14985	0.964	0.909	0.819	22575	21407	19654	16731
	4	18370	17716	16734	15098	0.964	0.911	0.822	23076	21875	20073	17071
949	1	18527	18100	17460	16392	0.977	0.942	0.885	23291	22066	20229	17168
	2	19034	18671	18126	17219	0.981	0.952	0.905	23137	21928	20139	17141
	3	19826	19535	19097	18369	0.985	0.963	0.927	22626	21494	19796	16965
	4	20670	20435	20081	19493	0.989	0.972	0.943	21900	20835	19238	16577
950	1	21538	21326	21008	20479	0.990	0.975	0.951	21556	20540	19016	16476
	2	22426	22224	21921	21416	0.990	0.977	0.955	21967	20953	19433	16898
	3	23412	23174	22818	22223	0.989	0.975	0.949	23316	22260	20677	18038
	4	24430	24090	23581	22731	0.986	0.965	0.930	26097	24918	23149	20201
951	1	25411	24923	24190	22969	0.981	0.952	0.904	29466	28079	25999	22532
	2	26202	25501	24451	22699	0.973	0.933	0.866	33016	31354	28861	24705
	3	26479	25683	24489	22499	0.970	0.925	0.850	36183	34228	31296	26409
	4	26926	26137	24953	22980	0.971	0.927	0.853	38725	36507	33180	27635
952	1	27004	26229	25067	23130	0.971	0.928	0.857	40391	37961	34317	28243
	2	26930	26321	25407	23884	0.977	0.943	0.887	40896	38387	34623	28349
	3	26904	26385	25605	24307	0.981	0.952	0.903	41344	38800	34985	28625
	4	26812	26315	25570	24328	0.981	0.954	0.907	41418	38859	35020	28621
953	1	26700	26232	25530	24360	0.982	0.956	0.912	41478	38926	35098	28718
	2	26699	26271	25629	24560	0.984	0.960	0.920	42130	39532	35634	29139
	3	27049	26674	26110	25172	0.986	0.965	0.931	42790	40157	36209	29627
	4	27326	27100	26761	26196	0.992	0.979	0.959	42824	40223	36321	29819

Column group headers: LIQUID ASSETS (million $); Less Reductions According to; ADJUSTED LIQUID ASSETS / UNADJUSTED LIQ. ASSETS; CURRENT LIABILITIES (million $).

TABLE III-4 (continued)

Year	Quarter	(1)	(2)	(3)	(4)	(5)	(6)	(7)	(8)	(9)	(10)	(11)
1954	1	27331	27229	27075	26819	0.996	0.991	0.981	43000	40478	36694	30388
	2	26939	26894	26826	26712	0.998	0.996	0.992	41883	39490	35899	29916
	3	26578	26529	26454	26331	0.998	0.995	0.991	40569	38346	35011	29454
	4	26535	26519	26495	26455	0.999	0.998	0.997	39972	37918	34838	29704
1955	1	26935	26675	26286	25636	0.990	0.976	0.952	39307	37371	34466	29625
	2	27692	27379	26911	26129	0.989	0.972	0.944	39846	37982	35186	30527
	3	28401	28009	27421	26442	0.986	0.965	0.931	40840	38994	36226	31612
	4	29164	28550	27629	26094	0.979	0.947	0.895	42361	40471	37635	32909
1956	1	29210	28567	27602	25994	0.978	0.945	0.890	43713	41696	38670	33627
	2	28737	27761	26297	23857	0.966	0.915	0.830	44997	42753	39387	33770
	3	27882	26833	25260	22639	0.962	0.906	0.812	46124	43647	39932	33739
	4	26953	25919	24368	21783	0.962	0.904	0.808	46933	44288	40321	33708
1957	1	26370	25355	23831	21293	0.962	0.904	0.807	48013	45190	40955	33896
	2	26049	25263	24085	22121	0.970	0.925	0.849	48958	46004	41572	34187
	3	25930	25262	24259	22588	0.974	0.936	0.871	49558	46544	42022	34487
	4	25709	25132	24265	22822	0.978	0.944	0.888	49343	46303	41743	34144
1958	1	25340	24932	24319	23298	0.984	0.960	0.919	48204	45225	40756	33308
	2	25079	24727	24199	23320	0.986	0.965	0.930	46878	44009	39707	32535
	3	24882	24531	24004	23126	0.986	0.965	0.929	45510	42764	38645	31781
	4	25161	24840	24358	23556	0.987	0.968	0.936	44567	41939	37997	31425
1959	1	26008	25608	25008	24008	0.985	0.962	0.923	45039	42481	38643	32247
	2	27159	26784	26221	25283	0.986	0.965	0.931	46685	44160	40373	34061
	3	28125	27704	27073	26021	0.985	0.963	0.925	48176	45618	41780	35384
	4	28577	28066	27299	26021	0.982	0.955	0.911	49885	47238	43267	36649
1960	1	28565	28007	27170	25774	0.980	0.951	0.902	51396	48614	44440	37484

TABLE III-4 (continued)

Year	Quar-ter	QUICK RATIO Actual	Col.2 + Col.9	Col.3 + Col.10	Col.4 + Col.11	CURRENT ASSETS (million $) Actual	Less Reductions According to: Col.3 Table 3	Col.5 Table 3	Col.6 Table 3	CURRENT RATIO Actual	Col.17 + Col.9	Col.18 + Col.10	Col.19 + Col.11
		(12)	(13)	(14)	(15)	(16)	(17)	(18)	(19)	(20)	(21)	(22)	(23)
1947	1												
	2												
	3												
	4	0.865				56840				2,782			
1948	1	0.850	0.861	0.880	0.921	58416	57737	56719	55022	2.760	2.872	3.064	3.471
	2	0.830	0.841	0.860	0.899	59947	59256	58221	56494	2.748	2.860	3.054	3.464
	3	0.810	0.824	0.847	0.896	61741	61079	60085	58430	2.735	2.853	3.057	3.492
	4	0.796	0.810	0.834	0.884	63154	62500	61518	59882	2.737	2.857	3.065	3.508
1949	1	0.795	0.820	0.863	0.955	64114	63687	63047	61979	2.753	2.886	3.117	3.610
	2	0.823	0.851	0.900	1.005	64683	64320	63775	62868	2.796	2.933	3.167	3.668
	3	0.876	0.909	0.965	1.083	64867	64576	64138	63410	2.867	3.004	3.240	3.738
	4	0.944	0.981	1.044	1.176	64870	64635	64281	63693	2.962	3.102	3.341	3.842
1950	1	0.999	1.038	1.105	1.243	65238	65026	64708	64179	3.027	3.166	3.403	3.895
	2	1.021	1.061	1.128	1.267	66700	66498	66195	65690	3.036	3.174	3.406	3.887
	3	1.004	1.041	1.104	1.232	69304	69066	68710	68115	2.972	3.103	3.323	3.776
	4	0.936	0.967	1.019	1.125	73439	73099	72590	71740	2.814	2.934	3.136	3.551
1951	1	0.862	0.888	0.930	1.019	78307	77819	77086	75865	2.658	2.771	2.965	3.367
	2	0.794	0.813	0.847	.919	83297	82596	81546	79794	2.523	2.634	2.825	3.230
	3	0.732	0.750	0.782	.852	87507	86711	85517	83527	2.418	2.533	2.733	3.163
	4	0.695	0.716	0.752	.832	90948	90159	88975	87002	2.349	2.470	2.682	3.148
1952	1	0.669	0.691	0.730	.819	93295	92520	91358	89421	2.310	2.437	2.662	3.166
	2	0.659	0.686	0.734	.842	94249	93640	92726	91203	2.305	2.439	2.678	3.217
	3	0.651	0.680	0.732	.849	95154	94635	93855	92557	2.302	2.439	2.683	3.233
	4	0.647	0.677	0.730	.850	95886	95389	94644	93402	2.315	2.455	2.703	3.263
1953	1	0.644	0.674	0.727	.848	96590	96122	95420	94250	2.329	2.469	2.719	3.282
	2	0.634	0.665	0.719	.843	97864	97436	96794	95725	2.323	2.465	2.716	3.285
	3	0.632	0.664	0.721	.850	99197	98822	98558	97320	2.318	2.461	2.722	3.285
	4	0.638	0.674	0.737	.879	99577	99351	99012	98447	2.325	2.470	2.726	3.301

TABLE III-4 (continued)

Year	Quar-ter	(13)	(12)	(14)	(15)	(16)	(17)	(18)	(19)	(20)	(21)	(22)	(23)
1954	1	0.636	0.673	0.738	.883	99572	99470	99316	99060	2.316	2.457	2.707	3.260
	2	0.643	0.681	0.747	.893	98798	98753	98685	98571	2.359	2.501	2.749	3.295
	3	0.655	0.692	0.756	.894	97812	97763	97688	97565	2.411	2.549	2.790	3.312
	4	0.664	0.699	0.761	.891	97770	97754	97730	97690	2.446	2.578	2.805	3.289
1955	1	0.685	0.714	0.763	.865	98388	98128	97739	97089	2.503	2.626	2.836	3.277
	2	0.695	0.721	0.765	.856	99963	99650	99182	98400	2.509	2.624	2.819	3.223
	3	0.695	0.718	0.757	.836	102197	101805	101217	100238	2.502	2.610	2.794	3.170
	4	0.688	0.705	0.734	.793	105116	104502	103581	102046	2.481	2.582	2.752	3.100
1956	1	0.668	0.685	0.714	.773	107886	107243	106278	104670	2.468	2.572	2.748	3.113
	2	0.639	0.649	0.668	.706	110438	109462	107998	105558	2.454	2.560	2.742	3.125
	3	0.604	0.615	0.633	.671	112530	111481	109908	107287	2.440	2.554	2.752	3.180
	4	0.574	0.585	0.604	.646	114192	113158	111607	109022	2.433	2.555	2.768	3.234
1957	1	0.549	0.561	0.582	.628	115953	114938	113414	110876	2.415	2.543	2.769	3.271
	2	0.532	0.549	0.579	.647	117470	116684	115506	113542	2.399	2.536	2.778	3.321
	3	0.523	0.543	0.577	.655	118663	117995	116992	115321	2.394	2.535	2.784	3.344
	4	0.521	0.543	0.581	.668	119070	118493	117626	116183	2.413	2.559	2.818	3.403
1958	1	0.526	0.551	0.597	.699	118144	117736	117123	116102	2.451	2.603	2.874	3.486
	2	0.535	0.562	0.609	.717	116986	116634	116106	115227	2.496	2.650	2.924	3.542
	3	0.547	0.574	0.621	.728	116083	115732	115205	114327	2.551	2.706	2.981	3.597
	4	0.565	0.592	0.641	.750	116051	115730	115248	114446	2.604	2.759	3.033	3.642
1959	1	0.577	0.603	0.647	.745	117961	117561	116961	115961	2.619	2.767	3.027	3.596
	2	0.582	0.607	0.649	.742	121314	120939	120376	119438	2.599	2.739	2.982	3.507
	3	0.584	0.607	0.648	.735	124385	123964	123333	122281	2.582	2.717	2.952	3.456
	4	0.573	0.594	0.631	.710	127316	126805	126038	124760	2.552	2.684	2.913	3.404
1960	1	0.556	0.576	0.611	.688	129878	129320	128483	127687	2.527	2.660	2.891	3.400

TABLE III-4 (continued)

		LIQUID ASSETS SALES				LIQUID ASSETS PLANT & EQUIPMENT OUTLAYS			
Year	Quar-ter	Actual (24)	Col.2 + Sales (25)	Col.3 + Sales (26)	Col.4 + Sales (27)	Actual (28)	Col.2 + Col. 15 Table 3 (29)	Col.3 + Col. 15 Table 3 (30)	Col.4 + Col. 15 Table 3 (31)
1947	1								
	2								
	3								
	4	0.116				2.031			
1948	1	0.113	0.109	0.103	0.092	1.994	1.918	1.805	1.617
	2	0.110	0.100	0.100	0.089	1.979	1.903	1.790	1.602
	3	0.107	0.103	0.097	0.088	1.995	1.923	1.815	1.634
	4	0.106	0.102	0.096	0.087	2.011	1.940	1.832	1.653
1949	1	0.106	0.104	0.100	0.094	2.108	2.060	1.987	1.865
	2	0.110	0.107	0.104	0.099	2.279	2.235	2.170	2.062
	3	0.116	0.114	0.111	0.107	2.528	2.491	2.435	2.342
	4	0.123	0.121	0.119	0.116	2.891	2.858	2.809	2.727
1950	1	0.128	0.126	0.124	0.121	3.197	3.165	3.118	3.039
	2	0.128	0.126	0.125	0.122	3.409	3.378	3.333	3.256
	3	0.125	0.123	0.121	0.118	3.452	3.416	3.363	3.277
	4	0.120	0.118	0.115	0.111	3.261	3.258	3.148	3.034
1951	1	0.114	0.112	0.109	0.103	3.098	3.038	2.949	2.800
	2	0.111	0.108	0.104	0.096	2.838	2.762	2.648	2.459
	3	0.111	0.107	0.102	0.094	2.619	2.540	2.422	2.225
	4	0.110	0.107	0.102	0.094	2.481	2.409	2.299	2.118
1952	1	0.111	0.107	0.103	0.095	2.386	2.318	2.215	2.044
	2	0.111	0.108	0.104	0.098	2.314	2.261	2.183	2.052
	3	0.110	0.107	0.104	0.099	2.318	2.273	2.206	2.094
	4	0.107	0.105	0.102	0.097	2.305	2.262	2.198	2.091
1953	1	0.104	0.102	0.099	0.095	2.286	2.246	2.186	2.086
	2	0.101	0.099	0.097	0.093	2.280	2.243	2.189	2.097
	3	0.100	0.098	0.096	0.093	2.275	2.249	2.201	2.122
	4	0.102	0.101	0.099	0.097	2.295	2.284	2.247	2.200
1954	1	0.103	0.103	0.102	0.101	2.315	2.306	2.293	2.271
	2	0.104	0.104	0.104	0.103	2.328	2.324	2.319	2.309
	3	0.105	0.105	0.104	0.104	2.340	2.336	2.329	2.318
	4	0.105	0.105	0.104	0.104	2.404	2.403	2.400	2.397

TABLE III-4 (continued)

Year	Quar-ter	(24)	(25)	(26)	(27)	(28)	(29)	(30)	(31)
1955	1	0.104	0.103	0.101	0.099	2.513	2.489	2.453	2.392
	2	0.104	0.102	0.101	0.098	2.599	2.570	2.526	2.452
	3	0.103	0.101	0.099	0.096	2.604	2.568	2.514	2.424
	4	0.102	0.100	0.096	0.091	2.549	2.495	2.415	2.281
1956	1	0.100	0.097	0.094	0.088	2.404	2.351	2.272	2.139
	2	0.096	0.093	0.088	0.080	2.195	2.121	2.009	1.822
	3	0.092	0.089	0.084	0.075	1.988	1.913	1.801	1.614
	4	0.088	0.084	0.079	0.071	1.803	1.733	1.629	1.457
1957	1	0.084	0.081	0.076	0.068	1.701	1.636	1.537	1.374
	2	0.082	0.080	0.076	0.070	1.633	1.584	1.510	1.387
	3	0.081	0.079	0.075	0.070	1.608	1.566	1.504	1.401
	4	0.080	0.079	0.076	0.071	1.611	1.575	1.520	1.430
1958	1	0.081	0.080	0.078	0.074	1.651	1.624	1.584	1.518
	2	0.082	0.081	0.080	0.076	1.778	1.753	1.715	1.653
	3	0.082	0.081	0.079	0.076	1.950	2.086	2.041	1.966
	4	0.083	0.081	0.080	0.077	2.201	2.173	2.131	2.060
1959	1	0.083	0.082	0.080	0.077	2.366	2.240	2.275	2.184
	2	0.083	0.082	0.080	0.077	2.453	2.419	2.368	2.283
	3	0.084	0.083	0.081	0.078	2.461	2.424	2.369	2.277
	4	0.085	0.083	0.081	0.077	2.368	2.326	2.262	2.156
1960	1	0.083	0.082	0.079	0.075	2.257	2.213	2.147	2.036

SOURCES:
Col. 1: See Appendix Table III-3B, Col. 8.
Col. 8: See Appendix Tables III-3B and III-3C, Current Liabilities = STL plus A/P plus FYTA
plus OCL.
Col. 12: See Table III-3, Col. 29.
Col. 16: See Table III-3, Col. 33.
Col. 20: See Table III-3, Col. 37.
Col. 24: See Table III-3, Col. 41.
Col. 28: See Table III-3, Col. 45.

actually observed. In circumstances where the hypothesized superior foresight prevailed, the ratio of quick assets to plant and equipment would have been higher. Hence, the actual magnitudes may depart markedly from desired magnitudes, contrary to an implicit assumption of the analysis.

Second, nonlinear responses may occur when ratios drop below a certain level. In a relative sense the difference between 1.6 and 1.4 in the liquid asset to plant and equipment ratio might not seem large but if a "critical value" of 1.5 is postulated, 1.4 in fact might be viewed as "intolerable."

Third, all appraisals of monetary policy depend in a most important way on the micro distributions. It is possible that the distribution of quick ratios, current ratios, and quick asset-sales turnover ratios, plus the other measures, change systematically over the cycle. For instance, even though the aggregate quick ratio deteriorates during the cyclical upswing, the effects of monetary policy might be much greater than those indicated if a few firms became progressively more liquid while the vast majority of firms became increasingly illiquid in the late recovery stage. It is to be hoped that subsequent analyses of the relationship between financial policies and investment will utilize micro distributions in addition to the aggregate figures.

V. MANUFACTURING INVESTMENT AND FINANCE IN THE LONG RUN

A. Introduction

As shown, a real financial squeeze often occurs towards the end of a business cycle recovery when fixed assets are being most rapidly accumulated. In particular, financial pressures would be distributed much more evenly over the cycle if retained earnings increased uniformly throughout the upswing instead of stabilizing early in the recovery. While monetary policy might alter this pattern, for example, by supporting an inflation in which price advances kept ahead of wage advances (a phenomenon much discussed in earlier business cycle literature under the heading of Forced Saving), it is unlikely that this would be attempted. Hence, in what follows, internal finance generated in the long run will be assumed to have similar cyclical characteristics as in the past. Given this continuity (an assumption to be relaxed in Section E) the effect of much higher interest rates in the long run will hinge primarily on three considerations—capital intensity, depreciation policy and, most crucial of all, rate of asset growth.

B. Capital Intensity

A reduction in capital requirements per unit of output characterized United States manufacturing from the 1920's to the 1940's according to the National Bureau of Economic Research Capital Markets Project. Thereafter the various capital output ratios remained approximately constant. Technological considerations probably dominated the trend. Should this trend resume, financial requirements would be correspondingly reduced.

A prolonged period of high interest rates would lead to the same qualitative conclusion according to classical capital theory. The widely accepted logic of capital theory suggests that less capital relative to labor will ensue from higher (relative) capital costs. Both technical factors as revealed in historical studies of the economy, and capital theory provide qualitative support for the belief that higher capital costs will, ceteris paribus, restrict capital accumulation and also corresponding financial needs. It should be noted that reduced investment and financing because of high interest rates is a consequence of monetary policy and a (qualitative) tribute to its effectiveness, unlike the other considerations under discussion which exogenously reduce dependence on capital markets and hence weaken the potential effectiveness of monetary policy.

C. Depreciation Expense

Increasing depreciation flows (see Section III-E) also suggest decreasing requirements for external finance by manufacturing concerns. Several years from now the vast preponderance of the capital stock will be made up of assets valued at high (relative to pre-World War II) postwar prices. This steady revaluation process, together with the more liberal depreciation provisions of the 1954 Internal Revenue Code, have already contributed to a marked upward shift in this component of gross corporate income. Once both effects have fully worked out, and assuming that depreciation allowances continue to be considered inappropriate sources for corporate dividends, a new equilibrium in the relation between internal and external finance should exist, bringing with it greater average insulation from external capital markets than prevailed in the past ten to fifteen years.

D. Rate of Growth

The most critical determinant of external financing is the rate of growth in assets and output. As already observed during periods of rapid cyclical expansion of fixed assets the financing problem is most severe and resort to external funds is at a maximum. While it would be extremely dangerous to impute this cyclical behavior to secular developments, a relationship between secular rate of growth and external financing can be theoretically established.[1]

---

[1]Edwin Kuh, Capital Stock Growth, Chapter 2, unpublished. The remainder of this section has been taken from Chapter 2 with slight modifications.

The growth model to be developed is derived from that of Evsey D. Domar in an article, "The Case for Accelerated Depreciation."[2] More elaborate or different models might be more cogant, although it is to be hoped that the relevant components have been assembled. The most basic assumptions of the model are:

(1) gross investment grows at a constant relative rate per annum; (2) the capital assets have a constant average length of life; and (3) straight line depreciation methods are used.

The first assumption, constant relative rate of growth per annum in investment, does not accord with the actuality of firm behavior, though the growth pattern does seem to provide a trend around which short-run, cyclical variations in investment occur. The second assumption is sufficiently convenient and relevant to merit its tentative acceptance. It embodies, of course, the famous "one horse shay" assumption that the productive capacity of assets are maintained at the same average level until the end of life. The fact that the following analysis is concerned with average length of life lends somewhat more credence to the proposition than would apply to an individual piece of equipment. The third assumption about straight line depreciation does violence to current practice, but may provisionally be accepted as a linear approximation. The results to be reported would differ quantitatively but not qualitatively if they were revised to incorporate current depreciation methods.

Let us introduce the following set of symbols:

K = Gross capital stock
I = Gross investment
P = Net profit after taxes
D = Dividends
E = External funds
F = Depreciation expense
R = Retained earnings
g = Rate of growth of all flow magnitudes
m = Average life of capital assets
p = Net profit rate $(P_t + K_t)$
r' = P/D = Actual divident payout rate
v = Present value of an annuity$\underline{3}/= \dfrac{1 - (1 + g)^{-m}}{g}$

[2] Evsey D. Domar, The Quarterly Journal of Economics, Vol. 37 (November 1953), pp. 493-519. This has been reprinted as Essay 8 in Essays in the Theory of Economic Growth, New York, 1957, pp. 195-222, see especially pp. 200-201. Also, Robert Eisner, "Depreciation Allowances,Replacement Requirements and Growth," American Economic Review, Vol. 42, No. 5 (December 1952), pp. 820-31.

[3] The annuity value enters into the series sum of equation (1) and has no significance other than serving as a convenient computational device.

On the assumption of a constant growth rate of investment,

$$(1) \quad K_t = I_t \sum_{n=1}^{m} (1 + g)^{-n} = I_t \left[\frac{1 - (1 + g)^{-m}}{g} \right] = I_t v .$$

Straight line depreciation is a constant fraction of the gross capital stock, namely the reciprocal of asset life and therefore can be expressed as:

$$(2) \quad F_t = \frac{K_t}{m} = \frac{I_t v}{m} .$$

We will adopt the assumption of a constant profit margin, which is plausible in a long-run context, although it is implausible cyclically.

$$(3) \quad P_t = p K_t = p I_t v .$$

The concept of a constant long-run payout will also be used here.

$$(4) \quad D_t = r'P_t .$$

$$(5) \quad R_t = (1 - r')P_t .$$

Combining (3) and (5), we find:

$$(6) \quad R_t = (1 - r')p K_t = (1 - r')p I_t v ,$$

where $(1 - r')p$ is the rate of retained profit on gross capital stock.

All that remains is the definition of total financing, which is simply:

$$(7) \quad I_t = R_t + F_t + E_t .$$

Substituting relations (2) and (6) into (7) for F_t and R_t, we have:

$$(8) \quad I_t = (1 - r')p I_t v + \frac{I_t v}{m} + E_t .$$

Dividing (8) through by I_t yields (9):

$$(9) \quad 1 = v \left[(1 - r')p + \frac{1}{m} \right] + \frac{E_t}{I_t} .$$

Finally, if we make the assumption that external funds too are obtained <u>on the average</u> at an exponential rate, the fraction $\frac{E_t}{I_t}$ will be constant through time for other given parameters also. Hence, equation (9) provides an expression for the proportion of funds originating respectively from retained earnings, depreciation and external funds.[4]

Table III-5 illustrates hypothetical growth rates and the corresponding fraction of funds obtained externally for a variety of different growth rates, profit rates, dividend payouts and depreciation rates.[5] While it would be useless to discuss at great length what the table reveals by itself, a few observations are in order concerning the values likely to be encountered when investigating actual data for manufacturing industry. For illustrative purposes, consider twenty-five year asset life as representative. Then, choosing a typical dividend payout of 50 percent, firms earning a 10 percent profit can grow slightly in excess of 7 percent per year without external financing. Many industries can reach or exceed the 10 percent net profit rate in boom years, but as a long-run average, 5 percent is a more reasonable figure when it is recalled that the relevant profit rate is net income after tax divided by gross fixed assets.[6] However, the 10 percent and 5 percent rates constitute a useful bracket. In the 5 percent profit rate situation, again for a 50 percent payout, firms can grow at about a 4 percent rate in the absence of external funds. To attain 9 percent growth, which is a very fast rate indeed, outside funds must be sought at a 35 percent ratio to the total of funds generated from all sources. Even with the

---

[4]If total, not just fixed assets are also growing at the same rate, then a further proportionality constant will be required, a point that should be mentioned for the sake of completeness.

[5]Whereas the original conception underlying this table can be found in E. D. Domar, op. cit., the variables selected are slightly different. Domar uses as a profit rate net income after tax and depreciation divided by net fixed assets, while we use the same profit numerator but gross fixed assets in the denominator. This construction is more practical for explaining gross asset growth, since the symmetrical treatment of net profit and depreciation lead to the ratio of gross retentions from net income and depreciation divided by gross fixed assets, a profit rate uninfluenced by arbitrary changes in the denominator resulting from changes in depreciation accounting methods. See equation (9) for the basic formulation from which values in Table III-5 have been derived.

[6]For all manufacturing, fourth quarter profit rates on an annual basis for the years 1954-57 were respectively, 10 percent, 13 percent, 12 percent, 9 percent. These rates are net profit divided by book value of gross fixed assets from various copies of the SEC-FTC publication, Quarterly Financial Report for Manufacturing Corporations. If these had instead been gross fixed assets at replacement cost, all the rates would have been less than 10 percent, although some high profit industries earning rates are substantially in excess of those cited here.

TABLE III-5

Growth Rates and Sources of Funds

Attainable Growth Rate	10% Profit Rate External Funds ÷ Total Funds for Alternative Dividend Payouts			5% Profit Rate External Funds ÷ Total Funds for Alternative Dividend Payouts		
	$r' = .80$	$r' = .50$	$r' = .30$	$r' = .80$	$r' = .50$	$r' = .30$
20-year asset life:						
1%	.00	.00	.00	.00	.00	.00
3%	.00	.00	.00	.11	.00	.00
5%	.13	.00	.00	.25	.07	.00
7%	.26	.00	.00	.36	.21	.10
9%	.36	.09	.00	.45	.31	.22
10½%	.42	.18	.02	.51	.38	.30
25-year asset life:						
1%	.00	.00	.00	.00	.00	.00
3%	.00	.00	.00	.13	.00	.00
5%	.16	.00	.00	.30	.08	.00
7%	.30	.00	.00	.42	.24	.13
9%	.41	.12	.00	.51	.36	.26
10½%	.48	.21	.04	.36	.44	.34
35-year asset life:						
1%	.00	.00	.00	.00	.00	.00
3%	.00	.00	.00	.17	.00	.00
5%	.20	.00	.00	.37	.12	.00
7%	.37	.00	.00	.50	.30	.18
9%	.49	.17	.00	.59	.43	.33
10½%	.55	.28	.08	.64	.50	.43

Note: Based on Equation 9.

extremely low dividend payout rate of 30 percent, a quarter of total funds necessary to finance a 9 percent rate of growth would have to come from external funds.

In summary, only if the rate of growth of output and investment proceed at very high rates, much higher than those observed in the past decade, will capital market contacts by manufacturing exceed present average levels.

E. Dividend Policy

The preceding discussion assumed that dividend policy remained essentially unchanged. This need not be so. Using the basic analytical framework devised by John Lintner,[7] it is possible that if the rate of growth were to increase rapidly, target dividend payouts and reaction coefficients would diminish, leading to a greater rate of retained earnings. It is entirely possible that the manufacturing sector would, given time to adjust, frustrate the potentially greater dependence on external capital markets which would be thrust ceteris paribus, upon it by a high rate of growth. We do not consider it unlikely that a prime consideration of many business concerns would be to keep external financing down to a pre-assigned magnitude, because of managerial distaste for external financing,[8] and also because present tax laws place a premium on using retained earnings instead of new equity issues.

---

[7]John Lintner, "Distribution of Incomes of Corporations Among Dividends, Retained Earnings and Taxes," Proceedings of the American Economic Review, Vol. 46, No. 2, May 1956. Lintner, through interviews and regression estimates has concluded that individual enterprises change their dividends according to the following equation:

(10) $\Delta D_t = c(D_t^* - D_{t-1}) + a.$

D_t^* represents the desired dividend and c is a reaction coefficient, assumed to be a positive fraction that reflects speed of adjustment. D* in turn is determined by the firm's desire to pay out a constant fraction of profits so that:

(11) $D^* = rP_t.$

We can rewrite (10) as:

(12) $D_t = c(rP_t - D_{t-1}) + a.$

Then

(13) $D_t = crP_t + (1 - c)D_{t-1} + a.$

[8]These reasons have been catalogued in Chapter II of Meyer and Kuh, The Investment Decision.

VI. PUBLIC UTILITIES AND CYCLICAL FINANCE

A. Introduction

Public utilities are a strong influence in both real and monetary capital markets and in addition possess unique institutional characteristics. As such, they warrant separate treatment from manufacturing.[1] Electrical and gas public utilities floated new securities equal or exceeding in value those of the manufacturing sector in nearly every postwar year as shown in Table III-6. Thus, unlike the manufacturing sector, public utilities rely heavily upon external financing, a fact attributable both to their history as a regulated industry and extremely heavy financial requirements imposed by the large quantities of fixed capital required per dollar of revenue.[2] Public utility assets, moreover, consist predominantly of plant and equipment with little extra for working capital.

In Section B, the cyclical record of postwar utility investment is presented. Generally speaking, the public utility investment pattern was cyclically uncorrelated with manufacturing investment in the trough and early upswing but coincided with peak levels of manufacturing investment at the end of a cyclical recovery. In Section C the impact of recent utility regulation doctrine is examined to discover how interest rate changes might affect utility tariffs. The remaining Sections, D and E, discuss the implications for investment behavior of the relatively small liquidity stock and the generally excellent capital market relations of the public utilities.

B. Cyclical Timing of Investment

The most outstanding cyclical attribute of public utilities postwar asset growth has been its comparative acyclical character (Appendix Charts III-2E and III-2G) and the corresponding pattern of its external financing (Appendix Charts III-7E and III-7G). Real output has grown steadily and rapidly with some diminution in the rate of growth towards the end of the present decade as can be seen in Appendix Charts III-2E and III-2G. In 1954, however, net capital raised by public utilities decreased from the preceding year, although total finance acquired (including that for retirement of securities)

---

[1] In addition to sources cited explicitly in the text, we have benefited greatly from discussions with Fred Morrissey, M. A. Adelman, and Morris Mendelson. They are in no way responsible for the constructions or misconstructions made of their remarks.

[2] A prime reference on asset acquisition and financing by public utilities will be found in a study by the National Bureau of Economic Research, Melville J. Ulmer, Capital in Transportation, Communications, and Public Utilities: Its Formation and Financing, Princeton, 1960.

TABLE III-6

New Capital Raised by Corporations, 1948-1959

Year	Total $ billions	Manufacturing $ millions	Manufacturing percent	Commercial and Miscellaneous $ millions	Commercial and Miscellaneous percent	Transport $ millions	Transport percent	Public Utilities $ millions	Public Utilities percent	Communications $ millions	Communications percent
1948	6,094	2,126	34.9	382	6.3	691	11.3	2,005	32.9	890	14.6
1949	5,001	1,347	26.9	310	6.2	784	15.7	2,043	40.9	517	10.3
1950	4,350	1,026	23.6	474	10.9	609	14.0	1,927	44.3	314	7.2
1951	6,672	2,846	42.7	462	6.9	438	6.6	2,326	34.9	600	9.0
1952	8,269	3,713	44.9	512	6.2	758	9.2	2,539	30.7	747	9.0
1953	6,959	2,128	30.6	502	7.2	553	7.9	2,905	41.7	871	12.5
1954	6,702	2,044	30.5	831	12.4	501	7.5	2,675	39.9	651	9.7
1955	7,009	2,397	34.2	769	11.0	544	7.8	2,254	32.2	1,045	14.9
1956	8,570	3,336	38.9	682	8.0	694	8.1	2,474	28.9	1,384	16.1
1957	10,747	4,104	38.2	579	5.4	802	7.5	3,821	35.6	1,441	13.4
1958	9,809	3,265	33.3	867	8.8	778	7.9	3,605	36.8	1,294	13.2
1959	7,591	1,941	25.6	812	10.7	942	12.4	3,189	42.0	707	9.3

SOURCE: Federal Reserve Bulletin, various issues, table entitled "New Security Issues." This table records new securities issued by corporations maturing in more than one year sold for cash in the United States. The data reported here are only for net proceeds intended for new capital, excluding net proceeds for retirement of securities.

far exceeded the previous year's long-term capital issues. The decline in net new issues (see Table III-6) continued into 1955, increasing only slightly in 1956. The drop from 1954, continuing for two more years, was not closely geared to the business cycle in this period. The growth in Telephone Company assets did not reflect business conditions (Appendix Chart III-2B) even though its output did (Appendix Chart III-1B).

An abrupt increase in new financing in 1957 and 1958, however, did coincide with a marked rise in plant and equipment outlays in 1957 and 1958. It is important to note, though, that investment outlays of the electrical utility industry appear to lag considerably behind the business cycle as measured by GNP. This stands in contrast to aggregate manufacturing plant and equipment outlays which coincides closely with levels of GNP.[3] As Murray Foss and Walter Leibowitz have observed:

> Since [public utility investment] programs require a longer-than-average time for completion, investment has at times lagged turning points in over-all investment; thus, in years following downturns and recoveries, capital outlays for electric facilities have given a contracyclical appearance. In 1958, for example, when total plant and equipment expenditures decreased about 1/6th, investment in electric facilities remained essentially unchanged; it declined by about 10 percent in 1959, however, when the cyclical recovery in other plant and equipment outlays was getting under way.

> Similarly, investment in the industry rose in 1949, when elsewhere it was declining, but decreased in 1950 when the over-all recovery in capital expenditures had begun. In the 1954 business recession utility investment fell and the decline continued in the recovery year 1955.[4]

Since the external financing of public utilities is a moderately constant proportion of total utility financing (Appendix Charts III-6E and III-6G), it follows that demands upon the capital markets in general follow the public utility fixed asset investment pattern. Hence, to the extent that a prime monetary policy objective is to damp cyclical fluctuations, the electric utility investment pattern is already basically favorable to that objective, except at cyclical peaks. Furthermore, the pattern appears to originate from a long gestation and planning period in investment expenditures. Variations

---

[3]See an excellent article on "Investment in Fuel and Power Industries," Survey of Current Business (June 1960), by Murray F. Foss and Walter Leibowitz, pp. 18-24.

[4]Foss and Leibowitz, op. cit., pp. 19-20.

in monetary policy therefore tend to exert a weak and unsure influence. Moreover, the public utility regulatory process and the manner
in which regulation relates to monetary policy tends to further weak-
en the relationship between public utility investment and monetary
policy.

C. Regulation

Generally stated, the purpose of public utility regulation is to
prevent the full exploitation of a local monopoly position. Therefore,
regulatory commissions strive to establish rates below the freely
chosen monopoly set of rates but high enough, in some sense, to
compensate the investors. The precise content of what constitutes
adequate compensation has had a long, tortuous and interesting
history in the law courts of this country. A most famous case at
the end of the last century, Smyth vs. Ames held that a utility is
entitled to rates which yield a "fair return" on the "fair value" of
its assets. In the ensuing decades much attention was focused on
valuation problems, and in addition, the question arose about what
constituted a fair rate. In general, the state regulatory commissions
agreed on some figure in the neighborhood of 6 percent on total
assets net of depreciation reserves. A drastic change, foreshadowed
in the 1923 Supreme Court decision in Missouri ex rel Southwestern
Bell Telephone Company vs. Public Service Commission was enun-
ciated in 1944 by the Supreme Court in Federal Power Commission
vs. Hope Natural Gas Company. This decision shifted regulatory
commission emphasis from valuation and the rate base to a more
systematic inquiry into what constitutes the "fair rate of return."
The fundamental change was that cost of capital became a dominant
rate level criterion. As one writer on the subject puts the matter:

> It (the Supreme Court) decided in substance that if rates
> produced revenues adequate to cover operating expenses, plus
> fixed charges on bonds and reasonable dividends on stock,
> with something more for surplus to maintain the financial
> integrity of the utility and to attract capital, they cannot be
> condemned as confiscatory.[5]

This shift in emphasis of regulatory proceedings did not eliminate
earlier arguments and problems concerning the rate base but the
1944 decision served to broaden the basis of information on which
regulatory decisions could be made.

In particular, it has become acceptable to many (if not all) state
public utility commissions for rate increases to be made in order

---

[5]Joseph R. Rose, " 'Cost of Capital' in Public Utility Rate Regulation," Virginia Law Review, Vol. 43, No. 7, p. 1081. The preceding
historical summary was also drawn from this article.

to pay for any increase in capital costs. This reorientation of public utility pricing doctrine has obvious implications for monetary policy. If interest rates rise sharply, it is now usually possible for the public utility to recoup the increased interest costs through higher rates. Although an administrative lag of a year to a year and a half may be involved, [6] the reasonable certainty that interest charges can be recouped will tend to encourage public utilities to ignore cyclical variations in interest rates. In short, utilities will not be too worried by higher interest charges if they can get rate increases on the basis of a demonstrated need to pay higher capital costs. They might further reason that interest rates are likely to go down during the next recession so that capital costs will then decrease. An advantage usually accrues to public utilities in these situations since effective pressures to decrease rates tend to be weak in comparison with pressures for increases.

A critical question remains to be answered. Will utilities in fact be able to recoup increased capital charges in higher rates, if granted by regulatory commissions? In short, is the price elasticity of demand for utility services greater or less than unity in the relevant range? Because public utility rates are typically held well below the maximum monopoly profit position and, in addition, there are few strong substitutes, at least in the short run, for most utility outputs, short-run demand elasticities will be small. A major exception is intra-utility competition between natural gas and electricity for certain purposes, although these high cross-elasticities will not greatly affect total demand for utility output or total assets needed in all utilities.

D. Liquidity

A long gestation period is a second important characteristic of capital formation in the electrical utility industry that suggests that the demand for monetary capital is likely to be highly inelastic with respect to interest rates. Once plans are made in an electrical utility, it is perfectly true that a variety of decisions can be altered if the level of business activity changes markedly. Michael Gort, in a review of the capital budget records of a number of electrical utilities, has shown that there is fairly close cyclical coordination in expenditures on generators, but not on the other principal

---

[6] The authors have not acquired enough information on the duration of this lag to have much faith in this estimate. All subsequent inferences dependent on the validity of this rough estimate must be qualified correspondingly. We believe the matter may be sufficiently important to warrant separate study.

categories of electrical utility hardware.[7] The fact remains, however, that internal liquid resources are small (See Appendix Charts III-9B, III-9E, and III-9G) and dividend payments highly regular (the utilities pride themselves on this stability which tends to keep down capital costs), so that the financial flexibility of electrical utilities is extremely slight. To put the matter more simply, when capital outlays are undertaken, corporate utilities simply must raise the funds either shortly in advance or concurrent with the acquisition of capital assets, given their liquid asset structures. Utilities frequently borrow short term to finance construction and then fund the short-term liability when a major project or series of projects have been completed.

E. Capital Market Relations

Utilities are frequent users of the capital market and nearly all of them have excellent bond ratings. Hence, so far as rationing is concerned, such excellent customers of long standing seldom are given a back seat in periods of financial scarcity. These relations are influenced by the fact that many state regulatory commissions forbid no-call provisions in bond issues, a restriction particularly distasteful to financial intermediaries like insurance companies, who will demand commensurately higher rates. Since utilities also appear quite willing to incur the interest charges, for reasons discussed above, and they are unlikely to be excluded from capital markets via rationing, the cyclical impact of monetary policy on plant and equipment outlays is likely to be negligible.

VII. LONG-RUN PUBLIC UTILITY PLANT AND EQUIPMENT
EXPENDITURES

A. Introduction

Section B below describes trends in the use of funds by the public utilities. Without exception, the public utilities have relied increasingly upon internal funds in current decades compared with the beginning of this century. In Section C, dealing with long-run price elasticities, a brief qualitative discussion suggests how unlikely it is that even much higher interest rates would lead to substitution away from aggregate public utility output.

Other factors also tend to minimize the likelihood that large increases in interest rates would appreciably curb utility investment

---

[7]Michael Gort, "The Planning of Investment: A Study of Capital Budgeting in the Electric Power Industry," Journal of Business, University of Chicago, Vol. 24 (April 1951), pp. 79-95; (July 1951), pp. 181-202. His findings are essentially confirmed by Foss and Leibowitz, op. cit.

outlays. One of these, discussed in Section D, is the further exploitation of large-scale production possibilities in electricity generation
which reduce average unit costs. A second, considered in Section E,
is that public utilities are required by law to produce service to
meet demands, so that it is unlikely that serious retardation in the
acquisition of assets will occur as a result of much higher interest
rates. It is possible, however, that some reduction in spare capacity
might ensue from much higher interest rates.

B. Historical Trends in Use of External Funds

Despite heavy dependence upon the capital markets (at least
relative to manufacturing) reliance on external financing by the
public utilities has declined secularly. A new, capital intensive industry will nearly always require relatively large amounts of external financing as an initial condition for acquisition of assets.
Thus, in the thirty-one year period, 1881-1912, electric utilities
met their financial needs 83 percent from external long-term financing and 8 percent from internally generated funds.[1] (The percentages, apart from rounding, do not add to 100 percent because of
short-term fund accruals.) From 1913 through 1937 new issues still
remained high, accounting for about 75 percent of total needs.
Throughout the period, nevertheless, the proportion of internal funds
grew as depreciation steadily increased in relative importance. In
the period 1938-50, net new issues were only 44 percent of total
finance flows while retained profits plus depreciation constituted
60 percent.

The picture is much the same for inter-city railroads, for recent decades a declining industry. Heavy resort was made to net
new issues in the early periods with total net new issues declining
and internal funds dramatically increasing in importance over time.
With some fluctuations, the same general pattern can be observed
for the telephone industry.

While the thirties tend to obscure the smoothness of the observed time series on financing, the observation holds that external
financing by public utilities has been decreasing over the long run.
A major reason for this is the rate of growth of assets, a point
developed by Domar.[2] Domar shows that when assets are growing
exponentially, the proportion of assets financed out of depreciation
will increase as the rate of growth declines. A somewhat different
reason for this relationship has been adduced by Ulmer, who argues

---

[1]Ulmer, op. cit., Table 47, page 151.
[2]Evsey D. Domar, "Depreciation, Replacement, and Growth," in
Essays in the Theory of Economic Growth, Essay 7, 1957, pp. 154-
194.

that capital consumption in excess of depreciation charges decreased rapidly throughout the period for all these industries.[3]

In addition, the rate of return in public service industries is calculated for regulatory purposes on a rate base which includes only the depreciated value of assets. This means that when net fixed assets are a relatively high proportion of gross fixed assets, the true financial rate of return or profit will be relatively high. The higher the rate of profit, of course, the easier it usually is to have internal financing. A consequence is that since the inception of effective regulation of the public utilities in the late twenties and early thirties, the profitability of these industries tends to rise, with a lag because of administrative delays, _after_ any extensive modernization or investment programs which reduce the _average_ age of physical assets. At those points in time just after extensive modernization, therefore, the availability of internal financing tends to rise at a time when demands for investment funds may be relatively low. Accordingly, it may be dangerous to generalize about trends in the ratio of internal financing to total financing until these regulatory influences "have stabilized." In particular, higher ratios of internal to external public utility financing in the fifties may be partly attributable to regulatory actions taken after the very large upsurge in public utility investment in the late forties and early fifties.[4]

While public utilities have increasingly relied on internal finance, especially from depreciation, currently a somewhat greater profit retention rate prevails than existed immediately after the war. Nevertheless, public utility retention rates, as shown in Appendix Charts III-4E and III-4G,[5] are extremely low compared with manufacturing.

Reasons underlying high dividend payouts appear to be twofold. First, some public utility commissions have objected to what they considered "excessive income retention" on the grounds that the

---

[3]See Ulmer, _op. cit._, pp. 158-173.
[4]On the other hand, a declining rate of growth in public utilities could well reverse this profitability picture in the future, assuming regulatory practice remains the same. A relative reduction in profitability induced by a slower rate of growth would, of course, at least partially offset the Domar effect, making it difficult to extrapolate future possibilities. However, a definite trend toward more internal financing is evident for all the public utilities, so that the effects of a changing rate base are insufficient to fully offset the results noted by Domar.
[5]Unlike the other utilities, the Bell System (Appendix Chart III-4C) steadily decreased its dividend payout.

investor should reap the benefit from funds which were generated
out of revenues paid for by the consumer. In Massachusetts some
utility rate cases in the past have used total invested capital net
of retained earnings as the base upon which earnings return was to
be computed, although this particular procedure has not, to our
knowledge, been followed elsewhere. Nevertheless, the implication
exists that unduly large retained earnings might not be considered
an allowable use of funds by the rate-making authorities.

A second reason for high dividend payouts depends on the cost
of capital. This controversial area in capital theory involves a
series of issues whose truth is not of concern here. The fact remains, nevertheless, that a number of utility companies believe
that equity costs of capital will be minimized by high dividend
payouts.

Furthermore, if the rate of growth of demand for assets remains
high, but at a continually decreasing rate, the results previously
cited from Domar (according to which depreciation assumes a
larger and larger fraction of gross capital outlays) support the
belief that historically observed trends might continue. Indeed,
depreciation has increased very rapidly postwar and for each utility
constitutes the preponderant sources of internal funds (See Appendix
Charts III-5B, III-5E, and III-5G). While insulation from capital
markets to the extent observable in manufacturing seems remote,
public utilities are likely to become increasingly less dependent
upon capital markets and will consequently pay less attention to
variations in monetary policy. This is one reason, although a secondary one, for supposing that over the long run public utilities will
not be strongly affected by behavior in interest rates, even should
such rates increase considerably.

C. Long-Run Price and Income Elasticities

If the general level of interest rates were substantially greater
than at present, say around 12 percent instead of less than half that
amount as in recent history, it might be expected that the relatively
capital intensive public utilities would develop tariff structures
that were more expensive relative to other prices in the economy
than is now the case. The process of adjusting utility rates to higher
financial costs would be subject to the administrative lag mentioned
earlier but once the transitional phase had passed, utility charges
probably would be adjusted upward relative to other prices.

It remains to be quantitatively established whether these higher
relative prices for public utility services would lead to large substitution away from utility consuming goods and hence to a reduction
in the demand for utility services, thereby substantially reducing
the demand for utility assets. Here we can only speculate, but these

speculations suggest that it is most improbable that relative price effects will have a major effect on total utility investment, even though it might influence its composition.

The presumption against significant reduction in quantity demanded over the long run because of higher relative prices stems primarily from the belief that even if the price elasticities were quite high on individual utility services, it seems unlikely that the total demand for all such services is very elastic. Since all the major public utilities are quite capital intensive, a shift from one to another (say from electricity to gas) should not greatly lessen total utility demand for physical assets. High capital intensities in the different competing utilities also insure that increased interest rates will tend to increase costs and prices among the different alternatives in roughly equal proportions.

D. Costs and Scale Economies in Electric Utilities

Foss and Leibowitz have found that "despite the sizable changes in materials and labor costs that occurred, the actual costs per unit of capacity addition in steam generating facilities declined somewhat from 1948-49 to 1956-57."[6] This particular result for generating equipment arose largely because costs per unit of output decrease as scale increases, and these large-scale plants have been installed in substantial quantities during the postwar period. There also appears to be considerable additional room for large-scale stations; for some time into the future these scale economies plus other technological advances might counterbalance, at least to some degree, any secular increase in the monetary cost of capital.

E. Demand-Output Relations

A unique characteristic of utilities is the requirement that they "must" provide service to all their consumers of a satisfactory quality more or less on demand. Hence, unless the rate structure becomes extremely unfavorable to the utilities, the rate of investment and corresponding finance will proceed in response to expected levels of quantities demanded. With higher interest rates, less capital intensive techniques would be utilized but, as already noted, the pricing characteristics of this market do not lead one to suppose that pressures in this direction would be overpowering. A number of investigators, including Modigliani and Kisselgoff,[7] have

---

[6]Foss and Liebowitz, op. cit., p. 21.
[7]Avram Kisselgoff and Franco Modigliani, "Private Investment in the Electric Power Industry and the Acceleration Principle," The Review of Economics, Vol. 39, No. 4 (November 1957), pp. 363-379.

found that the flexible acceleration principle explains plant and equipment investment in electrical utilities quite well. This is indeed as it should be, given the requirement that demand must be serviced.By the same token, general measures to curtail demand through reduction in personal income by fiscal policy or other measures would choke off some final demand and hence some utility demand for plant and equipment by increasing excess capacity.

APPENDIX

Tables and Charts

KEY FOR VARIABLES

ymbol	Number	Variable
	1	Net Sales
P	2	Net Profits after Taxes
E	3	Net Profits Retained in Business
E	4	Total Depreciation and Depletion
+ 4	5	Items 3 + 4
	6	Cash on Hand and in Bank
	7	U.S. Government Securities, Including Treasury Notes
+ C	8	Items 6 + 7
/R	9	Total Receivables
JV	10	Inventories
ther C.A.	11	Other Current Assets
FA	12	Net Total, Property, Plant, Equipment
ther NCA	13	Other Non-Current Assets
TL	14	Short Term Loans from Banks
/P	15	Advances, Prepayments by U.S. Government plus Other Notes and Accounts Payable
YTA	16	Federal Income Taxes Accrued
CL	17	Other Current Liabilities, plus Installments on Long Term Debt Due in One Year or Less
5 + Other NCL	18	Item 15 plus Other Non-Current Liabilities
TDB	19	Loans from Banks Due in more than 1 Year
LTD	20	Other Long Term Debt Due in More than 1 Year
	21	Capital Stock, Capital Surplus and Minority Interest

APPENDIX TABLE III-1A

SEC-FTC Quarterly Reports Data on Manufacturing Corporations
for Sample Revisions
(Current Million Dollars)

Year	Quarter	S (1)	NP (2)	RE (3)	DE * (4)	RE+DE (5)	C (6)	G (7)
1947	1	35,383	2,664	1,942	639	2,581	10,113	6,688
19	2	37,198	2,499	1,682	674	2,356	11,389	6,294
	3	37,956	2,436	1,636	704	2,340	11,596	6,411
	4	42,289	2,574	1,186	737	1,923	11,377	6,867
1948	1	41,415	2,895	2,045	775	2,822	11,395	6,726
	2	42,624	2,882	1,950	817	2,770	11,544	6,667
	3	44,345	2,953	1,967	852	2,821	11,739	7,030
	4	45,569	2,978	1,371	917	2,287	11,423	7,143
1949	1	42,213	2,461	1,532	934	2,466	11,362	7,406
	2	41,660	2,065	1,074	935	2,006	12,123	8,133
	3	42,360	2,376	1,501	935	2,435	12,726	9,210
	4	41,979	2,341	552	990	1,533	12,504	9,429
1950	1	42,741	2,471	1,481	997	2,476	12,098	10,106
	2	48,685	3,322	2,244	1,037	3,286	12,912	10,857
	3	54,830	3,850	2,499	1,081	3,588	13,934	11,910
	4	58,129	3,680	1,336	1,114	2,444	13,460	12,477
1951	1	60,821	3,397	2,213	1,124	3,341	13,550	12,538
	2	61,949	3,247	1,983	1,185	3,168	14,238	12,669
	3	58,920	2,477	1,239	1,235	2,474	14,229	12,705
	4	62,797	2,739	891	1,321	2,212	14,873	12,874
1952	1	60,576	2,562	1,303	1,282	2,585	14,262	12,160
	2	61,547	2,602	1,334	1,344	2,679	15,274	11,345
	3	60,983	2,600	1,368	1,394	2,762	15,268	11,562
	4	67,921	2,982	1,247	1,512	2,759	15,163	12,214
1953	1	66,582	2,869	1,600	1,517	3,117	14,362	11,611
	2	69,499	3,060	1,771	1,545	3,316	15,059	11,557
	3	67,341	2,904	1,658	1,590	3,248	15,210	13,019
	4	65,672	2,626	812	1,662	2,480	15,117	13,364
1954	1	61,925	2,635	1,325	1,658	2,987	14,184	11,809
	2	63,846	2,973	1,670	1,703	3,375	14,755	10,296
	3	61,910	2,709	1,361	1,733	3,099	15,304	11,484
	4	65,992	3,122	1,091	1,842	2,941	15,852	12,461

APPENDIX TABLE III-1A (continued)

Year	Quarter	(1)	(2)	(3)	(4)	(5)	(6)	(7)
1955	1	67,364	3,412	1,985	1,850	3,836	15,256	12,336
	2	71,953	3,975	2,542	1,936	4,475	15,482	12,595
	3	71,333	3,836	2,265	1,961	4,227	15,758	13,857
	4	75,996	4,271	1,845	2,048	3,898	15,907	15,443
1956	1	74,517	3,982	2,302	2,071	4,373	14,405	13,373
	2	76,958	4,246	2,508	2,115	4,623	14,603	11,581
	3	74,697	3,670	1,990	2,155	4,145	14,850	11,353
	4	81,084	4,255	1,996	2,256	4,252	15,762	11,885
1957	1	79,649	4,099	2,295	2,253	4,548	14,490	10,957
	2	80,943	4,072	2,255	2,316	4,571	14,669	10,229
	3	79,621	3,737	1,971	2,356	4,327	15,191	10,535
	4	79,826	3,530	1,354	2,443	3,797	15,501	11,263
1958	1	72,486	2,472	640	2,372	3,012	14,293	9,679
	2	74,593	2,840	1,052	2,426	3,478	15,042	8,811
	3	76,191	3,320	1,610	2,465	4,075	15,413	9,524
	4	81,856	4,036	1,986	2,547	4,533	16,002	11,878
1959	1	80,695	3,821	1,982	2,503	4,485	14,753	12,607
	2	88,369	4,858	3,002	2,595	5,597	15,076	13,383
	3	83,136	3,821	1,959	2,530	4,489	14,866	13,935
	4	85,617	3,828	1,477	2,652	4,129	15,276	14,411
1960	1	85,699	3,991	1,990	2,674	4,664	13,842	13,469

* Column 4: Total Depreciation and Depletion for 1947 and first quarter
of 1948 extrapolated linearly from later data.

SOURCE: Quarterly Financial Report for Manufacturing Corporations. Federal
Trade Commission, Securities and Exchange Commission.
The raw data were spliced by Mr. Locke Anderson, University of
Michigan. For the procedure used in splicing see Section II of
text.

APPENDIX TABLE III-1B

SEC-FTC Quarterly Financial Reports Data on Manufacturing
Corporations Adjusted for Sample Revisions
(Current Million Dollars)

Year	Quarter	G+C (8)	A/R (9)	INV (10)	Other CA (11)	NFA (12)	Other NCA (13)	STL (14)
1947	1	16,801	11,655	24,726	1,580	28,496	6,369	2,645
	2	17,673	11,509	25,388	1,286	29,998	6,592	2,301
	3	17,987	12,436	25,849	1,352	31,296	6,760	2,552
	4	18,218	12,473	26,990	1,440	32,714	7,342	2,892
1948	1	18,085	13,427	28,300	1,252	34,364	7,127	2,876
	2	18,165	13,528	28,951	1,335	36,503	7,531	2,700
	3	18,716	14,749	30,008	1,328	37,804	7,602	3,215
	4	18,512	13,811	31,075	1,374	39,997	7,857	3,219
1949	1	18,713	13,871	30,973	1,347	40,779	8,070	3,112
	2	20,196	13,342	29,456	1,260	41,386	8,601	2,446
	3	21,883	14,359	27,910	1,387	42,007	8,528	2,544
	4	21,887	13,307	28,316	1,271	42,922	8,463	2,544
1950	1	22,184	14,450	28,335	1,409	43,304	8,753	2,625
	2	23,750	15,878	28,946	1,526	44,159	8,809	2,424
	3	25,828	18,471	29,955	1,701	44,863	8,838	2,963
	4	25,957	19,505	34,265	1,596	46,424	8,925	3,779
1951	1	26,110	21,350	36,534	1,854	47,663	9,303	4,702
	2	26,914	21,223	39,918	2,007	49,523	9,701	5,177
	3	26,934	22,147	41,633	2,081	50,940	9,915	5,889
	4	27,747	21,859	43,396	2,086	53,077	9,980	6,412
1952	1	26,422	22,765	43,845	2,204	54,033	10,056	6,818
	2	26,618	22,111	42,961	2,186	55,771	10,256	5,974
	3	26,830	24,332	42,868	2,387	56,818	10,438	6,233
	4	27,377	23,851	44,324	2,463	58,438	10,162	6,568
1953	1	25,973	25,120	44,404	2,553	59,093	10,495	6,744
	2	26,615	24,937	44,944	2,477	60,209	10,592	6,437
	3	28,231	25,654	45,321	2,545	61,174	10,640	6,576
	4	28,483	23,149	45,433	2,469	62,824	10,434	6,253
1954	1	25,994	24,057	45,368	2,609	63,138	10,695	5,958
	2	25,047	23,838	44,188	2,805	64,345	10,732	5,147
	3	26,786	24,734	43,396	2,892	65,429	10,872	4,872
	4	28,313	24,344	43,995	2,712	67,123	11,063	4,559

APPENDIX TABLE III-1B (continued)

Year	Quarter	(8)	(9)	(10)	(11)	(12)	(13)	(14)
1955	1	27,593	25,871	44,166	2,872	67,140	11,512	4,786
	2	28,077	26,814	44,447	2,840	67,868	11,778	4,421
	3	29,621	28,837	45,119	3,168	69,047	12,074	4,690
	4	31,363	28,611	47,987	3,077	70,647	12,117	5,006
1956	1	27,778	29,962	50,268	3,573	71,710	13,361	6,055
	2	26,184	30,888	51,908	3,408	73,839	13,854	6,690
	3	26,203	32,805	52,718	3,386	76,092	14,443	7,018
	4	27,647	31,977	54,792	3,270	79,222	13,948	6,686
1957	1	25,447	33,500	56,095	3,585	80,687	14,708	7,839
	2	24,898	33,602	56,395	3,559	82,806	14,953	7,999
	3	25,726	34,426	56,117	3,614	84,645	15,260	7,618
	4	26,764	32,376	56,295	3,879	86,871	15,348	6,942
1958	1	23,972	31,615	55,222	4,115	87,627	16,022	7,232
	2	23,853	32,597	53,221	4,150	88,747	16,498	6,893
	3	24,937	35,095	52,112	4,128	89,401	16,802	6,391
	4	27,880	34,181	52,999	4,126	90,126	16,739	5,765
1959	1	27,360	35,800	54,592	4,813	90,734	17,531	6,535
	2	28,459	37,684	55,756	5,332	91,353	18,280	6,557
	3	28,801	38,609	55,796	5,351	92,596	18,854	6,727
	4	29,687	38,038	57,375	5,310	94,442	18,824	6,653
1960	1	27,311	39,223	60,102	6,179	95,361	19,570	7,887

SOURCE: Quarterly Financial Report for Manufacturing Corporations. Federal
Trade Commission, Securities and Exchange Commission.
The raw data were spliced by Mr. Locke Anderson, University of
Michigan. For the procedure used in splicing see Section II of text.

APPENDIX TABLE III-1C

SEC-FTC Quarterly Financial Reports Data on Manufacturing
Corporations Adjusted for Sample Revisions
(Current Million Dollars)

Year	Quarter	A/P (15)	FYTA (16)	OCL (17)	15+Other (18)*	NCL (19)*	LTDB OLTD (20)*	E (21)
1947	1	6,781	5,780	4,006	7,458	2,106	4,866	29,468
	2	6,826	6,345	4,197	7,545	2,209	5,085	30,441
	3	7,018	6,753	4,329	7,785	2,326	5,334	31,340
	4	7,986	7,174	4,156	8,810	2,464	5,631	32,071
1948	1	7,625	7,211	4,415	8,600	2,613	6,492	33,892
	2	7,819	7,321	4,445	8,853	2,839	6,416	34,986
	3	8,211	7,616	4,637	9,378	3,056	6,673	35,230
	4	8,711	7,837	4,444	9,752	3,316	7,153	35,913
1949	1	7,913	7,542	4,421	8,994	3,358	7,394	36,278
	2	7,630	7,080	4,513	8,761	3,148	7,795	37,182
	3	7,802	6,849	4,440	8,903	2,852	8,260	37,432
	4	8,060	6,422	4,282	7,310	2,289	8,781	38,341
1950	1	8,083	6,441	4,461	9,078	2,234	8,911	38,490
	2	8,999	7,045	4,848	10,051	2,146	8,894	39,126
	3	10,151	8,677	5,237	11,245	2,099	8,854	39,549
	4	11,669	11,745	5,242	12,879	1,987	8,982	40,604
1951	1	11,783	12,921	5,678	13,135	2,101	9,433	40,907
	2	12,586	13,876	5,876	14,065	2,257	10,091	42,070
	3	12,530	15,163	6,115	14,200	2,673	10,053	42,810
	4	13,684	16,493	6,014	15,296	2,677	10,672	43,482
1952	1	13,608	14,852	6,472	14,994	3,099	11,259	43,714
	2	13,692	12,960	6,907	15,047	3,344	12,144	44,225
	3	14,776	13,150	7,331	16,239	3,383	12,741	44,262
	4	16,057	13,067	7,208	17,460	3,519	13,496	44,628
1953	1	15,375	12,323	7,547	16,826	3,544	13,949	45,333
	2	15,528	12,208	7,969	16,924	3,502	14,555	45,471
	3	15,381	14,043	8,129	16,861	3,549	14,826	45,422
	4	15,156	13,959	7,668	16,664	3,284	14,987	45,946
1954	1	17,376	11,028	8,332	18,879	3,031	15,236	46,368
	2	15,417	8,723	8,385	16,853	2,798	15,679	46,794
	3	15,443	10,001	8,559	16,968	2,686	16,165	47,144
	4	16,663	10,803	8,621	18,199	2,694	16,182	47,195

APPENDIX TABLE III-1C (continued)

Year	Quarter	(15)	(16)	(17)	(18)	(19)	(20)	(21)
1955	1	16,580	9,496	9,174	18,321	2,735	16,923	48,746
	2	16,914	9,107	9,383	18,620	2,763	17,160	49,199
	3	17,210	11,433	9,521	18,983	2,887	17,389	49,819
	4	18,837	13,430	9,457	20,695	2,944	17,680	51,139
1956	1	18,158	11,237	9,992	20,192	3,211	18,065	52,290
	2	18,658	9,412	10,202	20,677	3,503	18,916	54,193
	3	19,087	10,763	10,495	21,122	3,722	19,557	54,974
	4	20,033	12,281	10,666	22,307	4,052	20,116	56,254
1957	1	19,644	10,669	11,610	21,601	4,064	20,842	57,030
	2	19,641	9,330	11,870	21,453	4,148	21,045	57,966
	3	19,452	10,483	12,212	21,435	4,097	21,678	58,561
	4	19,511	10,948	11,703	21,389	4,352	21,969	59,619
1958	1	17,726	8,593	11,657	19,791	4,397	22,251	59,978
	2	17,848	6,749	11,945	19,772	4,252	23,210	60,321
	3	18,314	7,633	11,955	20,334	4,235	23,839	61,000
	4	19,338	8,704	11,526	21,297	4,183	24,377	61,767
1959	1	19,535	8,675	12,350	21,522	4,104	24,561	62,658
	2	20,575	9,754	13,133	22,543	4,123	24,742	63,005
	3	19,941	10,319	13,268	21,985	4,187	24,950	63,809
	4	21,823	10,791	12,902	24,152	4,290	25,145	65,116
1960	1	21,432	9,907	13,916	23,830	4,338	25,326	65,888

* Columns 18, 19, 20: Long-term liabilities for 1947 broken down into bank
  loans and other according to their relative weight for 1948-49.

SOURCE: Quarterly Financial Report for Manufacturing Corporations. Federal
Trade Commission, Securities and Exchange Commission.
The raw data were spliced by Mr. Locke Anderson, University of
Michigan. For the procedure used in splicing see Section II of text.

APPENDIX TABLE III-2A

Quarterly Changes in Balance Sheet Items from SEC-FTC Quarter
Financial Reports Data on Manufacturing Corporations Adjust
for Sample Revisions
(Current Million Dollars)

Year	Quarter	S (1)	NP (2)	RE (3)	DE (4)	RE+DE (5)	C (6)	G (7)
1947	1							
	2	1,815	-165	-260	35	-225	1,276	-39
	3	758	- 63	- 46	30	- 16	207	11
	4	4,333	138	-450	33	-417	-219	45
1948	1	- 874	321	859	38	899	18	-14
	2	1,209	- 13	- 95	42	- 52	149	- 5
	3	1,721	71	17	35	51	195	36
	4	1,224	25	-596	65	-534	-316	11
1949	1	-3,356	-517	161	17	179	- 61	26
	2	- 553	-396	-458	1	-460	761	72
	3	700	311	427		429	603	1,07
	4	- 381	- 35	-949	55	-902	-222	21
1950	1	762	130	929	7	943	-406	67
	2	5,944	851	763	40	810	814	75
	3	6,145	528	255	44	302	1,022	1,05
	4	3,299	-170	-1,163	33	-1,144	-474	56
1951	1	2,692	-283	877	10	897	90	6
	2	1,128	-150	-230	61	-173	688	13
	3	-3,029	-770	-744	50	-694	- 9	3
	4	3,877	262	-348	86	-262	644	16
1952	1	-2,221	-177	412	-39	373	-611	-71
	2	971	40	31	62	94	1,012	-81
	3	- 564	- 2	34	50	83	- 6	21
	4	6,938	382	-121	118	- 3	-105	65
1953	1	-1,339	-113	353	5	358	-801	-60
	2	2,917	191	171	28	199	697	- 5
	3	-2,158	-156	-113	45	- 68	151	1,46
	4	-1,669	-278	-846	72	-768	- 93	34
1954	1	-3,747	9	513	- 4	507	-933	-1,55
	2	1,921	338	345	45	388	571	-1,51
	3	-1,936	-264	-309	30	-276	549	1,18
	4	4,082	413	-270	109	-158	548	97
1955	1	1,372	290	894	8	895	-596	-12
	2	4,589	563	557	86	639	226	25
	3	- 620	-139	-277	25	-248	276	1,26
	4	4,663	435	-420	87	-329	149	1,58
1956	1	-1,479	-289	457	23	475	-1,502	-2,07
	2	2,441	264	206	44	250	198	-1,79
	3	-2,261	-576	-518	40	-478	247	- 22
	4	6,387	585	6	101	107	912	53
1957	1	-1,435	-156	299	- 3	296	-1,272	-92
	2	1,294	- 27	- 40	63	23	179	-72
	3	-1,322	-335	-284	40	-244	522	30
	4	205	-207	-617	87	-530	310	72
1958	1	-7,340	-1,058	-714	-71	-785	-1,208	-1,58
	2	2,107	368	412	54	466	749	-86
	3	1,598	480	558	39	597	371	71
	4	5,665	716	376	82	458	589	2,35
1959	1	-1,161	-215	- 4	-44	- 48	-1,249	72
	2	7,674	37	1,020	92	1,112	323	77
	3	-5,233	- 37	-1,043	-65	-1,108	-210	55
	4	2,481	7	-482	122	-360	410	47
1960	1	82	163	513	22	535	-1,434	-94

APPENDIX TABLE III-2B

arterly Changes in Balance Sheet Items From SEC-FTC Quarterly
inancial Reports Data on Manufacturing Corporations Adjusted
for Sample Revisions

(Current Million Dollars)

Year	Quarter	G+C (8)	A/R (9)	INV (10)	Other C/A (11)	NFA (12)	Other NCA (13)	STL (14)
1947	1							
	2	872	-146	662	-294	1,502	223	-344
	3	314	927	461	66	1,298	168	251
	4	231	37	1,141	88	1,418	582	340
1948	1	-133	954	1,310	-188	1,650	-215	-16
	2	80	101	651	83	2,139	404	-176
	3	551	1,221	1,057	- 7	1,301	71	515
	4	-204	-938	1,067	46	2,193	255	4
1949	1	201	60	-102	- 27	782	213	-107
	2	1,483	-529	-1,517	- 87	607	531	-666
	3	1,687	1,017	-1,546	127	621	-73	98
	4	4	-1,052	406	-116	915	-65	
1950	1	297	1,143	19	138	382	290	81
	2	1,566	1,428	611	117	855	56	-201
	3	2,078	2,593	1,009	175	704	29	539
	4	129	1,034	4,310	-105	1,561	87	816
1951	1	153	1,845	2,269	258	1,239	378	923
	2	804	-127	3,384	153	1,860	398	475
	3	20	924	1,715	74	1,417	214	712
	4	813	-288	1,763	5	2,137	65	523
1952	1	-1,325	906	449	113	956	76	406
	2	196	-654	-884	-18	1,738	200	844
	3	212	2,221	- 93	201	1,407	182	259
	4	547	-481	1,456	76	1,620	-276	335
1953	1	-1,404	1,269	80	90	655	333	176
	2	642	-183	540	- 76	1,116	97	-307
	3	1,616	717	377	68	965	48	139
	4	252	-2,505	112	- 76	1,650	-206	-323
1954	1	-2,489	908	- 65	140	314	261	-295
	2	-947	-219	-1,180	196	1,207	37	-811
	3	1,739	896	-792	87	1,084	140	-275
	4	1,527	-390	599	-180	1,694	191	-313
1955	1	-720	1,527	171	160	17	449	227
	2	484	943	281	- 32	728	266	-365
	3	1,544	2,023	672	328	1,179	296	269
	4	1,742	-226	2,868	- 91	1,600	43	316
1956	1	-3,585	1,351	2,281	496	1,063	1,244	1,049
	2	-1,594	926	1,640	-165	2,129	493	635
	3	19	1,917	810	- 22	2,253	589	328
	4	1,444	-828	2,074	-116	3,130	-495	-332
1957	1	-2,200	1,523	1,303	315	1,465	760	1,153
	2	-549	102	300	- 26	2,119	245	160
	3	828	824	-278	55	1,839	307	-381
	4	1,038	-2,050	178	265	2,226	88	-676
1958	1	-2,792	761	-1,073	236	756	674	290
	2	-119	982	-2,001	35	1,120	476	-339
	3	1,084	2,498	-1,109	-22	654	304	-502
	4	2,943	-914	887	- 2	725	-63	-626
1959	1	-520	1,619	1,593	687	608	792	770
	2	1,099	1,884	1,164	519	619	749	22
	3	342	925	40	19	1,243	574	170
	4	886	-571	2,079	-41	1,846	-30	-74
1960	1	-2,376	1,105	2,227	869	919	746	1,234

APPENDIX TABLE III-2C

Quarterly Changes in Balance Sheet Items From SEC-FTC Quarter
Financial Reports Data on Manufacturing Corporations Adjusted
for Sample Revisions

(Current Million Dollars)

Year	Quarter	A/P (15)	FYTA (16)	OCL (17)	15+ONCL (18)	LTDB (19)	OLTD (20)	E (21)
1947	1							
	2	45	565	191	87	103	219	973
	3	192	408	132	240	117	249	899
	4	968	421	-173	1,025	138	297	731
1948	1	-361	37	259	-210	149	861	1,821
	2	194	110	30	253	226	-76	1,094
	3	392	295	192	525	217	257	244
	4	500	221	-193	374	260	480	683
1949	1	-798	-295	-23	-758	42	241	365
	2	-283	-462	92	-233	-210	401	904
	3	172	-231	-73	142	-296	465	250
	4	258	-427	-158	-1,593	-563	521	909
1950	1	23	19	179	1,768	-55	130	149
	2	916	604	387	973	-88	-17	636
	3	1,152	1,632	389	1,194	-47	-40	423
	4	1,518	3,068	5	1,634	-112	128	1,055
1951	1	114	1,176	436	256	114	451	303
	2	803	955	198	930	156	658	1,163
	3	-56	1,287	239	135	416	-38	740
	4	1,154	1,330	-101	1,096	4	619	672
1952	1	-76	-1,641	458	-302	422	587	232
	2	84	-1,892	435	53	245	885	511
	3	1,084	190	424	1,192	39	597	37
	4	1,281	-83	-123	1,221	136	755	366
1953	1	-682	-744	339	-634	25	453	705
	2	153	-115	422	98	-42	606	138
	3	-147	1,835	160	-63	47	271	-49
	4	-225	-84	-461	-197	-265	161	524
1954	1	2,220	-2,931	664	2,215	-253	249	422
	2	-1,959	-2,305	53	-2,026	-233	443	426
	3	26	1,278	174	115	-112	486	350
	4	1,220	802	62	1,231	8	17	51
1955	1	-83	-1,307	553	122	41	741	1,551
	2	334	-389	209	299	28	237	453
	3	296	2,326	138	363	124	229	620
	4	1,627	1,997	-64	1,712	57	291	1,320
1956	1	-679	-2,193	535	-503	267	385	1,151
	2	500	-1,825	210	485	292	851	1,903
	3	429	1,351	293	445	219	641	781
	4	1,246	1,518	171	1,185	330	559	1,280
1957	1	-689	-1,612	944	-706	12	726	776
	2	-103	-1,339	260	-148	84	203	936
	3	-89	1,153	342	-18	-51	633	595
	4	59	465	-509	-46	255	291	1,058
1958	1	-1,785	-2,355	-46	-1,598	45	282	359
	2	122	-1,844	288	-19	-145	959	343
	3	466	884	10	562	-17	629	679
	4	1,024	1,071	-429	963	-52	538	767
1959	1	197	-29	824	225	-79	184	891
	2	1,040	1,079	783	1,021	19	181	347
	3	-634	565	135	-558	64	208	804
	4	1,882	472	-366	2,167	103	195	1,307
1960	1	-391	-884	1,014	-322	48	181	772

SOURCE: See Appendix Tables III-1A, III-1B, III-1C.

APPENDIX TABLE III-3A

r Quarter Moving Sums and Averages for SEC-FTC Manufacturing
(Current Million Dollars)

Quarter	S (1)	N.P. (2)	R.E. (3)	DE (4)	RE DE (5)	C (6)	G (7)
1							
2	(Data recorded at latest quarter entering total or sum)						
3							
4	152,826	10,133	6,446	2,754	9,200	11,119	6,565
1	158,858	10,364	6,549	2,890	9,439	11,439	6,575
2	164,284	10,747	6,817	3,033	9,850	11,478	6,668
3	170,673	11,264	7,148	3,181	10,329	11,514	6,823
4	173,953	11,668	7,333	3,361	10,694	11,525	6,892
1	174,751	11,234	6,820	3,520	10,340	11,517	7,062
2	173,787	10,417	5,944	3,638	9,582	11,662	7,428
3	171,802	9,840	5,478	3,721	9,199	11,909	7,973
4	168,212	9,203	4,659	3,794	8,453	12,179	8,545
1	168,740	9,213	4,608	3,857	8,465	12,363	9,220
2	175,765	10,470	5,778	3,959	9,737	12,560	9,901
3	188,235	11,944	6,776	4,105	10,881	12,862	10,576
4	204,385	13,283	7,560	4,229	11,789	13,101	11,338
1	222,465	14,209	8,292	4,356	12,648	13,464	11,946
2	235,729	14,134	8,031	4,504	12,535	13,796	12,399
3	239,819	12,761	6,771	4,658	11,429	13,869	12,597
4	244,487	11,820	6,326	4,865	11,191	14,223	12,697
1	244,242	10,985	5,416	5,023	10,439	14,401	12,602
2	243,840	10,340	4,767	5,182	9,949	14,660	12,271
3	245,903	10,463	4,896	5,341	10,237	14,919	11,985
4	251,027	10,706	5,252	5,532	10,784	14,992	11,820
1	257,033	11,013	5,549	5,767	11,316	15,017	11,683
2	264,985	11,471	5,986	5,968	11,954	14,963	11,736
3	271,343	11,775	6,276	6,164	12,440	14,949	12,100
4	269,094	11,419	5,841	6,314	12,155	14,937	12,388
1	264,437	11,185	5,566	6,455	12,021	14,893	12,437
2	258,784	11,098	5,465	6,613	12,078	14,817	12,122
3	253,353	10,903	5,168	6,756	11,924	14,840	11,738
4	253,673	11,399	5,447	6,936	12,383	15,024	11,513
1	259,112	12,176	6,107	7,128	13,235	15,292	11,644
2	267,219	13,178	6,979	7,361	14,340	15,474	12,219
3	276,642	14,305	7,883	7,589	15,472	15,587	12,812
4	286,646	15,454	8,637	7,795	16,432	15,601	13,558
1	293,799	16,024	8,954	8,016	16,970	15,388	13,817
2	298,804	16,295	8,920	8,195	17,115	15,168	13,564
3	302,168	16,129	8,645	8,389	17,034	14,941	12,938
4	307,256	16,113	8,796	8,597	17,393	14,905	12,048
1	312,388	16,230	8,789	8,779	17,568	14,926	11,444
2	316,373	16,056	8,536	8,980	17,516	14,943	11,106
3	321,297	16,123	8,517	9,181	17,698	15,028	10,902
4	320,039	15,398	7,875	9,368	17,243	14,963	10,746
1	312,876	13,771	6,220	9,487	15,707	14,914	10,427
2	306,526	12,539	5,017	9,597	14,614	15,007	10,072
3	303,096	12,122	4,656	9,706	14,362	15,062	9,819
4	305,126	12,628	5,288	9,810	15,098	15,188	9,973
1	313,335	13,977	6,630	9,941	16,571	15,303	10,705
2	327,111	15,995	8,580	10,110	18,690	15,311	11,848
3	334,056	16,496	8,929	10,175	19,104	15,174	12,951
4	337,817	16,288	8,420	10,280	18,700	14,993	13,584
1	342,821	16,458	8,428	10,451	18,879	14,765	13,800

1, 2, 3, 4, 5: Obtained by taking four quarter moving sums of data in Appendix Table
        III-1A. Such procedure puts these "flow" magnitudes into annual rates.
6, 7: Obtained by taking four quarter moving averages of data in Appendix Table III-1A.
CE: Obtained by taking four quarter moving averages of data in Appendix Table III-1A.

APPENDIX TABLE III-3B

Four Quarter Moving Sums and Averages for SEC-FTC Manufacturi
(Current Million Dollars)

Year	Quarter	C+G (8)	A/R (9)	INV (10)	Other C.A. (11)	N.F.A. (12)	Other NCA (13)	STL (14)
1947	1							
	2	(Data recorded at latest quarter entering total or sum)						
	3							
	4	17,670	12,018	25,738	1,415	30,626	6,766	2,598
1948	1	17,991	12,461	26,632	1,333	32,093	6,955	2,655
	2	18,114	12,966	27,523	1,345	33,719	7,190	2,755
	3	18,296	13,544	28,560	1,339	35,346	7,401	2,921
	4	18,370	13,879	29,584	1,322	37,167	7,529	3,003
1949	1	18,527	13,990	30,252	1,346	38,771	7,765	3,062
	2	19,034	13,943	30,378	1,327	39,992	8,033	2,998
	3	19,826	13,846	29,854	1,342	41,042	8,264	2,830
	4	20,670	13,720	29,164	1,316	41,774	8,416	2,662
1950	1	21,538	13,865	28,504	1,332	42,405	8,586	2,540
	2	22,426	14,499	28,377	1,398	43,098	8,638	2,534
	3	23,412	15,527	28,888	1,477	43,812	8,716	2,639
	4	24,430	17,076	30,375	1,558	44,688	8,831	2,948
1951	1	25,411	18,801	32,425	1,669	45,777	8,969	3,467
	2	26,202	20,137	35,168	1,790	47,118	9,192	4,155
	3	26,479	21,056	38,088	1,885	48,638	9,461	4,887
	4	26,926	21,645	40,370	2,007	50,301	9,725	5,545
1952	1	27,004	21,999	42,198	2,095	51,893	9,913	6,074
	2	26,930	22,221	42,959	2,139	53,455	10,052	6,273
	3	26,904	22,767	43,268	2,216	54,925	10,183	6,359
	4	26,812	23,265	43,500	2,310	56,265	10,228	6,398
1953	1	26,700	23,854	43,639	2,397	57,530	10,338	6,380
	2	26,699	24,560	44,135	2,470	58,640	10,422	6,496
	3	27,049	24,891	44,748	2,509	59,729	10,472	6,581
	4	27,326	24,715	45,026	2,511	60,825	10,540	6,503
1954	1	27,331	24,449	45,267	2,525	61,836	10,590	6,306
	2	26,939	24,175	45,078	2,607	62,870	10,625	5,984
	3	26,578	23,945	44,596	2,694	63,934	10,683	5,558
	4	26,535	24,243	44,237	2,755	65,009	10,841	5,134
1955	1	26,935	24,697	43,936	2,820	66,009	11,045	4,841
	2	27,692	25,440	44,001	2,829	66,890	11,306	4,660
	3	28,401	26,466	44,432	2,898	67,795	11,607	4,614
	4	29,164	27,533	45,430	2,989	68,676	11,870	4,726
1956	1	29,210	28,556	46,955	3,165	69,818	12,333	5,043
	2	28,737	29,575	48,821	3,307	71,311	12,852	5,610
	3	27,882	30,567	50,720	3,361	73,072	13,444	6,192
	4	26,953	31,408	52,422	3,409	75,216	13,902	6,612
1957	1	26,370	32,293	53,878	3,412	77,460	14,238	7,058
	2	26,049	32,971	55,000	3,450	79,702	14,513	7,386
	3	25,930	33,376	55,850	3,507	81,840	14,717	7,536
	4	25,709	33,476	56,226	3,659	83,752	15,067	7,600
1958	1	25,340	33,005	56,007	3,792	85,487	15,396	7,448
	2	25,079	32,754	55,214	3,940	86,973	15,782	7,171
	3	24,882	32,921	54,213	4,068	88,162	16,168	6,865
	4	25,161	33,372	53,389	4,130	88,975	16,515	6,570
1959	1	26,008	34,418	53,231	4,304	89,752	16,893	6,396
	2	27,159	35,690	53,865	4,600	90,404	17,338	6,312
	3	28,125	36,568	54,786	4,906	91,202	17,851	6,396
	4	28,577	37,532	56,005	5,202	92,281	18,372	6,618
1960	1	28,565	38,388	57,382	5,543	93,438	18,882	6,956

SOURCE: Obtained by taking four quarter moving averages of data in Appendix
Table III-1B.

APPENDIX TABLE III-3C

our Quarter Moving Sums and Averages for SEC-FTC Manufacturing
(Current Million Dollars)

Year	Quarter	A/P (15)	FYTA (16)	OCL (17)	15+Other (18)	NCL (19)	LTDB OLTD (20)	E (21)	New plant & Equip. (22)
1947	1								
	2	(Data recorded at latest quarter entering total or sum)							
	3								
	4	7,153	6,513	4,172	7,900	2,276	5,229	30,830	8,702
1948	1	7,364	6,871	4,274	8,185	2,403	5,636	31,936	9,025
	2	7,612	7,115	4,336	8,512	2,561	5,968	33,072	9,154
	3	7,910	7,331	4,413	8,910	2,743	6,303	34,045	9,170
	4	8,092	7,496	4,485	9,146	2,956	6,684	35,005	9,134
1949	1	8,164	7,579	4,487	9,244	3,142	6,909	35,602	8,788
	2	8,116	7,519	4,504	9,221	3,220	7,254	36,151	8,352
	3	8,014	7,327	4,455	9,103	3,169	7,651	36,701	7,843
	4	7,851	6,973	4,414	8,492	2,912	8,058	37,308	7,149
1950	1	7,894	6,698	4,424	8,513	2,631	8,437	37,861	6,738
	2	8,236	6,689	4,508	8,836	2,380	8,712	38,347	6,578
	3	8,823	7,146	4,707	9,421	2,192	8,860	38,877	6,782
	4	9,726	8,477	4,947	10,813	2,117	8,910	39,442	7,491
1951	1	10,651	10,097	5,251	11,828	2,083	9,041	40,047	8,204
	2	11,547	11,805	5,508	12,831	2,111	9,340	40,783	9,233
	3	12,142	13,426	5,728	13,570	2,255	9,640	41,598	10,112
	4	12,646	14,613	5,921	14,174	2,427	10,062	42,317	10,852
1952	1	13,102	15,096	6,119	14,639	2,677	10,519	43,019	11,317
	2	13,379	14,867	6,377	14,884	2,948	11,032	43,558	11,641
	3	13,940	14,364	6,681	15,394	3,126	11,704	43,921	11,609
	4	14,533	13,507	6,980	15,935	3,336	12,410	44,207	11,633
1953	1	14,975	12,875	7,248	16,393	3,448	13,083	44,612	11,679
	2	15,434	12,687	7,514	16,862	3,487	13,685	44,924	11,710
	3	15,585	12,910	7,713	17,018	3,529	14,207	45,214	11,862
	4	15,360	13,133	7,828	16,819	3,470	14,579	45,543	11,908
1954	1	15,860	12,810	8,025	17,332	3,342	14,901	45,802	11,809
	2	15,833	11,938	8,129	17,314	3,166	15,182	46,133	11,570
	3	15,848	10,928	8,236	17,341	2,950	15,517	46,563	11,357
	4	16,225	10,139	8,474	17,725	2,802	15,816	46,875	11,038
1955	1	16,026	9,756	8,685	17,585	2,728	16,237	47,470	10,718
	2	16,400	9,852	8,934	18,027	2,720	16,608	48,071	10,654
	3	16,842	10,210	9,175	18,531	2,770	16,914	48,740	10,908
	4	17,385	10,867	9,384	19,155	2,832	17,288	49,726	11,442
1956	1	17,780	11,302	9,588	19,623	2,951	17,574	50,612	12,151
	2	18,216	11,378	9,793	20,137	3,136	18,013	51,860	13,090
	3	18,685	11,211	10,037	20,672	3,345	18,555	53,149	14,025
	4	19,059	10,923	10,339	21,075	3,622	19,164	54,428	14,954
1957	1	19,431	10,781	10,743	21,427	3,835	19,858	55,613	15,501
	2	19,651	10,761	11,160	21,621	3,997	20,390	56,556	15,950
	3	19,743	10,691	11,590	21,699	4,090	20,920	57,453	16,126
	4	19,537	10,358	11,849	21,470	4,165	21,384	58,294	15,959
1958	1	19,058	9,839	11,861	21,017	4,249	21,736	59,031	15,352
	2	18,634	9,193	11,879	20,597	4,275	22,277	59,620	14,108
	3	18,350	8,481	11,815	20,322	4,309	22,817	60,230	12,762
	4	18,307	7,920	11,771	20,299	4,267	23,419	60,767	11,433
1959	1	18,759	7,940	11,944	20,731	4,194	23,997	61,437	10,991
	2	19,441	8,692	12,241	21,424	4,161	24,380	62,108	11,073
	3	19,847	9,363	12,569	21,837	4,149	24,658	62,810	11,428
	4	20,469	9,885	12,913	22,551	4,176	24,850	63,647	12,067
1960	1	20,943	10,193	13,305	23,128	4,235	25,041	64,455	12,657

Col. 15 to Col. 22: Obtained by taking four quarter moving averages of data in
        Table III-1C.
Col. 22: Obtained by taking four quarter moving sums of data in Appendix Table
        III-9, col. 4
SOURCE: Obtained by taking four quarter moving averages of data in Appendix
        Table III-1C.

APPENDIX TABLE III-4

Natural Gas Pipeline Companies Annual Report Data
(Current Thousand Dollars)

Year	S (1)	NP (2)	RE (3)	DE (4)	RE+DE (5)	C (6)	G (7)
1947	370,100	64,955	20,668	34,165	54,883	86,842	20,630
1948	474,600	76,247	28,957	46,073	75,030	136,849	18,167
1949	549,500	78,329	26,908	53,510	80,418	205,269	17,821
1950	711,600	102,857	37,355	66,122	103,477	133,998	26,704
1951	923,000	123,416	47,426	90,672	138,098	153,125	15,607
1952	1,153,600	135,368	44,390	115,868	160,258	148,631	14,543
1953	1,426,700	155,729	44,371	133,164	177,535	167,077	51,105
1954	1,620,600	168,440	42,403	156,395	198,798	174,477	53,283
1955	1,908,400	221,786	70,613	174,355	244,968	207,457	40,309
1956	2,154,900	244,555	82,445	188,912	271,357	237,252	18,333
1957	2,438,400	258,555	81,261	215,912	297,173	254,212	19,957
1958	2,708,753	268,840	71,126	240,446	311,572	281,321	33,933

APPENDIX TABLE III-4 (continued)

Year	C+G (8)	A/R (9)	INV (10)	Other CA (11)	NFA (12)	Other NCA (13)
1947	107,472	43,758	22,435	None Recorded	1,081,275	39,515
1948	155,016	66,412	32,187		1,340,326	97,432
1949	223,090	68,980	34,240		1,745,175	97,847
1950	160,702	93,861	40,968		2,300,359	97,120
1951	168,732	119,224	57,579		2,989,524	120,840
1952	163,174	148,466	62,073		3,394,839	154,026
1953	218,182	170,364	63,136		3,897,293	195,601
1954	227,760	207,742	67,021		4,277,561	202,401
1955	247,766	242,017	65,159		4,599,213	240,070
1956	255,585	257,820	84,492		5,086,263	318,576
1957	274,169	301,767	126,336		5,868,637	582,869
1958	315,254	360,893	106,190		6,346,187	688,351

APPENDIX TABLE III-4 (continued)

Year	STL (14)	A/P (15)	FYTA (16)	OCL (17)	15+Other NCL (18)	LTDB (19)	OLTD (20)	E (21)
1947	None Recorded	41,491	40,365	2,881	88,022	None Recorded	572,881	433,579
1948		63,864	52,399	2,366	122,988		819,695	511,197
1949		73,690	52,193	2,097	156,089		1,131,312	622,438
1950		184,654	70,910	3,851	292,684		1,357,434	733,429
1951		278,971	101,869	6,317	412,684		1,798,240	877,314
1952		263,013	120,519	7,212	436,443		2,037,745	1,032,965
1953		249,178	154,128	7,203	445,449		2,384,516	1,239,097
1954		219,867	134,254	7,384	423,414		2,668,337	1,425,132
1955		336,387	169,590	12,731	525,655		2,769,337	1,521,269
1956		440,428	162,507	14,957	645,995		3,024,707	1,687,198
1957		467,206	152,328	19,127	749,386		3,725,348	1,957,419
1958		537,993	157,160	16,623	830,954		4,032,524	2,181,463

Column 1: Data refers to operating revenues.

SOURCE: Federal Power Commission Annual Reports on Natural Gas Companies.

APPENDIX TABLE III-5 ·

Privately Owned Class A and B Electric Utilities Annual Report Data
(Current Million Dollars)

Year	S (1)	NP (2)	RE (3)	DE (4)	RE+DE (5)	C (6)	G (7)
1947	4,291.1	642.7	148.6	376.1	524.7	562.6	310.7
1948	4,830.2	656.8	163.7	403.1	566.7	580.1	343.1
1949	5,068.7	757.3	204.3	431.6	635.9	590.1	345.5
1950	5,527.5	821.9	202.9	483.4	686.3	582.2	334.1
1951	6.058.5	814.2	162.8	525.6	688.4	575.6	419.3
1952	6,549.2	947.1	222.3	562.4	784.7	611.6	433.5
1953	7,136.3	1,030.2	249.8	618.0	867.8	608.1	326.3
1954	7,587.6	1,134.1	266.1	692.3	958.4	687.9	297.8
1955	8,360.4	1,244.1	301.9	766.6	1,068.5	678.4	337.5
1956	9,053.7	1,332.2	310.4	844.9	1,155.3	659.5	208.7
1957							
1958	10,194.8	1,518.8	384.9	994.3	1,379.1	720.6	192.8

APPENDIX TABLE III-5 (continued)

Year	C+G (8)	A/R (9)	INV (10)	Other CA (11)	NFA (12)	Other NCA (13)	STL (14)
1947	873.3	338.6	476.3	98.3	12,457.4	1,096.0	None Recorded
1948	923.2	406.7	593.3	62.0	13,897.5	1,154.6	
1949	935.7	426.9	489.6	46.5	15,558.2	1,272.4	
1950	916.3	508.5	586.1	47.2	17,055.7	1,234.9	
1951	994.9	533.1	717.3	62.2	18,637.5	1,234.5	
1952	1,045.1	588.9	741.2	67.4	20,623.8	1,255.2	
1953	934.4	608.2	762.4	72.1	23.146.5	912.0	
1954	985.8	665.7	709.4	75.9	25,340.8	1,009.1	
1955	1,015.8	748.0	725.2	78.3	27,303.0	932.9	
1956	868.2	808.2	835.0	106.0	29,483.8	937.2	
1957							
1958	913.3	925.8	804.3	129.3	35,282.1	1,008.1	

APPENDIX TABLE III-5 (continued)

Year	A/P (15)	FYTA (16)	OCL (17)	15+Other NCL (18)	LTDB (19)	OLTD (20)	E (21)
1947	458.4	551.8	150.1	No "Other NCL" Recorded	None Recorded	6,601.4	6,627.6
1948	614.9	590.3	108.3			7,718.7	6,965.3
1949	545.7	639.3	123.4			8,572.1	7,611.0
1950	595.8	748.4	124.2			9,188.6	8,267.4
1951	719.5	946.6	117.1			9,994.0	8,865.1
1952	785.1	1,078.2	142.8			10,809.4	9,751.4
1953	1,004.5	1,139.6	83.7			12,040.0	10,251.6
1954	986.2	1,154.8	104.7			13,322.2	10,961.0
1955	1,073.5	1,205.2	102.3			14,329.9	11,561.5
1956	1,339.5	1,172.2	115.6			15,231.2	12,206.7
1957							
1958	1,543.8	1,109.2	128.5 .			18,578.8	13,642.7

Column 1: Data Refers to total operating revenues.
Column 2: "Accounts Payable" include: Notes and Accounts Payable, Payables to associated companies, Dividends Declared and Interest Accrued. Interest accrued for 1947-53 was lumped with taxes accrued; it was estimated for these years using its proportion in 1953.

SOURCE: Federal Power Commission Annual Reports on Privately Owned Electric Utilities (Class A and B).

APPENDIX TABLE III-6

Bell System Annual Report Data
(Current Million Dollars)

Year	S (1)	NP (2)	RE (3)	DE (4)	RE+DE (5)	C (6)	G (7)
1947	2,224.6	161.2	-28.1	237.4	209.3	77.5	460.7
1948	2,624.8	222.4	19.3	278.1	297.4	86.3	376.9
1949	2,893.3	232.9	16.7	321.0	337.7	89.7	247.0
1950	3,261.5	347.0	98.7	333.8	432.5	95.2	289.3
1951	3,639.5	364.9	85.6	353.2	438.8	91.7	547.8
1952	4,039.7	406.7	86.9	381.7	468.6	103.7	689.8
1953	4,416.7	478.5	110.8	411.3	522.1	104.1	925.4
1954	4,784.5	549.9	134.6	447.6	582.2	99.2	887.8
1955	5,297.0	664.2	207.9	487.8	695.7	114.1	1,272.1
1956	5,825.3	755.9	239.1	535.2	774.4	114.4	1,207.8
1957	6,313.8	829.8	255.5	763.0	1,018.5	131.2	794.8
1958	6,771.4	952.3	340.5	843.0	1,183.5	137.0	1,206.5
1959	7,393.0	1,113.2	424.8	930.1	1,354.9		1,281.7

APPENDIX TABLE III-6 (continued)

Year	C+G (8)	A/R (9)	INV (10)	Other CA (11)	NFA (12)	Other NCA (13)	STL (14)
1947	538.2	270.5	135.7	54.9	4,975.4	417.2	None Recorded
1948	463.1	290.3	123.6	63.0	6,097.2	437.6	
1949	336.7	325.9	99.0	66.1	6,789.2	509.0	
1950	384.5	383.4	109.2	72.2	7,278.9	521.5	
1951	639.5	430.1	118.2	74.9	7,911.2	558.7	
1952	793.6	463.0	127.9	77.4	8,711.5	561.0	
1953	1,029.5	494.0	134.5	86.1	9,600.3	628.4	
1954	987.1	506.8	135.3	95.8	10,469.6	655.0	
1955	1,386.2	595.0	176.5	144.6	11,444.8	732.7	
1956	1,322.2	679.4	211.2	177.2	12,968.8	847.8	
1957	926.1	716.2	115.1	182.6	14,745.8	976.7	
1958	1,343.5	769.7	99.8	178.0	16,028.0	1,075.0	
1959		849.4	100.6	192.6	17,275.4	1,109.3	

APPENDIX TABLE III-6 (continued)

Year	A/P (15)	FYTA (16)	OCL (17)	15+Other NCL (18)		LTDB (19)	OLTD (20)	E (21)
1947	454.5	145.1	41.3	No "Other NCL" Recorded	None Recorded		2,759.1	2,661.4
1948	496.5	179.5	45.1				3,408.0	3,002.4
1949	516.2	207.5	45.0				3,655.0	3,342.9
1950	523.4	336.2	46.5				3,633.0	3,748.8
1951	618.5	448.3	63.0				3,707.3	4,351.2
1952	630.5	506.9	53.7				3,789.9	5,127.9
1953	729.9	584.7	41.1				4,188.7	5,689.2
1954	701.2	634.2	48.6				4,000.7	6,588.8
1955	897.5	707.0	51.2				4,375.6	7,366.7
1956	946.4	740.9	57.4				4,618.0	8,526.9
1957	947.5	755.6	60.6				5,688.0	8,643.0
1958	994.0	846.2	33.4				6,042.2	9,644.8
1959	1,089.9	870.8	49.3				6,432.3	10,010.0

Column 1: Data refers to net total operating revenues.
Column 15: "Accounts Payable" include: Notes and Accounts Payable, Advances and Customer Deposits, Dividends Payable and Interest Accrued.
SOURCE: American Telephone and Telegraph Company Annual Reports.

APPENDIX TABLE III-7

Manufacturing Index of Net Capital Stock, Production and
Capacity Utilization

r	Quar- ter	Index of Real Net Value of Manufacturing Structures & Equipment (1)	Index of Manufac- turing Production (2)	Rate of Change of Index of Manufac- turing Production (3)	Four Quarter Moving Sum of Rate of Change of Index of Manufacturing Production (4)	Index of Capacity Utiliza- tion (5)	Index of Capacity Utilization: Four Quarter Moving Average (6)
47	1	97.3	100.0	+8.3	-	102.8	-
	2	99.1	97.9	-2.1	-	98.8	-
	3	100.9	101.0	+3.3	-	100.1	-
	4	102.7	101.0	0	9.5	98.3	100.0
48	1	104.2	101.0	0	1.2	96.9	98.6
	2	105.6	102.1	+1.1	4.4	96.7	98.0
	3	107.0	104.1	+2.0	3.1	97.3	97.3
	4	108.4	101.0	-3.0	0.1	93.2	96.0
49	1	109.0	97.4	-3.6	-3.5	89.4	94.2
	2	109.5	90.3	-7.3	-11.9	82.5	90.6
	3	110.1	96.4	6.8	-7.1	87.6	88.2
	4	110.7	95.4	-1.0	-5.1	86.2	86.4
50	1	111.5	97.9	2.6	1.1	87.8	86.0
	2	112.1	107.2	9.5	17.9	95.6	89.3
	3	112.9	114.9	7.2	18.3	101.8	92.9
	4	113.5	116.4	1.3	20.6	102.6	97.0
51	1	114.6	118.5	1.8	19.8	103.4	100.9
	2	115.7	119.0	0.4	10.7	102.9	102.7
	3	116.8	119.0	0	3.5	101.9	102.7
	4	117.9	116.4	-2.2	0.0	98.7	101.7
52	1	119.0	116.9	+0.4	-1.4	98.2	100.4
	2	120.0	110.3	-5.6	-7.4	91.9	97.7
	3	121.1	124.1	12.5	5.1	102.5	97.8
	4	122.2	125.3	1.0	8.3	102.5	98.8
53	1	123.1	131.9	5.3	13.2	107.1	101.0
	2	124.2	130.0	-1.4	17.4	104.7	104.2
	3	125.1	129.1	-0.7	4.2	103.2	104.4
	4	126.2	117.8	-8.8	-5.0	93.3	102.2
54	1	126.9	120.6	+2.4	-8.5	95.0	99.2
	2	127.5	117.8	-2.3	-9.4	92.4	96.1
	3	128.1	119.6	1.5	-7.2	93.4	93.6
	4	128.7	121.5	1.6	3.2	94.4	93.8

APPENDIX TABLE III-7 (continued)

Year	Quar-ter	(1)	(2)	(3)	(4)	(5)	(6)
1955	1	129.5	131.9	8.6	9.4	101.9	95.5
	2	130.3	132.8	0.7	12.4	101.9	97.9
	3	130.9	135.7	2.2	13.1	103.7	100.5
	4	131.7	134.7	-0.7	10.8	102.3	102.5
1956	1	133.0	136.6	1.4	3.6	102.6	102.7
	2	134.4	133.8	-2.0	0.9	99.6	102.1
	3	135.6	139.4	4.2	2.9	102.9	101.9
	4	137.0	137.5	-1.4	2.2	100.3	101.4
1957	1	138.3	140.4	2.1	2.9	101.6	101.1
	2	139.5	137.5	-2.1	2.8	98.5	100.8
	3	140.8	139.4	1.4	0.0	99.1	99.9
	4	142.1	127.2	-8.8	-7.4	89.5	97.2
1958	1	143.3	123.4	-3.0	-12.5	86.3	93.4
	2	144.6	125.3	1.5	-8.9	86.7	90.4
	3	145.8	132.8	6.0	-4.3	91.1	88.4
	4	147.2	131.2	-1.2	3.3	89.2	88.3
1959	1	148.9	143.4	9.3	15.6	96.4	90.8
	2	150.7	150.3	4.8	18.9	99.7	94.1
	3	152.4	142.2	-5.4	7.5	93.3	94.6
	4	154.3	144.7	1.8	10.5	93.8	95.8
1960	1	156.0	150.3	3.9	5.1	96.3	95.7

Column 1: The index was constructed marking 1947 = 100. Only year-end figures were given by U.S. Income and Output; others were linearly interpolated.

Column 2: This index is based on the Index of Manufacturing Production (nonseasonally adjusted) of the F.R.B., making 1947 = 100. For periods when two F.R.B. indexes overlapped (i.e., 1952, Quarter IV, 1953, Quarters I, II and 1958, Quarter IV; Quarters I, II in 1959) the more recent index was used. The ratio of the new index to the old index during the period of overlap was used in the construction of the single index.

SOURCE: Data on Real Net Value of Manufacturing Structure and Equipment were obtained in U.S. Income and Output, U.S. Department of Commerce, Office of Business Economics, 1959.

Data on the Index of Manufacturing Production (nonseasonally adjusted) were obtained from issues of the Federal Reserve Bulletin.

APPENDIX TABLE III-8

Public Utilities Index of Production

Year	Electricity Index of Production (1)	Rate of Change of Index of Electricity Production (2)	Gas Index of Production (3)	Rate of Change of Index of Gas Production (4)	Bell System Index of Production (5)	Rate of Change of Index of Bell System Production (6)
1947	91	-	91	-	93	8.8
1948	101	9.9	102	12.1	101	8.9
1949	108	6.9	108	5.9	106	5.3
1950	122	13.0	126	16.7	114	6.7
1951	138	13.1	145	15.1	117	3.1
1952	150	8.7	157	8.3	120	3.0
1953	165	10.0	165	5.1	124	2.9
1954	176	6.7	181	9.7	129	3.8
1955	199	13.1	200	10.5	136	5.8
1956	218	9.5	218	9.0	144	5.7
1957	233	6.9	232	6.4	152	5.4
1958	243	4.3	243	4.7	159	4.5
1959	-	-	-	-	168	5.7

Columns 1 and 3: Federal Reserve Board Indexes of Gas and Electricity Production, 1947-1949=100.

Column 5: This Index (1947-1949=100) was constructed using as a measure of production the average daily telephone conversations during a year compiled by A.T. and T.

SOURCE: Federal Reserve Bulletin, American Telephone and Telegraph Company, Annual Reports.

APPENDIX TABLE III-9

Quarterly Comparison of Department of Commerce and SEC-FTC
New Plant and Equipment Outlays in all Manufacturing

Year	Quarter	ΔNFA (1)	DE (2)	NFA÷DE (3)	New plant & Equip. Expenditure (4)	Col.3 ÷ Col.4 (5)
1947	1					
	2	1,502	6,674	2,176	2,181	0.998
	3	1,298	704	2,002	2,148	0.932
	4	1,418	737	2,155	2,495	0.864
1948	1	1,650	775	2,425	2,201	1.102
	2	2,139	817	2,956	2,310	1.280
	3	1,301	852	2,153	2,164	0.995
	4	2,193	917	3,110	2,459	1.265
1949	1	782	934	1,716	1,855	0.925
	2	607	935	1,542	1,874	0.823
	3	621	935	1,556	1,655	0.940
	4	915	990	1,905	1,765	1.079
1950	1	382	997	1,379	1,444	0.955
	2	855	1,037	1,892	1,714	1.104
	3	704	1,081	1,785	1,859	0.960
	4	1,561	1,114	2,675	2,474	1.081
1951	1	1,239	1,124	2,363	2,157	1.096
	2	1,860	1,185	3,045	2,743	1.110
	3	1,417	1,235	2,652	2,738	0.969
	4	2,137	1,321	3,458	3,214	1.076
1952	1	956	1,282	2,238	2,622	0.854
	2	1,738	1,344	3,082	3,067	1.005
	3	1,047	1,394	2,441	2,706	0.902
	4	1,620	1,512	3,132	3,238	0.967
1953	1	655	1,517	2,172	2,668	0.814
	2	1,116	1,545	2,661	3,098	0.859
	3	965	1,590	2,555	2,858	0.894
	4	1,650	1,662	3,312	3,284	1.009
1954	1	314	1,658	1,972	2,569	0.768
	2	1,207	1,703	2,910	2,859	1.018
	3	1,084	1,733	2,817	2,645	1.065
	4	1,694	1,842	3,536	2,965	1.193
1955	1	17	1,850	1,867	2,249	0.830
	2	728	1,936	2,664	2,795	0.953
	3	1,179	1,961	3,140	2,899	1.083
	4	1,600	2,048	3,648	3,499	1.043
1956	1	1,063	2,071	3,134	2,958	1.059
	2	2,129	2,115	4,244	3,734	1.137
	3	2,253	2,155	4,408	3,834	1.150
	4	3,130	2,256	5,386	4,428	1.216
1957	1	1,465	2,253	3,718	3,505	1.061
	2	2,119	2,316	4,435	4,183	1.060
	3	1,839	2,356	4,195	4,010	1.046
	4	2,226	2,443	4,669	4,261	1.096
1958	1	756	2,372	3,128	2,898	1.079
	2	1,120	2,426	3,546	2,939	1.207
	3	654	2,465	3,119	2,664	1.171
	4	725	2,547	3,272	2,932	1.116
1959	1	608	2,503	3,111	2,456	1.267
	2	619	2,595	3,214	3,021	1.064
	3	1,243	2,530	3,773	3,019	1.250
	4	1,846	2,652	4,498	3,571	1.260

SOURCE: Col. 1:   See Appendix Table III-2B, Col. 12 - Col. 2: See Appendix
                    Table III-1A, Col. 4 -
          Col. 4:   Outlays for 1947-1955; Survey of Current Business, U. S.
          Department of Commerce, June 1956. Outlays for 1955-59; 1959 Statis-
          tical Supplement to the Survey of Current Business, U. S. Department
          of Commerce. Outlays for 1959; Survey of Current Business, U. S.
          Department of Commerce, February 1960.

APPENDIX TABLE III-10

Yearly Comparisons of SEC and SEC-FTC Long Term External
Finance in All Manufacturing

(Current Million Dollars)

ar	△OLTD (1)	△E (2)	△OLTD+E (3)	New Securities issued net of retirements(4)	Col. 4 ÷ Col. 3 (5)
48	1,522	3,842	5,364	2,126	0.396
49	1,628	2,428	4,056	1,347	0.332
50	201	2,263	2,464	1,026	0.416
51	1,690	2,878	4,568	2,846	0.623
52	2,824	1,146	3,970	3,713	0.935
53	1,491	1,318	2,809	2,128	0.758
54	1,195	1,249	2,444	2,044	0.836
55	1,498	3,944	5,442	2,397	0.440
56	2,436	5,115	7,551	3,336	0.442
57	1,853	3,365	5,218	4,104	0.787
58	2,408	2,148	4,556	3,265	0.717
59	768	3,349	4,117	1,941	0.471

URCE: Col. 1: Appendix Table III-2C, Col. 20.
       Col. 2: Appendix Table III-2C, Col. 21.
       Col. 4: Data obtained from several issues of the Federal Reserve
                Bulletin (Statistics on "Security Issues").

APPENDIX CHART III-1G

Pipeline Gas Companies
Percent Rate of Output Growth

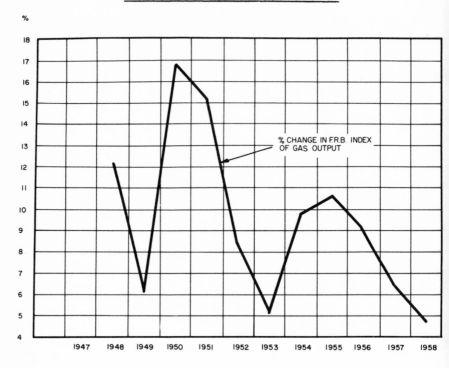

APPENDIX CHART III-2G

Pipeline Gas Companies
Plant and Equipment Expenditures

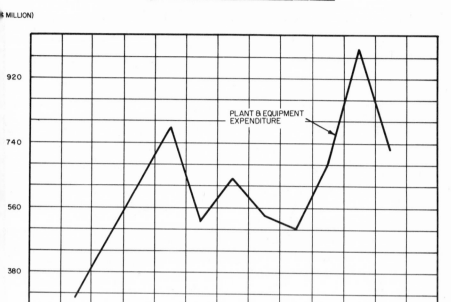

APPENDIX CHART III-3G

Pipeline Gas Companies
Liquidity Stock

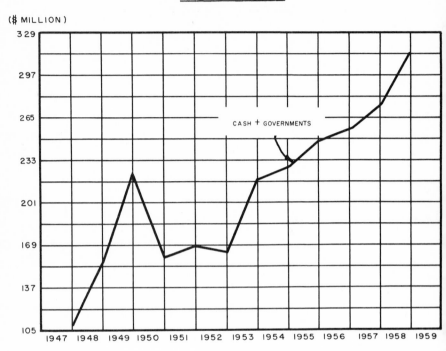

($ MILLION)

CASH + GOVERNMENTS

APPENDIX CHART III-4G

Pipeline Gas Companies
Profit Margin and Dividend Payout

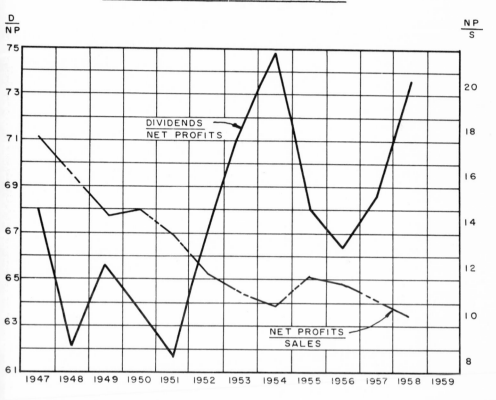

APPENDIX CHART III-5G

Pipeline Gas Companies
Internal Finance

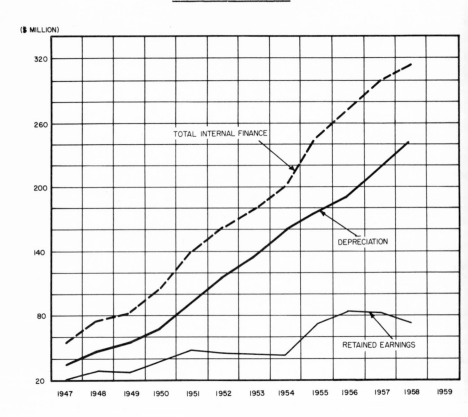

APPENDIX CHART III-6G

Pipeline Gas Companies
External Finance Fraction

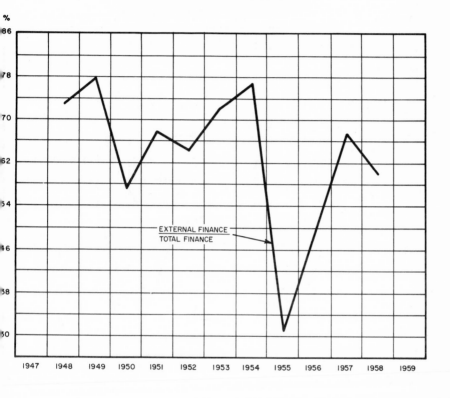

APPENDIX CHART III-7G

Pipeline Gas Companies
Total Finance

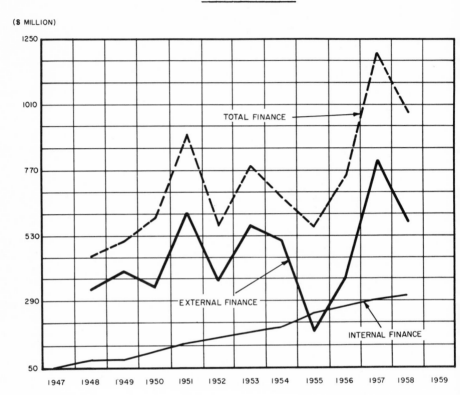

(**$** MILLION)

TOTAL FINANCE

EXTERNAL FINANCE

INTERNAL FINANCE

1250 · 1010 · 770 · 530 · 290 · 50

1947 1948 1949 1950 1951 1952 1953 1954 1955 1956 1957 1958 1959

APPENDIX CHART III-8G

Pipeline Gas Companies
Liquidity Ratios

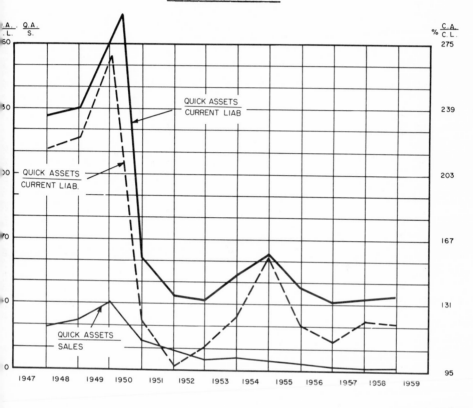

APPENDIX CHART III-9G

Pipeline Gas Company
Liquidity, Investment and Total Finance

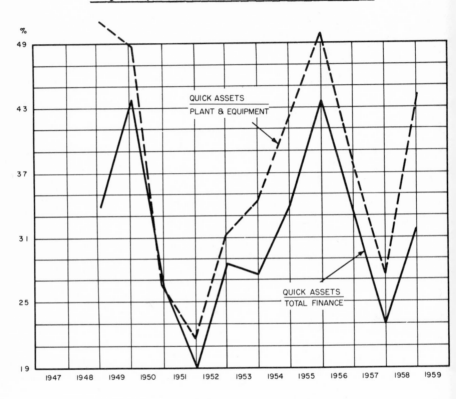

APPENDIX CHART III-1E

Privately Owned Electric Utilities
Percent Rate of Output Growth

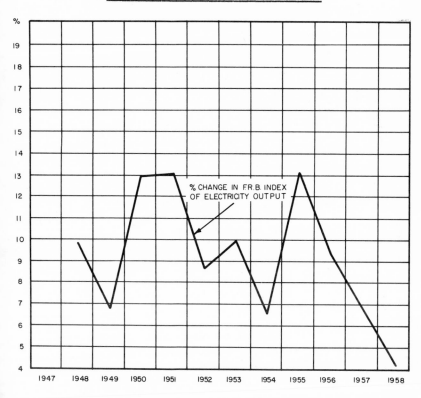

% CHANGE IN F.R.B. INDEX
OF ELECTRICITY OUTPUT

APPENDIX CHART III-2E

Privately Owned Electric Utilities
Plant and Equipment Expenditures

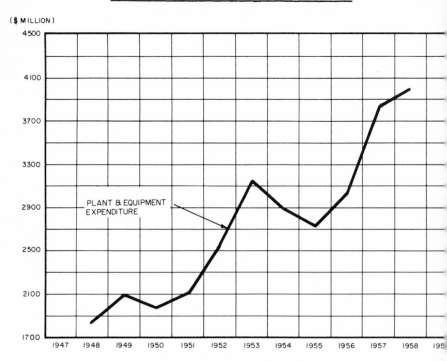

APPENDIX CHART III-3E

Privately Owned Electric Utilities
Liquidity Stock

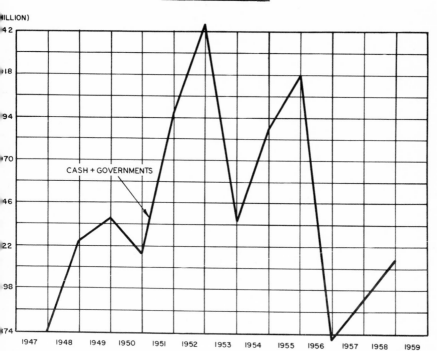

APPENDIX CHART III-4E

Privately Owned Electric Utilities
Profit Margin and Dividend Payout

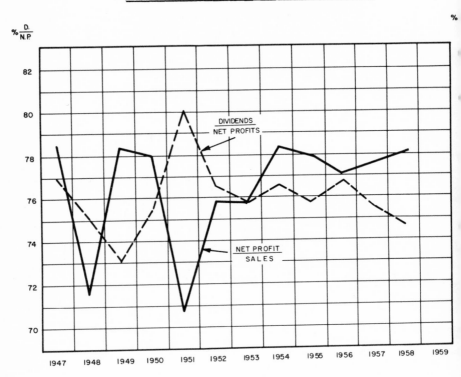

Privately Owned Electric Utilities, Internal Finance

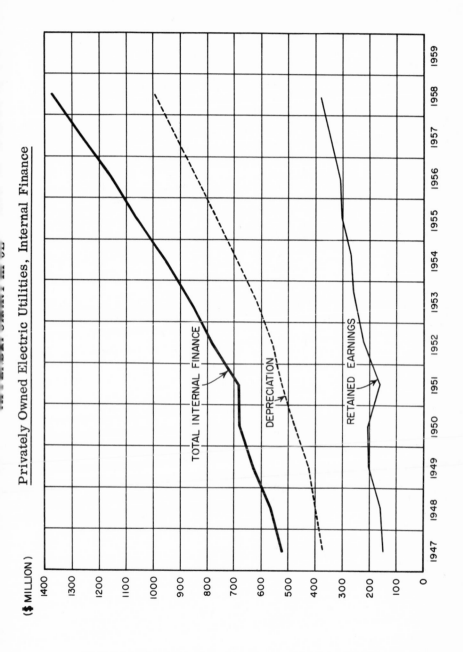

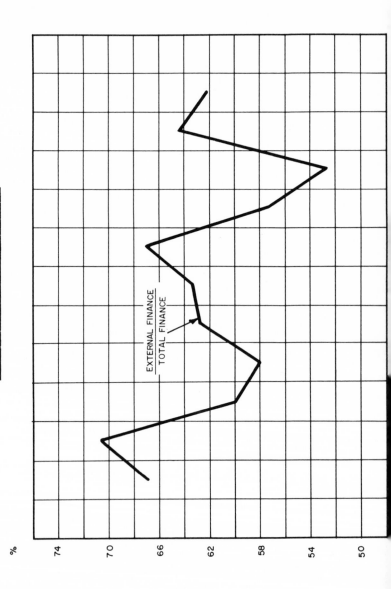

APPENDIX CHART III-6E
Privately Owned Electric Utilities
External Finance Fraction

APPENDIX CHART III-7E

Privately Owned Electric Utilities
Total Finance

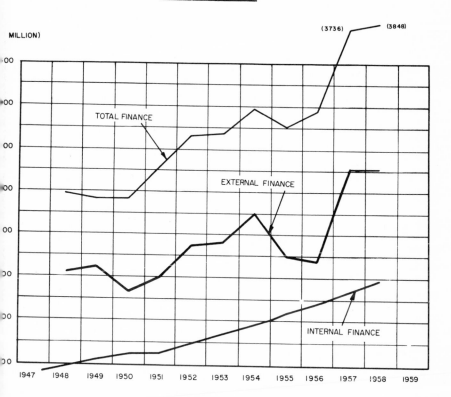

APPENDIX CHART III-8E

Privately Owned Electric Utilities
Liquidity Ratios

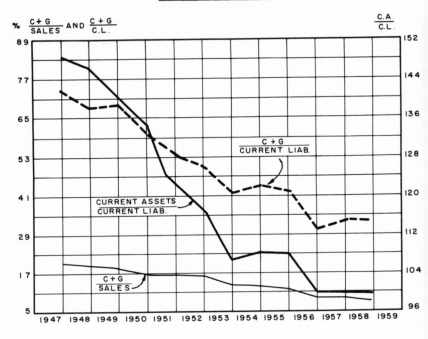

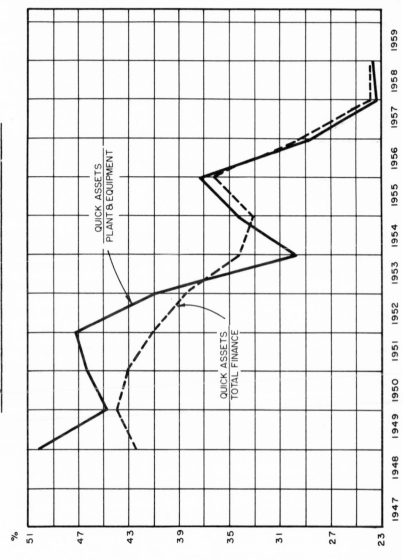

Privately Owned Electric Utilities
Liquidity, Investment and Total Finance

QUICK ASSETS
PLANT & EQUIPMENT

QUICK ASSETS
TOTAL FINANCE

APPENDIX CHART III-1B

Bell System
Percent Rate of Output Growth

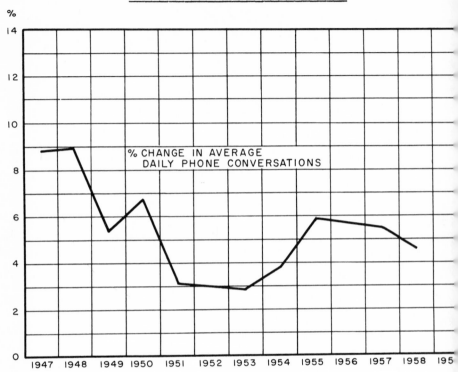

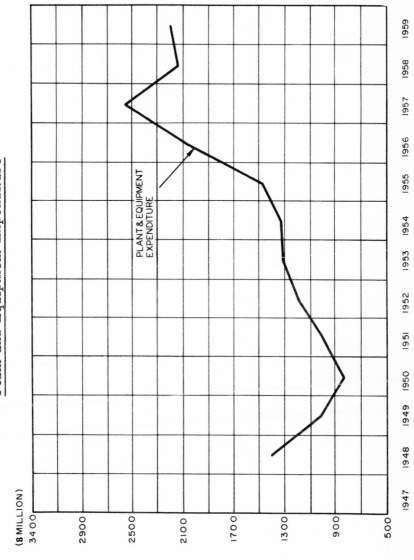

APPENDIX CHART III-2B

Bell System

Plant and Equipment Expenditure

APPENDIX CHART III-3B

Bell System
Liquidity Stock

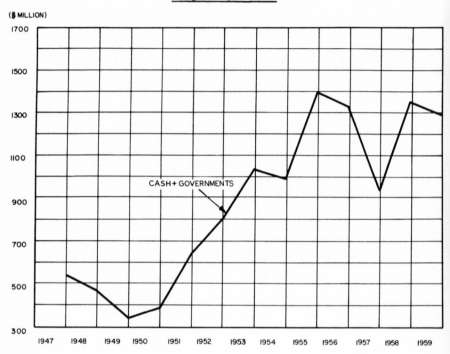

APPENDIX CHART III-4B

Bell System
Profit Margin and Dividend Payout

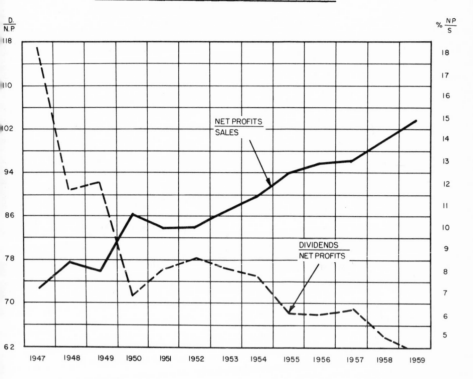

APPENDIX CHART III-5B

Bell System
Internal Finance

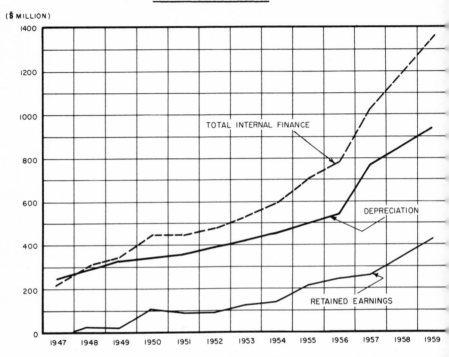

APPENDIX CHART III-6B
Bell System
External Finance Fraction

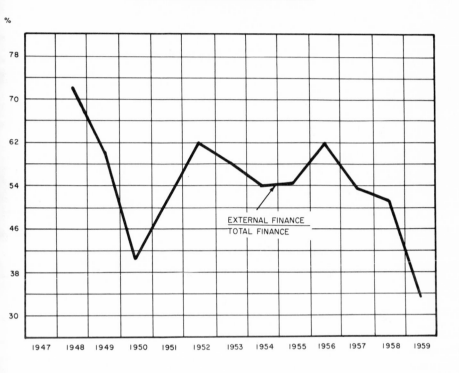

APPENDIX CHART III-7B

Bell System
Total Finance

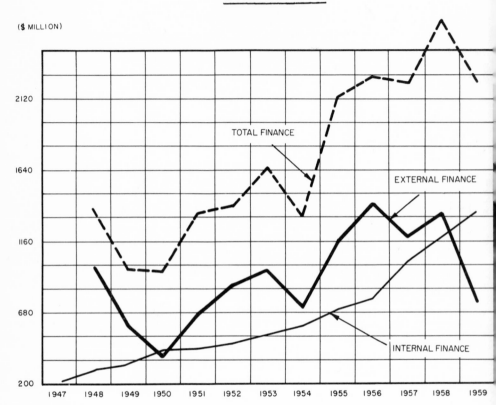

APPENDIX CHART III-8B

Bell System
Liquidity Ratios

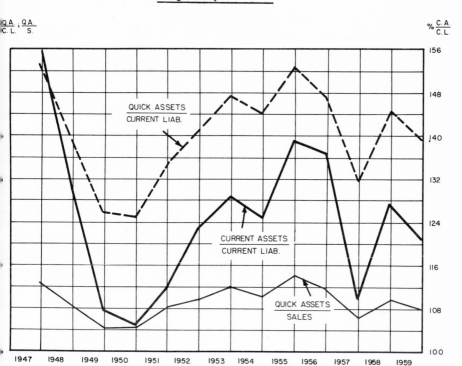

QA ; QA
C.L. S.

% C.A.
C.L.

QUICK ASSETS
CURRENT LIAB.

CURRENT ASSETS
CURRENT LIAB.

QUICK ASSETS
SALES

156

148

140

132

124

116

108

100

1947 1948 1949 1950 1951 1952 1953 1954 1955 1956 1957 1958 1959

APPENDIX CHART III-9B

Bell System
Liquidity, Investment and Total Finance

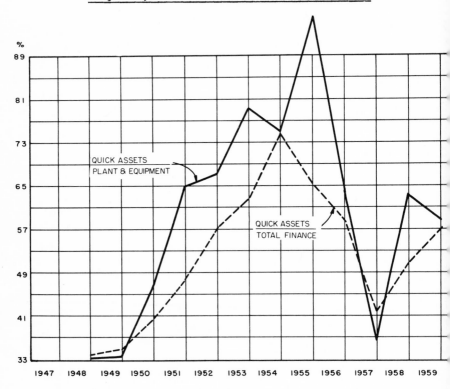

Research Study Four

DETERMINANTS OF RESIDENTIAL CONSTRUCTION:

A REVIEW OF PRESENT KNOWLEDGE

Leo Grebler
and
Sherman J. Maisel
University of California

I. INTRODUCTION

A. Purpose of This Paper

The objective of this paper is a comprehensive and critical review of the current state of knowledge of the determinants of residential construction. Such a review is a novel undertaking. Analysts of residential construction have presented their own findings, views and conclusions, with the usual amount of incorporation of related work by others. But none of them has attempted to bring together the substantial literature developed over the past 30 years, reviewed its contribution to knowledge, and identified the "dark corners" in theoretical concepts, data, and analytical procedures.

Meanwhile, the great public debates over housing problems during the past generation have centered on money. No matter how housing problems are defined, credit has been almost invariably singled out as the key to their solution. Most of the federal and other housing legislation enacted in the past 25 years has been designed to make external financing of housing more readily available or less costly to borrowers. Yet, after numerous governmental aids in operation for many years, the issue of money in housing is as lively as ever. Thus, our subject has significant policy implications, perhaps more so than the study of determinants of most other economic activities. A main task will be, therefore, to specify the current state of knowledge concerning the role of financial versus nonfinancial influences on residential construction.

Our review begins with a simple listing of the potential determinants of residential construction considered in past analytical work, and with a discussion of some problems of definition and classification encountered even in such a crude effort. It proceeds with a typology of analytical approaches to the problem. These items take up the remainder of this introductory chapter. The next chapter reviews the verbal or qualitative models of the residential construction market. Chapters III and IV are devoted first to a presentation and then to an extensive critique of the fairly large number of statistical-econometric models in existence. These are followed by materials which not only highlight the deficiencies of current knowledge but, we hope, will also represent a positive contribution to an improved understanding of the residential construction and total housing markets.

Because the federal credit programs in the housing sector are of such immense scope and are widely held to be of great significance in determining the amount and other aspects of residential construction, existing literature on their influence is discussed separately in Chapter VI. Chapter VII sketches out the wide range of economic and institutional factors affecting the availability and cost of credit for housing, which most of the analyses reviewed in this paper take as given rather than as something to be explained. This is a short excursion into an area really beyond the purview of our current subject and deserves more thorough consideration. The final chapter presents a summary and general appraisal of our findings.

B. List of Potential Determinants

The volume of nonfarm residential construction can conceivably be determined by a large number of factors. Those mentioned in most of the analytical work performed to date may be grouped as follows:

1. Changes in population
   a. Increases in population
   b. Changes in the age-sex composition
   c. Changes in the number, type, and size of households
   d. Internal migration and immigration
2. Changes in income and employment
   a. Total disposable personal income: past, current, expected
   b. Income distribution
   c. Employment and unemployment
3. Consumer asset holdings and their distribution, especially liquid assets and equities in existing houses

4. Changes in the prices of housing
   a. The price elasticity of housing relative to other prices
   b. The shape of the construction supply and cost curves
5. Relationship between occupancy costs and prices of dwellings
   a. Credit availability and the cost of credit
   b. Real estate taxes and operating expenses
   c. Depreciation
   d. Imputed costs of equity funds
6. Consumer tastes and preferences
7. Net replacement demand for dwelling units demolished or otherwise removed from the inventory less net conversions and mergers of existing units
8. Conditions in the existing housing supply
   a. Utilization of the housing inventory
      (1) Vacancies
      (2) Intensity of occupancy
   b. Prices and rents for existing dwelling units
   c. Quality, location
9. Reaction to changes in demand
   a. Builders' organization and profit expectations
   b. Investors' organization and profit expectations
   c. Market structure and market information

Analysis of the determinants of residential construction is complicated not only by the large number of potential forces impinging on this sector of the economy but also by interdependence of some of these factors. Thus, changes in income and income expectations influence the number of marriages and births and the ability of married couples, individuals and unrelated groups of individuals to establish households in separate dwelling units, all of which affect changes in the number and size of households. The utilization of the existing inventory is influenced by both demographic changes and changes in income, which also affect the prices and rents for dwelling units in the existing housing inventory. Prices and rents for new housing, as well as the availability and costs of borrowed funds, are not wholly independent of changes in aggregate income. And aggregate income which is considered one of the determinants of residential construction is, in turn, partially determined by the volume of such construction.

Analysis is further complicated by the fact that some of the listed factors may be more significant in determining long-run levels of residential construction, while others may have an important bearing on short-run changes—a distinction often not clearly specified or defined in the analytical work done to-date. A further distinction, also often neglected, is between the total housing market in which households demand dwelling units for occupancy and the construction market in which new units are demanded and built.

Moreover, some of the listed items may have a bearing only on the number of additional dwelling units demanded, while others affect total construction expenditures either because the number of units alters or the amount spent on each changes, and still others influence expenditures on both new and existing units. For example, a demand shift to larger or higher-quality units may raise construction expenditures without any increase in the number of new units built; or a decline in the number of new units demanded may be associated with no fall in total expenditures if construction costs, which are determined in nonresidential or nonconstruction markets as well as in the market for new housing, rise.

Finally, many investigators have found it necessary or useful to divide the determinants of residential construction into (a) those which affect the building of new houses for sale to owner-occupants and (b) those which affect the building of new rental housing. This distinction is considered important on the theory that the households demanding new owner-occupied houses behave more like consumers while the entrepreneurs building dwelling units for rent behave more like business firms.

Much of the research work on the subject has been concerned with selecting a few strategic forces among the multitude of factors which can conceivably determine the volume of residential construction, by either qualitative or quantitative methods, and with assigning weights to them through quantitative analysis. This approach has been dictated by the desire for relatively simple, workable models and by lack of adequate data for one factor or the other; and it has often been rationalized by assuming substitutability of some determinants for others. Thus, existing literature often merely mentions some of the potential determinants in our list without analyzing their effects on variations in the volume of residential construction in systematic or quantitative form.

Government housing programs are not specifically listed above as determinants of residential construction. For the most part, those programs are designed to increase the availability and reduce the cost of borrowed funds and are therefore subsumed under a listed item. To the extent that demolitions under the urban renewal program affect replacement demand, it is also subsumed under a listed item. Public housing programs clearly involving cash subsidies are usually not considered in studies of the determinants of residential construction, although they enter into projections of the construction volume required to meet housing "needs." Their volume depends on many factors not susceptible to economic analysis. Moreover, the volume of public housing has been so small

that its omission involves no serious error in historical analysis.[1]
The present review, then, addresses itself to determinants of what
is customarily labelled "private residential construction," although
such construction may be financed with loans insured or guaranteed
by governmental agencies or with mortgages purchased by the
Federal National Mortgage Association but originated by private
lenders.

The omission of governmental housing programs from our list
reflects the fact that these programs have rarely been systematically and specifically incorporated in analytical work on determinants of residential construction. Nevertheless, it will be
necessary for the purpose of this review to probe existing knowledge for what it reveals concerning the influence of government
programs on the level, composition, and short-term fluctuations
of residential building.

Our list of potential factors determining the volume of residential
building includes forces acting on both the supply of new dwellings
and the demand. Analytical work to-date, however, has been concerned mainly with demand. One can infer that this emphasis is
based on the notion that real resources for residential construction,
at least in the long run, are potentially available in such volume
that their supply will meet effective demand at current prices,
and that there are consequently no significant economic problems
other than price problems associated with the supply side. The
availability of land, building materials, labor, and contractors and
other entrepreneurs, as well as an effective market organization
that allows all these input factors to be brought together, is taken
for granted. This is a realistic assumption for a sufficiently long
period of our history, except for interruptions through wars and
their aftermaths. Existing literature usually deals with the supply
items in our list when it addresses itself to short-run changes.

C. Main Types of Analysis

Analytical work on the determinants of residential construction
can be divided broadly into two types:

1. Models based primarily on a verbal or qualitative analysis
   of the market. These models follow the classical tradition
   in economic analysis, being primarily descriptive and putting
   more or less stress on one or a few variables believed to

---

[1]Construction expenditures for public housing, including military
housing, equaled only little more than 3 percent of private residential construction expenditures during the postwar period 1946-58,
and they reached not more than 5 percent in any single year.

be significant. These variables are then analyzed on the basis of available statistics, assumed interrelationships, and logical reasoning. The mainly verbal models can be further separated into:

    a. Those which relate residential construction to housing market conditions, without specific consideration of factors external to the housing market.

    b. Those which take account of factors both external and internal to the housing market.

    c. Those which analyze residential construction in terms of secular trends, long swings, or short cycles.

2. Statistical models, primarily econometric, which attempt to account for specific quantitative changes in the volume of construction. They put numbers and values on the effect of specific variables and attempt to measure the extent of lagged relationships. These models can be further classified into:

    a. Those which primarily fit formal equations based upon a limited number of time series.

    b. Those which use a mathematical framework but fit the parameters by reference to various data, judgment as to important relationships, and a verbal analysis of significant changes.

The work described under 1a above has usually been performed by housing analysts who focus on the operation of the housing market as a whole. Most of the work under 1b and c has been done by general economists interested in business cycle analysis or the theory of investment. The models under 2 have been developed usually by economists aiming at econometric models for the entire economy or at general theories of demand.

Summarizing extensive pieces of analysis, sometimes of book length, is always a difficult undertaking. Faithful reproduction of an argument may require about as much space as the original work but would obviously make this report unmanageable. The briefing here employed involves losing or glossing over some of the more subtle points. In general, non-quantitative models are presented in outline form without reproduction of the statistical evidence occasionally used by authors to support them. In the case of econometric models, however, it is necessary to present the salient equations in full. In addition, the main econometric models have been tested in the light of currently available data, which are often revised and improved versions of those used by their authors, and the results of these tests are reported.

II. VERBAL OR QUALITATIVE MODELS

A. Residential Construction Related to Housing Market Conditions

One type of analysis concerns itself with the interaction between occupancy and price changes in the market for existing housing units and changes in the volume of construction. It recognizes that exogenous forces, such as population growth or increases in income, may determine both the changes of market conditions in the existing housing inventory and the volume of new construction. But interest here focuses on the way in which external forces work their way through the housing market and eventually cause new building to occur or cease, or expand or contract. This approach attempts also to furnish early housing market indicators considered to be useful for predicting changes in the level of construction.

Basic to this analysis is the common observation that the supply of housing units is relatively fixed in the short run, with annual new construction at most representing 3 percent of the standing stock. When exogenous forces produce an increase in demand for housing services, the first effect under usual market constellations is a greater occupancy rate. When the occupancy rate of the existing inventory reaches a critical zone, rents and house prices are bid up. When the resulting upward valuation of the housing stock leads to prices exceeding construction costs, new building in encouraged. When external forces produce a decline in demand for housing services, of course, the opposite forces are set in motion. In addition to general expositions of this type, there has been some empirical verification of the sequences of the processes described and of critical occupancy zones giving rise to changes in rents and house prices. (59, 17, 42, 14) [1]

This approach deals only indirectly with the determinants of residential building. It highlights the interrelationships between the over-all demand for housing and the amount of construction, but it gives little attention to the specific form in which demand is transferred from one market to the other or to the magnitudes of the resulting effects. Nevertheless, a particular aspect of interactions between the general housing market and new construction has a direct bearing on financial determinants of residential construction and is discussed below.

Housing specialists have never tired of spelling out certain undeniable facts on residential financing, that is, a mortgage loan at $4\frac{1}{2}$ percent interest for 30 years results in lower debt charges

---

[1]Numbers in parentheses refer to listings in the bibliography appearing at the end of this study.

than a loan at 5 percent interest with a maturity of 25 years, and so forth. Congressional testimony since the beginning of the thirties is replete with tables showing this kind of simple arithmetic. (2) (15) The implication is that more liberal financing terms will enable additional households to obtain new housing or better-quality housing, and this appears to be true when the individual family as demander for a housing unit is considered and other things are held unchanged. Aggregate economic effects of changes in the ease of borrowing, however, are not identical with the arithmetic effects on an individual family's ability to command housing.

Economists, of course, have always been aware of the relationship between changes in the general level of interest rates and changes in the value of capital assets, and of the processes through which easier credit terms are capitalized in the market for such assets. The application of this general principle to the housing market has been most clearly and consistently developed by Ramsay Wood, along these lines: Because the number of new houses available at any one time is very small compared to the existing total supply of housing, prices of new houses are determined to a very large extent by the prices of existing houses. Consequently, the prices of new houses cannot fall far below the prices of comparable old houses. If the costs of new houses to occupants were lowered by reduction of any cost component, financial or otherwise, speculative resale would develop. The market would evaluate the advantages of lower costs of the new houses against the existing stock of housing and the incomes prevailing in the community, and would equilibrate house prices on the principle that comparable houses command comparable prices. In practice, increases in land and construction costs would eventually absorb any initial difference between the cost to occupants of new houses and the market prices of existing houses. (59)

This line of analysis has been further, though somewhat sketchily, pursued by the same author in the development of a model to demonstrate "how changes in credit terms affect the working out of the forces of demand and supply" in the housing market. Among the conclusions relevant to this paper are: (1) easier terms will usually result in higher prices, (2) they will give an immediate advantage to only some bidders for houses, especially those who have few or no savings for downpayments, (3) they will put at a disadvantage bidders prepared to pay all cash or a large proportion of cash, (4) they will result in greater use of credit, and (5) the extent of credit liberalization will be limited by competitive demands for other funds—if these are strong, a sharp rise in the rate of return on mortgages will be required. (60)

A similar line of reasoning, developed by Ernest M. Fisher, takes its starting point from a simple conversion of the standard tables showing the results of changes in credit terms on mortgage debt charges. If it is arithmetically correct to say that a $4\frac{1}{2}$ percent, 30-year loan results in a lower charge than a 5 percent, 25-year loan, it is also arithmetically correct to say that, with a given debt charge, the first kind of loan gives the borrower command over a larger amount of funds with which to buy a house. In a sellers' market, the increased amount of debt that can be carried by a given debt charge under relaxed credit terms will tend to be absorbed in price advances rather than result in improved standards of housing (15). This reasoning implies that there are severe limits to an expansion of total residential construction through relaxed credit terms in periods of reasonably full resource employment.

In summary, the work discussed in this section is useful mainly in providing a framework for analysis of the processes through which stimulative or contractive forces work themselves out in the housing market as a whole. But the relationship between housing market processes and new construction is typically described only in general, qualitative terms. Moreover, there is a question of completeness even in terms of the limited objective of this type of analysis (see the framework of identities for the housing market in Section IV A). There is also doubt over the usefulness of the analysis for periods in which vacancy ratios and rents or house prices move within a narrow range.

The work on effects of changes of the ease of borrowing on the housing market, which has been associated with this approach, addresses itself specifically to financial determinants. Its main value lies in clarifying the impact of altered credit terms on prices for the existing housing stock and associated costs of resources used in residential construction. Here again, most of the analysis is in general, qualitative terms, and only an admittedly partial and merely illustrative model has been developed for tracing the effects of changing credit terms on the housing market and more specifically on the volume of residential building. The elaboration of such a model, cast in a form that lends itself to empirical tests of its validity, is a high-priority item in this area of research.

Some of the models discussed in this section fail to distinguish between short-run and long-term changes or to specify time dimensions. The implicit assumption of a nearly completely inelastic supply curve suggests that the models at best apply to the short run. To make them more useful for analysis, a great deal of additional information is required on the shapes of the supply curve in the markets for both existing housing and new construction. Moreover, the way in which these separate but interrelated markets react to demand movements warrants further investigation. Many of the stated results depend directly upon assumed demand curves, unspecified lags, and only partially tested relationships. The effects

of greater availability and easier terms of credit on new construction as against credit on existing property deserve more attention.
This kind of differentiation, partly fostered by federal housing
programs, prevailed through much of the postwar period. Consequently, the price and supply linkages between the markets for
new and existing construction may not have been as strong as some
of the analyses suggest. Also, the analytic framework does not
allow any quantification of the price effects of stimulative or contractive forces, including changes in the ease of borrowing, and
of the effects on the number of dwelling units built.

B. Residential Construction Related to External and Internal Factors

A few models analyze residential construction as a special
case of the general theory of investment and use variables both
external and internal to the housing market. Methodologically,
they tend toward an intermediate position between purely descriptive analysis and full-fledged quantitative models and attempt to
allow for structural and institutional characteristics of the housing
and construction markets.

Clarence D. Long, Jr., used such an approach in 1940 (31).
His work, however, applies investment theory to new private building as a whole rather than to residential construction, although
empirical materials are provided for the latter type as well as
nonresidential building. Because of this aggregation of activities
influenced by consumer demand and business demand, Long's application of investment theory is not sufficiently specific for inclusion
in the present report.

A specific model for residential construction within the framework of investment theory was more recently developed by James
S. Duesenberry. (12) This analysis deals not only with determinants
of residential building separately from other types of construction
but adopts the division between demand determinants for owner-
occupied and rental housing. Duesenberry takes his starting point
from the total demand for housing. The demand for single-family
dwellings by a population with given demographic characteristics
depends upon (1) aggregate income, (2) number of families, (3)
nonhousing assets, (4) housing assets, (5) prices of houses, (6)
level of rents, (7) prices of other goods, and (8) credit terms.
Duesenberry attaches particular importance to the amount of nonhousing assets as a determinant of the ability of potential buyers
to make downpayments — an item that has been the subject of an
independent, small-scale empirical investigation (43) — and to
credit policies which influence downpayment requirements. The
demand for rental housing depends on the same variables, "except
that assets are probably of little importance, and the signs of the
effects of rents and house prices are, of course, reversed."

After tracing the effects of changes in house prices and rents on changes in the rate of construction of single-family houses and apartments, and an analysis of supply factors (builders, material, and labor) and costs, Duesenberry concludes that, speculation aside, the rate of residential construction depends on the following factors: (1) rents and house prices relative to other prices, (2) vacancy rates for apartments and the ratio of demand to supply for single houses, (3) the number of speculative builders and the distribution of their assets in the case of single houses, (4) the total amount of assets in the community and the risk preferences of their owners in the case of apartment buildings, (5) the level of building and operating costs.

These factors are transformed into separate equation systems for single-house and apartment building under carefully defined equilibrium conditions. When the latter are dropped, there emerges a "dynamic system whose movements are ultimately governed by the movement of income and population." Erratic shifts in income and population or changes in the parameters of the system, however, may produce movements in the rate of building quite different from those of income. This observation leads to a descriptive discussion of housing cycles and the suggestion of two types of such cycles: (1) cycles with "normal relations" between housing investment and income movements. In these, housing investment follows income changes, but with different timing explained by lags and with stabilizing effects on total output; and (2) cycles in which structural changes in the housing industry itself, such as wartime backlogs and speculation, generate independent fluctuations which communicate themselves to movements of aggregate income.

In spite of conceptual neatness, the Duesenberry model suffers from several defects. The verbal statements emphasize lagged relationships but the equation systems fail to incorporate them in any specific form. Partly for this reason, it is never clear whether the analysis refers to the short run or long run. Moreover, the model is developed in terms of plausible rather than tested relationships. For example, the level of building costs is included among the independent variables determining the rate of residential construction, although several previous investigators have indicated in their models that costs are inconsequential. Also, no weights are given to the presumed independent variables. On more technical items, the model for total housing demand includes the "number of families" among the independent variables, and it is not clear whether the omission of the rather numerous households other than families is intentional. Likewise, single-family dwellings in that model are equated with owner-occupied dwellings, in spite of the fact that existing single-family houses are an important segment of the rental supply.

As for financial determinants, they are incorporated in Duesenberry's model for total housing demand and ingeniously linked to the amounts of housing assets and nonhousing assets in the hands of potential buyers of houses for owner-occupancy. But they are ignored in Duesenberry's rather extensive discussion of supply factors in new construction. The number of builders and the scale of their operations, for example, may be significantly influenced by the availability and ease of credit. Also, potential influences of credit on the demand for new construction are not specifically examined although they are obvious from the historical description of housing cycles in Duesenberry's work.

Another model of the "intermediate" type considered in this section has been suggested for short-run forecasting by John P. Lewis (30). In this case, the model is derived from a theory of investment by households in new housing and consumer durables on the ground that these investments have significant economic characteristics in common.

The starting point is a working estimate of the "normal physical requirements for new nonfarm dwelling units." The estimate takes into consideration "expansion requirements" composed of net nonfarm household formation, migration-induced increases in vacancies, net increases in second homes, and "replacement requirements." Among the latter, the rate at which residential units are withdrawn to make way for other urban land uses is a "powerful independent conditioner" of the demand for new housing.

According to Lewis, income has no stable, quantifiable short-run relationship to the demand for new residential construction. Support for this statement is found in a scatter diagram on spendable incomes per household and the amount of residential construction per household. Variations in mortgage credit terms, on the other hand, have a pronounced impact on short-run changes in the volume of residential construction. This point is illustrated by observations for the 1950's. Judgments on supply-price effects are suggested as modifiers of forecasts derived mainly from physical requirements and credit conditions. The remainder of Lewis' work concerns itself with lags and the problems involved in converting data on housing starts into construction expenditures.

Lewis has worked out an admittedly "opportunistic" procedure for forecasting rather than explanatory purposes. There is no question raised nor any pretense made about its applicability to conditions other than those of the 1950's. No effort is made to quantify the effects of the variables considered to be significant and, even if the limited objectives of this contribution are accepted, there is no way of telling how well the forecasting procedure would have "worked" for the period considered. The analysis provides no systematic link between the total demand for housing and the demand for new construction, nor does it discuss possible inter-relations between short-run and long-run changes in the level of residential construction.

The models discussed in this section include at least implicitly, but not in detail, the influence of fluctuations in the availability of construction financing on new residential building. This is also true of much of current commentary in the press and business journals. There is usually some reference to the impact on construction activity of changes in builders' ability to borrow, but the way and the degree in which these changes affect the volume of activity remain unspecified. This contrasts considerably with general business cycle theory in which the analysis of how the availability of producers' credit causes fluctuations in activity is prominent and fairly complete.

C. Secular Trends, Long Swings, and Short Cycles

Some of the literature on business and building cycles and one analysis of secular trends concern themselves specifically with determinants of residential construction. Other studies of cycles address themselves to purely descriptive analysis of relationships between business and building cycles or of leads and lags, without attempting to identify or quantify determinants of fluctuations in residential construction. These are omitted from the present review.

1. Secular trends

The work on secular trends, by Grebler-Blank-Winnick (18), takes its starting point from evidence that both gross and net capital formation in real terms between 1890 and 1950 showed arrested growth or actual decline. Moreover, the per capita value of resi-dential capital in constant prices fluctuated within narrow margins and in 1950 was only slightly larger than in 1890.

As for financial determinants of secular trends in residential construction, the analysis shows clearly (1) an increased tendency to debt-financing, (2) a rising ratio of net increases in residential mortgage debt to housing construction expenditures, and (3) great easing of credit between the twenties and early fifties in the form of lower interest rates, longer loan maturities, and larger loan-to-value ratios for first mortgages. The absence of a strong growth trend in real terms in the face of a trend toward easier external financing emphasizes the importance of nonfinancial determinants.

As for nonfinancial determinants, the analysis by Grebler, Blank, and Winnick deals separately with forces that have operated on the number of dwelling units built and on changes in real input

per new unit. In line with other investigations, the growth of nonfarm households emerges as main determinant of long-term trends
in the number of nonfarm dwelling units added to the supply. But
a large source of additions to the supply since the twenties were
conversions of existing structures rather than new construction,
with the result of a large gap between net increments to households
and the number of new units built. Because of an anticipated decline
in conversion potentials, the study projects re-establishment of
a closer long-run relationship between new dwelling units and
household growth in the period to 1975. While immigration until
the twenties has affected the level as well as the timing of new
housing construction, internal nonfarm migration apparently did
not raise significantly the level of residential building until 1950,
though it may do so in the future. Likewise, demolitions and other
withdrawals from the housing inventory have been insignificant
determinants of secular trends in new construction, but may become
more important mainly because of urban renewal, highway, and
other publicly aided programs.

According to Grebler and his associates, a strategic force in
the arrested growth of residential capital formation was a marked
secular decline in real input per new dwelling unit built, in spite
of the long-term rise in real consumer income. The factors producing this decline are identified and to some extent quantified,
but it suffices to say here that they are nonfinancial. The analysis
concludes with a strong presumption that housing has suffered a
secular decline in the consumer's scale of preferences and implies
that a reversal of past trends in residential capital formation
presupposes a reversal of consumer preferences - of which there
are some current indications but no conclusive evidence.

This analysis of secular trends has given rise to critical debate
too technical for inclusion in this review (44). For our purpose,
it is more important to outline the relevance of this work to an
evaluation of our financial system. During the 60-year period
covered by the analysis, there were great improvements in our
financial system generally and in the organization and practices
of residential mortgage lending specifically in terms of mobilizing
and channeling savings, adapting institutional policies to changing
demands exemplified by the increased desire for home ownership,
facilitating the inter-regional flow of funds, greater adoption of
the long-term amortized mortgage, and reduction in the cost of
mortgage financing. Some of these improvements were initiated
or strengthened by federal programs such as the Federal Home
Loan Bank System, the FHA, the veterans home loan program,
and the Federal National Mortgage Association. Yet, if the Grebler-
Blank-Winnick analysis is correct, the perfection of institutional
arrangements in mortgage finance seems to have failed to alter
an adverse secular trend. This finding may testify to the stub-

bornness of the underlying forces producing the trend, or, as some hold, to the remaining inadequacy of market devices for the financing of housing in some value-determined sense.

2. Long swings

Only a few analyses have come to grips with determinants of cyclical behavior in such fashion that they contribute to generalized knowledge of the determinants of residential building. By demonstrating that fluctuations in residential (or total) building exhibit characteristics as to timing and amplitude that cannot be explained by the course of general business conditions, the analyses have led to a search for presumably unique variables to which residential construction is responsive. The classic work of this type is Arthur F. Burns' "Long Cycles in Construction." (5)

Burns starts out by developing a model of the number of housing units built in a collectivistic, nonpecuniary economy (which precludes consideration of any financial determinants). Even in such an economy certain basic forces will produce long cycles. Among these are variability in the rate of population increase, inconstancy of housing standards, the immobility and durability of dwellings, and uncertainties of planning. Even small changes in the rate of population growth and in housing standards are apt to produce large variations in construction volume and shortages or surpluses which take a long time to correct. In a pecuniary economy, the influence of these basic forces is magnified by imperfect market information, psychological factors, market uncertainties, and changes in credit conditions, among other things. Market disequilibrium is normal. Because of the time required for the market to react to external forces, long cycles will result regardless of whether there are long cycles in the demand for the use of dwellings (such as may be associated with long swings in the rate of population growth or of immigration).

The analysis of how external forces such as changes in the rate of population growth work themselves out in the housing market is very similar to the work described earlier, and the previously noted limitations apply here. Except for general recognition that changes in credit conditions in a pecuniary economy will add to the potentials of long cycles, this approach allows no differentiation between nonfinancial and financial determinants. Its main value lies perhaps in the application of the "acceleration principle," in the sense that small relative changes in the strength of some of the underlying forces will produce very large changes in the volume of construction.

Another contribution in this group of literature is William H. Newman's systematic empirical analysis for the 1875-1933 period or subperiod (39). Newman concludes that:

1. Long swings in total building activity (of about 15-21 years duration), measured by building permit values, reflect long waves of population changes, which are accentuated by market imperfections producing delayed reactions to changes in underlying demand;

2. There is no consistent relationship between changes in income and long (major) building cycles;

3. Changes in building costs do not explain major building cycles;

4. Major cycles in building activity are not explained by changes in money-market conditions measured by fluctuations in high-grade bond yields;

5. The movement of net incomes from existing property shows a positive correlation with major swings in building activity.

Although these conclusions and the underlying data relate to total rather than residential building, there is at least a strong presumption that they are applicable to the latter. The finding under (4) has been reaffirmed for long swings in residential construction specifically by Grebler-Blank-Winnick (18), with ease of borrowing again measured by changes in the yields of high-grade bonds. Clarence D. Long, Jr., likewise finds no positive correlation of movements of mortgage interest rates and long building cycles (31).

A preview of Moses Abramovitz's current work on long waves in the rate of economic growth suggests that these long waves have been associated with great fluctuations in construction and specifically in residential building, which in turn have corresponded roughly with long swings in the rate of population growth. But it is too early to say whether Abramovitz's contribution will provide a generalized explanation of residential construction volume separate and apart from the relationship between long building cycles and long swings in the rate of economic growth (1).

3. Short cycles

William H. Newman's study, referred to earlier (39), addresses itself to short cycles in total building activity (averaging about 5 years) as well as long swings. He concludes that:

1. There is no consistent relationship between changes in income and short building cycles;

2. Changes in building activity are more likely to cause changes in building costs than vice versa;

3. A significant and systematic relationship between changes in bond yields and short building cycles suggests that expansion in building activity has been associated with greater ease of borrowing, at least in terms of direction of movement (rather than absolute levels).

Here again, there is a strong presumption that these conclusions hold for residential activity as well as aggregate building. More specific analyses of determinants of short-term fluctuations in residential construction have been undertaken for the period since World War II, mainly by Leo Grebler (17), Jack M. Guttentag (23), Saul B. Klaman (25), and Warren L. Smith (49). While these analyses differ on matters of emphasis and detail, they agree in the conclusion that short-run fluctuations in residential building have resulted mainly from changes in financial conditions labeled as ease of borrowing, availability of mortgage funds, or supply of mortgage credit. They agree also in linking the changes in financing conditions to the course of the moderate general business cycles that occurred during the periods of study. In the form of a synthetic description, the argument is about as follows: Changes in financing conditions have been greatly influenced by the level of general economic activity. When that level was rising and high, the expanded demand for funds by business, which is relatively insensitive to increased cost of borrowing, tended to reduce the availability of funds for housing, which is held to be unusually sensitive to changes in the cost of borrowing.[2] When there was slack in the economy at large and the supply of funds was ample relative to demand, credit for homebuilding and home purchase became more readily available. As a result, residential construction activity in the postwar period has shown a counter cyclical tendency or at least a strong lead in relation to general business fluctuations.

Analyses along this line employ various techniques in examining the possible effects of other than financial determinants on the short-term swings in residential building, such as household formation, income and employment, or prices. They agree in assigning to these determinants an insignificant, if any, influence on building fluctuations in the postwar period. They note at the same time that the dominant effects of credit factors on the cyclical behavior of residential construction may hold only for periods in which long-run demand forces were favorable to a high level of building activity and in which general business fluctuations were relatively short and moderate. Further, they concern themselves typically

---

[2] Cost of borrowing is defined broadly to include credit terms as well as interest rates. The latter are probably less important in determining the demand for new residential construction than are downpayment requirements and loan maturities.

with time lags between observed changes in the availability and costs of borrowed funds and in residential construction volume. One author concludes that the strategic financial factors in short-term swings of building activity have indeed been of a counter-cyclical character, but that actual construction expenditures varied in less than countercyclical fashion because of the time lags in the process of initiating and building residential projects (17).

The analyses differ in respect to the definition and measurement of credit variables; and one of them, by Guttentag, attempts an articulated distinction between credit availability, defined as varia-tions in the complex of lending terms (downpayment requirements, loan maturities, and interest rates), and the supply of credit or the schedule showing the amounts that lenders are willing to provide at various terms and interest rates (23). Guttentag stresses also that the countercyclical behavior of residential construction in the postwar period presupposed some inelasticity in the supply of credit. Another point of difference is found in the importance attached by various investigators to the inflexible interest rates on government-underwritten mortgage loans in producing the ob-served close association between changes in financial conditions and in the volume of residential building and the resulting counter-cyclical behavior of the latter. Likewise, there are differences in judgment as to whether the inflexible rates are necessary or desirable instruments of general economic stabilization policy. These matters will be discussed in Chapter VI which deals with federal credit programs.

The basic propositions offered by the analyses of short-term fluctuations in residential construction during the postwar period would bear further, more rigorous examination through quantitative factor analysis or econometric models. Much of the supporting evidence is descriptive and suggests general tendencies without allowing more definitive estimates of variations in the level of housing construction that may be associated with given changes in financial conditions. The often unavoidable use of "proxy" data for measuring the availability and costs of mortgage credit, in the form of bond yields and otherwise, points up the need for developing better direct data, especially data on changes in the terms and interest rates on conventional mortgage loans. Further research should also identify more specifically the basic demand conditions for housing under which change in the ease of borrowing becomes the strategic factor in short-term fluctuations of residential con-struction. It is not clear, for example, whether and to what extent the thesis would hold for periods of low or declining levels of consumer demand for housing associated with major, prolonged recessions, or with a high level of available vacancies. As this volume is being completed, a great deal of uncertainty has arisen over the stimulation of housing construction that may be expected

from the easing of credit during the recession of 1960-61, as compared to the experience observed in earlier postwar recessions.
This observation highlights the need for further study of the pre-
requisites in the economy at large, the financial markets, and the
housing market that have made the nearly countercyclical behavior
of residential building possible.

III. STATISTICAL-ECONOMETRIC MODELS

A. Advantages of the Econometric Approach

In recent years numerous econometric and statistical models
of the housing market have been developed. Some of these models
have attempted primarily to throw light on the construction market,
while others have been prepared as part of the larger task of building a model for the entire economy. What contributions do they
offer to a general understanding of the determinants of residential
construction?

While the advantages which economists hope to gain from this
approach are familiar, a brief discussion of the concepts and procedures will be useful. Econometric-statistical models summarize,
simplify, and express basic information in a form that brings out
essential interrelationships and allows them to be tested and
measured. As the previous section has demonstrated, verbal models
are often incomplete and both their content and their accuracy is
hard to test. A statistical model or framework, in contrast, lends
itself to completeness. One can see where gaps exist. Important
areas or essential relationships are less likely to be omitted. The
need for formal definitions and assumptions precludes the vagueness
and imprecision of many verbal theories (32, 33).

A statistical framework also allows quantification. Concepts can
be related to specific events. The parameters can be measured and
assigned exact weights. Available statistics can be employed more
fully and systematically. Perhaps more importantly, new series to
fill gaps can be defined and developed. The significance of data can
be estimated. Probability values can be assigned. The results of
predictions can be tested and, if errors are found, the model can be
corrected.

Because parts of a model can be stated in mathematical language,
a large number of diverse concepts can be treated in an integrated
form. Mathematics is a language developed for the logical expression and manipulation of relationships. Its use helps to ascertain
the complementary effects of many factors, a necessity in dynamic
analysis. What happens today is heavily influenced by past actions.
Delayed influence can be observed much more readily with the tools
of mathematics. Much of the search for a workable explanation of the
operation of the housing market is a seeking of lagged relationships.

The basic procedures and methodology of statistical and econc metric model-builders are simple. On the basis of an examination of past events, a theory is devised and formulated in mathematica terms. It is assumed that the data are related to each other ane reflect people's basic behavior patterns. An attempt is made by statistical procedures to uncover the underlying relationships The object is both to test and to measure the hypothesized structure

The relationships may be extremely complex. Some depene upon institutional and legal factors, such as the banking and mort-gage systems. Some are technological relationships, as the amoun of output that results from mixing certain labor, equipment, ane materials. Others involve tastes and group or individual reactions as, for example, the amount families are willing to spend for ren or housing expenditures and the estimates by investors of relative risks.

These behavior patterns are described in terms of functiona relationships. In the statistical or econometric treatment of models the exact form of these relationships is usually specified, ane statistical analysis (such as graphical correlation, least squares or maximum likelihood) is used to give them numerical values Verbal analysis, in contrast, usually indicates merely direction: and expected magnitudes.

The concepts of economic structure, constants, and variable: are related directly to the mathematical expressions from whicl the terms have been adopted. A simple model of a typical structura relationship for the residential construction market, expresse(algebraically, might take the form:

$$S = a + b_1 i + b_2 H + u$$

This states that housing starts (S) depend on the level of the interes rate (i), the number of households (H), and on certain disturbance: (u). These disturbances play a most significant part in the theor; and in the statistical estimation of the model. It is usually assume(that these disturbances occur with certain specified types of prob-ability distributions (52).

In addition to the disturbances which cause random movement: in the level of starts, two groups of relationships are expresse(in this equation. In the first place, the specific number of housin; starts in any period will depend upon the values of i and H. Sinc(these are expected to take different values at frequent intervals they are the variables of the relationship. The second group i: expressed by the small letters a, b_1, and b_2. They represent th(various institutional and behavioral relationships. These are calle(constants because in any short period, such as a year or two, the;

are not expected to vary. Over a longer period, however, these relationships can shift as human habits and institutions change. When analysts want to refer to the possibility of change in these relationships, they speak of them as "parametric constants" or more generally as "parameters" of the system. The econometrician attempting to specify the parameters, therefore, simply endeavors to measure the basic institutional and behavioral relationships. If he does so successfully, it enables him to state the direction and magnitude of changes in the dependent variable that will be caused by changes in an independent variable. Since these parameters express the underlying structure of the system, the concepts of a shift in the structure and alterations in the parameters are largely identical.

The econometric models attempt to explain why a variable (construction) assumes a certain value in a given period. The amount of construction is determined by its interrelationships with the other variables. It depends upon the behavioral structure of the economy and the values of the other variables. If the econometrician has specified the a's and b's—or the parameters—he can then explain how construction varies as the result of new values for the independent variables on the right-hand side of the equation. For example, as the level of the interest rate (i) or households (H) changes, the value of construction starts (S) will change. If the reaction takes time to occur, the change in the first variable leads that of the second, or the second lags behind that of the first. Since the dependent variable may also change as a result of shifts in the parameters (structure), this possibility must also be included in the analysis.

Problems arise if the theory or model explains changes in terms of "derived" rather than real relationships. Suppose that the value of S depends on Z, credit terms in general, instead of i, the interest rate. If for many periods i and Z move together (e.g., the movements in Z reflect solely interest changes because downpayments and loan maturities are not altered), predictions of S from i would be perfectly valid, even though the relationship between S and i is not the true causal but only a derived one. If, however, i and Z stop moving together, the predicted value of S based on i will be wrong. For accurate predictions, the model requires the parameter of Z or of i and the other credit terms to be separately stated. The general aim of the models is to find the true or invariant rather than the derived relationships. The more complete and exact one's knowledge of the real structure, the more likely are explanations and predictions to be valid.

The most common forms of statistical models in this field have been based upon a few aggregative time series and specify a small number of relationships from these rather limited data. While most of the discussion in the present section, since it reviews existing works, is concerned with these limited attempts at model-building, it should be made clear that other, more general econometric approaches are possible. A framework or model need not be complete in every detail. Its form and the information contained within it may allow the analyst to use judgment and to change parameters or estimate variables based upon logical assumptions. Some parts of the model may use exact statistical techniques such as time series analysis; other sectors may utilize parameters derived from cross-section analysis and surveys. When the structure shifts as a result of legal or institutional changes, the analyst may alter his equations in a formal or informal manner. The frequent variations in FNMA policy, for example, have effects that are unlikely to be measurable from annual data, but these could be inserted into a less rigorous model.

One important use of good models is to measure the effect of alternative assumptions or policy recommendations. The analyst can also use the model to test various orders of magnitude to see whether or not they would make significant differences in the predicted results (sensitivity analysis). As an example, only after one puts orders of magnitude on changes in household formation and the relationship of changes in the availability of credit to the cost of establishing a household is it possible to say whether credit changes are likely to have large or small effects on household formation.

To what extent the potentials of statistical-econometric models have been realized in existing studies of the determinants of residential construction remains to be seen when the results of these studies are examined later in this chapter. In addition, Chapter IV will review critically the procedural and statistical difficulties of the econometric approach as well as the quality of the data, which is so important to the success of econometric models.

B. Models Derived From Time Series Analysis

The number of econometric construction models based upon time series is fairly large. A partial listing includes the following:

I. C. F. Roos, Dynamic Economics. Bloomington, Indiana, 1934, Ch. VI.

II. L. J. Chawner, Residential Building, Housing Monograph Series, No. 1, U.S. National Resources Committee. Washington, D.C.: Government Printing Office, 1939.

III. H. W. Robinson, The Economics of Building. London: Staples Press, 1939.

IV. J. Tinbergen, Statistical Testing of Business Cycle Theories. Geneva: League of Nations, 1939.

V. J.B.D. Derksen, "Long Cycles in Residential Building." Econometrica (April 1940).

VI. L.R. Klein, "The Use of Econometric Models as a Guide to Economic Policy." Econometrica (April 1947).

VII. L.R. Klein, Economic Fluctuations in the United States, 1921-1941. New York: John Wiley and Sons, Inc., 1950.

VIII. L.R. Klein, another version of the above, in Conference on the Economic Outlook, University of Michigan Papers, November 1956.

IX. C. Christ, "A Test of an Econometric Model for the United States, 1921-1947," in Universities—National Bureau Committee, Conference on Business Cycles. New York: National Bureau of Economic Research, 1951.

X. J.M. Mattila, "An Econometric Analysis of Construction." Wisconsin Commerce Papers, Vol. IV, No. 1 (April 1955).

XI. V.L. Bassie, Economic Forecasting. New York: McGraw-Hill, 1958, App. C.

XII. George F. Break, The Economic Impact of Federal Loan Insurance. Washington, D.C.: National Planning Association, May 1961.[1]

As noted earlier, each of these works examines theoretical relationships explaining the behavior of the residential construction market and then utilizes statistical analysis—usually in the form of a multiple correlation regression equation—to specify these relationships in an exact numerical form. There is a fair degree of overlap among the analyses. However, some of them use different

[1]When this report was substantially completed, an additional relevant model was published by Richard F. Muth, "The Demand for Non-Farm Housing," as part of The Demand for Durable Goods (Arnold C. Harberger, ed.), The University of Chicago Press, 1960. Muth's approach differs from that of any of the models reviewed here and cannot be included in the general framework of equations established for the presentation and tests of these models. Time limitations did not permit the necessary considerable recomputation of his prewar data in order to discover whether his equations would be valid for the postwar period.

measures of the construction volume whose level they try to explain. They also differ in the influences they assign to the independent variables. In effect, each study offers a distinct picture of the structure of the market. For summary purposes, we have formed from these basic studies eight typical equations, each presenting a separate view of how the market operates. To simplify exposition, we utilize the following uniform nomenclature for the dependent and independent variables:

S = number of dwelling units started
D = volume of residential construction in constant dollars
D_1 = volume of construction of owner-type units
D_2 = volume of construction of rental-type units
r = consumer rent index
H = number of households
U = number of unemployed
C = costs of residential construction
C_2 = costs of construction of rental-type units
Y = disposable personal income in current dollars
Y_d = disposable personal income in constant dollars
i = bond yield rate
N = value of residential dwelling unit stock in constant dollars
P = consumer price index
Q = stock of dwelling units
Z = credit conditions

Lags are shown by subscripts.

The series used to measure these variables and their values are shown in Appendix A. These series differ somewhat from, as they differed among, the original studies upon which the equations are based, as is made clear in the later discussion of the problem of recomputation.

The general form and our discussion of these models is in each case based on an original work which most nearly typifies a certain approach. Since we are interested in a synthesis and general description, our exposition at times does not follow the exact analysis by the particular author whose study we cite as a typical example of the model. It should be noted also that in certain cases the housing equations were parts of a much larger and more complete model in the original works. In all cases, the equations must be understood as including a random disturbance term (u). It is assumed that, as a result of changes in these disturbances, the actual value of the dependent variable in any year may vary from that shown by the simple equation.

How does the residential construction market operate according to these various studies? What knowledge can be gained from them?

Equation 1.0:

$$S = a + b_1 r + b_2 C_{-1} + b_3 \Delta \frac{Yd}{H} + b_4 \Delta H_{-2}$$

This model states that the number of construction starts (S) in a given year depends upon the level of rents (r); the level of construction costs in the previous year (C_{-1}); changes in the per household level of income ($\Delta \frac{Yd}{H}$); and changes in the number of households two years previously (ΔH_{-2}).

J.B. Derksen (V) has worked out the theoretical reasoning for this type of relationship and has successfully fit parameters to it from the time series data. This model and a very similar one by Chawner (II) built upon the pioneering study in this field by Roos (I). The Roos study attempted to generalize from data available only in the city of St. Louis rather than from the more limited national data. It went somewhat beyond later analyses in utilizing certain nonlinear forms and in combining in the final equation several parameters developed from a series of sub-studies.

The theory behind this model states that construction starts should increase if either investors' incentive to build and operate tenant units rises, or if households increase and require more dwelling units, or if their income grows. The incentive to build (in reality, expected profits from building) is shown to depend upon the relationship between income and outlays in rental properties. This relationship should, in turn, depend upon the relative level of rents, costs of building, vacancies, and credit both in terms of costs and availability. On the basis of St. Louis data, Roos was able to develop parameters for each relationship hypothesized. Working with national series, however, Derksen found that some of the data used by Roos, such as vacancies, foreclosures, and the interest rate were either lacking or did not have significant regression coefficients and had little impact on the correlations. For this reason, equations of type (1.0) for national analysis reduce the incentive to invest to an assumed positive relationship to the level of rents and a negative one to costs. The final two terms of the equation show a relationship of starts to changes in income and in household formations.

As noted, Roos includes the credit factor specifically. Credit enters his system in three different ways. He considers it to play a role as (1) a determinant of the capitalization rate which investors would use in relating net income to capital costs, (2) a factor expressing the expectations of both investors and owner-occupants, and (3) an indication of the willingness of lenders to extend credit. In the absence of any direct measure of pertinent credit conditions, Roos used the foreclosure rate as a proxy variable to measure all the various aspects of credit changes. The foreclosure rate entered his system in a nonlinear form and was effective only between certain bounds. In one direction, its influence reached a maximum limit, while in the opposite it became inoperative. Since the 1940's, all fluctuations of the foreclosure rate have probably been beneath the minimum limit at which its influence, according to Roos' tests, would be felt. Consequently, an entirely new credit variable would have to be devised to fit his theory if his study were to be updated.

Equation 2.0:

$$S = a + b_1 \left(H - \frac{U + U_{-1}}{6}\right) + b_2 Q_{-1}$$

The second general equation states that starts (S) depend upon the number of households (H); upon the amount of unemployment (U); and upon the stock of dwelling units (Q). This equation in effect utilizes primarily the need for dwelling units by households as the basic explanatory factor. Changes in the incentive to invest or buy resulting from rent-cost relationships or credit conditions have been completely removed.

The demand for dwelling units arises from the relationship between the number of units in the housing stock of the previous year (Q-1) and the current number of households. This relationship can also be considered as the pressure of a vacancy factor. Its value falls the greater the vacancies. Households are adjusted by subtracting one-third of the average amount of unemployment in the current and preceding year, on the assumption that vacancy pressures are reduced if unemployment increases. This adjustment concept was introduced by Bassie (XI). He argues that unemployment is both a more sensitive and a more useful economic indicator for housing demand than income. A family's demand for a dwelling is unlikely to disappear if its income is reduced by a small percentage. On the other hand, if its income is nearly wiped out because of unemployment, a more drastic and immediate contraction of housing demand will occur. Bassie found little difference empirically between including a separate parameter for unemployment and utilizing it to adjust households directly. He also found as high correlations with this simpler model as were developed by those who introduced cost and similar independent variables, as in Equation 1.0.

Equation 3.0:

$$D = a + b_1 Y_d + b_2 \frac{r}{c} + b_3 N + b_4 \Delta H$$

This equation introduces a new dependent variable. Instead of attempting to explain the number of dwelling units started, this relationship is concerned with the amount spent for construction of dwelling units (D). In effect, this model attempts to explain both the number of units built and the average amount of dollars spent per new unit. In the form used in this and the following equations, estimated expenditures in current prices are corrected by a cost index so as to arrive at expenditures in constant prices.

The theory behind this model and a summary of computations utilizing it can be found in the studies of Mattila (X) and Break (XII). Comparison shows that the relationships hypothesized are in effect a combination of Equations 1.0 and 2.0. The incentive to invest and to purchase is represented by the parameters of a rent to cost ratio $\frac{r}{c}$ and of personal disposable income (Y_d). The need for dwelling units by households is introduced again through the change in the number of households (ΔH) and the existing stock (N), but the stock in this case is measured in constant dollar values instead of numbers of dwelling units. Some of the relationships would appear to be more directly concerned with the cause of changes in the value of units and others with the cause of changes in the number of units demanded. Statistically, of course, it is impossible in this equation to differentiate between these separate relationships.

Equation 4.0:

$$D_1 = a + b_1 \frac{r}{c} + b_2 (Y_d + Y_{d-1} + Y_{d-2}) + b_3 \Delta H$$

This equation states that the dollar volume (corrected for cost changes) of construction of owner-type units (D_1) depends upon ($\frac{r}{c}$), the ratio of rents which households would have to pay for rental units to the price of buying a house (represented by a cost index). The second major influence is held to be disposable income (Y_d), averaged over several years to take into account the need for ac- cumulating a downpayment. Finally, the equation includes the net change in the number of households. In effect, this item measures part of the need for additional units while the previous variables influence both the average value and the number of dwellings constructed.

Equation 4.0 is taken directly from Klein (VII) who has presented a large group of residential construction equations as part of his general models of the American economy. Since the housing equa- tions are merely part of an over-all structure, one cannot assume that they would necessarily have been presented as actual models of the housing market. They do, however, add to the general array of possible approaches. This and the following equation differ from the other models by attempting to explain the construction demand for owner-type and rental-type units separately. They are based on the assumption that home buyers behave more like purchasers of other durable consumer goods and, therefore, the theory required is that of household behavior. Rental units are constructed for profit and as a business; therefore, a theory based upon that of the firm is needed. Klein desired to include among his variables the financial costs of home-ownership since they are clearly a major item for the average household, but was deterred by the absence of data.

Equation 5.0:

$$D_2 = a + b_1 r_{-1} + b_2 (C_2)_{-1} + b_3 (C_2)_{-2} + b_4 i + b_5 (\Delta H)_{-1}$$

This equation complements the preceding one by expressing the demand for rental construction. The dollar volume of construction of rental units (D_2) is held to be dependent on investors' profit considerations. Expected profit is assumed to depend on last year's rents (r_{-1}), and on anticipated price changes based on a comparison of lagged costs (C_2). The equation also uses bond yields (i) as a factor expressing the competitive position of other investments. In addition, the factor of household formation is included, as in the previous equation. Neither 4.0 nor 5.0 includes a direct measure of the existing housing stock.

The Klein model for rental units adopts largely the earlier work of Roos and Tinbergen (IV) who also placed a great deal of emphasis on interest and prospective profits as determining the incentive to build. It may be noted that interest cost has been left out of most of the previous models because of the unavailability of data on mortgage interest rates. Klein uses the bond yield as a measure of the relative attractiveness of investments other than rental housing.

Equation 6.0:

$$D = aN_{-1} + bY_d$$

This is a simple equation for predicting the value of residential construction, somewhat equivalent to equation 2.0 for starts. It assumes that the value of construction is related to current income levels (Yd) and in addition to last year's depreciated value of the housing stock in constant dollars (N_{-1}). The equation is found in the Klein models of the economy, updated by Goldberger and aided and maintained by Suits (VIII).

Equation 7.0 has two forms:

$$S = a + b_1 \left(\frac{Yd}{c}\right)_{-\frac{1}{2}} + b_2 \Delta H - b_3 N_{-1} - b_4 Z_1 \qquad (7.1)$$

$$S = a + b_1 Yd_{-1} - b_2 \frac{c}{p} + b_3 \Delta H - b_4 N_{-1} - b_5 Z_2 \qquad (7.2)$$

Equation 8.0 is the directly related value equation, also in two forms:

$$D = a + b_1 \left(\frac{Y}{c}\right)_{-\frac{1}{2}} + b_2 \Delta H - b_3 N_{-1} - b_4 Z_1 \qquad (8.1)$$

$$D = a + b_1 Yd_{-1} - b_2 \frac{c}{p} \quad b_3 \Delta H - b_4 N_{-1} - b_5 Z_2 \qquad (8.2)$$

These equations are taken directly from Break's study (XII). Break attempts to build upon all the previous models and to introduce at the same time credit specifically. He utilizes graphic multiple correlation and a wide number of variants for both the dependent and independent variables. The advantage but also disadvantage of graphic correlation is that it enables one to give major weight to the simple zero-order correlation between the dependent variable and the independent variable in which he is primarily interested. At the same time, when there is high multicollinearity between the various independent variables, the weight assigned to the primary independent variable by this method will be high. The parameters are unlikely to specify the exact structure of the system.

Break uses as his dependent variables the number of dwelling units started (S) and the annual level of construction expenditures (D). He also attempts to measure the influence of credit on average expenditures per unit $\left(\frac{D}{S}\right)$ but his coefficients are not significant. He measures his dependent variables both directly and also on a per-capita basis but finds little or no advantage in the use of per-capita data.

In contrast to the previous studies, Break divides his sample period into two parts, 1925-41 and 1948-56, and fits separate equations to each segment. There are two primary reasons for his use of separate periods. First, equations covering the entire period do not give a good fit to the separate parts. Second, there is a very basic shift in the primary independent variable—credit—between the two periods.

In both equations of type 7.0 and 8.0, the first independent variable used by Break is the relative ability to purchase houses, similar to the reasoning of previous models. Break measures this influence in two ways. First, he divides disposable income in current dollars by a housing cost index $\left(\frac{Yd}{c}\right)$, as in equations (7.1) and (8.1).

This shows the year-to-year changes in the amount of income related to housing prices, and no other cost or income factor need be included. Second, he includes disposable income in constant dollars (Y_d) and at the same time the relative movement of housing costs or prices to all consumer prices $(\frac{c}{p})$, as in equations (7.2) and (8.2).

The next two independent variables are identical in all these equations and are similar to those in previous models. They are household formation in the current year (ΔH) and the previous year's value of the housing stock in constant dollars (N_{-1}).

It is the importance and variety of expression given to the final independent variable, credit (Z), that distinguishes Break's work from the earlier models. The credit variable for the period 1925-47 is based upon the mortgage credit studies of the National Bureau of Economic Research. Weighted average interest rates, maturities, and loan-to-value ratios are formed from the NBER samples of loans made by life insurance companies, commercial banks, and savings and loan associations. These three series are then combined into one composite "terms of credit" variable in the following manner:

$$Z = \frac{\text{interest rate}}{\text{maturity} \times \text{loan-to-value ratio}}$$

A rise in interest rates will raise the value of this variable, while an increase in either the length of maturities or the loan-to-value ratio will decrease it. Thus the higher this index the tighter are credit terms, and vice versa. The index had maximum values of 1.42 in 1925 and 1.46 in 1933 (see Appendix A). It fell rather steadily from 1933 to 1940 to reach .47 and was at .40 in 1947. It fell steadily from 1925 to 1929, moved up sharply in 1930 and again in 1933, and then declined steadily though not evenly until 1940. As would be expected, the index shows little or no response to short-term credit changes in this period.

For the period 1947-57, Break has developed his own measure of credit conditions based upon the same formula. The index is based upon published data for FHA and VA loans and upon separate data for conventional loans. Because these series vary substantially among themselves, the weights used in combining them give different results. Break is not willing to assume that any single series is correct. Instead, he utilizes four separate series in which the variables are either sensitive or insensitive, cross-classified by stringent or liberal. The insensitive and stringent series varies in the 11 years between .48 and .39 with a maximum annual drop of .06 in 1953-54. The sensitive and liberal series varies in the same period between .47 and .28 with a maximum drop of .09 in 1953-54.

The difference in these separate measures of credit conditions produces a range of Z coefficients in Break's actual computations of his equations. The most sensitive series has a coefficient only about a third as large as the most insensitive. In all cases, the coefficient has a negative sign, indicating that tighter credit terms cause a drop in the number of starts or the volume of construction.

C. Tests of the Time Series Models

In the previous section, we have described eight basic models found in the econometric studies which utilize aggregate time series for fitting their parameters. On the whole, these models follow a similar general pattern. They tend to include as one demand factor the need for units caused by household formation or by the ratio of total households to total dwelling units. They also contain other economic variables including a measure of general ability to purchase or spend usually through some expression of disposable income, and an incentive factor usually in the form of a rent-cost relationship. They discuss the possibility of other variables and different lags, but generally obtain high correlations with the few variables for which data are available.

The theory behind the models is of a fairly high order. In certain cases it may not be clear exactly which market is under consideration, but on the whole the models are primarily concerned with explaining or predicting the volume of residential construction either in terms of units or real values. As we shall see, major questions arise with respect to the procedures used. Nevertheless, the examples cited are well-conceived attempts to apply the particular methodology involved.

To determine the usefulness of these studies for analysis, explanatory prediction, or policy decisions, we must test each of them against theory and against each other. Such tests of models are not common. With a few exceptions, equations have been completed, offered as possible structures, and then forgotten. While it is clear that a record of consistency or of success in prediction would not necessarily mean that the models actually described the true determinants of residential construction, the opposite result would clearly indicate some difficulties in concept, procedures, or data. By testing the models, one may expect to achieve greater knowledge of the market and obtain leads for developing better models in the future.

For the tests we have compared one or more of the published equations for each model with a newly fitted or recomputed equation for the same model. Only the most recent ones (6.0, 7.0, and 8.0) could be used in their published form. Recomputation was required for several reasons:

(a). Data for additional years have become available. The number of original observations was small. Prediction should be improved if more observations are added, and many of the difficulties discussed in the following part should be reduced as the number of degrees of freedom increases. Most of the construction market models were based primarily upon the period 1920-40, although some have also used a varying number of postwar years. We have recomputed equations (1.0) to (5.0) for the period 1920-40 plus 1950-56. All models exclude the war period, but we have also excluded the years 1946-49 when demand and supply were in very serious disequilibrium.

(b). The data have been subject to periodic revisions. Estimates of the dollar volume of residential construction, personal income, and the stock of housing have all been revised drastically since the original work on these equations was performed.

(c). Periodically, new and better series become available. The Bureau of the Census has issued a new series on household formation. The Department of Commerce has issued a new series on volume of construction in constant dollars. Grebler, Blank, and Winnick (18) have made new estimates of the value of the housing stock in constant prices.

Under the logic of econometric model-building, all of the revised series, new series, and additional years should be included in the algebraic fitting of the equations in order to get the best possible description of the structure of the market. The recomputations enable us to test the models under the best conditions. In some cases, however, the method of estimation may not be as satisfactory as in the original studies. When the housing equation was part of a model of the whole economy or of the entire construction industry, maximum likelihood methods could be used on the full set of equations. In the recomputations, only a single equation is used, and the recomputed equations have been fitted by the least-squares method.

Types of Tests

Three different types of tests are applied to the models: (1) Tests of internal consistency and of agreement with the initial assumptions of the theory; (2) success in extrapolating within the tolerance limits of the fitted equation; (3) success in prediction compared to other methods (7).

As for the first type of test, each previously fitted equation in effect claimed that it described properly in terms of signs, elasticities, and magnitudes the market relationships it found in theory. If this claim is valid, a mere recomputation of the equation with additional data should not significantly alter the description. After we have recomputed the model, we ask the following questions: (a) Are the coefficients still statistically significant?; (b) Are the signs of the coefficients still in the same direction as in the original equation and the author's discussion thereof?; (c) Is the index of correlation still significant? What changes have occurred in the index?; and (d) What has happened to the relative size of the coefficients?

If the revised model still describes the market approximately as it was described in the original, the size of the elasticities and the magnitudes of the coefficients should be about the same. On the other hand, if there is a vast difference between the fitted equations, then the system has failed to describe the structure of the market accurately, or a structural shift may have occurred. If the magnitude of these shifts is large, the system in its existing form has been unable to deal with the problems of structural change.

As for the second type of test, it is possible to determine whether the deviations between predicted results and actual figures for an additional period could have arisen purely as a result of chance. If the deviations could have resulted from sampling variance, there is no internal evidence that the model is incorrect. The model has described the new period equally as well as it described the sample period.

For this test, we derive from our data the standard error of the forecast. This does not depend, as does the standard deviation of the regression line (standard error of estimate), wholly upon the past data in the sample period, but depends in addition upon the values that the variables take in the new period. The question is whether the predicted values differ significantly from the actual values, given the level of the variables in the year of prediction and the variance of the disturbances in the period originally included.

As for the third test, even if the predicted value does fall within the limits of the model, we still may ask whether or not the prediction is as good or better than that which could be obtained in other ways. The standard errors of a forecast tend to be large, particularly if the values of the variables differ considerably from their means for the sample period. As a result, the prediction may be consistent with the model but still not very useful.

A simple method for this test is to compare the results of a statistical-econometric model with those of "naive" forecasts or those of forecasts based upon less rigorous or judgment methods.

We compare the predictions made by the recomputed models for the years 1957 and 1958 with two "naive" forecasts and also with the "projections" published in the preceding year's November issues of Construction Review, a joint publication of the Departments of Commerce and Labor.

The first "naive" model is simply a forecast of no change. How does the prediction made by each of the equations compare with a model which assumes that the level of output in 1957 would be the same as in 1956 and that 1958 would be the same as 1957? The second "naive" model is based upon the assumption of constant year-to-year change. It predicts that 1957 will vary from 1956 to the same degree and in the same manner as 1956 varied from 1955.

We discuss these tests for each of the models separately. For the first five models for which we have recomputed the equations, we show the new coefficients and the predictions made from them for the years 1957 and 1958. We also compare their predictions with the reported values, the expected variance in the forecasts, and the predictions made by the naive models and the official fore-casters. Tables IV-1 through IV-8 summarize the comparisons of the different predictions for 1957 and 1958.

For equations 1.0 to 5.0, we show in Charts IV-1 to IV-6 the relationship between the individual independent variables and the dependent variable. From these charts, it is possible to see how much of the year-to-year variation comes from each independent variable, how the estimated variable differs on a year-to-year basis from the actual, and how the relationships appear to have changed over time.

Tests of Equation 1.0

The estimated coefficients for equation 1.0 based upon the most recent data are:

$$(1.0) \quad S = -861.8 + 9.911\,r + 2.373\,c_{-1} + .2643\left[\Delta\frac{Y_d}{H}\right] + .4665\Delta H_{-2}$$
$$ (1.419) \quad (1.219) \quad (.0630) \quad\quad\quad (.0960)$$
$$\overline{R} = .96 \quad\quad \overline{S} = 104.8 \quad\quad d = 1.336$$

In the study by Derksen, the related equation had the values:

$$(1.1) \quad S = -545 + 16.3\,r - 8.56\,c_{-1} + 5.80\,\Delta\frac{Y_d}{H} + .44\Delta H_{-2}$$
$$R = .96$$

Equation 1.0 is based on data for the periods 1920-40 and 1950-56, while 1.1 in contrast contains only data for 1914-38. Also, in

CHART IV-1

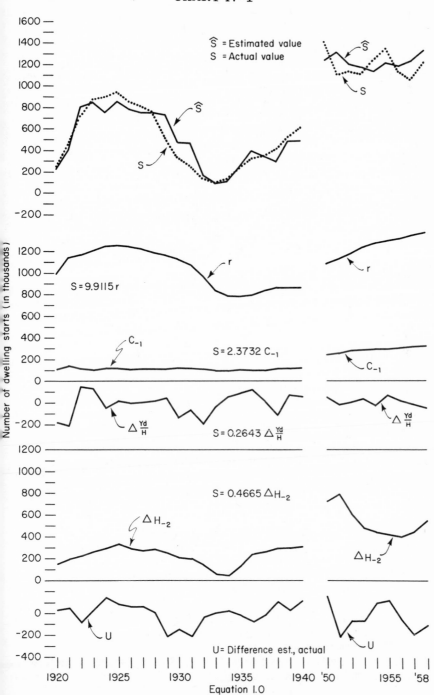

Number of dwelling starts (in thousands)

$\widehat{S}$ = Estimated value
S = Actual value

$\widehat{S}$

S

S = 9.9115 r

r

r

C_{-1}

S = 2.3732 C_{-1}

C_{-1}

$\triangle \frac{Yd}{H}$

S = 0.2643 $\triangle \frac{Yd}{H}$

$\triangle \frac{Yd}{H}$

S = 0.4665 $\triangle H_{-2}$

$\triangle H_{-2}$

$\triangle H_{-2}$

U

U

U = Difference est., actual

1920   1925   1930   1935   1940 '50   1955 '58

Equation I.0

equation 1.0 the average household income change $\left[\Delta\frac{Yd}{H}\right]$ is in constant dollars and refers to the difference between the current and previous year's income. Derksen, on the other hand, working before the period of large price changes, did not find it necessary to use price-corrected income figures (Equation 1.1). He also used the income change between the current year and the following year, but this is not useful for prediction. This income variable plays a relatively small role in both equations. The remaining variables are the same, but in the interim major revisions as well as additions of data have occurred for all series.

In the recomputed model, equation 1.0, we see a high correlation $(\bar{R})$ but a fairly large standard error of estimate $(\bar{S})$. The signs of the cost coefficient disagree with the theory. Higher costs, instead of reducing the number of starts, tend to raise starts. On the other hand, the cost coefficient is statistically the least significant.

All of the other coefficients in equation 1.0 are both significant and have the right sign. When we examine the Beta coefficients or the weights of each of the variables in terms of their own standard deviations, we find that the movements in the rent index and in household formation each account for about one-third of the movement in starts, with costs and income splitting the remaining third. The manner in which the year-to-year movements in each of the variables are related to changes in starts is shown in Chart IV-1. From this it is evident that movements in rents and costs tended to be gradual and primarily influence the general level of the estimates. Year-to-year fluctuations are related primarily to movements in incomes and household formation.

According to the bottom section of Chart IV-1, the errors in the estimates which reflect the disturbances in the basic data are far from random. The disturbances tend to be positive for a string of years, then turn negative for a period, and so forth. In effect, the disturbances appear to be auto-correlated. It therefore appears plausible that they contradict one of the basic assumptions of the statistical methodology (52). A test of the null hypothesis that the disturbances are independent can be obtained through the Durbin-Watson coefficient (shown as d) in the data under equation 1.0. This test proves to be inconclusive, $d = 1.34$. This statistic falls within the bounds (in this case 1.03-1.85 at the 5 percent significance level) for which no clear answer is possible (13).

To examine one possibility of correcting for the probable auto-correlation, even though we recognized that many equations already used transformed variables, we calculated all of the equations both in their original terms and also after transforming each of the variables to a first difference of that shown in the basic

TABLE IV-1

Equation 1.0
Dwelling Unit Starts
(In Thousands)

	Predictions		Absolute Deviation		Percent Deviation		Forecast of Direction of Movement	
	1957	1958	1957	1958	1957	1958	1957	1958
Actual Values	1,042	1,209						
Naive Model, No Change	1,118	1,042	+ 76	-167	+ 7.29	-13.81	No	No
Naive Model, Constant Change	907	966	-135	-243	-12.96	-20.10	Yes	No
Official Projections	1,000	1,100	- 42	-109	- 4.03	- 9.02	Yes	Yes
Original Econometric Model	n.a.	n.a.	n.a.	n.a.	n.a.	n.a.	n.a.	n.a.
Recomputed Econometric Model (Standard Error of Forecast)	1,220	1,311	+178 (119.6)	+102 (116.5)	+17.08	+ 8.44	No	Yes

model. An example of a transformed and recomputed equation is shown as 3.0 - A in Table IV-3 (this is the case where the greatest change in d took place as a result of the transformation). The transformations made no appreciable difference in the accuracy of the predictions or in the ability to forecast turning points. The statistic "d" stayed in the same approximate range in each case.

What happens when our various tests are applied to the recomputed equation? First, comparison of the old and new coefficients shows that the primary variables, rents and household change, maintain their same approximate weights and sign. The sign of costs is altered, and the weight of the income variable decreases sharply. The $\bar{R}$ which results from the recomputed equation is high, and the "b" coefficients are significantly larger than their standard errors. On the other hand, one cannot put too much faith in these measures because both serial correlation and multicollinearity appear to be present. The presence of these two factors leads to an underestimate of the standard errors and, as a result, the usual tests for the significance of the coefficients may be invalid.

Second, how does the new equation work in predictions? For this test we examine the comparisons in Table IV-1. The average error of the recomputed econometric model in the two years was 140,000 units. The percentage deviation of the prediction from the reported actual value was 12.72 percent. Even though large, these errors were not outside the normal tolerance limits which might be expected since the standard error of the forecasts averaged 118,000. The model correctly predicted the direction of change in 1958 but not in 1957.

The econometric model was very poor for 1957. While it was not too good for 1958, it was better than any of the others. It did considerably better than the constant change model in terms of percentage deviations. In magnitude of error, it was somewhat poorer than the "no change" model, but that model cannot predict a change. The best of these predictions by far was the official one. The official projection correctly called the turns in both years, and its average error was only about half that of the others.

Tests of Equation 2.0

The estimated values for the coefficients of equation 2.0 are:

$$(2.0) \quad S = 71.65 + 156.8\ (H - \frac{U + U_{-1}}{6}) - 117.2\ Q_{-1}$$
$$ (15.6) \phantom{\ (H - \frac{U + U_{-1}}{6}) - } (14.7)$$
$$\bar{R} = .94 \qquad S = 139.8 \qquad d = 1.52$$

For Bassie's somewhat related study, the equation reads:

$$(2.1) \quad S = 302 + 172 \left(H - \frac{U + U_{-1}}{6}\right) - 150\,Q_{-1}$$

$$R = .95$$

This second equation is offered as an empirical forecasting model and not as a structural model of the market. This limited objective enables Bassie to justify the use of independent variables which differ somewhat from those based upon theory and from those used in the recomputed equation 2.0. For households (H), he uses the number of married couples. These, during much of the period, were closely correlated with the number of households, but in recent years the ratio of married couples to households has changed. For the stock of housing, Bassie chains the BLS starts less estimated demolitions to the 1940 Census. His estimate of nonfarm housing stock at the beginning of 1955 is about 6,000,000 below our estimate based upon the Census of 1950 and the National Housing Inventory of 1956 (See Q in Appendix A). Because equations 2.1 and 2.0 use data of different dimensions, the coefficients of equation 2.1 must be inflated to make the two comparable. When the coefficients of equation (2.1) are corrected to approximate what they would be for the units used in our recomputation, the equation reads:

$$(2.2) \quad S = 330 + 200 \left(H - \frac{U + U_{-1}}{6}\right) - 162\,Q_{-1}$$

Clearly, there has been a decided change in the parameters. The recomputation (2.0) gives a considerably smaller weight to the negative influence of the existing housing stock. In effect, the re-computed model states that vacancies have a much smaller influence on construction than in the inflated original formulation (2.2).

The correlation coefficients of the two models are about the same. The signs of the regression coefficients have not changed and both coefficients are statistically highly significant.

Examination of Table IV-2 shows that the recomputed model (2.0) has done relatively well in its predictions for 1957 and 1958. The direction of change was slightly wrong for the first year and correct for the second. The result is 8.2 percent too high for 1957 and off 3.9 percent for 1958. The average percentage error for the two years is 6.1 percent. This is nearly twice as good as the best naive forecast and somewhat better than the official projection. The average standard error of the forecast was 157,000 units, far larger than either error.

Table IV-2 also shows a 1957 and 1958 prediction from Bassie's original equation (2.1), but the attempt may suffer slightly from

TABLE IV-2

Equation 2.0
Dwelling Unit Starts
(In Thousands)

	Predictions		Absolute Deviation		Percent Deviation		Correct Forecast of Direction of Movement	
	1957	1958	1957	1958	1957	1958	1957	1958
Actual Values	1,042	1,209						
Naive Model, No Change	1,118	1,042	+ 76	-167	+ 7.29	-13.81	No	No
Naive Model, Constant Change	907	966	-135	-243	-12.96	-20.10	Yes	No
Official Projections	1,000	1,100	- 42	-109	- 4.03	- 9.02	Yes	Yes
Original Econometric Model	1,127	989	+ 85	-220	+ 8.16	-18.20	No	No
Recomputed Econometric Model	1,127	1,062	+ 85	- 47	+ 8.16	- 3.89	No	Yes
(Standard Error of Forecast)			(155.6)	(158.6)				

a possibly incorrect interpretation of the author's description of his series. These predictions, based on his equation and attempting to use his series, are relatively better than the ones Bassie obtains for 1954 and 1955. Even so, the table shows that the predictions from equation (2.1) are poorer than the simplest naive model, and are much worse than either the Commerce-Labor projections or those from the recomputed model.

An examination of Chart IV-2 which charts the year-to-year estimates of Equation 2.0 gives a clearer picture of how this system functions. Because the number of both households and dwelling units have increased steadily, both these variables rose in every year except for 1930-33 when the rise of unemployment exceeded the growth of households and caused the first variable to turn down. A predicted change in starts occurs when the rate of growth of households exceeds that of dwelling units (or vice versa) or when unemployment alters decidedly. In fact, the changes in the relationships of the two independent variables during the postwar period have been rather small. As a result, the maximum year-to-year variation in equation's (2.0) estimate of starts has been 9 percent while the average year-to-year movement of the estimate was 2 percent. Alterations in actual starts averaged 10 percent. Starts have fluctuated around the level of the equation's estimates. When starts did not change much, or rose towards previous heights as in 1954 and 1956, this equation did an excellent forecasting job. In 1950, 1951, and 1955, when starts varied more widely, the predictions were poor.

As one would expect from examining Chart IV-2, serial correlation is again present. The value of d for equation (2.0) is 1.52. From this fact and the figure, one might conclude that, because each year's prediction depends so greatly on recent levels, forecasts from constantly recomputed equations should be quite good. The theory behind the model is quite similar to, and not necessarily better than, that of the naive models. There is little evidence of consistency in the value of the coefficients or reason to believe that they give a proper description of the underlying structure of the market.

Tests of Equation 3.0

The estimated values for equation 3.0 are:

$$(3.0) \quad D = -19.857 + .1350\, Y_d + 8.413\frac{r}{c} + .0057\,\Delta H - .0831\,N$$
$$ (.0189) \quad\ (.9264) \quad (.0021) \quad\quad (.0281)$$
$$ \overline{R} = .95 \quad\quad \overline{S} = 1.26 \quad d = 1.318$$

CHART IV-2

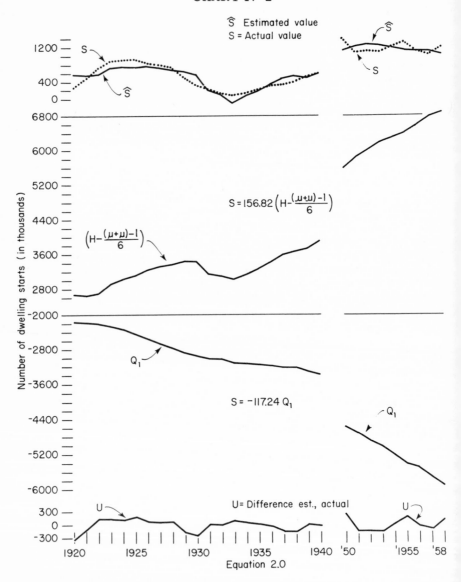

Equation 2.0

Mattila in his study has presented coefficients for this equation and some related ones:

$$(3.1) \quad D = -10.810 + .1463\,Y_d + 10.65\frac{r}{c} + .0030\,\Delta H - .1368\,N$$

$$\qquad\qquad\qquad (.035) \qquad (2.3) \qquad (.001) \qquad\qquad (.027)$$

$$\qquad R = .71 \qquad S = 1.11 \qquad \frac{\sigma^2}{\sigma^2} = 1.233$$

Equation (3.1) is estimated by the limited-information-maximum-likelihood method from a system of five equations. It is based upon the period 1919-41 and 1946-50.

$$(3.2) \quad D = -9.0539 + .1887\,Y_d + 5.39\frac{r}{c} + .0004\,\Delta H$$

$$\qquad\qquad\qquad (.036) \qquad (2.0) \qquad (.003)$$

$$\qquad\qquad - .1232\,N + .2138\,Z_1$$

$$\qquad\qquad (.050) \qquad (.123)$$

This equation is estimated by the least squares method for the period 1920-41. It includes the credit variable Z_1 in the form discussed previously in the presentation of equations 7.0 and 8.0.

$$(3.3) \quad D = -5.414 + .1663\,Y_d + 7.51\frac{r}{c} - .1570\,N$$

$$\qquad\qquad\qquad (.031) \qquad (1.5) \qquad (.027)$$

$$\qquad R = .86$$

Equation (3.3) is also estimated by the least squares method with observations for 1920-41.

In equations 3.1, 3.2, and 3.3, the series for income, rents, and costs are in 1939 prices while the series on the value of the housing stock is in 1926 prices. In 3.0, all values are in 1947-49 prices. In the recomputation, the Boeckh cost index has been substituted for the American Appraisal Co. index, the latest Department of Commerce estimates for income and households have replaced those used by Mattila, and the Grebler-Blank-Winnick estimates of the value of the stock of housing those by Goldsmith. All indexes substituted are of roughly the same orders of magnitude as the original ones.

The recomputation in equation 3.0 has improved the correlation compared to that obtained in 3.1. The signs of the coefficients all remain the same. Each of the regression coefficients in 3.0 is still statistically significant, and the relative amount of deviation remains about the same as in the original published forms. When the magnitude of the coefficients in the original and the recomputed equations is compared, however, sizable changes appear to have occurred. The Mattila equation (3.1), transformed approximately to the same base and units as the recomputed equation (3.0), reads as:

$$(3.4) \quad D = -21.62 + .1463\,Y_d + 10.65\left(\frac{r}{c}\right) + .0060\Delta H - .1368\,N$$

The coefficient of the rent-cost variable in the recomputed equation is about 20 percent smaller than in 3.4 (the transformed values of 3.1), the coefficient of the housing stock variable is about 40 percent less, that of income about 10 percent less, while the household formation coefficient is about the same size. An examination of the data shows the reason for these variations. Mattila used the 1946-50 period in his computations. This was a very disturbed period in which household formation was unusually high, while the stock of housing, after the depression and the war-imposed halt of construction, was low. In recent periods, both of these have returned to more normal levels. As a result, the shift in the period used for fitting the equations results in a decided change in the coefficients.

Mattila encounters the same type of difficulty when he recomputes his equations using slightly different periods and variables. Thus, in comparing 3.2 and 3.1, he notes that the coefficients of income (Y_d) and dwelling units (N) are remarkably similar. On the other hand, the rent-cost coefficient in 3.2 is only half the previous one, the importance of household formation (ΔH) practically disappears, and the sign of the credit variable (Z_1) is the opposite of what one would expect from the theory. Because the coefficients of H and Z_1 were not statistically significant and because of multi-collinearity, Mattila removed them to obtain equation 3.3. This is a cross between our equations 3.0 and 6.0. In equation 3.3, the size of the coefficients is decidedly different from 3.0 and, in addition, one variable has been entirely removed.

Again, this general equation to explain the value of construction clearly does not meet the test of consistency. How good is it on prediction (Table IV-3)? The problem of household formation from 1946 to 1950 apparently accounts for the extremely poor results of attempting to explain 1957 and 1958 from model 3.1 (the original econometric model in Table IV-3) which was published as recently as 1955. In the post-sample period, the rate of household formation fell while the value of the housing stock rose rapidly. Since the latter had a negative coefficient in the original model, the combination led to a considerable underestimate of the value of residential construction. While the estimate from Mattila's equation would have to be adjusted more carefully to account for changes in the data, the error would probably range around 50 percent. As one would expect, equation (3.0), after recomputation, yields a much better prediction for 1957 and 1958. It is nearly 10 percent too

Equation 3.0
Volume
(Billions of Dollars)

	Predictions		Absolute Deviation		Percent Deviation		Correct Forecast of Direction of Movement	
	1957	1958	1957	1958	1957	1958	1957	1958
Actual Values	12.90	13.55						
Naive Model, No Change	13.65	12.90	+ .75	- .65	+5.81	- 4.80	No	No
Naive Model, Constant Change	12.22	12.15	- .68	-1.40	-5.27	-10.33	Yes	No
Official Projections	13.20	13.36	+ .30	- .19	+2.33	- 1.40	Yes	Yes
Original Econometric Model	6.74	5.25	-6.16	-8.30	-47.75	-61.25	Yes	No
Recomputed Econometric Model (Standard Error of Forecast)	14.13	13.00	+1.23 (1.446)	- .55 (1.483)	+9.53	- 4.06	No	Yes

Equation 3.0-A
Volume
(Billions of Dollars)

	Predictions		Absolute Deviation		Percent Deviation		Correct Forecast of Direction of Movement	
	1957	1958	1957	1958	1957	1958	1957	1958
Actual Values	12.90	13.55						
Naive Model, No Change	13.65	12.90	+ .75	- .65	+ 5.81	- 4.80	No	No
Naive Model, Constant Change	12.22	12.15	- .68	-1.40	- 5.27	-10.33	Yes	No
Official Projections	13.20	13.36	+ .30	- .19	+ 2.33	- 1.40	Yes	Yes
Original Econometric Model	6.74	5.25	-6.16	-8.30	-47.75	-61.25	Yes	No
Recomputed Econometric Model (Standard Error of Forecast)	13.83	12.48	+ .93 (1.446)	-1.07 (1.483)	+ 7.21	- 7.90	No	No

high for 1957, and off 4.0 percent for 1958. Its average error for
the two years is 6.8 percent. This is not quite as good as the first
naive forecast but better than the second. On the other hand, the
results are poorer than the average error of 1.87 percent achieved
by official projections of the judgment type. The latter correctly
predicted the direction of movement in both years, while the econometric model on this count was wrong for 1957. The model was
well within a single standard error of forecast, as was the previous
one.

Chart IV-3 makes it clear that the so-called incentive to build
variables Yd and $\frac{r}{c}$ have moved in opposite directions. Their shifts
in over-all level have been far more important than their year-
to-year changes. The same is true for the stock of housing (N).

In the postwar period it has been primarily the erratic growth
of income and of households that has led to the year-to-year movements in the estimated volume of construction from Equation 3.0.
Again the Durbin-Watson coefficient (d = 1.318) and Chart IV-3
indicate the possibility of serial correlation. Equation 3.0-A, the
first difference form of equation 3.0, is as follows:

$$(3.0\text{-A}) \quad \Delta D = -.2018 + .1152\,\Delta Y_d + 3.5453\,\Delta\frac{r}{c}$$
$$(.0346) \qquad (1.4088)$$
$$+ .0010\,\Delta^2 H - .0105\,\Delta N$$
$$(.0020) \qquad (.0808)$$

$$\bar{R} = .66 \quad \bar{S} = 1.21 \quad d = 1.6404$$

We see (and the same general picture holds for all of the first
difference transformations) that the coefficient of correlation falls
sharply. The signs and general relationship among the regression
coefficients do not change. In this case, the last two coefficients
which appeared just significant in the original equation are now
considerably below any of the usual levels thought of as significant.

The transformation does succeed in removing some of the serial
correlation. The d now equals 1.6404, while the upper bound (at
the 5 percent significance level) at which one would conclude that
no positive serial correlation exists is 1.75. Chart IV-4 shows
the considerable difference resulting from the transformation.
According to Table IV-3, however, no improvement is made in
predictions from this transformed model, and this is also true
for the other equations. One forecast is better and one worse. The
average for the two years is not quite as good as for Equation 3.0,
and the one success in predicting the turn is lost.

CHART IV-3

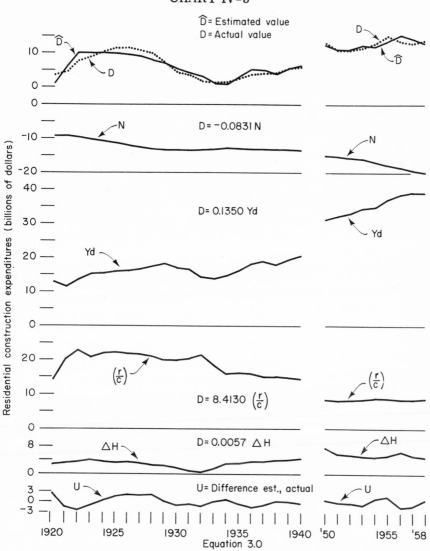

$\widehat{D}$ = Estimated value
D = Actual value

$D = -0.0831\,N$

$D = 0.1350\,Yd$

$D = 8.4130\left(\frac{r}{c}\right)$

$D = 0.0057\,\triangle H$

U = Difference est., actual

Residential construction expenditures (billions of dollars)

Equation 3.0

CHART IV-4

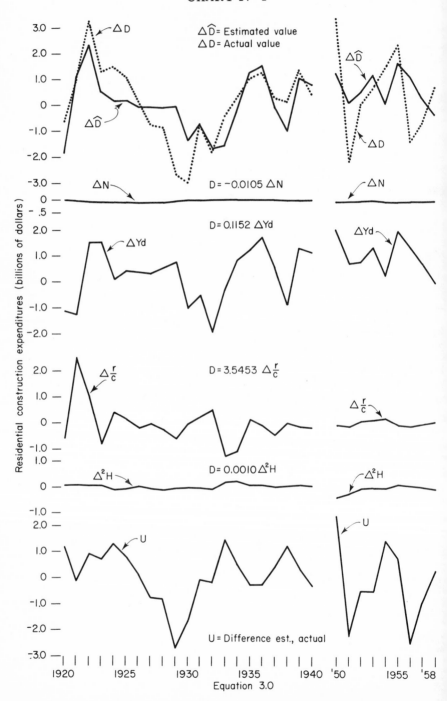

Equation 3.0

Tests of Equation 4.0

Equation 4.0 has the values:

(4.0) $D_1 = -18.68 + 4.76 \left(\frac{r}{c}\right)$

                  (.655)

         $+ .023 (Yd + Yd_{-1} + Yd_{-2}) + .0073 \Delta H$

         (.002)   (.001)

   $\bar{R} = .97$ $\bar{S} = .89$ $d = 1.944$

This equation, it will be recalled, differs from the previous ones by attempting to separate the demand for owner-type and rental-type units, even though the separation is necessarily less than exact.

When Klein (VI and VII) published an equation of this type, the values were:

(4.1) $D_1 = -7.49 + 3.14 \left(\frac{r}{c}\right)$

                (.52)

        $+ 0.02 (Yd + Yd_{-1} + Yd_{-2}) + .0039 \Delta H$

       (.003)   (.0005)

    $\bar{S} = 0.21$ $\dfrac{\delta^2}{\sigma^2} = 1.80$

A recomputed version with two additional years was published by Christ (IX):

(4.2) $D_1 = -2.65 + 1.80 \left(\frac{r}{c}\right)$

               (.8)

       $+ .0061 (Yd + Yd_{-1} + Yd_{-2}) + .0015 \Delta H$

      (.004)   (.005)

   $S = .36$

Equation 4.1 used observations for the period 1920–41, Equation 4.2 added 1946–47, and Equation 4.0 used 1920–41 and 1950–56. In addition, the bases of the indices were changed and some were rather completely revised. If the bases of 4.1 are revised to agree approximately with 4.0, its values become:

(4.3) $D_1 = -14.98 + 3.14 \left(\frac{r}{c}\right)$

       $+ .02 (Yd + Yd_{-1} + Yd_{-2}) + .0078 \Delta H$

It is clear that in the original equation (4.1) and the recombination by Christ (4.2) the parameters are quite far apart. The addition of 1946 and 1947 causes each parameter to shift by magnitudes of from nearly 2 to 30. The income coefficient becomes not significant and the rent-cost variable is barely significant. The comparison is much better between our recomputation (4.0) and the original equation (4.1). The coefficient for the rent-cost variable has increased by about 50 percent and the income variable also shows a sharp increase in importance. All coefficients remain decidedly significant, their signs agree with the theory, and the correlation is very high.

When the Christ recomputation was tested for the year 1948, it overestimated the amount of production by about 10 percent. This was slightly better than the no-change naive forecast and somewhat worse than the constant-change forecast for that year. Because of the long time that has elapsed since the Klein model was computed and because of some decided differences in the form the series now take, we have not attempted to calculate a prediction for 1957-58 from models 4.1 or 4.2.

Table IV-4 shows that the prediction from the recomputed model (4.0) are poor. They overestimated the amount of production by from 14 to 16 percent in both years. This was far worse than the average errors of under 6 percent for the two naive forecasts and under 5 percent for the official projection. The predictions were at about 1.5 times the standard errors of forecast from the actual for both years. In effect, then, this equation was about the poorest of all. It was, however, still well within the limits of sampling variability. This brings out again the large range of predictions possible within the limits of sampling variability, given the variance of the sample period.

From Chart IV-5 we observe the same type of relationships noted previously. The incentive and ability to purchase variables $\frac{r}{c}$ and $(\mathcal{E}Yd)$ both move steadily. Their levels shift during the war in opposite directions, but average out in a higher rate of expenditures. It is primarily the change in households that causes the year-to-year movements in the estimates. In this case, there is no evidence of serial correlation—the statistic d equals 1.944.

In recent years, the predictions failed to show actual decreases in the volume of construction when they occurred, and the year-to-year estimates tended to vary far less than the actual values.

Tests of Equation 5.0

Equation 5.0 is complementary to equation 4.0. This equation attempts to explain the volume of expenditures for construction of rental-type units.

TABLE IV-4

Equation 4.0
Owner-Type Volume
(Billions of Dollars)

	Predictions		Absolute Deviation		Percent Deviation		Correct Forecast of Direction of Movement	
	1957	1958	1957	1958	1957	1958	1957	1958
Actual Values	10.87	10.92						
Naive Model, No Change	12.11	10.87	+1.24	- .05	+11.41	- .46	No	No
Naive Model, Constant Change	10.81	9.63	- .06	-1.29	- .56	-11.81	Yes	No
Official Projections	11.66	10.69	+ .79	- .23	+ 7.27	- 2.11	Yes	No
Original Econometric Model	n.a.	n.a.	n.a.	n.a.	n.a.	n.a.	n.a.	n.a.
Recomputed Econometric Model	12.61	12.41	+1.74	+1.59	+16.01	+14.56	No	Yes
(Standard Error of Forecast)			(1.011)	(1.037)				

CHART IV-5

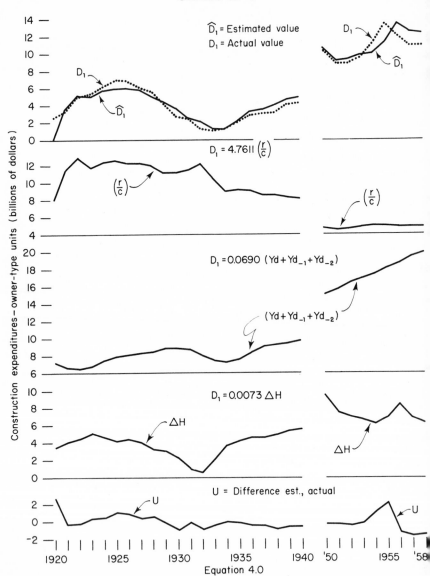

Equation 4.0

Its values are:

(5.0) $D_2 = -4.551 + .087r_{-1} - .0027(c_2)_{-1}$
                   $(.0080)$ $(.024)$
          $-.052(c_2)_{-2} + .0030\Delta H_{-1} - .237i$
          $(.026)$ $(.0005)$ $(.146)$
          $\bar{R} = .94$ $\bar{S} = .49$ $d = .928$

This type of equation in Klein's work (VI and VII) was:

(5.1) $D_2 = -1.99 + 2.93r_{-1} + .16(c_2)_{-1}$
                   $(.39)$ $(.53)$
          $- .44(c_2)_{-2} + .0013\Delta H_{-1} - .25i$
          $(.52)$ $(.0006)$ $(.07)$
          $\bar{S} = 0.25$ $\dfrac{\delta^2}{\sigma^2} = 2.16$

In the recomputation by Christ (IX) it read:

(5.2) $D_2 = -1.79 + 3.05r_{-1} + .04(c_2)_{-1}$
                   $(.36)$ $(.5)$
          $- .53(c_2)_{-2} + .0011\Delta H_{-1} - .25i$
          $(.5)$ $(.0005)$ $(.06)$
          $\bar{S} = .25$

If the parameters are shifted for equation 5.1 to account for changes in base years so as to agree approximately with 5.0, it becomes:

(5.3) $D_2 = -4.40 + .0505r_{-1} + .0012(c_2)_{-1}$
          $- .0033(c_2)_{-2} + .0029(\Delta H)_{-1} - .551i$

The process of recomputation has again caused decided changes in the parameters. The effect of movements in household formation remains about the same. The importance of rent movements becomes slight and that of interest charges is cut in half. On the other hand, movements in costs become considerably more important and last year's costs now are found to have a negative effect on construction. This may be considered a movement towards greater logic, but the significance of last year's costs remains low. The coefficients for costs lagged two years and for the interest rate are also not large compared to their variances.

Table IV-5 shows the relationship of the different forecasts. All did extremely poorly in 1957, but the econometric model was the best of a poor lot. A decided shift took place in the rental-type

CHART IV-6

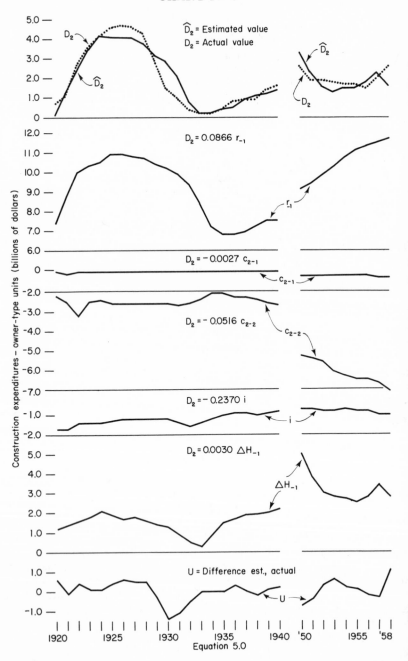

Equation 5.0

TABLE IV-5

Equation 5.0

Rental Type Volume
(Billions of Dollars)

	Predictions		Absolute Deviation		Percent Deviation		Correct Forecast of Direction of Movement	
	1957	1958	1957	1958	1957	1958	1957	1958
Actual Values	2.03	2.63						
Naive Model, No Change	1.54	2.03	-.49	-.60	-24.14	-22.81	No	No
Naive Model, Constant Change	1.41	2.52	-.62	-.11	-30.54	- 4.18	No	Yes
Official Projections	1.54	2.67	-.49	+.04	-24.14	+ 1.52	No	Yes
Original Econometric Model	n.a.	n.a.	n.a.	n.a.	n.a.	n.a.	n.a.	n.a.
Recomputed Econometric Model (Standard Error of Forecast)	2.29	1.56	+.26 (.562)	-1.07 (.569)	+12.81	-40.67	Yes	No

market in 1957. Whether this was a basic shift in the structure or simply a reaction to changed variables is not certain. In any event, the amount of this type of construction increased by nearly a third, and all of the forecasting methods missed the major change. In 1958, the official forecasters were able to take account of the new situation and they did very well. The econometric model on the contrary slipped badly. Its movement in the wrong direction resulted from a sharp change in prior costs and household formation. These led to a prediction of a decrease in construction whereas it actually rose sharply. Even so we note that this error was not beyond that which might have been expected on a random basis. The validity of the standard error is, however, again called strongly into question by the high amount of serial correlation d = .928.

Tests for Equation 6.0

Equation 6.0 uses merely the incentives to build variables without the households or household change variables. This model was computed in the form:

$$\frac{D}{N_{-1}} = a + b\frac{Y_d}{N_{-1}}$$

Its parameters as presented by Suits, in the University of Michigan 5th Annual Conference on The Economic Outlook in November 1956, were:

(6.0) $D = .066\,(Y_d) - .021\,N_{-1}$
             (.006)   (0.006)

The observations covered the years 1928–41 and 1948–56.

In attempting to recompute this equation we obtained a somewhat similar form, but its predictions were far worse than those of the original model. Since Suits has published predictions for both 1957 and 1958, we decided to utilize his own predictions (Table IV-6). For these years, the equation did a fair job of prediction, with an average error of 7.4 percent as compared with errors of 1.87 percent in the official projection and slightly over 5 percent for the no-change naive forecast.

It is clear that this model, with its two variables, is subject to large shifts depending upon the accuracy of the estimated independent variables. As is brought out later, both of the variables used have actually experienced major changes over time and are subject to biases in the period under consideration. The problem of serial correlation is again great. The value of the stock of

Table IV-6

Equation 6.0
Total Volume
(Billions of Dollars)

	Predictions		Absolute Deviation		Percent Deviation		Correct Forecast of Direction of Movement	
	1957	1958	1957	1958	1957	1958	1957	1958
Actual Values	12.90	13.55						
Naive Model, No Change	13.65	12.90	+ .75	- .65	+5.81	- 4.80	No	No
Naive Model, Constant Change	12.22	12.15	- .68	-1.40	-5.27	-10.33	Yes	No
Official Projections	13.20	13.36	+ .30	- .19	+2.33	- 1.40	Yes	Yes
Original Econometric Model	13.90	12.60	+1.00	- .95	+7.75	- 7.01	No	No
Recomputed Econometric Model	n.a.	n.a.	n.a.	n.a.	n.a.	n.a.	n.a.	n.a.

housing (N) grows continually. One would expect an equation of this type to do a better job of prediction than of explanation, and this is what happened for the years covered.

Equations 7.0 and 8.0

A different method was adopted for testing these equations. The equations have just been computed by Break (XII) and he has tested them carefully. Thus, it appears sufficient to report his results. In the case of equation type 7.0 for estimating starts, there are three separate equations and the credit variable assumes several values. The two credit coefficients shown here are the extremes.

$$(7.1.1) \quad S = 5.6 \left(\frac{Yd}{C}\right)_{-\frac{1}{2}} + 1.0\,\Delta H - 5.0\,N_{-1} - \frac{50}{150}\,Z_1 \quad (1925\text{-}41)$$

$$\bar{R} = .90$$

$$(7.1.2) \quad S = 9.0 \left(\frac{Yd}{C}\right)_{-\frac{1}{2}} + .05\,\Delta H - 4.5\,N_{-1} - \frac{1000}{3100}\,Z_2 \quad (1948\text{-}56)$$

$$\bar{R} = .81$$

$$(7.2) \quad S = 5.0\,Yd - 20\frac{C}{p} + .05\,\Delta H - 4.5\,N_{-1} - \frac{1000}{3100}\,Z_2 \quad (1948\text{-}56)$$

Obviously there was a decided shift in these parameters between the two periods 1925-41 and 1948-56. In the earlier period, Break shows an income elasticity about triple that of the later periods. Household formation is important in the first period but shows little or no influence in the postwar years. The existing stock of housing has roughly the same weight in both periods. On the other hand, the importance of credit is 10 to 20 times as large in recent years as it was in the interwar period.

The effect of introducing the credit variable in comparison to equation 1.0 is to reduce greatly the importance of household formation and to lower somewhat the cost or price elasticity. Comparing the equations, we find that, because of multi-collinearity, we really obtain no knowledge of which variables are basically significant. This observation is reinforced by an examination of the standard errors of the coefficients for the credit variable. The standard errors vary between "not significant" to "just significant" at the .05 level.

When we review the equations for expenditures on residential construction 8.0, we find similar results:

$$(8.1) \quad D = 0.1 \left(\frac{Y}{C}\right)_{-\frac{1}{2}} + .002\,\Delta H - .01\,N_{-1} - \frac{11}{28}\,Z_2 \quad (1948\text{-}56)$$

$$(8.2.1) \quad D = .03\,Yd_{-1} - .002\frac{C}{P} + \frac{.01}{.02}\,\Delta H_{-1}$$

$$+ .00\,N_{-1} - 0.6\,Z_1 \qquad\qquad (1925\text{--}41)$$

$$(8.2.2) \quad D = 0.1\,Yd_{-1} - .16\frac{C}{P} + .002\,\Delta H$$

$$- .01\,N_{-1} - \frac{11}{28}\,Z_2 \qquad\qquad (1948\text{--}56)$$

Again, there is a sharp change between the periods, with the importance of household formation decreasing radically. There also is the same abrupt increase in the importance of the credit variable. Compared to other studies, credit has again replaced household formation and the stock of housing as the dominant variable. While it is possible that these changes reflect basic shifts in the economy, it appears more likely that the alterations result primarily from the statistical techniques used. Because of inter-correlation between the independent variables, these estimated parameters are not stable.

Break has undertaken a series of tests in which he attempts to determine whether or not the equations account for the changes in the dependent variables between two periods. As noted previously, the equations based on observations for 1925-41 did not hold after the war, and this is the reason for dividing the sample period.

The results of his tests are found in Table IV-7. An examination of the table shows that, for every period except the final one, the direction of change was correctly predicted when both the least sensitive and the most sensitive credit variable was used. With only two exceptions, however, the equations failed to predict the full magnitude of the change. The equations with the most sensitive credit variables did better in every year than those with the other credit variables, since they showed more change and thus came closer to the correct amount.

Given a median number of about 1,050,000 starts in the years predicted, the average percentage error for the equations with the most sensitive credit variable would be from 7 to 20 percent. For the least sensitive, the percentages would run from 10 to 30. For construction expenditures, the absolute values averaged about $9.6 billion. The errors here would average between 1 and 15 percent for the most sensitive credit variables and between 5 and 25 percent for the least sensitive. The largest errors occurred in the last estimate, that for 1955-57, the only one which went beyond the sample period.

TABLE IV-7

Break's Tests of Equations Type 7.0 and 8.0

Equation	Period	Actual Change	Equation with Most Sensitive Credit Variable		Equation with Least Sensitive Credit Variable	
			Prediction	Error	Prediction	Error
		(000 Starts)				
7.1.1	1933-41	+525	+575	+ 50	+480	- 35
7.1.2	1948-50	+440	+260	-180	+165	-275
7.2	1948-50	+440	+194	-246	+ 99	-341
7.1.2	1950-52	-280	-178	+102	-108	+172
7.2	1950-52	-280	-206	+ 74	-136	+144
7.1.2	1953-55	+240	+161	- 79	+141	- 99
7.2	1953-55	+240	+157	- 83	+137	-103
7.1.2	1955-57	-318	-160	+158	- 70	+248
7.2	1955-57	-318	-210	+108	-120	+198
		(Billions of dollars in 1947-49 prices)				
8.2.1	1933-41	+4.8	+4.5	-0.3	+3.2	-1.5
8.1	1948-50	+3.5	+3.1	-0.4	+2.0	-1.5
8.2.2	1948-50	+3.5	+3.6	+0.1	+2.6	-0.9
8.1	1950-52	-2.4	-2.3	+0.1	-1.4	+1.0
8.2.2	1950-52	-2.4	-2.2	+0.2	-1.3	+1.1
8.1	1953-55	+3.4	+2.6	-0.8	+2.2	-1.2
8.2.2	1953-55	+3.4	+3.3	-0.1	+2.9	-0.5
8.1	1955-57	-2.5	-1.4	+1.1	-0.2	+2.3
8.2.2	1955-57	-2.5	-1.1	+1.4	+0.1	+2.6

There is but slight evidence from these data that equations of type 7.0 or 8.0 have done any better in passing the tests for either consistency (based on the differences between the two periods) or prediction than did the previous ones. The measurement of serial correlation has not been performed specifically for these equations. Since they are based on approximately the same variables as the previous equations, however, the same statistical problems must exist.

IV. CRITIQUE OF STATISTICAL-ECONOMETRIC MODELS

The discussion of the advantages, uses, and problems of econometric demand estimation has taken place on several levels (7, 10, 29, 58). Much of it is concerned with the general applicability of the method, assuming the availability of the required information. As is proper, such discussion deals primarily with the development of scientific tools. Only little attention has been given to the results achieved in the application of the tools so as to determine their usefulness in practice. Virtually no work has been done on the relationship of the basic assumptions to the real economy.

In this review, we are concerned with judging the present usefulness of the econometric approach compared to others, given our existing state of knowledge, and also with the type of data and procedures which would be necessary to improve it. Listing certain variables as dominant causes and assigning quantitative weights to them may give an appearance of reality to these studies, but it does not mean that the actual market structure has been revealed.

The previous section in which we tested the time-series equations raises serious doubts over their present usefulness for analysis. We shall now summarize the results and at the same time examine further some of the problems which must be met if econometric models are to be used more effectively. The summary will be under four headings: The structure and its consistency; the predictions; procedural and statistical difficulties; and data deficiencies.

A. The Observed Structure of the Market and the Consistency of the Observations

If one could accept the equations as true descriptions of the market, what would they reveal? The eight models discussed show a market in which the amount of construction is determined by a small number of independent variables, each operating in a simple, uncomplicated form. When the coefficients of these few variables are determined through regression, they "account" for 90 percent or more of the changes in construction volume which occurred in the sample period.

Almost all models include one or more variables which are expected to measure the willingness, ability, or desire of households or firms to construct dwellings. Foremost among these is some measurement of real income. When included, income appears to have a positive and fairly significant influence on construction. Income elasticity measured at the means is 2.0 to 3.0, i.e., a 1 percent rise in real personal disposable income is related to a 2 or 3 percent rise in the amount of building. While the movements of real income are not extreme, changes of as much as 10 percent between two years are not uncommon. In recent years, income has most frequently varied by 3 or 4 percent a year. The income variable, therefore, would explain construction variations in the vicinity of 10 percent between adjacent years.

The incentive to build is also hypothesized as being influenced by rents and by costs. Higher rents lead to more construction demand. Higher costs should have the opposite effect. In several cases, the rent index is divided by costs to get a measure of their joint change. In some cases, costs are used to correct incomes—in effect putting incomes on a real basis.

The influence of rents directly or of rents divided by costs is in the proper direction in every case. Costs by themselves have the wrong sign in recomputed equation 1.0 and in the original equation 5.1. The rent coefficients tend to be large and significant. In most cases, they carry the largest beta weights of any variable. On the other hand, as is evident from the Charts, the rent indexes rarely show much year-to-year variation. Their main impact is to differentiate the levels for each decade. The cost variables tend to be small, are not very significant, and carry but small weights.

Other variables measure the impact of household formation and of the stock of housing. The coefficients of these variables have the correct sign in all cases. An increase in households raises the level of construction, while more units or greater value in the stock tend to diminish it. The significance of these variables changes a great deal from equation to equation. Except for income, they form the entire list of variables in equations 2.0 and 6.0, but in the final groups 7.0 and 8.0 they almost disappear. Most equations show construction volume increasing about 0.5 percent for each 1.0 percent change in household formation. As pointed out in the next section, this indicates either large effects of new building on vacancies, or a large volume of replacements, or serious errors in the results.

Changes in credit conditions do not appear in most models. The interest rate was used in early versions of 1.0 and 3.0 prepared by the original authors. It had disappeared by the final version either because of signs disagreeing with the theory or a low level of significance. It does appear in equation 4.0 but has a rather unimportant influence. Only in equations 7.0 and 8.0 does credit have the proper sign and appear significant. Because of the way in which these equations are constructed, credit plays a major role. In the postwar versions of equations 7.0 and 8.0, a 1 percent change in the terms of credit causes a 0.5 to 1.5 percent change in construction, i.e., the credit elasticity of construction was between 0.5 and 1.5. The credit index changed by 5 to 30 percent per year, depending upon which form is used. As a result, movements in the credit variable account for annual shifts of 10 to 30 percent in total construction. This would be large enough to explain most year-to-year shifts in the postwar markets.

While this brief review indicates that the models offer some insight, as yet they cannot be said to have proved much. None of the time series models really meets satisfactorily the criterion of furnishing numerical values for all the rather intricate relationships that a well constructed, complete theory of construction appears to demand.

Furthermore, because of the statistical problems to be discussed shortly, the stability and consistency of the various coefficients is not great. The coefficient of correlation is high no matter which equation is used. For short periods, forecasts turn out to be better the fewer the variables introduced.

In every case, additional years caused decided changes in the parameters. In a few cases, the movement was sufficient to alter the signs. In others, the weights of the separate independent variables altered considerably. As indicated later, there is good reason to believe that these shifts reflect problems of statistical procedures and data biases. The time-series models in their present forms give only a general indication of some of the variables probably at work in the market.

3. The Ability to Predict

The tests of the ability to predict did not prove that the basic procedures used in the econometric analyses were wrong. Almost all equations obtained high correlations and significant regression coefficients for the sample period. Nor was there a failure to forecast within the expected tolerance limits. The predictions tended to fall within the 95 percent fiducial limits established by the variance of the sample period, and in several cases well within a single standard error.

On the other hand, the tests indicated that the predictions from the models were not very useful. Errors tended to be as high or higher than those in simpler or judgment procedures. The difficulty in forecasting arises from the fact that, even though the correlations are high, the standard errors still run from 10 to 15 percent at the means. When fiducial limits are set for individual years, the variance of single observations is introduced and the wider part of the tolerance bands must be used because the independent variables in the most recent years are far above their means. As a result, the possible range of predictions arising from sampling variance alone is very wide even if the structure were to remain unchanged.

Moreover, all of these attempts to measure the variance are likely to be incorrect. They are based upon assumptions of randomness and lack of correlation in the residuals. This is not the case, as is revealed by examination of the estimates and by the evidence of serial correlation in the errors. As is well recognized, economic phenomena which arise from the basic functioning of the economy do not vary in a random manner. The presence of serial correlation is one of the factors tending to give better predictions than one might expect if the disturbances were random. When an equation has been recently computed, it should be expected to give adequate predictions for a year or two if the economy changes only slowly. This accounts for some of the occasionally successful predictions from the naive models and judgment forecasts. We saw in the discussion of rental-type housing (5.0) that, when a decided change occurred in this market in 1957, all types of forecasts failed dismally.

Because a forecast is not too difficult when the economy is moving slowly or well within its previous limits, the simple test of predictions is not sufficient to enable us to say that an equation has really described the market. In fact, the tables in the preceding chapter show that the two simplest equations (2.0 and 6.0) did the best job of prediction for 1957 and 1958, even though neither makes the claim of really describing adequately the manner in which the market works or how the market would be influenced by changes in structure or in variables subject to outside forces.

The previous tables compare the ability of the various equations to predict. Some of their results are summarized in Tables IV-8 and IV-9. Table IV-8 shows the success of the various techniques in forecasting the direction of the next year's movement. (It will be recognized, as is made clear in Table IV-9, that only four types of predictions were made in each year. Two sets of econometric models were used to forecast starts and two for total volume.) The "no change" model by definition failed to show the direction of movement. The "constant change" model correctly predicted the direction half of the time, as did the recomputed econometric models. The official predictions were successful in direction in 6 out of 8 cases.

TABLE IV-8

Success in Predicting Direction of Movement
in 4 Series in 1957-1958

	Number of Successes	Number of Failures	Successes as % of Total
No Change Model	0	8	0
Constant Change Model	4	4	50
Official Projections	6	2	75
Econometric Models*	6	6	50

* Based on Recomputed Equations 1.0 to 5.0 and 3.0 - A.

TABLE IV-9

Rank and Magnitude of Percentage Deviations
Forecast From Actual 1957-1958

Item	Year	No Change Model	Constant Change Model	Official Projections	Econometric Models
Starts	1957......	2	4	1	3[a]
	1958......	3	4	2	1
Volume	1957......	3	2	1	4[b]
	1958......	2	4	1	3
Owner Type	1957......	3	1	2	4[c]
	1958......	1	2	3	4
Rental Type	1957......	2 1/2	4	2 1/2	1[d]
	1958......	3	2	1	4
Total		19 1/2	23	13 1/2	24
Means Percentage Deviation:	1957......	12.16	12.33	9.63	12.45
	1958......	8.57	11.60	3.51	16.84

[a]Average of equations 1.0 and 2.0
[b]Average of equations 3.0 and 3.0-A
[c]Equation 4.0
[d]Equation 5.0

The critical year for predictions was 1957 when the number of starts dropped by 7.3 percent compared to 1956 and the constant dollar value fell by 5.8 percent. Of the econometric models, (2.0) and (4.0) correctly predicted the direction of change. The judgmen projections correctly predicted the continued fall in starts, tota and owner volume, but failed to forecast the upturn in the construction of rental-type units.

Table IV-9 ranks the various predictions (using an average of the two econometric models for starts and volume). For 1957 the official projection ranked first for two predictions and was second, or tied for second, for the others. The econometric model show one first, one third, and two fourths. In terms of the average percentage error for 1957, the official projections were off 9.6 percent while all of the others were off slightly over 12 percent.

In 1958, the direction of construction changed. The officia projections caught the changed direction in all but one case (and that may result simply from a difficulty of interpretation). Thei average margin of error was only 3.5 percent. The econometri models also predicted the direction of change correctly except for rental-type housing. It was the major error in this category tha raised its average error so high.

It should be made clear that our test of ability to predict i only one of many possible types. In view of limited resources and degrees of freedom, the test has been performed here for only two years, and it is possible that a longer series of prediction would make such tests carry greater weight. It also is clear tha even if a method is successful at predicting, it may tell little o nothing about the structure of the system—which is our primar interest. Thus, even if the "constant change" model had been suc cessful in both years, it could not be used to explain the construction market. The same is true of the official projections, because the did not show the reasoning behind their estimates. On the othe hand, it is possible that the official forecasters had at least a intuitive idea of how the system worked and that they used thi intuitive model in their projections.

This comment underlines again the fact that it is the successful description of the system which is being sought. The problem of forecasting and of description are far from identical. However it is still true that one test of a good description is that it be usefu in predicting.

C. Procedural and Statistical Difficulties

Careful consideration of the procedures used in the equation shows that they fail to meet the basic requirements worked ou n statistical theory for obtaining the numerical coefficients of the heoretical models. The users of these procedures are perfectly ware of the shortcomings, but they have felt that it was better o try to utilize the existing information than give up the task as opeless. There was always hope that, even though the statistical heory could not be exactly followed, in practice the gaps would ot affect the usefulness of the results. It was also recognized that dequate information on the problems which required solution would ever be forthcoming unless attempts were made to work with the rocedures at hand.

As our review suggests, this approach has had disappointing esults. Until data are improved and are made available for more eriods, or until other less rigorous procedures are developed o utilize existing data, it appears unlikely that equations suitable or use in current analysis or prediction can be worked out. What re some of the procedural and statistical difficulties which must e solved?

1. Lack of sufficient observations and multicollinearity

A major problem of analysis arises from the fact that the exist-ng annual time series are simply too short to specify with any egree of reliability or consistency the parameters of all the ariables which economic theory and qualitative observation inform s are likely to play an important role in determining demand. Our data cover at a maximum 30 usable years. The interrelationships re so complex and changes so frequent that these limited data annot specify the structural relationships statistically.

A theoretical exposition of relationships in housing will rapidly st from 10 to 15 variables considered basic in shifting demand. The theory underlying the models requires that the structural ystem include all variables which have a dominant influence. nexpressed influences must be minor or random. However, the tatistical methods used to-date are limited to 4 or 5 variables. The majority of models 1.0 to 8.0 used only 3 or 4 independent ariables.

The reasons why so few variables are used are well known. or a variable to appear significant it must move separately from ne others enough times to be "found" statistically. Also, sufficient bservations are needed to give reliability to the results. These wo problems are usually discussed under the heading of degrees f freedom and multicollinearity.

A good introduction to the problem of too few observations and nsufficient degrees of freedom is furnished by Snedecor (51):

One should be increasingly cautious of analyzing more variables in small samples. The reason is readily explained by an appeal to the geometry of regression, but we shall have to start with two variables. In a plane, two pairs of observations fix a linear regression, all additional pairs being available not only for improving the regression but for an estimate of error as well. In three-space the required number of triplets of observations to fix a regression plane is three. The analogy may be extended to four and more variables despite the limitations of our three-dimensional world. A regression in six variables would fit perfectly (R - 1) six sets of observations, leaving no information about error.

If two explanatory series varied exactly together, multicollinearity would exist. The required six points to fit our function would not be available. There would be only five, since one point would have two observations. There would be no method for differentiating between the two explanatory series with parallel movements. As Tinbergen says (53):

> The "best" fit could therefore be obtained with each of an infinite number of different combinations, in which one series would successively be substituted to a larger and larger extent for the other. The two regression coefficients of these two series would be entirely indeterminate; only some combination of them would be determinate.

Even if the two series were not perfectly correlated, but only somewhat correlated, a loss of points needed to determine the regression would occur. Additional difficulties results from the fact that, with many inter-related series, there is a tendency for a few to blanket the rest though all are important causally.

If the independent series were not completely correlated, the necessary regressions might be obtained in time by increasing the number of observations. Unfortunately, this cannot be done by using annual data in the housing market because the observations are limited. This leads to an impasse. On a priori grounds, ten or a dozen series appear to affect the dependent variable—housing demand. However, this cannot be shown by statistical methods since use of any four or five series gives nearly perfect correlation. Yet, for analysis or policy one cannot be sure that these series are more important than the rest.

The high correlation coefficients and so-called significant regression-coefficients are not suitable measures of the reliability of the choice of variables, for we obtain equally valid results with a wide variety of totally dissimilar equations or theories. We are able to "prove" statistically that completely unlike theoretical structures rather fully describe the housing market. We are not able to choose among the different explanations. The tests of consistency and predictions offered but slight aid.

2. Use of improper indexes, annual data, and nonbasic series

The models of the construction market discussed so far utilize as independent variables and therefore as explanations some of the primary series which should in turn be explained if we are to have basic knowledge of how the market works. For example, household formation was accepted as an exogenous variable in all of the models. Yet, as our discussion in the next chapter will indicate, this is a major factor which must be explained. Similarly, costs and rents are considered exogenous or predetermined. Again, the housing market analyst must be concerned with how changes in costs and rents result from market interactions as well as with the question of how the market reacts to them. Variables such as vacancies and demolitions which may be extremely important never appear in the models.

The indexes used in the time series models are highly aggregated. Maisel and Winnick (34) have shown that family size, the life cycle, and education or occupation all have some influence on housing expenditures. There have been decided shifts in the distribution of these factors over the period covered by the time series. It is well recognized that the necessary adjustments for these shifts can be made, but this has not been done to date.

The logic of the procedures for finding the true structural equations requires that, if a non-measurable element is found or basic shifts in the economy take place, these should be accounted for by the addition of a new parameter. This has not been done in any of the models discussed, even though significant alterations have occurred in building, selling, and financing houses in the period since 1920, which is covered by the series. These changes are among the factors which cause the data shown in the Charts of Chapter III to disagree so markedly with the concepts underlying the basic statistical theory.

In addition, all of the studies have used annual time series. This automatically leads to a large loss of information compared to monthly or quarterly data. Clearly, a sharp drop in the number of observations occurs and with a large loss in degrees of freedom. Consequently, the chance of observing statistically relevant variables is sharply reduced.

Most equations are based upon lagged relationships. Lags are unlikely to occur exactly evenly on a one or two year basis. If shorter periods were used, it might be possible to estimate the lags more exactly. An examination of the data shows frequent sharp shifts within the course of a year. The annual data may average two or more distinct types of movements. A very significant clue to the relationships involved may be completely obscured as a result of this averaging process. For example, important credit shifts may not appear at all in the data if the period of high or low interest rates existed only from the middle of one year to the middle of the next—yet such changes have been frequent in recent years.

3. Estimating the economic relationships

If the model were properly specified and if sufficient data covering the proper periods were available, problems would still arise in the statistical estimation of the economic relationships. The statistical tools of regression require certain very basic properties to apply within the data being analyzed if the procedures and statements formulated from them are to be valid. These properties deal primarily with the form of the disturbances or residuals from the basic relationships and also with the form of any errors of observation in the variables.

We have already discussed the presence of multicollinearity in the data and of serial correlation among the disturbances. It is also probable that other assumptions concerning the form and variance of the disturbances are wrong. In addition, as we shall see, the basic time series are known to be biased and they contain large errors of observation.

Volume of construction, rents, costs, and income may all be jointly determined. If so, the proper model may be a set of simultaneous equations rather than the simple ones used in the previous chapter. In such a mutually-determined system, the disturbances are not independent of all the explanatory variables. As a result, the method of least squares may be biased. Other forms of estimation called maximum likelihood estimates must be used. In the original studies, some relied upon least squares while other did use the more complex forms of estimation.

In the recomputed equations of Chapter III, it was simply assumed that in each case construction was the dependent variable. In effect, it was implied that the influence of housing construction in a given year on income, costs, rents, and household formation was so slight as to allow it to be neglected without serious consequences. This is obviously not completely true, and for costs and at times households it may be decidedly false. To the extent that the form of the original models would lead to different estimates, the recomputed models may not be adequate tests.

Even if a different form of estimation were chosen, however, the data differ so widely from the basic statistical assumptions that both biases in the coefficients and errors in the estimates of variance are most probable. These factors may account for the changes in the coefficients as well as for some of the wide variances observed.

4. Linearity of the variables

The time series used are also assumed to act in a linear manner. This assumption is almost necessary for the estimates to be made at reasonable cost. At least for some of the series, however, the assumed linearity is probably incorrect. For income, as an example, Maisel and Winnick (34) found a much better fit using the logs of both income and expenditures for their cross-section data. Such corrections could be used in the time series data but have not been commonly made.

For credit, the problem of non-linearity is still more complex. Here there are conflicting effects on monthly payments of changes in interest, loan maturity, and downpayments. An examination of a mortgage payment table shows that this function is extremely complex. There is no logical reason for assuming that a single linear relationship will be satisfactory, particularly if the availability of housing credit as a result of competition with other markets must also be taken into account.

Many of these defects can be removed by the use of a less formal structure. A major advantage of using a more complex but less mathematically determined structure is that qualitative judgment can be used to shift the parameters and to take account of problems of aggregation and institutional and similar changes. Parameters can be estimated from surveys or other cross-sectional data. The effect of specific laws, events or changes in institutions can be introduced. Data covering odd periods or related variables can be utilized.

In light of the procedural and statistical problems, little credence can be given to the explanations of the housing market offered by existing econometric models. The unsolved problems are simply too great. They are compounded by the deficiencies of the data themselves.

D. Data Deficiencies

The data which have been utilized for the fitting of the parameters in existing time series equations do not meet the minimum criteria of the theories. The errors are not small, randomly distributed, and equal to zero. Instead, they tend to be large and biased.

Major areas which should enter the models are left out because they are entirely void of data. In addition, past attempts at obtaining numerical equations for the models have utilized the existing data in a rigid procedure which requires an entirely different order of data and which could not be expected to yield useful results.

Because hopes for the future usefulness of the econometric method depend either upon developing techniques for the existing data or upon developing data to fit the potential techniques, the data problems are considered in some detail.

There is tendency in much statistical research to accept as valid any published index, especially if it bears the imprint of a government agency. Lip service is paid to the possibility of error in such indexes, but for easily understood reasons the researcher seizes upon them as a means of solving the problem of data. Thereafter they are treated as gospel, without further consideration of their actual worth. Obviously, however, the validity of any results in econometric analysis depends entirely upon the accuracy of these basic indexes.

It is also sometimes assumed that, even though the particular series are obviously in error or do not measure what they are supposed to measure, they still can be used as a form of proxy variable which will show the fluctuations and magnitudes of change even though at the wrong level. Such an assumption may be correct for short periods, though even here careful examination must be made of the probability that the movements may not be of the proper magnitude or in the correct direction. The assumption is almost certain to be incorrect for the long periods covered by the series, for most series have been derived by different methods for several sub-periods. Their coverage changes. There is a constant effort to improve the series and to make them more representative. When these changes occur, past data are usually adjusted to the new techniques for a few years, but not for many. As a result, a typical series will be at one level, then will shift to another, and so on. This is demonstrated most clearly by the major dependent variables—housing starts and residential construction expenditures.

1. Housing starts and construction expenditures

Construction data are among the poorest parts of this country's major economic statistics. This has been recognized by all specialists concerned with their gathering, by congressional investigations of our statistical system, and by independent consultants asked to suggest methods of improvement. The series suffer from poor techniques,. sloppy workmanship, infrequent bench marks, poor coverage, and most other deficiencies which can be found in statistics. The net result is that the data fail to measure to some unknown degree what they are supposed to represent. The amount of difference between the series and the true facts has shifted from period to period. There are biases which, because they are correlated with movements of the independent variables such as credit and income, probably produce incorrect estimates.

The Census counted all dwelling units in 1956, 1950, and 1940, on a complete or sample basis. It also counted all occupied dwelling units in 1930 and 1920. If the last two are adjusted upward by an allowance for vacancies, we can derive an estimate for all nonfarm dwelling units on census dates. These are the figures found in the estimates of dwelling unit stocks in Appendix A (Q). The difference between the stock at each census date gives the total change in dwelling units standing. For the period 1920-30, Wickens made some estimates of demolitions and structural conversions, and the remaining change in the stock distributed annually according to building permit fluctuations appears as part of the official series on housing starts.

During the 1930's, the Bureau of Labor Statistics began to issue estimates of starts based on permit data. Basically, the concept of the series is simple. The number and value of residential building permits have been reported to the Bureau of Labor Statistics by most permit issuing agencies. The BLS, in addition, has conducted independent sample surveys to ascertain (1) the relationship of permit data to actual construction both in numbers and value, and (2) the number and cost of units and of additions and alterations in non-permit areas. The independent surveys are small and subject to large errors. An additional problem arises from the growing use of independent surveys over the past 10 years as the meagerness of the previous estimates became apparent. Consequently, the gap between the real magnitudes and the estimates may have been closing at some unknown rate and by fits and starts.[1]

Between 1930-40, 1940-50, and 1950-56, the BLS estimates of housing starts probably accounted for only 75, 70, and 80 percent, respectively, of the reported net change in units standing after liberal allowances for conversions and demolitions. Instead of

---

[1]Since this report was written, the Bureau of the Census has taken over the responsibility for issuing estimates of housing starts. Their initial publication on this topic indicates the seriousness of the problems raised here, plus others. There is not yet any official revision of starts prior to 1959. (Cf. U.S. Department of Commerce, Bureau of the Census, Construction Reports—Housing Starts (20-11 (Supplement) May 1960.)

considering the monthly and annual data as information to be blown up and used for interpolation, the BLS has attempted to explain most of the variations as resulting from differences in definitions. The discrepancy between net changes in stock and housing starts became particularly clear after the 1956 National Housing Inventory by the Census, which was so designed as to yield a more exact measurement of the amount of new construction since 1950. As a result, there is now fairly general agreement that the BLS data underestimated residential construction by 15-20 percent between 1950 and 1956. The underestimate in previous periods may have been even larger because sample surveys for non-permit areas were few or nonexistent.

In summary, one procedure was used for estimates between 1920 to 1930, another from 1930 to 1947, and still another with significant year-to-year alterations between 1947 and 1957. Thus, the reported annual movements may well reflect changes in methodology almost as frequently as they reflect real movements of the market.

Similar reservations hold for the estimates of residential construction expenditures. In the first place, these are derived from the estimated number of housing starts, which were found to be subject to substantial margins of error, and from building permit valuations. Second, the empirical basis for "phasing" the expenditures, i.e., distributing the total over the construction period, has been very weak. Third, the estimates of expenditures on additions and alterations, which form a basic part of total expenditures and have accounted for 5 to 10 percent of the total, have been quite arbitrary. In recent years, a few independent surveys indicated that the guesses on this item were likely to be far off the mark, and the estimates for the postwar period were finally revised by up to 165 percent. This raised the estimates of the total volume of residential construction by 10 to 20 percent. The readjustment was only extended back to the end of World War II. As a result, the levels of the series must be 10 to 20 percent apart. There is also no real evidence as to whether the reported year-to-year changes have any relationship to reality.

2. The rent indices

Almost all of the time series equations use an index of rent as one of the main independent variables. It is assumed that the price of houses and the price of housing services influence the number built and the expenditures by owner occupants. At the same time, investment theory indicates that rents as incomes should influence investment in rental units.

Most analysts recognize that the rent component of the BLS Consumer Price Index does not meet the requirements desired in a price index. The BLS index is supposed to measure only the changes in the costs of similar rental units used by moderate income families over time and makes no claim to represent the general price or cost of housing services. Because the BLS series is the only easily available official index, however, it is used in most cases as a proxy variable. It is included on the assumption that its movements will reflect in a general way the changes in prices and incomes which are generally desired by theory. Maisel (35), Winnick (56), and Reid (45) have shown that this assumption is false. The rent index should not be expected to move in the same manner as housing prices or shelter rents. All evidence points to the fact that they have not moved together.

This lack of correspondence does not necessarily result from failure of the BLS to measure what it has set out to do—although this certainly is one possible cause of the problem. Both Maisel and Winnick have shown that, even if the BLS data are accepted as reliable, the rent index cannot be used for the purposes desired. The BLS, as an example, indicated an increase of 20 percent in rents between 1940 and 1950 for 31 major cities covered, while the Census for the same period reported increases in median rents of 54 percent for the 1940 inventory and 61 percent for all rented units.

Some differences arise because the BLS samples only units occupied by moderate income families in particular urban places. There are strong indications that changes for the non-sampled population may have been greater than for the sampled units. Much more important is the fact that the BLS theoretically samples similar units while rents actually paid reflect sharp changes in the composition of the inventory. Market conditions alter the units offered for rent. For most analytical purposes the resulting rent changes are what should be measured. The differences between rent indexes and house prices are even greater, for much the same reasons.

Finally, even if the rent indices measured correctly changes in amounts paid, they would not measure movements in income from rental properties. As a number of studies indicate clearly, net income is far more volatile than gross income (rent levels). The situation is analogous to income and profits for firms. The measurement that is of interest in investment theory is usually that for net rents or profits, not the gross amount which the rent index attempts to measure.

3. Cost indices

Cost indices play three important roles in the time series equations. In several formulations, costs are related to specific items such as wages, incomes, and rents, on the assumption that opposing movements will indicate shifting profits and therefore willingness to supply more or less space. In other systems, costs are used to correct estimates in current prices in an attempt to put all series on a constant price basis. Finally, costs are used in some equations as a proxy variable for missing price indices.

No matter how cost indices are used, the same difficulties arise. The construction cost indices usually exclude builders' profits and often overhead charges, or a constant percentage is added for these items. Yet, frequently the series is included in the equation in order to measure exactly these excluded items. More important, most cost indices are simply a weighted average of national prices and wage rates (and often nominal ones at that). Usually, the indices do not take into account changes in efficiency or productivity. They vary in the number of materials and labor skills covered and in the degree to which the weights are based on specific skills rather than generalized sub-units. The weights are usually unchanged, or changed little, over the entire period covered.

The Boeckh cost index, which is generally considered to be the best available and was used in the previous computations, has all of these faults. The index for residences was gathered for 4 cities up to 1933 and for 20 cities since that time. It measures changes in costs for a typical brick and frame house in each city. On theoretical grounds one would not expect this index to measure very accurately changes in the costs determining current construction expenditures. The dollar volume of residential construction is affected strongly by regional shifts, changes in the type of houses built, and changes in equipment and materials. The whole familiar index number problem of substitution for high price items arises. The Grebler-Blank-Winnick study (18), as well as other investigations, has shown major shifts over time in all of these factors. Further, the influence of most of them may change with cycles and credit conditions, as well as secularly. Thus, the impact of credit on tract building and on the ratio of metropolitan to nonmetropolitan units may strongly influence the amount of expenditures but not the cost indices. As a result, changes in the cost-corrected indices reflect biases from the correction procedure as well as alterations in demand.

As an indication that these problems are not minor, Colean (8) has shown that two cost indices based upon theoretically the same concepts and methods but using different weights of materials and labor and obtaining their quotations in separate parts of the country showed differences in movements of 20 to 30 percent in a 4-year period.

4. Stock of housing and vacancies

The problems of these series are interrelated, as are their derivations. Basic information is contained in the decennial Census and in a few vacancy surveys taken by WPA in some cities during the 1930's and again by the Bureau of the Census since 1955. Consequently the interpolations between the census dates are extremely crude. Yet, it is the movements between the dates and not their levels that assign values to the fitted parameters.

Some of the problems of estimating the housing stock are clear from our previous discussion of the series on housing starts. In effect, one must assume that the BLS data on starts correctly estimate the year-to-year changes in the number of houses constructed even though they miss the proper level. One must also assume that variations in the number of net conversions, demolitions, and units added and lost through other means follow the fluctuations in housing starts. This appears a rather illogical assumption, because on a priori grounds one would expect some form of lagged relationship.

According to Newcomb (38), an investigation by the War Production Board found little or no relationship between BLS reports of starts and actual net additions to the housing stock. Using 1935-39 = 100, the BLS index varied between 26 and 143 during the 1930's. The WPB estimate of additions to the stock varied only between 55 and 115. The lows and the peaks were in different years and the actual direction of change differed in 4 of the 9 years. Too little is known about the two conflicting estimates to judge their relative reliability.

In any case, it is clear that the BLS series of starts must be blown up in some form to estimate the annual changes in the total stock. This was not done in most of the previous models based on time series. We have corrected the stock figures in this manner in our recomputations when we used the number of units in the stock as a variable. We have not recalculated the estimated value of the housing stock in this same manner, because there is virtually no knowledge of what values to assign to the non-BLS reported units.

We will not elaborate on the problem of depreciation estimates for the value of the housing stock. The tremendous variations in estimates of depreciation and the lack of real knowledge are discussed in detail in the primary source for this series, Grebler-Blank-Winnick (18).

5. Households

For household estimates between 1920 and 1940, the problems are similar to those of housing stock estimates. Again, bench-mark figures can be derived for the census years. Interpolations are based upon annual series for marriages, divorces, and deaths.

There is no annual information on separations, doubling and un-doubling of married couples, or the number of households other than husband-wife units. Again, an assumption must be made that these vary in accordance with reported marriages, although we know from the postwar period that this is far from true.

In the Census series on households (used in Appendix A), an effort has apparently been made to derive the number of households from estimates of the stock of dwelling units. From what we now know of the BLS series on starts that was used to derive the dwelling stock estimates, this attempt may have selected the wrong dependent variable. It might have been better to adjust the estimated stock to estimated households, rather than vice versa.

In the past few years, better estimates of households, the stock of dwelling units, and vacancies have been prepared, yet all attempts to reconcile the three have met with failure. This failure results from the fact that all the series have extremely large sampling variations, and it is particularly serious when estimates of fluctuations in growth are involved. Maisel, in a separate study, has found that no firm statements can be made about year-to-year variations in households (and probably not in vacancies either) (36). Although annual fluctuations in the number of households as high as 70 percent or more have been reported, they still fall well within the expected probable sampling variability and could be zero.

6. The interest rate

Some of the series used in econometric models have certain peculiarities which frequently cause them to be employed incorrectly. The most important of these pertain to the mortgage interest rate. The interest rate is incorrectly used primarily for three reasons: (1) Researchers take a bond yield or similar published index to reflect changes in the mortgage rate; (2) they fail to differentiate between the contract or face rate and the effective rate of interest; and (3) they combine rates quoted on first mortgages covering varying percentages of value and types of appraisals into a single series, although separate interest rates may apply for each loan-to-value ratio.

The disparity between movements in mortgage rates and those of interest rates applying to bonds or other marketable securities is too familiar a phenomenon to require comment. Area differentials and the stickiness of local mortgage interest rates have been stressed by most researchers into the money market. Whatever the reasons, interest rates on mortgages have changed less frequently. The use of other interest time series to approximate the changes that have occurred in the mortgage market gives a totally false picture of timing and magnitude (8).

On the second point, while theoretically the contract and effective rates of interest can be separated with ease, it is almost impossible to do so in practice, especially if the researcher wants to ascertain changes in the effective rate of interest over time. The effective rate is larger than the contract rate because additional expenses are incurred such as legal costs, fees and brokerage or renewal commissions. Variations between the two rates, even on first mortgages, might total 20 to 25 percent, while on second mortgages the effective rate might easily run from 200 to 400 percent of the contract rate. Even more important, the contract rate cannot be used as an approximation of the effective rate because the differences between them vary widely depending on the state of the money market and the business cycle. Almost no information is available on effective mortgage rates charged, except for a few spot studies in particular cities at certain times.

A final error is the assumption that an index of mortgage rates can be obtained without considering the percentage of equity behind each loan. This is especially true when comparisons are made between pre-FHA and post-FHA rates. Previous to FHA, mortgages were frequently for short terms and unamortized. In addition, the first mortgage normally covered only 50 to 60 percent of value, with remaining external funds often obtained through costly second mortgages. As a result of FHA mortgage insurance and VA guaranty for high-percentage first mortgages and perhaps also because lenders have altered their evaluation of risk on conventional loans, there has been a general upward shift in loan-to-value ratios. Mortgage interest rates in recent years therefore have applied to a much larger proportion of high-percentage first mortgages than in the prewar period. Neither the mortgage interest rate series nor the proxy series used in most models reflect adequately the effects of this drastic change on mortgage borrowers' outlays. They also fail to reflect the opposite effects on borrowers' outlays of the more general adoption of regular amortization.

The information on housing credit conditions has improved fairly rapidly in recent years. The studies of financial markets and institutions by the National Bureau of Economic Research have produced a large amount of data mainly for the prewar period. The FHA and VA reports have added to our knowledge of the postwar period. (These sources of information are utilized in the derivation of series Z in Appendix A.) As indicated earlier, however, most credit changes are nonlinear. They affect availability as well as rates. They can be handled far better by judgment on movements of the parameters than by an attempt to obtain an exact, fixed credit index.

7. Summary of data problems

There is no need here to discuss the problems of basic statistical series such as those for disposable income and unemployment.

It may just be noted that each revision of these indices has caused major changes in the parameters of the econometric equations.

The problems raised by the errors, biases, and shifting levels of all of these series are especially great, and the difficulties magnified, when the statistical procedures require a long string of consistent data, as is true for all studies based on annual time series. The problems are less severe in a series of monthly or quarterly data covering only 5 or 6 years, yet the number of observations is as great as that for much longer annual series. Progress can perhaps be made by developing models for a limited number of years but using monthly or quarterly figures although such data increase the problems of serial correlation.

Also, new data can be developed. For example, there are probably enough indications of price changes from various sources in recent years to splice together an acceptable price index, though this would be a time-consuming and arduous task. Such series would come closer to indexes of the GNP type in which it is difficult if not impossible to specify reliability. Still, in practice, indices derived by judgment may be more valid than some of the existing series which follow standard procedures but suffer from methodological and reporting difficulties.

The next chapter presents several examples of series which are needed for improving the analysis of determinants of residential construction. The data contained in these series are only illustrative. If an effort were made to obtain more information, however, most if not all of them could be as accurate as the data used in many other economic analyses.

Our observations on data problems show again why the existing econometric models cannot be accepted as suitable for much exact analysis. Even though at first appearance they seem an improvement over verbal models by attempting to be complete and quantified, they are not in practice. Their greatest value lies in offering leads for future work.

V. BUILDING BLOCKS FOR AN ECONOMETRIC-JUDGMENT MODEL

In Section I-B, we pointed out that existing verbal and econometric models included nine major determinants of residential construction, and that most of these in turn consisted of several minor ones. The verbal models as a rule dealt with only one or a few of these. The econometric models, because of a limited number of observations and other data problems, tended to utilize only three or four variables. The number of variables made but little difference in the accuracy of predictions. None of the models offered a very satisfactory basis for current analysis. They tended to be either too limited or inaccurate.

One of the authors of this paper has had under preparation an econometric-judgment model of the residential construction market.[1] While this model and particularly the data in it are still in preliminary form, it may be useful as a framework for further research work in this area. A complete formal framework of the housing and construction markets can serve a useful purpose even if the data at the moment are not sufficient for fully adequate quantification. The situation is analogous to the widespread use of econometric-judgment models for analyzing and forecasting movements of the GNP. A framework for the market can indicate probable relationships. It can show the difference between reactions in the housing market where rights to the occupancy of dwelling units change hands and reactions in the construction markets where new buildings are offered and demanded. In the construction market, a complete framework can differentiate between factors that primarily affect the number of dwelling units built and forces that influence the price or value of the average unit.

Our previous discussions have indicated how these various concepts have been confused and intermingled in existing theories. The reasons for confusion are not hard to find. Similar variables affect each market. For example, income or credit may influence the demand for all dwelling units, may alter the number of units started, and may change the amount spent for each unit. For analysis, it is usually necessary that these effects be kept separate. Such separation becomes far simpler if a complete framework is available that shows clearly and exactly what relationships exist and how each variable can cause separate reactions. Even if it is only a statement of identities, a framework enables the analyst to categorize and file facts under their proper heading.

The concept of Gross National Product has become almost universal in use and has lead to significant attempts to test pertinent theories, better data, improved classifications, and more accurate forecasting. A similar framework is needed to perform the same functions for the housing market.

A. The Framework

The necessary identities in the housing market are simplest to see if we consider first only the market for the number of dwelling units. Here by definition we find that:

---

[1] This material draws in significant sections on the preliminary draft of an article by S. J. Maisel, "A New Model of the Construction Market."

$$S_1 = H_1 + V_1$$

Where S_1 = the number of dwelling units existing in a period
H_1 = the number of households in a period
V_1 = the number of vacant dwelling units in a period

We also know that:

$$S_2 = H_2 + V_2$$

Subtracting we have:

$$S_2 - S_1 = (H_2 - H_1) + (V_2 - V_1)$$

or $\Delta S = \Delta H + \Delta V$

We also know, however, that:

$$\Delta S = C - D$$

Where C equals the number of new dwelling units constructed and D the new increase or decrease in the housing stock from demolitions and net conversions. D can be either positive or negative. By subtracting we find that:

$$C = \Delta H + \Delta V + D$$

This identity tells us that the number of new units constructed in a period must exactly equal the change in the number of households, plus the change in the number of vacant units, plus the net number of units demolished or converted.

While this is only an identity, it is very useful as a starting point for analysis. Any variable that influences the number of new housing units built must alter one of the items in this equation. The effects of prices, incomes, and credit do not operate separately and directly on construction demand. They influence first one of the categories in the above equation, just as in income analysis they must influence the equation: GNP = consumption expenditures +investment + government expenditures. If a variable has little or no influence on H, V, or D, it cannot have a significant influence on the number of units constructed. As a corollary, the impact of any variable such as income or credit must be measurable through its influence on any or all of these items.

It is of interest to establish the approximate magnitudes of the last equation covering all dwelling units (farm as well as non-farm) for the one period in which fairly good data are available,

1950 through 1956, between the decennial housing census and the National Housing Inventory of 1956:[2]

	C	=	ΔH	+	ΔV	+	D
Total	10,920,000	=	7,050,000	+	2,310,000	+	1,560,000
Annual rate	1,620,000	=	1,050,000	+	340,000	+	230,000

According to these figures, net household formation equaled 65 percent, increases in vacancies equaled 21 percent, and units removed from the stock equaled 14 percent of total new construction.

For many analytical purposes, we are also concerned with the changes in the value of the housing stock and the value of new construction. For these items, a similar set of relationships exists:

$$\text{Value}_1 = S_1 \cdot E_1$$

Where S equals the number of dwelling units in the stock and E equals their average value. The average value depends upon the net housing expenditures of the average family, real or imputed. It also depends upon the existing capitalization rate for these expenditures. Thus, the average value may shift either because households change their expenditures or because of an altered capitalization rate. Credit may act on either expenditures or the capitalization rate.

Similarly: $\text{Value}_2 = S_2 \cdot E_2$

Then, by subtraction, $V_2 - V_1 = (S_2 \cdot E_2) - (S_1 \cdot E_1)$

Also:

$$\underset{a}{S_2 \cdot E_2} = \underset{c}{(C \cdot E_C)} - \underset{d}{(D \cdot E_D)} + \underset{e}{[\Delta E (S_1 - D)]} + \underset{b}{(S_1 \cdot E_1)}$$

or (a) the total value in the second period equals (b) the value in the first period plus (c) the value of all units constructed during the period, less (d) the value of all units demolished, plus (e) the change in the value of the stock which remains in existence.

---

[2]These figures are approximate. The Census data are based on samples and reflect also a great deal of difficulty with enumerator bias in applying the definitions of household and dwelling unit. As a result, the separate Census enumerations of the same population may vary by 500,000 to 1,000,000 dwelling units. The figures in this section are illustrative only. They are based in part on assumptions and should not be used outside the context of this section and its analysis.

By substitution we find that:

$$\Delta Value_{2-1} = (C \cdot E_C) - (D \cdot E_D) + [\Delta E (S_1 - D)]$$

According to this equation, in order to explain the change in total value from period 1 to period 2, one must explain the change in the number of units C-D, plus the unit prices of new dwellings, the prices of those removed, and in addition the revaluation of the stock which remains. Again, a change in supply and demand must influence either the number of units or their average value or both. The variables which affect units and values must be clearly differentiated since their impact varies greatly, even though some variables, such as changes in prices or credit conditions, may affect both.

Here, too, it is possible to put approximate numerical values to this equation for the period between April 1, 1950 and December 31, 1956. On the first date, there were about 45,980,000 dwelling units valued at $224 billion, or an average value of $4,900 per unit. By December 31, 1956, the value of the housing stock had nearly doubled. There were about 55,340,000 dwelling units valued at $431 billion, or an average value of $7,790 per unit.[3]

The net change in value of $207 billion resulted from (a) the construction of 10,920,000 new dwelling units with an average value of $11,900 each for a total of $130 billion; (b) the net demolition of 1,600,000 units with an average value of $2,900 or a total loss of $5 billion; and (c) an average increase in value of $1,850 for each of the 44,420,000 units remaining in the stock between the two periods, for a net increase in their value of $82 billion. In terms of the previous equation we find:

$207 billions   (10.9 . $11,900) - (1.6 · $2,900) +
                    (44.4 · $1,850)

$Value_{2-1}$ =   [C (in millions) . E_C]- [D (in millions) · E_D] +
                    [(S_1 - D) (in millions) . E]

---

[3] These approximate values were obtained by dividing all dwelling units into those in nonfarm detached single-unit structures occupied by their owners and all others. The median value of the owner-occupied single units was reported by the Census and was multiplied by the total in this classification to obtain the total value for the class. The mean value of "all others" was assumed to be 100 times the monthly contract rent reported by the Census for nonfarm tenant occupied units.

It becomes clear from the above that an explanation of the market for housing and for residential construction really involves three tasks. First, what causes the increase in the total number of housing units demanded $\Delta S = C - D = \Delta H + \Delta V = D$? As we shall see shortly, in equilibrium this equation may be considered a true causal relationship which explains the movements in both the total housing market and the construction market. However, in a disequilibrium situation, no causal relationships can be attributed. Second, what causes the increase in the average value per unit $E_2 - E_1$? Third, how is this increase distributed between the average value E_C of new units and changes in the average value of existing units ΔE? The change in average value of existing units may reflect expenditures or altered capitalization rates. It may reflect a change in real values or only money prices. There should also be some relationship between the changed value of existing units and the cost of new construction.

B. Equilibrium Versus Dynamic Models

In the housing market, we encounter the usual problems of a failure of agreement between the comparative statics-equilibrium models, in which we normally couch our theoretical analysis, and the actual dynamic path to equilibrium which is measured in our statistical data. There may also be significant differences between the short-run and long-run influences of many of the independent variables.

Because of the durability of houses and because of poor market information, it is frequently assumed that the periods of disequilibrium may be unusually long and may account for some of the major production fluctuations. This failure to achieve equilibrium readily is one of the basic causes of the unique fluctuations in the housing market commented on at length by Duesenberry (12), Long (31), Derksen (11) and others.

The housing market will be in equilibrium when every household has one or more (seasonal, etc.) dwelling units of the type and quality it demands. Not every existing dwelling unit will be occupied since there will be a normal number of vacancies exactly justified by the frictions of the market. At a later period, as a result of new values for the independent variables (population, income, credit, costs, etc.), a new equilibrium will be required. More households will exist and will demand units; the quality or value of the units demanded will differ; the normal number of vacancies may rise or fall with shifts in tenure, migration, credit and market conditions. At the same time, the number of units in the supply will have altered because of demolitions, conversions, etc. The quality of the housing stock will have changed because of depreciation, deterioration, additions, alterations, and repairs. As the framework outlines, a new equilibrium taking account of all of these changed variables and desires will be achieved through the proper amount and type of new construction and through changes in the value of the existing stock. When we use the term construction demand, we usually refer to the need for units to bring about this new equilibrium.

We may want to describe and analyze either the short-run or long-run changes in equilibrium, depending on the length of time between observations and on factors which cause the changed values for the independent variables. Thus, for credit we may wish to describe the effect on short-run equilibrium of the month-to-month or quarter-to-quarter results of Federal Reserve actions to change the ease of credit. On the other hand, we may be interested in the long-run effects of altered institutions and attitudes towards mortgage investment. We normally think of long-run changes as the slower, more gradual movements which result when tastes, population, productivity, and institutions alter. The short-run movements result when income, prices, credit, or expectations fluctuate.

In the housing market, all existing units are in the supply but are not necessarily occupied. Available statistics do not tell us whether the market is in equilibrium or not. New construction may have failed to adjust the total supply to the desired or scheduled movements of demand. The number of dwelling units or their value may be above or below the equilibrium level. Usually, this disequilibrium will create a situation in which the actual number of vacancies does not equal the normal number. Some people may be holding vacancies unwillingly. At other times, the number of vacancies may be too low for a properly functioning market. In either case, disequilibrium exists and there will be pressures pushing the market away from the existing situation.

It is also possible that some people may occupy units of the wrong type, size, or quality. They may choose not to move and not to adjust their expenditures to changed conditions because of an insufficient supply or because they cannot readily liquidate their existing housing investment. Rarely, as during a war, there may be doubled-up families who would demand dwelling units under the prevailing economic conditions but cannot obtain them because of controls.

It is entirely possible that in the housing market—similar to that for corn-hogs, inventories, and others—equilibrium is rarely achieved. The lags in adjustment of supply to demand may lead to constant over- and undershooting of the desired equilibrium and to continuous fluctuations. The econometric models have demonstrated that, given particular values of the parameters, such a search for equilibrium may be a normal feature of residential construction. As a result, we must recognize that reported changes in the volume of new construction may reflect two entirely different types of movements.

In the first place, construction may be required to reach a new equilibrium resulting from movements in the independent variables, such as income, employment, credit terms, population, costs and prices. These variables alter household formation or the rate of demolitions and conversions or the desired number of vacancies. A usable theory should explain the variations in construction demand resulting from each of these factors. In the second place, however, the recorded changes may reflect in part variations from scheduled demand. The actual amount of new construction may have exceeded or lagged behind the volume required to reach the new equilibrium. Because of market imperfections, for example, builders or investors may err in judgment and dwelling units may be added for which there is no demand. They make up an undesired inventory. Their supply pressure in subsequent periods may cause the rate of construction to fall below the rate at which new demand is growing. Statistical movements will tend to fluctuate around real demand, but not necessarily in a regular or random manner.

The measured changes reflect both desired and unwanted additions to the supply as well as errors in measurement. An important function of a workable theory is to recognize this fact. Analysis should explain each type of movement. None of the previous theories has attempted to do so, although some have noted the importance on theoretical grounds of these separate factors.

C. Illustrative Analysis of Housing Demand and Supply 1950-1959

As an indication of the empirical use of a more complete framework of the residential construction market, we present Table IV-10. This is an extremely rough estimate of what may have happened to construction demand and supply over the past ten years and should be considered as illustrative only. If similar data for the housing market and information on all related independent variables were available on a quarterly basis, one would be able to test suggested theories with far greater success.

This table suffers from many of the data problems noted in Chapter IV, plus significant sampling errors and the fact that the estimates are extremely crude. We have not had the time or resources to mine fully even the existing data. However, until the data system has been vastly improved it is unlikely that the type of information required will be available in such form as to allow exact statistical manipulation, mathematical fitting of parameters, and so forth. Table IV-10 and the tables which follow indicate the types of data required and illustrate a form of presentation believed useful for analysis based on judgment which utilizes available information on size and relative magnitude of the possible relationships.

The first two columns indicate the number of housing units started and completed each year. The third column, which is simply the difference between the first two and which attempts to measure the number of units under construction, calls attention to the fact that a lag exists between starts and the number of units actually added to the inventory. The change in units under construction appears to account for a large share of the year-to-year shifts in construction starts, which many analysts have tried to explain in terms of more basic demand determinants.

The column "net loss from stock," or the result of net demolitions and conversions, is one about which almost nothing is known. The only available data are fragmentary estimates of various types of losses and gains contained in the National Housing Inventory covering the period between April 1950 and December 1956. For want of any better data on the distribution over time of this variable, we have assumed a rough correlation in time between losses from the stock and completions.

Completions less net losses show the net increase in the stock (column 5). Additions to the housing stock seem to be more stable than the series on starts, although part of this apparent stability may arise from our assumptions.

Column 6 shows the changes in households as enumerated by the Census and adjusted to an annual basis for this table. The Census uses a sample survey and covers changes in various 11- to 13-month periods usually ending in March or April. These estimated changes differ over time because of alterations in population movements, in the social and economic determinants of household formations, and in statistical variances arising from survey and estimating techniques. A more detailed examination of these variations and the problems which arise in using them for statistical analysis are described in a recent article by Maisel (36).

In the following sections we shall examine the columns separately and relate them to the previous discussions of the major determinants of construction demand, with emphasis on the types of functional relationships that might exist between the movements of these items and the independent variables.

1. Household formation

The column on household formation shows sharp movements. As Maisel indicated in his lengthier discussion of this series (36), part of the movement appears to result from sampling variance and part from social and economic processes. It is most difficult to determine which particular movements arise from which cause.

During this period, changes in household formation accounted for not quite two-thirds of housing starts based upon present Census concepts. As for household formation, slightly over 50 percent came from demographic factors. This means that only one-third of construction can be accounted for by these factors. The explanation of the remainder must be sought elsewhere.

How can we account for the fact that household formation was nearly double the population change standardized for movements in age-sex ratios? One factor at work appeared to be a definite shift in social forces. In economic theory, this would be listed and discussed as a structural change. The number of nonmarried household heads has been rising rather steadily, and the age at marriage has been falling. Both earlier marriages and more single-person households appear to be occasioned by a change in tastes and attitudes as well as economic factors. These two items account for most of the increase in households from social and economic forces.

The effect of economic conditions on the rate of household formation is less certain. Various theories have been developed attempting to show that income, credit, and costs of housing could all influence this rate. In extremely crude tests by Maisel, quarterly changes in unemployment appear to cause variations in the rate of household formation. A correlation exists between changes in unemployment and the marriage rate. Further, the number of doubled-up couples probably varies with income fluctuations. The time series models may also be interpreted as lending some credence to the view that income influences household formation, and Bassie's results (3) can be interpreted as another indication of this relationship.

Credit terms could influence the number of new households either through the size of the downpayment or as a determinant of rents and the monthly payments of owners. The various theories give no indication of the magnitude of changes in households that could be expected from this factor, and Maisel found no correlation in his tests. On the other hand, Break's results might indicate that credit variations play some significant role in determining when households are formed.

Most newly formed families rent, but if a significant number should prefer to remain doubled-up until they accumulate a downpayment, changes in downpayment requirements would have a direct effect on household formation, which would appear statistically as a correlation between easier credit and more households. There is no indication, however, that required downpayments are a really significant factor in the rate of doubling-up. This rate has been declining through the period covered, and the number of doubled-up couples in recent years has been very small.

To measure another type of effect of credit and other costs and prices on household formation, we must be able to estimate the cost or price elasticity of household formation. Is it likely to be large or small? Again, we have but little empirical evidence. We know that interest and amortization outlays form about half to two-thirds of rents or the financial costs of house ownership. In turn, rent is only one—although a major—cost in establishing a household. The impact of altered credit terms is rather immediate in changing the financial costs of newly-bought owner units, but probably much delayed for rental-type units and, of course, barely touches existing mortgage contracts. As rough order of magnitude, a half-percent change in interest may alter the costs of maintaining a separate household by 3 to 5 percent. If we accept the most sensitive credit indexes of the type constructed by Break, terms of credit might increase or decrease the costs of maintaining a separate household by 5 to 10 percent.

How likely is a change in costs of this magnitude to cause households to form or consolidate, and what speed or reaction would be expected? It appears that the psychic costs of merged households are high and also that market reaction to changed credit conditions is considerably delayed. On the other hand, even if the cost elasticity for total households was small, it might still cause a considerable impact on net household formation. The fact that no such relationship has been found empirically may mean either that the data are faulty or that the coefficient for the credit terms variable with respect to household formation is really extremely small. Clearly, a need exists both for better theory and data.

Most of the equations and theories which have used household formation as an independent variable are not sufficiently specific on this item. We need to understand why household formation fluctuates. While many theories seem to have assumed that household formation is subject to economic influences, the reasons and expected magnitudes for such impacts particularly in the case of credit have not been spelled out. The only positive results seem to indicate that the formation of nonfarm households is influenced by fluctuations in income or unemployment. The theory of how or why other economic factors change the number of households remains in a primitive state. Furthermore, there have been few attempts to differentiate between demographic, social, and economic forces.

2. Net loss from the existing stock

This factor, which includes conversions and demolitions, is estimated to have equaled about 11 percent of total construction in recent years.[4] Prior to the National Housing Inventory of 1956, there was virtually no reliable information on its magnitude. It has frequently been assumed that between 1930 and 1950 the number of conversions and other gains were so large that they greatly reduced the demand for new construction by adding many more units to the existing stock than were lost from other causes.

We still have little or no information on what accounts for these movements in the stock. Table IV-11 is based upon rather crude estimates developed by Maisel for the Senate Subcommittee on Housing (37). The table has been altered to show additions from other sources not included in the original study. The table reveals that important segments of demolitions and other losses can be considered as primarily exogenous. This would be true of fires, flood, clearance for highway construction and urban redevelopment, and probably for demolitions to use the site for other private improvements. Such exogenous causes of removals must be estimated for their impact on the demand for new housing units, but they need not be explained by a model of the housing market. The model should explain, however, why the rate of net conversions varies, and it should deal with the relationship between the actual physical destruction or temporary abandonment of housing units and their period of economic usefulness.

The literature on conversions does not reveal much about the forces explaining this activity or accounting for its apparently significant variations over time. Many model builders seem even unaware of the importance of this factor, as well as of other atypical additions to the housing stock. Grebler-Blank-Winnick, however, stress the significance of conversions in their analysis of secular trends. (18) Some estimates of housing needs attempt to account for conversions as a function of style and the number of older houses. A few spot studies indicate that such a relationship need not exist. Many so-called conversions appear in nearly new houses. It is also possible that the rate of reported conversions is related to the formation of other than husband-wife households. Measurement in this whole area is highly inadequate. There is neither positive nor negative evidence of any relationship between short-run fluctuations in the rate of conversions and

---

[4]In Tables IV-10 and IV-11, new housing units of the non-Census type are treated as offsets to losses. On page 557 and in other data taken directly from the National Housing Inventory of 1956, these additions are shown as part of new construction.

changes in the economic variables, except for the general impression that conversions were unusually high during the Great Depression. Additions also came from trailers, dwellings in previously nonresidential structures and other units not shown in the series on "starts." These probably move in relation to other construction, but again there is no information on the timing of their changes.

Existing theories have given greater attention to the causes and the timing of the demolition of units for economic reasons. In fact, an assumption of some type of replacement cycle plays a significant role in many of the housing cycle theories. Other works recognize, probably more realistically, that demolitions are based primarily upon economic and not on physical factors. This concept then leads to the idea of a rising rate of demolitions and abandonments as income and credit factors become more favorable.

It would be possible to erect a rather complex theory of demolitions, but it could not be tested with existing data. Furthermore, such a theory does not seem necessary or useful for explaining either short-run or moderate-run changes in demand. Observation, a few available statistics, and Grebler's study of the Lower East Side of Manhattan have indicated that fluctuations in the rate of demolitions due to endogenous housing market forces play but a slight role in demand.

In conclusion, current estimates of conversions and of demolitions and other losses as well as of increases in the stock of dwellings from other sources are important for an understanding of the total housing market. The impact of these items on supply and demand is large and subject to great variations over time. Their neglect has caused significant gaps and errors in existing theories. On the other hand, until more current observations are available, there is but a slight basis for developing a theory to explain and predict demand movements from these sources. It is possible, for example, that demolitions and conversions follow a fairly steady trend and do not fluctuate greatly, but it is also possible that they move, as we assumed, with starts or completions. In the latter case, simple lagged parameters would suffice to account for the total effect of this entire sector in any econometric models developed in the future.

3. Changes in vacancies

The idea that changes in vacancies have a significant influence on construction demand is implicit in most of the econometric models and some verbal models. The influence of vacancies on demand is introduced through a relationship between the number of households and dwelling units. The importance of this factor is made explicit in Bassie (3), Rapkin-Winnick-Blank (42), Duesenberry (12), and others. Actual data on vacancies, however, have been almost nonexistent until very recently. As a result, the theory of how this influence is felt and how it can be measured is not made clear in the models which depend on algebraic use of existing data to illustrate their theories and measure parameters and relationships. The inability or failure to measure and include changing vacancies directly in their theories may be one of the primary reasons why these models fail to describe the structural relationships of the market.

In an attempt to explore the significance of vacancies, Maisel has developed a rather arbitrary and primarily illustrative measure of changes in different types of vacancies between 1950 and 1960 on an annual basis (Table IV-12). Between January 1, 1950 and December 31, 1959, the increase in existing vacancies (other than units under construction) is estimated to have been 3,660,000 equaling about 26 percent of the total units constructed during this period, or about 30 percent of the net additions to the stock of dwelling units in existence. Of the total, the increase in (a) normal vacancies, as defined later, accounted for 2,290,000 units. The increase in (b) vacant dilapidated or other marginal units enumerated was 330,000. The increase in (c) unwanted or excess vacancies equaled 1,040,000, which included a shift from a deficit to a surplus in this category. Finally, the increase in (d), the inventory of units under construction not included in the above total, was 170,000. As would be expected, this last factor did not play a significant role in the total changes in demand for the entire period, but it was extremely important in the year-to-year fluctuations.

(a) <u>Normal vacancies</u>. We divide normal vacancies into three types: (1) Dwelling units available for sale or rent which are needed for flexibility in the housing market. (2) Units held off the market awaiting occupancy, under repair, awaiting owner's decisions, etc. (3) Seasonal units.

The definition of normal vacancies is far from simple. From a macro-point of view, some vacancies in the housing market are necessary. An intolerable situation would exist if people had no choice when they wished to migrate or change their accommodations for other reasons. While the individual landlord may want to minimize his own vacancies, aggregate supply and demand should adjust so as to leave the desired normal vacancies. The resulting equilibrium price makes it worthwhile for the individual to hold his share of vacancies for whatever brief period is required on the average.

TABLE IV-10

Illustrative Estimate of Changes in Housing Demand and Supply, 1950-59
(Thousands of Dwelling Units)

Year	Starts (1)	Completions (2)	Under Construction (3)	Net Loss from Stock (4)	Net Gain in Stock (5)	Change in Households (6)	Change in Vacancies (7)
1950	1,650	1,430	+220	-150	1,280	1,100	180
1951	1,290	1,470	-180	-150	1,320	890	430
1952	1,330	1,310	+20	-140	1,170	840	330
1953	1,300	1,315	-15	-140	1,175	620	555
1954	1,440	1,370	+70	-150	1,220	810	410
1955	1,570	1,505	+65	-155	1,350	1,000	350
1956	1,320	1,445	-125	-155	1,290	850	440
1957	1,190	1,255	-65	-125	1,130	840	290
1958	1,380	1,285	+95	-125	1,160	890	270
1959	1,550	1,465	+85	-130	1,335	920	415

Basis of Estimates: The number of starts is based upon an inflation of BLS reports by 18 percent for 1950-56 and 14 percent in 1957 and 1958. Completions are based upon starts lagged six months. Net loss in stock is an independent guess based partly upon NHI data. Changes in households are from Census Current Population Reports (P20-Nos. 94 and 103), with 1955 and 1956 smoothed. The change in vacancies is the residual. Starts are based upon the present Census concepts as defined for Series C-20. Other additions to the housing stock are shown as offsets to losses in the column "net loss from stock."

TABLE IV-11

Illustration of Net Losses From the Existing Housing Stock

April 1, 1950 - December 31, 1956

Annual Rates

Demolitions

Temporary public housing	-50,000	
Clearance for public housing	-15,000	
Title 1, urban renewal clearance	- 5,000	
Highway clearance	-15,000	
Other demolitions	-85,000	
Subtotal		-170,000

Conversions and mergers

Conversions	+110,000	
Mergers	-100,000	
Subtotal		+ 10,000

Other changes

Additions	+220,000	
Fires, floods, & other casualties	- 20,000	
Other losses	-190,000	
Subtotal		+ 10,000
Total annual losses		-150,000

Source: Estimated from 1956 National Housing Inventory, Vol. 1 and other data. Cf. S. J. Maisel, "Importance of Net Replacements in Housebuilding Demand," Study of Mortgage Credit, op. cit. which contained estimates for nonfarm changes.

TABLE IV-12

Illustrative Estimate of Vacant Dwelling Units
January 1, 1950 – January 1, 1960
(Thousands of Units)

	Held Off Market	Seasonal	Available Own or Rent Normal	Deficit (-) or Excess	Dilapidated	Total Existing Vacancies	Under Construction	Total Existing And Under Construction
Total Jan. 1, 1950	700	960	1,050	-320	450	2,840	605	3,445
Annual Changes								
1950	50	50	30	30	20	180	+220	400
1951	110	140	30	100	50	430	-180	250
1952	80	110	30	70	40	330	+20	350
1953	150	170	30	150	50	550	-15	535
1954	140	80	30	130	30	410	+70	480
1955	220	-	30	80	20	350	+65	415
1956	90	170	30	70	80	440	-125	315
1957	80	180	30	0	0	290	-65	225
1958	40	30	30	170	0	270	+95	365
1959	100	-	30	240	40	410	+85	495
Total Jan. 1, 1960	1,760	1,890	1,350	720	780	6,500	775	7,275

Basis of Illustrative Estimate: The changes in Total Vacancies and in Units Under Construction are taken from Table IV-10. Percentage distributions are based on Census, Current Housing Reports – Housing Vacancies, Series H-111, for 1955-60. The averages for the four quarters centered on January are used. These are inflated approximately 10 percent to agree with totals in the column "Total existing vacancies." This is made necessary by the fact that, depending upon which Census survey is used, different estimates of the total number of all dwelling units and of vacant units result. The estimates for 1951-54 are interpolations. The sharp year-to-year changes in some of the subcategories probably reflect sampling variations.

It is possible that the normal vacancy rate should fluctuate with economic variables. The cost and ability to hold units vacant varies somewhat with credit and prices. The number of units held off the market should vary with turnover. We lack precise knowledge of how or why such changes occur. Only recently have measures been developed of actual variations in the different categories of vacancies that may be used as the basis of some theoretical reasoning.

Because of the paucity of data, we have defined the "normal" sector of units available for rent or sale in a rather arbitrary way. We consider as normal vacancies equal to 1.8 percent of the total nonfarm housing stock to allow for units for rent, and equal to 0.5 percent of the total stock to allow for owner-type units available for sale. These assumptions are roughly equivalent to a normal available vacancy rate of 5 percent for tenant-type and 1.0 percent for owner-type units, but the exact percentage will vary slightly depending upon the relative share of each type of unit in the total market. We have also assumed that all vacant seasonal units are used for seasonal purposes and that therefore 100 percent vacancy as defined by the Census is normal for this group. Further, we count all units vacant and reported held off the market as normal vacancies.

The reasons for separate normal ratios for rental-type and owner-type units are well known. Most sales of existing houses are made while the previous owner still occupies the unit. Many moves are for the purpose of adjusting expenditures and house size to new family tastes. In these cases, it is usually not worthwhile to incur the costs of vacancies in order to make the move. Other owner-type units become vacant as families are dissolved or as they move to other areas. In the case of migration, home owners have usually a strong incentive to sell before they vacate their units so as to be able to buy a house in their new location. There are also new units held vacant when they are completed and first offered for sale. Altogether, the owner-type vacancies under normal circumstances should be comparatively small. This is reflected in the above assumption and in the meager data underlying the illustrative Table IV-12.

The rental market has a considerably larger volume of normal vacancies. It is harder to rent units when they are still occupied. The rate of turnover is much higher than in owner-type units. Somewhat higher vacancies do not disturb investors since investments in apartments are usually made on an assumption of 5 to 10 percent vacancy rates. For all of these reasons, an assumed normal vacancy rate for these units of 5 percent of the rental housing stock or 1.8 percent of the total stock does not seem too high.

There are a large number of units held off the market at any time. The estimate of this number according to the Census has both a large sampling and enumerator variance. Units are held vacant that have already been sold or rented as the new owner prepares to move. Some units are purchased for the purpose of being demolished. Other units may get tied up in estates. There are many other reasons why at any time a normal percentage of all units should be in this category. Table IV-12 estimates that roughly 1.5 percent of all nonfarm units were held off the market and normally vacant in 1950. During the next ten years, the number of units in this category increased by more than a million, and their share in the total nonfarm dwelling unit stock rose to 3.0 percent.

Seasonal units are those held for occupancy in resorts, etc. Even if they are occupied on a seasonal basis when the enumerator appears, they are supposed to be counted as vacant, while the household's primary home is shown as occupied. On the other hand, if the identical unit is occupied on a year-round basis it drops out of the seasonal stock. The number of seasonal units demanded again is primarily a function of tastes, incomes, etc. However, the number may vary somewhat as demand pressures on the stock cause some of them to be reclassified from seasonal to regular use and vice versa. Table IV-12 indicates an increase of nearly one million units of this type in the 1950-59 period. They accounted for nearly 3.1 percent of the stock at the beginning of 1960.

Clearly, the increase of 2,290,000 units in our assumed normal vacancies from these three sources during the 1950-59 period equaled a significant part of the total increase in the stock. Without more data, we cannot know whether or not all of this increase was really a normal and a desired one, or whether the increase followed the path assumed in the table. It is possible that both the increase in the total and the annual fluctuations were much larger than illustrated, with the result of severe pressures on the construction market in different periods. Again, we lack both data and a testable theory.

(b) Dilapidated vacancies. This is another category where both large enumerator and estimating problems exist. It is supposed to include only units fit for use and repairable. Those units which are unfit for use are designated as "other losses" from the dwelling unit stock even though they are still standing. Some observers feel that dilapidated vacancies have little or no impact on the market. Others believe that the market will react in the same way to them as to other vacancies and that even the units enumerated as unfit for habitation might enter the supply if either a housing shortage or a depression should occur.

(c) <u>Excess or subnormal inventories of vacancies</u>. We have noted that, because of lags in the adjustment of starts to the total demand for housing, vacancies may rise above or all below the desired amount. A disequilibrium situation can occur. If demand exceeds supply, vacancies are below normal, prices rise, and new construction is stimulated. In the opposite case when supply exceeds demand, excess vacancies appear. To liquidate the excess, the amount of construction will fall below that required by the demand from new household formation and net withdrawals from the housing stock. The amount of disequilibrium which can exist will depend upon the reaction time of the system. One of the major determinants of the amplitude of building fluctuations may be the amount by which these excess inventories vary from normal.

Rapkin-Winnick-Blank (42) and Duesenberry (12) provide good descriptions of why reaction lags should exist and why vacancies should fluctuate over and under the normal amount. As the time required to sell or rent increases, owners may still attempt to get their initial price even though it means holding units vacant for somewhat longer periods than normal. The market is so imperfect that no one can be certain that the equilibrium price has altered until it is tested carefully. As this period of testing lengthens, an undesired inventory is held by those waiting to rent or sell. When owners finally sense that the equilibrium has altered and builders feel that the current volume of new construction cannot be marketed, there will still be a considerable period until this knowledge spreads, is taken into account by investors and builders, and alters the construction level. In the meantime completions will continue at a high level and excess inventories will grow even larger. Finally, in order to allow disposal of the unwanted units, construction will have to drop below the normal amount.

This is a typical example of what happens to goods with so-called long gestation periods. Demand increases. Many entrepreneurs build to meet the demand. They overshoot the mark because of the length of the planning and production process or because of poor market information. Building remains above the proper rate until the existence of excess units is generally recognized and the number of units started curtailed. There are indications that this lag is much larger and more serious for rental-type units than for those built for sale to owners. For the latter, the production time is shorter and market information is somewhat better than for rental units. In addition, builders' working capital and credit limit severely the number of unsold owner-type units they can hold.

The theory indicates that changes in credit, income movements, and price expectations can each lead to positive or negative changes in these undesired inventories. Stringent credit, price declines, and dropping income should all decrease construction for inventory even before the full gestation period is completed and excess stocks are experienced. On the other hand, an increase in any or all of these variables should raise the number of units under construction and may lead to too high a level of production.

The observed correlation between income, credit, prices, and construction starts in the time-series models may well be accounted for, at least in part, by these movements in vacant units in contrast to actual shifts in basic demand for housing. Increased construction associated with a shift in an economic variable may reflect the building up of inventories and not a change in final demand. If we could measure the movements in this inventory directly and over shorter periods, we would be able to estimate the separate effects of credit, income, and costs on final demand and on inventory fluctuations. We would then have a much greater chance of finding the true structural parameters of the system.

In Table IV-12, the column giving the excess or deficit in vacancies available for rent over and above those considered normal shows a steady increase in the total. In some years, the rise in this inventory was very large. The year-to-year changes in the rate at which this inventory increased do not, on the whole, appear excessive, but they were sizable compared to the annual movements of starts.

The decade of the fifties began with an estimated deficit of 320,000 units vacant and available to own or rent. There was a true housing shortage. From the beginning of the period, completions exceeded current demand. In 1953 the amount added beyond current demand was 150,000 dwelling units. In that year, the deficit in our assumed normal vacancies disappeared. The total of excess units continued to build up through 1957, but at a slower rate. In 1957, starts and completions were both low. The total excess is estimated to have been at 300,000 dwelling units and there were no additions to this stock. In the following year construction turned up sharply. The table indicates that the undesired inventory more than doubled in 1958-59. The increase of 240,000 in 1959 was the largest of the decade.

The average change in the rate of accumulation between each set of years was approximately 60,000, with a maximum change in the rate of 170,000 occurring between 1956 and 1957. While the accumulation appears related to the changes in starts and completions, there is no simple correlation. There is also a major problem of identification of the direction of influence. Since this table is extremely crude, it cannot be used to analyze the causal relations. It does, however, indicate the important part that changes in the undesired inventory may play in any market model.

(d) <u>The inventory under construction.</u> Usually the concept of vacancy is applied only to completed units. For analytical purposes, however, it is necessary to pay much more attention to the units under construction. This is an inventory of work in progress. Its economic effects are similar to inventories in other industries. It is well recognized that manufacturing inventories show the sharpest fluctuations of all related parts of the economy. Construction inventories shift in the same rapid manner. They contain a variable amount of investment depending on their size and have the same economic effect on employment, income, etc. as any other type of inventory. Dwelling units under construction are even more significant than other inventories because so much of the common analysis has been in terms of housing starts. Plans and expectations have been based on movements in the series of starts. When construction is measured in starts, units under construction are counted as part of the total supply. As can be seen from Table IV-12, the short-term alterations in this inventory are extremely significant—a phenomenon similar to that experienced in other types of investment.

For our estimates, we have assumed that units are "under construction" for six months after they have been started, and that half the starts of any year are not completed until the next, while our estimate of the stock of units is lagged six months behind starts. On these assumptions, Table IV-12 indicates that the inventory of units under construction shifted by nearly 400,000 in the unusual period 1950-51, and by between 130,000 and 190,000 in the years 1955-58. The movements in this inventory in most periods could account for the largest share of fluctuations in the series on starts.

The changes in the pipeline of construction are a typical case of the acceleration principle. As demand increases, investment in units under construction expands. If final demand stops growing and a constant number of new units are being sold, the units under construction will hold constant. The number of starts, however, will fall since some units were started in the first period to fill the pipeline.

As is true for any inventory, the units under construction are related to sales. Builders will try to maintain a certain ratio of units under construction to sales. In a market with rapid turnover, they may raise this ratio. Efficiency is better with a higher ratio, and builders will feel that risks are low. As sales begin to fall, risks increase and builders will cut the ratio and reduce the units under construction by even more than final demand. This inventory may be particularly affected by builder's expectations and by credit. It is quite possible that the major fluctuations of the past few years have been keyed closely to the willingness of builders to expand and contract their inventories as the available construction credit and financial commitments have altered. This possibility also appears

to be amenable to econometric analysis if reliable quarterly data
on units under construction, financial commitments, and ease of
credit were available. This again is one area of significant relations almost entirely neglected in the previous models.

To summarize this section, it was shown that between two
equilibrium points the number of units started will be equal to the
increase in households, the amount of units needed to replace the
net losses, if any, from the existing stock, and the desired increases in vacancies. In any period, however, the actual number
of units started will vary from the equilibrium amount depending
on fluctuations in the level of undesired vacancies and of units
under construction.

A complete theory attempting to evaluate actual or potential
changes as a result of movements of any of the independent variables must explain their equilibrium impact on household formation,
on the desire to convert, demolish, or abandon units, and on the
normal vacancy level. In addition, it is possible that a change in an
independent variable may cause a significant movement away from
equilibrium through a temporary increase in the undesired inventory or that under construction. The duration or amount of this
movement from equilibrium will depend on the interacting forces
of the independent variables as well as on the technological and
institutional structure of the market.

Most existing theories have attempted to throw light on one or
a few reactions of the market to a small selected group of variables.
This is not surprising given the limited availability of data. If the
guesses of Tables IV-10 to IV-12 are anywhere near right, however,
a satisfactory solution requires a more comprehensive approach.
Examining Table IV-10 again, we see that demographic forces,
social, and economic influences on household formation, changes
in vacancies, and changes in units under construction each may have
played an important and varying role in the annual fluctuations
of the number of starts. The impact of the independent variables
must be analyzed in terms of each of these factors.

D. The Determinants of the Average Expenditures Per Unit
Constructed

In addition to explaining the factors which influence the number
of dwelling units started or constructed in any period, a satisfactory
theory for the residential construction market should explain what
determines the average amount of expenditures per new unit and
also the expenditures for capital improvements, i.e., "additions
and alterations." This area has had the least analytical work and

remains the most underdeveloped part of residential construction theory. Of the models discussed earlier, only Break's (4) attempted to deal with it directly, but he obtained no significant relationships from his data. Several of the econometric models attempted a partial explanation by combining in their reasoning and parameters a discussion of the determinants of starts and expenditures. The verbal models by Wood (59), Grebler (17), Rapkin-Winnick-Blank (42), Fisher-Fisher (14) and Duesenberry (12) also deal in some sense with this problem by pointing out that the movements in the price of and expenditure for existing housing are major determinants of the price of and amounts spent for new units. Supply in the construction market also is assumed to affect the price of both new and existing units.

Much of the literature on the effect of credit changes on building volume assumes a particular form of relationship between the markets for new and existing construction, although the form in most cases is not made wholly explicit. Such assumptions are necessary because the analysts usually deal with the role of credit in the entire housing market and then attempt to show how credit changes influence construction.

Robinson (46), Maisel (32,33), and Smith (50) have developed a formal framework for the relationships between the markets for new and existing housing and have attempted to work out some but not all of their interactions. (Both markets can, of course, be further subdivided by tenure, location, ownership, size, etc., but for simplification all of these can be aggregated initially into single markets.) Their basic models describe a situation in which the equilibrium of supply and demand in both the housing market (for occupancy) and in the market for new construction are determined simultaneously.

In equilibrium, a number of dwelling units are demanded and supplied for occupancy at definite prices, which determines the value of the housing stock, i.e., $S_1 . E_1$ (units times average value), as explained in Part A of this chapter. When the independent variables change, a new equilibrium will be reached at a value $S_2 . E_2$. This new value depends partly on the changes in the number of units demanded, as described in the previous part of this chapter, and partly on the change in the average value per unit.

What causes households to desire to occupy a house worth E_2 on the average instead of E_1? Part of the new equilibrium will depend on movements of the demand curve resulting from changes in income, credit, and taste. Part will depend on movements of the supply curve for existing units, which is affected by demolitions, abandonments, conversions, and alterations. Part will depend on the supply curve for new construction. The equilibrium level of new construction and its price are determined simultaneously with the supply changes in the existing stock and its average price.

As an example of these changes, it was noted in Part A that, according to a crude estimate, the average value of all dwelling units rose by $2,900, or about 60 percent between 1950 and 1957. At the same time, the total value of the housing stock rose by $207 billion. Of this amount, over 60 percent was accounted for by new units constructed, while nearly 40 percent was attributable to revaluations and additions and alterations in the existing stock, after accounting for withdrawals from the stock. At the same time, the index of the cost of new residential construction increased by 20 percent, and that of rents by 22 percent. The average amount spent per unit constructed rose somewhat more than the reported increase in construction cost or rent.

Such movements in value can be due to either a change in prices or a change in the real quantity of housing services rendered by the stock. A complete theory of construction should deal with both aspects. How do changes in the independent variables, such as credit and income, affect the quantity of housing services demanded and supplied in the average dwelling unit? How do these changes affect the price of the average dwelling unit?

In the present framework, we shall consider only the factors altering the real value, or the quantity of services per unit. The effect of credit and other changes on prices is also significant, but price movements depend more on the supply curve than on the demand curve. If a theory can explain changes in the equilibrium level of value, then the division between movements in real terms and those in prices will depend on the shape of the supply curve and the way supply reacts to the same independent variables. The division of money value into its components may be considered as subsidiary to the determination of what causes value changes, although it is clearly of utmost significance for specific policy recommendations.

Before proceeding with a discussion of the determinants of the demand for different quantities (or real values) of housing services in a dwelling unit, housing services need to be defined. There are many dimensions to real housing values. A change in the real value of housing services can take any of the following main forms: (a) the amount of space; (b) the finish of the space; (c) the amount and quality of equipment; (d) the utility of the space (design); (e) the prestige status of the space; (f) its relationship to community facilities, transportation, etc., and (g) the amount of required current maintenance and repairs (one can substitute current costs for initial costs).

The amount a family will have to pay for its housing will differ depending upon how much it receives along each of these dimensions. Clearly, each household may purchase and receive varying amounts of services along each line depending upon its composition, tastes, income, and other circumstances. The present analysis, however, addresses itself to the forces which cause the amount of services demanded by the average family to vary. This average is a vector which merges all of these dimensions.

We shall discuss this problem in three separate parts. The first two deal primarily with the average real value demanded in the over-all housing market, while the last relates the change in the equilibrium value demanded in the total market to the amount of residential construction supplied.

1. What resources will a family allocate to its housing?

The theory of the resources a family will allocate to housing is a special case of the general theory of household demands. A family's expenditures are held to depend on its tastes, income, prices, assets, and other variables. The general theory is well developed. Most discussions of the consumption function and most empirical work on expenditure patterns apply. Many of the expenditure studies, such as those by Lewis, Allen and Bowley, Prais and Houthakker, Wold, the National Resources Planning Board and others, give estimates of the income elasticities of housing expenditures. Other studies also give information on the influence of other variables on housing expenditures. Thus, Maisel and Winnick (34) consider not only the influence of income, but such variables as family size, age, race, education, occupation, and location. They conclude that most of these variables do influence expenditures, but that the range of tastes is wide and that lags in adjustment are considerable.

Very little work has been done on the price elasticity of housing expenditures. Some authors have argued that price elasticity should be high, while others hold it to be low. Outside of econometric models in which both the number and the average value of housing units reflect rather high estimated price elasticities, the few studies of this matter tend to find a low price elasticity.

While there has been considerable debate over the role which assets play in general consumption, this is not true of the analysis of housing expenditures, with the exception of Duesenberry (12) and a brief mention in Klein (28). This may be a serious defect. Assets may play a major role in determining a family's housing expenditures. Relevant assets are of two types, each with a separate impact: (a) financial, and (b) specific housing assets.

Most analysts stress the influence of lack of financial assets on housing expenditures. It is assumed that lower downpayments remove a financial disability and thereby allow a household to increase the current resources it devotes to its housing. A household can purchase a house at an earlier time than would be possible otherwise, or it can buy a more expensive house. This increase in real housing values purchased, brought about by the removal or reduction of the need to save a downpayment, is believed by many to be the primary justification for governmental programs in the housing market.

Analysts have paid less attention to the importance of existing housing assets in determining present and future expenditures. Yet, such assets may influence spending more than other assets or required downpayments. Except at infrequent intervals, most people do not re-examine the value of their housing assets to determine whether or not too large or too small a share of the family's wealth is devoted to housing. Families tend to occupy more expensive houses than they would do otherwise when the value of their existing housing assets has been increasing. However, there are great lags and much inertia in the market. There also seems to be a tendency for money received from the liquidation of housing assets to be reinvested in upgraded family housing rather than for other purposes. At least in recent years, the housing press has frequently commented on the use of money received from the sale of houses as a downpayment on more expensive houses.

In summary, we can say that the theory of the resources a family will devote to housing has been rather well articulated with the exception of the relationship of assets to expenditures. Tests have been performed of the relationships with income, demographic, and status variables but not as frequently with price and credit. While significant relationships have been found, they are not in a form which can easily be used for analysis or prediction. The relationships are primarily developed from cross-section data with all their inherent problems, and their variances tend to be large. No effort has been made to gather all of the existing data into a model which would predict the exact influence on total housing expenditures of these variables.

2. The division of the homeowner's shelter costs

Shelter costs are extremely difficult to measure for the average owner of a house. A certain amount of capital is invested in each dwelling unit, both from the individual's and the aggregate point of view. However, the cost of living in a dwelling with a given capital value will vary from period to period depending upon the cost of capital (the interest rate or yield on real-estate equities) and upon real depreciation after adjustment for price changes. The annual costs of shelter will be much higher for a house with a specified amount of capital if that capital could be producing a 10-percent yield in other uses instead of a 2-percent yield. In the same manner, if rapid style and neighborhood changes reduce the utility of a given house, living in it will cost its owners more per period than if its capital value remains constant or declines very slowly.

What is the relationship between these real costs of shelter and a household's decision to allocate a certain percentage of its current income to shelter? In the first place, its shelter expenditures cover both the initial cost of the dwelling and current expenses such as real-estate taxes, maintenance, and utilities. Other things equal, a rise in these expenses will mean that less money is available to pay for the initial expenditure on the dwelling, and vice versa.

A second relationship appears to depend upon how the owner measures his shelter costs. He has a choice of allocating his shelter expenditures either in terms of their financial drain on his budget or by attempting to impute and weigh his real costs for the period. Given a decision to allocate a certain share of a family's current income and assets to housing, the amount and quality of shelter purchased may vary greatly depending upon which type of costs is considered pertinent. This is obvious when a comparison is made between a household occupying a dwelling for which it owes a lender 100 percent of the value and one occupying an identical house, but with a 50-percent loan on similar payment terms and identical taxes and operating expenses. If the consumer considers only his current debt charges, the first family would judge that it was allocating twice as much income to its dwelling as the second, and even if it considers its total financial outlays including real-estate taxes and operating expenses, the first family would still judge that it was allocating substantially more to its dwelling than the second. The real costs, however, would be identical.

Changing credit conditions alter both the financial and real shelter costs, although most analysts have stressed the former. Assume an owner can borrow 100 percent of the price of a house. Any movements in the interest rate will vary both his real and financial costs to the same degree. The more resources the owner has to pay the lender for interest upon the amount borrowed, the less can be used to increase the quantity of housing purchased. Of course, if competitive interest rates were imputed, a change in the interest rate would affect his real costs to the same extent even if he had no loan. Most people, however, intuitively believe that a household will lower the amount of housing capital purchased more if interest as part of a financial payment rises than if higher interest costs are simply imputed on its own equity.

Higher loan amortization payments are also assumed to lower the amount of housing capital purchased. This follows partly from the consideration of a household's current financial outlays. A family will allocate only a certain share of its income to its shelter payments even though these may include a large share of forced saving through amortization payments which exceed the loss in capital values. The average family is limited in its power to save and will usually allocate less to real shelter costs if it is forced to accumulate an equity in its dwelling. In this view, a family will give greater weight to its financial than its real costs.

There have been but few tests of how the average family alters its real housing expenditures when financial payments change, even though a fair amount of data are available. The tests which have been performed, however, seem to indicate that households occupy more housing space and use more housing capital when credit terms are easier. Again, the tests have not been frequent enough, or have not been analyzed sufficiently, to estimate the size of the parameters or to utilize this knowledge in a working model.

3. The division of additional consumer spending on housing between new construction and appreciation of the existing stock.

The previous two parts discussed the question why demand for quantity of housing services per dwelling unit varies. The average household determines to allocate more or less resources to its housing because of a change in income, tastes, credit, etc., or the amount of resources which can be devoted to the dwelling alters because complementary payments such as taxes, utilities, interest, or amortization are changed. In addition, to determine the equilibrium position resulting from such shifts in demand one must know the shape of two supply curves, that of the housing market and that of the construction market.

At one extreme, if the housing supply curve were completely inelastic and no construction could take place, all additional expenditures resulting from positive changes in income and taste or easier credit would go to the owners of the existing supply. Their receipts would increase. The additional receipts would be capitalized. The higher value of the existing stock would all appear as a price rise and capital gain for existing owners. At the opposite extreme, all of the additional expenditures might be used to purchase additional dwelling values created through new construction.

The actual adjustment of equilibrium at least in the short run will be complex and will occur along several channels. The housing stock and the demand may be constantly striving to achieve equilibrium. However, because of neighborhood loyalties, costs of transfer of owned properties, and market imperfections, the adjustments within the existing stock are slow. Maisel and Winnick (34) discuss this problem at length and show that, as a result of these rigidities, the variations in the type of dwellings that households of similar income and other characteristics occupy are very wide at any time. The lags in adjustment to changed variables are great.

What are the various methods of adjustment, assuming real increases in value and not price rises? Additional quality may be obtained by investing more resources in existing units through alterations and additions. These will raise the average real value of existing units. Other adjustments will come from building more expensive new units. Finally, part will come through making obsolete existing units, removing them completely, and replacing them.

The shape of the supply curve, and the manner in which it affects revaluation of the stock in contrast to new investment, have been discussed by Duesenberry (12), Fisher (15), Wood (59), and Maisel (32,33), but there is no consensus of opinion. Moreover, little attention has been given to the obsolescence and abandonment of housing units when households decide to increase the average real value of their dwellings. Much of the literature assumes — but the assumption is rarely made explicit – that such a shift in household demand will make an additional number of existing units obsolete. As a result, units will be abandoned and replaced by new housing of a more expensive type. Our discussion of net losses from the housing stock pointed out that, at least to date, there is little indication that this form of adjustment has been at all important. We also noted, however, that part of the increase in units held off the market might be attributed to this cause. Some observers go farther and hold that adjustments through demolitions of existing units should rarely be necessary. They believe that a desired supply can be achieved most efficiently except in unusual circumstances by constructing (a) the total number of units required by new households, vacancies, and exogenous losses as outlined in the previous part but with a minimum number of units made obsolete, and (b) altering the existing stock to increase its quality (50). If such assumptions are correct, a shift in the demand for quality, or quantity of services, per unit will increase the average expenditures per new dwelling, but will have slight impact on the number of units demanded. If these assumptions are wrong, then a change in quality demanded, in addition to increasing average expenditures, will affect the number of units by increasing the losses from the existing stock.

In summary, the question of what influences the amount which an average household will allocate to shelter has been discussed at considerable length in the literature on demand in general and on housing. The form of several of the specific relationships has been tested, and the parameters have been estimated. While the role of credit in this process has been considered, the tests of this variable

are less numerous and less specific. Other variables, including the
critical one of price, have had even less empirical research. No
general summary exists of present knowledge in the form of a
working model.

Practically no work has been done on the relationships between
altered total housing expenditures, resulting from changes in income or credit or similar independent variables, and revaluation
or additions and alterations in the existing stock and new construction. On this point, there are basic and significant conflicts between
the assumptions used by various students in their analysis of the
market.

VI. FEDERAL CREDIT PROGRAMS AS DETERMINANTS

Considerable literature exists on the effects of federal housing
programs on the composition of residential construction and on
short-term fluctuations. Most of it is of the verbal-qualitative
type. With one exception, the statistical-econometric models at
best concern themselves with the effects of changes in credit conditions generally, without attempting to examine and quantify the
component sources of such changes. The long-run impact on the
level of construction has had relatively little attention. Yet, whether
the extensive housing aids offered by the federal government have
helped raise the level of new construction or accelerate the growth
of the housing sector would seem to be a strategic question.

A. Level of Construction

Only two studies have been specifically concerned with the effect of federal housing programs on the level of housing construction in the postwar period. One of these, by R. J. Saulnier, concludes
that, in spite of the governmental efforts to stimulate residential
construction through easier mortgage credit, building activity was
actually less in the boom years following World War II than might
have been expected in view of the trends in population and family
formation. This conclusion is based on a comparison of a single
"boom" year in residential construction, 1950, and of the 1948-50
period with 1925 and 1923-25, respectively. The ratio of nonfarm
housing starts to the housing stock, to the increase in nonfarm
population, and to the increase in nonfarm families was substantially lower in the recent than in the earlier periods. Likewise,
construction expenditures in constant prices were much less when
related to population and family increases. Construction costs and
housing prices, on the other hand, rose much more sharply in the
recent postwar period than in the twenties. Thus, "the period after
World War I, lacking the urgent stimulation of liberalized home
mortgage credit, not only produced relatively more housing but did

so virtually without cost and price inflation, though building costs
rose slightly in what was a period of sagging price levels for the
economy generally; the post-World War II expansion, on the other
hand, which was relatively modest as compared with the demographic trends of the period, was characterized by a marked inflation of building costs and housing prices." (47) The implication
is that federal credit aids have had the effect of pushing up house
prices rather than expanding the level of housing construction.

These conclusions can be questioned on several grounds. First,
the analysis sets out to determine the impact of the federal credit
programs on the volume and price of residential construction, but
ends up at best with determining the effects of the postwar trend
toward more liberal credit terms (compared to the prewar period).
The changes in housing credit terms, however, may have been,
and most probably were, occasioned by much more pervasive
forces than the federal programs. Among these were the supply
of funds relative to demand, the general monetary and fiscal
policies affecting the supply-demand relationship and, more specifically, such matters as the pegging of federal securities prices until
the Treasury — Federal Reserve Accord of 1951 and the desire and
relative ability of financial institutions to shift from federal securities to mortgage loans and other investments with higher net yields.
Granting that any impact of the federal housing credit programs on
the level of residential construction would have operated for the
most part through the channel of credit terms, nothing can be said
specifically about such an impact so long as influences of the programs are not segregated from other influences affecting credit
terms. At best, it seems plausible that aggregative or average
"credit terms" would have been less favorable to mortgage
borrowers by some unknown quantity if it had not been for the
federal programs.

The second reason for questioning the validity of the analysis
is that a comparison of the performance of an economic sector in
two relatively short periods nearly a generation apart requires consideration of secular trends. Indeed, Saulnier's finding of a lessened
response of housing output to differences in credit terms is consistent with the secular trends shown by Grebler and his associates (18). Third, the comparison of the post-World War II period
with the twenties ignores the effect on the demand for residential
construction of the marked shift from unamortized or partially
amortized housing loans to fully amortized mortgages. "The almost
universal inclusion of payments on principal in debt service has
raised periodic outlays substantially at any given level of interest
rates and has tended to absorb (in terms of cash accounting) much
of the advantage to borrowers resulting from the lower interest
rates and longer contract terms of recent periods." (18) Fourth,
demand and supply in the housing market during the 1948-50 period

were probably in much greater disequilibrium as a result of war effects than they were in 1923-25, Saulnier's reference period. Residential construction was more severely restrained in World War II than in World War I, and for a much longer span of time. Likewise, the burst of household formation after the recent war may have been relatively greater than after our involvement in the earlier war. Fifth, some of the underlying data are questionable. The Census Bureau's postwar sample data on the increase in non-farm families, for example, involve such a large margin of error that the Bureau itself warns against reliance on the year-to-year changes used by Saulnier in part. Ratios of housing output to increases in nonfarm population ignore the substantial decline in the average size of households between the periods considered. As indicated in Chapter IV, the basic series on starts were derived by entirely different techniques. As a result, differences in levels of 20 percent or more may simply reflect sampling variations.

Finally, more evidence would seem to be needed for isolating the effects of the federal credit programs or, for that matter, of more liberal credit on construction costs and housing prices. The much greater increase in costs during the period after World War II in comparison to the twenties can be observed for private non-residential construction, for which there have been no federal aid programs of any consequence, as well as for residential building. This observation suggests that the causes of cost-rise differentials between the two periods may be more complex, or one would need to demonstrate that the federal housing aids were the main factor in bidding up the prices of resources used for both residential and other construction. And differential movements of relative prices in the two periods examined by Saulnier, such as construction costs relative to nonfarm wholesale prices or consumer prices, may have been in any event more relevant to his argument than absolute price movements.

The second attempt to evaluate the effects of the federal aid programs on the level of postwar residential construction, by Break (4), has led to conclusions quite different from those of Saulnier. Break estimates that "the postwar impact of the FHA and VA programs would be approximately 130,000 additional houses a year or greater annual expenditures on new dwelling units (in 1957-58 dollars) of $1.4 billion. Most of our estimates, however, fell within a higher middle range, indicating a stimulus to the housing industry of as much as 375,000 to 500,000 additional dwelling units a year or, in dollar terms, some $4 to $5.5 billion." Without the governmental assistance, it appears according to Break that housing starts and residential construction expenditures in constant prices would have been at least 10 percent, and possibly as much as 30-40 percent, below their average 1948-56 level.

Break arrives at these conclusions by employing two statistical procedures. First, he develops the econometric model described in Chapter III. This model, it will be recalled, attempts to measure the sensitivity of residential construction to changes in mortgage credit terms and assigns a large weight to the credit variable for the postwar period, in contrast to the years 1925-41. As a minimum, according to this study, it would appear that a 0.1 decline in the composite terms of credit variable in the postwar period stimulated the construction 150,000 new dwelling units and the expenditure of one billion or more in terms of 1947-49 prices. Next, he measures the impact of federal loan insurance on mortgage credit terms by comparing composite series of average interest rates, maturities, and loan-to-value ratios on conventional home loans and on FHA and VA home loans. The spread between the two series serves as a measure of the impact of federal loan insurance programs. Break recognizes the complex interrelations between the conventional and government-underwritten mortgage lending markets which may affect the spread and make it a less than perfect yardstick. He is also aware of the weakness of existing data on conventional lending terms. Nevertheless, he is satisfied that the procedure yields acceptable results.

If Break's procedures are accepted, his conclusions seem impeccable. As was pointed out in Chapter III, however, Break's model is subject to reservations. Moreover, his estimates of the influence of federal credit programs are presented in such wide ranges that their usefulness is severely limited. The upper ranges of his estimates of the impact of federal credit programs claim that practically all FHA and VA underwritten activity has been a net addition to residential construction that would not have occurred without the programs — a finding which is difficult to accept on commonsense grounds. Also, none of his studies of the influence of mortgage credit terms on the average expenditure per dwelling unit in constant prices indicated a high degree of sensitivity to credit changes, which, as he notes, is not consistent with his estimates of the influence of the composite terms of credit variable on the number of new dwelling units built and on the aggregate expenditure on such units. Thus, Break's pioneer attempt at measurement through often ingenious procedures still leaves a great many questions unanswered.

Another observation relevant to the impact of federal housing programs on the level of new construction pertains to the disproportionate share of new construction (as against existing property) in FHA and VA operations. For the entire market in houses for owner-occupancy, it is roughly estimated that at least two existing homes have been bought in the postwar period for every new home purchased. In contrast, more than half the number of FHA mortgages on homes in the postwar period and more than 60 percent of the number of VA home loans closed since 1949 were on new construction.

The disproportionate share of new construction in the FHA and VA programs is explained by a variety of circumstances. Throughout the existence of FHA until the Housing Act of 1957, maximum loan-to-value ratios and maximum loan maturities were more favorable for mortgages on new construction. In the case of both FHA and VA, the property and neighborhood standards of the agencies have been such as to exclude much of the existing housing supply. The appraisal practices of the agencies may also have militated against existing property. Finally, sellers of existing homes often find it more difficult to wait for the rather lengthy processing of papers by FHA or VA than do builders and therefore prefer to sell to purchasers using other means of financing. Whatever the reasons, one would assume that the greater use of FHA and VA financing in new rather than in existing construction should have discriminated in favor of new building.

B. Composition of Construction

The main questions on the influence of federal housing programs on the residential construction "mix" pertain to the distribution of new construction (a) over houses for owner-occupancy and rental housing, (b) over various price and rental ranges, and (c) over various geographic regions.

As for sales and rental housing, many housing specialists have expressed the view that FHA, largely oriented toward the support of single-family house construction, and the veterans housing program, which is solely geared to helping veterans acquire homes for owner-occupancy, have served to accentuate the building of houses for sale to the detriment of new housing for rent. The proportion of rental units to total housing starts has indeed been much lower in the recent postwar period than in any other period of comparable length for which records are available. After a careful study, Louis Winnick has concluded: "The spectacular shift to single-family houses is basically a reflection of consumer preferences, exercised within the present range of housing choice. A long period of prosperity has enabled most consumers to realize the urge for ownership. But prosperity is not the sole reason. Without government credit aids, the single-family housing boom could not have reached its recent proportions". (57)

To the extent that the federal insurance programs have favored single-family house construction, they may also have contributed to the great postwar growth of suburbs at the expense of less intensive growth or actual stagnation of central cities. And the postwar migration to suburbia may have tended to raise the level of total construction by leaving pockets of unused or underutilized housing in central city areas or by accelerating demolitions in such areas.

As for the influence of federal programs on price ranges of new housing, the 1950 Census of Housing and the 1956 National Housing Inventory have demonstrated that FHA and VA financing has been used primarily by families in the middle-income brackets and for the purchase of medium-priced houses. The share of FHA and VA loans in the acquisition of low-priced homes by lower-income families has been small compared to the share of conventional loans, as has been their share in the high-price or high-income market. Although the 1956 data shown in Table IV-13 relate to both new and old houses, they are in all probability also applicable to new homes alone.[1] The concentration of FHA and VA activity in the medium-price and medium-income groups is probably due in large part to the fact that lower-priced houses often do not meet the construction and locational standards of the mortgage insurance agencies. Other reasons may be the limited accessibility to FHA and VA financing in small or remote localities in which lower-priced houses are more common, and the less intensive use of such financing for the purchase of existing property. No analytical work of any consequence has been done on the position of rents in FHA rental housing projects in the hierarchy of rents in new rental construction or the total rental housing stock.

As for the regional distribution of new construction, the federal credit programs (the Federal Home Loan Bank System, the Federal National Mortgage Association, and FHA and VA operations) are generally credited with having facilitated the interregional flow of funds. Legal prohibitions of the acquisition of out-of-state or nonlocal mortgages by most types of institutional lenders do not apply to FHA and VA loans. Moreover, the federal insurance or guaranty has transformed the residential mortgage into a more

---

[1] For a summary of 1950 data, see Grebler-Blank-Winnick, op. cit., pp. 150-153. Also, the median family income of owner-occupants was reported in the National Housing Inventory of 1956 as follows: $6,178 for purchasers with FHA loans, $5,854 for purchasers with VA loans, and $5,677 for purchasers with conventional loans. The median ratio of purchase price to income was 1.9 for owners having FHA and VA mortgages and 1.7 for owners having conventional loans (first mortgages with no second mortgage). See also R. J. Saulnier's Introduction to J. E. Morton, Urban Mortgage Lending: Comparative Markets and Experience for the National Bureau of Economic Research (Princeton: Princeton University Press, 1956), p. 6.

TABLE IV-13

Distribution of Purchase Prices of New and Old Single-Family Houses Financed with Mortgage Loans, by Type of Mortgage Financing, 1956

Purchase Price Class	FHA and VA First Mortgages[a]		Conventional First Mortgages[a]		FHA and VA as Percent of Total in Each Price Class
	Number	Percent	Number	Percent	
Less than $4,000	61,099	1.3	838,665	15.6	6.7
$4,000 to $5,999	214,852	4.7	704,371	13.1	23.4
$6,000 to $7,999	568,410	12.3	733,732	13.6	43.7
$8,000 to $9,999	921,174	19.9	615,103	11.4	60.0
$10,000 to $11,999	995,348	21.5	540,956	10.0	64.8
$12,000 to $13,999	956,029	20.7	487,625	9.0	66.2
$14,000 to $16,999	585,327	12.7	488,961	9.1	54.5
$17,000 to $19,999	193,937	4.2	312,503	5.8	38.3
$20,000 or more	125,635	2.7	671,909	12.5	15.8
Total Reporting	4,621,811	100.0	5,393,825	100.0	46.2

[a]With no second mortgage

Source: "Financing of Owner Occupied Residential Properties," 1956 National Housing Inventory, Vol. II, U.S. Department of Commerce, Bureau of the Census, Washington, D.C.: 1958, Table 5. Data relate only to reported cases. Because they are derived from a sample survey and the number of "not reported" cases varies greatly between purchase price classes, the data must be used with caution but they are indicative of general tendencies.

standardized instrument that lends itself more easily to transactions over wide distances. Thus, mutual savings banks and other lenders in the East buy FHA and VA loans in the West and South even though they cannot or will not purchase conventional mortgages on property in these areas. In the case of the Federal Home Loan Bank System, the consolidated obligations of the Banks are typically sold in capital-surplus areas while most of the proceeds usually are used for advances to members of the System in capital-deficit areas. A similar function is performed by the Federal National Mortgage Association whose mortgage purchases have been concentrated in the West and South (18, 27). Also, the loan participation program authorized in 1957 for insured savings and loan associations makes it possible for institutions of this type in capital-deficit areas to sell participating interests in areas with surplus funds. Several studies have noted a narrowing over time of regional interest-rate differentials for residential mortgage loans and attributed this change in part to the federal instrumentalities (18, 27, 47).

None of the research work to-date has addressed itself to the question paramount from the viewpoint of this report, to wit, whether compositional changes in residential construction attributable to the federal programs have resulted in increases in the aggregate level of this type of construction. Some of the studies, though, indicate a presumption that they did.

C. Effects on Stability and Instability

The great volatility of housing starts under the FHA and VA programs in the postwar period has long been the subject of debate among housing analysts and general economists. The facts are clear. Year-to-year changes in the volume of starts under these programs have been much greater than other starts, which have been financed with conventional loans or full cash. This observation is illustrated in Table IV-14. Similar differences can be observed in related financial data. The estimates in Table IV-14 reveal also that housing starts under the VA program have been more volatile than those under the FHA program. This difference in relative instability reflects at least in part the greater administrative discretion of the FHA in adjusting maximum interest rates to market conditions under legal interest rate ceilings, while adjustments of the VA rates required congressional action which was taken belatedly or not at all. A more extensive treatment of the reasons for differences in the volatility of FHA and VA activity can be found in several analyses, for example, (25) and (49).

Aside from the facts, two main issues are involved. One is the role of inflexible interest rates on government-underwritten mortgages in producing the pronounced fluctuations in starts under the federal programs. The other pertains to the desirability of

TABLE IV-14

Privately Owned Permanent Nonfarm Dwelling Units Started,

By Type of Financing, 1951-1958

| Year | Total | Under Government Programs | | | Other Financing[a] |
		FHA	VA	Combined	
1951	1,020,100	263,523	148,634	412,157	607,943
1952	1,068,500	279,901	141,274	421,175	647,325
1953	1,068,300	251,969	156,616	408,585	659,715
1954	1,201,700	276,307	307,038	583,345	618,355
1955	1,309,500	276,695	392,870	669,565	639,935
1956	1,093,900	189,341	270,675	460,016	633,884
1957	992,800	168,423	128,302	296,725	696,075
1958	1,141,500	397,500	295,400	692,900	744,000

[a]Conventional mortgage financing or all cash. Since this column is a residual, the full impact of any errors in estimated starts is reflected in these totals.

Source: Housing Statistics, Housing & Home Finance Agency, Washington, D.C. The series on housing starts was revised substantially in 1959, and the new estimates are not comparable to the ones used in the above table. In the absence of official revisions for prior years at the time of this writing, it seems best to limit the data to the period ending in 1958.

maintaining inflexible rates as an instrument of economic stabilization policy, in view of the observation that the administered rates
have contributed to the restraint of housing construction in periods
of business expansion accompanied by increased levels of interest
rates, and to its stimulation in periods of business recession and
easier credit.

Many analysts have attributed the "feast and famine" in govern-
ment-aided activity solely or mainly to the ceilings on the maximum
interest rates on FHA and VA loans. According to this reasoning,
lenders have usually withdrawn from the FHA and particularly the
VA market during periods of generally rising interest rates when
net yields on government-underwritten mortgages, because of legal
or administrative limits on interest rates, became less attractive.
Discounts on government-underwritten mortgages to provide yield
flexibility have been at best highly imperfect substitutes for more
freely adjustable interest rates, and even discounts have at times
been regulated under legislative mandates. Conversely, when the
general level of interest rates was falling or low, lending on FHA
and VA mortgages was greatly stimulated (9, 41).

A modified version of this position has been presented by Grebler
(19, 20). According to this view, the interest-rate ceilings have been
only one, though perhaps the most important, of several conditions
contributing to instability in the federally-assisted housing sector.
Another factor has been the source of demand for FHA and VA loans.
Much of this demand comes from groups of consumers who are in the
market only when the most liberal terms permitted under the
programs are available, and drop out when they are not. In other
words, the FHA and VA programs meet to some extent demands
which are activated only in periods of easy credit. Still another factor may be the mortgage insurance feature itself, which reduces
the effectiveness of the risk deterrent in periods of acute competition for investment outlets. In this view, even completely free interest rates on government-underwritten loans would merely reduce
but not eliminate the greater volatility of government-underwritten
activity.

An even more qualified position is taken by Guttentag (23). According to this analysis, the maintenance of fixed maximum interest
rates did not constitute a significant restraint on total mortgage
lending during the postwar periods of decline in residential building
which Guttentag studied (through 1956), because the supply of
mortgage credit was very inelastic in some of these periods and
because builders could absorb discounts (providing lenders with
competitive yields) in others. The inflexible rates probably served
to intensify fluctuations in the supply of mortgage credit to some
extent, but their importance in this respect has been greatly exaggerated. An extension of Guttentag's analysis to the period after

1956 would be useful in testing its validity but is outside the purview of this report.

As for the desirability of maintaining the inflexible rates for countercyclical purposes, some economists have argued that the policy pursued to-date should be continued in the interest of general economic stability. The following statement is perhaps the most articulate expression of this position (49).

"The fact is that monetary policy appears to have had more effect on residential construction than on anything else in the last few years. There may also have been significant effects on capital expenditures by smaller business concerns and on debt-financed expenditures by state and local governments, but even here the evidence is not entirely clear or convincing. If interest rates on government-supported mortgages were made flexible, I believe one of the major mechanisms by which monetary policy exerts its effects on the economy would be eliminated and the effectiveness of monetary policy as a means of promoting economic stability would be significantly reduced.

"I would therefore favor retention of the interest rate ceilings. However, provision must be made for adjusting these ceilings as underlying conditions change." (Smith, Study of Mortgage Credit, p. 263)

Others have held that the rigid interest rates on FHA and VA mortgage loans have subjected the housing sector to excessive fluctuations impairing the continuity and efficiency of production and that completely free or more flexible rates would reduce the degree of instability in this sector of the economy.[2] The termination of fixed rates would at least remove the paradoxical situation that governmental interference, which is supposed to benefit the housing sector, at times operates unintentionally as a potent restrictive force in disfavor of housing. Moreover, if it is considered desirable for economic stabilization purposes to restrain government-sponsored residential construction, it would be preferable to do so through deliberate changes in downpayment requirements and maximum loan maturities, rather than through the operation of legal maximum rates which were never designed to perform economic stabilization

---

[2] In addition, it is argued that the inflexible rates fail to protect would-be borrowers because these face the alternatives of obtaining no loans on the prescribed rates or conventional loans on less liberal terms. Guttentag, however, holds that the policy of rigid rates has been in the best interest of home buyers (23). The present report concerns itself with the effects of housing credit programs on stability and instability, leaving aside the welfare argument.

functions (19, 20). A similar view has been expressed in a staff
report for the Joint Economic Committee (9, 41): "The question is
whether it would be better to keep the present interest rate limitations, recognizing them frankly as a selective credit control, and
manipulating them accordingly, or to adopt another kind of selective
regulation in the form of variable controls over downpayments and
maturities of mortgages. On balance, it would probably be preferable to eliminate the interest rate ceilings and adopt the other form
of controls, since the interest rate ceilings have peculiar allocational
effects."

At times, discretionary powers of federal housing and other
governmental agencies have been used for the purpose of restraining
and relaxing housing credit. This was the case during the Korean
hostilities when the maximum permissible terms for government-
underwritten mortgage loans were tightened, other administrative
actions taken to curtail housing credit extended by federal agencies,
and the terms on conventional real-estate loans controlled by Regulation X under the authority of the Defense Production Act of 1950.
Essays by Saulnier and O'Leary on the experience with this type of
selective credit control come to about the same conclusions (41a
and 48). The cutback of residential mortgage lending and building
activity was less than desired and anticipated by policy-makers.
This was largely the result of three factors. Drafting Regulation X
was a novel undertaking and under the law required industry con-
sultation, and thus took an unusual amount of time. Partly because
of this delay, a large number of transactions was exempt from the
regulation because of prior financing commitments under more
liberal terms. Finally, early congressional relaxations of the restraints blunted the effectiveness of such controls. As for the future
(peacetime) application of such controls, Saulnier suggests that "it
would seem sufficient. . . to administer the loan insurance and loan
guarantee programs so as to prevent them from acting in a procyclical fashion. For true contra-cyclical influence shall have to
depend, it would seem, on the more traditional techniques of central
banking control." O'Leary adds that enforcement would always be
exceedingly difficult as the residential mortgage business is ingenious in discovering new ways to operate, although adjustments of
credit terms on FHA (and presumably VA) loans, which can be made
promptly without advance notice, can be more useful.

The view that the restraints in the Korean period were relatively
ineffective is not shared by Guttentag (23). According to his analysis,
the restrictions were responsible for the termination of the 1949-
50 expansion in construction and mortgage lending, notwithstanding
the initial accumulation of commitments exempt from the regulations. This difference in appraising the effectiveness of the restraints, however, may be narrowed down to the question whether
the curtailment of activity met the anticipations of policy makers,

which Saulnier and O'Leary deny and which Guttentag does not raise, or whether the restraints produced a substantial though delayed reduction in activity, on which all observers agree. In his extensive analysis of the controls, Guttentag concludes also that they bore more heavily on new than on existing housing, on government-underwritten than on conventional mortgages and, within the government-underwritten sector, more on VA loans than on FHA loans.

A few years after the Korean hostilities, in 1955, selective credit controls were again used in the housing sector, in the form of restraints on the terms of government-underwritten mortgage loans, restraints on Federal Home Loan Bank advances to member savings and loan associations, and warnings of the Federal Reserve Bank of New York against excessive "mortgage warehousing" loans by commercial banks. These actions, as well as subsequent relaxations in 1956 and 1957, have been subjected to extensive analysis by one of the authors of this review (19, 20). He concludes that the selective regulations, together with other forces, made a moderate and short-lived contribution to the restraint of homebuilding and helped correct maladjustments in the housing and mortgage market inherited from the 1954-55 expansion of residential construction. These results were over and above those obtained from the general policy of credit restraint and reinforced the latter. Delays in policy formation, a large number of previous commitments exempt from the regulations, the moderate extent of the restraints, and early relaxations militated against more substantial effects. Also, the experience seems to support the view that the use of selective controls for moderating an apparently unsustainable expansion in one economic sector is difficult if not impossible while the economy generally is still sluggish. The imposition of major selective housing credit controls in mid-1955 coincided with but did not precede the adoption of a clear-cut policy of general credit restraint.

The relaxations of housing credit in 1956 and 1957, in the face of continued and strengthened policies of general credit restraint until the fall of 1957, helped cushion the decline in residential construction, mainly by counteracting the temporary demise of the veterans home loan program, which resulted from the fact that the legal maximum interest rate had become noncompetitive. In addition to relaxations and withdrawals of previous restraints, the federal government offered positive relief to the housing sector mainly through large purchases of mortgage loans by the Federal National Mortgage Association. The analysis concludes that the relief actions for housing are unlikely to have occasioned an appreciably greater severity of general credit restraints than would have been the case otherwise, or that they caused the policy of restraint to fall far short of its objective. The relief actions were of limited magnitude and became largely effective in 1957 when over-all demand pressures on resources were already subsiding.

Finally, Break's work referred to at several points (4) gives an affirmative answer to the question whether the FHA and VA loan insurance programs have tended to stabilize employment, aggregate output, and prices. (He does not concern himself with their effects on stability of residential construction itself.) He argues, first, that the programs are potentially capable of exerting a stabilizing influence on the economy as a whole. The most obvious way in which this potential can be realized is by varying the maximum permissible loan maturities and loan-to-value ratios so as to restrain housing activity during periods of general economic expansion and stimulate it during periods of contraction. Such deliberate policy does not discriminate against housing since it only moderates but does not eliminate the long-run stimulating effects of the government programs on the housing sector - a position also taken by Grebler (19, 20) and others. Second, Break attempts to demonstrate that the federal mortgage insurance programs possess built-in countercyclical powers. One of these stems from the cyclical changes in loan default risks which are protected by insurance. The other results from the relatively inflexible maximum interest rates in government-underwritten mortgages. Third, Break analyzes the short-term behavior of mortgage credit terms during the postwar period and concludes that changes in these terms have in fact been countercyclical. By using the framework of his econometric model, he explains much of the cyclical fluctuations in residential construction since World War II in terms of these changes rather than other factors such as income, unemployment, or household formation. This part of his work confirms in quantitive fashion the more general analysis outlined in the section on short cycles in Chapter II-C.

Break concedes that it is impossible to isolate the short-term influence of FHA and VA mortgage insurance from that of general monetary and fiscal policies. In view of the built-in stabilizing potentials of the programs and the occasional use of discretionary changes in FHA and VA maximum terms, however, his analysis leaves a strong presumption that the programs have had an appreciable stabilizing effect on total economic activity.

VII. LOOKING BEHIND THE CREDIT VARIABLE: A BRIEF COMMENT

At many points, this paper has identified the role assigned by various analysts to credit as a determinant of residential construction. No matter how changes in the availability and terms of housing credit may be measured, it is clear that they are determined

in financial markets in which there are many competing demands
for funds as well as general supply functions. The availability and
terms of housing credit are also influenced by the structure of
competition among lenders and by monetary and fiscal policies
which affect the ease of borrowing generally but may have different
degrees of impact on various sectors of the economy. Moreover,
housing credit has at times been subject to selective credit regulation.

Basically, analysts concerned with determinants of residential
construction have treated the availability and terms of housing
credit as an independent variable and, when they consider it a significant variable, have struggled with the problem of identifying and
using data appropriately expressing changes therein; but they have
not, in turn, attempted any systematic explanation of changes in this
variable itself. This is a self-imposed and necessary limitation in
any model of any kind pertaining to an economic sector. For that
matter, even models for the U. S. economy as a whole are typically
weak in establishing systematic links between the "real" or output
accounts of the economy and its financial accounts.

By the same token, systematic consideration of the pervasive
economic and institutional forces acting on the availability and
terms of housing credit is outside the purview of this paper. Descriptive and analytical materials on these forces are provided in
two recent, major studies (23, 25). Nevertheless, it is not amiss to
add at least a brief comment and a few questions.

What is the position of the housing sector in the capital markets?
Is there any evidence in support of the view, held by some housing
specialists and by many builders but also found among legislators,
that the housing sector is somehow at a disadvantage in the allocation of funds through the financial markets? The available data on
the share of residential mortgage financing in the total uses of
capital funds do not furnish any conclusive evidence on this point.
The data at best show a statistical position of housing credit demands actually met in relation to other credit demands actually
met, but they cannot reveal whether a given share of housing credit
in the total is "adequate" or reflects a strong or weak position of
housing in the capital markets. Nevertheless, it will be useful to
indicate some orders of magnitude.

According to Klaman, the net flow of funds into residential
mortgages from 1948 to 1957 equalled 38.5 percent of the total net
flow of funds into capital market securities, including corporate
securities, state and municipal and federal obligations, and mortgages. "Over the full decade...residential mortgages were the
largest investment outlet in the capital market, ...absorbing nearly
$88 billion of funds, compared with $70 billion for corporate

securities, $34 billion for state and local government securities,
and $20 billion for nonresidential mortgages." (26) Klaman's data
show also large year-to-year variations in the share of residential
mortgages in total net capital flows, ranging from 50.0 percent in
1950 to 30.4 percent in 1952.

According to one of the statements on uses and sources of funds
developed in recent years, the net flow of funds into residential
mortgages from 1947 to 1957 equalled 31.4 percent of the total
capital funds available from savings sources including savings
institutions and other nonbank sources of funds. Here again, the
annual share of residential mortgages varied between a low of 18.7
percent in 1949 and a high of 36.4 percent in 1957 (40).

Differences in the level of the ratios between these two studies
are explained mainly by differences in the definition of the capital
market. Among other things, Klaman includes only debt instruments
in his uses of funds whereas the other study includes corporate stock
as well. An analysis by Arnold E. Chase, based on a more narrow
definition of available savings, shows that the ratio of the residential
mortgage debt outstanding to savings held by financial institutions
increased steadily from 32 percent in 1947 to 56 percent in 1956.
In 1921-29, the same ratio rose from 42 percent to 62 percent (6).
Finally, the residential mortgage debt in 1955 equalled 27.1 percent
of the estimated residential wealth in that year, as against 14.3
percent in 1945, 19.2 percent in 1939, and the previous high of 24.0
percent in 1933, so far as can be determined from available bench-
mark data (27).

The position of housing credit in the capital markets can be
influenced by many economic as well as institutional factors. Among
these may be the relatively small scale of individual credit transactions, especially in the case of home loans, and the resulting high
cost of originating and servicing mortgage loans. Also, the majority
of residential builders are in the small business class, and the complexities inherent in the financing of the construction process may
be compounded by the general financing problems of small businesses with typically small working capital in relation to total
financing requirements. Further, housing is said to be still more
dependent on local savings and local suppliers of funds than are
other economic sectors, especially corporate business and governments. Its access to the national capital market has been improved
through the Federal Home Loan Banks and the Federal National
Mortgage Association, which can issue large blocks of their obligations backed directly or indirectly by residential mortgages, but
there remains a question whether and how institutional arrangements for tapping that market may be strengthened. There is a
related question about the extent and effects of the interregional flow
of funds and the desirability of removing legal and institutional

obstacles, especially for conventional mortgage loans which are less marketable than government-underwritten paper.

Except for savings and loan associations, all principal portfolio lenders on residential mortgages have substantial alternative investment outlets. In perfect markets, one would assume that the choice of investment outlets in these cases will be conditioned by expected net yields commensurate with risk evaluations. But this principle can be modified by desired mortgage-asset ratios (quite apart from legal investment limitations), which may change over time. Whether mortgage investments fluctuate with the net inflow of total savings and repayments into financial institutions or in response to altered institutional notions of balanced investment portfolios can make a great deal of difference to the amounts made available for residential financing. Even relatively small changes in desired mortgage-asset ratios of major groups of institutions can produce large shifts and substantial instability in the amount of external funds available for housing. In the case of the larger life insurance companies, the net yield principle is also modified by the need for maintaining an efficient nation-wide organization for acquiring mortgage business. Thus, investment preferences can turn in favor or disfavor of housing within certain unknown limits of net yield differentials between residential loans and other investments after allowance for risk.[1] In the postwar period, the allocation of funds to the housing sector has been also influenced greatly by the maximum interest rates on FHA and VA loans, which at times were noncompetitive with interest rates on other investments.

The position of housing credit in capital markets may also vary with general business fluctuations and the monetary policies associated therewith. Thus, it has been alleged that tightening credit has a disproportionately severe impact on the housing sector, in large part because of the unusually great dependence of this sector on external funds.[2] There is at least a strong presumption that easing

---

[1] The most comprehensive, though still impressionistic consideration of these matters can be found in Saul B. Klaman, The Postwar Mortgage Market, op. cit. Klaman mentions also the "human factor," mainly the strength and seniority of the head of the mortgage department.

[2] According to estimates for the postwar years through 1955, about 70 to 75 percent of the funds used in the acquisition of new residential construction had been borrowed. A similar proportion probably holds for the purchase of existing homes. On the other hand, only 35 percent of the total funds used by corporations from 1948 to 1957 came from external sources. For new construction, see Grebler-Blank-Winnick, Capital Formation in Residential Real
(Footnote continued on following page.)

credit may also have a disproportionately favorable effect on housing. Evidence on this point is only sketchy. Further, statistical observations and analyses of the cyclical relationships between the supply of mortgage credit and residential construction usually are based on the actual flow of mortgage funds and ignore fluctuations in advance commitments which are a highly important determinant of changing production schedules of builders. This omission reflects in part the but recent evolution of the commitment technique in mortgage lending (27) and the limited and often belated information available on the volume of commitments.

Finally, the availability, cost, and terms of housing credit are influenced by the complex legal procedures associated with mortgage lending and foreclosure in case of default, and by the competitive structure of local mortgage markets. As for legal procedures and their costs, the active interest developed during the thirties in the simplification and unification of widely varying state real-estate mortgage and foreclosure laws and in the reduction of excessive foreclosure expenses and redemption periods has waned under the influence of the postwar prosperity. As for the competitive structure of local mortgage markets, the paramount question is whether there are significant elements of oligopoly, such as a highly differentiated product, a small number of competitors, a dominant position of one lender or of a groups of institutions of the same type (assuming less vigorous intra-group than inter-group competition), non-price competition, and insufficient market information available to borrowers or even lenders. Are there marked differences in competitive market structure between large and small communities, or between credit for older and new houses, or single-family homes and rental projects? To what extent and with what lags are adjustments to changing money market conditions made in terms of mortgage interest rates or non-interest charges, loan maturities, downpayment requirements, or appraisals? Only a handful of systematic studies of local mortgage markets have been made (16, 21, 22, 54, 55), and we can be sure of but one thing: knowledge in this area is at least as imperfect as the market itself.

(footnote 2 continued)
Estate (Princeton University Press, 1956), Appendix M and Table 80. As for the purchase of both existing and new homes, a survey taken in the fall of 1956 showed that 84 percent of the home owners who had purchased their houses between January 1954 and August 1956 had incurred mortgage debt (National Survey of Households, in Consumer Instalment Credit, Board of Governors, Federal Reserve System, Part I, Vol. 2, Section IV, Table C-2). This percentage is consistent with similar figures reported for several postwar years in the Consumer Finance Surveys.

VIII. SUMMARY

Our review of current knowledge of the determinants of residential construction has produced somewhat disappointing results. Neither the verbal-qualitative propositions on how the market for residential building operates nor the statistical-econometric models developed to-date have produced a complete, internally consistent, and accurate framework that would allow a theory of market behavior to be tested and provide a basis for reasonably dependable prediction. Moreover, the available data themselves are in many respects faulty and often unusable for empirical tests of theoretical statements, and much of the information needed for such tests is yet to be developed.

Lest our critique of current knowledge in this field appear unduly harsh, it should be added that the work under review is the product of but one generation. Scholarly investigation of the housing market, new residential construction, and mortgage and construction financing was virtually nonexistent before the 1930's, and most of the statistical series have been devised and to some extent improved since that time. As a result of diligent data collection and pioneering analytical work, we are currently at least much more aware of the complexities of the market, and of the theoretical, statistical, and procedural pitfalls in trying to understand it, than was the case a generation ago. There has been substantial progress, but the point is that the advance of knowledge to-date has not been commensurate with the importance of public and private decisions bearing on the housing sector of the economy, especially in view of the scope of federal housing programs and their interrelationship with monetary and fiscal policies.

This summary will first attempt a general appraisal of our findings in respect to the main nonfinancial forces considered to be determinants of residential construction, and then discuss separately the financial determinants of this activity.

A. General Appraisal

At the start of our examination of the determinants of residential construction, we saw that the forces considered by analysts to impinge on this economic sector could be divided into 9 major groups, some external and other internal to the housing market. Our review has made clear that most of these forces have been examined over and over again and from many points of view, but with greatly varying degree of concentration and specificity.

The verbal-qualitative propositions on determinants of residential construction, whether they concern themselves merely with interactions between the total housing market and new construction, or with the whole array of factors influencing the volume of residential building, or with long and short cycles and secular trends, suffer from several debilities. They are usually incomplete or offer no proof of their completeness. They are based upon insufficiently specified assumptions on the shape of demand and supply curves. They are rarely stated in terms that lend themselves to quantitative analysis and empirical tests. They give at best indications of the general direction of market movements in response to changes in a limited number of variables, but not of the magnitude and time dimensions of the movements. They have added mainly to our general knowledge of how external forces, such as changes in credit conditions or variations in consumer income, may work themselves out in the housing and construction markets.

The statistical-econometric approach lends itself to more complete, inclusive, and quantitative statements with more definite time dimensions and estimates of leads and lags. But both internal analysis of the econometric models and comprehensive tests of their results - the first tests undertaken in this field - revealed the potential advantages to be largely illusionary. Almost all studies used only a few of the potential determinants of residential construction and attempted to explain most market movements by the particular ones they had selected, often from the opportunistic viewpoint of data availability. Also, many of the studies failed to differentiate clearly between variables that affected the total demand for housing initially and therefore construction demand as a derived factor, and variables influencing the amount of construction directly. In addition, technical procedures often were found to be faulty. Great differences in results arose from attributing improper weights to certain factors because of an incomplete system, or from errors in judgment, or from mistaken ideas of the validity and meaning of data. None of the existing studies was in a finished enough state to use it for a full analysis of the market or for predicting the impact of any particular variable. They lacked completeness, accurate measurement of parameters, and frequently even the necessary assumed form of the relationship between a variable and construction starts or expenditures. If the ability to predict is used as a criterion of "success" of econometric models, the results are far from flattering to this method. Most of the econometric models did worse in this respect than the "naive" forecasts or judgment projections which our tests employed for comparison.

Our critique of past analytical work has led us in Chapter V to suggest some new directions for future research. These involve, among other things, the development of a more complete framework of identities in the housing market, which would enable the analyst to consider factors now often ignored or cast aside as unimportant, such as changes in the quantity of the standing stock of housing caused by demolitions and conversion or merger of existing dwelling units.   Our suggestions also highlight   the   need   for explaining household formation, which emerges as a strategic factor in most of the existing models but is practically always treated casually as an independent variable requiring no further analysis. Other points to be considered in future research will become apparent as we turn to a summary examination of what our review revealed in respect to each of the main determinants of residential construction.

1. Changes in population

The growth of population appears to be related to residential construction primarily through its impact on the number and type of households. The general identities shown in Chapter V make it clear, and most theories agree, that the largest share of the demand for the construction of new dwelling units would be explained if we could accept household formation as an exogenous variable or if a model were sufficiently accurate to predict household formation correctly. The number of new households formed each year would exactly equal the demand for new construction if the number of vacancies remained constant and the net losses from the housing stock were zero.

The number and types of households, however, cannot be completely explained in terms of demographic changes. There are important economic and social forces which alter the number of households formed from a population of given size and age-sex distribution. Household formation has a price, credit, and income elasticity requiring analysis if its influence on residential construction is to be fully understood. The influence of changes in these elasticities probably differs greatly in the short and long run.

Various studies point out that population changes may have some influence on vacancies and net losses from the housing inventory. Large-scale migration, for example, may lead to excess vacancies and abandonment of units in certain areas and greater aggregate demand. None of the data examined revealed much influence of this type to-date. Also, changes in the number, type, size, and location of households have been shown to influence average expenditures per unit. The exact parameters of these influences on expenditures have not been consolidated into a single estimating series.

2. Changes in income and employment

Most of the theories agree that both income and employment have a direct relationship to household formation. Movements in these factors cause the number of households formed from a given population structure to fluctuate. Bassie and Maisel independently have estimated that in the short run household formation will fluctuate by 10 to 20 percent of the movements in unemployment rates.

Most of the studies of household budgets show that the income elasticity of current housing expenditures is about 0.5. The controversies over the consumption function and household expenditure theory in general apply equally to this analysis. There is but little agreement as to what measures of income and expenditures apply. Some critics hold that the information from the budget studies in their present form does not measure the relevant variables. There have been no adequate tests of what an income elasticity derived from household budget studies means for the total expenditures on housing over time nor, as reiterated so repeatedly, has this elasticity been applied to analysis of the demand for new construction.

In addition, certain of the gaps noted under the previous variable (population) apply to income and employment, as well as to most of the other potential determinants of residential construction. Thus, several analytical statements discuss but none of them attempt to estimate the impact of variations in income and employment on vacancies or on net losses or increases in the housing stock resulting from demolitions, conversions and similar internal changes. Moreover, when a relationship between income and the value of occupied dwelling units is established, present analyses do not permit its transformation into a form that would measure directly the influence of income on construction expenditures.

3. Consumer asset holdings

The main analysis of asset holdings has been concerned with downpayment terms in the purchase of houses for owner-occupancy. There is general agreement that lack or paucity of assets makes the required amount of downpayments important. There is also some indication that the increase in equities of existing houses brought about by price increases in the postwar period has probably led to greater expenditures on housing. However, the intricate relationships between varying downpayments and monthly debt payments and their effects on consumer decisions in the purchase of houses have been left largely unexplored.

4. Changes in the prices of housing

The analysis of price as a determinant of residential construction has taken several approaches. One of these is the proposition that changes in relative housing prices could cause movements in household formation. It is, of course, also possible that prices other than those for housing could have a similar impact through the "Pigou-effect," by altering the real value of assets and income. In existing econometric studies, neither factor shows any clear indication of great importance.

Another proposition states that relative prices appear to influence the value of housing demanded. On this point, assumptions are usually made with but slight empirical verification that housing has an inelastic price demand. As a result, an increase in the relative price of housing would increase the total amounts expended, but would also decrease somewhat the quantity purchased. There would be a substitution in favor of other goods, but presumably not enough to lower total expenditures on housing.

Other price studies have been concerned with the shape of the housing supply curve. Several of those primarily attempting to analyze credit impacts assume a very inelastic supply curve and, as a result, conclude that credit liberalization is ineffective because, while it increases demand, it does not raise the volume of housing offered. The studies usually fail to show the exact manner in which demand changes resulting from easier credit work their way through the existing housing stock and then affect new construction, although a promising first step in that direction has been noted.

In contrast, other analyses assume that, at least in the long run, housing prices must be competitive with the general economy. As a result, the supply price in construction will not depend on the specific demand in this field, but instead on the over-all level of wages, profits, etc. Some also hold that the impact of easier credit is to make the short-run supply curve of new building more elastic. If so, the results of easier credit in most circumstances would be the opposite of those assumed by the previous group of studies.

5. Relationships between occupancy costs and prices of dwellings

A major factor under this heading is the impact of credit, discussed in the next part. There is general agreement that real estate taxes and operating expenses are competitive with the sums which can go to the purchase of a dwelling for owner-occupancy or investment. As a result, movements in these costs tend to be directly reflected in total shelter expenditures and in the sums available to pay for the dwelling.

In theory, variations over time among real, imputed, and financial ownership costs should have an immediate and large impact on the amount of current housing expenditures and on their relationship to the capital value of the dwelling. While the theory on this point is rather simple, little is known about the variables the average family or mortgage lender takes into account in making decisions.

6. Tastes or consumer preferences

The part played by tastes is generally accepted. One of the analyses included in our review has emphasized the possibility of a decreased preference for housing over the long run, and there has been some discussion of a recent reversal in consumers' attitudes. Again, but little study has been given to the formation of tastes for housing, the relative position of housing in the preference scales of different groups of consumers or various types of households, and possible means of influencing attitudes toward housing if such action should be desired.

7. Losses from the housing stock

There is fairly general agreement that net losses from the stock increase by an equivalent amount the demand for new construction. The data in Chapter V, while very sketchy, indicated that the importance of endogenous losses to the market seems to have been overemphasized. From 1930 to 1950, there were probably net gains rather than net losses from demolitions, conversions, abandonments, etc. Since that time, there seem to have been net losses but they appear to result from exogenous forces. To what degree net losses are primarily exogenous and how significant economic replacement demand may be is debated at some length in the literature. But the entire problem of how changes in the demand for occupancy affect losses and additions to the stock without new construction still remains to be worked out.

8. Market movements about equilibrium

Some of the theories, especially those of the verbal type, consider the probability that some of the variations in construction activity may result from market movements about equilibrium rather than changes in basic demand and supply forces. Shifting undesired vacancies and overbuilding or underbuilding due to profit expectations or credit changes or imperfect market information may account for substantial portions of the fluctuations in residential construction and probably depend on the structure of the market. These factors have all been worked out rather completely in theory but have rarely if even been quantified. Chapter V attempted to illustrate the possible magnitude of these movements during the 1950's. It appears that the year-to-year shifts in vacancies and units under construction in many instances have been enough to account for much of the annual movements in starts. The model is far from satisfactory, however, because there is not sufficiently accurate information to show what exact relationships, magnitudes, or time dimensions are involved. At the present time, this type of research work serves mainly as a warning against considering all market movements to reflect changes in basic demand and supply, as many models do.

B. The Impact of Credit Changes

We can utilize the framework developed in Chapter V to indicate where changes in credit terms appear to have a significant effect and where they do not. According to this framework, any effects of changing credit terms can be divided into those (1) altering the equilibrium demand for new units to be constructed, (2) those causing the number of units constructed to lead or lag the equilibrium demand, (3) those causing changes in the value of construction per unit, and (4) those changing supply and related factors. The latter concern the impact of credit changes on the supply curve for construction through their influence on the scale of builders' operations, the availability and cost of construction financing and similar matters which are beyond the scope of this paper.

1. The equilibrium demand for new units

Most of the verbal and econometric models list credit as a probably important determinant of how many new units will be demanded in equilibrium. The verbal statements fail to show precisely how and in what magnitude changes in credit terms influence equilibrium demand. The quantitative studies in econometric models, with the exception of Break's, fail to demonstrate any great significance of this variable. Since most of the live controversy over credit in housing seems to be fought on the assumption that the number of units demanded depends largely on the availability and cost of credit, this is an astonishing result. If correct, it would leave us with the presumption that the influence of credit changes lies mainly in generating movements in the demand for units about the equilibrium level and in altering the average value of units constructed (see the next items).

Chapter V specified the ways in which credit can influence the equilibrium demand for new units. Changes in credit terms must alter either the number of households, or the level of normal vacancies, or the net losses from the housing stock. The unanswered question is whether and to what degree any of these influences have actually been present.

Household formation might be increased if more liberal credit terms were granted in the form of lower downpayments or monthly financial charges. This effect would occur if the inability to buy instead of rent restrained marriages or kept household groups doubled up with others. Most analyses suggest that such an effect would be relatively minor. As for the impact on normal vacancies of easier credit, it appears probable that owners would be more willing to hold vacancies for a longer period if financing was easy, but no attempt has been made to measure this influence. On the other hand, they may hold more undesired vacancies if credit is tight.

The question of demolitions or abandonments resulting from easier credit also remains without quantitative answer. Here, however, some theorists appear to believe that credit has a major impact. As easier credit becomes prevalent, households can afford more quality generally and additional consumers can shift from renting to owning, which is usually associated with improvements in housing quality. As a result of these forces, additional dwelling units of the lowest quality will presumably be abandoned and eventually demolished.

2. Movements of demand for units about equilibrium

There is general agreement that credit changes may cause sharp fluctuations in the construction market about the equilibrium level. Less stringent credit can lead builders or investors to start more units. Lower downpayments cause tenants to purchase their own houses. The number of units under construction increases and eventually the undesired inventory of vacancies starts to rise also. Construction is expanding while this inventory expansion is under way. Eventually the excesses have to be worked off and construction falls below real demand.

The question as to whether credit-induced fluctuations increase or decrease economic instability is but slightly related to whether or not the changing credit terms are moving the market closer to or farther away from the equilibrium level. The equilibrium rate of construction need not be stable. Conceivably, a series of disequilibrium rates might be more stable than a series of equilibrium ones. As an example, if changes in income cause household formation and demolitions to increase sharply, credit changes choking off some of the rising demand and releasing it at a later period might increase the stability of production. In this connection, it may be noted that there is a better chance for more stringent credit terms in the housing sector to result in deferral rather than permanent loss of demand than is true for many other kinds of demand. Few homes are bought on impulse. Consumers are slow to adjust the quality of their housing accommodations to changes in their income or asset holdings. The time when a family purchases a home is conditioned largely by the family life cycle in which a span of one or two years is negligible. Consequently, most of the demand eliminated by credit restraint is likely to reactivated when financial conditions become more favorable to borrowers.

3. Changes in the average value of units constructed

There is again general agreement that the terms of credit alter the amount a family can and probably does spend for housing. Periodic debt payments are competitive with original capital expenditures on the dwelling. The lower the effective interest rate and the longer the loan maturity, the more can be spent on the acquisition price of houses. Since owners tend to occupy better housing than tenants, the same factors, by increasing home ownership, lead to higher-quality housing.

The great debate in this area is over the question how much of the higher expenditures is absorbed by price increases and how much results in additional real values. There is again agreement that the division depends upon the complicated interactions of supply and demand in the existing stock and the supply curve for new construction, but there is wide disagreement over the magnitudes involved and, worse, there are few solid facts for analysis.

C. Federal Housing Credit Policies

The absence of dependable analysis of the impact of credit changes on residential construction is, of course, reflected in the state of knowledge concerning the influence of federal housing credit programs and policies. To measure this influence, it is necessary not only to determine the over-all impact of altered credit terms but also to devise a method for isolating the effects of housing credit programs from those of general changes in the availability and cost of credit. Only one analyst, Break, has attempted this task; and his results indicate, first, that the federal programs in the postwar period have raised the volume of construction substantially above the level that would have been obtained without them and, second, that they have contributed to the cyclical behavior of residential construction conducive to over-all economic stability. The first finding is presented in such wide ranges as to leave the debate over price versus volume effects of the federal programs largely unsettled, except for its challenge to the extreme position that there have been no volume effects. The second finding is consistent with existing qualitative analyses.

Credit policy decisions in the housing field, finally, may have dimensions other than their effects on housing demand and the supply of new construction, with which this paper has been mainly concerned. Changes in housing credit terms may affect, among other things, the level of savings, the total amount of credit demanded, the income of borrowers and lenders, and the volume of nonresidential construction. These interrelationships between the housing sector and the total economy are mentioned here as a reminder that changes in housing credit, and in federal policies to occasion such changes, have general economic implications far beyond those encompassed in the analytical framework of most of the literature discussed in this paper.

APPENDIX A

Statistical Data Used in Tests

of Econometric Models

APPENDIX TABLE IV-A1

Testing of Econometric Models -- Basic Data

	S	D	D_1	D_2	r	$\wedge$H	C
Year	Non-Farm Dwelling Starts (Thousands of Units)	Expenditures on Residential Construction (Billions of 1947-49 $)	Expenditures on Owner-Type Units (Billions of 1947-49 $)	Expenditures on Rental-Type Units (Billions of 1947-49 $)	Housing Rent Index (1947-49 = 100)	New Non-Farm Household Formation (Thousands)	Cost Index for Single Family Residences (1947-49 = 100)
1917	-	-	-	-	-	277.5	-
1918	118	2.31	-	-	78.8	332.0	39.6
1919	315	4.02	3.06	.96	85.3	411.0	46.0
1920	247	3.40	2.67	.73	100.2	474.0	59.3
1921	449	4.42	3.29	1.13	115.1	556.0	47.6
1922	716	7.67	4.95	2.72	118.5	618.5	43.8
1923	871	8.96	5.37	3.59	121.6	701.0	49.1
1924	893	10.45	6.20	4.25	125.9	626.5	48.4
1925	937	11.51	6.95	4.56	126.4	571.5	47.9
1926	849	11.57	6.88	4.69	125.2	598.0	48.4
1927	810	10.82	6.17	4.65	123.2	545.5	47.7
1928	753	9.96	5.67	4.29	120.3	456.0	47.9
1929	509	7.25	4.32	2.93	117.4	426.0	50.0
1930	330	4.26	2.76	1.50	114.2	312.5	48.7
1931	254	3.49	2.47	1.02	108.2	136.5	44.9
1932	134	1.66	1.30	.36	97.1	88.5	38.0
1933	093	1.24	1.06	.18	83.6	288.5	38.0
1934	126	1.51	1.28	.23	78.4	506.0	41.3
1935	221	2.51	2.11	.40	78.2	567.5	40.3
1936	319	3.75	2.93	.82	80.1	626.0	41.7
1937	336	4.02	3.10	.92	83.8	632.5	46.6
1938	406	4.15	3.25	.90	86.5	666.0	48.0
1939	515	5.49	4.11	1.38	86.6	741.5	48.9
1940	603	5.91	4.34	1.57	86.9	768.5	50.5
1947	-	-	-	-	-	1,325.2	-
1948	932	9.64	8.14	1.50	100.7	1,539.0	104.8
1949	1,025	9.48	7.54	1.94	105.0	1,695.3	102.1
1950	1,396	13.02	10.45	2.57	108.8	1,295.7	107.7
1951	1,091	10.79	8.86	1.93	113.1	1,027.0	116.0
1952	1,127	10.77	8.89	1.88	117.9	953.4	119.1
1953	1,104	11.37	9.54	1.83	124.1	909.3	121.2
1954	1,220	12.78	11.08	1.70	128.5	857.0	120.3
1955	1,329	15.08	13.41	1.67	130.3	941.8	123.9
1956	1,118	13.65	12.11	1.54	132.7	1,152.8	129.4
1957	1,042	12.90	10.87	2.03	135.2	947.7	131.8
1958	1,209	13.44	10.58	2.86	137.7	863.2	133.0

APPENDIX TABLE IV-A1 (continued)

C_2	Y	i	N	$\frac{r}{c}$	$(H - \frac{U+U_{-1}}{6})$	Q	Z
Cost Index for Apartments Etc. (1947-49 = 100)	Disposable Personal Income (Billions of 1954 $)	Corporate Bond Yields (per cent)	Stock of Residential Structures (Billions of 1947-49 $)	Ratio of Index of Rents to Costs	Households Less Unemployed Jan. 1	No. of Available Dwelling Units July 1 (Millions)	Index of Composite Terms of Credit
37.1	113.1	-	-	-	-	-	-
42.2	108.1	-	110.02	1,990	-	18.22	-
47.9	106.7	6.27	110.63	1,854	16.70	18.46	-
61.3	97.0	7.08	110.24	1,690	17.05	18.57	+
49.2	85.8	7.04	111.95	2,418	16.93	18.82	+
46.2	99.0	5.95	116.63	2,705	17.29	19.27	+
51.1	112.4	6.04	122.49	2,477	18.60	19.99	+
50.2	113.4	5.80	129.64	2,601	19.35	20.86	+
50.6	117.1	5.47	137.43	2,639	19.85	21.75	1.42
51.0	120.3	5.21	145.03	2,587	20.71	22.69	1.41
50.3	123.2	4.97	151.88	2,583	21.24	23.54	1.34
50.5	127.9	4.94	157.88	2,511	21.50	24.35	1.28
51.7	134.9	5.21	161.13	2,348	21.98	25.10	1.26
50.9	126.1	5.09	161.55	2,345	21.92	25.61	1.36
46.9	121.4	5.81	161.45	2,410	20.09	26.08	1.34
40.0	104.6	6.87	159.59	2,555	19.78	26.45	1.33
41.1	102.1	5.89	157.37	2,200	19.27	26.64	1.46
45.2	109.2	4.96	155.45	1,898	19.89	26.77	1.21
44.5	120.0	4.46	154.55	1,940	20.83	26.95	0.89
45.8	134.9	3.87	154.84	1,921	21.84	27.27	0.85
51.1	139.5	3.94	155.38	1,798	22.96	27.29	0.74
53.2	131.9	4.19	156.06	1,802	23.40	28.21	0.61
53.9	143.2	3.77	158.01	1,771	23.84	28.79	0.58
54.8	153.1	3.55	160.30	1,721	24.99	29.53	0.47
91.7	201.1	-	-	-	-	-	-
103.5	211.5	3.08	165.58	.961	-	-	0.48**	0.47***
104.8	213.8	2.96	169.90	1,028	34.29	38.81	0.44**	0.35***
109.6	231.0	2.86	177.71	1,010	35.83	40.19	0.40**	0.28***
118.0	237.0	3.08	183.15	.975	37.39	41.57	0.42**	0.34***
122.0	243.6	3.19	188.35	.990	38.65	42.98	0.47**	0.43***
125.8	255.0	3.43	193.87	1,024	39.63	44.34	0.45**	0.39***
126.8	256.9	3.16	202.64	1,068	40.47	45.71	0.39**	0.30***
130.6	273.4	3.25	213.51	1,052	40.96	47.20	0.39**	0.28***
137.0	284.2	3.57	222.72	1,025	42.03	48.74	0.40**	0.34***
141.1	290.1	4.21	231.09	1,025	43.17	50.14	0.44**	0.39***
143.6	289.3	4.16	238.56	1,035	43.80	51.43	*	-	-

Sources of Data

S   Nonfarm Dwelling Starts.
       1920-1956 Table A-1, Page 254, Eleventh Annual Report—
                 1957, Housing and Home Finance Agency
       1957-1958 Housing Statistics, May 1959.

D   Expenditures on Residential Construction measured in 1947-
       49 dollars.
       1920-1954 Table 10 A, Page 40, New Private Construction in
                 1947-49 Prices, "Construction Volume & Costs
                 1915-1956," Supplement to Construction Review,
                 U.S. Dept. of Commerce.
       1955-1958 Construction Review, October 1960.

D_1 Expenditures on Owner-Type Units measured in 1947-49
       dollars. Based on the percentage of total derived from ratio
       of single-family dwelling starts to total starts lagged six
       months.
       1918-1956 Table A-1, Page 254, Eleventh Annual Report—
                 1957, Housing & Home Finance Agency, and Table
                 10, Page 40, "Construction Volume & Costs
                 1915-1956," Supplement to Construction Review.
       1956-1958 Housing Statistics, May 1959.

D_2 $D - D_1$

r   Housing Rent Index (BLS Consumer's Price Index).
       1920-1957 Table A-23, Page 264, Eleventh Annual Report—
                 1957 Housing & Home Finance Agency
       1958 Housing Statistics, May 1958.

ΔH New Nonfarm Household Formation.
       1919-1958 Estimated number of households from Table 2,
                 Page 6, "Current Population Reports," Series
                 P-20, No. 92, March 5, 1959. Data are interpolated
                 to put on January 1 basis.

U   Unemployment.
       1929-1958 Table D-17, Page 158, Non-Institutional Popula-
                 tion & Labor Force, "Economic Report of Presi-
                 dent," January 1959. For 1948-1957, new def-
                 inition was used.
       1920-1928 S. Lebergott's annual estimates of unemployment
                 in U.S. 1900-54, in The Measurement and Be-
                 havior of Unemployment, National Bureau Eco-
                 nomic Research - Princeton University Press,
                 1957.

C   Cost Index for Single-Family Residences (Boeckh).
       1920-1956 Table 14, "Construction Volume & Costs 1915-
                 1956," Supplement to Construction Review, U.S.
                 Dept. of Commerce
       1957-1958 Housing Statistics, May 1959.

C_2 Cost Index for Apartments, Hotels, Office Buildings (Boeckh).
          Same as for C

Y_d Disposable Personal Income
          1929-1957 Table II-1, Personal Income and Its Disposition,
                    "U.S. Income & Output," A Supplement to Survey
                    of Current Business, Nov. 1958.
          1918-1928 Table B, National Income and National Product,
                    Page 959, F. Dewhurst, America's Needs and
                    Resources (1955, The Twentieth Century Fund).
                    Adjusted to 1954 Base.

i Corporate Bond Yields
          1919-1958 Moody's Bond Yields Composite Average of
                    Yields on Corporate Bonds in Percent. Moody's
                    Industrial Manual 1957 Blue Pages a 18, a 19.

N Stock of Residential Structures measured in 1947-49 dollars.
          1918-1953 Table D-1, Cumulated Estimates of Non-farm
                    Residential Wealth - Page 360, Grebler-Blank-
                    Winnick - Capital Formation in Residential Real
                    Estate, adjusted to 1947-49 base.
          1954-1958 Estimated by formula as detailed in basic source.

$\dfrac{r}{c}$ Ratio of Index of Rents to Costs.

$(H - \dfrac{U + U_{-1}}{6})$
          Households less unemployed.
          Total households from ΔH, plus 1/3 average of U and U_{-1},
          present and preceding year's unemployment.

Q Number of Available Dwelling Units.
          For Census years the housing stock was estimated from the
          decennial censuses of 1930, 1940, and 1950, plus the National
          Housing Inventory for 1956. The annual figures were inter-
          polated by the percentage movements shown in the Bureau of
          Labor Statistics estimates of dwelling units starts lagged by
          six months. The estimates for 1957 and 1958 used the same
          blow-up ratio required for the period 1950-56.

Z Index of Composite Terms of Credit.
          1925-1957 Based on G. Break's unpublished study for the
                    National Planning Association, Tables A-2 and
                    A-4, ** = Insensitive and stringent.
                    *** = Sensitive and liberal.

REFERENCE NOTES

1. Abramovitz, M. Testimony in Employment, Growth, and Price Levels, Hearings before the Joint Economic Committee of the Congress, 86th Cong., 1st Sess., April 7-10, 1959.

2. Abrams, Charles, and Morton Schussheim, "Credit Terms and Effective Demand for New Housing," Study of Mortgage Credit (Subcommittee on Housing of the Senate Banking and Currency Committee, 85th Congress, 2nd Session, Washington, December 22, 1958), Tables 62 and 63, p. 83.

3. Bassie, V. L., Economic Forecasting. New York: McGraw-Hill, 1958, Appendix C.

4. Break, George F., The Economic Impact of Federal Loan Insurance. Washington, D.C.: National Planning Association, May 1961.

5. Burns, Arthur F., "Long Cycles in Residential Construction," in Economic Essays in Honor of Wesley C. Mitchell. New York: Columbia University Press, 1935.

6. Chase, Arnold E., "Supply and Use of Mortgage Funds, 1920-1929 and 1947-1956," Monthly Labor Review, October 1957. Chase's definition of savings includes savings accounts in savings association, mutual savings banks, commercial banks, postal savings, and credit unions.

7. Christ, C., "A Test of an Econometric Model for the United States, 1921-1947," in Universities — National Bureau Committee, Conference on Business Cycles. New York: National Bureau of Economic Research, 1951.

8. Colean, Miles L., American Housing. New York: The Twentieth Century Fund, 1947, p. 191, Appendix B, pp. 352-360.

9. For example, see Miles L. Colean, "A More Effective Mortgage Insurance System." Study of Mortgage Credit, op. cit., pp. 295-296.

10. Cowles Commission, Statistical Inference in Dynamic Economic Models. New York: John Wiley and Sons, Inc., 1950.

11. Derksen, J. B. D., "Long Cycles in Residential Building." Econometrica (April 1940).

12. Duesenberry, James S., Business Cycles and Economic Growth. New York: McGraw-Hill, 1958, Chapter 7.

13. Durbin, J., and G. S. Watson, "Testing for Social Correlation in Least Squares Regression, I and II," Biometrika, Vol. 37, (1950) and Vol. 38 (1951).

14. Ernest M. Fisher and Robert M. Fisher, Urban Real Estate. New York: Henry Holt and Co., 1954, Chapters 9 and 10.

15. Fisher, Ernest M., Urban Real Estate Markets: Characteristics and Financing. New York: National Bureau of Economic Research, 1951, Chapter 4.

16. Gillies, James, and Clayton Curtis, Institutional Residential Mortgage Lending in Los Angeles County, 1946-1951. Los Angeles: University of California, Bureau of Business and Economic Research, 1956.

17. Grebler, Leo, "The Housing Inventory — Analytic Concept and Quantitative Change." American Economic Review, Vol. XLI, No. 2 (May 1951).

18. Grebler, Leo, David M. Blank, and Louis Winnick, Capital Formation in Residential Real Estate. Princeton: Princeton University Press for National Bureau of Economic Research, 1956. See Table 73 and pp. 252-260.

19. Grebler, Leo, Housing Issues in Economic Stabilization Policy. New York: National Bureau of Economic Research, Occasional Paper 72, 1960.

20. Grebler, Leo, "The Role of Residential Capital Formation in Postwar Business Cycles." Conference on Savings and Residential Financing, sponsored by the United States Savings and Loan League, 1959.

21. Gregory, Paul M., "Imperfect Competition in the Mortgage Market." The Southern Economic Journal, Vol. X, No. 4 (April 1944), p. 278. The article draws on the author's "The Worcester Mortgage Market" (unpublished doctoral dissertation, Clark University, 1942).

22. Hurff, George B. et al., Residential Mortgage Financing, Jacksonville, Florida, First Six Months of 1950. Housing and Home Finance Agency, Housing Research Paper 23, December 1952.

23. Guttentag, Jack M., Some Studies of the Post-World War II Residential Construction and Mortgage Markets. Unpublished dissertation, Columbia University, New York, 1958. See also Guttentag's article "Credit Availability, Interest Rates, and Monetary Policy," The Southern Economic Journal (January 1960).

24. Guttentag, Jack M., "Mortgage Warehousing." The Journal of Finance (December 1957).

25. Klaman, Saul B., "Effects of Credit and Monetary Policy on Real Estate Markets: 1952-1954," Land Economics (August 1956).

26. Klaman, Saul B., "The Availability of Residential Mortgage Credit," Study of Mortgage Credit, op. cit. pp. 189-199.

27. Klaman, Saul B., The Postwar Residential Mortgage Market. New York: National Bureau of Economic Research, Chapter 4, pp. 33-38; Chapter 7, pp. 93-95; Table 3-1, 1961.

28. Klein, L. R., Economic Fluctuations in the United States, 1921-1941. New York: John Wiley and Sons, Inc., 1950.

29. Koopmans, T., "The Logic of Econometric Business-Cycle Research." Journal of Political Economy (April 1941).

30. Lewis, John P., Business Conditions Analysis. New York: McGraw-Hill, 1959, Chapter 20.

31. Long, Clarence D., Jr., Building Cycles and the Theory of Investment. Princeton: Princeton University Press, 1940.

32. Maisel, S. J., An Approach to the Theory and Problem of Analyzing Housing Demand. Unpublished dissertation, Widener Library, Harvard University, 1948.

33. Maisel, S. J., Fluctuations, Growth and Forecasting. New York: John Wiley and Sons, Inc., 1957.

34. Maisel, S. J., and Louis Winnick, "Family Housing Expenditures — Elusive Laws and Intrusive Variances," in Consumption and Saving. Philadelphia: University of Pennsylvania, Wharton School of Finance and Commerce, Vol I, pp. 359-436.

35. Maisel, S. J., "Have We Underestimated the Increase in Shelter Rent?" Journal of Political Economy (April 1949).

36. Maisel, S. J., "Changes in the Rate and Components of Household Formation." Journal of the American Statistical Association (June 1960).

37. Maisel, S. J., "Importance of Net Replacements in Housebuilding Demand." Study of Mortgage Credit, op. cit., pp. 32-42.

38. Newcomb, R., and H. C. Kyle, "The Housing Crisis in a Free Economy." Law and Contemporary Problems (Winter 1947), p. 188.

39. Newman, William H., "The Building Industry and Business
     Cycles." The Journal of Business. Chicago: University of
     Chicago Press, Vol. V., No. 4, July 1935.

40. O'Leary, James J., "Postwar Trends in the Sources and Uses
     of Capital Funds," Study of Mortgage Credit, op. cit., pp. 253-
     283. O'Leary's figures are those developed by the Life Insur-
     ance Association of America.

41. O'Leary, James J., "The Effects of Monetary Policies on
     the Mortgage Market." The Journal of Finance (May 1958)
     pp. 176-187. Similar views are expressed in the Staff Report
     on Employment, Growth and Price Levels. Joint Economic
     Committee, December 24, 1959, p. 393.

41a. O'Leary, James J., "The Effects of Monetary Policies on
     the Residential Mortgage Market." Study of Mortgage Credit,
     op. cit.

42. Rapkin, Chester, Louis Winnick, and David M. Blank, Housing
     Market Analysis. Washington: U. S. Housing and Home Finance
     Agency, December 1953.

43. Rathbun, Daniel B., "Liquid Assets: A Neglected Factor in
     the Formulation of Housing Finance Policies." The Journal
     of Finance (December 1952).

44. Reid, M., "Capital Formation in Residential Real Estate."
     The Journal of Political Economy (April 1958), and a rebuttal
     and further discussion in the December 1959 issue of the
     Journal. For a critique of the "Change in Taste" argument,
     see also Richard F. Muth, "The Demand for Non-Farm Hous-
     ing," published in The Demand for Durable Goods, ed. by
     Harberger, 1960, pp. 29-96.

45. Reid, M., "Increase in Rent of Dwelling Units from 1940 to
     1950." Journal of the American Statistical Association (June
     1959).

46. Robinson, H. W., The Economics of Building. London: Staples
     Press, 1939.

47. Saulnier, R. J., Harold G. Halcrow, and Neil H. Jacoby, Federal
     Lending and Loan Insurance. Princeton: Princeton University
     Press, 1958, pp. 336-347; pp. 351-352.

48. Saulnier, R. J., "An Appraisal of Selective Credit Controls."
     American Economic Review, Papers and Proceedings, (May
     1952).

49. Smith, Warren L., "The Impact of Monetary Policy on Residential Construction, 1948-1958." Study of Mortgage Credit, op. cit.. This volume includes various other papers, notably by Saul B. Klaman and James J. O'Leary, dealing with the same subject.

50. Smith, Wallace F., An Outline of the Housing Market, with Special Reference to Low-Income Housing and Urban Renewal. Unpublished Ph.D. dissertation, University of Washington, 1958.

51. Snedecor, G. W., Statistical Methods. Ames, Iowa: Iowa State College Press, 1946, 4th edition, p. 359.

52. Theil, H., Economic Forecasts and Policy. Amsterdam: North-Holland Publishing Co., 1958, Chapter 6, Part 2.

53. Tinbergen, F., Statistical Testing of Business Cycle Theories. Geneva: League of Nations, 1939, p. 29.

54. U. S. Housing and Home Finance Agency, Small City Mortgage Market: Hagerstown. Washington, D.C.: Housing Research, Housing and Home Finance Agency, 1951.

55. Wendt, Paul F., and Daniel B. Rathbun, The San Francisco Bay Area Residential Mortgage Market. Berkeley: University of California, Bureau of Business and Economic Research, 1951.

56. Winnick, Louis, American Housing and Its Use. New York: John Wiley and Sons, Inc., 1957, Appendix B.

57. Winnick, Louis, Rental Housing. New York: McGraw-Hill, 1958, p. 237; Table 1.

58. Wold, H., Demand Analysis, New York: John Wiley and Sons, Inc., 1953, particularly Part I.

59. Wood, Ramsay, "Housing Needs and the Housing Market," Housing, Social Security, and Public Works. Board of Governors of the Federal Reserve System, Postwar Economic Series, No. 6, June 1946.

60. Wood, Ramsay, "Credit Terms and the Effective Demand for New Housing." Study of Mortgage Credit, op. cit., pp. 39-45.

Research Study Five

THE IMPACT OF MONETARY POLICY
ON STATE AND LOCAL GOVERNMENT
EXPENDITURES IN THE UNITED STATES

Charlotte DeMonte Phelps[1]
Cowles Foundation for Research
in Economics

I. INTRODUCTION

The purpose of this paper is to assess the impact of monetary policy on state and local government expenditures in the United States. The question is apt because the state-local sector finances a large part of its capital outlays by borrowing.[2]

-----

[1]I gratefully acknowledge the help of the following people on the research underlying this paper: C. A. Hall, A. M. Okun, F. E. Morris, D. Netzer, E. S. Phelps, R. C. Pickering, and H. W. Watts. I also wish to thank the organizations which gave me financial assistance: The Cowles Foundation for Research in Economics at Yale and, of course, the Commission on Money and Credit.

[2]The Census definition of capital outlays, used throughout this study, includes outlays for land, equipment, existing structures, and construction. Amounts for additions, replacements, and major alterations to fixed works and structures are counted as capital outlays, but expenditures for repairs to such structures are considered current operation expenditures.

State and local governments derive current revenues from three sources: taxes, service charges, and intergovernmental aid. If expenditures exceed current revenues, they can bridge the gap by increasing the volume of understanding debt and/or by drawing down the volume of cash and security holdings. Seldom does a state or local government have an unplanned expenditure gap; i.e., an operating deficit. Rather those state and local governments which borrow use this method intentionally to finance capital improvements.[3] In 1958 for example, the state-local sector increased the volume of outstanding debt by $5.1 billion, borrowing $8.3 billion and retiring $2.6 billion.[4] About three-quarters of the new debt was allocated to capital outlays for education, highways, and local utilities.

Table V-1 shows the postwar history of state and local expenditures, revenues, and changes in outstanding debt.[5] Over the postwar period, revenues tripled and expenditures quadrupled. In the early postwar years, the expansion was generated by the backlog of unfilled needs carried over from the depression and war years. However by the early fifties, the increased demand for services reflected primarily the growth and changed geographical location of the population, together with the desire for a higher standard of public services.

In the first postwar year--1946--cash balances accumulated during the war made it possible to finance the small volume of expenditures and to decrease the volume of outstanding debt. After the initial postwar readjustment, state and local governments financed 10.8% (weighted average of 1948-60) of their total expendi-

---

[3]Some states have financed veterans' bonuses by borrowing. This is the only major exception to the practice of restricting debt finance to capital outlays.

[4]The difference between borrowings less retirements and the increase in outstanding debt is a statistical discrepancy.

[5]The financial balance equation is: revenues plus increase in debt equal expenditures plus increase in cash and security holdings. It should not be expected that the increase in debt equal expenditures minus revenues. Governments may borrow to increase cash and security holdings. In effect, this happened in 1948, 1952, and 1953. The fact that state and local governments often restrict the uses of revenues obtained from different sources makes it likely that cash balances will increase at the same time that debt is increased. If a government sets up separate Fund Accounts for utilities and general revenues, it may, for example, borrow to finance utilities expenditures while it runs a surplus in the General Fund. The fact that borrowing sometimes precedes expenditures by a substantial length of time also makes possible the simultaneous increase of debt and cash balances.

tures by increasing outstanding debt. There seems to have been no trend toward increasing reliance on debt finance, measuring reliance by the ratio of increase in debt in total expenditures or to capital outlays. The debt reliance ratios are shown in Table V-1.

The debt reliance ratios evidence some sensitivity to changes in business conditions and monetary policy. After the Treasury-Federal Reserve Accord of 1951 the ratios increased when credit conditions eased and declined when credit conditions tightened. Figure V-1 shows the yields on long-term U. S. Government bonds and state-local bonds from 1951 through 1960. The 1952-53 tight money period overlapped the calendar year, so that it cannot be said on grounds of monetary sensitivity whether the ratios in 1952 should have been higher or lower than the ratios in 1953. However 1954 has been characterized as a year in which easy credit conditions were the prevailing influence, and in that year the ratio of increase in debt to total expenditures and the ratio of increase in debt to capital outlays were the highest of the post-Accord period. Credit conditions gradually tightened from 1955 through 1957, and the debt reliance ratios gradually fell over this three-year period. In 1958 when credit conditions eased again the debt reliance ratios rose. The ratios in 1959 and 1960 did not behave as expected.

The body of this paper is devoted to an analysis of other types of data which reflect the impact of monetary policy on state and local government expenditures. The focus is on the sensitivity of capital expenditures because it is assumed that they absorb the brunt of any adjustment to changes in credit conditions. Section 2 outlines a model of the decision process which controls the planning and execution of state and local capital expenditures. Section 3 is devoted to a summary and criticism of previous empirical studies of the impact of monetary policy on state and local borrowing and construction. The model provides a framework for evaluating these studies. Section 4 summarizes the results of the author's study of the sensitivity of municipal capital expenditures to tightening credit.[6] Some of the hypotheses suggested in the model were tested in this study. In Section 5 some hypotheses are offered to explain the difference between previous findings and the author's.

II. A MODEL

To analyze how changes in credit conditions may affect the volume and timing of state and local capital expenditures, it is useful to date the period for which expenditures are planned and to divide

---

[6]Charlotte DeMonte Phelps, "The Impact of Tightening Credit on Municipal Capital Expenditures in the United States," Yale Economic Essays, Fall 1961. The model presented in Section 2 is discussed in more detail in the essay.

TABLE V-1

Revenues, Expenditures, and Change in Outstanding Debt
of State and Local Governments: 1946 – 1960
(In Millions of Dollars)

(1)	(2)	(3)	(4)	(5)= (4) ÷ (2)	(6) = (4) ÷ (3)
Year Revenues	Total Expenditures	Expenditures for Capital Outlays	Increase (+) or Decrease (-) in Debt	Debt Reliance Ratio	Debt Reliance Ratio
1946 15,983	14,067	1,305	-754	-5.4%	-57.8%
1948 21,613	21,260	3,725	1,841	8.7%	49.4%
1950 25,639	27,905	6,047	3,116	11.2%	51.5%
1952 31,013	30,863	7,436	3,065	9.9%	41.2%
1953 33,411	32,937	7,905	3,612	11.2%	46.6%
1954 35,386	36,607	9,125	5,149	14.1%	56.4%
1955 37,619	40,375	10,705	5,336	13.2%	49.8%
1956 41,692	43,152	11,407	4,601	10.7%	40.3%
1957 45,929	47,553	12,639	4,171	8.8%	33.0%
1958 49,262	53,712	13,986	5,148	9.6%	36.8%
1959 53,972	58,572	15,351	5,923	10.1%	38.6%
1960 60,277	60,999	15,104	5,845	9.6%	38.7%

Source: U. S. Department of Commerce, Bureau of the Census.

FIGURE V-1

Yields on Long-Term U.S. Government Bonds and State-Local
Government Bonds: 1951-1960

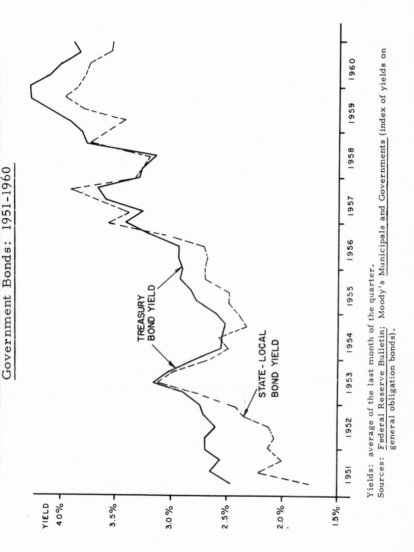

Yields: average of the last month of the quarter.
Sources: Federal Reserve Bulletin; Moody's Municipals and Governments (index of yields on
general obligation bonds).

the decision process which controls the planning and execution of plans into four stages: (1) the initial formulation of expenditure plans for t_1 and t_2, (2) the authorization of expenditures planned for t_1, (3) the review and execution of expenditures authorized for t_1 and (4) the review and revision of expenditures planned for t_2.[1] Stages (1) and (2) occur within one fiscal year which may be designated t_0. Stages (3) and (4) occur within one fiscal year--t_1. The duration of stages (1), (2) and (4) is less than a year.[2]

Assume that in t_0 officials plan capital expenditures for periods t_1 and t_2 on the basis of an anticipated time path of the interest rate over future periods. The interest rate on which officials base their plans is the rate which they expect to pay when they sell a long-term bond to finance the planned expenditures. For simplicity assume that they expect the interest rate in t_0 to prevail in future periods. If the interest rate in t_0 is high, officials will wish to finance only a small part of the improvement program by borrowing and to defer many outlays until they have accumulated reserves to finance them.   The opposite is true if the interest rate is low. A high interest rate also means that the volume of capital improvements which they can purchase with any given budget is smaller than with a low interest rate.

In t_0 officials submit plans for t_1 to the city council or state legislature to be authorized (approved), but they leave plans for t_2 tentative.[3] Once bond financed expenditures are authorized, the finance officer is free to initiate preparations for the actual bond sale (drafting a prospectus, advertising the sale, etc.).

In t_1 officials review plans in the light of conditions which have developed since the initial formulation of plans. Changes in priorities of proposed projects, changes in expected tax revenues and changes in credit conditions, for example, may prompt them to make revisions.

If credit in t_1 is tighter than it was in t_0, officials review the courses of action open to them if they are to carry out expenditures in t_1 as authorized. Assuming that some bond financed expenditures have been authorized and that preparations for sale have been begun, they can either proceed as planned or postpone the bond sale and

---

[1] The definition of the period "t" is adaptable to any specified planning period. It is convenient to think of the period for which plans are made as a fiscal year.

[2] In equation (2) Section 4, the authorization stage is of three months duration.

[3] In the case of bond financed expenditures, sometimes authorization by public referendum is required by law.

secure temporary finance to make necessary cash outlays. Which, if any, of these courses is feasible depends on five factors: (1) legal restrictions on the bond sale, (2) the government's policy of timing the bond sale with respect to the scheduled initiation of construction, (3) arrangements for the substitution of revenues within and between separate Fund Accounts, (4) the ability of the government to borrow short term externally, and (5) the ability of the government to increase taxes or service charges to cover additional interest payments.

After considering the feasible alternatives, officials ask whether the most acceptable of them--i.e., the least costly action--is preferable to postponing or cutting back the level of capital expenditures in t_1.[4] Notice that the choice is whether to postpone or cut back the level of total capital expenditures, not just the level of bond financed expenditures. The relative prices and priorities of the improvements determine which shall be postponed or cut back.

Whether officials prefer to carry out expenditures as planned depends on the proportion of capital expenditures they have planned to finance from bond sales, the magnitude of the change in the interest rate between t_0 and t_1, and officials' expectations concerning the level of the interest rate in t_2.

Officials also review plans for expenditures in t_2 in the light of tighter conditions. Whether they prefer to leave the volume of expenditures planned for t_2 unchanged depends on the same factors which affect their preference to carry out, postpone, or cut back the actual level of expenditures in t_1.

If, to make a different assumption, credit conditions ease in t_1 as compared with t_0, officials consider whether to carry out expenditures in t_1 as planned, to accelerate expenditures planned for t_2 to t_1, or to increase expenditures in t_1. They also decide whether to increase the level of expenditures planned for t_2.[5]

Officials can accelerate or increase expenditures in t_1 either by selling bonds sooner than planned or by securing temporary finance. Which of these courses is feasible depends on the first four factors which limit the ability of officials to execute an expenditure plan

---

[4]Special meanings are intended for the words "postpone" and "cut back." Expenditures which are postponed are included in plans for a future period. Expenditures which are cut back are withdrawn once and for all from the planning horizon.

[5]The term "increased" expenditures denotes the addition of expenditures which were not included in the original plans made in t_0.

when credit tightens. It also depends on the length of time necessary to introduce a new item into the current budget.

Whether it is preferable to accelerate or increase expenditures rather than carry out expenditures as planned depends on the degree of reliance on debt finance, the magnitude of the decrease in the interest rate between t_0 and t_1, and expectations concerning the future course of the interest rate. In addition, it depends on the opportunity to invest bond sale proceeds temporarily. Even if officials decide to accelerate a bond sale which is earmarked to finance expenditures planned for t_2, they may prefer to invest the proceeds rather than use them to accelerate expenditures. Their decision depends on their evaluation of the benefits of having the project completed sooner than planned as compared with the benefits of having the interest earned on the investment to spend on future projects. By accelerating a bond sale, officials increase budgeted revenues by the difference between the savings from the lower interest rate and the cost of holding the debt longer.

III. PREVIOUS EMPIRICAL STUDIES

The first studies of the impact of monetary policy on state and local government expenditures focused on periods of tightening credit and utilized bond sale postponement data. They broke into the decision process at the time when the bond sale was planned-- some time after the authorization of expenditures--and followed it for a specified period to determine whether the bond was sold as planned or was postponed. It is clear from the description of the decision process in Section 2 that the execution of authorized expenditures need not be postponed even though the bond sale is postponed and that even if the bond sale is not postponed plans for future expenditures may be cut back. Therefore the empirical results of these studies should be viewed only as a first approximation to the estimation of the sensitivity of state and local expenditures to tightening credit.

Richard C. Pickering collected and analyzed bond sale postponement statistics from the financial press for May, June, and July 1953, a period during which the Bond Buyer's Index of Yields on Twenty Bonds rose 39 basis points or 15 percent.[1] He drew his observations of planned issues from bond sale advertisements,

---

[1] Richard C. Pickering, "Effects of Credit and Monetary Policy since Mid-1952 on State and Local Government Financing and Construction Activity," unpublished manuscript which reflects the personal views of the author and not necessarily those of the Board of Governors of the Federal Reserve System with which he is associated, April 1955.

whether or not the planned date of sale was included in the advertisement. He followed up all issues for which no bids were received, all bids were rejected, or the sale was not completed on the scheduled day to see whether they were actually sold later privately or publicly. The par value of the issues he followed up was $339.2 million; the number of issues was 34. Over half of the number of issues were sold thirty days or less after the initial offering date, and two-thirds of the dollar volume were sold in that period. Only two issues were delayed six months and none longer than that.

Pickering tabulated the credit ratings of the bonds in his sample. Half had ratings of A or lower and almost half had no ratings. There are two hypotheses which could explain why borrowers with low credit ratings postponed more bond sales. One is that municipalities with lower credit ratings are subject to a larger absolute increase in the cost of borrowing than municipalities with high credit ratings.[2] The other is that municipalities with low credit ratings find it more difficult to raise additional revenues to cover increased interest costs than municipalities with high credit ratings. A common characteristic of low rated municipalities is a high debt to assessed valuation ratio, i.e., a narrow margin for increasing tax revenues.

Pickering also tabulated the type of collateral used to secure bonds in his sample. One third by value and number were revenue bonds. However 80 percent by value of the bonds not successfully reoffered in May, June, and July were revenue bonds. He also observed that the number of revenue bonds was smaller relative to the total number of bond sales during the tight money period than during the preceding and subsequent easy money periods. These findings could be masking the same explanatory factors as the credit rating findings, because revenue bonds as a group are rated lower than general obligation bonds. But they may reflect the fact that it is easier to raise additional revenues to cover increased interest costs on tax financed projects than on self-supporting projects.

Frank E. Morris conducted two studies of bond sale postponements based on financial press data different from those used by Pickering. The first of these studies covered the third quarter of 1956, a period which experienced roughly the same increase in bond yields as the 1953 period Pickering studied.[3] Morris drew obser-

---

[2] The hypothesis that when credit tightens the net interest cost increases more on low rated bonds than on high rated bonds was confirmed; see C. D. Phelps, op. cit.

[3] Frank E. Morris, "A Measure of the Impact of Tight Money on the Volume of Long-term Municipal Issues during the Third Quarter," IBA Statistical Bulletin, No. 1, October 1956 (Investment Bankers Association of America, Washington, D. C.)

vations of planned sales from reports which included the planned date of sale and observed actual dates of sale from press reports. On this basis he recorded 119 issues aggregating $175 million which were not sold on their initial offering dates. Of these 78 issues totaling $136 million were not sold during the quarter.

The similarity between the degree of stringency in May, June, and July of 1953 and the third quarter of 1956 suggests that there should be similarity in the response of state and local governments to credit conditions in the two periods. One measure of this response, the ratio of the par value of bonds not sold on their initial offering dates to the value of total bond sales during the quarter, was 21 percent in the 1953 quarter and 15 percent in the 1956 quarter.[4] Another measure, the ratio of the par value of bonds not sold during the quarter to the value of total bond sales during the quarter, was 8 percent in the 1953 quarter and 11 percent in the 1956 quarter. A possible explanation of the higher initial postponement ratio in 1953 and the higher final postponement ratio in 1956 is that the brunt of the interest rate increase came in the early part of the 1953 quarter, allowing more time for initial postponements in 1953 and overstating the effect of final postponements in 1956. All things considered, the data suggest a similarity of response.

Morris' second study of bond sale postponements covered the nine month period, July 1, 1956 through March 31, 1957.[5] In it he defined a postponement as a bond which was actually offered but not sold during the period. In other words, he observed plans at a later stage in the decision process than in his earlier and in Pickering's study. He found that $539 million (12 percent of the value of scheduled offerings) were not sold on their initial offering dates and $321 million (7 percent of the value of scheduled offerings) remained unsold at the end of the period.

He classified final postponements according to the type of collateral used to secure the bonds and the proposed use of the bond sale proceeds. He found that 13 percent of the revenue bonds offered during the period were postponed while only 5 percent of the general obligation bonds offered were postponed, a substantiation of Pickering's findings on the greater sensitivity of revenue bonds

---

[4]The par value of postponements taken as a ratio of the par value of issues scheduled during the quarter would have been a better measure for comparing the response in the two periods. Because neither Pickering nor Morris reported scheduled offerings, the value of actual sales as given by The Bond Buyer was substituted as a basis for comparison.

[5]Frank E. Morris, "A Study of Municipal Bond Sales Postponed during the Past Nine Months," IBA Statistical Bulletin, No. 3, April 1957.

to monetary policy.[6] With respect to the purpose classification, he found that 33 percent of road and bridge bonds offered during the period were postponed. There was relatively little difference among the postponement ratios of the other purposes which ranged from 1 percent to 7 percent. The fact that two large revenue bonds totaling $100 million accounted for half the value of the postponed road and bridge bonds suggests that the same underlying causes were responsible for the high incidence of postponements for revenue bonds and road and bridge bonds. However Morris interpreted the findings on the purpose classification as showing that state and local governments gave road and bridge construction lower priority than other types of construction and therefore postponed road and bridge bonds while selling bonds for other purposes as planned.

John A. Cochran conducted a study of bond sale postponements during 1955, 1956, and the first half of 1957.[7] He drew observations of planned and actual bond sales from press reports. He counted as planned sales all new issues of $6 million or over for which "some specific authoritative published information was uncovered which demonstrated the clear intention of floating the bond issue on or around a certain future date" and defined an initial postponement as a cancellation, substitution of alternative means of finance, or reduction in size of $6 million or more which was not followed by a flotation in the same month in which it was scheduled for sale. He found that initial postponements for the entire period amounted to $2.3 billion, that total postponements amounted to $3.8 billion, and that net initial postponements amounted to $1.5 billion.[8]

Cochran's data on initial postponements can be compared with Morris' nine month study of postponements. The ratio of initial postponements to planned offerings as measured in dollar value for the nine month period July 1956 through March 1957 is 15 percent according to Cochran's data and 12 percent according to Morris' data. These estimates are fairly close considering that Cochran included larger-size bonds in this sample than Morris and that Cochran defined initial postponements in terms of a longer

---

[6]These postponement ratios are based on the value of the bonds.

[7]John A. Cochran, "Postponement of Corporate and Municipal Bond Issues, 1955-57," unpublished manuscript which reflects the personal views of the author and not necessarily those of the Federal Reserve Bank of New York with which he was then associated, August 1957.

[8]Total postponements were defined as initial postponements plus issues postponed more than once during the two and one-half year period. Net initial postponements were defined as initial postponements less issues which were successfully reoffered during the two and one-half year period.

length of time between planned and actual sale dates than Morris. The former difference in data tends to make Cochran's estimates of postponements higher than Morris', while the latter tends to bias his estimates below those of Morris.

There are several problems in conducting an empirical study of bond sale postponements, problems which Pickering, Morris, and Cochran handled differently. The first problem is a consequence of the nature of the data. The plans for bond sales reported in the financial press are not equally certain or firm. Therefore one drawing on this source must decide which of the reports to use as observations of planned sales. Should admittedly uncertain plans for sale be lumped together with firmer plans for which the sale date has been set? Should subjective data (intentions to float a bond as reported in an interview or in a public speech) be pooled with objective data (lists of bonds for which the sale date has been set)? Pickering and Morris adopted the objective criterion, while Cochran relied heavily on subjective data. Morris used the narrowest definition of certainty.

A similar problem arises in connection with finding out when a planned issue was actually sold. Many postponed issues are eventually sold by private negotiation rather than by auction as planned. In these cases, actual sale may never be recorded in the press. To find out whether and when the actual sale took place may require contacting the underwriter or the borrower. In the studies discussed, only Pickering went to the trouble of tracing privately negotiated sales.

Another problem is defining the length of time which should elapse between the planned and actual sale date before a postponement should be recorded. Should a bond sale be considered postponed if it is sold a day, a week, a month, two months, or six months later than planned? Pickering and Morris defined initial postponements as bonds not sold on the scheduled day. Morris defined final postponements as bonds not sold during the period investigated. Such a definition of a final postponement may either overstate or understate the duration of the postponement depending on when it occured in the period.[9] The most accurate way of measuring a final postponement is by the number of days (or months) that elapse before the bond is successfully reoffered.

The last major problem is whether to measure the volume of postponements by the number of issues or the dollar value of issues. The dollar value was the measure most commonly used for several

---

[9] The inaccuracies of the postponement measures made it difficult to compare the bond sale postponement studies.

reasons. It permits recording a reduction in the amount of a planned issue as a postponement, a common response of large borrowers to a tight money policy. If part of a planned issue is sold on schedule and part is not, it permits distinguishing between the two courses of action. The last reason is that it gives more weight to large size issues, the dominant forces in the market. However, both measures are desirable in order that the differential effects of monetary policy on large as compared with small borrowers can be investigated.

Morris and Pickering next tackled the problem of relating changes in the volume and timing of bond sales to changes in the volume and timing of construction over the entire monetary cycle. Morris compared the cyclical movements of state and local government bond yields with the cyclical movements of the dollar value of actual bond sales, contracts awarded and construction put in place by state and local governments from 1952 through 1959.[10] He found that the bond yields followed the contour of the general business cycle as defined by the National Bureau of Economic Research reference cycle dates, while the bond sales, contracts awarded, and construction put in place series showed a moderate countercyclical pattern. Both construction series lagged the bond sale series. From the deviations above and below the trend line, he estimated that about 10 percent of bond sales, 5 percent of contracts awarded, and slightly less than 5 percent of construction put in place were shifted from the final stages of the boom to the recession and recovery periods.

What inferences may be drawn from these findings? First and most important, they support the hypothesis that state-local construction is sensitive to interest rate movements and credit conditions. Second, the evidence that the construction series lagged the bond sale series, suggests that most state and local governments follow the policy of timing bond sales in advance of construction. Last, the fact that the amplitude of the fluctuations in the construction series is less than the amplitude of the fluctuations in the bond sale series suggests that state and local governments do manage to find ways to carry on expenditure plans in spite of bond sale postponements and that they do not use all the proceeds of accelerated bond sales to accelerate the rate of construction. However it also reflects the fact that state and local governments do not finance all construction by borrowing.

Because school and water and sewer plant construction may be considered more urgent than other types of construction, Morris

---

[10]Frank E. Morris, "The Impact of Monetary Policy on State and Local Governments: An Empirical Study," Journal of Finance, XV (May 1960), pp. 232-249.

separated out these three purposes from the aggregated series to see whether they were less sensitive to interest rate movements. He pooled the water and sewer data because they are related purposes. He found that neither the school series nor the water-sewer series were sensitive to interest rate movements, while the residual exhibited greater sensitivity than all purposes combined. It would have been interesting if he had separated out the road and bridge category, for it is possible that the fluctuations in the residual were dominated by the fluctuations in road and bridge bonds. The hypotheses explaining why particular categories of bonds exhibit greater or less sensitivity to interest rate fluctuations than other are subject to confirmation by studies which relate changes in the volume and timing of bond sales and construction to the reasons for changes.

A significant deficiency of the approach Morris adopted is that it does not enable distinguishing between postponements in expenditures due to tight money and advances in the timing of expenditures due to easy money. Both are lumped together as shifts.

Pickering did not lump postponements and advances together.[11] He measured the volume of construction expenditures which were postponed when credit tightened in the latter half of 1957 and the volume of construction expenditures which were accelerated when credit eased in the first half of 1958. The study was based on data obtained in a survey of state and local finance officers. The officials interviewed were selected on the basis that their cities or states issued bonds during the first half of 1958. They were asked when they had originally planned to sell the bond which put them in the sample. If they sold the bond later than they planned, a bond sale postponement was noted; if they sold the bond earlier than they planned, a bond sale acceleration was noted. Additional questions were asked to determine whether and why officials did or did not delay (accelerate) expenditures when they postponed (accelerated) bond sales.

Pickering found the 9 percent of the bonds sold in the first half of 1958 had been postponed from the preceding tight money period because interest rates were too high and 2 percent were sold in this period because of the easy credit conditions. He found that about 17 percent of the bond sale postponements resulted in postponements in construction and that none of the bond sale accelerations resulted in accelerated construction. To put his findings in Morris' terminology, he found that about 2 percent of construction

---

[11]Richard C. Pickering, "State and Local Government Bond Financing During the First Half of 1958," unpublished manuscript which reflects the views of the author and not necessarily those of the Board of Governors of the Federal Reserve System, May 1959.

was shifted from the final stages of the boom to the recession and recovery periods.

Pickering also explored the extent to which state and local governments used temporary finance to carry on construction in spite of bond sale postponements and the extent to which they put the proceeds of accelerated bond sales in temporary investments. He found that the use of temporary finance, principally short-term bank notes, prevented construction delays in the case of about 40 percent of total bond sale postponements. He found that all bond sales which were accelerated due to monetary conditions were either invested in short-term Treasury bills or in time deposits. Only when bond sales were accelerated due to the completion of plans sooner than expected was the rate of construction accelerated.

Pickering's method of sample selection and his measure of planned expenditures biased his estimates of postponements. By limiting the sample to governments which sold bonds in the easy money period, he excluded those which postponed projects in the tight money period and did not reschedule them when credit eased. By using data on planned bond sales to represent planned bond financed expenditures he provided no way of estimating the volume of expenditures which were cut back before the bond sale was planned.

Both Morris' and Pickering's studies give the erroneous impression that the only effect of monetary policy is to shift the timing of expenditures from tight money periods to easy money periods. To estimate the volume of expenditures that are cut back when credit tightens and the volume of new projects that are scheduled when credit eases, it is necessary to get data on planned expenditures, not planned bond sales. By the time officials plan the actual date of a bond sale, engineering and architectural specifications for construction are generally underway, if not completed. Therefore postponement of a bond sale seldom means cancellation of a project. Officials are more likely to cut back plans at an earlier stage of the decision process--before expenditure plans are authorized.

Another limitation on both studies is their focus on construction expenditures. While it is true that the majority of long-term bonds are used to finance construction, many governments have some arrangements for the substitution of revenues within and between separate Fund accounts. It is of interest to know whether they use these arrangements to adjust to changes in monetary policy. Do they, for example, borrow temporarily from appropriations for equipment purchases in order to carry out construction plans on schedule when credit tightens? Officials may prefer to vary the timing of cash purchases rather than the timing of contracts, because drawing up a contract involves a complicated multi-stage decision process.

Another facet of the adjustment process which neither Morris nor Pickering investigated is the extent to which current tax financed expenditures are postponed or cut back when credit tightens and accelerated or increased when credit eases. Arrangements for the substitution of revenues between the General Fund and Bond Funds open up the possibility of altering the timing of tax financed expenditures in order to carry out bond financed expenditures on time. Even without these arrangements, it is possible that officials will prefer to cancel some tax financed authorizations in order to issue a bond as planned and keep expenditures over the planning horizon within the budget constraint.

At the planning stage of the decision process, the method of finance is not legally tied to a particular project. Therefore officials may cushion the impact of tightening credit by switching some projects from debt finance to pay-as-you-go finance. This question is outside the scope of both previous studies because they did not investigate the impact of monetary policy on the planning of expenditures prior to their authorization.

A comparison of Morris' and Pickering's construction studies shows their estimates of the percentage of bond sales shifted from the later stages of the boom to the recession and recovery periods are very close: 10 percent and 11 percent respectively. Morris' and Cochran's bond sale postponement studies, which covered periods which roughly coincide with the expansion phase of the business cycle, tend to corroborate an estimate in the neighborhood of 10 percent. However, the range between Pickering's and Morris' estimates of the percentage of construction shifted from the later stages of the boom to the recession and recovery periods is fairly broad: 2 percent to 5 percent. The research discussed in the next section was designed to shed more light on the area needing clarification.

IV. THE IMPACT OF TIGHTENING CREDIT ON MUNICIPAL CAPITAL EXPENDITURES

a. The Approach

The approach of this study was shaped by the conception of the governmental decision process described in Section 2 and by the fact that when credit tightens some governments experience larger increases in the cost of borrowing than others. A cross section of data on state and local government bond interest rates and municipal capital expenditures drawn from the 1955-57 period of tightening credit were analyzed to answer two questions: (1) Which types of bonds become relatively more expensive to issue when credit tightens? and (2) Do those municipalities which have planned or authorized the financing of capital expenditures by bonds which have become relatively more expensive to issue, postpone and cut back a larger proportion of total capital expenditures than other municipalities?

In order to answer the first question the bonds were typed according to seven characteristics which were hypothesized to define the structure of state and local government bond interest rates. These characteristics, which may be viewed as measures of different kinds of risks, are: maturity, optional feature, credit rating, size of issue, type of collateral, type of issuing agency, and purpose of issue.[1]

Two general hypotheses were tested by means of multiple regression analysis. The first was that the structure of interest rates results from investors trading off risk against the rate of return, the consequence being that low risk bonds bear low interest rates and high risk bonds bear high interest rates. The second hypothesis was that the compensation investors demand for incurring a given risk varies with changes in monetary conditions. When credit tightens investors demand a higher rate of return on all state and local government bonds, but they demand a greater increase in the return on high risk bonds than on low risk bonds.

In order to answer the second question two broad hypotheses were also tested. The first was that the proportion of total planned capital expenditures that is postponed and cut back is positively related to the increase in borrowing costs experienced between the initial formulation of plans and the revision of plans. The second was that the proportion of total authorized capital expenditures which is postponed and cut back is positively related to the increase in borrowing costs experienced between the authorization and execution of expenditures.[2] Alternative measures of the increase in

---

[1]Because the structure of interest rates is multi-dimensional, in order to study the effect of one of the characteristics on the interest rate it is necessary to use a method of analysis which holds the values of the other characteristics constant. Some previous researchers dealt with this problem by selecting for study a sample of bonds for which at least some of the variables were constant. See Roland I. Robinson, The Postwar Market for State and Local Government Securities, A Study by the National Bureau of Economic Research (Princeton: Princeton University Press, 1960) and articles by Frank E. Morris in the Investment Bankers Association's Statistical Bulletin. In the author's study multiple regression analysis is used to separate out the effects of each of the characteristics on the interest rate and to analyze the impact of monetary policy on the structure of interest rates.

[2]The focus was on the response of expenditures planned and authorized for one year--1957. Therefore it was impossible to distinguish postponements from cutbacks.

borrowing costs--the absolute increase and the relative increase--
were used because it was not known whether a given absolute increase causes fewer postponements and cutbacks in a city which
initially expected to pay a high interest rate than in one which expected to pay a low interest rate. The responses of current tax
financed and bond financed expenditures were examined at both the
planning and the execution stages of the decision process.

How were the question 1 hypotheses related to the question 2
hypotheses? To test the question 2 hypotheses it was necessary to
have estimates of the interest rates on which officials based
planned, authorized, and actual expenditures. The results of the
tests of the question 1 hypotheses led to an equation which was used
to provide the needed estimates.

The use of this equation rested on the assumption that the interest
rate on which officials based planned, authorized, or actual expenditures was equal to the market rate currently paid by other cities
floating bonds with the same characteristics as the bond issue which
they contemplated. It was assumed that officials expected the current
interest rate to prevail at the anticipated date of the bond sale.

Why was this equation used to estimate each city's borrowing
costs? Why weren't the rates on comparable bond issues sold at the
time officials made plans, authorizations, and actual expenditures
used? The answer is that it was not until the hypotheses suggested
by previous studies were tested that it was known which characteristics affect the cost of borrowing.

Why weren't the interest rates paid by each city on the bonds it
sold during the planning and authorization periods used to estimate
the rates on which its officials based planned and authorized expenditures? There are two reasons. One is that cities adapt the
types of bonds they issue to their needs so that they often do not plan
to issue the same type of bond as they are currently selling. The
other reason is that many cities do not sell bonds every year, and
therefore in a random sample of cities some will not be selling a
bond currently.

Another possible question is why the interest rate on the bond
each city actually sold to finance authorized expenditures was not
used to estimate the interest rate at the time expenditures were
made. The reason is that the timing of the bond sale is affected by
the volume and timing of expenditures which are themselves guided
by fluctuations in the price of municipal bonds. Therefore the rate
of interest on the actual bond issue reflects the response to credit
conditions rather than the condition causing the response.

For all these reasons the testing of the question 1 hypotheses and the resulting equation for estimating the cost of municipal borrowing were both a precondition and an integral part of studying the interest elasticity of municipal capital expenditures.

In this study some areas were explored which Morris and Pickering did not chart. The principal innovation was the estimation of changes in capital expenditure plans which are made in response to tightened credit at different stages of the municipal decision process. Of secondary importance was the use of data on total (bond financed and tax financed) capital expenditures, not just bond financed construction expenditures.

Some of the criticisms leveled at Morris and Pickering are also applicable to this study. Specifically cutbacks and postponements are still indistinguishable. All that can be said is that a lower level of expenditures at a later stage of the decision process reflects both cutbacks and/or postponements. However it is important to realize that the measures of planned and authorized expenditures used in this study permit the measurement of more cutbacks than previous studies. Pickering used planned bond sales as a proxy for planned expenditures, but plans for bond sales--in the sense that the date is set--are usually made subsequent to the planning and authorization of expenditures. Morris measured postponements and cutbacks from the cyclical pattern of actual expenditures. Who knows what the pattern of actual expenditures would have been had monetary conditions been different?

While an attempt was made to measure the substitutability between tax financed and bond financed expenditures, no attempt was made to measure the substitutability between construction expenditures and other types of capital outlays. However it does seem an improvement over previous research that reductions in all types of capital outlays were recorded.

Of course the fact that all the data were taken from a period of tightening credit means that this study contributes no information about the impact of monetary policy on the shift of municipal capital expenditures from a period of tightening credit to a period of easing credit.

b. Nature of the Data

The question 1 hypotheses were tested with data on 2,000 bonds issued by states and other local governments besides municipalities. This was done to provide a large sample for studying the effects of investor risk on the cost of borrowing and to ascertain whether other levels of government are treated by the market in the same way as municipalities. The final equation for estimating the cost of borrowing contains the answer to investors' preferences concerning the type of issuing agency and makes it possible for other researchers to estimate the rate of interest used by other levels of government in planning, authorizing, and executing capital expenditures.

Several private firms—Moody's and Standard and Poor's being most widely known—rate state and local borrowers according to their ability and willingness to repay loans. All state government and most local government bonds that are rated by Moody's enjoy one of the four top ratings (Aaa, Aa, A, and Baa); for the most part lower ratings are assigned to foreign government bonds. Bonds rated below Baa were excluded from the question 1 sample because there are so few of them. Unrated bonds were also excluded because the credit worthiness of the governments which issue them varies so widely.

The data on planned, authorized, and actual capital expenditures used to answer question 2 were obtained through a mail survey of the 148 United States cities which keep capital budgets and whose bonds are rated Baa or better by Moody's. The survey was limited to cities whose bonds are so rated because the question 1 sample was restricted in that way. The survey data make it possible to investigate some of the questions unanswered by previous studies.

Capital budget accounts are kept for all types of capital outlays--land and equipment as well as construction. Most cities keep separate accounts for bond financed and tax financed expenditures. Therefore capital budget data are ideally suited for an investigation of the impact of monetary policy on all types of capital outlays and of the incidence of monetary policy on tax financed expenditures relative to bond financed expenditures.

The capital budget data have the additional advantage of being objective. When asked for capital budget data, all officials respond from a uniform frame of reference and can date their decisions.

The limitations imposed on the survey population necessitate two assumptions if the sample inferences are to be applied to the population of all municipal borrowers. First it must be assumed that cities which keep capital budgets respond to changes in monetary conditions in the same way as cities which do not keep capital budgets. There is no evidence to controvert this assumption. However the kind of capital budget which shows long-term plans over five or six years constitutes an advanced administrative technique. Cities in the survey which use such a budget may not therefore be representative.[3]

---

[3]The term capital budget is used in two senses. It is sometimes (Footnote continued on following page.)

Second it must be assumed that cities which issue bonds with no credit rating or a rating below Baa respond to tightened credit in the same way as cities which issue bonds with one of the four top ratings. The assumption that credit rating does not affect a city's response to monetary policy (except through the interest rate) is built into the regression model and therefore the exclusion of some credit ratings does not introduce another limitation. However the exclusion of cities that issue unrated bonds may bias the results on the side of less sensitivity to interest rate changes because municipalities which issue unrated bonds generally rely less on debt finance.

c. Conclusions

The tests of the question 1 hypotheses resulted in the following equation:[4]

(1) $N = -2.311 - .069M + .030GM + .068O_1 - .294GR_1$
              $(.015)$ $(.005)$ $(.017)$ $(.009)$

              $-.222GR_2 - .111GR_3 + .0016S - .178C_1$
              $(.006)$ $(.005)$ $(.0007)$ $(.021)$

              $+ .161A_1 + .106A_2 + 1.710G$
              $(.027)$ $(.023)$ $(.056)$

$S_u = .277$

$R^2 = .832$

$N =$ "net interest cost," the interest rate on municipal bonds

$M =$ maturity

(footnote 3 continued)
used to describe a long-term capital improvement program, i.e., a five or six year projection of capital expenditures. It is also used to designate that part of the current budget which deals with capital outlays. Accounting for capital outlays in the current budget is a standard operating procedure. Data taken from long-term capital improvement programs were used to measure the impact of tightening credit on the planning of expenditures. Data taken from current budgets were used to ·measure postponements and cutbacks of authorized expenditures.

[4]This equation with $A_1 = 0$ was used in the tests of the question 2 hypotheses to estimate the interest rates on which officials based planned, authorized and actual expenditures.

O = optional feature: O = 1 callable
                        O = 2 non-callable (omitted
                                        category)[5]

R = credit rating   R = 1 Aaa

                        R = 2 Aa

                        R = 3 A

                        R = 4 Baa (omitted category)

S = size of issue

C = collateral   C = 1 general obligation bond

                        C = 2 revenue bond (omitted category)

A = issuing agency   A = 1 counties, municipalities and
                                special districts

                        A = 2 school districts

                        A = 3 states, authorities, and
                                commissions (omitted
                                category)

G = the long term U.S. Government bond rate, the index of
    monetary conditions

The first general hypothesis dealing with question 1--that the
structure of state-local interest rates results from investors
balancing different types of risk against the rate of return--was
confirmed by the sample of state and local government bonds sold
during the 1955-57 period of increasing credit restraint. The coefficients estimated by equation (1) indicate that low risk bonds bear
a lower rate of interest than high risk bonds. They show that interest
rates on short-term bonds are lower than rates on long-term bonds
for all values of the long term U.S. Government bond rate greater
than or equal to 2.30 percent; that interest rates on non-callable
bonds are lower than rates on callable bonds; that interest rates on
bonds with high credit ratings are lower than interest rates on bonds
with low credit ratings; that interest rates on small bonds are lower
than rates on larger bonds; that interest rates on general obligation

---

[5]One category is omitted from each of the classifications because
only n-1 are independent.

bonds are lower than rates on revenue bonds; and that interest rates on state bonds are lower than rates on local government bonds.

The data did not support the hypothesis that the cost of borrowing varies according to the purpose for which the funds are intended; i.e., that investors consider bonds issued for certain purposes especially risky.[6] They also showed no difference in the interest costs borne by school districts as compared with the costs borne by municipalities and other local governments.

The second general hypothesis--that monetary policy has a differential impact on the structure of interest rates--was also confirmed. However in this sample it was possible to measure the differential impact within only two of the six risk categories--maturity and credit rating--without running into problems of multicollinearity. The hypothesis that a given increase in the Government bond rate causes a larger increase in the interest rate on long-term state-local bonds than on short-term bonds was confirmed, whether the increase was measured in absolute or relative basis points. The hypothesis that a given increase in the Government bond rate results in a larger increase in the cost of issuing low rated bonds than in the cost of issuing high rated bonds was confirmed only when the increase was measured in absolute basis points. The percentage increase in the cost of issuing low rated bonds is less than the percentage increase in the cost of issuing high rated bonds.

The results of the tests of these hypotheses provide the information for determining which types of bonds become relatively more expensive to issue when credit tightens. If the increase in borrowing costs is measured in absolute basis points, it is long-term low rated bonds which become relatively more expensive to issue. If the increase is measured in relative basis points, it is bonds which have less risky characteristics in all categories except maturity that become relatively more expensive. A given absolute increase in borrowing costs results in a larger percentage increase in the cost of issuing bonds with initially low interest rates than bonds with initially high rates.

The results of the tests of the question 2 hypotheses suggested that, among municipalities which have planned or authorized the financing of some capital expenditures by long-term borrowing, an increase in the municipal bond rate affects the planning and execution of capital expenditures differently.

---

[6]The purpose variable was excluded from equation (1) because it did not reduce the variation in the state-local interest rate by a statistically significant amount.

At the planning stage of the decision process, a tightening of credit has a negligible impact on total capital expenditures. The regressions of planned current tax financed expenditures and planned bond financed expenditures on the increase in the municipal bond rate indicated that municipalities cushion the impact of tightening credit by increasing reliance on tax finance and decreasing reliance on bond finance.

The hypothesis was confirmed that, at the execution stage of the decision process, municipal officials postpone and cut back the total volume of actual relative to authorized capital expenditures to a greater extent the greater is the relative increase in their borrowing costs. However tests showed that when credit tightens the proportion of authorized bond financed expenditures and the proportion of authorized tax financed expenditures that are postponed and cut back are each statistically insignificant when measured separately. The author's interpretation of these findings is that officials distribute the burden of adjustment to tighter conditions between tax financed and bond financed expenditures, achieving the objective of staying within the budget constraint while making the adjustment in each expenditure category relatively easy to bear.

The hypothesis that tightening credit causes postponements and cutbacks of actual relative to authorized total expenditures was not confirmed when the increase in borrowing costs was measured in absolute terms instead of relative terms. However this does not cast doubt on the inference that tightening credit has an impact on the execution of total authorized expenditures. Apparently it means that in this sample large absolute increases in the interest rate were correlated with initially high interest rates so that, while some cities cut back and postponed expenditures, there was little or no correlation between the magnitude of cutbacks and postponements and the absolute interest rate increase.

In the tests of the hypotheses about the impact of tightening credit on the planning of expenditures, it made little difference whether the increase in the interest rate was measured in absolute or relative terms. This was because in this sample those cities which experienced the largest absolute increase in borrowing costs between planning and revising plans also experienced the largest relative increase.

The question of the relative versus the absolute increase in the interest rate as alternative explanations of the proportion of expenditures that is cut back and postponed is important in analyzing the incidence of tightening credit on different kinds of state and local borrowers. For example, if the absolute increase offered the better explanation of the observed response to tightening credit, it could be inferred that, other things being equal, cities with low credit ratings are "hit harder" by tightening credit than cities with high credit ratings. If the relative increase offered the better explanation, the opposite inference would be justifiable. In view of the fact that the absolute increase offers the better explanation of the variation of some dependent variables and that the relative increase offers the better explanation of the variation of others, further research on the "absolute-relative" question would be desirable.

d. <u>An Estimate of the Impact of Tightening Credit on the Execution of Total Authorized Capital Expenditures</u>

Equation (2) resulted from the tests of the hypotheses about the impact of tightening credit on the execution of total capital expenditures:

$$(2) \quad \frac{A_{t_0} - E_{t_1}}{A_{t_0}} = 19.30 + 1.15 \frac{N_{t_1} - N_{t_0}}{N_{t_0}}$$

where A = total authorized capital expenditures
E = total actual expenditures
N = "net interest cost," the municipal bond rate
t = period during which expenditures were authorized or executed

Equation (2) is used below to estimate the impact of tightening credit on the aggregate of municipal capital expenditures in the United States in 1957 and 1959. These estimates should be viewed with caution because equation (2) is based on a small sample (21 municipalities) obtained from a selected population with the broad population of municipalities and the standard error of estimate (20.94) is rather high.[7]

Moody's index of yields on general obligation bonds is taken as a rough approximation of the average interest rate on which municipal officials base authorized and actual expenditures.[8] It is assumed that officials based authorized expenditures for calendar 1957 (59) on the average rate during the last quarter of 1956 (58). It is also assumed that they continually adjusted actual expenditures to changes in the interest rate so that the average interest rate prevailing at the time expenditures were actually made is represented by the average

---

[7]See Section 4b, p. 26.
[8]Equation (1) is not used to estimate the N's, because it is applicable only to individual borrowers.

rate during 1957 (59).[9] Using these definitions the estimates of N are as follows:

$$N_{56} = 3.36\% \quad (N_{56} - N_{57})/N_{56} = 5.95\%$$

$$N_{57} = 3.56\%$$

$$N_{58} = 3.62\% \quad (N_{58} - N_{59})/N_{58} = 3.31\%$$

$$N_{59} = 3.74\%$$

All municipalities in the United States actually spent $3,653 million on total capital outlays in the fiscal year ending in 1957. In 1959 they spent $3,253 million.[10] If a rather bold simplifying assumption is made that all municipalities have a fiscal year that coincides with the calendar year, this information can be used in equation (2) to solve for authorized expenditures and the volume of expenditures that were cut back and postponed.[11] The resulting solutions are:

$$A_{56} = \$4,404 \text{ million} \qquad A_{56} - E_{57} = \$1,151 \text{ million}$$

$$A_{58} = \$4,750 \text{ million} \qquad A_{58} - E_{59} = \$1,097 \text{ million}$$

Notice that not all these postponements and cutbacks are attributable to tightening credit. Had there been no change in credit conditions over the periods considered, officials would still have postponed and cut back about 19 percent of total authorized expenditures.[12] In 1957 the 6 percent increase in borrowing costs prompted officials to postpone and cut back an additional 7 percent of expenditures. In 1959 the 3 percent increase in the municipal bond rate caused officials to postpone and cut back expenditures by an additional 4 percent. This means that the volume of postponements and cutbacks due to tightening credit was about $302 million in 1957 and $181 million in 1959.

---

[9]These assumptions were also used in the estimation of the regression coefficients.

[10]Compendium of City Government Finances in 1959 (Washington, D.C.: U.S. Department of Commerce, Bureau of the Census).

[11]The fiscal year followed by municipalities is not standardized. If the survey sample is representative, probably around half have a January–December fiscal year; and the other half a July–June fiscal year.

[12]Delays in the preparation of engineering and architectural specifications and in land acquisition are some non-monetary factors that cause postponements of expenditures.

V. CONCLUSIONS

Pickering and Morris found that from 2 percent to 5 percent of state and local construction expenditures was shifted from periods of tightening credit to periods of easing credit. The present author found that from 4 percent to 7 percent of municipal capital expenditures was postponed and/or cut back due to tightening credit. The differences in the estimates could be attributable to any of a number of factors. One possibility is that municipalities or local governments are more sensitive to monetary policy than state governments. (They are subject to larger increases in borrowing costs when credit tightens.) Another is that the volume of expenditures that is cut back (dropped altogether) is considerable. Still another possibility is that the volume of non-construction capital outlays that is postponed and/or cut back is large.

Research Study Six

DETERMINANTS OF THE VOLUME AND COMPOSITION
OF SAVING WITH SPECIAL REFERENCE TO
THE INFLUENCE OF MONETARY POLICY

Irwin Friend*
University of Pennsylvania

INTRODUCTION

The primary purpose of this paper is to highlight what we do and do not know about the determinants of saving with particular emphasis on the influence of monetary (and debt management) policy. This potential influence of monetary policy on saving via changes in interest rates, in liquidity or in other financial conditions can be studied either by analyzing the relationship of these financial variables to saving propensities of the different sectors in the economy so that only the supply of saving is considered; or the relationship of these variables to the demand for saving (viz., investment propensities) can be analyzed at the same time so that the implications of monetary policy for the joint determination of the level of saving and investment can be more fully appraised. It is intended to concentrate on the supply side in this paper since other papers in this series are covering the demand for saving. However, some attention will be paid to the demand side, i.e., to the influence of monetary policy on investment propensities, for two reasons: Policy will frequently be concerned with affecting the level of real saving and investment (presumably jointly determined by the schedules of

---

*I am indebted to my colleague, Professor Jean Crockett, for her valuable comments.

saving and investment propensities); and much of the data available for testing the relationship of saving to other variables measure the intersection of saving and investment schedules and may or may not represent saving schedules.

Before discussing the influence of monetary policy on saving, it will be desirable to consider as background material the general state of existing knowledge on the nonfinancial as well as financial determinants of saving. A summary statement on the current status of over-all theory and data relating to the main determinants of saving is provided in the first section of this paper.

The second section of this paper presents both a specific review of economic theory relating interest rates, liquidity and other financial variables to saving and a fairly comprehensive analysis of the correspondence between such theory and the empirical evidence. The third and final section is a summary of findings and statement of implications.

While much of the analysis will refer to total saving, i.e., to income less consumption either of some economic unit or of the nation as a whole, this paper will also cover the components of saving, i.e., the changes in individual items of assets less liabilities whose sum is equal to total saving. (More precisely, saving can be defined either as income less consumption or equivalently as the change in assets less liabilities apart from balance sheet revaluations or capital transfers from one economic unit to another.) As is customary in such analysis, saving includes net investment in capital goods and in financial claims but not in human capital or in research. The only significant ambiguity that arises in the definition or measurement of private saving relates to net investment in consumer durables which is treated as consumption in the official national income statistics of the United States but is frequently considered as saving in economic analysis. Another difficulty of measurement involves the treatment of government net investment in capital goods as consumption in these same statistics. Where any statement in this paper depends to any important extent on the precise treatment of consumer durables or of government investment in capital goods, that fact will be indicated.

It might be noted that most of the paper is based on prior work by many different people, but as will be indicated later some of the results are new. Where gaps existed and could be bridged -- at least in crude fashion -- without much effort or time, an attempt was made to do so. However, in such cases, the procedures followed could rarely be satisfactory, and the gaps that remain are more impressive than those that have been filled in.

I. GENERAL STATE OF KNOWLEDGE ON DETERMINANTS OF SAVING

Economic theory generally emphasizes the dependence of saving on income, interest rates, wealth or net worth, and tastes, all measured in real terms. Income is considered to be the primary determinant of saving, with higher income closely associated with higher saving. While current income is of special importance in this connection, past incomes and expected future incomes may also exert a significant influence on current saving. The relation between saving and wealth, for given income, is not normally considered so important as the income effect but for a specific economic unit higher wealth is generally believed to be associated with smaller needs for additional wealth, with higher spending potential and hence with lower current saving. The wealth effect on current saving is likely to be particularly significant when past saving decisions have not been voluntary, so that for example the assets accumulated are higher than desired at a given level of income, or when substantial unanticipated changes in assets or in income occur, so that assets again are considered excessive (or deficient) relative to income. However, the wealth effect might be expected to depend not only on the level of net worth but also on its composition, with financial and especially monetary assets likely to have a larger negative influence on saving than nonfinancial assets, particularly if saving is defined to exclude net investment in consumer durables.

The implications of theory for the influence of interest rates on saving are more controversial and will be considered in a later section. It might be noted here, however, that interest rates are regarded as the basis for converting current saving (or abstinence from current consumption) into a larger amount of future consumption so that if the general price level is expected to change, interest rates will either have to be adjusted for the rate of such change, or the relationship between present and expected future prices introduced as another economically relevant variable affecting saving behavior. In addition to interest rates and expected prices, related credit conditions (viz., down payments and maturities) also affect the ease of enhancing present or near-term consumption at the expense of future consumption.

The basis for the presumed importance of income, and to a lesser extent of assets and interest rates, lies in the underlying motivation for saving by an economic unit. Apart from such mechanical factors as the lag of consumption behind income, saving is motivated by the desire and conditioned by the ability to set aside current income for future use, whether for specific consumption or investment or for general contingencies. This general motivation gives rise to several specific reasons for saving: to smooth out or otherwise adjust consumption over a planning period which is longer than the period for which saving is being measured; to provide protection in connection with uncertainty about future income and needs; to receive an interest or other return on assets; and to leave an estate or to provide for one's heirs.

While these economic reasons for saving imply that income must play a central role in determining the volume of saving, they are not adequate for specifying the form or precise nature of the relationship. Clearly, the nature of the relationship between saving and current income will depend, at least to some extent, not only on the other economic variables specified but on the correlation between current income and expected future income, on preference between consumption today and tomorrow (including consumption of one's heirs), and on the assessment of and reactions to uncertainty.

Moreover, noneconomic influences characterizing different socio-economic groups, as well as individuals within the same group, are important in determining "tastes" or attitudes towards consumption and saving, and thus play a substantial role in determining the volume (and composition) of saving. Japan is a much poorer country than the United States, but the typical Japanese family seems to have a very much higher saving-income ratio (and a considerably different composition of saving). Such "noneconomic" differences in saving behavior among groups are presumably not congenital but reflect attitudes instilled by the dominant social institutions, as exemplified by the supposed influence of the Puritan ethic in the earlier history of Western nations or by government propaganda and moral suasion during wartime.

So far we have been discussing the broad determinants of saving for an economic unit such as a household or a business firm. (The third major economic sector, viz., government, is motivated by similar but also by other factors, including those associated with economic stabilization and development.) In generalizing these results to the economy as a whole, there are two qualifications to our previous analysis. First, the relation of saving to income and other variables for the country as a whole will depend not only on the micro-relations characterizing saving of different groups but also on the distribution or relative importance of these groups in the population.

For example, abstracting from uncertainty, if the level of income and the size and age composition of the population remain fairly stable, the dissaving of the retired would be expected to offset the saving of younger persons so long as estates are neglected or remain constant in size. Under such circumstances, the annual saving of an individual family during the working life of its head or dissaving after the head's retirement can be determined by its average income, length of life, and working span, while the national saving is, of course, zero. If income increases steadily but the size and age composition of the population are stable and estates can be neglected or bear a constant relation to income, the level of national saving is related to the annual rate of change in national income. Or if income per consumer unit remains constant but the number of consumer units increases, the level of national saving is related to population growth.[1]

Second, it should be noted that measures taken to increase the propensity to save of an economic unit or group may under certain circumstances decrease income and hence saving for the country as a whole. If for any given level of aggregate income, savers collectively want and attempt to save more than investors collectively want to invest in capital goods, the level of the national income and probably also of saving will decline. However, it is not necessarily true that steps taken to encourage saving will decrease income and saving since a higher propensity to save might increase desired investment either indirectly through lower interest rates or directly through encouraging more investment on the part of savers. In a full employment or inflationary situation, a rise in the propensity to save as a result of a change in tastes might be expected to be associated with more investment and saving rather than with lower real income or with the same investment and saving and stable prices; the reverse, i.e., less investment and saving, might be expected in a situation already characterized by deflationary tendencies. The result depends not only on the state of the economy but also on the means utilized to influence saving; thus, specific monetary and debt management policies or other measures which stimulate saving and discourage investment might easily bring about lower rather than higher saving. It may be unnecessary to point out that if a higher rate of saving and investment for the economy under full-employment conditions can be achieved, the rate of economic growth will be increased correspondingly.

Relation of Total Saving by Major Economic Groups to Nonfinancial Variables

With this brief theoretical background, we can now turn to the main empirical findings of studies relating saving to income and other nonfinancial variables. According to the official Commerce national income statistics which go back to 1929, total net saving has averaged 9 percent of the national income since World War II, about the same as in 1929 and 1941 but significantly higher than in any of the other prewar years 1930-40, a period which reflected of course relatively depressed economic conditions. The concept of saving referred to in these statistics excludes net investment in consumer durables (other than housing) and net government investment in

---

[1] Irwin Friend and Irving B. Kravis, "Consumption Patterns and Permanent Income," American Economic Review (May 1957), p.537.

capital goods. Longer-run estimates from 1897 through 1949 by R. W. Goldsmith, which are conceptually more inclusive than the Commerce series, show little change over this period in the ratio of total net saving to the national income.[2] The Goldsmith figures point to an average national saving ratio inclusive of consumer durables and government investment of one-eighth the national income during "normal" periods, i.e., exclusive of war and deep depression years.

Perhaps the most interesting development in recent saving behavior, according to the Commerce statistics, was a sharp rise in the personal saving-income ratio during 1951 to a higher level which has been maintained since that time. To a considerable extent this may have reflected a downward movement in the ratio of net investment in consumer durables to personal disposable income, once the more pressing wartime induced shortages had been filled, and a shift from such investment to other forms of saving. The personal saving-income ratio in recent years -- close to 7.5 percent under the Commerce definition -- has definitely been higher than in the earlier peacetime years covered by the Commerce series but is probably not much different from the average in the decades prior to 1929. (The comparison of the recent Commerce series with the published Goldsmith data for pre-1929 years has been facilitated by new preliminary estimates of personal saving for 1950-56 kindly made available by Dr. Goldsmith. However, such a comparison is still quite tenuous in view of the incomparabilities of the two sets of data and the especially dubious nature of some of the earlier figures.)

It is interesting to note that while there has been a significant rise in the official personal saving-income ratio in recent years, there has been no corresponding rise in the ratio of total saving to the national income. The offsets have been a significant decline in the ratio of personal disposable income and corporate income after taxes to the national income, a decline in the corporate saving-income ratio, a slight decline in the ratio of corporate income after taxes to personal disposable income -- the latter of which is associated with a lower propensity to save, and finally a decline in government saving (or rise in dissaving).[3] The corporate saving-

---

[2]R. W. Goldsmith, Study of Saving in the United States, Vol. I, (National Bureau of Economic Research, Princeton University Press, 1955).

[3]The national saving-income ratio, i.e., the ratio of national saving to the national income or net national product, can usefully be regarded as the sum of three products--the product of the ratio of personal saving to personal disposable income times the ratio of such income to the national income, and corresponding products for the corporate and government sectors.

income ratio in recent years -- above 40 percent without inventory valuation adjustment but not much different from 40 percent with that adjustment -- has on an adjusted basis been fairly close to though probably somewhat above the average level characterizing earlier peacetime and prosperous decades in our history. (In view of the substantial rise in personal tax rates applicable to dividend income, a larger increase in the corporate retention ratio might have been expected in recent decades.) The share of both personal and corporate income after taxes in the national income has of course declined over the past half century.

According to the official national income statistics, individuals' or personal saving -- defined to include saving by noncorporate farm and nonfarm enterprises, nonprofit organizations, private pension, welfare and trust funds as well as by consumers, but not net investment in consumer durables or government insurance and pensions -- has accounted for some two-thirds of the total with corporate saving accounting for most of the remainder. While these figures as well as all others in this paper refer to net saving unless otherwise noted, it may be remarked that corporate gross saving is relatively more important than their net saving, accounting for about half of total gross saving according to the national income statistics. Government saving -- defined in these statistics as surplus or deficit on income or product account and including government insurance and pensions but excluding net investment in capital goods -- has been relatively small on the average except for large wartime deficits. The conceptually different Goldsmith data, which include government net investment in capital goods as government saving but classify government insurance and pensions as individuals' saving, indicate that from 1897 to 1949 individuals on the average accounted for roughly 70 percent of total net saving, corporations for 20 percent and government for 10 percent. However, after 1950 the Goldsmith data show a marked decline in the share of government saving to well under 5 percent of the total. On the other hand, if government insurance and pension funds are considered as part of government saving, the Goldsmith data would imply a government share in total saving of roughly 10 percent in recent years as compared with 15 percent in the immediate postwar period.

It should be stressed that a substantial though, in view of the inadequacies of the available data, indeterminate proportion of individuals' saving seems to be attributable to noncorporate nonfarm businessmen, with some data suggesting that this proportion may amount to one-third or more, while other entrepreneurial personnel -- including farm operators, owner-operators of small incorporated businesses, independent professional men, and business managers and officials -- also account for a significant fraction of individuals' saving.[4] Thus on the Commerce definition of saving at least half of the total seems to be attributable to corporate or non-corporate business units or entrepreneurial groups. It is interesting that the apparently high rate of saving by businessmen can be explained only in part by their higher reported income and may reflect the stimulation of direct investment outlets, greater uncertainty and some understatement of income and perhaps also innate psychological influences. The declining entrepreneurial share in total personal income over the past half century may help to explain the relative constancy in the over-all personal saving-income ratio in spite of the rise in income. The admittedly inconclusive data available indicate that a high proportion of the cyclical fluctuations in the total of individuals' saving relative to their income may be explained by the movements in entrepreneurial saving, and even more fragmentary evidence suggests that saving and investment by entrepreneurs may be of the same general order of magnitude.[5]

Upper income groups generally, totally apart from their occupation, seem to have a higher than average propensity to save and account for a substantial proportion of all saving. A careful analysis of the most recent consumer survey data on saving -- covering 1950 -- suggests that whereas saving (defined approximately as in the national accounts) was negative for persons whose current income after taxes for the year was less than $1,000, the saving-income ratio rose to 5 percent for family incomes between $4,000 and $5,000 and to over 30 percent for incomes above $10,000, with the last group accounting for 4 percent of the population but for 58 percent of total saving by families (including single persons).[6] If personal saving is adjusted to include net investment in durables, a pro rata share of corporate saving based on market value of stock owned, or a pro rata share of capital gains and losses, the 1950 saving-income ratios of all income groups were raised markedly but the income concentration of saving was not greatly changed. However, in view of the major deficiencies in the survey data on saving, the above statements about the saving behavior of different income groups in the population -- like those about different occupations or other groups of individuals -- cannot be considered as definitive and the estimates presented are subject to a very substan-

---

[4]Irwin Friend and Irving Kravis, "Entrepreneurial Income, Saving and Investment," American Economic Review (June 1957), pp. 269-301; and Irwin Friend and Stanley Schor, "Who Saves?" Review of Economics and Statistics (May 1958), p. 234.

[5]"Entrepreneurial Income, Saving and Investment," op. cit.

[6]"Who Saves," op. cit., p. 239.

tial margin of error.[7] Even less can be said with any certainty about secular and cyclical variation in the saving behavior of the different income groups.

Some analysts have seriously questioned the finding that the upper income groups have a higher propensity to save relative to income than other groups, maintaining that the average propensity to save out of "permanent" (average, discounted, expected) income is constant for the different income groups.[8] According to this hypothesis, the reason that consumer survey data seem to show a contrary result is that actual income as measured in surveys is a composite of permanent and transitory income, with the latter positively correlated with measured income and completely or almost completely saved. The permanent income hypothesis has been useful in stressing that the saving-income ratio may not be so sensitive to rising incomes as the raw survey data suggest and that the propensity to save out of income changes considered by the recipient as permanent or long-run may be substantially different (and is probably lower) than the propensity to save out of other income changes regarded as more transitory or short run. However, virtually all direct tests seem to point to a significant correlation between the saving-income ratio and income class, regardless of the steps taken to minimize the influence of transitory income. New data, derived from a continuous panel rather than from a single cross-section of households, will be required to resolve this issue finally.

The only other potentially important economic determinant of personal saving which has been investigated in detail through analysis of consumer surveys is asset position, particularly liquid assets but also debt, value of house and other durables.[9] In many of these

[7] The absence of reliable data on the distribution of individuals' saving among the more important groups in the population (especially broad income and occupation classes) is one of the more shameful gaps in our economic information.

[8] See particularly Milton Friedman, A Theory of the Consumption Function, National Bureau of Economic Research, 1957 and Franco Modigliani and Richard Brumberg. "Utility Analysis and the Consumption Function," Post Keynesian Economics, ed. K. K. Kurihara, New Brunswick, N.J., 1954. For other points of view, see "Consumption Patterns and Permanent Income," op. cit., and various papers in the Oxford Statistical Bulletin (May 1957), and in Consumption and Saving, Vols. I and II, University of Pennsylvania, 1960.

[9] See Lawrence R. Klein, "Statistical Estimation of Economic Relations from Survey Data," Contributions of Survey Methods to Economics, (New York: Columbia University Press, 1954); Jean Crockett and Irwin Friend, "A Complete Set of Consumer Demand Relationships," Consumption and Saving, op. cit., Vol. I; and Harold Watts and James Tobin, "Consumer Expenditures and the Capital Account," Consumption and Saving, op. cit., Vol. II.

studies, liquid assets may be a proxy for total assets with which it is probably closely correlated. Generally these studies show that, for given income, liquid assets tend to be negatively correlated with saving (defined to exclude durables), and to a lesser extent stocks of durables and debt positively correlated with saving, but the overall influence of these variables does not appear to be impressive. The liquid assets effect which seems the strongest of these turns out to be significant only for the lower income groups. However, there is every presumption that the available consumer survey data are completely inadequate for stuying assets (and liabilities) effects since differences in asset position among families reflect variation in past saving behavior and tastes as well as the impact of changes in the level and structure of assets on a typical family or group of families. Time series analysis, which has serious deficiencies of its own for this purpose, also has shown the same kind of qualitative influence of liquid assets on personal saving, but as will be indicated subsequently estimates of the quantitative importance of this influence has been extremely variable to say the least.

The remaining influences on individuals' or personal saving behavior which have received some attention in the literature relate either to financial variables to be discussed in a later section of this paper, other demographic or sociological variables (e.g., family size, age, race, home ownership, and region) which are not very important from the viewpoint of policy implications, and psychological or institutional variables about which not very much can be said. Some of the demographic or sociological variables (such as home ownership and race) which earlier studies of survey results suggested had a significant influence on saving behavior turn out to be less important than previously thought when other relevant variables are held constant or when the survey data are roughly adjusted for known biases.[10] The psychological or institutional variables which seem to have the most obvious impact on saving behavior have to do with cultural differences among peoples whose genesis and influence it is difficult to explain. Whether high or low saving rates among nationals of other countries persist when they migrate to the United States, it is not possible to say.

More important, we do not know whether it is feasible to influence the rate of personal saving (out of disposable income) substantially in a democratic society by psychological or institutional measures except in periods of stress when moral or legal coercion can be exercised effectively, but there is some reason to believe that institutional changes may be effective in this respect. There is some presumption that the growth of compulsory government insurance

---

[10]See "Who Saves?", op. cit., p. 230, and "A Complete Set of Consumer Demand Relationships," op. cit.

schemes in the mid 1930's might be expected to have lowered the reported rate of personal saving, which is defined by Commerce to exclude government insurance, and to have increased the more relevant ratio of personal saving plus such insurance to income, though there is no convincing evidence either for or against this thesis. The rapid growth of quasi-compulsory private pension funds in the early 1950's coincided, in part probably accidentally, with an increase in the reported rate of personal saving which is defined to include such funds, and here it seems quite plausible (though again not conclusive) that the effective rate of personal saving was increased somewhat.

It is more questionable whether the rate of saving can normally be affected appreciably by exhortation or even by high pressure "sales" campaigns. There is no evidence that exhortation to increase saving in the United States in recent years, or even to buy savings bonds, has been particularly successful. Nor does a similar but more concerted effort to increase saving by the government in India seem to have been much more effective. On the other hand, the rapid growth in net purchases of U.S. investment company stocks (largely mutual funds) since the early 1950's undoubtedly reflects not only the favorable economic environment and stock market psychology but also the intensive sales campaign carried on by the industry involved. There seems little doubt that sales effort in this industry has paid off handsomely, and it is interesting to note that there is a significant direct relation between the growth of individual investment companies and the percentage sales charge levied on investors.[11] The question which cannot be answered with our present information is the extent to which money invested in mutual funds would have been saved in any event, but presumably not all of it would have been saved in the absence of the sales effort which was expended and the associated increase in purchases.

Given the central importance which economic theory and empirical data attribute to income in the determination of saving both for a single economic unit and in the aggregate, and the essential role played by this saving-income relationship in many theories of aggregate income determination, it is not surprising to find that a substantial amount of research effort has been expended in attempting to estimate the value of the marginal propensity to save out of aggregate income for the personal and corporate sectors of the economy. Such attempts have largely been directed to time-series data in spite of the small number of independent observations they provide, since the basic question at issue is how saving may be

---

[11]This finding is noted in A Study of Mutual Funds by Irwin Friend, F. E. Brown, Edward S. Herman and Douglas Vickers. (Washington, D.C.: U.S. Government Printing Office, 1962.)

expected to change as income changes over time (rather than from one economic unit to another).

Two general approaches have been taken each with its own advantages and disadvantages: first, to relate either annual or at times quarterly personal or corporate saving to income after taxes and to any other variables considered significant over some fairly long period (typically from 1929 though occasionally from the turn of the century) without specification of other relevant relationships in a complete economic model; second, to specify a complete economic model where the values of the marginal propensities to save obtained from the saving or consumption relationships are influenced by the rest of the model. In both approaches, a stable saving function is typically assumed, i.e., the marginal propensity to save and the influence on saving of any other variables specified are assumed to remain the same over the time period covered. For the most part, survey or cross-section data are used more as a general check on the degree of confidence that can be placed in the time-series results rather than as a more reliable substitute. In spite of the advantages of cross-section data in making available a large number of independent observations, in isolating income from correlated non-income effects, and in holding constant supply considerations, the difficulties of inferring intra-personal behavior over time from inter-personal comparisons at a point of time have greatly impaired the usefulness of these data and are likely to continue to do so until continuous panel data are available.

The estimates of the marginal propensity to save out of personal disposable income have varied rather widely, depending not only on the specification or nonspecification of the model but on the assumed functional form of the relationship between saving and income, on the other variables introduced into the analysis, including whether a distinction is made between short-run and long-run propensities, on the definition of saving, and on the period covered. It may be noted that distinctions between short-run and long-run saving propensities, which as might be expected typically show larger short-run values, may simply imply a lag of consumption behind income or may reflect differences between the effects of transitory and more permanent changes in income. Several recent studies differentiating between short-run and longer-run propensities have indicated a short-run marginal propensity to save out of personal disposable income, or more precisely the ratio of the annual increment in saving associated with an annual increment in income, of .45 or more, and a long-run marginal propensity to save of .25 or less. One of these studies was based on an econometric model using Commerce national income data from 1929 to 1950 (exclusive of World War II years) and on a personal saving or more accurately a consumption function relating saving to nonfarm and farm entrepreneurial income as well as to other personal disposable income, to consumption lagged one year to allow for the persistence of consumption habits, and to liquid assets (with explicit allowance for population and price); a second analyzed the same relationship but without incorporating it in a complete economic model; and still a third related the current year's personal saving or rather consumption to a weighted average of the current year's and sixteen previous years' income (using price deflated per capita figures) based on the Goldsmith series for peacetime years in the first half of this century, with the data determining the weight to be attached to each of the years' incomes and with the weighted incomes supposedly representing an empirical approximation of "permanent" income.[12]

The first two of these relationships -- based on the same type of "absolute" income hypotheses -- not surprisingly point to a similar short-run or year-to-year marginal propensity to save out of personal disposable income, about .45 with the recent distribution of income among farm and nonfarm entrepreneurs and other individuals; but the third -- based on a "permanent" income hypothesis -- indicates a significantly higher short-run propensity, .71 if no adjustment is made for the more comprehensive definition of saving employed and probably about .70 with such an adjustment.[13] The long-run marginal propensity to save, i.e., the total and not only the current increment to personal saving which results from an annual increment to income, is about .25 according to the two absolute income relationships and considerably lower, .12 on the broader definition of saving but probably about .10 on a basis comparable with the .25 figure, according to the permanent income relationship.

---

[12]The first of these relationships may be found in L. R. Klein and A. S. Goldberger, An Econometric Model of the United States (Amsterdam, 1955), pp. 51 and 90; the second in Karl A. Fox, "Econometric Models of the United States," Journal of Political Economy (April 1956), pp. 128-142; and the third in A Theory of the Consumption Function, op. cit., p. 147. Klein and Goldberger also present a revised model incorporating data for 1951 and 1952 into the 1929-50 relationships which has the effect of increasing moderately both the short-term and long-term marginal propensities to save.

[13]A rough recomputation of the Friedman time-series relation of consumption to permanent income for this paper redefining consumption to include gross expenditures on consumer durables, but using the same weights for current and past years' incomes and the same time period, implies a k or long-run consumption-income ratio of .90, a short-run ratio of .30, and hence corresponding saving ratios of .10 and .70. It may be noted that extending the time period through 1956 but more important making several technical changes in the estimation procedure, including the use of income for 8 instead of 16 previous years, reduces these saving ratios further to .06 and .68 respectively.

Still another relationship was computed for purposes of this paper between per capita deflated saving (exclusive of consumer durables) and both disposable income and consumption lagged one year on the basis of two bodies of data and periods: the first based on the Goldsmith series for the period 1898-1956 (excluding 1917-18 and 1942-45) yields a short-run marginal propensity to save of .35 and a long-run propensity of .08; the second based on the Commerce series for 1929-59 (excluding 1942-45) yields corresponding propensities of .33 and .13. Both but particularly the latter give a very good fit to the data including those for recent years. It may be noted that, other things being equal, the smaller the marginal propensity to save the greater will be the effect on the national income of an increment in investment or in government expenditure.

Other time-series relationships between personal saving and income and other variables (such as liquid assets, entrepreneurial as distinct from other income, change in income from the preceding year, etc.) but which do not distinguish in the same manner as the relationships previously described between short-run and long-run effects, yield a diversified harvest of marginal propensities. However, several of those relationships which were most successful in predicting the level of saving in recent years—such as the deflated per capita regression between saving and income and liquid assets— indicate a marginal propensity to save out of disposable income close to .25 and hence quite close to other absolute income long-run results described above [14] The marginal effect of liquid assets on personal saving indicated by these and other relationships is even more variable and more open to question on statistical and conceptual grounds, with the only consensus that liquid assets (in real terms) are negatively correlated with saving and do not have so strong an effect as income on short-run variations in saving.[15]

The preceding discussion suggests that earlier analyses of the historical data have not led conclusively either to a particular value or a narrow range of values of the marginal propensity to save out of personal disposable income. This is almost equally true of the year-to-year as well as the long-run marginal propensity to save,

---

[14]Irwin Friend with the assistance of Vito Natrella, Individuals' Saving (New York: John Wiley & Sons, Inc., 1954), pp. 140 ff. This estimate is also quite close to the long-run income coefficients of saving implied by the Crockett-Friend and Watts-Tobin analyses of the 1950 BLS consumer survey or cross-section data (see Consumption and Saving, op. cit., Vols. I and II).

[15]The Klein-Goldberger relation previously referred to points to a "marginal propensity to save" out of liquid assets of -.024, the Friend relation to -.11, and some more recent studies to -.22 or even higher negative values (e.g., see Arnold Zellner, "The Short Run Consumption Function," Econometrica, 25 (1957), pp. 552-567).

though there is of course some presumption that the annual marginal propensity to save out of that year's increment in income is greater than the long-run propensity. Moreover, the historical relationships do not do a particularly good job in forecasting the more significant changes in saving behavior, as for example occurred in 1951, indicating either that saving relationships are not particularly stable over long periods of time, or cannot explain short-run movements, or that the influence of all relevant variables has not been adequately introduced or assessed. Fortunately, an examination of the data from 1951 on suggests a fairly stable personal saving-income relation in recent years. The annual ratio of personal saving to disposable personal income as measured by Commerce has for nine years remained extremely close to its average level of 7.4 percent. Any plausible estimates of the year-to-year marginal propensity to save in this period seem very much lower than those discussed previously. However, while the recent year-to-year marginal propensity to save out of disposable income seems quite low (i.e., in the neighborhood of .074), the corresponding propensity to save out of the Gross National Product is of course much higher (.64 according to a simple complete model which relates change in consumption to change in income, treats nonconsumption expenditures as autonomous and has an average absolute error of less than 1 percent in estimating consumption over the past decade).

In addition to the studies which have suggested that the annual marginal propensity to save may be significantly larger than the corresponding long-run propensity, there have been studies investigating the possibility that the marginal propensity to save out of incomes of different degrees of "permanence" or "transitoriness" may be quite different. This is a possibility of great potential importance for policy purposes since various fiscal and monetary measures might affect permanent vs. transitory incomes quite differently. According to the recent permanent income theory, transitory income is completely saved (including net investment in durables as saving) so that temporary tax relief to stimulate consumption which would increase permanent income only to a modest extent might have comparatively little effect at least on nondurable goods and services. While the tests of this hypothesis are still not conclusive, in part because of the difficulty of defining transitory income in any satisfactory operational way, some very recent studies have cast considerable doubt on the assumption that a more transitory income receipt is automatically or on the average associated with substantially higher saving than a more permanent receipt of this same size.[16]

---

[16]See in particular the study by Ronald Bodkin, "Windfall Income and Permanent Income," which concludes that there is no evidence
(continued on following page)

The marginal propensity to save for U.S. corporations as a whole is much higher than for individuals. One of the best known corporate saving functions relating corporate saving to profits after taxes (both adjusted and unadjusted for inventory gains and losses) and dividends lagged one year, for the period 1918-41 except for two years -- 1936 and 1937 -- subject to an undistributed profits tax, indicates a short-run or year-to-year marginal propensity to save of .85, and a long-run marginal propensity of .50 or less (depending on whether an adjustment is or is not made for inventory profits).[17] Updating this relation and recomputing the results for the period

---

(footnote 16 continued)

that the marginal propensity to consume out of the particular windfall tested (the National Life Insurance Dividend of 1950) was particularly different from that of ordinary income, the critical comments in this study by Milton Friedman and the rejoinder by Bodkin, in Consumption and Saving, Vol. II, op. cit. Another study in this volume by Harold Watts and James Tobin on "Consumer Expenditures and the Capital Account" obtains from a different type of analysis a short-run income coefficient for saving which is definitely lower than a long-run coefficient and seems to be in the direction but not in the amount predicted by the permanent income hypothesis. Still a third study in Vol. I of this series by H. S. Houthakker and John Haldi, "Household Investment in Automobiles: An Intertemporal Cross-Section Analysis," suggests that for automobiles "the marginal propensities to invest out of permanent and transitory components [of income] are of the same order of magnitude."

[17]John Lintner, "Distribution of Income of Corporations Among Dividends, Retained Earnings and Taxes," American Economic Review (May 1956). Similar relations, including an additional variable representing accumulated undistributed profits, incorporated by Klein-Goldberger into the complete econometric model mentioned previously, show about the same short-run marginal propensity for the peacetime years during the period 1929-50 but a much higher long-run marginal propensity of .80; when the years 1951 and 1952 are added the short-run and long-run propensities are reduced somewhat but the coefficient of the lagged dividend variable has a sign contrary to expectation and an extremely large standard error. (See An Econometric Model of the United States, pp. 51 and 91.) An updating and recomputation of the Lintner regression for purposes of the present paper gives the following corporate saving relation derived from unadjusted I.R.S. data: $S_t = 1,174 + .836\pi_t - .624D_{t-1}$ where the data are measured in millions of dollars and S, π and D refer to annual saving, profits after taxes and dividends, the multiple correlation coefficient is .94, the standard error of estimate is $766 million, the standard error of the coefficient of π_t is .07, and that of D_{t-1} is .08.

1923-56 (omitting 1936-37 and 1942-45) yields only a slightly different short-run marginal propensity (.84) but a moderately higher long-run value (.57). Surprisingly enough, in view of the much greater availability of cross-section data for corporations than for individuals or families, there has been comparatively little analysis of corporate propensities to save from such data. However, the cross-section results which have been published, based on quite inadequate materials, point to similar high short-term marginal propensities to save (though on the average perhaps somewhat lower than in the time-series data) but to higher long-run propensities than the time-series data.[18]

Relation of Components of Saving to Nonfinancial Variables

Generally speaking, much less attention has been devoted by economists to the determinants of the components of saving, i.e., the changes in the individual items of assets and liabilities, than to the determinants of total saving for any economic unit or sector. There are several reasons for this state of affairs: It is the act of saving rather than any specific change in assets or liabilities of an economic unit which is regarded as financing directly or indirectly the investment of that or some other unit; all realized saving adds to wealth; and, perhaps most important, the different forms of saving are considered as essentially competitive with or substitutable for one another rather than with items of consumption, so that it is easier to predict total saving than its components and changes in one component of saving tend to be offset by changes in another component.[19]

The discussion of the determinants of the components of saving in this paper will be restricted to the individual's or personal sector of the economy where it is of most interest. Tables VI-1 and VI-2

---

[18]Such results for the United Kingdom and the United States are presented by S. J. Prais, "Dividend Policy and Income Appropriation," in Tew and Henderson, Studies in Company Finance (New York: Cambridge University Press, 1959). The U. S. results discussed by Prais were obtained from S. P. Dobrovolsky, Corporate Income Retention 1915-43, National Bureau of Economic Research, 1951. An analysis of cross-section data in the food and steel industries carried out at the Wharton School shows that in recent years such data imply the same high marginal propensity to save in the short-run, viz., about .85, and unlike the other cross-section data cited by Prais a rather low long-run propensity to save. However, the use of continuous cross-section data raises both long-run and short-run propensities.

[19]It might be noted that the composition of saving might better be termed the disposition of saving and perhaps most accurately designated as the distribution of changes in earned net worth among specific items of assets and liabilities.

TABLE VI-1

RATIOS OF COMPONENTS OF PERSONAL SAVING TO DISPOSABLE PERSONAL INCOME FOR SELECTED PERIODS, 1900-1956 (GOLDSMITH DATA)

Period[a]	Currency and Demand Deposits (1)	Time and Saving Deposits[b] (2)	Saving & Loan Associations and Credit Unions (3)	Cash and Deposits (and Saving & Loan) (1 + 2 + 3) (4)	Private Life Insurance (5)	Private Pension and Retirement Funds (6)	State and Local Government Pension and Retirement Funds (7)	U. S. Government Pension and Retirement Funds (8)	Corporate (and Foreign) Stock (9)	Corporate (and Foreign) Bonds (10)
1900-09	.022	.035	.001	.058	.008	--	--	--	.028	.019
1920-29	.015	.036	.008	.058	.013	.001	.001	.001	.030	.022
1946-50	.003	.011	.008	.021	.020	.004	.003	.013	.010	-.003
1951-56	.005	.014	.016	.035	.020	.008	.004	.009	.010	.002

Period[a]	State and Local Government Obligations (11)	U. S. Government Bonds (12)	Net Investment in Non-Farm Residential Construction (13)	Net Change in Non-Farm Residential Mortgages[c] (14)	Net Investment in Consumer Durables (15)	Net Change in Consumer and Other Debt[c] (16)	Net Investment in Non-Farm Unincorporated Business (Including Non-Residential Construction)[d] (17)	Net Investment in Farms[e] (18)	Borrowing on Securities[c] (19)	Total Personal Saving[f] (20)
1900-09	.003	-.001	.021	.005	.015	.004	.001	.003	.004	.110
1920-29	.007	-.015	.037	.014	.022	.006	.006	-.002	.005	.116
1946-50	.003	.002	.022	.026	.046	.015	.007	.002	-.001	.114
1951-56	.005	.001	.034	.033	.027	.014	.005	--	.002	.118

[a] The estimates for 1900-09 and 1920-29 were obtained from R. W. Goldsmith, A Study of Saving in the United States, Volume I; the saving estimates for 1946-56 were kindly supplied by Dr. Goldsmith and represent some revisions in his 1946-49 published series, and an extension of his earlier work to 1956; the income estimates for 1946-56 were obtained from the U.S. Department of Commerce, Survey of Current Business, after checking these data with the published Goldsmith series (through 1949) for comparability.

[b] Farm bank deposits prior to 1923 are divided in the same ratio as in 1923. In any event they are quite small.

[c] Positive values represent dissaving. In Column 14, increases in mortgages owned by individuals have been subtracted from increases in mortgages owed by individuals. A similar procedure has been followed in Columns 17 and 18. For the years 1946-56, the mortgages owned by individuals are divided in the same ratio as in the earlier estimates for the 1946-49 period.

[d] Nonfarm nonresidential construction, producer durables, inventories, less nonfarm mortgage debt on nonresidential structures, and debt to banks and other institutions.

[e] Farm construction less farm mortgage debt.

[f] The sum of the components presented in earlier columns will not add precisely to the total indicated in Column 20.

TABLE VI-2

RATIOS OF COMPONENTS OF PERSONAL SAVING TO DISPOSABLE PERSONAL INCOME FOR 1946–59 (S. E. C. AND DEPARTMENT OF COMMERCE DATA)

Year	Currency and Demand Deposits (1)	Time and Saving Deposits (2)	Saving & Loan Association Shares (3)	Cash and Deposits (Including Saving & Loan) (1 + 2 + 3) (4)	Private Insurance Reserves (5)	Insured Pension Reserves (6)	Non-Insured Pension Funds (7)	Investment Company Shares (8)	Other Preferred and Common Stock (9)	Corporate (and Foreign) Bonds (10)
1946	.032	.033	.007	.072		.021	.002		-	
1947	-.001	.013	.007	.019		.021	.002		.004	
1948	-.014	.004	.006	-.004		.020	.002		.006	
1949	-.012	.005	.008	.001		.020	.003		.004	
1950	-.014	-.002	.007	.023		.019	.004		.003	
1951	.018	.008	.009	.035	.014	.004	.006	.002	.006	-.001
1952	.012	.018	.013	.043	.016	.005	.006	.003	.004	.002
1953	.002	.017	.014	.033	.015	.004	.007	.002	.002	.001
1954	.004	.017	.017	.038	.016	.005	.007	.002	.001	-
1955	-	.012	.017	.029	.015	.004	.008	.003	.001	.004
1956	-.003	.013	.015	.033	.015	.005	.008	.003	.002	.001
1957	-.004	.020	.015	.031	.011	.005	.009	.003	.001	.001
1958	.008	.025	.019	.052	.012	.005	.009	.005	-.002	.006
1959	-.002	.013	.021	.032	.011	.005	.011	.005		.005

Year	State and Local Government Obligations (11)	U. S. Savings Bonds (12)	Other U. S. Government Securities (13)	Net Investment in Nonfarm Homes (14)	Net Change in Mortgages on Nonfarm Homes (15)	Net Change in Consumer Debt (16)	Net Change in Securities Loans (17)	Net Changes in Tangible Assets Less Changes in Other Debt [b] (18)	Total Personal Saving (S. E. C.) (19)	Total Personal Saving (Commerce) (20)
1946	-.001	.008	-.019	.016	.023	.014	-.017	-.002	.075	.084
1947	.002	.012	-.005	.028	.027	.017	-.003	-.004	.041	.028
1948	.005	.008	-.001	.036	.025	.013	-.001	.025	.058	.058
1949	.002	.008	-.001	.031	.022	.014	-.001	.013	.043	.045
1950	.002	.001	-.002	.049	.035	.018	-.001		.049	.061
1951	.002	-.002	-.004	.039	.029	.004	-.001	.019	.088	.078
1952	.004	-	.001	.037	.027	.018	-.003	.007	.080	.079
1953	.007	.001	-	.037	.029	.014	.002	.016	.084	.079
1954	.003	.002	-.006	.041	.035	.004	.003	-.002	.064	.073
1955	.006	.001	.006	.049	.043	.022	.002	.003	.066	.064
1956	.005	-	.006	.041	.035	.011	-.003	-.002	.075	.064
1957	.007	-.006	-.010	.036	.025	.008	-	-.008	.075	.075
1958	.004	-.002	-.010	.036	.029	-	.001	-.016	.069	.074
1959	.007	-.005	.031	.045[c]	.039	.018	.001	(n. a.)	(n. a.)	.069

[a] From U.S. Securities and Exchange Commission, Statistical Bulletin and U.S. Department of Commerce, Survey of Current Business.

[b] Net change in tangible assets of nonfarm and farm unincorporated enterprises and of nonprofit institutions less increases in debt of these groups to corporations and financial institutions.

[c] Depreciation estimated.

(which are based on different source materials employing different concepts) present some summary statistics showing the trend in the ratio of selected components of personal saving to personal disposable income in the first half of this century and in the past decade. Changes in total cash and deposits (including deposits and shares in savings and loan associations) have represented a lower proportion of income in recent years than in earlier prosperous periods -- with savings and loan associations showing an increase, but all other cash and deposits showing a decrease relative to income. Saving in the form of private life insurance increased markedly in relation to income until some time in the 1930's and then stabilized, except for insured pension reserves which did not level off until the 1950's; annual increments to noninsured private pension and retirement funds continued to increase throughout the period. Saving in U.S. Government or state and local pension and retirement funds has of course been higher in the period after World War II than in prior years.

Individuals' net purchases of corporate stock have constituted a substantially lower ratio of income in recent years than either in the 1920's or earlier in this century, with investment company shares constituting the great bulk of such purchases in recent years. The ratio of their purchases of corporate (and foreign) bonds has also declined substantially; their relative purchases of U.S. Governments are slightly higher than in the 1920's and their relative purchases of state and local obligations not much different from the earlier period. Of particular interest is the very substantial increase in individuals' net purchases of U.S. Government securities other than savings bonds in 1959, apparently partly at the expense of corporate securities but much more at the expense of financial deposits other than those in savings and loan associations. Net investment (i.e., expenditures less depreciation) in housing constitutes about the same proportion of income as in the 1920's but the recent rate of increase in mortgage debt has been higher. Net investment in consumer durables was unusually high relative to income in the first few years following World War II, but since 1951 has been at about the same level as in the mid- and late 1920's; the rate of increase in consumer debt has, however, been somewhat greater in the more recent period. Finally, net investment in unincorporated enterprises did not appear to be much different relatively in recent years than in the corresponding earlier periods, though the available data in this entrepreneurial area are extremely weak so that not much confidence can be placed in these results.

It might be noted that some of the more interesting changes in the composition of personal saving over the past half century or so may partly reflect changes in the distribution of income among different income classes. Though other factors -- supply as well as demand -- are obviously also involved, the apparent trend towards less concentration of total income among the upper income groups may help to explain the significant drop in the relative importance of net purchases of corporate securities and cash and deposits (other than in savings and loan associations) and the rise in the relative importance of insurance, pension funds, and consumer durables.

The difficulties in separating the influence of demand conditions for particular kinds of assets and liabilities from supply conditions is even more formidable than for saving as a whole. Thus in the case of total saving, in the absence of a complete economic model, it is generally assumed that the saving schedule (as a function of income and related variables) is more likely to be stable over time than investment so that the intersections of the two schedules depicted by time-series saving or investment data may be taken as an approximation of a saving schedule. For specific components of saving, i.e., for changes in particular assets or liabilities, such an assumption may well be more tenuous. It might be reasonably satisfactory for items like private life insurance but less satisfactory for items like cash and securities (though many economists consider that the real amount of cash balances is determined in the long-run by the public's demand). In view of the potential substitutability of one form of saving for another, it is not surprising to find much greater difficulty in explaining variation in most important components of saving than in saving as a whole.

Theoretical considerations suggest that the components of saving are influenced by the same set of economic variables which affect total saving, with income, interest rates, wealth or net worth, and price expectations as well as tastes, all of potential importance. In this case, not only the level but the structure of interest rates, not only wealth as a whole but the stock of wealth in the form of the particular component being studied or of closely related components, and not only over-all price expectations but those relating to the asset or liability item in question, would be expected to have a significant influence on the demand by savers (or by asset and liability holders) for specific assets and liabilities. Clearly, the relative yield and costs -- adjusted for any differential taxation -- may play a major role in choosing among different forms of assets and liabilities. Furthermore, if a relatively unfavorable trend in prices of a particular type of asset is in prospect, or if for some other reason holdings of this asset are larger than desired relative to income or to other assets, an attempt will be made to reduce such holdings.

The major motives for saving mentioned earlier in this paper in connection with the discussion of saving generally will, of course, not have the same impact on different forms of saving. Thus liquid assets, common stock and net investment in durable goods are imperfect substitutes for providing protection to cover different kinds of uncertainty or even for adjusting consumption over a long planning period under conditions of certainty. Moreover, the ready availability of certain media of investment (e.g., mutual investment companies), other institutional considerations and noneconomic influences may play a major role in the composition of saving.

In view of the myriad influences determining the relative importance of the different components of saving, it is fortunate for the analyst that there seems to be a high degree of substitutability among these components. Specifically, both cross-section and time-series analysis indicates that, for a given level of income, a high level of saving in one type of asset (or liability) tends to be associated with a low level of saving in other types, and that there seems to be much more substitutability or competitiveness in this respect between different forms of saving than between these saving items and consumption.[20] It is desirable, however, to consider briefly the major determinants of the different components of saving both because the substitutability among them is not complete and it is important for some purposes to know the factors responsible for the substitution which takes place.

Cross-section analysis of survey results indicates that, as might be expected, cash and deposits and net business investment are more sensitive to changes in income than items like insurance, net investment in owned dwellings, net investment in consumer durables and consumer credit.[21] In the former items, the average saving-income ratio rises markedly with income, while in the latter there is not much change in the saving-income ratio over a broad range of incomes. Surprisingly, securities do not fall in the former category though this may reflect deficiencies in the survey data. It may be noted, in view of the earlier discussion of permanent vs. transitory income effects, that in the Wharton School-Bureau of Labor Statistics "Study of Consumer Expenditures, Incomes and Savings," an analysis of families with a three-year span of constant incomes in 1950 (with income in 1949 about the same as in 1950 and expecting 1951 income to be about the same) does not modify substantially these conclusions about the relative effect of family income level on the ratio to income of the different components of saving. Another analysis of these same 1950 data indicates that saving in a particular form tends to be related not only to income but also negatively to the level of assets in that form at the beginning of the period and positively to the initial level of other assets; this analysis explains a much higher proportion of the cross-section variation in total saving

---

[20]Irwin Friend and Robert Jones, "The Concept of Saving," Consumption and Saving, op. cit., Vol. II.

[21]E.g., see "Who Saves?" op. cit.

and in durable goods purchases than in the financial components of saving.[22]

A time-series analysis of the 1897-1956 Goldsmith data and of the more recent Securities and Exchange Commission-Commerce 1951-59 data relating annual changes in each of the components of saving in Tables VI-1 and VI-2 to changes in personal disposable income shows very little short-run correlation between saving and income for most of these components. There is of course more correlation between the level of these components of saving and income, but even here the correlation is generally lower than for total saving. The correlation between forms of saving and income is somewhat higher for investment in tangible goods than for financial items such as cash and deposits and securities. The very low correlation between cash and deposits and income and between securities and income is moderately improved when cash and deposits and securities are combined, reflecting the substantial degree of substitutability between these two categories of saving. The relation between insurance and income is more stable than for most financial assets with a moderately high correlation when a time trend is introduced. Movements in mortgage or in other consumer debt cannot be explained at all satisfactorily by income alone; presumably the explanation would be substantially improved if expenditures on housing or on other durables during the period, the level of relevant debt at the beginning of the period, and credit terms were taken as additional independent variables.

There have been a few intensive time-series studies of the demand by savers for several types of assets and liabilities -- notably money (usually defined as currency plus demand deposits), investment in homes, consumer durables and consumer credit -- but generally speaking they do not provide very useful new insights into the nonfinancial factors affecting the composition of saving. Thus permanent income has been used to help explain fluctuations in the real demand for money; the number of married couples, the stock of houses, and unemployment to explain the demand for housing; consumer inventories at the beginning of the year and income variables as well as relative prices and average credit terms to explain the demand for automobiles and, to a lesser extent, other consumer durables.[23] The influence of financial factors on the composition of saving will be discussed further in the next section.

---

[22]"Consumer Expenditures and The Capital Account," op. cit.
[23]E.g., see Milton Friedman, "The Demand for Money: Some Theoretical and Empirical Results," American Economic Review (May 1958), pp. 525-7, and comments by James S. Duesenberry, pp. 528-9; V. Lewis Bassie, "Factors Affecting Construction," Economic Forecasting (New York: McGraw-Hill, 1958), pp. 678-80; Daniel B. Suits,

(continued on following page)

II. FINANCIAL DETERMINANTS OF SAVING

Traditionally, the interest rate for complex of rates) has been considered to be the most important financial determinant of saving. However, prices, liquidity of assets and non-interest terms of credit are additional financial variables which might significantly affect saving. Monetary and debt management policy can influence these variables in a variety of ways. Thus, an increase in the nominal supply of money by open-market operations would almost certainly lower interest rates, would have some tendency to raise prices, might lower or raise the real value of private wealth (since the influence of lower interest rates would tend to offset that of higher prices), and would have an indeterminate effect on the liquidity of assets or more precisely on the relative importance of monetary vs. non-monetary assets (with equity issues of particular significance in the latter category). Both the real national income and total saving (and investment) would probably be raised if the period in question was characterized by a significant amount of unemployment, while total saving might be raised even if the past period was one of full employment. However, the precise effect of such monetary measures on saving in the economy will depend on the sensitivity of saving to income, interest rates and asset effects, and to changes in expectations relating to prices as well as to these other variables; to the sensitivity of investment to these variables; and to the supply and demand relations characterizing both monetary and non-monetary assets. All of these aggregate or macro-effects will depend in turn on the corresponding micro-effects for major groups in the population and on the relative weights of groups with different saving, investment and asset holding propensities.

In addition to the many instruments of monetary control directed at the supply of money and hence credit conditions in general, there have of course been instruments directed at specific kinds of credit (viz., housing, consumer durables, and securities, with only the latter currently operative), while such other measures as public debt policies can affect the maturity composition of the national debt and hence the differential between short- and long-term interest rates and the liquidity of privately held assets. It may be unnecessary to point out that public debt policies by the Treasury associated with the disposition of a surplus or financing of a deficit can also affect the supply of money.

(footnote 23 continued)
"The Demand for New Automobiles in the United States 1929-56," Review of Economics and Statistics (August 1958), and comments by Marc Nerlove in the Review of Economics and Statistics (February 1960).

While there exists a rather impressive theoretical literature on the relation of financial variables to saving and related magnitudes, theory does not give an unambiguous answer to many of the more important questions and in some instances does not even give qualitative answers to the most basic questions. The initial theoretical problems which will be considered in this connection relate to saving at the micro-level, i.e., to the saving behavior of individual households, business firms, and governmental units. A further set of theoretical problems relates to macro-behavior, i.e., to the relevant behavior of the economy as a whole, reflecting not only the aggregation of the micro-relationships between saving and the variables to which it is related but also the specification of the other economic relations necessary for the joint determination of all of these interdependent variables. For example, it is by now well recognized that an increase in saving propensities by any large sector in the economy -- i.e., an increase in the amount it will want to save at a given level of real income, assets, interest rates, etc. -- will probably be self-defeating in an economy marked by deflationary tendencies since an increase in desired saving is likely to be associated under these circumstances with lower income and hence lower aggregate saving.

At the micro-level, there is still no generally accepted theory of even the qualitative relation between saving and interest rates. A rise in interest rates might increase the propensity to save of a household or other economic unit by encouraging them to refrain from consumption and thereby acquire assets permitting a higher consumption at some future time. However, to the extent that the purpose of saving is to smooth out lifetime consumption, there would be no permanent effect of higher interest rates. Moreover, an increase in interest rates might conceivably lower saving by providing a desired standard of living or any other objective of saving (such as for estate purposes) with the accumulation of a smaller amount of assets than would otherwise be necessary. In other words, the substitution effect or the relatively low (high) price of future consumption implied by high (low) interest rates points to a positive relation between saving and interest rates, while the income effect or the opportunity for both more present and future consumption offered by high interest rates points to a negative relation. Another potentially significant influence of higher interest rates on the saving of an economic unit is the wealth effect, i.e., the lower capital values of non-monetary assets might stimulate saving. On the other hand, higher interest rates might foster increased dissaving by the aged to the extent that their wealth is in the form of assets which will benefit by the increase in yields. Finally, to the extent that saving of a household or a firm is motivated by investment plans, higher interest rates might discourage both investment and saving.

It is easy enough to proliferate the kinds of considerations relevant to the determination of the theoretically expected relation

between saving and interest rates for a "representative" household
or other economic unit -- with expectations as to future income,
interest rates, and consumption needs all obviously important.
However, there does not seem to be much point to this since, as
noted earlier, theory does not give a convincing answer even to the
nature of the qualitative relation between these two variables. For
an average household, my own judgment (which may not be too different from that held by most economists) is that saving might be
expected to be positively but not very strongly related to interest
rates, in the sense that a very large increase in interest rates
would be required to stimulate saving to any marked degree. For an
average business firm, I would expect the relation to be again positive but still not very strong. On the one hand, business firms
probably have greater latitude in adjusting the dividend rate to assumed changes in their financial needs than households have in adjusting their standard of living, and the firms are more likely to be
aware of and act on interest rate changes. Higher interest rates and
tight money are likely to be associated with capital rationing in a
period when investment opportunities look attractive and this might
well induce greater business saving. On the other hand, it can be
argued that, to the extent business saving is for the purpose of direct
investment and investment is made less (more) desirable by higher
(lower) interest rates, an increase (decrease) in rates may deter
(stimulate) investment and hence saving -- though from an economic
point of view such saving behavior might be considered irrational.
For government, the other major sector in the economy, it seems
doubtful at the state and local level that interest rates have much
direct effect on saving (i.e., surplus or deficit on current account)
though they may influence both taxes and expenditures, and the timing
of investment may be affected fairly appreciably; at the national level
the effect is presumably even less.

In aggregating the saving behavior of these "representative" economic units to obtain an over-all relation of saving to interest rates
and other relevant variables, perhaps the most important question
that arises is the effect of changes in interest rates on the distribution of income among groups in the population with different propensities to save out of income. If, for example, higher interest rates
imply a redistribution of income in favor of upper income groups,
one could argue that the national saving would be increased as a
result. Unfortunately, satisfactory information on the effect of
changed interest rates on income distribution or on the relation
between income distribution and saving is not readily available.
Proponents of the recently developed permanent income theories of
saving, discussed in an earlier section of this paper, would deny
there is any significant relation between income distribution and
saving, though my own view (and I believe the consensus of opinion)
is that other factors being equal high income groups tend to save a
larger proportion of their income than other groups.

Other potentially significant effects of higher interest rates on the distribution of income among different economic groups and hence on total saving propensities of the population as a whole include a possible redistribution in favor of the older groups of families, including those still employed as well as those retired, and perhaps a redistribution in favor of households (with saving normally in excess of investment) as contrasted to business firms (saving less than investment).[1] The first of these effects might be reasonably neutral with respect to the aggregate relation of saving to income but the second should tend to lower the aggregate propensity to save in view of smaller marginal rate of saving by households than by firms. When all these income redistributional effects are viewed together, it is my impression they do not have a major influence on the impact of interest rate changes on the aggregate saving function. On the other hand, it is possible that they do.

Much more important than aggregation problems in going from micro-relations between saving and its determinants to a system of macro-relations specifying the level of national saving (as well as income, interest rates and other relevant variables) which will be realized in a period of time is the nature of the economic model specified, i.e., the particular variables assumed to be significant and the functional relations assumed to exist among them. While the previous discussion suggests that there is a moderate positive functional relation between saving and the level of interest rates so that consumption is negatively related to such rates, theoretical considerations point even more strongly to a negative relation between investment propensities and the level of interest. Since realized saving and investment must be equal in any period for the economy as a whole, the level of realized saving (in real terms) may be raised, unchanged or lowered by measures taken to lower (or raise) interest rates depending on the nature not only of the saving (or consumption) and investment functions but also of the supply and demand relations for both monetary and non-monetary assets (and on any other relations necessary for the determination of the variables involved in the saving and investment functions). As suggested earlier, it is generally agreed that in a depressed economy, lower interest rates (initiated, say, by open-market operations) would probably have little effect on the amount of desired saving at given levels of income, but would stimulate investment and hence raise

---

[1] To the extent that interest rates influence government taxes and expenditures, the redistribution of income between the public and private sectors may also affect the relation of aggregate saving to income.

the level of national income and aggregate saving and investment.[2] In a "full-employment" economy (assured, say, by a sufficiently high level of private demand or by appropriate fiscal policies) lower interest rates induced by a higher supply of money might again tend to raise aggregate saving (or the ratio of saving or investment to income), though in such an economy unless anti-inflationary fiscal measures are taken the major impact of more money after an initial and perhaps temporary reduction in interest rates would be higher prices which might and might not redistribute incomes in such a way as to stimulate saving and "permanently" reduce the rate of interest.

It should be obvious from the foregoing discussion that the macro-effect of changes in interest rates on saving will depend on the reasons responsible for these changes. Thus, though there are differences in opinion about the desirability of certain objectives and the quantitative effectiveness of various kinds of monetary and fiscal policies towards these objectives, it seems likely that it is economically possible through a combination of such policies to achieve both reasonably full employment and virtually any desired ratio of aggregate saving (or investment) to the national income.[3] It might be noted that this possibility is independent of the level of government expenditures. For example, if changes in tax policy undertaken to achieve full (or high-level) employment at reasonably stable prices do so at the expense of a desired over-all investment-income ratio, a combination of cheaper money and more taxes should make possible the continuance of full-employment with more saving or investment and less consumption.[4]

---

[2]Some attempts to reconcile the "classical" and "Keynesian" viewpoints on the influence of monetary policies on saving and on other relevant aspects of models of income determination include: J. R. Hicks, "Mr. Keynes and the Classics," Econometrica (April 1937); Oscar Lange, "The Rate of Interest and the Optimum Propensity to Consume," Economica (February 1938); and more recently Don Patinkin, Money, Interest and Prices, (Chicago: Row Peterson and Co., 1956); and J. R. Hicks, "A Rehabilitation of Classical Economics?" The Economic Journal, (June 1957).

[3]See Paul A. Samuelson, "The New Look in Tax and Fiscal Policy," Federal Tax Policy for Economic Growth and Stability, Joint Committee on the Economic Report, November 9, 1955, pp. 232-33.

[4]If for example there are only two policy instruments, changes in the nominal supply of money (M) and changes in the tax function T(Y) which is levied solely on households (where Y represents the national income), then full employment Y_1 at reasonably stable prices can probably be achieved through changing T(Y) alone though M can also be changed to affect i (the interest rate), C (consumption), and I (investment). Full employment $Y_1 = C_1 + I_1$ (postulating no government expenditures for convenience), but the ratio $I_1/Y_1 = K_1$ whereas the

(continued on following page)

The theoretical role of the other financial variables which potentially affect saving -- viz., prices, valuation and liquidity of
assets, and non-interest terms of credit -- will be discussed only
briefly. Higher prices (i.e., for commodities) would, other things
being equal, lower the value of assets or at least of monetary assets
and hence from this viewpoint seem to discourage consumption and
encourage saving. Moreover, higher prices would, other things being
equal, increase the demand for nominal cash balances for transactions purposes and, unless the demand for speculative balances
were decreased as much or more, this would increase the interest
rate and perhaps further encourage saving. However, the other things
involved are rarely equal. As was pointed out earlier, monetary
policy which might be responsible for higher prices might also tend
to be associated with lower interest rates which might discourage
saving -- at least at a given level of income. Higher prices, particularly if re-inforced by low interest rates, should raise the value
of equity securities which can have a substantial impact in further
discouraging saving -- again at a given level of income. Perhaps
more important, rising prices may result in expectations of a further
rise so that the saving propensities of non-entrepreneurial households would again be diminished, a point which has been greatly
publicized in recent years. On the other hand, the redistribution of
real income effected by rising prices might well favor economic
groups such as entrepreneurs and the upper-income brackets who
have higher than average saving propensities, and even without such
redistribution both corporate and noncorporate entrepreneurs might
under the circumstances described be motivated to invest and hence
save more than formerly. While the above arguments which largely
apply to the micro-level appear inconclusive as to net effect, in a
macro-context they would normally seem to imply a positive relation
between prices and real aggregate saving, at least where there is

---

(footnote 4 continued)
desired ratio $I_2/Y_1 = K_2$. Now, if we assume the simple relations
(again for convenience) $\Delta C = a \Delta M - c \Delta T$ and $\Delta I = b \Delta M - d \Delta T$,
then the two conditions to be met by monetary and fiscal policy are
(1) $I_2 = I_1 + b \Delta M - d \Delta T = K_2 Y_1$, and (2) $\Delta Y = \Delta C + \Delta I = a \Delta M -
c \Delta T + b \Delta M - d \Delta T = 0$, from which we can obtain the required tax
and monetary changes. It might be noted that ΔM would be expected
to affect ΔI more than ΔC, and the reverse would be true of ΔT;
moreover, while ΔS would be positive and equal to ΔI, this would
reflect the influence of increased government saving and not of increased private saving. Many problems have of course not been
touched upon, including the determination of the required parameters, the difficulty of keeping prices in line, the theoretical possibility that extreme and for other reasons inadmissible values of
i or T would be required (if, e.g., the marginal efficiency of capital
were to become zero), the implications of any desired progressive-
ness of the tax structure on I, etc.

unemployment of resources and price rises are not of the type which lead to a complete loss of confidence in the monetary system. It is of course obvious that the price level is influenced not only by monetary measures, but also by fiscal, price-wage and other policies and institutional arrangements.

Sufficient attention has probably already been paid to the impact of valuation and liquidity of assets on saving in view of the little that can be said on this score. The valuation of at least monetary assets and securities (which is a function of interest rates as well as commodity prices) will tend to be inversely correlated with the propensity to save out of a given level of income, while more liquid assets -- e.g., as a result of open-market operations -- would be expected to have the same type of effect on saving as assets with a higher valuation.

The expected nature of the influence of non-interest terms of credit on saving is quite close to the direct interest effects previously described. In general, easier terms of credit -- such as more credit available at the same interest rates, lower down payments, or longer maturities -- have effects similar to lower interest rates in deterring saving at the micro-level, but probably normally raising aggregate saving at the macro-level if economic resources are otherwise not fully employed. The influence on saving of down payments and maturity terms, which presumably have their major impact on expenditures for consumer durables, might be expected to depend to a greater extent than for other credit terms on the definition of saving used, i.e., whether it is inclusive or exclusive of net investment in such goods, and on the time span covered.

Relation of Total Saving by Major Economic Groups to
Financial Variables

While empirical studies have on occasion indicated a significant influence of interest rates on investment propensities, they have never to my knowledge indicated a correspondingly significant effect on saving propensities. However, in view of the central importance of this effect in our analysis of the financial determinants of saving, and in view of the recent availability of a longer time span of data and new theories of saving behavior, an attempt has been made in this paper to test further the relation of saving to interest rates.

Two bodies of data were utilized to analyze the relation of personal or individuals' savings to interest rates, the Goldsmith annual series from 1897 to 1956 (inclusive and exclusive of net investment in consumer durables) and the Commerce national accounts annual data from 1929 to 1959, omitting the years 1917-18 and 1941-47. First, several relationships of the type described in

Section 1 were fitted between personal saving and disposable income: viz., between change in saving and change in income; between the level of saving and income and liquid assets, all in price deflated per capita terms; between the level of saving and income, change in income and time, with the relevant variables again in price deflated per capita terms; between saving and entrepreneurial and non-entrepreneurial income, previous year's consumption, liquid assets, and population, with all variables except the last price deflated; and between price deflated per capita saving and a weighted average of the current year's and previous year's income, with the data determining the weight to be attached to the different years' incomes. As pointed out earlier, the last of these relationships has been adduced as an empirical approximation of the relation between saving and "permanent" income.

Second, deviations of observed saving from the level implied by these relationships were related to Moody's Aaa corporate bond yields[5] in two different ways; i.e., the deviation of saving from "expectation" to the level of yields (in some cases with allowance for a possible time trend), and changes in the saving deviation to changes in yields either during the same year or the preceding year. These relationships between personal saving, or that part of it unexplained by other factors, and interest rates were as often in the wrong as in the right direction, and the relationships as a whole were not statistically significant.[6] Similar negative results are obtained if we confine our attention to the relation between personal

---

[5]The Moody's data were carried back prior to 1919 on the basis of the 20-year corporate yield series cited in Historical Statistics, 1949, U. S. Bureau of the Census, p. 279, by adjusting upward the level of the latter by the average difference between the two series in the later years. It has not been possible to adjust these or other bond yields in this paper for the trend in commodity prices which presumably influence expected future prices.

[6]The one apparent exception is the regression of the deviation in saving (exclusive of consumer durables) from the level implied by "permanent income" on the level of yields, where the yield coefficient is statistically significant at the 2σ level and is positive (i.e., has the right sign) but the coefficient of determination is only .12.

The corresponding regression for saving inclusive of net investment in consumer durables, which is the definition implicit in the usual formulation of the permanent income hypothesis, does not yield a statistically significant yield coefficient and the coefficient of determination is .02. It may be noted, however, that if these results are taken at face value, they would seem to imply that a change in interest rates is to some extent negatively associated with net investment in durable goods and associated positively with saving exclusive of consumer durables.

saving and interest rates in years of high employment or in recent years only. One piece of evidence arguing in favor of a positive relation between saving and interest rates at high levels of income is the conjunction of a higher ratio of saving (exclusive of consumer durables) to income and higher interest rates in the period after 1950 compared to the early post-World War II years, but the unprecedented liquidity and deferred demands of the immediate postwar period seem to offer a more plausible explanation of the low personal saving rate. Nor does it appear likely that a different statistical treatment of the saving-interest rate relation or the use of other bond yield series would alter these conclusions.

The evidence against an important interest rate effect on saving propensities is admittedly far from convincing. Thus it is quite possible that the saving relations tested reflect a mixture of interest effects on saving and investment propensities in spite of the fact that individuals' saving and either individuals' or aggregate investment can differ greatly. Even where the national income is held reasonably constant at high employment levels, high interest rates may discourage investment more effectively than they encourage saving or discourage consumption and so be associated with low aggregate investment and saving; or on the other hand high interest rates may reflect in part deliberate action by the monetary authorities to discourage high aggregate investment in inflationary periods when the marginal efficiency of investment is unusually high and so tend to be associated temporally with aggregate saving which is high in spite of the level of interest rates. One theoretically appropriate way of disentangling these effects would be to specify and test the relevant "complete" economic model, but such attempts as have been made have not been successful in detecting significant interest rate effects.[7] Another and in many respects more promising method of attempting to isolate interest rate from other effects on personal saving would be through the collection of new household survey data on a panel basis, where the subjective reactions and objective responses to interest rate changes could be obtained for different types of families.

If attention is directed to data for other countries as well as for the United States, there does not seem to be any significant relation between the personal saving-income ratio and interest rates of those countries for the same time period, whether or not an attempt

---

[7]It may be noted that there is no obvious reason why the specification bias in estimating the effect of interest rates on consumption from a single least square regression coefficient of consumption on income and interest rates or from a typical simplified "complete" model is likely to introduce a positive bias into an otherwise negative relation between consumption and interest rates or a corresponding negative bias into the saving relation.

is made to hold constant the influence of the national income.[8] These results may, of course, reflect the complicating influence of cultural and institutional factors and differences in the marginal efficiency or productivity of capital in the different countries. The personal and total saving-income ratios were higher than in the United States for well over half the countries covered in this analysis. When the relation between the personal (or total) saving-income ratio and interest rates is analyzed for each of three foreign countries -- Japan, the United Kingdom, and West Germany -- over the past decade to keep cultural factors reasonably constant, only for the United Kingdom is there definite evidence of a positive relation between personal (but not total) saving and interest rates. For the United Kingdom, the relation between the total saving-income ratio and interest rates can be carried back to 1870 but in this case there is no positive correlation between these two variables.

For U.S. corporations as for individuals, the empirical evidence gives little support to the thesis that interest rates affect saving propensities. Thus deviations of actual saving from the level predicted by the basic corporate saving function discussed in Section 1 (with annual dividends determined by profits after taxes and preceding year dividends) had virtually no correlation, or more precisely a statistically insignificant negative correlation, with Aaa bond yields for the period 1918-56 covered in the analysis. For the United Kingdom also, there seems to have been an insignificant negative correlation between corporate saving and bond yields over the past decade.

The empirical evidence on the effect of other financial variables on the saving of households and business firms is equally unsatisfactory. The apparent negative influence of liquid assets on saving has been discussed in Section 1, but it should be pointed out again that such assets to a considerable extent may serve as a proxy variable for total assets so that it is quite difficult to isolate the magnitude of the effect of liquidity per se. It is virtually impossible from the available data to isolate the differential effect on saving of varying degrees of liquidity, as exemplified by the distinction between

---

[8] The countries included in an analysis of the relation between the personal saving-income ratio and long-term Government interest rates for 1957 were Australia, Belgium, Canada, Costa Rica, France, India, Ireland, Netherlands, New Zealand, Japan, Sweden, United Kingdom, the United States, and West Germany. A similar analysis was made of the national saving-income ratio for Belgium, Canada, Denmark, India, Ireland, Italy, Japan, Netherlands, Norway, Portugal, United Kingdom, the United States, and West Germany. In both instances the correlation between saving and interest rates was negligible.

cash and Government securities or between bills and bonds. While price expectations would be expected to affect saving propensities, there seems to be no evidence that this effect has been significant in the United States, and the relatively high rate of saving of recent years occurred during a period when the dangers of prolonged inflation were probably as widely publicized as any in our history. Rapidly rising and high stock prices have sometimes been cited as one important reason for the low personal saving-income ratio of the late twenties, but whether or not this is true seemed to have no comparable effect in the late fifties. If saving is defined to include net investment in consumer durables, fluctuations in the terms of credit have had a more obvious impact on the composition of saving than on its total; however, the picture is somewhat different for saving exclusive of consumer durables since the liberalization of credit terms has been associated at least in the shortrun (notably in 1955) with more investment in consumer durables and less in other forms of saving.[9]

Relation of Components of Saving to Financial Variables

In discussing the theoretically expected influence of interest rates and other financial variables on the composition of saving, it may be noted again that in large part this can be considered the same as the influence of these variables on the disposition of existing as well as new assets (and liabilities) among different forms. However, in analyzing the composition of saving, the focus of interest is ordinarily on the changes in assets and liabilities abstracting from any price revaluation. The relative demand for a particular component of saving or type of asset will presumably depend in the first instance on the comparative yield of that asset (or inversely on cost in the case of a liability). A higher yield on time or savings deposits, shares in savings and loan association, or on bonds would be expected, other things equal, to attract funds into that medium whether or not the total of saving (in all forms combined) for any of the economic units involved is or is not increased. For some kinds of assets, the concept of yield has to be interpreted somewhat differently from that relevant to a fixed-interest-bearing obligation: for common stock, expected yield and perhaps more important price expectations constitute the relevant variable; for consumer durables other than homes, the usual yield concept is not very useful, though prices and price expectations play a somewhat analogous role. Where comparative yield or rate of return is important, this relates not only to the current value of this variable but also to

---

[9] It should be unnecessary to add that this does not imply more liberalized terms alone accounted for the higher automobile sales in 1955.

expectations of future return. Clearly, investors do not rush to buy bonds at higher current yields if much higher rates of returns seem imminent.

We cannot of course abstract from conditions on the other side of these supply-demand relations for particular types of assets in appraising the influence of any financial variable on the aggregate change in that asset. Thus expansionary open-market operations will be reflected in an increase in the public's monetary assets and in many periods of time even in an increase in the real value of monetary assets. Similarly, it is impossible for the buying public (for convenience considering only a closed economy) to purchase more stock issues on balance than corporations issue, though experience indicates there is no corresponding limitation on the market price of existing stock issues. More generally, the ready availability of diverse kinds of institutional media for saving may obviously have a major impact on the amount of realized saving in that form.

The evaluation of different kinds of risk and considerations of convenience also play a major role in the demand for particular types of assets. For example, attitudes towards the cyclical risks of stock ownership seem to have changed markedly in recent years, apparently at least in part as a result of an unprecedented record of economic stability. Less money may have been demanded by the public (totally apart from the restrictions on the supply side) because of this greater attractiveness of other assets, but certain minimal amounts would presumably be required not only for convenience or need for transactions purposes but also for precautionary purposes to avoid certain types of risk.

The theoretical role of the influence of non-interest terms of credit on the composition of saving is fairly straightforward. Easier terms of credit applicable to a particular type of asset should, at least in the short run, increase effective demand for that asset, and net investment in such assets should be enhanced at the macro as well as micro level.

An analysis of the relation of the components of saving to interest rates, analogous to that already described for saving as a whole, indicates that such rates or relative yields do not seem to explain a high proportion of variation in the components of saving left unexplained by income but as might be expected do explain a somewhat higher proportion of such variation than for saving as a whole. In other words, higher interest rates on interest-bearing financial deposits or bonds do attract a flow of funds from non-interest bearing deposits, even though total saving may not be increased, as illustrated by the dramatic rise in individuals' net purchases of U.S. Government securities in 1959 associated with a sharp rise in their yields at the same time that the over-all personal saving-income

ratio declined somewhat. It has not proved possible, within the
limitations of the analysis carried out, to explain nearly as high a
proportion of the variation in components as in total saving (in
view of the much more important role of income in the determination of total saving and the more important role of supply considerations and special demand factors in the determination of some of
the components of saving). Net investment in housing does not seem
strongly affected by interest rates, but this may well reflect the
deficiencies in the simple uniform analysis followed for the different components, which among other things uses general rather
than specific interest rates and does not distinguish between the
supply of and demand for mortgage funds. Net saving in the form of
common stock other than investment companies, which is measured
as the net increase in issues (less the net amount purchased by
groups other than domestic individuals), is probably greatly limited
by supply considerations at least in the short run, with substantial
fluctuations in demand along a relatively stable supply curve
determining the short-term level of stock prices. Individuals' net
accumulation of shares in investment companies, which has been
larger in recent years than for all other common stock combined,
is much less inhibited by supply considerations since such shares
effectively represent tap issues available at prices determined by
the ordinary market forces. It is interesting to note therefore that
the forthcoming Investment Company Study referred to earlier
indicates a fairly strong positive correlation between annual changes
in the net sales of mutual fund shares -- the largest sector of the
investment company industry -- and the approximately concurrent
changes in stock market prices.

There seems little doubt from a casual inspection of developments over the past decade that credit terms apart from interest
rates play an important role in the determination of at least the
timing of net investment in consumer durables and housing. While
no special analysis to determine the quantitative importance of
specific credit variables such as down payment or maturity was
made for purposes of this paper, reference may be made to other
studies which indicate a major impact of these variables on annual
net investment in automobiles.[10] The unavailability of funds for

---

[10]Thus the Federal Reserve Board study of Consumer Instalment
Credit, Part IV, "Financing New Car Purchases," A National Survey
for 1954-55, 1957, pp. 4-5, notes that "Approximately one-half of the
instalment buyers in 1954-55 said that they would not have bought the
new car they did at the time if substantially larger down payments or
shorter maturities had been required." Marc Nerlove, in "Professor Suits on Automobile Demand," Review of Economics and Statistics (February 1960), pp. 102-104, derives elasticities of new car
purchases with respect to average contract duration of .6 to .7 from
time-series data for the period 1929-1941 and 1941-1956.

FHA and VA mortgages as a result of limitations on the rate of interest charged has frequently been cited as a significant deterrent to investment in housing in several postwar years and there seems little doubt that other changes in the ease of borrowing have also markedly affected at least the timing of such investment.

III. SUMMARY AND IMPLICATIONS

This paper has been primarily concerned with the determinants of saving in the U.S. economy, with special attention to financial determinants. Such saving has amounted to roughly 10 percent of the national income, somewhat lower than the average in a number of other countries for which data are readily available. The two private sectors in our economy, i.e., households (including nonprofit organizations) and business firms, account for virtually the entire national saving, with government saving relatively unimportant. The latter has represented anywhere from 0 to 15 percent of total saving depending on the treatment of government net investment in capital goods and government pension and retirement funds; in recent years the government share in saving has been zero or negative on the narrow definition and 10 percent on the broadest definition. Though data on unincorporated business saving are quite poor, it appears that corporate and noncorporate business saving together may be at least as large as saving by nonbusiness households.

For economic units in each of the two private sectors, saving during a period seems to be determined largely by income and tastes, with the real value of initial assets and, even more so, the level of interest rates and other financial variables appearing to play a lesser role. The opportunity for more profitable, or otherwise desirable, direct investment probably also plays a significant role in the saving behavior of business firms. Perhaps the most important difference in the relation of saving to income among major groups in the U. S. economy is the much higher propensity to save by business firms than by other groups; there is also evidence that upper income groups (who are generally the upper wealth groups) tend to save a higher proportion of their income than other households, though the quantitative importance of the latter finding has recently been questioned. As a result, the distribution of income among different groups in the population as well as the level of income can have a considerable effect on the aggregate amount of saving associated with a given total of income.

While government saving as usually defined has not been substantial in the United States in spite of high tax revenues, any national government obviously has wide latitude not only for channeling command over real resources or income to government through taxes but also for saving a higher (as well as lower) proportion of such income than would otherwise be saved by the private sectors in the economy. For example, even treating social insurance funds as part of individuals' saving, the Japanese government seems to have saved from 20 percent to 30 percent of their current revenue and to have accounted for between 20 percent and 30 percent of the national saving for every year from 1952 through 1957 (the last available) and for a much higher proportion in the earlier reconstruction years. The government saving-income ratio in Japan is significantly higher than the household ratio though not so high as the corporate ratio. In West Germany, the ratio of government to total saving was even higher during this period, averaging 35 percent to 45 percent from 1952 through 1958 depending on whether social insurance funds are excluded or included in the government sector. The United Kingdom seems much closer to the United States in this respect than to Japan and West Germany.

In view of the basic importance of income in the determination of the level of saving, measures taken to influence private saving by operating on tastes, assets or interest rates without regard to income effects may be self-defeating. Thus in a period marked by a considerable amount of unemployed resources, measures taken to encourage saving by government or private exhortation or by monetary policies designed to raise interest rates might be expected, in the absence of offsetting measures, to lower income and hence aggregate saving by lowering spending not only on consumption but on investment. The level of interest rates it may be noted seems likely to have a greater impact on planned investment than on planned saving. However, while interest rates (and other terms of credit) may not affect saving propensities very greatly, they do have a marked impact on the composition of saving, with savers not too surprisingly preferring assets with higher yields and lower costs or easier credit terms.

Assuming a period marked by full employment and inflationary pressures, a rise in the propensity to save induced by measures which do not correspondingly depress the propensity to invest might be expected to be associated with more aggregate investment and saving rather than with lower real income. Such measures might include new savings media (sometimes with a considerable element of forced savings such as pension funds) or the more general availability of existing savings media (e.g., mutual funds) or various forms of exhortation to save (or decreased advertising designed to encourage spending), but without more aggressive measures by the government it is difficult to have a major short-run effect on saving propensities. It might be noted that even in the type of full employment situation predicated, monetary (and debt management) policies which stimulated saving moderately and discouraged investment drastically might bring about lower rather than higher saving. In any case, increased savings propensities however achieved and tighter monetary policies regardless of their direct influence on saving will of course help to contain inflationary pressures.

While this paper has been more concerned with the influences which make the level of saving what it is rather than with optimal criteria for what the level should be, some consideration might be given to the latter problem. Presumably our basic economic objectives include reasonably full employment or the maintenance of a high level of output in an economy marked by freedom of choice, with the national income relatively immune from depression, and a high rate of economic growth. Other economic or related equity objectives may include a desired level of communal consumption and investment, which in the United States means a democratically determined volume of government expenditures; and, at least as much for equity as for economic reasons, certain desired characteristics of the after-tax distribution of income and reasonable stability of prices. Our record of performance in the period after World War II is one of reasonably full employment for the longest period in our history associated with a ratio of aggregate saving or investment to income which compares favorably with past periods; and there seems to be no obvious reason why this record cannot be maintained. We have had a larger amount of upward price instability than may have been desirable or necessary, but there seems to have been some improvement in this situation during recent months.

A major question relevant to optimal saving behavior which has been increasingly raised in recent months, however, is whether our rate of economic growth has been as high as is desirable. In an economy operating at a high ratio of capacity, this depends to a large extent on the ratio of aggregate private and public saving or investment to income and on the state of technology. Many poorer nations, including democratic as well as totalitarian countries, have been saving much higher proportions of their income and enjoying higher rates of economic growth -- reflecting their higher saving rate but also their ability to take advantage of improved technologies in more economically advanced countries. Even in the United States the average productivity of new business investment (or the reciprocal of the capital coefficient) seems to be so high that from a national point of view a dollar of saving flowing into such investment may produce a social annuity of close to 20 percent of the investment per annum. It might be noted that this figure is much greater than the average return to individual savers or even to individual investors on an after-tax basis.

In determining the desirability of more aggregate saving and investment from the point of view of the economy as a whole, obviously it is not adequate to know the past productivity of new investment since it is the future productivity which is relevant and this presumably is related to the growth of technology and is a declining function of the amount of new investment for any given technology. Moreover, in addition to productivity, the optimal amount of saving will depend on the psychological or subjective discount factor relevant to the comparative evaluation of a dollar of future vs. present consumption, and on the relation of utility of the volume of consumption during a given period.

If it is desired in the light of an evaluation of these circumstances to increase our present national saving-income ratio, this probably can be accomplished by several combinations of fiscal and monetary policy designed to increase public or private saving and investment. One possible approach would be to encourage private investment by relatively easy monetary or credit conditions throughout the cycle, and to encourage consumption during recessionary periods and saving during inflationary periods by appropriate fiscal policy, though such measures could raise a number of political and economic problems including that of income distribution. Another possible approach is to use selective fiscal policy instead of or together with monetary measures to stimulate investment (public as well as private) over the entire cycle, with fiscal policy again used to increase saving in the boom and consumption in recession. If it seems desirable to encourage private saving over the entire cycle, without discouraging investment via higher interest rates, additional help might be provided by institutional changes which would make readily available different saving media geared to the needs and tastes of specific sectors in the population.